S0-ATO-761

LIFE'S ULTIMATE QUESTIONS

BY THE AUTHOR

A Guide to a Christian Philosophy of Religion (Four Volumes)
A Guide to Religious Authority and Biblical Interpretation in the Thought of John Calvin
Questions People Ask About a Christian Philosophy of Religion (Two Volumes)
Religious Authority, Biblical Interpretation, and the Modern Mind
Theology and Contemporary Art Forms
Demons, Demons, Demons
Why Christians Fight Over the Bible
Christ and the New Consciousness
Christianity and Contemporary Art Forms
Nineteenth Century Devotional Thought (editor)
Makers of the Modern Theological Mind: Paul Tillich
What is Christian Doctrine?
The Lion and the Lamb: The Book of Revelation for Today
Life's Ultimate Questions

LIFE'S ULTIMATE QUESTIONS

A Contemporary Philosophy of Religion

John P. Newport

WORD PUBLISHING
Dallas · London · Sydney · Singapore

LIFE'S ULTIMATE QUESTIONS

Library of Congress Cataloging-in-Publication Data

Newport, John P., 1917–
Life's ultimate questions : a contemporary philosophy of religion / John P. Newport.
p. cm.
Bibliography: p.
Includes index.
ISBN 0-8499-0498-6
1. Christianity—Philosophy. 2. Bible—Philosophy. I. Title.
BR100.N53 1989
201—dc20 89-5843
CIP

Printed in the United States of America

1 2 3 9 AGF 9 8 7 6 5 4 3 2

To Eddie Belle

Encourager, Enabler, and
Companion of the Years

Contents

Preface

This work, like all books of its type, grows out of a particular religious and intellectual odyssey. At the same time, it must take its place among the variety of approaches to reality that are available in a pluralistic world. As one who stands in the tradition of religious liberty and religious freedom, I hope I can face plurality with strong convictions and yet with humility and a refusal to force or intimidate. I also hope I have learned from alternative approaches.

Although this book is written from a particular perspective—that of evangelical Christianity and the biblical worldview—I would hope it is not just "a sequence of straw ideas easily knocked down by a highly selective treatment of the biblical perspective," as Yale Divinity School Professor Robert Calhoun once described the work of a prominent theologian. Still, because a writer's background and belief structure inevitably color a work of this kind, it should be helpful to relate in some detail the immediate and more distant background of my personal pilgrimage as it pertains to the writing of this book.

1. The Immediate Background

In the mid-1970s, I left my teaching position at Southwestern Baptist Theological Seminary to become the Chavanne Professor of Religious Studies at Rice University in Houston, Texas. One of my former graduate students, who had become minister of a large Houston church, asked me to present to his congregation a series of Sunday evening talks in which I related the biblical worldview to eleven of life's ultimate or crucial questions. He also asked that I contrast the biblical view with alternative approaches. (Through the years I have continued to learn from laypersons in the congregations of various denominations where materials in this book have been presented.)

The response to this series was excellent, and so I used the material in developing a similar course at Rice for undergraduates. But this was quite a different situation, as the detailed religious biographies I required of my students showed.

For whereas the church members had been sympathetic toward the biblical approach, the Rice students were far from convinced.

As would be understandable at a scientifically oriented university, a number of the students had embraced a "scientific" or rationalistic worldview. They did not see the biblical worldview as a viable option, because some Christians they had known had displayed an obscurantist or irresponsible attitude toward the disciplines of science and philosophy. Other students, those of a more religious temperament, had reacted against the orthodox approach to the Bible and had become interested in a non-Christian mysticism or some form of the occult. Some students had been "turned off" by television evangelists and egocentric religious leaders, whom they saw as using religion to further their own purposes or prejudices. And still other students were suspicious of the biblical worldview because they saw Christians as preoccupied with rigid conventionality and devotion to the minutiae of propriety.

I found a similar response to the biblical worldview among some of the Rice faculty members. One prominent scientist on the faculty, for instance, said he had never been shown that the biblical worldview could be satisfactorily related to developments in the natural and social sciences.

My interest in relating the biblical worldview to life's ultimate questions resulted in a number of requests from colleges and universities to lecture on this subject. Foundations with evangelical concerns, such as the Staley Foundation, used me in their programs. With the help of doctoral students at Rice University and Southwestern Seminary, I began to explore these areas in some depth—and the result is this book.

2. The Larger and More Distant Background

But in a way, of course, the ground for this book was broken long before I started teaching at Rice—or even at Southwestern. I was reared in a devout Christian home. My parents and grandparents placed the highest priority on their evangelical heritage and on moral and spiritual values. During my college days, I prepared for the study of law, acquiring at the same time a broad liberal arts background. On a national debate tour, however, I stayed in fraternity houses to save housing expense, and in those weeks I came to believe that America's greatest need was in the moral and spiritual area. This led me to shift vocations and prepare for the Christian ministry. In my subsequent years of study at Southern Baptist Theological Seminary, I emphasized biblical study and was deeply involved in experiential Christianity.

After finishing a doctorate in biblical studies at Southern, I became minister of a church across from a college campus. There, as I would discover later at Rice, some of the students and professors were reacting against various types of religious orthodoxy. They were seeking assistance in relating the biblical worldview to the wider currents of intellectual and religious life. Teachers asked for help in relating their biblical faith to their specific disciplines. In the wider academic world, advanced scientific views and the modern historical model of explanation in terms of origins were seen by some to be replacing backward religious views. In the graduate schools which they were attending, the teachers were told that to be "scientific" they must specialize and eliminate religiously derived principles from their disciplines.

These experiences and requests impressed me with the need for evangelical scholars to become active and competent in the fields of philosophy of religion, philosophical theology, and Christian apologetics. I resigned my church and traveled to Europe to begin a program of doctoral study in these areas.

At the University of Edinburgh, I studied under controversial and yet stimulating teachers such as John Baillie, John Macmurray, James Stewart, William Manson, J. H. S. Burleigh, Tom Torrance, and O. S. Rankin. Visiting lecturers who were equally stimulating were Reinhold Niebuhr and Emil Brunner. At the same time, through Charlotte Chapel Church, InterVarsity Christian Fellowship, and visits to Tyndale House in Cambridge, I maintained active ties with the more conservative Christian approach in Great Britain. During this same general period, I engaged in a program of study at the Universities of Basel and Zurich in Switzerland. Notable professors of influence were Oscar Cullmann, Karl Ludwig Schmidt, Karl Barth, and Emil Brunner. Professor Cullmann, especially, helped me see the relevance of the broad biblical vision for basic philosophical problems—as G. Ernest Wright and Frank Cross would do later.

Returning to the United States, I continued my interest in the subjects covered in this book while teaching at Baylor University, New Orleans Baptist Theological Seminary, and Southwestern Seminary. A major breakthrough came when I received a Rockefeller grant to study the relationship between Christianity and culture at Harvard University and Harvard Divinity School in the late 1950s. Here I confronted firsthand the questioning by linguistic analysts of the validity of religious language. In courses at Boston University, I reacted to the Personal Idealism of Peter Bertocchi and the Brightman school. At Harvard I said yes and no to the teachings of Paul Tillich. (Later, I would write a book on Tillich.) New insights came from the lectures of Richard Reinhold Niebuhr (the son of H. Richard Niebuhr and nephew of Reinhold Niebuhr), Paul Lehman, John Wild, Dean Sam Miller, George Buttrick, James Luther Adams, and Arthur Schlesinger, Jr. I was introduced to situation ethics by Joseph Fletcher. Especially helpful in the biblical field were G. Ernest Wright, Frank Cross, Krister Stendahl, and Amos Wilder.

To help prepare for an evangelical dialogue, I became actively identified with the conservative Christian community in Boston through the Tremont Temple and Park Street churches and through Gordon College. As an associate fieldwork director for the Boston University School of Theology, I made regular visits to the more liberal churches in New England and noted the contrast with the conservative groups. The tension was heightened as I became a participant in numerous dialogue sessions in Cambridge and Boston. (I was billed as a "Constructive Evangelical.")

I learned much from these sessions. For one thing, I learned that simple answers do not suffice for complex questions. I also learned much about conservative cultural obscurantism, as well as the way more liberal groups tend to dissipate the faith in order to accommodate modernity.

Still another sabbatical, in the mid-1960s, found me at Union Seminary in New York City, which at that time was the most controversial and yet one of the most stimulating theological centers in the United States. I was well acquainted with this school, because in the late 1940s and early 1950s I had done research there for my Ph.D. thesis. At Union, I received helpful insight from visiting professor Abraham Joshua Heschel, one of the world's eminent Jewish scholars, and from Reinhold Niebuhr. New insights also came from John Macquarrie, W. D. Davies, Tom Driver, James Muilenburg, Samuel Terrien, Daniel Day Williams, John Bennett, and Roger Shinn.

As will be noted in the book, I have given considerable attention to the alternative views of world religions. My interest in this subject began when I was at Harvard. Robert Slater, the Director of the Center for the Study of World Religions at Harvard, as well as Huston Smith at Massachusetts Institute of Technology, showed me the importance of understanding world religions in a rapidly developing planetary culture. When Robert Slater transferred to Hindu Benares University in Benares, India, I arranged to go there and to other parts of the Far East to study world religions firsthand. I am indebted to Professor Slater and to missionaries in Thailand, Hong Kong, Taiwan, Korea, and Japan for their help. Tucker Calloway and Robert Culpepper were especially helpful during my stay at Seinan Gakuin University in Japan.

A crucial breakthrough in preparation for this study also came at Harvard, where I began a dialogue with G. Ernest Wright. He had been reared in a conservative Presbyterian home and had become a world-renowned scholar in Old Testament and archaeology. Beginning his teaching career in Chicago at McCormick Seminary, he had become concerned with the relation of the biblical worldview to basic philosophical problems. Brought to Harvard by President Nathan Pusey in the 1950s to help reinvigorate Harvard Divinity School, he had maintained an ongoing dialogue with his colleague, Paul Tillich, whose ontological approach in Wright's opinion was not adequate to express the biblical worldview. Wright opened up to me the importance of the Old Testament for life's ultimate questions. This broad concern transcended his particular perspective on "salvation history."

Before I left Cambridge, Professor Wright called me to his home. His concern was to develop a more adequate approach to the teaching of philosophy of religion in evangelical seminaries. He contended that there is a unique biblical approach to classic philosophical questions. Together we discussed how this approach could be developed and implemented. Many of the ideas in this book had their origin in that session.

After leaving Harvard to return to my teaching at Southwestern Seminary, I sought to implement the approach Professor Wright and I had discussed. I enlisted the help of doctoral students in researching topics and persons related to this new approach. I also wrote an article entitled "Biblical Philosophy and the Modern Mind," which created considerable discussion among philosophy of religion teachers who read the article. I was encouraged that Eric Rust, originally trained in Old Testament and science in England, was sympathetic with this approach and was writing extensively in this area. Further graduate work in philosophy led to a thesis in the area of linguistic analysis and religious language. Especially helpful at this time were Ted Klein and A. C. Garnett. And my involvement with the consultations sponsored by the Lily Foundation to explore the area of theological education and the arts also contributed to the development of my thought in this area.

At Southwestern Seminary, we invited lecturers from the evangelical community who were helpful in dialogue and in their teachings—and these, too, contributed to the ferment of ideas which eventually resulted in this book. These scholars included James I. Packer, George Ladd, Colin Brown, Daniel Fuller, Millard J. Erickson, Culbert Rutenber, Robert Johnston, Carl F. H. Henry, Gordon Fee, Richard Lovelace, David Hubbard, Lewis Smedes, Richard Mouw, Donald G. Bloesch, Ronald Enroth, George Schweitzer, R. T. Kendall, Bernard Ramm, F. F. Bruce, G. R. Beasley-Murray, J. Edwin Orr, Hendrikus Berkhof, Bruce Metzger, and Robert Mounce. Other stimulating lecturers who came to Southwestern and were helpful in this study included Martin Marty, Will Herberg, Frank Cross, James McCord, Wolfhart Pannenberg, William Foxwell Albright, Stanley Hauerwas, Bruce Larson, J. V. Langmead Casserley, F. W. Dillistone, Stephen C. Neill, and Gabriel Fackre.

It is obvious, then, that this book has developed out of a rich and varied background. The approach could be called "semipopular." The wide acceptance of my recent book on the Apocalypse, *The Lion and the Lamb,*[1] has encouraged me in the use of this format.

I have purposely dealt in some detail with contemporary controversial problems which relate to life's ultimate questions. Hopefully this book will be helpful to pastors, church staff members, lay people, and missionaries, as well as teachers and students in colleges and seminaries.

The intellectual and practical context at Southwestern Seminary, where I am vice president for academic affairs, provost, and professor of philosophy of religion, has been very helpful. I am grateful to Russell Dilday, president of the seminary and professor of philosophy of religion, who has encouraged me in this project. Professors Yandall Woodfin, L. Russ Bush, and James Denison in the Department of Philosophy of Religion at Southwestern have been important persons in the framing and development of my thought. Professor Niels Nielsen, Jr., chairman of the Department of Religious Studies, Rice University, was a significant person in the development of this study in its early stages.

Norma Haynes, my administrative associate, has been supportive and helpful. Special appreciation is in order for Susan Lafferty, who is a gifted secretary and constructive critic. I would also like to thank Carey Moore, senior academic editor at Word Publishing, who provided encouragement and brought the book to publication. I am especially indebted to Anne Christian Buchanan, whose perceptive and critical editing of the manuscript provided the basis for revision. Above all, I express appreciation to my wife, Eddie Belle, who has undergirded this project in many ways and who, more than anyone else, has made this study possible.

1

The Importance of Applying the Biblical Worldview to Life's Ultimate Questions

I. Why Is It Important to Study Life's Ultimate Questions?

1. A Built-In Need

Human beings, as opposed to animals, have the capacity for self-awareness or self-transcendence. This means that built into the nature of men and women is a concern with certain fundamental or crucial questions about the nature of human life—its ultimate meaning and destiny. To be human is to make value judgments—decisions about what we should do, decisions about good and evil and right and wrong, decisions about how we will lead our lives.[1]

According to Harvard professor of divinity Gordon Kaufman, addressing ultimate questions is a necessity for thinking persons. And this has been true through the ages; as long as humans have existed, we have asked ultimate or crucial questions. Sometimes we have asked these questions openly—as in the case of Plato, Aristotle and Descartes. At other times the questions have been dealt with implicitly or indirectly, as in the myths of the ancient Greeks, Assyrians, or Egyptians.[2]

2. A Heritage of Concern

Throughout history we can find examples of how the world's peoples have been concerned with ultimate or crucial questions.

The Hindus, for example, have been concerned through the ages with questions of evil and guilt. This can be seen in the formulation of the law of karma, or retribution, which is related to their teaching about reincarnation. According to this view, sin must be paid for either in this life or a future one.

Zoroaster, the Persian prophet of the seventh century B.C., had as his overwhelming concern the question of the origin of evil. A century later, the Hindu prince Gautama, later to be called the Buddha, became concerned with the problem of suffering as he observed the poor people in his father's kingdom.

The ancient Greek philosophers addressed life's ultimate questions in a variety of ways. The Stoics, for example, were occupied with the problem of how to deal with suffering in a practical way, while their counterparts, the Epicureans, saw happiness and pleasure as an answer to the question of life's meaning. Socrates and his follower Plato were preoccupied with the question of the objectivity of truth and morality in a world of relativism and cynicism—as well as the problem of life beyond death and the problem of evil. And Aristotle, the successor to Plato, was concerned with tragedy, evil, and morality.

In the fifth century A.D., as the Roman Empire was collapsing, Augustine became concerned with the meaning and purpose of history. Later, during the Middle Ages, Anselm concerned himself with the place of reason in the Christian faith, while Thomas Aquinas was concerned with how to relate the faith to the rapidly growing Islamic world.

Martin Luther in the sixteenth century grappled with the question of how to deal with guilt and become right with God. And among the concerns of Luther's fellow reformer John Calvin was the relationship of Christianity to culture and to the political community.

In the eighteenth century, Immanuel Kant sought to explain how moral experience—the inner pressure of the conscience, or the sense of oughtness—implies freedom and the reality of God and immortality. For Sören Kierkegaard in the nineteenth century, the chief concern was how to overcome the wrongful dominance of reason in the Christian life. Karl Marx was concerned about the meaning of history as it related to economics. Martin Heidegger in the twentieth century was concerned with the importance of seeing life in the light of death.

3. A Contemporary Quest

These examples show us that thinkers over the centuries have continued to ask life's ultimate questions. Some observers today contend that these broader questions of philosophy (including religion) are outmoded and will gradually disappear. A realistic observation, however, will show us that this approach is too shallow. The religious and metaphysical impulse—our concern with ultimate questions—is too deeply true to our nature to be permanently displaced.

Besides, as Robert Bellah and his colleagues point out, religion and metaphysical concerns are *not* dying out in today's world. On the contrary, the rapid spread of Islam, the rise of new religious groups in Japan, and the religious resurgence in China as well as in North America, all point to a continued and vital interest in life's ultimate questions.[3]

This came home to me when I conducted three study trips to mainland China in the early 1980s. It is ironic that, despite the Communist antipathy to religion, Christianity has not died out in China since the Communist takeover in 1949; rather, it has grown by leaps and bounds. Chinese leaders have had to come to grips with this development. They are now modifying the Marxist line that religion is an "opiate of the people" and are pointing out that, in many cases, religion has helped the people to be better workers.

Even if concern about life's ultimate questions is as great today as it was in earlier ages, the *particular* questions that capture the imaginations of men and women may be different. For just as different questions are more important to us at different times in our lives or under different circumstances, different questions may also dominate during particular times of history.

Paul Tillich points out, for example, that in the early years of Western Civilization a crucial question was that of light for the darkness of ignorance. In the Middle Ages, a primary question was forgiveness, because of a widespread sense of guilt. In the twentieth century, a crucial concern relates to the lack of meaning —the profound and widespread sense of meaningless that permeates the lives of many in our culture and around the world.

But there are other questions as well. Langdon Gilkey contends that the character of everyday experience reveals such contemporary crucial questions. Today's so-called secular man is "bugged" with ultimate questions just as were people in earlier centuries. People today realize their limits and have a sense of anxiety, alienation, and guilt.

According to Gilkey, we can see this concern about ultimate questions beneath the surface of various cultural developments. Our obsession with youthful appearance and beauty, as evidenced by the size and power of the cosmetics and health-club industries, is rooted in our concern for our finiteness—we are afraid to grow old. We carefully avoid the subject of death—as seen in the genteel euphemisms of the funeral industry. This can be seen as an indication of our unwillingness to face the fact of our own mortality. And the offices of psychiatrists and psychologists are flooded with people who are bothered by a serious sense of anxiety. Many say this is evidence of a concern about meaning—both for their individual lives and perhaps for the larger purposes of history and life itself.[4]

Definitions

1. *Philosophy.* The term *philosophy,* in its historical and traditional sense, means the love or pursuit of wisdom. In the Greek sense, wisdom implies not only wide knowledge, but also sound judgment about the values of different things in life.

Philosophy, as used in this study, also involves an attempt to account for the nature of existence as a whole. It interrelates the various disciplines, such as theology, history, science, linguistics, and so forth. When we think of philosophy, we commonly mean a very general perspective on things which is likely to affect the outlook or emotional attitude of those who accept it and also to influence their conduct. The *Shorter Oxford Dictionary* defines philosophy as "that department of knowledge which deals with the general causes and principles of things." This definition substantially follows Plato.

Philosophy is thus a worldview which affects practical life. The philosophical method is commonly held to involve the clarification and analysis of the broad concepts of philosophy.

Reference will be made to various classical divisions of philosophy—such as philosophy of history, aesthetics (philosophy of beauty), philosophy of language, philosophy of religion, philosophy of science, epistemology (theory of knowledge), and philosophy of moral judgment (ethics)—in appropriate sections of this study.

2. *Metaphysics.* In the work of Aristotle, the general term *philosophy* covered all that now would be called science. In order to distinguish this broad concern from the original Platonic understanding of philosophy, he called Plato's view "first philosophy" or "metaphysics"—as opposed to "physical science." Thus the term *metaphysics* is almost synonymous with the original meaning of philosophy. In this sense, metaphysics seeks to interpret, organize, and relate the diversity of experience into a comprehensive whole.

In the twentieth century, many philosophers have rejected the idea of a transcendent dimension to reality—or at least reject the possibility of knowing this reality or speaking of it. This challenge to traditional philosophy, metaphysics, and theology will be discussed in chapter 3.

3. *Worldview (German: Weltanschauung).* The term *worldview* is used in the sense described by the prominent German philosopher Wilhelm Dilthey (1833–1911). Dilthey affirmed that philosophy must be defined as a comprehensive vision of reality that involves the social and historical reality of humankind, including religion. A worldview is thus the nature and structure of the body of convictions of a group or an individual. (A conviction means a person's persuasions concerning the meaning of life.)

A worldview, defined in simple terms, is a concept which includes all dimensions of reality, from the existing individual to the universe itself. The worldview of a person or a group is that which brings integration—a comprehensive interpretation—to life. Worldview includes a sense of meaning and value and principles of action. It is much more than merely an "outlook" or an "attitude."

It is important to note that each person's worldview is based on a key category, an organizing principle, a guiding image, a clue, or an insight selected from the complexity of his or her multidimensional experience.

4. *Philosophy of Religion.* Philosophy of Religion is the branch of philosophy that concentrates on thinking or reflection about religion. It is occupied to a large extent with the consideration of reasons for and against various fundamental religious beliefs. Matters considered include arguments for the existence of God, the nature and significance of religious experience, the nature of religion, the relationship between religion and science, the nature of revelation, the place of religion in human culture as a whole, the logical analysis of religious language, and the nature and the significance of religious symbolism. These topics all grow out of a single enterprise—the rational scrutiny of the claims of religion.

A highly developed religion presents us with a number of important claims on our belief, our conduct, and our attitudes and feelings. It gives answers to questions concerning the ultimate source of things, the governing forces in the cosmos, the ultimate purpose of the universe, and the place of man in the scheme.

The primary purpose of this book is to develop a philosophy of religion that is based not on classical categories, but on the human experience of ultimate questions—those issues that raise themselves over and over in life because they touch on matters that are basic to life itself.

5. *Biblical Worldview or Biblical Philosophy.* A biblical worldview, philosophy, or metaphysic is informed by key categories derived from biblical materials. The biblical materials themselves are not a metaphysical system. However, they contain an implicit metaphysic or comprehensive view of reality. The biblical worldview is built upon the events recorded and interpreted in the biblical materials. Crucial categories which inform a biblical model of metaphysics are the categories of incarnation, personalism, singular history, creation, freedom, and purpose.

II. What Basic Considerations Undergird the Importance of Applying the Biblical Worldview to Life's Ultimate Questions?

1. The Universality of Faith Principles

Upon analysis, it is evident that all worldviews and philosophies are based on certain presuppositions and key ideas—either explicit or implicit. The key principle in a particular worldview or philosophy is derived predominantly from some specific and dominant type of experience which is in the individual's background —whether it be intellectual, aesthetic, moral, or religious.

Since there are so many key principles and experiences, there are many worldviews or religions or philosophies. In the secular world, for example, there are people who do not raise the ultimate questions of life from the standpoint of a transcendent reality. Furthermore, the resources for their solution are not found in a trans-human power such as the Holy breaking into life through special revelation, in sacred archetypes, or in an eternal order.

These secular people contend that they find the truth about themselves and the world in art, logic, scientific investigation, or political activities. These activities, they say, reveal "the way" to give their life significance and purpose.

But even such secular "solutions" to life's ultimate questions arise from a dominant experience. According to prominent British philosopher Dorothy Emmet, metaphysical theories or worldviews always involve judgment. These theories are compositions born in particular types of selective experience. The great philosophers, in other words, did not cast around looking for some interesting idea on which to construct a theory or worldview; rather, they were charged with a sense of the importance and significance of some spiritual or intellectual experience. The excitement of this experience drove them on to attempt to give intelligible form to other reaches of experience with reference to this basic insight or experience.[5]

Plato, for example, found his metaphysical key in an intuitive perception of the intelligible beauty of eternal forms. This key led Plato to emphasize the importance of geometry. But the excitement inspired by the contemplation of the beauty of pure form was not described by Plato in cold abstractions. Rather, his description took on the imaginative clothing of myth; to him, pure form became *eros* (desire love) moving between heaven and earth. For Plato, eternal patterns or forms were more real than the experienced forms of human life.

Aristotle drew his analogy from physiological desire, which he saw as a manifestation of the human drive toward completion. In terms of this view, the microcosm (particular) experience within the universe becomes an analogy of the macrocosm (universal) experience. For Aristotle, our basic drive in life is occasioned by the Prime Mover (God), because the Prime Mover is the supreme object of desire.

The key for René Descartes was found in his discoveries in coordinate geometry. Gottfried Wilhelm von Leibniz found his key idea in the algebraic model. For Kant, the key was the moral experience of obligation; for Herbert Spencer, it was evolution; for Samuel Alexander, it was the drive toward higher levels which he saw in nature.

In other words, according to Emmet, metaphysical theories are seeking to say something about the ways reality transcends experience in terms of the relations found *within* experience. As coordinating and unifying analogies, these theories or models seek to relate diverse types of experience by extension of a key idea derived from some predominant intellectual or spiritual experience or insight.

Claremont philosopher John Hutchison agrees with Emmet. He asserts that faith (in God or a substitute god) is universally human—that to act is to have faith in the assumptions on which one acts. There is thus a *faith principle* in every philosophy or worldview, in the precise sense that embedded in its foundation are some significant principles which the philosopher assumes rather than proves.

Modern logic has taught us that one cannot prove anything conclusively. Every proof or argument begins with certain assumptions or "primitive propositions." At times the thinker may not be aware of the assumptions which lie at the foundation of his system or worldview and which give decisive guidance to his thinking. But such lack of awareness does not prevent the assumptions from operating.

Some philosophies and worldviews give their faith principle more open or explicit expression than others. Some try to suppress their faith principle entirely, but such denial merely forces it underground, perhaps to be discovered by future generations. (Often in the history of thought the unconscious assumption of one philosopher becomes the object of critical study of another.)[6]

For Hutchison, this means that all philosophies, despite their claims to objectivity and openness, are actually theologies in disguise. Philosophers who disparage belief in the gods of specific theologies actually do so because of their previous commitment to the "reasonable" God of their own covert or hidden theology.[7]

All of this means that the individual thinker is logically prior to his thoughts.

Thought begins with the thinker who has faith principles, presuppositions, and key ideas.

In a broad sense, then, we can say that there are no psychological or philosophical atheists. All persons have a central loyalty or a key experience which gives them a framework of orientation—a "god," if you will.

2. The Validity of Acknowledging Faith Principles

What all this means in terms of life's ultimate questions is that it is not only valid, but also preferable, for a person to acknowledge frankly the peculiar presuppositions on which his or her viewpoint is based. When a person is frank about his or her presuppositions or key ideas that person is freed from a false need to be "objective" and will be able to address the basic questions of existence more effectively.

Gordon Kaufman contends that there is no thinking that does not emerge from a concrete point of view. This means that the Christian's admission of his point of view is more honest than, and just as valid as, many philosophers' claim to impartiality.[8]

According to William Hordern, analytic philosophy, which is prominent in philosophical circles today, is a valuable tool that can be used by Christians to show unbelievers the nature of their own "faith" commitment. Through the analysis of language, unbelievers can be shown that, despite their claim to be purely rational, their reasoning actually begins on a convictional basis—just as Christianity does.[9]

Following the approach suggested by Hordern, Claude Tresmontant, who is active in the National Center of Scientific Research in France, has shown that although Marxism claims to rest on positive (practical, provable, material) sciences alone, it makes assertions which are, strictly speaking, metaphysical and are beyond the assertions of positive science. For example, Marxism teaches formally and dogmatically that the world is uncreated, self-created, eternal, and impotent in time and space. To hold such a view is to take up a metaphysical position based on a faith presupposition.[10]

As we have indicated, no one can fail to take up a metaphysical position—whether explicitly or implicitly. If we search in the nooks and corners of the thought of a rationalist or positivist thinker, we will almost certainly find that latent philosophical assumptions soon appear. (For example, one person who claimed to be a rationalistic scientist revealed himself at heart to be something of a pantheist—one who identifies God with nature—as well as having a special attraction to Indian mysticism.) We can no more get away from metaphysics or a worldview based on faith than we can avoid living in a universe governed by such laws as gravitation.

3. The Need for a Distinct Biblical Worldview or Philosophy

If this is true, then it is clearly preferable to admit one's faith assumptions honestly and to examine what they mean in terms of how they speak to life's ultimate questions. From a Christian perspective, this means the conscious development of a distinct biblical philosophy or worldview.

This is especially important because the Bible contains certain important ideas that may not be adequately expressed at all in another metaphysic—for example, Platonism cannot do justice to the biblical ideas of creation and incarnation. Consequently, conversion to Christianity requires conversion to a biblical metaphysic or worldview.

A critical examination of how the biblical worldview approaches life's ultimate questions is also important because of the tendency for the distinctive biblical worldview to be distorted or confused by alien worldviews. This has happened many times over the centuries.

For example, Greek philosophy has so dominated Western thought that it has also penetrated much of Christian thinking and distorted many of our ideas about the biblical view. It is a self-contradiction, for example, to fuse Aristotle's idea of God—the Eternal Introvert, self-absorbed and self-contained—with the Hebrew view of a temporal creator, a busy interposing power who brings about righteousness in the hurly-burly of history, or with the Christian conception of a loving Father who shares in the grief of his children.[11] And yet many Christians are Aristotelian in their view of God simply because they have absorbed that outlook through their culture and have never questioned whether their view of God is truly biblical.

4. Evangelical Neglect in Developing a Distinctive Biblical Worldview

Richard Cunningham, while on sabbatical at Cambridge University in England, was introduced to an Anglican philosopher of religion by his title: Professor of Christian Philosophy at Southern Baptist Theological Seminary. The Cambridge philosopher replied wryly, "Oh! I didn't know Southern Baptists were interested in philosophy."[12]

Unfortunately, there is more truth than poetry in this statement. On the whole, evangelicals have resisted submitting the claims of their faith to the scrutiny of reason or developing a distinctive biblical worldview or philosophy.

There are several important reasons for this. One is that evangelical growth in the eighteenth and early nineteenth centuries was largely based on "awakenings" or "revivals" which tended to emphasize emotion and the will more than the intellect.[13] Then, beginning in the latter part of the nineteenth century, a second factor appeared—one which has dominated the intellectual energies of conservative thinkers up to the present day. This is the struggle over biblical inerrancy, occasioned by the development of post-Enlightenment critical methods and by an increase in our historical knowledge.[14]

In any case, many Christians who are gifted intellectually, and who have encountered God through faith, have rightly interpreted the Christian faith from the biblical revelation. However, because of the aforementioned factors, they have resisted subjecting their faith to any kind of philosophical reflection or aligning it with any philosophical point of view. They have emphasized religious language which is devotional and worshipful, and they have been satisfied with an inner assurance of the truth of their faith. Their Christian faith is primarily existential, engaged, committed, and involved. They are wary of any emphasis that would either assess their faith critically or seduce it into what they see as an abstract reflection by vain philosophy.[15]

There is still another reason why evangelicals have tended to neglect the development of a distinctive biblical worldview or philosophy: In many cases, they have been excluded (or excluded themselves) from the mainstream of philosophical thought.

In recent decades, influential philosophers have argued that it is unacceptable to attach the qualifier *Christian* or *biblical* to the words *worldview* or *philosophy* and have suggested that any Christian assumptions within the philosophical arena are improper. From this perspective, Christian philosophy is either theology masquerading as philosophy or corrupted philosophy. This group does recognize that there are Christians who are philosophers, but they contend that there is no distinctive Christian or biblical philosophy as such.[16]

The forerunners of this contemporary perspective are numerous in modern philosophy. For example, Descartes established philosophy on a rigorous rationalistic basis independent of the biblical revelation. David Hume, with his empirical skepticism, ruled out metaphysics and cognitive religious claims. Responding to Hume's challenge, Kant restricted knowledge to the phenomenal world—the world known by the senses. He held that we cannot know "things in themselves" or comprehend transcendent reality. Metaphysics and religious concepts, for Kant, had only a regulative purpose—that of providing a unified worldview or a basis for a practical moral life.

With certain exceptions such as Georg Hegel, most nineteenth-century Continental Christian thinkers, including Kierkegaard, Friedrich Schleiermacher, and Albrecht Ritschl, did not emphasize metaphysics or broad worldviews. And in the twentieth century, Analytical Philosophy, which has become a dominating force in Anglo-American thinking, has generally attempted to restrict philosophy to the task of analyzing our thought processes and language and has attacked the possibility of a broader worldview. This means that in many of the leading Western centers of philosophy, the philosophy departments have not made a place for Christian philosophizing or even for a broader approach to the philosophy of religion.[17]

I found this to be true when I investigated the Ph.D. program in philosophy at Harvard. In my interviews with philosophy department leaders, I found that they were primarily concerned with symbolic logic and language analysis. They had little concern for the broader metaphysical concerns—the ultimate questions—which were my primary interest. (The one exception in the Harvard philosophy department at that time was John Wild, who had broader metaphysical interests.)

In any case, because of their own attitudes and because of the dominant attitudes in philosophical circles, Christian scholars in general and evangelicals in particular have neglected the development of a biblical worldview or a philosophy adequate to their own background and vision. Could we not say that the entire Christian movement has thus been impoverished?[18]

III. What Is the Distinctive Nature of the Biblical Worldview or Philosophy?

British philosopher H. A. Hodges claims that in many cases the biblical worldview is not something non-Christians have seen and rejected, but something they have never seen—or have only glimpsed from afar. According to Hodges, an important challenge is to make the biblical worldview visible and to help people to see it as a distinctive and comprehensive way of seeing life and reality and answering life's ultimate questions.[19]

1. Definition of the Biblical Worldview or Philosophy

The biblical philosophy or metaphysic or worldview is the systematic development of one alternative in the philosophical, metaphysical, and religious quest. The Hebrew-Christian community, in the midst of many rival interpretations, was led to accept the teaching that God voluntarily revealed himself in mighty deeds and words through particular historical events and people.

G. Ernest Wright contends that this historical grounding is unique among religions—that the Bible is the witness to the only religious movement in history that centers its case squarely in history and its inspired interpretation. According to the biblical worldview, there is only one arena where ultimate meaning is to be found—the arena of the human struggle for civilization. Nature in itself does not contain ultimate meaning, although it can point to that meaning. Human beings cannot find authentic meaning through their elaborate attempts to get beyond or out of history. Rather, certain key events have been selected which are unique, remarkable, and unrepeatable—and which, when interpreted under divine inspiration, hold the clues to meaning.[20]

To a follower of Plato or to a believer in the Hindu worldview, the notion that ultimate reality can best be known through particular spatio-temporal occurrences is a contradiction and a scandal. The concern of a Platonic philosopher and of certain Hindu thinkers is to get away from the particulars and move into the realm of universal spirit.

According to the biblical worldview, however, a personal revelation through particular circumstances of time and space is the only way to become acquainted with the sovereign, free, and personal God and his purposes. Particularity, far from being a scandal, has the highest metaphysical credentials—for God himself is a particular, a Person. So, for the biblical worldview, the starting point is in revelation which comes through particulars—not through philosophical reasoning, religious intuition, divination, or human religious consciousness.

It is a biblical conviction that God entered history in divine acts and raised up men to interpret the significance of these acts. In the Old Testament we see the beginning of this revelation as the living God revealed himself, his will, and his way in contrast to the nature gods commonly worshiped in ancient times. A continuation and fulfillment of this revelation is seen in the New Testament, where the religions and philosophies of the day were either judged or transformed.

2. The Presuppositions of the Biblical Worldview

A careful study of the Bible emphasizes that despite its rich diversity it is based on a common set of presuppositions or philosophical assumptions. For example, the Bible is personal and not abstract. The primary emphasis from beginning to end is relations between persons, as seen in such key words as *purpose, loyalty, love*, and *promise*. The Bible is also personal in tone; it speaks with a richness of feeling that is very different from the abstract laws and structures of science. The ultimate priority in the Bible is what has been called the "life-world" or *Lebenswelt*. This attitude, which includes a concern for global meaning or transcendence, is only one example of the unique world of biblical attitudes, perceptions, and modes of understanding which we intend to explore.

Hodges contends that the *basic* presuppositions of the Bible could be united under the term *Abrahamic theism*. The New Testament insists again and again that Abraham is a model for Jew and Christian alike and that the true Christian is the spiritual child of Abraham. This means that the story of Abraham as interpreted in Romans and Hebrews gives us a standard by which our attitude toward life is to be regulated.[21]

Abraham was a man who committed himself unconditionally into the hands of God. This attitude presupposes a great deal. It presupposes not merely that God exists—a question which philosophers have debated at length—but also that he is of a certain character. It presupposes that God has control of the world and the course of events in it, that he exercises control in a purposeful way, and that human beings have a place in his design. Furthermore, it assumes God communicates with humans in ways which they can legitimately understand as commands and promises and by which their lives can be guided. This is the set of presuppositions that comprise Abrahamic theism. To work out the implications of this view in detail, showing how it applies to life's ultimate questions, is a basic concern of this study.[22]

According to Tresmontant, when Abraham left Ur of the Chaldees and ceased to worship the moon and the stars and sacrifice to the idols of his fathers, and when he started for a country which he knew not, he brought about what is seen by many as the greatest and most decisive revolution for the human race. Here we have an intellectual revolution, a liberation, an unprecedented act of free thought, and a rejection of pagan myth. Here is an effort to use reason under God's guidance—undoubtedly an important revolution.[23]

The pagan nations (then and now) sought the absolute or the divine in the material universe or in the invisible world. Israel knew that God must be sought elsewhere and in other ways. Israel alone among the nations dared to say that the world is not divine and not uncreated. Thought has never been so bold, so blasphemous, in relation to the ideas of the holy and the meaning of life then commonly held.[24]

3. The Importance of Defining and Preserving the Biblical Worldview

It should be helpful at this point to present the views of four representative Christian scholars on the constructive nature of the biblical worldview and its importance. It is noteworthy that they represent varied countries and backgrounds, but concur on the importance of developing and maintaining a distinctive biblical worldview.

(1) The Emphasis of Dooyeweerd. Herman Dooyeweerd, the late professor of the philosophy of law in Amsterdam, points out that historically the biblical worldview (in its New Testament form) was proclaimed in an intellectual world already deeply marked by Greek thinking, with its characteristically dualistic worldview. Some early Christians believed that the best alternative to the dominant way of thinking was to reject any relationship to secular thought. An extreme example was Tertullian's sharp distinction between Athens, standing for the wisdom of the world, and Jerusalem, standing for the wisdom that comes from God.

Because human reason ever seeks to assert its proclaimed autonomy, Dooyeweerd sees a continuing tendency for the Christian mind to accommodate itself to the world. This means that those who wish to remain true to the fullness of the biblical worldview must do more than properly relate their hearts to God; they must also seek a biblically directed global vision of the world and life. This means they must constantly guard against the dilution of biblical truth. It is important that those of us who seek to live under the biblical worldview commit ourselves to constantly reforming our thinking by consciously bringing it under the Word of God and allowing that Word itself to provide the framework out of which we develop our thought.[25]

(2) The Emphasis of Barth. Karl Barth, one of the twentieth century's most important Protestant theologians, stresses that the Christian worldview must come from the Bible and not from any ontological or philosophical system. Of course, Barth is well aware that no worldview is independent of philosophical assumptions—that when a human being starts to think or speak, he thinks or speaks philosophically. But Barth asserts that the philosophy must serve the purposes of the biblical worldview rather than dictating the nature or the form of the Christian perspective.[26]

When certain philosophical presuppositions distort the Christian worldview, says Barth, they must be avoided; in other words, philosophy is a good servant but a bad master. We must avoid foreign importations that would cause us to have the wrong cultural or philosophical preunderstanding. Although the Christian thinker cannot be free and detached from such preunderstanding, it is essential that the basic procedures and principles of the biblical worldview not depend on commitments that are not authenticated by Scripture.

(3) The Emphasis of Berkouwer. Gerrit C. Berkouwer, a well-known Dutch theologian, is even more sensitive than Barth to the dangers of using philosophical

categories which are alien to the biblical worldview. According to Berkouwer, each person who professes to follow the biblical worldview is to be judged in terms of the degree to which the Word of God controls and directs his thought, whatever the terminology may be.[27]

(4) The Emphasis of Niebuhr. Reinhold Niebuhr, a foremost American leader in the field of Christian ethics, stresses an understanding of and preservation of the essential Hebraic nature of the biblical worldview. The Christian worldview is commonly believed to be a joint product of Hebraic and Hellenic cultures. But as Niebuhr notes, this is true only in the sense that, beginning with the Johannine literature in the Bible, the Christian worldview sought to come to terms with the Greek concept of the permanent structure in things. This means that the Christian view embodies in its own life the permanent tension between the Greek and Hebraic ways of apprehending reality.

But this does not change the fact that when it is true to itself the Christian worldview is Hebraic rather than Hellenic. It believes in a personal God even though such a belief would be an embarrassment to the Greek philosophers. It has, as has Judaism, the sense of a covenant community based on commitments and memories of past revelations. It also relies on these historic revelations to penetrate the divine mystery rather than upon an analysis of the permanent or "eternal" structures from which the temporal events flow.

The Christian worldview is, therefore, Hebraic rather than Hellenic in its essence, even though in popular piety the Greek idea of the immortality of the soul has usurped the Hebraic idea of "resurrection of the body."[28]

4. The Historicity of the Biblical Worldview

(1) The Emphasis of Albright. Undergirding what we have seen about the distinctive biblical worldview is the work of the late William Foxwell Albright, who stressed the historical context of the biblical worldview. Albright, a prominent archaeologist associated with Johns Hopkins University, claimed that the literature of the Bible is unique in the world's cultural history in that it builds its worldview on God's revelation in a people's history as interpreted theologically. Here is presented not a God of philosophy who is to be comprehended solely in terms of general principles expounded by a reasoned logic, but a God of history—one who is to be known primarily in the testimony to his activity which biblical people saw as the explanation for their own history.[29]

The knowledge of the biblical God is therefore "historical" knowledge. It is best expressed in the dialogue of events and in the revealed understanding of the meaning of the human struggle in the otherwise meaningless chaos of human triumph and defeat, war and peace, righteousness and unrighteousness.

This concept of revelation in history led Israel to preserve, to collect and ultimately to write down her historical traditions. The Israelites were the first people in world history so to do in this fashion. Israel's knowledge of God, therefore, led her to an interest in history. This was true because God had chosen the forms of history as the way in which he revealed himself to her.[30]

Biblical archaeology is a research tool of the historian who wishes to fit our knowledge of biblical literature squarely within the context of its time, its geography, its climate, and its historical and cultural setting. This means that the biblical literature then becomes an integral, not a separate, part of human history. The work of biblical archaeologists has borne remarkable fruit in our time. Biblical teaching has been revolutionized. The Old Testament particularly has taken on fresh and exciting life as a piece of insightful literature.[31]

All of this means that the biblical worldview is inseparable from history. This fact requires of the careful student an act of self-transcendence whereby he or she can reconstruct and participate in both the biblical events and their interpretation. In more traditional language, this means that the biblical student must comprehend both the Event and the Word which expounds it.[32]

The basic thing that can be said about the God of the Bible concerns his historical actions. Through these actions and an inspired interpretation of their meaning, he has created a new people who have placed acknowledgment of his sovereignty and calling to his service as the meaning and content of their life. There is no other realm of knowledge except the historical available to us whereby this God is to be known. This means that the first thing to be said about God is the "historicity" and "time-full" character of the knowledge that we have of him. The Bible is the basic testimony to this new reality and the fountain of the religious movements that have emerged from that reality.

This revelation that comes to us from the Bible cannot be characterized primarily as a *torah* (law) or as a logical treatise. It also cannot be seen as an otherworldly mythology encased within an outmoded geography of the universe. Instead, the historical character of the Bible and its revelatory events strike deep within the human soul at the springs of human action. The Bible thus brings about a comprehensive vision and a restructuring of the self within a new historical community.[33]

Thus we see why the confession of God's activity in the Bible must not be wrenched apart from history; to do so would leave it almost completely a cultic myth divorced radically from concrete reality. Our interest in the "facts" of the Bible is not to be dismissed as foolish historicism or a pedestrian preoccupation with "facts"; we should not be embarrassed by wanting to know exactly what happened. We must not allow the "history of salvation" to become nonhistorical or resort to a certain type of subjective existentialism in order to make the Bible relevant.

If we follow the Bible, history cannot be evaded. The question of humankind's crucial problems and existential concerns can never be solved apart from the context of society, history, and the struggle of civilization to be civilized—all of which we find in the Bible. The sovereignty and revelation of God in the biblical context is encountered precisely in this wide human and historical context.[34]

(2) The Emphasis of Cohen and Heschel. The work of Arthur A. Cohen and Abraham Heschel underscore Albright's emphasis on the historicity of the biblical worldview.

For Cohen, the biblical faith affirms that God is manifested in history through the transmitted word—both the unforgettable memories rehearsed in worship and the written legacy. God is never manifested in generalities. He may be transcendent and distant, but he is always a God of history. The biblical view is thus related to sacred history or covenant people. As biblical people, we set ourselves to follow the God who has revealed himself to us in time and history and inspired words.[35]

Abraham Heschel points out that the biblical prophets did not speak of "being" and "becoming" and "form" and other generalities, as did many of the Greek philosophers. Rather, the prophets gave orations about widows and orphans, about the corruption of judges, about the affairs of the marketplace. Some might feel that the prophets were thus making much ado about paltry things and using excessive language about trifling subjects. Some would ask what it matters if somewhere in ancient Palestine poor people have not been treated properly by the rich. So what if some elderly women found pleasure and edification in worshiping the "queen of heaven"? Why such immoderate excitement? Why such intense indignation? The answer is that God reveals himself through such concrete stuff. The biblical worldview deals with universals through particulars.[36]

According to the biblical view, as opposed to the view of the Greeks, human beings know God by a direct encounter in history. God is not a static being whom we come to know by discursive argument. Rather, God meets men and women in history as a living personal God who lays claim on them. We know God as we respond to his revelation in Event and Word. Saving knowledge comes by the obedience of faith, by will, and not just by reasoning. As men do the will of God, they know (John 7:17). Such knowledge is brought to a focus in Jesus Christ, in whom God personally enters history to redeem us from our self-centeredness and sin.

5. The Narrative and Cultural/Linguistic Nature of the Biblical Worldview

(1) Story Emphasis. The concepts which constitute the biblical worldview are related in narrative or story form. Many today believe Auguste Comte was wrong when he said that science supersedes a religion which comes to us in the story form.

Enlightenment thinkers such as Comte believed civilization had outgrown stories—that narratives are irrelevant to truth and truth is irrelevant to narratives.[37] In contrast to such thinking, today there is a strong emphasis among responsible biblical scholars on Christian narrative theology. This emphasis undertakes to explore and proclaim the stories of Christianity.

For such an approach, the first task is to uncover the stories which show what the biblical key words mean. But the narrative theologian emphasizes not the doctrines of the Bible, but the narratives which form those doctrinal traditions.[38]

According to Roman Catholic scholar Terrence Tilley, human experience is inherently durational or time-oriented. If this is true, how can we talk about our experience? The answer fits perfectly: in narratives. Because stories portray experience in and through time, stories are the most fitting way to tell of human experience.[39]

(2) Importance of the Cultural/Linguistic Framework. George Lindbeck, the prominent Yale professor, contends that a religion such as Christianity should be viewed as a cultural and/or linguistic framework or medium that shapes the entirety of life and thought. Like a cultural language, the biblical religion is a communal phenomenon that shapes the subjectivities of individuals. It comprises a vocabulary of discursive (explicit) and nondiscursive (ritual, etc.) symbols, together with a distinctive logic or grammar in terms of which this vocabulary can be meaningfully utilized.[40]

The primary function of the Bible, from Lindbeck's perspective, is to reveal the character and to offer an identity description of an agent, namely God. The Bible does this not by telling what God is in and of himself, but by recounting the interaction of his deeds and purposes with those of humans in their ever-changing circumstances. These accounts reach their climax in what the Gospels say of the risen, ascended, and ever-present Jesus Christ, whose identity as the divine-human agent is enacted in the stories of Jesus of Nazareth. The climax, however, is logically inseparable from what precedes it. The Jesus of the Gospels is the Son of the God of Abraham, Isaac, and Jacob.[41]

The primary focus in the Bible is not on God's being in and of itself, for that is not what the text of the Bible is primarily about. Rather, the focus is cultural—it is on how life is to be lived in the realities of this world in the light of God's character—as this is pictured in the stories of Israel and of Jesus. The intention of the perspectives obtained from the biblical worldview should in every case be to describe life and reality in ways conformable to what these stories as a whole indicate about God and his purpose.[42]

For example, the biblical view calls for churches that will socialize their members into an outlook which supports concern for others rather than just for individual rights and entitlements. Churches should also emphasize a sense of responsibility for the wider society rather than just for personal fulfillment.

(3) The Role of the Biblical Worldview in Shaping the Cultural Future. Cultural historians point out that the Bible has shaped the imagination of Western civilization. If this is true, then the West's continuing imaginative vitality and creativity may well depend upon the existence of Christians and churches for whom the Bible is not simply a classic among others, but the definitive and guiding dynamic of their lives.

This means that, in the long run, those who represent the biblical worldview will be practically relevant to the degree that they do not first ask what is either practical or relevant, but instead concentrate on their own biblical outlook and form of life. Although practical efficacy is not the priority purpose of the biblical faith, practical and effective good works of unforeseeable kinds flow from faithfulness to the biblical faith. It was these good works rather than an intentional effort that caused biblical religion to help produce democracy and science as well as other values which we treasure in the West. In a similar unplanned way, biblical religion can help save the world civilization from the demonic corruption of these same values.[43]

Lindbeck concludes his emphasis by stating that becoming a Christian involves learning the story of Israel and Jesus well enough to interpret and experience oneself in one's world in terms of that story. Biblical religion is above all an external influence that molds and shapes the self and individual experience, rather than an expression of a preexisting self or a preconceptual experience.[44]

Lindbeck also emphasizes that the cognitive or intellectual aspect of biblical religion, while important, is not primary. The proclamation of the gospel, as a Christian would put it, is first of all the telling of the story; explaining or analyzing the story is secondary. However, this proclamation gains power and meaning insofar as it is embodied in the total dynamics of community life and action—including cognitive activity.[45]

The biblical worldview thus constitutes a unified view that provides an approach and answer to life's ultimate questions. According to Hodges, the biblical worldview is a considerably more far-reaching system of ideas than non-Christians or indeed many Christians realize, and it cannot be expressed, explained, or defended in a few words. By "far-reaching," Hodges means that it makes a difference to our overall conception of reality—not merely of certain aspects of our existence. If a person becomes a Christian, his or her entire conceptual framework will be altered first; changes of detail will follow from this.

Even nature will be seen differently—not that Christians have different formulae for the laws of nature, but that Christians have different ideas of what these laws represent. The same is true of all human activities and values. Thus the adoption of the biblical worldview represents a total change—intellectual as well as moral.[46]

Because this is true, according to Lindbeck, the method we should use in presenting the biblical worldview resembles ancient catachetical teaching more than modern translation. Instead of redescribing the faith in new concepts, this method seeks to teach the original language and practices of the religion to potential adherents.

Pagan converts in the early centuries did not, for the most part, first completely understand the faith and then decide to become Christians. Rather, they first decided, and *then* they understood. They were first attracted by the Christian community and form of life. When they made their commitment, they submitted themselves to prolonged instruction in which they practiced new modes of behavior and learned the stories of Israel and the fulfillment of these stories in Christ.[47]

From Lindbeck's perspective, today many of the churches which profess to hold the biblical worldview accommodate the prevailing culture rather than shape it. They cater to majority trends. This makes it difficult for the churches to attract serious students even from among their own children.

Thus it is important for Christians, if they would fulfill God's purposes and even survive, to form communities that strive without traditional rigidity to cultivate and understand the biblical worldview and learn to act accordingly. As we shall see, one of the important tests of the adequacy of the biblical worldview is in the area of performance. The ultimate way of testing the merits and demerits of the biblical worldview is performance.[48]

IV. What Are the Essential Features of the Distinctive Biblical Approach to Reality Which Have Implications for a Comprehensive Worldview or Philosophy?

The Bible has several emphases which have philosophical or worldview implications. In considering these, however, we must remember that the biblical philosopher does not have the same responsibilities as a theologian. He is not primarily doing the detailed dogmatic work of the theologian. Rather, he finds certain basic ideas within the biblical revelation to be philosophically valuable because they allow him to deal constructively with various broad and ultimate concerns. The biblical philosopher thus seeks to use revealed ideas philosophically and attempts to justify them for their philosophical power.[49]

Leonard Hodgson has noted that philosophically potent ideas may come from religious prophets as well as from professional philosophers. To dismiss an idea because it may originate in the biblical revelation is to commit the genetic fallacy (downplay an idea because of its origin). The basic question about any philosophic insight is not where it comes from, but whether it more fully illuminates, interprets, and integrates life's ultimate questions. The work of the biblical philosopher, like that of any other philosopher, must be judged on its own philosophic merits or weaknesses.[50]

1. Teachings Related to the Nature of Humankind

The biblical view sees humans as made in God's image, with the capacity to respond to God and live in fellowship with him. Even though men and women have used their freedom to rebel against God and thus are fallen creatures, they are still responsible; their humanity has not ceased to exist.

However, human reason is distorted. Furthermore, humanity's problem is basically rebellion against God, not just ignorance. The cross of Christ, which provides the key to the whole pattern of biblical events, is a revelation of this rebellious and sinful state. This means that neither argumentation nor good works, neither discursive logic nor moral righteousness, can deliver men and women from sinful pride. Sin is not just bound up with a person's sensuous nature; it penetrates the inner sanctuary of the spirit. Human beings cannot escape their love of self, and they consequently find themselves prisoners of their own egocentrism.[51]

2. Teachings Relating to the Nature of God

The dominant biblical teaching about God is that he must be conceived as fully personal. Throughout the Bible there are detailed descriptions of the personal nature of God, including his personal will and purpose in the acts of creation and redemption. The Incarnation is the unique and final disclosure of

God's personal nature, as well as the unveiling of the true personal being of humankind.

The dynamic living God revealed in the Bible is in marked contrast to the static "God of Pure Being" expounded in many classic philosophical systems.[52]

3. Teachings Related to the Doctrine of Creation

Creation out of nothing is basic to biblical thought. In the biblical view, God is not conditioned by preexistent material or by creative patterns independent of himself from which he chooses in creating.

The doctrine of creation out of nothing also draws a sharp distinction between God and the world. It clarifies that the world is not an overflow from God's nature, but distinct from him and made by him. The biblical view thus dismisses both pantheism (the belief that God and nature are one) and dualism (the belief that reality is made up of two opposing forces, as good and evil, God and Satan), which will not ultimately be reconciled as acceptable views. Creation out of nothing also points to a personal mystery in God that cannot be contained in human or empirical (experience-based) categories.[53]

The biblical view of creation stresses God's sovereignty over the physical process and its total dependence upon him. It points to the transcendence of God, which must not be obscured by any view of his immanence.

A corollary of creation out of nothing is continuous creation. This points toward God's continuing acts of historical creativity.[54]

4. Teachings Related to the Doctrine of Knowledge

When it comes to knowing God in a saving relationship, the Christian begins not with rational arguments or mystical experience, but rather with a confrontation in human history. God has not chosen to disclose the depths and fullness of himself as the end point of a rational argument or in a mystical identification available in unredeemed humanity's subjective depths. Instead, he has chosen to make his final revelation of himself in and through certain particular historical events. These include an exodus of a slave people from Egypt and the vicissitudes of their subsequent history as interpreted through the prophetic consciousness. And his climactic act of disclosure was incarnational—he chose to reveal himself through the life, death, and resurrection of an humble carpenter.[55]

E. Y. Mullins, the prominent Southern Baptist theologian of the first half of the twentieth century, once challenged the followers of Scottish Common-Sense Realism who implied that human reason comes before faith or revelation. Mullins conceded that human rational ability is generally trustworthy in many areas of life. However, in relation to the ultimate issues of life, reason is so clouded by rebellion and sin that it must have special revelation.[56]

In the biblical view, the knowledge of God is found in obedience to God's personal revelation. The personal self-disclosure of God in revelatory events must be received by men and women in faith, which involves the will as well as the mind and emotions. This response of the whole person is expressed in a person's life and produces changed patterns of living.

5. Teachings Related to the Doctrine of History

The Bible has a strong emphasis upon the significance and the purposive nature of history. The divine purposes in history grow out of God's nature—his personal love and concern. God's personal purpose determines the way he relates to his personal creatures in and through the historical process.[57]

The biblical view, however, does not make history the ultimate reality. History is not synonymous with God, and its process is not regarded as the development of the divine life. God is immanently active in history, but he is also other than and beyond history.[58]

6. Teachings Related to Ethics

Morality from the biblical perspective is empowered and guided by a covenant relationship with a holy and loving God. Ethical decisions are made in relation to the principles found in God's progressive revelation to man as recorded in the Bible and centered in Jesus Christ. Related themes are intentional community and voluntarism. Voluntarism and freedom of worship imply that the church and state should be separate.

For a biblical philosopher, these biblical emphases need to be organized in a way that will construct a distinctive worldview or philosophy. It makes no sense to think of convinced men and women living lives based upon their shared convictions, yet engaging in no reflection upon them. We must combat the wrong kind of anti-intellectualism, which has recurred from earliest times in Christianity and has often characterized evangelicals. Of course, differing contexts and methods provide a lively dialogue even among those who in some measure share the biblical vision.[59]

V. How Can Evangelicals Develop the Biblical Teachings into a Comprehensive Worldview or Philosophy Which Deals with Ultimate Questions?

1. The Appropriateness of Identifying a Biblical Worldview or Philosophy

It is important to note that the biblical approach to ultimate questions has much in common with the approaches of other constructive philosophers who share the perennial philosophical concerns—life's ultimate questions.

Philosophy has traditionally concerned itself with two different tasks—the critical and the constructive. The *critical* task emphasizes a range of questions concerning the relationship of our thought and language to reality, truth, and fact. It involves analyzing our intellectual tools and thinking processes.[60]

On the other hand, the traditional *constructive* task of philosophy seeks to integrate all of our knowledge in an inclusive and comprehensive understanding of reality. As I have indicated, much modern philosophy has ignored or minimized the constructive task and confined itself to a critical role; for example, analytical philosophy has largely restricted philosophy to the critical analysis of language. But biblical philosophy calls for the Christian to think constructively as well as critically—to consider the inclusive dimensions of existence and being, including life's ultimate questions.[61]

As I have also indicated, biblical philosophers venture beyond the work of most theologians in that they seek to deal with life's ultimate or broad questions —those related to science, culture, world religions, and other areas of experience that are of interest to philosophy. The biblical philosopher will also deal with the question of truth in relation to the religious experience of humanity and the total sweep of human experience. He will seek to show the explanatory power of the biblical worldview in the larger context of ontology (the study of the nature of being) and metaphysics.[62]

We have already pointed out that some seventeenth- and eighteenth-century thinkers, as well as some contemporary secular philosophers, question the idea of a distinctly Christian or biblical philosophy. This concern has even been raised by Christian thinkers.

The Yale philosopher, John Smith, himself a Christian, has some misgivings about a so-called biblical or Christian philosophy. He wonders if there is a unique Christian approach to central philosophical issues and questions.[63]

Smith is at least partially correct in that the prefix *Christian* or *biblical* is not significant for many areas of philosophy. There is no specifically Christian logic, philosophy of science, philosophy of economics, aesthetics, and so forth. However, the biblical worldview has implications for any one of these areas.[64]

In contrast to Smith, however, it is our contention that many philosophical or ultimate questions may be illuminated by assumptions and insights taken from the biblical revelation. To call this approach biblical philosophy is not basically different from identifying other individual philosophies by the commonalities they share in a general philosophical method—empirical, analytical, naturalistic, idealistic, and so forth. The qualifiers clearly indicate that such philosophies work within distinctive methodological parameters.[65]

2. The Unity and Uniqueness of the Biblical Worldview

Today we are much more aware of the theological diversity of the Bible than we once were. As a result of this diversity, some scholars suggest that many different philosophies appear in the Bible, and that to select one of them and label it "biblical" is arbitrary.

A leading spokesman for a biblical philosophy is Edmond L. Cherbonnier of Trinity College in Connecticut. Cherbonnier contends that there is a basic metaphysical unity in the Bible. He examines the unspoken philosophical assumptions which the Bible makes when it is not talking philosophy at all, which is a large percentage of the time. When these assumptions are examined, they comprise a remarkably consistent worldview spanning over a thousand years and including scores of writers. It is this overall unity of philosophical or metaphysical outlook which can be designated as "biblical."[66]

Cherbonnier also affirms that the biblical worldview is unique, and he offers six key points in which the biblical description differs from the classical Greek or Hindu perspectives.

First, God is pictured as a free agent in interaction with other real free agents. This emphasis upon free agents can be seen in three ways. God is a definite agent who takes purposeful, determinative action—as seen in the salvation events recorded in the Bible. The biblical God is also shown to be a free agent in that he is portrayed as a "Being among other beings." An abstract entity beyond particularity does not exercise freedom. Another way God is pictured as a free agent is in the Bible's use of anthropomorphic language—talking of God in human terms. This anthropomorphic language highlights the types of activities in which a free agent engages.[67]

In the *second* place, in the biblical worldview, the knowledge of God is not immediate. It must be mediated to man by God or by one of his agents.

Third, salvation as portrayed in the Bible is not simply the realization of an already existent state of identity with God.

Fourth, the individual who is saved is not involved in an isolated experience which has no ramifications for others.

Fifth, love is not the desire for unity, that is, only the longing toward identity with God. Rather, love is the dynamic for the relation between singular persons. Love does not just seek to merge the self in a mystical relation with God. Rather, love leads to an outgoing relationship to others in fellowship and service.

The *sixth* emphasis is probably the most incompatible point in relation to the Greek view. It affirms that in the Bible intellectual "knowing" is not primary. Knowing is conditioned by another factor: the will. Thus, the important element in knowledge is not the identity of subject and object, but the orientation of the heart and the will of the knower.[68]

John Wild of Harvard, Northwestern, and Yale undergirds the emphasis of Cherbonnier. He points out how the Greek tradition is deeply ingrained in our psyche and how it tends to subordinate personal faith in the concrete world of human existence to the objective universe of reason. This Greek view is poignantly expressed in Plato's famous image of the cave, in which the temporal world is compared to a gloomy underground cavern and concrete experience is compared to a fleeting succession of shadows that poorly reflect the "real life" of eternal forms or ideas.[69]

In the light of this understanding, we can better understand Paul's bitter condemnation of "philosophy and vain deceit" (Col. 2:8) and "the wisdom of this world" (1 Cor. 1:20). These passages are not condemnations of philosophical understanding in general, as they are often supposed to be. Rather, Paul was opposing the pretentious claims of Greek rationalism which was the dominant philosophy of his time. According to Paul's biblical understanding, this Greek transcendental claim of reason was pure foolishness.[70]

3. The Call for Comprehension and Appropriation of the Biblical Worldview

The biblical worldview requires that we become deeply involved historically. This includes an intellectual and volitional involvement in Israel's history amidst the imperialistic struggles of the ancient nations and in the life of the early Christian church, as well as in our own time and history. There is no "beyond" to which we can go for primary knowledge. There is no arena of logic which contains or adequately states the case. There is no mystical exercise which by itself alone provides the key to understanding. We know God by participating in his purposes and making the biblical worldview our own.

The Bible as historical testimony does not exhaust or even penetrate the mystery of ultimate power and meaning. Yet it does claim to reveal God as he would be known as our God. As such, the Bible serves as a pair of spectacles—not to see all knowledge, but to see meaning, value and purpose by faith in what otherwise would be meaningless, valueless confusion.[71]

4. The Usefulness of Certain Aspects of Other Philosophical Systems

The biblical worldview is both distinct and unique. However, it is possible for the biblical philosopher to selectively utilize, while critically evaluating from a biblical worldview perspective, certain aspects of philosophical systems developed since the ancient Greek period—ideas which coordinate with or are complementary to the biblical worldview. Chief among these systems are idealism, materialism, naturalism, existentialism, and process thought.

(1) Idealism, Materialism, and Naturalism. A generation ago, leaders assumed that idealist philosophies (those emphasizing that the basic reality is spirit) were the most appropriate vehicles for expressing biblical truth. Recent work among religious thinkers has questioned this approach and reappraised the religious value of other philosophies, such as naturalism (the view that nature is all-inclusive) and materialism. These schools of thought have taught us much about the irreducible reality and significance of time and matter. This reappraisal has come precisely at the moment when a new reading of the Bible and its view of life have underscored the same themes.

As has been recently shown, the biblical worldview, in its emphasis upon the reality and importance of all aspects of creation, advocates a *relative* materialism.[72] In fact, idealism's distinction between appearance and reality is closer to the views of Oriental religions and Greek philosophies than to the biblical religion, which is metaphysically realistic in its outlook. However, many systems of idealism do contain the concepts of freedom and responsibility, which do better justice to the facts of human life than the frequently naïve views of some forms of naturalism and materialism.

Far from undermining the distinctiveness of the biblical worldview, the new understanding of its relationship with other philosophies actually undergirds our affirmation of the uniqueness and importance of the biblical emphases. The biblical worldview includes the valid truths of many of the alternative philosophies and worldviews of our time. Furthermore, it combines them in a unique way which is appropriate to a revealed and normative worldview.

Nevertheless, if we take biblical concepts as the foundation of our metaphysical view of reality, other popular worldviews must be excluded—at least in their totality. For example, even though the biblical worldview might utilize certain naturalistic elements, a completely naturalistic worldview must be excluded. This is true because such a view restricts reality to the system of observable nature and restricts possible occurrences within reality to what conforms with its fixed laws. Materialism as a total view is even more emphatically opposed by biblical revelation. Also, most forms of idealisms are excluded because they tend to deny the reality of the material world and the transcendence of God.[73]

(2) Realism, Subjective Idealism, and Existentialism. Perhaps the most compatible type of metaphysic as far as the biblical worldview is concerned is some form of realism—one that includes a supernatural dimension rather than limiting itself to nature.

It must be emphasized that the biblical worldview has a basic objectivism—it assumes that there are objective measures of the true, the good, and the right. The God who is the center of the worldview revealed in Scripture is capable of emotion and action, but he is also fully perfect and complete and thus in a sense unchanging. This means that his nature and revelation reflect norms and values that have permanence. Love, truth, and honesty are enduringly good. This is true because they correspond to the unchanging nature of God.

The biblical worldview also sees truth as unitary. God and reality are what they are, independent of anyone's perceiving, understanding, appreciating, or accepting them. The knower's reaction to truth is important, but the truth is not dependent upon that reaction. This excludes any type of extreme subjective idealism, as well as certain aspects of existentialism. The reason for this exclusion is the fact that some versions of these views place too much emphasis on a person's subjective ability or right to determine truth apart from the objective truth related to God.

John Macquarrie believes that there are several major philosophical perspectives available today from which Christians can learn. He feels that Heidegger's brand of existentialism, in particular, proposes a view which, of all current Western reflections on man, stands nearest to the Christian doctrine of man. However, Macquarrie does qualify this claim, for Heidegger does not speak of God or humankind as the Bible does.[74]

In an earlier generation, E. Y. Mullins showed the ability to weigh emerging philosophies in order to sift out the good and discard the useless as he "redeemed" those new ideas and methods for Christian purposes. He was careful not to identify himself unreservedly with every contemporary philosophical movement. However, he was willing to admit special indebtedness to a particular viewpoint or thinker.[75]

(3) Process Thought. For the past forty years, there has been a group of Christian thinkers in this country engaged in the task of interpreting Christianity by

the use of such concepts as "becoming," "process," "change," "participation," "organic," "emergence," and "the dynamic." Known as process theologians, these thinkers have adopted their technical terms from the process philosophy of Alfred North Whitehead.

Christian philosopher Eric Rust affirms their efforts to deal seriously with the universe as a dynamic process. Rust appreciates their concept of interrelatedness, their openness to novelty and future creative possibilities, and their rejection of a mind-matter dualism. He also finds some contributions in the process descriptions of God as operating within the dynamic process of the universe through the persuasion of love, and the dynamic nature of the divine perfection which allows God to be enriched by the natural process.

But at the same time, Rust levels criticism at some of the basic categories of the process thinkers. He especially criticizes the Whiteheadians' use of an organic rather than a personal model, claiming that this organic model creates problems for their understanding of God and of human personhood. Their stress on God's immanence and the organic nature of God does not make a sufficient distinction between God and the world. And their disavowal of an absolute creation makes it difficult for them to preserve the balanced values of the biblical view. (Whitehead, for example, postulates creativity as a primordial reality and then defines God and the world as mutually necessary—God requires the process quite as much as the process requires God.) In this sense, process thought offers only a finite God rather than one who is absolute over creation. He is a God who directs but does not create the process.[76]

Although Whitehead seems to leave open the possibility of personal immortality, he more explicitly speaks of human persons enduring only as memories within the ongoing becoming of God. A biblical personal conception of God and man requires more than that.[77]

VI. What Are Representative Methods of Comparing the Validity of the Various Worldviews?

In an increasingly pluralistic world, it is important to establish methods of comparing worldviews and ways of undergirding our conviction concerning the normativity and superiority of the biblical worldview.

If we grant that the biblical worldview and other worldviews are unique, each with its own autonomous context of meaning, which of the distinctive worldviews, religions, or philosophical systems is the most adequate? What are the criteria for establishing the validity of a worldview? And why would we accept the biblical worldview rather than other alternatives?

Admittedly, factors other than rational ones are important in leading people to build their lives around a certain worldview. But these factors do not displace the necessity of sound reasoning. Even though religious commitment is passionate, it should not dispense with careful reasoning. Even the apostle Paul, an ardent partisan of the biblical worldview, made it clear that he was "appointed for the defense of the gospel" (Phil. 1:16).[78]

Through the centuries there have been notable leaders who have sought to establish the superiority of the biblical worldview in their own particular contexts. Notable are Justin the Martyr and Tertullian in the second century, Augustine in the fifth century, Anselm and Aquinas in the Middle Ages. In their own way the sixteenth-century Reformers were apologists for the biblical worldview. In the seventeenth and eighteenth centuries, Blaise Pascal and Joseph Butler were influential.[79]

The twentieth century has also seen notable Christian scholars who have set forth methods of comparing and evaluating alternative worldviews. These modern apologists usually ask the following questions about a worldview: Does the view fit the facts? Does it make sense? Does it have individual and cultural relevance? Does it adequately answer life's basic and ultimate questions?[80]

It should be helpful at this point to describe the methods of some representative twentieth-century apologists. Most of these scholars utilize the verification method, which involves both logical consistency and factual adequacy. They also point out that an adequate view must satisfy the whole person, not just certain aspects of existence. It must also meet people's deepest psychological needs and resolve their moral predicament.[81]

1. The Method of Carl F. H. Henry

According to Henry, every worldview begins with certain presuppositions or assumptions. Some assumptions are more adequate than others, and all assumptions are subject to consistent investigation by reasonable minds.

Henry's guiding instrument for separating adequacy or truth from inadequacy or error is the law of noncontradiction, a basic law of logic since the days of Aristotle. On this basis, Henry insists that the most promising first principle for any thought system is Christian theism. In the Bible, God has given us a revelation of himself which, when examined by the laws of reason, stands up better than any other basic assumption. From Henry's perspective, furthermore, by using the law of noncontradiction, all nonevangelical stances can be shown to be contradictory and therefore false.[82]

Henry also affirms that Christianity alone can resolve the individual's moral predicament.[83] In the social area he claims that Christianity alone can furnish adequate moral standards and moral power.[84]

2. The Method of Arthur Holmes

Respected Wheaton College philosopher Arthur Holmes contends that philosophers draw the "root metaphors" of their perspectives from some common area of human experience. For example, some use mechanistic, idealist, or organismic models. For the Christian, meaning is disclosed most fully and clearly not in some universal form of ordinary experience, but in the unique event, recorded in the Bible, of the Incarnation. New Testament writings elaborate on an enriched conception of God and of man and history that is made possible by Christ's coming. It is this perspective, subjectively embraced in believing, that the Christian philosopher deliberately confesses in his metaphysical explorations.[85]

For Holmes, there are three basic criteria of truth. First is a criterion of *personal disclosure value*. Does a particular worldview open up a new understanding of the meaning of life and the purpose of life and history?

Second is a criterion of *empirical fit*. The perspective one lives with must do more than give personal disclosure value; it must also fit the facts of experience and fit them well.

The third criterion is that of *logical coherence*. An adequate philosophical or worldview perspective must have power to integrate, to reveal the oneness in the many and to show intelligible order in diversity and change.

In addition to these three criteria of truth, Holmes suggests that faith and devotion are not to be coerced by argument. They are rather to be brought out by the witness of God's Spirit to the bearing of Jesus Christ and the gospel on the felt needs of a person. If a person is to know God for himself, it will be a response to God's personal disclosure which goes beyond the communication and proclamation of truth and involves the application of divine grace to man's deepest needs.[86]

3. The Method of Cherbonnier

Cherbonnier contends that to affirm the uniqueness of the biblical worldview is not to deny its reasonableness. In fact, the way to preserve the uniqueness of the biblical worldview is precisely to demonstrate its superior reasonableness. However, to show the biblical view superior requires the use of the enduring contributions of the Greek genius to human thought. In other words, the principles of clarity, coherence, and consistency must be utilized.[87]

The primary function of the biblical worldview and of biblical language is to convey the truth concerning the things of God's revelation so that this truth might be known by human beings. But these concepts, "know" and "the truth," must be understood within the biblical perspective. For a primary function of biblical language is related to knowledge. The biblical view of knowledge emphasizes knowledge of a person, not just abstract knowledge that comes through sensory experience. It should be noted, however, that the biblical revelation does not have its basic foundation in myth, because it has a strong referential function which distinguishes it from myth. It primarily refers to the redemptive acts of God in history.

In the biblical vocabulary, the presupposition of the existence of God is not questioned. But the Bible does give a valid type of verification of its worldview —not a scientific verification in the narrow sense, but an existential or experiential verification that comes through confrontation with a Person. This is a verification which is consistent with the basic premises of the biblical faith. Whether we wish to call this "empirical" or experience-based with John Macmurray is a matter of little consequence if we recognize that the term *experience* is broader than just sensory experience.

4. The Method of Frederick Ferre

But is there a way to evaluate worldviews or metaphysical systems more systematically? Frederick Ferre, well known in American philosophical circles for his work in philosophy of religion, believes there are both internal and external criteria which can be used. Internal criteria relate to the internal structure of the worldview itself. External criteria relate to ways practical life is influenced by the worldview.

The first of the internal criteria is *consistency*—the absence of logical contradiction among the symbols in the system. Consistency is a necessary but not a sufficient condition for acceptance of a metaphysical system.

The second internal criterion is *coherence*. It is not sufficient for the symbols in a system merely to be consistent; they must also be coherent. Coherence means a genuine unity and an interrelatedness—an absence of fragmentation—among the components of a system.

In addition, if the biblical worldview or any other worldview is to be judged as empirically meaningful, it must meet external criteria. The first external criterion is *applicability*. A view must be capable of illuminating experience naturally and without distortion. It must ring true to life.

But beyond applicability is a second external criterion—*adequacy*. A worldview must in theory be capable of accounting for *all* possible experience. A view which can tie together a large sweep of experience with less distortion than an alternative view must be graded higher and hence be regarded as preferable to the other. An adequate worldview will be able on the basis of its key concepts to interpret all experience without oversight, distortion, or the need to explain certain discrepancies away.[88]

5. The Method of Dorothy Emmet

Dorothy Emmet echoes Ferre in contending that certain criteria can be applied to justify holding a particular worldview—and up to a point her categories correspond to those of Ferre.

First, she says it must be possible to show that a *coherent* perspective can be developed in terms of the basic idea or chief concept of a worldview. At this particular point Emmet shows that a metaphysical worldview is quite important for a thinking person. A metaphysical theory provides form, and without form nothing can be grasped—without form we have only a vague multiplicity of confused impressions. There is an exhilaration and satisfaction about achieving a form in which to express a person's experience or basic idea, even if the form must needs be a simplification of the original experience.

According to Emmet, a second criterion can be applied. A key idea of importance can claim support from the fact of its *comprehensiveness*—its ability to coordinate a wide range of diverse facts and experiences in a coherent form. It must be possible to show that the world can be ordered from that perspective; and that when it is so ordered, light will be thrown on types of experience other than that which forms the matrix or basic concept from which the metaphysical view is developed.[89]

Beyond this, there is a further suggestion that a metaphysical theory, while not capable of absolute demonstration, should commend itself as self-evident to the civilized minds of the age. *Self-evidence* means that a theory uncovers absolute presuppositions. Furthermore, a theory is self-evident when it has a creative and stimulating influence on the intellectual imagination of the age in its literary, religious, political, and social life.

It is also important to suggest that the theory or worldview will not commend itself if the attempt to order experience from a particular perspective leads to obvious distortions or to dislocations or inconsistencies within the worldview itself. The demand for *systematic unity* is in itself a check on the vagaries of mere subjectivism.

But systematic unity need not mean forcing all experience into the straitjacket of a preconceived body of ideas which admits no further development. An adequate worldview must remain open and admit to unsolved problems or even aspects of reality which cannot be brought completely under its categories. For example, it must not do violence to the empirical propositions of science and common sense within their own limits, i.e., working according to their own experimental methods.

In other words, according to Emmet, no worldview or metaphysical theory can be sustained which does not respect empirical propositions in their own sphere. But an adequate worldview can set these patterns in a wider context of interpretative theory without distorting their essential character and thus give a synoptic vision.[90]

6. The Method of Reinhold Niebuhr

Niebuhr's entire apologetic task was directed toward establishing the relevance and superiority of the biblical understanding so that it may be an available resource of insight, redemption, and healing. It is Niebuhr's contention that although the Christian revelation is given *to* experience and not derived from it, nevertheless its truth can be validated or confirmed in experience. The truth of the biblical worldview is not entirely verified by rational proof, but a limited rational validation of the truth of this view is possible. This validation has both negative and positive aspects.[91]

Normally, rational analysis of the limitations of "worldly wisdom" will not of itself persuade one of the truth of the biblical way. Acceptance of the Christian way is always a gift of grace, a mystery which is not subject to manipulation. However, if one is to make room for Christianity in the world, it is important to puncture the idolatrous pretentions of a culture, awaken it from its complacency and interpret the significance of its despair. When forms of worldly wisdom are shown to provide an inadequate interpretation of the total human situation, biblical understanding secures a limited negative validation—as well as a fresh relevance.

This engagement of the "wisdom of the cross"—the faith which "is perplexed but not in despair"—with the "wisdom of the world" is of special significance to a generation which has moved so rapidly from optimism to pessimism and from complacency to despair. This neither proves the truth of the biblical worldview nor makes it acceptable. However, if the engagement is real and vital, the Christian faith can be shown to involve a wisdom which makes sense out of life on a different level than does worldly wisdom.

The positive apologetic task is not a different task from the negative one, but is simply a different thrust of the one and the same task. The positive approach consists of correlating the truth apprehended by faith in repentance with truths about life and history gained generally from experience. Insofar as this shows the Christian faith to be a more adequate source and center for interpreting life than alternative interpretations, such a correlation can be said to validate the truth of the Christian faith.[92]

7. The Method of Edward Carnell

Edward Carnell, the late president of Fuller Theological Seminary, is recognized in evangelical theological circles as a significant Christian apologist. He was chosen to represent the conservative perspective in the widely heralded dialogue with Karl Barth at the University of Chicago in 1962. According to Carnell, one of the main reasons we cannot by rational means alone prove the truth of the biblical way to a person outside the faith is that such a person's criteria of judgment must be changed before he or she can accept that truth. Accepting the Christian way brings a radical change in a person's set of values, and things that were formerly thought to be valuable and significant are now seen as worthless (Phil. 3:7–8). Until this change has occurred, it is difficult to persuade a person that Christianity is superior to his or her present frame of reference.[93]

When first confronted with the Christian faith, the person whose first allegiance is to economic success will undoubtedly want to know, "Will it make me more wealthy?" To the person who worships pleasure, the acid test will be "will I have more fun?" The person who worships science will want to know what scientific problems the Christian faith can help to solve.

So each person from his particular perspective scans the Christian faith and asks if it can meet his or her present wishes, desires, and values. This can create a serious temptation to the Christian. Today there are many who are ready to give a glib "yes" to such questions. "Become a Christian," they say, "and you will become happy, healthy, wealthy, and popular. You will also have peace of mind and serene security." In short, unbelievers are promised that Christianity will give them everything that they have wanted most.

Carnell contends that we can create a deeper appreciation for the biblical worldview by revealing the weaknesses of alternative worldviews than we can by making promises that are contrary to the nature of the faith. In fact, one of the tasks of a Christian apologist is to show the weaknesses of alternative worldviews and to lay bare what is left if the Christian worldview is abandoned in favor of another option. Carnell draws on Kierkegaard at this point. Kierkegaard was so skillful in this approach that he established a dialectic of despair which revealed that the Christian way is the only valid option—one must either swim with Christianity or sink into despair.

Carnell, too, believes that by analyzing and evaluating the alternative worldviews he can lay bare their inadequacies. The way of pleasure, for instance, ends in boredom, frustration, guilt, and exhaustion. Following materialism or Marxism means a loss of moral and spiritual realities, and a person with eternal potentialities can never finally be satisfied with materialism.

The same is true with a positivism which states that the only reality is that which can be verified by physical observation. In such a case, the loss of metaphysics means a loss of a transcendent standard of ethics. Man is reduced to a one-dimensional being participating in only one environment.

And then there is the option of rationalism. But human beings are more than reason; reason cannot satisfy the inner longings of human hearts. And secular humanism, with all of its emphasis on human dignity and welfare, cannot solve the problem of guilt and man's moral impotence. And finally, the way of secular existentialism leaves us in subjectivism, because there is no transcendent and objective referent outside of the self.

The historic Christian worldview does not denounce pleasure, economic security, wisdom, or authority. Rather, if it is grasped in its fullness, it answers humankind's basic religious needs. After realizing the basic weaknesses of alternative worldviews, a person should be more open to the glories of the biblical worldview.[94]

As has already been indicated, persons will change their organizing principle and thus their worldview, or exchange it for another worldview, only when they have a new encounter with reality in which new experience is gained which cannot be comprehended or adequately interpreted in the old worldview. In traditional religious language, coming to this point is called "conversion."[95]

But it should be mentioned that conversion can occur in the broader sense of changing worldviews as well as in terms of a personal religious conversion. In fact, a personal conversion to Jesus Christ should lead to a reevaluation of the larger aspects of a person's worldview—in other words, a conversion of the will should lead logically to a conversion of philosophy.

8. Summary

By way of summary, we must reiterate the consensus of almost all biblical apologists—that the biblical worldview cannot be proved in the way that a mathematical equation can be proved. However, as we have indicated, a systematic and consistent approach can present a strong verification of the basic premises of the Christian worldview.

We can begin by applying the test of coherence to the Christian worldview—placing major assumptions side-by-side to see how they cohere with each other or hang together. If they do not basically contradict, they are shown to be coherent and consistent. And, of course, the Christian insists that the biblical viewpoint is coherent, that the Christian way is rational because it is rooted in the rationality of God and his creation.

Although the biblical worldview cannot be perfectly verified according to reason, we believe we do have rational probability—that the Christian worldview offers a way of life that reason shows to be the most probable of all alternatives. Existentially or experientially, it offers full assurance of the reality of personal redemption when surrender is made to the Savior. The total impact of the evidence of religious experience—the moral experience of humankind and revelation in history—presents a strong case for the Christian worldview.

In this study we will attempt to show that the answers given to life's ultimate questions by the biblical worldview surpass in a comparative and experiential testing the answers given by alternative philosophies and religions. As we have already indicated, from a negative perspective, other worldviews and philosophies give an inadequate interpretation of the total human situation. From a positive perspective, the biblical worldview is more comprehensive, creative, and consistent.

In the chapters to come, we will affirm that the biblical worldview sees life as a whole and in greater depth than any other worldview. The biblical worldview —far from being irrelevant to the twentieth century—is indispensable. It is our contention that the basic and crucial philosophical and religious questions being raised in the world today can find a saving and fully adequate answer only in the perspectives, directives, and saving experience provided by the biblical worldview.

VII. What Is an Appropriate Order for Dealing with Life's Ultimate Questions?

Since this study emphasizes the biblical worldview in relation to life's ultimate questions, we propose to deal with life's crucial questions in the order in which they were faced by the people of the biblical community as they moved through history. This order should help preserve the durational, history-centered, and narrative nature of the biblical worldview.

First is the question of the meaning of history. In biblical history and today this is of primary concern. The significance and uniqueness of the biblical view of history can be seen only when it is contrasted with the pessimistic-cyclical views of history and the more modern inevitable-progress views. As we will see, the strengths of the progress views, including the Marxist view, are actually latent in the biblical worldview.

Second is the question of the meaning of religious language in general and biblical language in particular. God revealed himself in historical events and their interpretations as recorded in the Bible. Is the language of the Bible metaphoric or factual or both? How can we say that the Bible is valid and meaningful? How can one understand and utilize the archaic language of the Bible in a modern scientific world?

The third and fourth questions relate to the creation of nature and humankind and deal with the relationship between science and religion and miracles, providence, and intercessory prayer.

The fifth and sixth questions concern the way in which God exercises sovereignty over the world. This involves the problem of Satan's revolt and humankind's revolt and the consequences of these rebellions, as well as the problem of the demonic and personal evil and suffering.

The seventh question is the universal concern about death and the life beyond.

The eighth question concerns the nature of religious experience and mysticism and the meaning, significance, and destiny of the followers of non-Christian world religions.

The ninth question seeks to find an appropriate answer to the relationship of reason and faith and revelation.

The tenth question is concerned with human morality, freedom, and the moral argument for God.

The eleventh question relates to the meaning of beauty, aesthetics, and culture and the relationship of this meaning to the knowledge and service of God.

VIII. What Is an Appropriate Method for Presenting and Sharing a Worldview?

In this chapter, we have noted methods of comparing worldviews. In a pluralistic world it is important to enter into the marketplace of ideas and share our deepest convictions about why we think that the biblical worldview alone will furnish the pattern for the scattered pieces of the jigsaw puzzle of life and bring meaning, purpose, empowerment, and hope to human existence.

In recent years, our world has grown "small" through the advance of communication, technology, and travel. And in this new "small" world, many people other than Christians are seeking to share their deepest convictions and meaning systems and to convert people to them. Because of the United State's experience as a "melting pot," she has developed a unique method for handling this diversity of worldviews.

This basic method for dealing with religious diversity has its roots in two historical traditions. One is the idea that America is God's new Israel—a nation of destiny. This emphasis had its immediate origin in the Puritan adaptation of certain emphases of what might be called the "right wing" of the Protestant Reformation. In the nineteenth century, it was translated into a popular concept known as "manifest destiny," the belief that the United States, because of its founding in a pristine land by religiously oriented people, was a nation chosen by God to reflect his moral and spiritual purposes and share them with the world.

A second tradition is of more immediate relevance in an America and a world that has become pluralistic in terms of religious and philosophical perspectives. This tradition is related to the idea of religious freedom and tolerance toward religious and cultural pluralism. This aspect of the American worldview came from Roger Williams and was influenced by the "left wing" of the Protestant

Reformation.[96] In essence, it held that, while religious ideas and communities are important, human sin and finiteness made it impossible for any one group to represent the absolute truth. Therefore, religious communities were to share their vision by persuasion and incarnation rather than by utilizing civil powers to enforce their basic ideas or worldviews.

This basic concept developed historically into an understanding that deep religious conviction could not be enforced through political means. And this understanding was woven into the very fabric of the nation's government. Such a creative approach ensured that harmony could be preserved amidst the deep-seated diversity of the United States. The biblical worldview, for example, could be zealously propagated without government persecution or direct government help. The biblical faith could freely proclaim and share its highest insights, yet it must preserve a humble and contrite recognition that all actual expressions and formulations of religious faith are subject to historical contingency and finiteness. In other words, biblical people could hold and witness to their ultimate religious convictions with a sufficient degree of humility in order to allow them to live peacefully with those who have other convictions.

Many wise Christian leaders have pointed out that this American way is actually in keeping with the Judeo-Christian interpretation of sin. According to this tradition, pride and self-centeredness constitute the essence of sin. An authentic biblical faith, therefore, should encourage humility.[97]

Reinhold Niebuhr has gone so far as to show that the unique American way of government was actually developed to facilitate this unique American way of life. In the executive, legislative, and judicial balance in the American government, freedom to propagate a view is allowed, and yet there is a methodology established to keep any one group from dominating in an improper way. There is a system of checks and balances.[98]

For almost thirty years I have spent my Thanksgiving holidays with international students at various conferences across the country. I always try to explain to these students from countries across the world about our American way, including our concept of religious liberty.

I tell them that I am glad to be a part of the religious group which took the initiative in sending James Madison to Congress to help frame and urge the passage of the Bill of Rights, which guaranteed religious freedom. I tell them of the excitement of a free and diverse society that is filled with vitality and spiritual challenge. I point out that one reason we can have international student conferences where all viewpoints are discussed and shared is that we do not fear truth. Although the biblical worldview has been dominant in our heritage, we do not fear openness and testing. Any worldview or philosophy of religion which is based on truth and reality and not just on inheritance or establishment should prosper in a context of openness and testing.

Although I apologize to the international students for the fact that American Christians have often distorted this biblical worldview and have not lived up to its ideals, I share with them how important I think it is to the American way and how important it is to me personally. Because I am finite, and because I believe in religious freedom, I would not seek to use political, economic, or psychological pressure to force them to accept this view which has been such an important part of the strength of the American way and which means so much to me.

But I also tell them that I would be remiss unless I shared with them my conviction that the biblical worldview is the most adequate view to answer life's crucial questions. Furthermore, I share with them how the biblical view undergirds the belief in the worth and dignity of persons. It provides a motivation for education and scientific research. It justifies and sustains a visionary and noble humanitarian program. In addition, it provides an answer to the longings for ultimate meaning and salvation and moral power for individual life and for the cosmic process.

At such meetings I call for the students to work for universal religious freedom. In such a context, we can use sharing, incarnation of the teachings of our faith, and reason to commend our worldviews. We should accept a worldview, not just through birth or convenience, but because of careful and prayerful examination.

2

The Biblical Worldview and the Meaning of History

I. Why Is the Question of the Meaning of History Important?

1. The Importance of Personal Concern

Consciously or unconsciously, all of us are concerned with the crucial question of the meaning of history. This is true because convictions about what the past was about and where the future is going—in other words, philosophies of history—can drastically affect, for good or ill, the self-understanding of individuals, nations, and civilizations.

The question of the meaning of history becomes especially important during times of personal and world crisis. For during those times when the world seems to be erupting or falling down around us, it is natural to question the significance of events past and present—to ask, "Is there any meaning to my life in particular and to history in general?"

2. The Importance of Determining the Most Authentic and Constructive View

Next to a general concern is the related question of which is the true or most authentic, constructive, and creative view of the meaning of history. And this is a crucial question, for the twentieth century has seen several rival interpretations of what history means and where it is going.

The Nazis, for example, had a definite and conscious view of the meaning of history—one which appealed tremendously to German youth in the 1930s. When I was studying in Switzerland just after World War II, I roomed with Martin Neiden, who described to me how as a teenager he had been caught up in the Nazi Youth Movement. He grew up in the chaos of the 1930s in Germany, after Germany had been defeated in World War I and was undergoing runaway inflation and economic depression. In this time of despair, Hitler introduced to the German people a philosophy of history which he promised would give their lives meaning and purpose. Hitler convinced young people that they were an important part of history; in fact, he promised that their achievements would determine the course of history for a thousand years.

During my stay in Switzerland, I saw young communists march in the streets of Zurich with their red flags, shouting "Working Men of the World Unite!" Thanks to Karl Marx, the communists in every part of the world claim that they have the key to the march of events in our time. They deny that there is anything absolute or transcendent in human life and thought, and they decry religion, but they believe that they have reached a scientific understanding of the process of history. The Marxists see capitalism and communism locked in mortal combat, but they believe that in the conflict, by an inexorable necessity built into the structure of history, communism must prevail.

This communist view is not only a way of looking at history, but also a way of furthering history. Thousands of intellectuals and millions of workers have shown themselves willing and eager to invest their all in this gospel. It has apparently given to some of them a new sense of meaning to life. It has also inspired in them the assurance that they are acting in unison with vast historical forces which are moving irresistibly to a predestined goal. This goal is the classless society, Paradise Regained, and the liberation of the masses from their chains.

Those of us who embrace the biblical tradition have rejected the Nazi and communist interpretations of history, but what have we offered in their place? Can we give to the peoples of the world an interpretation of the human drama that will give meaning, dignity, and direction to their personal lives and provide them with a worthwhile task to perform and a cause to serve?

Many of us believe it is a tragedy of our time that, although we have in the biblical approach to history a view that can match and surpass the Marxist interpretation, we have failed to cherish it. We are neither teaching the biblical view to our children nor propagating it as we should. Could this be because we have never fully understood this dynamic biblical approach to this crucial question? In any case, it is important that we examine more closely the crucial question of the meaning of history.

II. How Would You Define History and Classify Approaches to History?

1. The Definition of History

Before we examine various alternative views of the meaning of history and present the biblical view, it is important to set forth a working definition of the word history.

We will primarily follow Webster in his definition that history is "a systematic *written* account of events" or "a branch of knowledge that records and explains the character and significance of past events." This definition implies that history has both an outer and inner side.

The fact that history is "written" implies, in the words of Rust, that "history is a remembered past." It is not just the totality of happenings in any particular epoch—but those happenings which have passed through the human mind and been retained in the memory because a significance or a meaning has been read into them.

Furthermore, a historian, in his search for meaning in the past, is not concerned with every type of human event. The historian's field of interest is that of human events which possess a significance for communal life. History is concerned with individuals living in community and not with isolated units. The events retained in history are those which have repercussions upon an entire historical group.

This is not to imply that the individual does not count in history. But it does suggest that the individual gains historical significance by his relationship—positive or negative—to a societal group. The great figures of history have found their place in the remembered past for one or both of two reasons: (1) They created a crisis which profoundly affected the future life of a historical society, and/or (2) they helped shape a society and make it conscious of its historical mission. For example, both Augustus Caesar and Napoleon have special historical significance. But they are significant primarily because they symbolically represent their community and shaped its direction.[1]

Our own individual experiences illustrate how history is a record of past human actions which have had social significance. For example, I am a part of the history of Louisville, Kentucky; New Orleans, Louisiana; Jackson, Mississippi; and Waco, Houston, and Fort Worth, Texas. And yet I doubt that my name will be in any of the history books of these cities. Why? Because my actions will not be deemed by those who write history to have been of enough social significance to have a place in the history of these cities.

2. The Two Major Approaches to History

(1) The Approach of the Scientific or Technical Historian. Simply speaking, the study of history can be approached from one of two different directions. First, there is the approach of the technical or empirical historian. As a professional, the historian aims at impartiality. He uses scientific methods to seek the truth as far as it is discoverable. In order to do this, he must carefully investigate manuscripts, tablets, monuments, inscriptions, and other data which the archaeologist or the anthropologist may put at his disposal. He gathers materials, scrutinizes them, and discards what appears to be false. Only when he has completed these activities is he ready to put it together into a coherent whole.

This attitude toward the historical task has existed since the early Greeks, whose history writing was characterized by a spirit of empirical investigation. Herodotus, for example, adopted as his explicit method the interrogation of eyewitnesses to the events he wished to describe.[2] However, it is generally accepted that the scientific age of history was inaugurated by the German historian Leopold von Ranke, who undermined the credibility of various authors of the Renaissance by exposing inaccuracies in their accounts.

Once the scientific era of historiography (the study of the discipline of history) was underway, total reconstructions of historical theory often were needed, for in many cases the alteration of single facts transformed the entire story.

The scientific approach to history calls for objectivity, accuracy, and unbiased investigation. It challenges the notion that history is written to justify causes, pointing out that the function of history is not to write romantic summaries of past periods of time, but to reconstruct the past events as accurately as possible.

According to this concept, the writing of history is to be governed by tough, critical, empirical rules. All the sciences are to be utilized by the historian for whatever information they may supply. Special attention is given to documents not intended to be historical documents—for example, diaries, letters, memos, ledgers, and import lists—and whenever possible the historian is to work from original documents rather than second-hand reports. (It was from this last emphasis that the science of archiving developed late in the nineteenth century.)[3]

It should be noted, however, that even a scientific approach to history can never be as absolute and precise as natural sciences such as physics and chemistry. Historical evidence is never absolute; events of the past cannot be reproduced as they actually occurred. History rests largely on probability. It is a peculiar science, in that it depends so much on truths which can only be discovered and verified by insight, sympathy, and imagination. Even when historical evidence is obtained scientifically, the historian has to interpret the evidence. Thus, even the approach of the technical historian has some hidden philosophical implications.[4]

(2) The Approach of the Philosopher and Theologian. The second possible approach to history is one that goes beyond the technical or the scientific approach. For despite the contributions of the technical historian, there will always be the cry for an interpretation of the human drama that does more than uncover and analyze the facts. People who are struggling with the meaning of events in their lives want more than arid discussions about the date and documents; they want to hear an interpretation of the majestic issues that relate to humanity's larger destiny. Technical proficiency does not necessarily make scholars skilled at such a task—any more than it renders them skilled at making love or choosing a spouse. The question of *meaning* in history calls for a more philosophical or theological approach.

As intimated earlier, this desire for a "philosophy of history" rather than a "scientific" history is especially strong in times of crisis. For example, the philosophical and theological *City of God* was Augustine's answer to the crisis of the sack of Rome in A.D. 410. The crisis of World War I led Oswald Spengler to write his answer in *The Decline of the West.* People in crisis are concerned with the whence, whither, and why of themselves and society as well as the substance of events.

Now, this doesn't mean that the task of the technical historian and that of the philosophical historian are mutually exclusive. On the contrary, the philosopher or the theologian at the beginning admits his debt to the scientific historian. He must build on facts. He must come to terms with the basic, tough, empirical, critical, and sifted rules developed in modern scientific historiography. The philosopher or theologian also heeds the generalizations and predictions which the technical historian has made.

But for the fullness of commentary on the drama of human life in time, the philosopher or theologian attempts to go beyond scientific technique, to stand back and see the landscape as a whole. And for the sum of our ideas and beliefs about the march of the ages, this is the approach that is needed. To decipher the ultimate question of the meaning of history, we need the prophet, the philosopher, and the theologian.

Indeed, we decide our total attitude to the whole of human history when we make our decision about our religion or philosophy or worldview. In fact, it is the combination of history with a religion or its equivalent that generates power and fills the story with significance.[5]

When looking at history, the philosopher or theologian seeks the broader interpretation. He or she asks questions such as: What is the ultimate significance of history? Is history merely the result of chance or inexorable Fate, or is it a divine drama with a plot, a plan, or a goal? Is there a hidden master Dramatist? These questions are significant and vitally related to human life and destiny, to our highest hopes and deepest fears. For if there is no purpose, how can we do anything but despair?[6]

It can be said that every person has a philosophy of history—a viewpoint from which he or she interprets life. This viewpoint may be only semiconscious; it may be vague, superficial, and unorganized. So the question is not, Shall I have a philosophy of history?—but rather, What sort of philosophy of history shall I have?

(3) The Biblical Example of a Philosophical or Theological Approach to History. The biblical view, of course, is an example of the second approach to history—the philosophical/theological approach. The Bible makes the bold assertion that the tiny slender stream of biblical history provides the meaning of that wide river we call world or universal history. According to the biblical worldview, the key to all of history is to be found in the series of events that comes to a climax in the incarnation, death, and resurrection of Jesus Christ.[7]

Of course, scientific history has no way of speaking to certain events contained in biblical history. Genesis 1–3, for example, tells of the creation of the world, the pristine relationship between God and humanity, and the initial breakdown of that relationship. Clearly, these chapters are not history in the professional or scientific or technical sense.

Historians work with historical data of all kinds—manuscripts, inscriptions, archaeological reports, and so on—and attempt to make a meaningful interpretation of these data. From the scientific point of view, then, if there are no data, there is no writing of history. And there can be no data in the technical historical sense when it comes to the statements in Genesis 1–3.

In the deeper sense, however, Genesis 1–3 is history. From a biblical point of view, the world was created in space and time. Humanity did appear as God's creature. There was the event of sin and the resulting conflict between humanity and God. Genesis deals with real events and real space and in real time, just as does scientific history, but it deals with those kinds of events that elude technical scientific history. (Problems related to the biblical view and scientific data concerning prehistory—dinosaur bones, radiocarbon dating, dates for the first man, etc., will be discussed in chapter 4, "The Question of Science and the Biblical Worldview, with Special Emphasis on the Origin and Development of the Earth and the Human Race.")

In fact, Genesis deals with prehistory, which is history which occurred before the usual means of writing history existed and which therefore needs a special classification or a special category. It has been suggested that Genesis 1–3 is prophecy in reverse—God's gift of the ability to see into the past. Just as the prophets spoke of future judgment and salvation in terms of Hebrew culture, concepts, and history, so the writer of Genesis spoke of events that occurred long before recorded history.

(A pioneer in this line of thinking was Jay Kurtz, who wrote in the nineteenth century. He reasoned that just as God enabled the prophet to write of the future by use of his present culture, God could enable the biblical writer to write of the past by the same means. Thus the Creation account is a projection in reverse. It is the prophet looking backward by the use of the cultural grid of his time.[8])

The purpose of Genesis 1–3 is basically theological. Its chief significance is to show that sin had its origins with the very first human beings (Homo sapiens)—that Creation, the origin of the human race, and the emergence of sin are all bound together in one history. For this reason, although Genesis 1–3 is real history, it is a genre of history that is not manageable by the ordinary methods of technical historiography.

We who hold the biblical account to be historically valid should not seek to oppose technical history nor try to spare the Bible from scientific scrutiny. We object, however, when the scientific explanation claims to replace the biblical witness.[9]

For example, the Persian king Cyrus, as a human figure, is open to the usual methods of the technical historian. However, Cyrus's role as a shepherd of God is known only by divine revelation (Isa. 44:28). It is history interpreted theologically, and is beyond the reach of scientific history. Similarly, Daniel's four kingdoms have been the proper subject of historians writing on world history, but their role in the preparation for the Messiah and his kingdom is known only from the standpoint of a divine interpretation made known through divine revelation.[10]

In a similar fashion, all aspects of the life of Christ which have to do with life in ancient Palestine are open to the scrutiny of scientific history. However, all aspects of the life of Christ which are the products of the act and agency of God are known only through divine interpretation.

The events in the life of Christ are indeed history—they occurred; they have space and time coordinates. We must neither minimize the "eventness" of this history nor dilute the revealed character of the divine interpretation. Both event and interpretation are hard data, and we do justice to biblical history only as we hold firmly to both.

That Jesus Christ the man was crucified under Pontius Pilate deserves a place in every book on world history. But it is an equally hard datum of biblical history that on the cross he died for the sins of the world. Both the historical death and the revealed interpretation are firm realities of biblical history.[11]

Biblical history also includes what we call consummation or the final events. The consummation relating to the second coming of Christ forms a special problem, since it has not yet occurred. But the end of history, like the beginning, is an integral part of biblical history and cannot be sacrificed without compromising its integrity.

The biblical accounts of both the beginning and the end were written by certain historical projective techniques. The future in the Bible is also written by means of an alphabet of apocalyptic symbols. This in no manner detracts from the actuality or the "eventness" of the end of time as described in the biblical accounts.

Christians accept the credibility of biblical events such as the resurrection of Jesus Christ because up to a point we can pursue their space-time coordinates. But we also accept them because they fit into the total panorama of redemptive history as we understand it. And we are also led by the Spirit of God into the acceptance of the total corpus of scriptural revelation.[12]

III. What Are Representative Examples of the Cyclical View of the Meaning of History?

Because views about history affect all of us—including historians—it is important to understand the various competing ideas about history and its meaning. Of course, there are as many philosophies of history as there are philosophies, but fortunately these tend to fall into patterns. Six basic categories or classifications can be distinguished, of which the oldest and one of the most influential is the pessimistic-cyclical view.[13]

1. The Origin of the Cyclical View

Mircea Eliade, the late professor of the history of religion at the University of Chicago, called the circular or pessimistic-cyclical view the "Myth of Eternal Return." It was widely held in ancient China, India, the Middle East, and the Greco-Roman world. D. W. Bebbington describes this approach to history as comparable to a pattern of cycles.

Undoubtedly, this school of thought was influenced by the life cycle of an individual from birth to death. Since most of the people in the ancient world were agricultural, they also saw the yearly rhythm of the seasons reproduced on a larger and grander scale in history. On the basis of both of these analogies, people tended to see history as constituting a cyclical, repetitious pattern.[14] (Some of the views grouped under this pattern or category have other dimensions. The cyclical concept, however, is present in each view to a greater or lesser extent.)

2. The Chinese View of the Circular Pattern of Dynasties

On a recent trip to China, I was reminded of the fact that in ancient days the Chinese saw history in terms of the cycle of the rise and fall of dynasties. For centuries, the Chinese accepted a belief in an ideal of a stable moral and political order that was based on the writings of Confucius. Those persons aspiring to public office would read the Confucian classics in order to discover general principles of ethics and government. A departure from these principles would lead to what they called the withdrawal of the mandate of heaven and the decline of a dynasty. A return to Confucian principles, however, would lead to a renewal. Thus they saw the historical process as a series of repetitive cycles.[15]

3. The Hindu and Buddhist View of Cosmic Cycles

(1) The Hindu Version. The *Puranas,* widely read religious writings of India, teach that the universe passes through cycles of enormous proportions. The basic cycle of twelve thousand years consists of four "ages," each of which is preceded by dawn and followed by twilight. (These twelve thousand years are divine years and equal to 4,320,000 human years.) After an entire cycle of twelve thousand years, the universe falls into chaos and a new cycle begins. The process is endless.

Since the cycle is perpetual and inevitable, what matters in life is not to perform great or good deeds within the historical process, but to escape from the historical process. Meaning can be found only beyond history in the eternal sphere. According to Hindu understanding, then, there is no point in seeking guidance about the future from the past, as the Chinese attempted to do.[16]

The Hindu cycle theory is also closely related to the Hindu doctrine of karma, or rebirth and reincarnation. According to this doctrine, both the individual and the universe go through cycles of rebirth, and salvation consists in achieving Nirvana, or escape from the repeated process.

(2) The Buddhist Version. Buddhist scholars accepted the traditional Hindu view of the historical process. They compared the great cycle of twelve thousand years to a wheel with twelve spokes. Along with the Hindus, there was a sense of resignation in the face of the transience or brevity of this present cycle.[17]

(3) The Implications of the Hindu-Buddhist View. The Hindu-Buddhist outlook grants that one must live in history but sees history itself as barren—its ambiguities unconquerable and its motion aimless. In fact, true reality is not to be associated with time or the temporal flux. For this reason, there is little emphasis on recording or remembering events.

This view does include recognition of and deep compassion for the universality of suffering. However, it also tends to breed passivity; it calls for people to retreat from a reality which it feels powerless to transform. Therefore, there is less impulse to channel history in the direction of universal humanity and justice.

Hindus and Buddhists tend to see history not as progress, but as deterioration, decay, and corruption. By mystical union with the ultimate, one overcomes not reality, but one's own involvement in reality.[18]

4. The Pessimistic and Cyclical Emphases of the Middle East

(1) The Ancient Persian Version. Ancient Persia was influenced by the pessimism of the cyclical view of India. There was a Persian concept of four successive ages of history, symbolized by gold, silver, steel, and a mixture including iron. The declining value of the metals symbolized the progressive decadence of history. Unlike India, which saw fresh cycles taking place, the Persians had no doctrine of eternal recurrence. At the end of the metal age there would be judgment and a universal cataclysm.[19]

(2) The Babylonian Version. A cyclical pattern of history was also held by the Babylon empire in its early years. The past was seen as a cyclical pattern of happiness and disaster as dynasties rose and fell. This view was similar to the Chinese model. The future was seen as obscure and erratic.[20]

5. Pessimistic, Cyclical, and Timeless Views of the Ancient Greeks and Romans

(1) The Ancient Greek Version. The Greek poet Hesiod, of the eighth century B.C., was the earliest ancient Greek writer to describe something like a philosophy of history. He wrote of a race of heroes which began with the gold race and ended with the race of iron. There was an overall pattern of increasing decadence symbolized by metals of decreasing worth.

There is also evidence, in this earlier period, that Greek life was bound to the rhythms of nature such as the changing seasons. This view was similar to that of other Near Eastern cultures. (The Hebrews, with their historical concern, were the exception.) The well-being of the people, according to the earlier Greek view, depended upon the proper relation to the forces of nature, which were personified and deified as goddesses and gods.[21]

(2) The Cyclical Emphases of Plato and Aristotle. Although Plato and Aristotle had little interest in history, they did write of the "Great Year," that return to an ideal era which was a part of a cycle in the historical process. Plato also recognized the cycle in the changing seasons.

Pythagoras, who had lived in the sixth century B.C., had taught that the cycle of the historical process would end in a catastrophe but then be repeated in identical form. In his *Timaeus* and other writings, Plato gave a fuller expression of this view and argued for a periodic destruction of civilizations by catastrophic happenings such as floods. Out of these catastrophes, only the illiterate and uncultured members would survive to start a fresh turn of the repetitious wheel of time.[22]

A related view held by Aristotle saw the Great Year as a part of a cycle of civilization which was separated from other cycles by a partial world disaster, which ruined culture but permitted the continuity of the human race.

For the Greeks, therefore, time was a circle, a periodical repetition of the same thing. Even the life of the human soul was involved in this cycle of "coming-to-be and falling away," of birth and death, growth and decay.

(3) Plato's Negative View of Time. Under the influence of their classic philosophers, such as Plato, the ancient Greeks became philosophically oriented;

they sought to discern structures in reality and to come to an understanding of the forms which govern the changing processes.

Time takes on a negative character. The Greek view of the future is closed. Time as a cycle of recurrence excludes the emergence of novelty in the world. The present thus loses its decisive character, because nothing done in the present could possibly contribute to anything new in the future.

For the Greeks, time is also destructive—a curse. Salvation, then, must consist of an escape from the world of time and flux into a world where time does not exist. Blessedness is in the timeless Beyond. The idea that redemption is to take place through divine action in the course of events in time is totally alien to the Greek mentality.

This viewpoint, first expressed by Plato, found ultimate expression in the mysticism of Plotinus in the third century A.D. In this view, a brooding fate, a sense of downfall, hung over history. In addition, history was dominated, like nature, by the circular motions of the heavenly bodies. The cycles in the heavens meant a repetitive chain of cycles in the story of the race. History and time were seen as a meaningless repetition in which nothing is ever accomplished; the work of successive generations creates a glorious structure, which perishes as the movement of history turns full circle.

(4) The Cyclical View of the Stoics. During the later Greek classical period, and later in the Roman empire, Stoicism was the most popular of all the philosophies. It was in its fully elaborated Stoic form that the doctrine of historical recurrence was most widely accepted by thinkers.[23]

The pessimistic element was especially dominant in the Stoic view of history. Chrysippus, who taught at Athens in the late third century B.C., held that after fire had consumed the earth, there would be a new world. He said that there will be another Socrates and another Plato and that each man will have the same friends. According to Chrysippus, this restoration would take place not once, but many times; all things would be destroyed and restored eternally.

The Roman philosopher, Seneca, who lived during the time of Christ, also accepted the view that human life is periodically destroyed and civilization begins again. He believed that each cycle begins with a golden age of innocence and simplicity, but that then the arts, inventions, and later the luxuries lead to progressive deterioration and eventual destruction. In Seneca's view, fate, or *moria,* which is the fixed order of the universe, must be accepted with resignation.

All this was the background of the belief of Marcus Aurelius, the Roman emperor and Stoic who taught that nothing in the world could be truly new. Everything was a repetition of what had passed in a previous age of the world.

This concept of eternal recurrence encouraged the attitude for which Stoics are best remembered—their self-disciplined acceptance of all that happened in a spirit of resignation. This view has even come to be called a "philosophical" attitude, because Stoics have been taken to be typical of philosophers. Both this teaching about history and the spirit of resignation resemble the Hindu views of life and history.[24]

(5) The View of the Greek and Roman Historians. In a broad sense, there is nothing to indicate that Herodotus wished to break with the Greek circular view of history. And although Thucydides, the other eminent historian of ancient Greece, devised an ingenious method for checking the validity of evidence, he displayed no strong sense of the grand pattern in the historical process. He was, like the classical Greek philosophers, really concerned with the eternal order; to him, historical particulars merely illustrated the universal and unchanging ideas which constituted reality. For Thucydides, as for Marcus Aurelius, history could come up with nothing that was drastically new. This is in contrast to the biblical view, which holds that history as it moves onward reveals novelty.[25]

Tacitus, the great Roman historian, also subscribed to the idea that everything, including social history, moves in seasonal cycles. For Tacitus, as for many before and after him, the rhythm of the natural world caused him to see the past as a process of recurrence.[26]

6. The Influence of the Ancient Pessimistic-Cyclical View of History

(1) Lack of Hope in History. All through the ancient classical period, the widespread consensus was that history was on the downward part of its cycle. The significant mark of these cultures is the lack of hope and a sense of nostalgia for a past "Golden Age." Not even advances in what they knew as science or technology had a qualifying effect on this pessimism, which is reflected in Paul's reminder to Gentile Christians in Ephesus: "Wherefore remember, that ye being in time past Gentiles . . . having no hope" (Eph. 2:11–12, KJV).

The only hope which was held out was the salvation that was to be found in the soul's *present contact* with the unseen world—not in the future. Thus the real hope is not *over* there in the future, but *up* there in the unchanging eternal world. Salvation was seen as an escape into the eternal world here and now—not looking forward into the future.[27]

Paul Tillich calls the Greek view of history a tragic interpretation of history. This is because history was seen by the Greeks as an eternal cycle of genesis, greatness, decay, praise of great moments (the heroic), and forlornness about the destructive end of all things. The whole cycle is determined by fate, and there is no hope of either an immanent or a transcendent fulfillment in history. In other words, there is no forward-looking and dynamic philosophy of history in Greek thought.[28]

(2) Greek Influence on the Hebrews. The Hebrews, as we shall see more fully, found a stay for their souls not in the contemplation of a timeless realm above the process of events, but in the hope of a more blessed future—and this remained the dominant aspect of their outlook. However, the Greek influence can be found in the Book of Ecclesiastes. Koheleth, the "gentle cynic" who is the author of this book, states, "Vanity of vanities . . . ; all is vanity. What profit hath a man of all his labor which he taketh under the sun? One generation passeth away, and another generation cometh; but the earth abideth for ever. . . . There is no new thing under the sun" (Eccles. 1:2–3, 9).[29]

The view held by Ecclesiastes arose in Hebraic culture during a period when the disappointment over unrealized messianic hopes filled the Hebrews with great perplexity. Thus Koheleth interprets history in terms of the classical Greek concept of recurrence.[30]

(3) Influence on the Concept of Permanent Structures of Reality. The cyclical emphasis in the thought of the Greeks and the Romans was not without positive effect. Among the Greeks in particular, it contributed positively by leading to a concern for the permanent structures of reality.

Since they did not know what to do with time, the Greeks turned their attention to the search for those forms and ideals which were beyond time—eternal, not subject to change. These ideas included the heroic virtues extolled by Homer, the laws or judgments set forth by Herodotus, and the laws of political behavior analyzed by Thucydides, as well as the forms of geometry and the eternal ideals of Plato.

Behind the immediate phenomena of flux, or unrest, the Greeks saw a fundamental equilibrium in the cycle of recurrence. To them, wisdom consisted of knowing that equilibrium and of coming into harmony with it—realizing that the locus of the real and the significant was not in history but in this timeless realm of the forms. The Greek genius flowered in philosophy and provided Western thought with its basic conceptual tools for rational understanding. This is in contrast to the Hebrews, who emphasized the importance of God's actions in history and the religious, ethical, and personal importance of time and history.[31]

7. The Cyclical View of Nietzsche

Although pessimistic-cyclical views of history were more pervasive in ancient times—at least in the West—they have also been held by several influential modern thinkers and writers.

One of these was Friedrich Nietzsche, who wrote during the last part of the nineteenth century and who, particularly in *Thus Spake Zarathustra,* taught a belief in eternal recurrence. Nietzsche's explicit purpose was to dismiss the Christian view that history was guided toward a specific goal by the divine will. His view was close to nihilism; he denied all meaning to history, stating that "the eternal hourglass of existence is turned over and over—and you with it, a dust grain of dust!"[32]

8. The Cyclical View of Spengler

(1) Life and Writing. An even more influential modern example of the pessimistic-cyclical theory of history is that of Oswald Spengler. Born in 1880, Spengler was an unknown teacher of mathematics in Munich until he startled the intellectual world with his book, *Decline of the West.* This two-volume work was originally conceived before World War I and completed in 1917, although it was not published until after the war.

(2) Basic Concepts. Spengler's basic view of history is similar to that of the Greeks—indeed, he bases his view or theory on an analysis of Greco-Roman

culture, although he offers comparative data from all great human cultures. But Spengler's view differs from the Greek in that it is dressed up in biological garb. In his construct, every culture is a unique organic structure which grows and then decays like any other plant or animal. Like any organism, it is subject to a natural term of years. It is born, lives, and dies—it has physiological limits.

To Spengler, there is no continuous and universal world culture. History is pluralistic, or made up of many cultures; there is no single straight line of development.[33] Each culture passes through four fairly distinct stages, which are roughly analogous to the seasons or to life stages of a human being.

First comes spring, or childhood, the time of the germination of life and of early growth. In this period, people live close to the soil, and mythology and religion are born.

The second, or summer, stage of a culture is the stage of blossoming or youth. It is the prime of life—a time of ripening consciousness. In the case of Western civilization, this time occurred during the Renaissance and the periods of reformation.

The third stage of a culture is comparable to autumn—the time of ripest maturity which soon will fade into decline. The autumn stage is marked by the rise of cities and commerce. Science and philosophy begin to overshadow religion and to sow the seeds of skepticism and revolution; the emphasis is on rationalism and enlightenment.

Then, finally, comes the winter stage—the period of the freeze, of old age and death. In this period, quality is replaced by quantity, beauty is replaced by utility, and the war lords come to inherit the earth. This is the stage of a materialistic world outlook, a period of science, utility, prosperity, and war.[34]

(3) Spengler's Analysis of Western Civilization. From a cultural analysis that is both startling and revealing, Spengler concludes that the European-American civilization which dominates the globe has reached its full growth and begun the dying process.

Each successive culture, according to Spengler, is an organism that carries within itself a distinctive principle. World history is the collective geography of such cultural organisms. When one culture dies, it gives birth to another culture in which the same process will be repeated. All human dreams and achievements make no lasting contribution to the human story, but die along with their culture.

Spengler believed that the great and determinative forces of history belong to the subrational sphere and consist of the cosmic forces of race, blood, sex, and an instinctive will to power. These forces shape and use the intellectual and spiritual activities of humanity. Human beings are unable by their own thoughts and aspirations to stem the inexorable movement of their own cultural epoch to its predestined end. Therefore, wisdom lies in realizing at what stage of growth or decay our culture has arrived and in allowing ourselves to embody the historical destiny in our decisions and actions. To oppose the inevitable is sheer folly.[35]

Spengler argues that "all world-improvers, priests and philosophers are unanimous in holding that life is a fit object for the nicest meditation. However, the life of the world goes its own way and cares not in the least what is said about it." The spiritual ideals, moral principles, religious beliefs, and artistic standards held by any particular culture are mere surface affairs.[36]

(4) Strengths and Weaknesses of Spengler's View of History. Spengler's view, by showing the possibility of cultural decline, is helpful in that it stirs us out of smug complacency. It undergirds the truth of the Christian doctrine of sin. It also shows a need of deep-seated spiritual revival if decline and fall are to be counteracted.

However, there are many weak points to be found in Spengler's thought. For example, he presses a biological analogy to the point of making it a law. He ignores freedom and personal decision—the possibility, borne out by experience, that a person *can* rise above environment. He depreciates reason and ideals, in comparison with instinctive feeling, more than is justified. And he overemphasizes the sexual drive and racial identification, which are indeed important, but not all-important or all-dominating, as Spengler states. (It may also be said that Spengler's view helped prepare the way for the Nazis.)[37]

9. An Evaluation of the Cyclical View of History

No fully articulated cyclical view of history is popular in the West today. Yet the cyclical theory remains a powerful influence in the West, as well as in other parts of the world. For example, dynastic cyclical patterns persist in contemporary Chinese historiography, despite Western and Marxist influence. Camus, the French author who died in 1960, revived the ancient Greek cyclical view in his popular book, *The Myth of Sisyphus*. The Hindu and Buddhist views are still widely taught by various contemporary groups which are influential in the United States and in Western Europe as well as in many countries of the Far East. The cyclical view of history is far from dead.[38]

As we have already indicated, there are serious problems in any form of this theory of history. The golden age is conjured up by people eager to escape, if only in imagination, to a better world. Primitivism, which is another name for the idea of a golden age, is a form of idealization of the past which overlooks the absence of evidence that any such age existed. It is not surprising that this view has seldom commanded the allegiance of historians.[39]

There is also the problem of lack of evidence for any theory of repeated cosmic cycles. The apparent evidence that once attracted men to the cycle theory of history was derived from the astronomical observations of the ancient East and the Mediterranean worlds. Modern astronomy has clearly shown that Plato was mistaken about the existence of a Great Year of the heavenly bodies. It also seems fair to suggest that he and others of his time were equally mistaken about the existence of equivalent cycles in world history.

The most plausible form of the cyclical theory is the idea which postulates a pattern in the rise and fall of dynasties, nations, or civilizations. There is a certain amount of truth in this idea. Nations do become more powerful, then grow weak once more. But it is difficult to prove any consistent similarities between the various instances of decline that would establish a regular pattern. Nations lose power for particular, distinctive reasons as well as for reasons that can be generalized and which would apply to all nations in history.[40]

The most pervasive and negative influence of the various varieties of the cyclical theory of history is its pessimism. The outlook is dark for those who believe history has declined from a golden age, that the cosmos will be destroyed without any better replacement, or that any ruling house or society is bound to come to nothing. People who hold this view tend either to give themselves up to pessimism, as did Hesiod and Spengler, or to cultivate an attitude of resignation, as did the Stoics.

Thus we see that an unmodified cyclical view leads to a sense of the ultimate futility of human existence. This is in contrast to the biblical view of history, which has given Western civilization its remarkably widespread conviction that the future offers hope.[41]

IV. How Would You Describe and Illustrate the Inevitable Progress View of the Meaning of History?

The inevitable progress view of history first appeared in the seventeenth century and has had a powerful influence on certain areas of contemporary thought. Rather than seeing history as a series of repetitive cycles, those who hold the inevitable progress view see history as moving forward in a straight line—or, more precisely, an upward spiral—and improving steadily as it goes along.

This view of history has been closely connected with the Enlightenment emphases on reason, science, and the perfectibility of the human race. It does not recognize God as the guide of history; rather, it sees human beings, through reason, and/or the power of evolution as being the agents of forward movement through time. This view was strongly stimulated in the early nineteenth century by the success of science and Darwin's theory of biological evolution, but it had its roots in earlier centuries.

The story of the gradual emergence of the belief in progress from the end of the seventeenth century forward and of its development through the eighteenth and nineteenth centuries has been definitively told by J. B. Bury in his book, *The Idea of Progress: An Inquiry into Its Origin and Growth*, which was published in 1920.[42]

1. The Biblical Influence on the Inevitable Progress Approach to History

In some ways, the inevitable progress view of history can be seen as a heretical child of the biblical tradition. The perspective of the inevitable progress view preserves the biblical pattern of history unfolding in a straight line, although it largely ignores the biblical views of creation, incarnation, and final judgment.

One aspect in particular of the biblical tradition was picked up by those who held the inevitable progress view of history—hope for the future. The biblical religion was deeply concerned with the promises made by God to his people.

The Hebrew nation was taught to look forward in keen expectancy to a better, even a triumphant future. The messianic prophets also fostered hope in the expectation that the Messiah of the Davidic line would restore the royal house and introduce a glorious new era. The religion of the Hebrews was thus from the beginning a religion of hope. The Hebrews lived on hope, and the whole orientation of their thought was toward the future.

The New Testament also encouraged the idea of progress and the forward look, although it maintains that the turning point of history which in the Old Testament had been an anticipated event was now a reality. The new age of which the prophets had spoken had now actually dawned in Jesus Christ, and the Christian church was moving in this new age.

Many believe that the idea of inevitable progress could not have grown up other than on ground prepared for it by the biblical teachings. Strains of the Christian influence are still influencing the people who hold the inevitable progress view of history today. In fact, some have said that the inevitable progress view of history is a Christian heresy. At any rate, it is a lopsided emphasis—the development of one aspect of biblical truth to the neglect of other aspects.[43]

2. The Idea of Progress through Revolutionary Rationalism

(1) The Views of Francis Bacon and Descartes. The earliest form of the inevitable progress view of history was revolutionary rationalism, a concept which first appeared in the early part of the seventeenth century. Two important thinkers who influenced the development of the revolutionary rationalism view were Francis Bacon, who initiated the new development in British thought, and René Descartes, who influenced Continental thinking.

Both Bacon and Descartes believed that in their time the world was standing on the threshold of new knowledge that would be brought about by human reason, and each was as excited as the other by the prospects of the enlightenment which would thus be brought about. Both of these men thought of their own time as revolutionary in the sense that it would mark a break with the longstanding traditions of the past. They also probably hoped that the enlightenment they dreamed of would be achieved in the very near future.

(2) The View of Condorcet in France. By the eighteenth century in France, the idea that unaided reason could be trusted to further progress was becoming more open and widespread. Added to this emphasis on reason was disdain for the past—it was expected that the newly won rationality would work a radical change in history. The French philosophers of this period gave past history a great deal of attention, but only for the purpose of showing its crimes and follies and pointing the way to a new future.

An example of this attitude can be seen in the work of Marie Jean Antoine Nicolas Caritat, Marquis de Condorcet, who was an encyclopedist and a friend and biographer of Turgot and Voltaire. Condorcet wrote his *Sketch of a Historical Picture of the Progress of the Human Spirit* in 1793. In it, the past history of humanity is regarded as a long line of continuous and uninterrupted progress.

In Condorcet's view, history begins with an age of barbarism, in which human beings are distinguished from the brutes only by their better bodily organization. From that point, history is divided into nine stages, each of which is marked by a definite advance in knowledge and enlightenment. From this survey, Condorcet claims to derive his conviction of the inevitability of human progress throughout future time unless some cosmic catastrophe should intervene. He then proceeds to a prophetic account of the future tenth period. The dominant notes of this period will be equality and perfectibility both of nations and of classes. There is also the perfectibility alike of knowledge, virtue, and bodily condition. Condorcet gives us a complete version of the eighteenth-century doctrine of inevitable progress as it was worked out in France.[44]

(3) The American View. For many reasons, the view of inevitable progress found early and ready acceptance in America. This is partly because the American nation was born in the seventeenth and eighteenth centuries, when this view of history was being formulated. Furthermore, the open frontier and the mobility of American life seemed to give tangible signs of progress, inclining Americans toward this faith. So, from the days of Thomas Jefferson and Ralph Waldo Emerson to John Dewey in the early twentieth century, the idea of inevitable progress has had a large and ardent following in America.

3. The Idea of Progress through Evolutionary Positivism

(1) The View of Comte. In essence, the idea of positivism is that all knowledge is based on observation, experiment, and the ascertaining of scientific laws. The idea of evolutionary positivism is that throughout history humankind has been progressing toward the point where positivism is recognized and accepted as the foundation of all thought.

Auguste Comte was one of the originators of this approach, which was the next phase in the development of the doctrine of inevitable progress. Comte's fame rested primarily on his *Positive Philosophy* (1830–42), which was a rework of a course of lectures delivered in Paris.

In the past, according to Comte, human consciousness has passed through three stages. First, there was the *theological* stage—the stage of childhood—in which all phenomena are attributed directly to God. During this stage human beings were religious and theological in their thinking. They looked for final causes and sought for the supernatural origin and final purpose of their world.

Second, there was the *metaphysical* stage—the stage of youth—in which there was still a search after primary causes conceived as abstractions. During this stage man was still concerned with the same issues of the origin and final purpose of the universe, but at the level of reflective thought.

The third stage is the *positive*—or adult—stage, in which it is recognized that the only knowledge possible is that of the relation of observed facts. At this time, science achieved ascendancy, and humankind became positivistic in its thinking. The origin and goal of the universe ceased to be a live issue. Rather, human beings confined themselves to empirical investigation of observable facts and their relationships.

According to Comte, this third stage was where civilization had come in his time. In his view, theology and metaphysics had been left behind, and understanding and control were still progressing in each science as observational and correlating techniques improved. Eventually, he believed, all phenomena and their relationships would be understandable, and the questions which man could legitimately ask (questions about observable facts and their relations) would be answered.

Comte believed that the earlier theological and metaphysical stages were necessary to human development in order that human beings might know the legitimate limits of their knowledge and therefore of their understanding and control of the world. He was even prepared to admit the value of Christianity and the part it had played in the progress of the race. Yet he denied the claim of Christianity to represent ultimate truth. That claim was reserved for his own scientific creed.

Comte also believed that whereas in earlier years scientific progress had been more marked in the natural sciences, in the next stage of the evolutionary advance humankind must turn its scientific techniques upon the moral and social sphere. This view greatly influenced the French sociologist Émile Durkheim and, through Durkheim, the development of sociology as a discipline.[45]

Interestingly enough, Comte himself became dissatisfied in later years with the dry and detached tone of his earlier writings. And he found an outlet for his changed perspective in the organization of a new religion, which he called the Positivist Church of Humanity. He produced a positivist calendar of "saints" who had worked for human progress. He also composed a positivist catechism and declared in 1857 that he would in the future sign circulars as "High Priest of Humanity." Comte even claimed that he had entered a new phase in his career—that whereas in the first stage he had been the new Aristotle, now he was the new Saint Paul![46]

What Comte did not realize was that his own cultic progress was simply a secularized version of the eschatological faith of the Roman Catholic Church. In fact, his doctrine has been called "Catholicism minus Christianity." In seeing that a religion of some kind is essential to the social structure, he was in fact acknowledging that the so-called theological stage was not and never could be really passed by in the development of mankind. Even scientific positivism could not do away with those ultimate questions which human beings raise and seek to answer in their religious consciousness.[47]

It should be noted that Comte's new religion of humanity was embraced in many parts of the world. In Brazil, for example, particular members of the upper class who wished to mark their independence of mind by breaking with the Catholic church were attracted to the Religion of Humanity. The Brazilian flag bears to this day the positivist motto, "Order and Progress."[48]

Comte was one of those responsible for the active thread of the idea of progress in the mid-nineteenth century. In fact, declares J. B. Bury, Comte "did more than any preceding thinker to establish the idea of progress as a luminary which could not escape man's vision."[49]

(2) The English Approach. With the development of the popular press in England, the idea of progress and rationalism in general—and the concept of evolutionary positivism in particular—spread to the lower social groups. The desire to improve themselves and so to push forward the advance of civilization became the accepted attitude of the skilled workers of Great Britain and their friendly societies and mechanics' institutes. To them, the Great Exhibition in the Crystal Palace of London in 1851 became a visible proof that technology and prosperity were advancing together. The exhibition aroused something like a national celebration of the possibilities of progress both in the material and moral realms.[50]

(3) The Influence of Darwin. The influence of Charles Darwin's concept of organic evolution on modern thought has been widely recognized. However, as John Baillie points out, the modern idea of progress did not originate as an extension of the doctrine of organic evolution. Actually, the reverse is nearer the truth. As we have seen, Comte began the publication of his positivist philosophy in 1830, and by the middle of the century his ideas had been absorbed into the thought of the English rationalists. It was in such a climate that Darwin published his *Origin of Species* in 1859.

Thus we see that the nineteenth-century discoveries in the biological field were themselves stimulated by the prior existence in the minds of the earliest investigators of the ideas of development mediated to them by the followers of Comte. However, the idea of biological evolution, when it did appear, resulted in a strong reinforcement of the idea of inevitable progress.[51]

In the early nineteenth century, the scientific mind was beginning to be open to the possibility that species, instead of being fixed, were subject to a process of development from the simpler to the more complex. The significance of Darwin lies partly in the fact that he brought forward new evidence of such development, as well as codifying existing evidence more completely than anyone had done before him. However, his chief significance is in the fact that he posited a means whereby such development might take place—the principle of natural selection. The only progress promised us through the operation of this principle is the progressive replacement of those forms of organic life which are less able to cope with a given environment.

As we will see, the notion of evolution soon began to expand from the biological to the historical and ethical spheres. Furthermore, there was little hesitation on the part of scholars to draw from this extension beyond biology to further encourage their hopes of progress.[52]

(4) The View of Herbert Spencer. The most influential exponent of the conception of evolution, covering the inorganic, organic, and the "superorganic" fields, was Herbert Spencer. He had confidently adopted the evolutionary hypothesis even before Darwin provided it with causal explanation.

In his *Social Statics,* published in 1851, Spencer affirms that advancement of any kind is due to the working of a universal law. By virtue of this law, advancement must continue until the state we call perfection is reached.

Progress, therefore, is not an accident, but a necessity. As surely as a blacksmith's arm grows large and the skin of a laborer's hand becomes thick, Spencer said, the things we call evil and immorality must disappear, and humanity must become perfect.

It is generally conceded that Spencer is more responsible than any other single writer for the tendency to convert the doctrine of evolution into an instrument of unbridled optimism and inevitable progress.[53]

4. The Idea of Evolutionary Progress Related to the Development of Ultimate Reality, or God

In the early years of the twentieth century, the concept of evolution was destined to find a still bolder application—the suggestion that ultimate reality is itself subject to an evolutionary progress. According to this view, progress does not eventuate under the eyes and by the prevenient and sustaining power of a God who is eternally perfect and complete in himself. Rather, God himself is also progressing. This view was suggested and taught by a number of thinkers.[54]

(1) Henri Bergson. According to early twentieth-century French writer Henri Bergson (1859–1941), the basic fact of all experience is change. Reality, therefore, is to be understood on the model of process and change, which is basically evolutionary. "Becoming"—not being—is the essential mark of ultimate reality.

Unlike the classical Greeks, however, Bergson did not think of becoming as a cyclical process. Instead, it is a directed process of development in which time is meaningful and fundamental. In addition, Bergson regarded reality as a process in which an all-embracing life-force is creatively active.

Bergson rejected the biblical perspective of the balance between the transcendence and immanence of God. Rather, in his view, God is exclusively the immanent life-force. In religion, said Bergson, human beings intuitively unite themselves with the life-force (*élan vital*) and with the founder of love, which is God. The goal of human existence is thus mystical union with God or the *élan vital.*[55]

(2) Samuel Alexander. Another significant thinker in this tradition is Samuel Alexander, who has been called a naturalistic, emergent evolutionist. In *Space, Time and Deity,* he affirms that the space-time continuum—the basic system of three physical dimensions (spatial dimensions) and a fourth temporal dimension (time)—is the single primordial matrix out of which the whole process of the universe emerges. This infinite space-time matrix is the ultimately reality, and all beings, deity included, are dependent upon it.

"Nysus," an immanent striving or urge toward higher levels, pervades the space-time matrix, although time is the creative principle of movement basic to it. This process has a single definite direction toward the production of progressively higher values. The direction, however, is not, as Christianity has taught, given to the process by a transcendent God who himself is above the process. Rather, direction is inherent in the process itself as the "nysus," which we may doubtless take as the equivalent of Bergson's *élan vital.*[56]

It is clear that, if we follow this view, we can no longer conceive of progress as occurring within or against the background of an ultimate reality which is not itself subject to change. In Alexander's view, reality itself is evolving. And God is neither the transcendent author of evolution nor even the immanent "nysus" that pushes it forward. God is himself a product of evolution or, rather, "One that will be."

Critics of this approach have asked where this new dynamism or urge or driving force comes from, since in Alexander's model there is no reality outside the process from which it could proceed. Alexander replies that we must accept its appearance with what he calls "natural piety" and ask no further questions. To this assertion, W. R. Matthews has replied with the wry comment that "we may suspect that natural piety is commended to us lest, pushing our questions beyond the appearance of things, we should be led to supernatural piety."[57]

(3) Lloyd Morgan. Lloyd Morgan, another prominent early twentieth-century thinker, represents the more "idealistic" wing of the emergent evolution group. He differs from Alexander in holding that to explain progress we must posit not only a force acting from below (an "urge"), but also a force acting from above (or an "attraction"). In his 1923 book, *Emergent Evolution*, Morgan describes this activity which draws us on as God. This means that in Morgan's view, something more than Alexander's "natural piety" may be permitted us.

According to Morgan, if there is a deity in the universe in the normally accepted religious sense of the term—that is to say, as the creator of first cause and so on—that deity is the space-time continuum itself. This neutral stuff would appear to contain all the potentialities for subsequent emergents. Out of it the "nysus" toward deity emerges, and the dynamism of time is a generator of all qualities. Like Bergson and Alexander, Morgan would deny a transcendent god who is logically and chronologically prior to the space-time universe.[58] (The biblical view, in contrast, insists that God is not only logically prior to the space-time universe, but also stands related to it as Creator.)

(4) Alfred North Whitehead. The ideas of Alfred North Whitehead, who was active until the mid-twentieth century, may be regarded as the culmination of the speculative tradition whose course we have been following—that of the emergent evolutionists. Whitehead's view is called Philosophy of Organism. In *Process and Reality*, Whitehead rejects the traditional idea that process has its place only within or against the background of a timelessly perfect ultimate reality. Rather, he states as a metaphysical principle that "the very essence of real actuality—that is, the completely real—is process." The process is itself the actuality and requires no antecedent's static cabinet (or transcendent God). Thus the process must be inherent in God's nature, whereby his nature is acquiring realization.[59]

According to Whitehead, there are two aspects to God's nature. First, there is the *primordial* nature of God. God is not *before* all creation, but *with* all creation. Moreover, God is *deficient* in his primordial nature. In the abstraction of his primordial actuality, we must ascribe to him neither fullness of feeling nor consciousness.

But, second, there is the *consequent* nature of God. The completion of God's nature into a fullness of physical feeling is derived from his activity in history. His derivative nature is consequent or dependent on the creative advance of the world or history.[60]

In the teachings of Whitehead, we do not have the self-sufficient transcendent deity of Christian theism. Rather, we have an evolving deity dependent for consciousness upon the process of nature in history. He gives to the process its subjective aims, and he is for it "the great companion—the fellow sufferer who understands."

Indeed, the world creates God as much as God creates the world. God and the world are mutually necessary. God provides the rational ground for the world through his vision of the eternal objects and thus supplies the process with an aesthetic order. But, on the other hand, the world makes possible the consequent nature of God; it makes it possible for the deity to become conscious. God is not the first cause of the world, the creative and efficient ground of all actuality. He is dependent on the world for his own completion.[61]

From a biblical perspective, Whitehead's greatest weakness is that he does not really ascribe personal being to God. He never escapes his naturalistic presupposition, and therefore his god cannot escape the process and transcend it.

And yet, allowing this basic weakness, Whitehead does offer some valuable insights which correct what has been the dominant Christian view of deity since the medieval period. In his involvement with the world process, Whitehead's deity is much nearer the biblical disclosure than the common conception of God. Whitehead's understanding of God's relation to the world as one of persuasion and not power says much to those who seek to express God's essential being as love. And his emphasis on God's involvement in the process reminds us that the God of the Bible is a living God, not the static perfection of Greek thought.[62]

5. The Idea of Progress as the Outworking of a Rational Process (G. W. F. Hegel)

The most impressive attempt of speculative philosophy to explain *a priori* the course of development which history *must* follow was made by G. W. F. Hegel in the early nineteenth century. Hegel became the dominant philosophical mind in Germany after he succeeded Johann Gottlieb Fichte in the chair of philosophy at the University of Berlin in 1818. Hegel's lectures on the *Philosophy of History* were put together by his admirers and published after his death from cholera at the height of his fame.[63]

(1) The Pattern of History as a Reflection of the Working of the Rational Mind. For Hegel, the real world is secondary to the mind, and ultimately the mind is the only reality. Hegel's stress on the concept of mind came from his belief that the particular human mind is the manifestation of the eternal mind, which in Hegel's thought is the equivalent of God. In knowing the world, the human

mind creates the world, because the human mind is part of the great creative mind, or God. Hegel is therefore classified as an absolute idealist; he believes the ideas of the mind are wholly responsible for the external world.[64] Since for Hegel the rational is the only reality, all the historical process must conform to the laws of logic. Hence, the rational pattern of history does not have to be discovered by historians following empirical methods; it can be demonstrated by metaphysics or, in Hegel's language, logic. Whereas the working historian is concerned with particular facts, the philosopher is concerned with those necessary laws of logic which govern the course of historical development.[65]

(2) The Dialectical Pattern. The pattern to be discovered in the world, therefore, is the same pattern that operates in the mind. Both patterns are called the "dialectic," which is perhaps the best known feature of Hegel's system. In the historical process, as in logic, a moment or occurrence (thesis) is succeeded by its opposite (antithesis), which in turn is succeeded by the unification (synthesis) of the opposites. This unity or synthesis then becomes the first moment of a new phase.

According to Hegel, this triadic pattern can be regularly discerned in various sections of world history. The thread of linear progress runs through the pattern of history. There is confidence in a goal being achieved, and this goal embraces a firm scale of values.[66]

For Hegel, there is a grand design behind the contradictions of history, and that design is a self-realization of what he calls the Absolute Idea (or the World Spirit or the Rational Spirit—Hegel uses these terms interchangeably). In history, the Absolute Idea is spelling itself out logically in time, giving itself concrete historical existence in a myriad of subjective centers of human consciousness and objectifying itself in the processes of nature. In this movement, reason moves on a triumphant course. The struggles and decisions, victories and defeats of individuals are of consequence only as manifestations of the inner dialectic of the Absolute as it determines itself in time. They are tools in the hands of God, the Absolute Person, and are subject to the power and cunning of reason.[67]

(3) The Application of the Pattern to History. In Hegel's model, the historian's task is to supply empirical confirmation of the logician's *a priori* dialectical scheme. But Hegel himself goes beyond logic to apply his dialectical notion to the actual process of world history.

In the beginning, according to Hegel, political organization took the form of despotism of the oriental type—in which only one person (the despot) was free. Next, by way of antithesis, came the Greco-Roman extension of freedom to all citizens (but not to slaves). Finally, there came the synthesis, which in Hegel's mind was the fulfillment by the Germanic nations of the Christian ideal of the infinite value and freedom of every individual—the historical self-realization of the Absolute Idea. Thus a culmination of world processes was to be found in the perfection of the political developments of the Prussian state about 1830.

It should be noted that, although the movement of historical development as Hegel understood it was from East to West, apparently Hegel never contemplated the possibility that the process would continue its Western course and cross the Atlantic. The provincial character and limited dimensions of Hegel's logic eventually became apparent, although in its day it served the purpose of bolstering the myth of Prussian greatness.[68]

(4) The Claims of Hegel's Views. Hegel himself said that his philosophy had made articulate the spiritual content of the Christian religion. In his view, Christianity in the past, by its naïve and childish dogmas, communicated truth pictorially to minds which hitherto were incapable of understanding his philosophy of the Spirit. However, when the significant elements of religious faith are freed of emotional and mythical entanglements, they support the view that the Absolute Idea controls history. According to Hegel, religion at root is an immature form of speculative reason.[69]

In the Hegelian view, history has no ultimate reality. It contains nothing which the mind cannot already grasp and is merely an illustration of what the thinker knows already in principle. History is simply an illusionary reflection of an impersonal rational reality.[70]

(5) The Implications of Hegel's View. When Hegel made historical facts only transient individualizations of an eternal and unchanging idea, he dismissed the need for a special revelation in history. He also cut out any element of the personal in decision making and any consciousness of the otherness of God. History itself is merged into God, or the Absolute Idea, and personal freedom and responsibility are merely illusions. Humankind thus becomes identified with absolute spirit as a concrete manifestation of it.[71]

The virtue of Hegel's system is that it did attempt, even though it failed, to give significance to historical development. It recognized the presence of a dialectical tension between certain elements and of some form of directed and purposive movement in the temporal order. Hegel attempted to find significance for time by seeing eternity as strung out in a succession of concrete manifestations like a string of beads.

However, Hegel's system failed in giving significance to historical development because it could only conceive an impersonal absolute as the ultimate reality for which time had no real significance. As with Plato, so with Hegel there is no real reason why there should be any history at all. If human beings already possess within their own reason that eternal idea which is unfolding itself in time, why should there be any history at all?[72]

(6) The Influence of Hegel's View. Although it may seem strange to us today, Hegel's influence was considerable. In the area of theology, the Tübingen school applied his dialectic to the history of the early church, and much arbitrary and biased biblical criticism was the result. In England during the latter nineteenth and early twentieth centuries, a remarkable renaissance of Hegel's idealism occurred under the leadership of T. H. Green, Edward Caird, F. H. Bradley and others. And Hegel also had considerable influence during that same period in the United States, where the St. Louis School of Philosophy was dominated by his viewpoint.

As we will see, and as is well-known, Hegel's philosophy exerted its most enduring influence through the teachings and activities of Karl Marx. Marx found that Hegel's logic of history could be diverted to form the basis of Marx's dialectical materialism.[73]

6. General Weaknesses and Strengths of the Inevitable Progress View of History

(1) Weaknesses. It should be helpful to suggest some weaknesses of this view, seen as a broad movement, which has had so many advocates in history and has been so influential in the history of the past several centuries.

First, the concept of inevitable progress as determinative law does not apply to an area where human personalities of free intellect are involved. If human behavior is largely under the control of at least partially free intelligence, can any direction of history be inevitable?

As we have noted, Hegel was a dominant leader in the inevitable progress view of history. He especially tends to minimize the individual and ignores the personal in its full range of relationships. He also ignores human freedom in any real sense, and he reduces the reality of human estrangement and alienation to a necessary stage in the logical dialectic of spirit.

Second, the inevitable progress view doesn't adequately address the inherent evil in humanity. To use biblical parlance, with all of their idealisms and structures of improved social justice, human beings remain sinners in their innermost nature. However much outward history may manifest an improvement in outward structure, inner history discloses the same pattern of sinful rebellion. Pride, arrogance, and sensuality still remain. The bias to evil remains in the human heart and, as history progresses, expresses itself in the new ways that civilization provides.[74] (A glance at the twentieth century, with its specters of the Holocaust and nuclear destruction, gives a quick lie to the idea of inevitable progress.)

Third, if the final goal of history—perfection or utopia in the inevitable progress view—is only realized at the *end* of the process, there is an element of injustice about the whole idea. Since this view does not allow for resurrection, those who have gone before will have no share in the fruit of their striving and the city of their dreams.

The only way out of this problem is to merge the individual into the solidarity of the race and thus deny human personality its true significance. However, as long as men live, justice will demand that those of every generation shall be able to fulfill their historic destiny and share in the meaning of history. To satisfy the cravings of the human soul, the consummation of history must lie beyond history in the new heaven and the new earth, so that those of all ages may share in its glory.[75]

(2) Strengths. Despite its weaknesses, however, the inevitable progress does contain certain elements of truth.

First, in the case of scientific knowledge (and science has always been a key emphasis of this view of history), continual progress does seem to be a reliable pattern. Indeed, one of the primary traits of scientific knowledge is that it is cumulative or progressive in nature. Thus inherently scientific knowledge grows or has the real possibility of growth in the course of time.

Second, social progress is possible, although it is limited. The application of science to society in certain clearly specified ways has resulted in an enormous increase in the amount of physical power available for human use. Such a growth may be called technical progress. In the technical sphere, the tools employed by man at various stages reveal a steady improvement from the clumsy ax of the stone age to the latest refinements of scientific genius.

There is also possible progress in devising social and political arrangements to control certain perennial human impulses and the problems arising from them. The creation of democratic forms of government constitutes a device for checking human power impulses and giving institutional expression to cooperative impulses. There is evidence of some progress over the centuries in social idealism, economic orders, and techniques for civilized life.[76]

Third, the kernel of truth in progress is that human life in history has serious and genuine significance. Stated theologically, human life in history has significance for God. Life in history is not to be regarded as a mere vestibule to eternity, or as an appearance of some timeless or eternal substance. It has, rather, its own significance.

But this truth can, we believe, be stated more adequately (which is to say more in keeping with the facts of existence as men encounter them in active daily life) in traditional biblical terms rather than in terms of the progress philosophy. The Christian emphasis on creation and incarnation suggests that human history has meaning for God in terms of divine will and purpose. God is involved in history. Furthermore, the temporal processes of nature and history are meaningful to God as the arena of God's grace and his self-giving, creative love.[77]

V. How Would You Describe the Importance, Basic Ideas, and Influence of the Marxist View of the Meaning of History?

1. The Importance of Marxism

The writings of Karl Marx have proved to be the most challenging critique of Christianity to emerge in the twentieth century. More intellectuals have been lured away from religion by the logic and clarity of Marxist arguments than through any other scholarly instruments. The appeal of the socialist movement generated by Marxist thinking has captured the allegiance of more oppressed industrial workers and impoverished peasants than any option of hope which has been provided by democratic capitalism. And though Karl Marx himself despised the Christian belief system, liberation theology—which is quite powerful in South America and in some Third World countries—has even sought to integrate Marxist revolutionary ideology with the Christian belief system.

Thus it should be fair to state that the Communist movement constitutes the most serious threat to the continued existence of traditional Christianity since the forces of Islam marched to the gates of France and of Vienna in the eighth century A.D. It is also fair to state that Marxist thought has provided the most popular ideological alternative to the Christian faith since the Renaissance.[78]

2. The Basic Idea of the Marxist View of History

Essentially, the Marxist view emphasizes that history is determined primarily by economic forces. The final goal toward which history moves is capacity production of material goods in a classless society. Once this goal has been attained, other values which are commonly considered as spiritual will automatically arise to make man's life a time of peace and happiness in which the greatest pleasure will be enjoyed by the greatest number. The means provided in the course of history for attaining this goal is the class revolution or revolt of the working classes of society.[79]

3. Important Influences on the Development of the Marxist View

(1) Karl Marx's Personal Pilgrimage. Karl Marx was born in 1818 in the Prussian Rhineland, where French influence was quite strong. He was born Jewish and was descended from a long line of rabbis, but his father was a lawyer. When Marx was six years old, the family became Christian, and he was reared a Protestant, though very early in his life he abandoned religion altogether.

Marx was a student during a time of intense intellectual activity in Germany. This intellectual ferment was passed on to the young people, and philosophy played a large part in their education. Marx's Ph.D. thesis in philosophy, which he wrote while studying in Germany, compared the natural philosophy of Democritus and Epicurus.

In 1842, Marx joined the staff of a newspaper in Cologne. He next went to Paris to study socialism. Here he met French socialist leaders and renewed his acquaintance with Friedrich Engels, the German socialist writer who had a manufacturing interest in England. Had it not been for Engels, Marx might have remained a purely academic thinker. Engels interested Marx in the British capitalist system, and this interest led Marx into research of a more concrete nature.

In 1845 Marx was expelled from Paris at the request of the Prussian government. He went from there to Brussels, Belgium, and then, in 1849, to England, where he existed on financial help from his friend, Engels. He used his time writing, organizing the international revolutionary movement, and pursuing the many feuds to which these activities led. He spent much of his time seated inconspicuously in the library of the British Museum, analyzing human history from an economic perspective.

Marx's pamphlet, *The Communist Manifesto,* which was the first statement of the principles of modern communism, was published in February 1848. Another crucial book, *Das Capital,* was published in 1867 and has become the bible of the Communist Party.[80] Both books were edited and published by Engels.

Karl Marx died in 1883. Over his grave, Friedrich Engels pronounced an oration in which he declared that Marx's work in the field of social science was equal to Darwin's in that of natural science. At any rate, Marx was fully as influential as Darwin in shaping modern history.

(2) The Influence of Hegel. Hegel's philosophy of history emphasized the dynamic process of history as moving toward inevitable fulfillment in Hegel's own time in Germany. Hegel saw no reason for expecting any basic revolution in the institutional life of Western man or in the country of Germany.

People in the Western world were entranced by Hegel's speculative idea that all history was a spiritual process in which human beings cooperated and that the process had reached its culmination in nineteenth-century Western civilization.

Marx, as a student of philosophy in Germany, where Hegel was teaching, was intrigued by Hegel's profound speculations on the nature of history. But Marx could not accept Hegel's emphasis that no more radical changes were necessary in the structure of human society. So Marx reversed Hegel's view of reality, making *matter*, rather than mind or spirit, the only reality. However, he borrowed Hegel's dialectical principle and his idea of historical evolution and development, adjusting Hegel's system to fit his own thought. Thus modern Communism through Marx is indebted to Hegel.[81]

(3) The Influence of Feuerbach. In Marx's expositions of his views on the historical process, the starting point is that man is the maker of his own history. This proposition emerged largely from Marx's encounter with the thought of the mid-nineteenth-century German thinker, Ludwig Feuerbach.[82]

According to Feuerbach, religion's apprehension of the infinite is really humankind's apprehension of the depths of their own self-conscious being. The idea of God arises out of the situation in which human beings see their own unlimited nature in objective terms and conceive of this as separate from themselves. In other words, religion is humanity's own actual nature, contemplated as another being; humans project their own image on the backdrop of the universe. Thus the actual person is the only true God to himself.

Feuerbach held that this atheistic viewpoint is the only true historical perspective. When humankind adopts this viewpoint, it becomes free to develop inherent qualities of its own essential being. Man's historical salvation consists in realizing this false projection of God.

Marx also picked up from Feuerbach a basic materialism, a view that the only reality is material. In this view, man is especially what he eats. At the practical level, according to Feuerbach, the affirmation of God's existence makes no difference to historical life. No practical consequences flow from intellectual speculation about a supreme being.

In Feuerbach, the idea of the process of history has descended from the level of Hegel's self-determination by the rational spirit to the level of determination by the natural. The way was thus prepared for Karl Marx's dialectical materialism.[83]

(4) The Influence of the French Revolutionary Tradition. Marx's time in Paris was important in that it served to bring to light the prophetic side of his personality. While in Paris, Marx came into contact with men who regarded philosophical theorizing as merely a step to practical political action. They were instrumental in bringing him to the point of actively working toward revolution instead of simply writing philosophy about it.

4. Key Elements in the Marxist View of History

(1) History Is the Story of Class Conflict. By studying the economic and social institutions of Western civilization from the sixteenth to the nineteenth centuries, Marx hoped to discover a pattern of history which would serve to guide the working-class revolution, which he was convinced was in the making. The result of his thinking about society, institutions, and history was the formulation of a philosophy of history known as dialectical materialism. We are primarily interested in this phase of his work.

According to Marx, the pattern of change which can be observed in Western civilization is rooted in the structure of history itself. Marx rejected the basic principle of Hegel's philosophy of history—that the dynamic changes wrought in history were dependent upon a spiritual force, the Absolute Idea. Instead, Marx claimed that economics determine the process of history—that the economic techniques developed in a society for assuring man's survival determined the patterns of that society, including the way its citizens think and the way they rationalize their behavior.

Like Hegel, Marx identified stages in the formation of society. And he claimed that at certain points in history the development of the mode of production outpaces changes in the political and legal structures of society. With the change of the economic foundation, the entire superstructure is more or less rapidly transformed,and an epoch of social revolution begins. Such social revolutions separate the stages of history.

In each stage, according to Marx, the division of labor gives rise to conflicts between social groups having different modes of production. These social groups are the "classes" of Marxist thought—in each stage, the ruling class is the one that controls the dominant mode of production.

Marx identified Asiatic, ancient, feudal, and bourgeois periods as historical phases that had already emerged in his day. He believed the bourgeois stage would be the last in which there is class conflict, for it would be superseded by a revolution with the proletariat in the vanguard. This revolution, in turn, would usher in the classless society.[84]

For Marx, economic forces do not exist as entities separate from their practice in history. Human activity is, in his view, essentially concerned with production; therefore, humans are essentially economic beings. Consequently, economic developments must depend upon human decisions. The processes of history, according to Marx, are determined by no agency other than humankind.

Laws for Marx can be equated with tendencies. What people have freely done in a previous generation has turned the historical process in a certain direction. A Marxist law is no more than a description of the way in which human possibilities happen to have worked out. Marx never deviated from his initial premise that humankind, not fate or law, is the maker of history.[85]

(2) Ideologies as Instruments of Oppression. The concept that ideologies are instruments of oppression became central in Marx's thinking. In his view, every political or economic system creates an ideology to legitimize its existence. Ideologies are of great significance in that they not only convince the ruling class of its right to rule, but they also convince the oppressed social class that the political and economic systems are functioning in its best interests.

In Marx's view, the most common ideology is a theological system which makes the ruling elite appear to be ordained of God and decrees the government, which serves its purpose, to be of divine origin. But Marx also made a strong case for the claim that all philosophical systems, like theological ones, are only inventions on behalf of the ruling classes. Through philosophy, the dominant classes make their control of society and their unfair appropriation of the wealth generated by industrial production seem reasonable and right.[86]

5. Influential Later Developments in the Marxist View of History

(1) The Views of Vladimir Ilyich Lenin. The Russian revolutionary leader Lenin openly recognized Marx's theory of history as the kernel of his own thought. However, he believed that the years before and after the Russian revolution demanded the making of history rather than concern with its nature. Lenin studied Russian and international capitalism and wrote short works on the political demands of the hour in preparation for leadership in the 1917 revolution in Russia.[87]

(2) Western Thinkers Influenced by Marx. In the face of the failure of communist revolutions outside of Russia following World War I, Western Marxism withdrew from its seemingly futile political activity and devoted itself primarily to philosophy. Thinkers in this tradition explain the nonrevolutionary attitude of the proletariat as a result of cultural dominance exercised by the ruling class.

In Germany, the Frankfurt School devoted itself to the elaboration of Marxist theory. Founded at the University of Frankfurt in 1923 to promote Marxist studies, it functioned there until the Nazi takeover forced it to move to the United States in 1933. It returned in 1950 to Germany, where it is still active.

This group pointed out the importance of Hegel's influence on Marx. It also emphasized the importance in Marxist thought of the human condition. In recent years, frustrated with civilization's apparent failure to achieve Marx's goals, the Frankfurt School grew quite pessimistic about the course of history, dismissing progress as a hallucination.[88]

(3) Recent Soviet Thought. In a handbook on *Historical Materialism* published in 1973 for Western consumption, Soviet Marxists emphasized their

confidence in progress. They defined the pattern of history as a forward movement along an upgrade leading from a lower state to a higher one. Whereas recent Western Marxism sees little hope for the future, recent Soviet Marxism seems to be quite hopeful.[89]

(4) French Thinkers. Outside of Russia and her communist satellites, probably the greatest impact of Marxist philosophy has been in France. The Marxists there interpret the French Revolution as a bourgeois uprising against a feudal nobility. To a quite remarkable extent, the debate about the French Revolution in France takes place on Marxist premises.[90] Marxists are quite active and influential in French political and educational circles.

6. Secular Criticisms of the Marxist View of History

In the past century, many secularly based criticisms of the Marxist view have been elaborated. Critics of Marx's ideas have observed, for example, that history has not worked out in the twentieth century as Marx predicted. The working class has tended to be nationalistic rather than international in its outlook as Marx expected, and worldwide revolution of the proletariat has not occurred.

Historians have been able to offer considerable evidence pointing to the fact that certain corrective techniques built into the system of capitalism have upset Marx's predictions. In many capitalistic countries, for instance, the particular genius of democracy for reconciling differences between classes has precluded violent revolution. Marx could not foresee the flexibility with which capitalism would adapt itself to changed conditions.[91]

Another common criticism of Marxist thought is that the many-sided cultural achievement of humankind cannot be explained simply in terms of economics alone, and the idea of production is not adequate as the ultimately determining element in history. For example, it is difficult to believe that great works of Western art simply reflect the way men and women labor for food, clothing, and shelter.

It seems fairly evident today that Marx's emphasis on production as an all-embracing explanatory factor in history was mistaken. His view was, after all, an intuition arising from a desire to respond to Hegel. Thus it was the fruit of reaction against a particular idealist philosophy, not the result of mature reflection on world history.[92]

Finally, critics of Marxism point to the negative results of its dominance in societies where it is the dominant social system. It is ironic that the Marxists, in order to achieve the society whose goal is total freedom, have fostered more enslavement and mind control than all the totalitarian movements that have gone before.[93]

7. Representative Christian Criticisms of the Marxist View

There are also many specifically Christian criticisms of Marxism. For example, Marxism displays an incredibly naïve view of human sin and a lack of understanding of forgiveness. This can be seen especially in the Marxist characterization of human evil as avarice or lust for property, which Marxists believe could be eliminated by eliminating private property entirely. This view, while it is strikingly similar to the biblical view that evil stems from arrogant pride, is simply not adequate to explain the tenacity of evil in civilization.

If private property is seen as the locus of evil, then it may be legitimately concluded that if private property is abolished, evil will be eradicated. The activities of the current Soviet rulers are sufficient refutation of this point. Their activities are also incidentally an unwitting verification of the traditional Christian view of sin as pride or arrogance!

Marxism also deliberately aims at destroying eternal truths. Marx believed moral judgments lacked an objective foundation and hence were meaningless. Marx's friend and publisher Engels particularly delighted in his rejection of absolute truth. Marxism, therefore, has been left with no objective moral standard by which to assess historical events.

Christians have also pointed out that, although it is deliberately antireligious and attacks religion as a major instrument of oppression, Marxism holds a number of quasi-religious pretensions. It rejects faith in an absolute God, but it substitutes faith in a utopian materialism—the revolutionary future which Marx saw as superseding all previous class structures and resulting in an ideal future.[94]

Christians also indicate that faith in God and Christianity do not inevitably make for economic, social, and political reactionism. Christian faith affords the possibility and necessity of radical change and growth, in addition to an appropriate preservation of tradition and the continuity of a stable order. Both stability and change are equally necessary for a truly human civilization. This mysterious unity of tradition and renewal is the only hope in a world in which dogmatic conservatism and dogmatic revolutionism have brought about a tension that spells disaster.

Another weakness of Marxism from a biblical perspective is its failure to provide a hope for any fulfillment beyond time. Humankind, as made in God's image, is more than a one-dimensional creature.

8. Lessons to Be Learned from Marxism by Christians

Even though Karl Marx directly opposed the biblical view, there is much Christians can learn from both Marxist ideas themselves and from the way those ideas have been applied in societies around the world.

For example, Christians should listen to the Marxists in recognizing the importance of economic factors in human decisions and in the life of social groups. If Christian faith is to survive, Christianity must be a religion in which the material and the spiritual are firmly held together as they are in the Bible.[95]

Christians must recognize the need to mend our own weak spots. There is some truth in the Marxist view that in many cases our religion, like law and ethics, is a rationalization of our own interests. It is important for Christians to use the valid aspects of Marx's critique of bourgeois Christianity to purge ourselves of those accretions to our faith that are alien to the essence of the biblical message and only serve our social class interests.

In addition, Christians should note the importance of propagating a dynamic and prophetic Christian philosophy of history. One criticism of Christians in the past centuries is that they have not seen, as Marx saw, that the whole order of society can be changed. Traditionally, Christians have been quick to mobilize against particular evils, but we have been slower to identify more central evils of false philosophies and a false understanding of the nature of society.[96]

In a way, the great success of twentieth-century Marxism demonstrates how much human beings need a definite and total philosophy of life—and how much they need hope for the future. Christians, who know that life in Christ offers just such a total philosophy and such a dramatic hope, should beware of selling the gospel short.[97]

Christians can learn from Marxists in seeing opportunity in social injustice and the problems of the people of the world. Industrial civilization has enormously increased the general welfare of mankind, yet it has not solved the grave problems of inequality. The Marxists have an astonishing capacity for detecting discontent and grievances arising from inequality and injustice in any part of the world and turning this unhappiness to their own purposes. Could not the same problems of inequality and injustice provide fertile ground for showing Christ's reconciling love and the gospel's deep concern for justice?[98]

Marxism shows the power of a strategic and dedicated minority. However, this does not mean that all political minorities are Marxist! Our reaction to Marxist abuses must not cause us to identify all political reforms with communism. Similarly, the totalitarianism of many Marxist states should remind Christians of the necessity of constantly evaluating the dominant group—even if the dominant group is Christian—for abuse of power is not solely a Marxist transgression.

Even though we must avoid overreacting to Marxism, we must also be prepared to defend ourselves against seduction by Marxist philosophy. In particularly, we must guard against those who would make Christianity into nothing more than another form of the communist revolution. We must recognize that the good communism has actually done in a country has often been an entering wedge for evil. The Marxist can point to a record of significant achievement in the area of material and technical gain, but too often this has been the opening for a total dictatorial control in the country.

Finally, with the Marxists, we must remember that the purpose of a worldview is not just to understand the world, but also to help change it. With Archbishop William Temple, we must note that in its radically historical nature, Marxism shows its deep indebtedness to the biblical view of history.[99] We must retain our deep appreciation of the grounding of our own tradition in the particulars of history and its ongoing emphasis on justice.

A basic conclusion for Christians when studying the various views of history is that history cannot change its nature by itself, because human beings cannot change their sinful nature by their own powers.

There will indeed be an end of history, but when it comes it will not be the result of inevitable progress or man-made efforts or revolutionary tumult and bloodshed. The final end of history will be by the act of that transcendent God with whom finally we all have to do, and who acts redemptively within the process of history. In the interim between the present and the final stage of history, Christians must seek, with God's guidance and power, to realize on earth as much of the biblical pattern of justice and love as possible.

VI. How Would You Define and Illustrate the Intuitive or Subjective Approach to History (Historicism)?

Historicism is an influential modern approach to history. It began its development in the eighteenth century, largely as a German reaction to the idea of inevitable progress that had grown up in France and Great Britain. It became influential in the United States in the latter part of the nineteenth and early twentieth centuries.[100]

1. The Key Ideas of the Historicist View

(1) Cultures Are Molded by History. The central idea in historicism is that all cultures are molded by history. The very word *historicism* provides witness to this conviction that the customs and beliefs of any group are the products of the group's historical experience. According to this view of history, everything people know, including all they understand or think they understand about God's dealings with human beings, is forged in a particular historical setting and bears the unique imprint of that setting. (For example, the teachings of Socrates could be propagated only in the free and democratic atmosphere of Athens.) Customs and beliefs are like flowers that will flourish only in a particular soil. The explanation of why different nations have different approaches or distinctives lies chiefly in language; the way a nation speaks determines its stock of ideas.[101]

In the United States, for example, one by one the most advanced thinkers in each of the social disciplines became acutely conscious of the historical origin of culture. This is to say that they came to see that all creations of the human mind and heart are products of the historical process that fashioned them. These thinkers noted that all ideas, values, institutions, and behavior patterns known to humanity are produced by human beings and therefore bear the imprint of the historical setting in which they emerge.

The starkness of this new—or at least new degree of—historical consciousness was captured by Justice Oliver Wendell Holmes. He stated that the law, which for centuries had been thought to embody timeless principles of justice, is in fact only a shrewd prediction of what a judge will do next. The same unflinching relativism was expressed in sociology by the German thinker Max Weber, in philosophy by John Dewey, in history by James Harvey Robinson, in political science by Charles Beard, and in anthropology by Franz Boas. By the 1920s, the assumption that all knowledge, including all forms of religious knowledge, is fashioned wholly from the materials of human history, had come to be the hallmark of the modern mind.[102]

It is argued by some that the rapid deepening of historical consciousness during the late nineteenth and early twentieth centuries was to some extent a direct product of economic and social turmoil. For example, America had become a welter of contending factions and diverse cultures. In such a setting, it was difficult not to recognize the profoundly historical nature of the real world.[103]

The most striking social change was the relentless pressure of immigration. Another pressure that prompted thoughtful people to reassess older assumptions was the fragmentation of life in the cities. Shifting patterns of education in the latter years of the century also fostered recognition of the pluralistic character of the world. These social pressures helped to nurture the conviction that cultural patterns are fluid and relative and pluralistic—and, therefore, historically created.[104]

(2) The Importance of Intuition or Empathy. A second concept in historicist thought is concerned with how we appreciate groups other than our own. Historicism deals with the question of how we can break out of our own thought-worlds in order to penetrate the thought-world of other places and times. The historicist answer is that we have a faculty of intuition. A human being enjoys a gift of empathy for other human beings that allows him or her to grasp the significance of what others do.

Historicists call this process of intuition "understanding"—or, in the German, *Verstehen*. This is a form of interpersonal perception that goes beyond the rational. It is not achieved by reason, for in the historicist view reason is fit for investigating only the nonhuman world. The technique of intuition enables us to overcome the barriers that separate us from other parts of the human world. Understanding is the distinctive method of the historical sciences, which are the disciplines that study humankind.

These two key ideas of historicism both bear the marks of reaction against the Enlightenment. The very idea that all cultures are molded by history is a contradiction to the idea of progress, for it implies that there is nothing linear about history. The idea of a goal of history, such as human perfection, which is often held by those who advocated the inevitable progress view, is absent from historicism.

In addition, the historicists differ from the advocates of inevitable progress in that they deny that reason is the measure of humankind. Reason, they argue, is incapable of grasping the significance of human behavior; only a special intuitive faculty is capable of that. To the historicist, reason is not all-powerful, just as the idea of progress does not sum up the significance of the past.[105]

2. The Key Advocates of the Historicist View

(1) Giovanni Vico of Italy. A forerunner to later historicist thinking was Giovanni Battista Vico, an eighteenth-century Italian thinker who was one of the first to recognize the "inner" aspect of historical thinking.

According to Vico, we first do critical sifting of historical evidence and arrive at a mass of historical facts, which represents the outer side of historical events. However, we cannot have the certainty about these facts that a natural scientist has about his data. We need to penetrate to the inner side, to the motives and intentions, feelings and aspirations of those who participated in these events and whose actions, corporate and individual, constituted these events. According to Vico, to understand history we have to get "inside the skin" of those human beings whose actions were crucial in the historic past.

To an important extent, the past is beyond observation and experiment. Therefore, to understand its inner side we must utilize imagination. The historian has a common nature uniting him or her with the persons being studied. History is thus able to penetrate to the inner depths, whereas science has to be satisfied with the external and the phenomenal.[106]

(2) Leopold von Ranke of Germany. In Germany the dominant leader of the historicist approach was Leopold von Ranke. Von Ranke emphasized that the historian's mind must penetrate to the inward nature of events, and that intuition enables the historian to divine the essence of the past. Although he did believe in intensive research, he was chiefly interested in getting into the inner nature of the historical facts.[107]

(3) Wilhelm Dilthey of Germany. Wilhelm Dilthey, a significant German philosopher of the first decades of this century, was the most important later historicist. He elaborated and developed the historicist notion of intuition. His view is that history is concerned with the understanding of human action by methods different from those of the natural sciences. The laws of science cannot grasp the particular features of any instance of human behavior, because behavior is charged with intention, and human intention can only be intuited. The process of understanding, according to Dilthey, is not just an irrational jump of feeling but an intelligible method, guided by principles which Dilthey called "hermeneutics."[108]

Dilthey was influenced by the early nineteenth-century theologian Friedrich Schleiermacher, who contended that biblical verses must be understood in their context. Dilthey likewise emphasized that human action can be grasped only in its context. This was Dilthey's doctrine of the "hermeneutical circle": a part must be understood through its setting in the whole.[109]

Thus we see that Dilthey tended to minimize inference—reasoning on the basis of evidence—as a means of understanding and instead to emphasize intuitive insight. In his view, understanding involves a direct awareness of the inner through the outer. Through intuition, historical events as actions become transparent and the inward motivation is laid bare. Thus, the historian identifies himself with the past and actually relives its inner side.[110]

(4) R. G. Collingwood of England. A similar, although less carefully worked-out, historical approach was developed at Oxford University by R. G. Collingwood, who died in 1943. Collingwood's papers on the subject were published after his death as *The Idea of History.*

For Collingwood, the historian must penetrate beyond the external facts of an event to its inner reality—to the thought of the person in the past—and totally identify his or her mind with the persons he or she is studying. Historical events are unique in having an internal aspect that can be mentally reenacted. Hence this task of studying the inner reality of events is unique to the historian. Events of nature have nothing but an outer reality, so the natural scientist is excluded from exploring the mental world of humankind. The contrast establishes for Collingwood that history has its own distinctive methodology.[111]

3. The Influence of the Historicist View

In Germany, the historicist stress on the corporate personality of the nation helped to form the foundation of Hitler's philosophy. In Nationalist Socialist thought, the nation was defined less in terms of language than of race. However, the ideas of the nation's central role in history and its superiority to normal moral conventions bear the marks of the historicist style of thinking.[112]

Thus historicism has deeply affected the way history has been written from the early nineteenth century onward. It has affected almost every field of human thought. Dilthey's method was taken up by Martin Heidegger, whose *Being and Time* (1927) became the early classic of existentialism. In the United States, historicism influenced the thought of prominent theologians such as Augustus H. Strong, who died in 1921. Strong struggled to hold together his conservative Christian faith and the radical assumptions of historicism. The same problem bedeviled conservative thinkers of all kinds.[113]

4. Strengths and Weaknesses of the Historicist View

(1) Strengths. According to Eric Rust, in order to acquire historical knowledge we do have to penetrate the outward actions and understand motives and intentions. Inference, sympathy, and imagination all play their part in an accurate understanding of past events. Imagination fuses our hard intellectual labor and our inferences and endeavors to knit them together. Yet even this is not enough; an intuitive capacity often provides the historian with the final key. Historical understanding thus involves the disciplined and critical use of reason, sympathetic and imaginative reconstruction, and intuitive insight.

Rust notes, however, that the issue of objectivity must also be emphasized. The historian does not create the past; there is a givenness—an objective reality—about the events with which he or she deals. Therefore a historian must be careful not to let intuitive assessment of a past event interfere with the objective reality of that event—as far as this objective reality can be critically determined from available data.[114]

(2) Weaknesses. To a great extent, the main historicist idea—that human groups are molded by history—is undeniable. But historicism takes a further step. It tends to hold that the flux of history eliminates any constancy in human actions in history; it minimizes the idea that there is such a thing as

human nature. But surely humans in different times of history have the same types of motives, the same order of feelings, the same types of thinking. Surely there are some things all human beings have in common!

In this aspect, historicism has overreacted against the Enlightenment. Certainly, the Enlightenment notion that man is defined totally by his power of reason is inadequate. But this does not mean that all human characteristics are determined by circumstances. Historicism underestimates the extent to which human nature is constant.[115]

The historicist idea of how we obtain knowledge of the past is also questionable. The historian, it is said, can intuit the mental world of people long dead. But at this point, a historian's creativity may lead him or her astray. There is no objective criterion in the historicist approach for determining how accurately the historian reflects the past.

Historicism has also been fertile soil for dangerous doctrines—such as National Socialism, as noted above. The Nazis were able to exploit the image of a unique and glorious German past that German historicists had created.

The problem here is that historicism concentrated attention on the idea of the nation as a unique cultural system functioning independently of any universal code of conduct. This approach provides fertile ground for the right-wing tendency to glorify whatever is traditional about a culture.

The historicists also often argued that it was their duty to promote with a single eye the greatness of a nation such as Germany. This was to transform the commitment of historians into an unchangeable ideological straitjacket that restricted their critical powers. In Germany, for example, the criticisms by historians of other nations were ruled out of court because they "could not express the spirit of Germany." Hence, the deeds of the German state were seen to be beyond debate.

Unfortunately, historicism has tended to collapse into historical relativism and to undermine its own premises. Because there was no ground for preferring one custom to another, one moral code to another, or even historicism to another worldview, the whole historicist perspective stood revealed as an arbitrary preference. For this reason, confidence in historicism as a way of understanding history has declined in the twentieth century.[116]

VII. How Would You Define and Evaluate the Futurology Approach to History?

When I moved to Houston, Texas, and assumed a position at Rice University, I found that the concept of "futurology" was everywhere in the air. The original futurology group, the Club of Rome, met in Houston. Various Rice University departments sponsored futurology lectures. I attended the Fourth International Congress of Religion, Architecture, and the Arts, which emphasized futurology. Although the novelty of this dramatic movement has worn off, interest continues in both popular and scholarly circles. In recent years, futurology has become identified for some with the "New Age" movement.

This futurist movement has significance for contemporary approaches to history. It also undergirds in some ways the biblical view of history.

1. Definition and Approach of Futurology

Futurology or futurism is the catch-all term applied in the United States to organized, institutionalized programs, as well as individuals, whose major activity is concerned with the study of the future. Futurologists attempt to develop an analytical model of what is presently taking place and from there, on the basis of available data, try to forecast what might happen in the future. Scientific futurists understand their task as basically observing present trends and then, by means of extrapolation, projecting what would happen if these trends were to continue.[117]

Because present trends are so diverse and complex, such analysts commonly project alternative futures, called "futuribles." Different futures are possible, we are told, and it is up to us to decide which of the alternative futures we wish to actualize.[118]

The belief is that if we use scientific procedures to gain an understanding of the forces determining the present, we will have the information to decide and so control our own destiny, so that our world will be guided into a truly human future. We need, says Alvin Toffler, understanding, decision, and control. Diagnosis precedes cure.

Futurology, then, is a new synthesis of varied disciplines. It is closely related to history, but it involves a projection into a new time dimension. It is also related to cultural anthropology, theoretical sociology, social philosophy, and theology of history. It uses mathematical probability and deals with all aspects of the human future. Futurology is cross-disciplinary—a team venture. It also attempts to address both short-range and long-range developments.

2. Reasons for the Rise of Futurology

Why, in our times, has there arisen this serious movement, which uses the best available statistical techniques, computer data, and methods of social analysis?

Down into the nineteenth century, the time span of important social and technological change was longer than that of a single human life. Change occurred too slowly for most people to be aware of it. In the twentieth century, however, and especially in the atomic age, universal basic change has been occurring within less than one generation. The rapid expansion of scientific frontiers has created both new problems and the means of solving old ones. It has created concern or anxiety about the future as well as equipment, such as computers, that can help us study it.

3. Leaders in Futurology

Through media emphases a number of futurologists have become well known. Some of the better known futurologists include Alvin Toffler, a social critic who has written *Future Shock* and *The Third Wave*; Daniel Bell, a sociologist who has written *The Post-Industrial Society;* and Marshall McLuhan, a communication theorist who has written *The Gutenberg Galaxy.*

Fred Polack is a political figure in Holland who is author of *The Image of the Future.* Kenneth Boulding, an economist, has written *The Meaning of the Twentieth Century.* Biologist Paul Ehrlich, the author of *The Population Bomb,* has stated his futuristic concerns on network television. R. Buckminster Fuller is an architect and designer who has written *Operating Manual for Spaceship Earth.* Herman Kahn is a physicist who has written *The Year 2000.*

In addition to individuals, there are a number of organizations that are seminal in the futurist movement. Most of us have heard of the Club of Rome, with their publication entitled *The Limits of Growth.* The World Future Society publishes a journal called *The Futurist.* And there are a number of well-known think tanks, such as the Hudson Institute and the Rand Corporation, that specialize in the study of the future.

4. The Types of Futurology

Futurologists have been divided into certain categories or types. There are the optimists, who presuppose a qualitative change in human society or human nature or human consciousness. These draw on nineteenth-century forerunners such as Auguste Comte and Karl Marx, who predicted utopian futures based on qualitative change in society.

Marshall McLuhan is one of these optimists; he foresees an electronic unity which will undergird human progress. Psychologist B. F. Skinner anticipates progress through psychological conditioning, accomplished by gifted psychologists who should dominate society.

Then there are the technocratic optimists, who assume that many basic human problems (as defined by humanists) can be solved by technology. A basic representative is Herman Kahn of the Hudson Institute, who edited *The Next 200 Years.*

Closely related to the optimists are the "optimists beyond pessimism." These people see a cultural or ecological catastrophe leading to a new super civilization, which will be built from the ashes of our present order. An example is L. S. Stavrianos, who wrote *The Promise of the Coming Dark Age.*

Pessimists are also to be found among futurologists. There are the cultural pessimists who see certain trends in society leading to a total collapse of civilization. Jacques Barzun could be put in this category, along with people like Malcolm Muggeridge in his earlier writing. There are the scientific pessimists, who see current trends in the ecosystem leading to catastrophe unless those trends are reversed. The Club of Rome reflects this view in its book *Limits to Growth,* as does Paul Ehrlich in *The Population Bomb.*

Pessimism has increased in recent years because of failures in utopianism even while some of its goals were apparently succeeding. An example is the welfare state, which is a reality in some countries—such as Sweden—but which has not brought overall happiness to the large majority of its people. In addition, the prevalence of Freudian psychology has emphasized the dark underside of the human personality and tended to reduce belief in the possibility of a perfectly rational and ordered future society.[119]

5. The Importance of Futurology

It is widely accepted that futurology has great importance, for we tend to be pulled toward our images of the future. Fred Polack makes a good case for the fact that what people think will happen has a definite impact on what does happen.

This fact underscores the necessity of hope for the future. Psychoanalyst Erich Fromm maintains that without hope directed toward a positive future, the present becomes unlivable. In the same vein, James Cone suggests that if the future is not meaningful, "all is despair." Furthermore, it is hope in the face of an open future that makes freedom possible. Without it, we are in bondage to past traditions and present predicaments.

There are other facets of the importance of futurology. Considering the future tends to give us perspective. It heightens imagination and identifies crucial areas for future action. Futurology is also a testing ground for alternative philosophers, philosophies, or worldviews. And people in the biblical tradition suggest that it awakens many to the validity of biblical insights.[120]

6. The Attitude of the Biblical Worldview toward Futurology

As several biblical thinkers have pointed out, in many ways the basic outlook of futurology is congenial to biblical concerns. The conscious purpose of most future planners is, in general, consistent with Christian emphases—opposition to war and oppression, disease, poverty, discrimination and dehumanization.

The biblical worldview is certainly congenial to the idea of expectation and hope for the future; in this way it agrees with some of the emphases of the futurological optimists. In fact, people in the biblical tradition believe that the projection of a positive and realistic image of the future is one of the important contributions of the biblical worldview to today's civilization. And as we have seen, such a positive image gives human beings a sense of purpose and expectation; it pulls a civilization forward and gives hope. In the words of Daniel Bell, "in the end, it is moral ideals . . . that shape history."

At the same time, the biblical worldview identifies with many of the concerns of the pessimistic futurologists in being acutely aware of negative trends in modern society and the possible shadowy side of the world to come. Because Christians know the reality of sin that permeates every phase of our personal and corporate activities, we can understand sin's capacity to darken future developments as well. We can well understand the need to study possible future problems—excess free time, boredom, increased alcoholism and drug use, pollution, and the widening of the gap between rich and poor. We must be at work to ensure that the forces of dehumanization do not swallow up positive humanizing influences in the future.

It should be noted that a number of Christian scholars are writing in this area. Representative authors include Tom Sine, Stephen Travis, Os Guinness, and Ted Peters. Organizations such as the Billy Graham Center have sponsored consultations on futurology. More recently, evangelical Christians are seeking to evaluate from a biblical perspective futurology concepts which have been absorbed by New Age leaders. In its effort to transform individuals and society and bring about a utopian era, the New Age movement has sought to replace both secular humanism and the traditional biblical teachings with mystical enlightenment and even occult practices.[121]

The last word for those who hold the biblical worldview is that the future ultimately lies beyond human efforts. A positive future involves more than technology or political development; it involves renewal and conversion. Many Christian young people in their professional lives are engaged in the ideal of furthering economic and scientific progress. But the biblical worldview also calls in a more fundamental sense for renewal through divine resources.

The unique contribution of the biblical view toward the study of the future is its vision of a kingdom that is rooted in the past, is present, and is in the future as well. In this way, the biblical faith is closely related to the concerns of the futurologists—in fact, in many ways it is an adequate futurology in and of itself.[122]

VIII. What Is the Biblical View of the Meaning of History?

1. Old Testament Teachings on History

(1) The Centrality of History. All peoples of the world have a history of sorts —whether recorded by the written word or passed on by oral tradition. All peoples, at least in civilized areas, have their monuments, their stories of great deeds, and their annals and chronicles. However, as we have seen, the sense that events in time have significance and purpose is not universal. In our civilization, this urgent sense of purposive history is part of the Jewish religious heritage.

As we have already indicated, most of the world's early religions tended to see history as cyclical and events in time as only poor reflections of the real world, which was considered to be "up there." There was little sense of the unfolding of events through the ages according to a plan or temporal order, little sense that events in the temporal world had significance or meaning. In the early days of civilization, history was not taken seriously—except by the Hebrews.

At the very beginning of Israel's historical consciousness stands Abraham as an example and a symbol. He was called from the astrological naturalism of Ur of Chaldees and started on his way to Canaan. And while on his way, at Haran, he received a second call to a purposive future that would involve all nations (Gen. 12:1–3; Acts 7:4). In these calls and Abraham's response, humanity was emancipated from nature by the challenge of God who calls and asks for a definite response. This God of Abraham goes before humanity through time, pointing the way. There is no cycle. History is not a matter of chance or inflexible fate, but rather a place of human freedom and responsibility—the place of God's calling.[123]

The understanding of the purposive nature of history, then, began with Abraham. However, the concept of history in its fully developed sense is a product of the prophets of Israel. Indeed, Israel's uniqueness as a nation lies in the demand of the prophets for obedience to the Creator God who had called Israel to his purpose.

The prophets had an approach to life which takes time with radical seriousness. It understands the past in terms of God's creativity and promise. It understands the future in terms of God's ultimate victory over evil. This view understands the present in terms of that past and future, demanding obedience and repentance from apostasy.[124] The prophet thus was the interpreter of history; it was in history that he found revealed God's will, judgment, and redemptive purpose.

The Hebraic mind, as it is described in the Bible, sees all history as a great and meaningful process under the control of the God who is the Lord of history. In the beginning, the process was seen as concerning only the Hebrew people, but by the time of the prophet Amos, the vision was universal—the God of Israel was seen as the Lord of people everywhere (Amos 6:14, 9:8). To the Hebrews, history is of one piece—the single great drama under one Lord. Thus we have emerging the idea of the unity of history as *world* history.[125]

(2) The Purposeful Nature of History. According to the Old Testament Hebrews, because history is under the control of God, it has purpose—it is moving toward a goal. The past itself showed purpose, and the past contained promises which could be fulfilled only in the future. God's purposes are effected, with time, in and through history. The salvation that is promised as the ultimate validation of life is inaugurated in history, although its fulfillment and consummation will be beyond time as we know it now. From this point of view, earthly history takes on a meaning and seriousness that are completely absent where the biblical influence has not been felt.

Although the prophets were to articulate the Hebrew sense of history, it is clear that the origin of the biblical sense of history is connected with one particular event, which was indelibly imprinted into the spirit of Israel: the deliverance from slavery in Egypt. The remembrance of this intervention through the Passover festival formed the center of Israel's worship.

God's deliverance from Egypt was not a goal in itself. Rather, it was meant to be a leading into the Promised Land. Thus, even the forty years between the Exodus and the final entry into the Promised Land were goal-directed and purposeful.

But history did not stop upon the arrival in Canaan; it continued to move toward a climax—the kingdom of David. It soon became clear, therefore, that the entry into the Promised Land was not an actual fulfillment of history. This is true partly because progress was hindered by Israel's unfaithfulness, and partly because God's final goal is much broader than Israel at first understood.

For the same reason, the climax under David and Solomon is not an end either. The line of Israel's history declined to include the Exile, but the major prophets in the later historical books described God as continuing with his care and guidance throughout his people's struggle. In the midst of all that was contrary to their expectation, they began to wait for a new Anointed One from the house of David—to look forward to the messianic age, in which God's leading of his people would reach its goal.

Actually, the person and work of Jesus Christ cannot be understood apart from this beginning of the concept of history with the Exodus. Matthew, especially, who writes for Jews, makes this plain. Christ was called from Egypt (2:15), went through the waters, journeyed through the desert, and made a covenant on the mountain. And when he died, he gave his life as a Passover Lamb whose blood would save Israel and whose death would mean the exodus from the house of slavery for all nations.[126]

The pervasive importance of the Exodus and of historical thinking in the national and religious life of Israel is strikingly seen in the way in which Israel transformed the festivals of the seasons into ceremonies commemorating historical events.

The Feast of Unleavened Bread, Pentecost, and the Feast of Tabernacles were all originally festivals of the agricultural seasons. They were used by the Near Eastern nature religions to insure fertility by means of proper seasonal observances. These festivals were, of course, attractive to the Israelite after they settled in Canaan and adopted agriculture as a means of livelihood. Yet in adopting these nature festivals, the Israelites changed them into celebrations of historical events from Israel's past. The Feast of Unleavened Bread became connected with the Exodus, and Pentecost was related to the giving of the Law at Sinai. The Feast of Tabernacles was related to the sojourn in the wilderness. This same historical concern transformed the sprinkling of blood on the lintel from an ancient rite warding off evil demons into the Passover celebration of Israel's deliverance from Egypt and the slaying of the Egyptian firstborn. Such a radical change of the meaning of the nature festivals highlights the radical difference between the Hebrews and the other Near Eastern peoples, including the Greeks.[127]

(3) Orientation toward the Future. Above all, it is the Hebrew sense of a hopeful future that characterizes this unique understanding of history. For most of the pagan world, there was nothing that time could bring but a turn of the wheel of fortune and a recurrence of the never-ending cycle of history. We can thus understand the profound sense of melancholy that pervaded the best of pagan spirituality and even left traces in the book of Ecclesiastes.

In Israel, however, time was seen as potentially open. It is important to stress *potentially*, however, for Israel did not have the nineteenth-century view of necessary or inevitable progress. The new was not built into nature, from which it emerged developmentally. On the contrary, the new depended entirely on the inscrutable, although faithful and creative, power of God.

(4) How God Works in History: An Elected People in a Covenant Relationship. It was a fundamental Old Testament idea that, although God had many people, he reserved a special place for Israel—he had *elected* them to be the conduit of his blessings to all other nations (Gen. 12:1–3). This sense of election is an important clue for the understanding of the meaning and significance of Israel and the biblical view of history.

Many through the centuries have objected to this idea of Israel's election. They say that a God of love and justice could hardly exhibit such favoritism. But we must remember that Israel paid a terrible price for this election. They were not elected just to receive a special privilege. God was in constant conflict with the desires of Israel. Amos 3:2 states "you only have I known, therefore I shall visit upon you all your iniquities."

It is also true that Israel was not chosen because of merit. Then why did God choose Israel? The doctrine of election is traced to the promise of God to Abraham, the patriarch of the Hebrew people. And this promise is set in the total plan of history. Man and woman had been driven from Paradise because of their rebellion against their Creator. As a result, civilization became corrupt. So in the election of Israel God was seeking to answer the plight of humanity.[128]

Not all of the biblical writers saw clearly the universal aim of God for Israel nor the mission of Israel for the saving of the nations. Yet all the biblical writers were conscious of the responsibility that is coextensive with Israel's privileges.

It should also be remembered, of course, that even though Israel was the elect nation, it was not unique in being used by God to execute his purposes. At times God used pagan nations and individuals as well. Even Assyria was a rod of God's anger against Israel.[129]

The concept of election found its concrete expression in the Old Testament concept of covenant. God in his grace offered a covenant to Israel. It had the advantages for Israel of an inheritance; security from enemies; and law, order, and inner peace. But it also meant an obligation: to obey God and to reflect his nature and character. This covenant was not to be seen as a legal burden, because the law and its guidelines were based on an act of God's grace for the good of the people.[130]

This covenant or agreement between God and Israel resulted in a unique people with a unique outlook that set them apart from other peoples of their day. For example, in Israel there was an equality of persons under the law, and the poor, weak, and defenseless received special consideration. Inherent in Hebrew understanding was that God was for the weak—a terror to the rich and wicked.[131]

Even when Israel selected a king, as did the other countries, they looked upon him differently than other countries looked upon their kings. Israel's king was considered adopted as God's son—the "anointed one"—to protect the people from enemies and secure righteousness in the social order. When the current kings betrayed this trust, it was said that God would raise up a future Anointed One who would fulfill the theological conditions on which the monarchy rested.

Kingship, for the Hebrews, was not divinely ordained as a primary office. Rather, the kingship was introduced as an emergency measure. The ideal or normative period was the time prior to the kings, when the Israelites lived directly under God, with judges raised up to lead the people in emergencies.

Even after the kings were established, the prophets maintained their right of criticizing the kings. And the people at certain times had to rebuild their community without a king, even as they had in the wilderness period. This prepared the way for the "new king" of the "New Covenant."[132]

(5) The Old Testament View as Foundational to the New Testament View. In summary, we see that the doctrines of election and covenant gave to Israel an interpretation of life and a view of human history which are absolutely fundamental to an understanding of the Christian view of history and to Christian theology. This is especially true when these emphases are seen with Christ as their fulfillment.

In fact, we cannot understand the New Testament view of history if we refuse to listen to the Old Testament emphases. The Old Testament played an important role in the life of Jesus and in the hearts and minds of the apostles. It is not possible to accept the New Testament teachings concerning the relationship of God and history without accepting in principle the related witness of the Old Testament.

It was in the Old Testament that the biblical doctrine of history was born. Actually, the development of such a set of ideas is quite remarkable, because the polytheistic cultures that surrounded Israel had little sense of the significance of history; their life was based on nature and its cycles. However, under the guidance of God's revelation, Israel had little interest in nature except as God used it in his historical acts to reveal himself and accomplish his purpose. The God of history was unaffected by the cycles of nature.

The sense of the movement of history toward a future goal where past and present find fulfillment is the source of the New Testament view and the modern conception of history in the West.[133]

2. New Testament Teachings on History

(1) Unity of History. The New Testament sees the unity of history in the continuing and purposeful working of God in the progression of events (2 Cor. 5:18–20). The characteristic biblical approach to time is contained in the Greek word *kairos* (Gal. 4:4), not the word *chronos,* which refers to time in the sense of passing minutes and days. *Kairos* is bound up with the biblical phrase, "the fullness of time," which refers to "filled time"—time replete with happening and meaning.

From the biblical perspective, history can be divided into periods, each centering in a special *kairos* or manifestation. However, each *kairos* only gains its true significance by its relation to the central *kairos,* which is the life, death, and resurrection of Jesus. To this central event in the series of times each *kairos* of the Old Testament points forward in promise, and each *kairos* of the present period points back in fulfillment.

Thus Augustine, Francis of Assisi, Luther, Calvin, John Wesley, and William Carey make, each for his own period, the *kairos* of the hour in reinterpreting Christ, who is the midpoint of all history and of each succeeding generation.[134] Using Christ as the central point of history in their particular period of opportunity, Christian leaders through the centuries have confronted men and women with the absolute demand and final grace of God as he has revealed himself in this great act of redemption.

The ebb and flow of history around each such *kairos* indicates that it is preceded by a period of decay and expectation and followed by a period of reception and the inclusion of new insight and religious experience into the divine purpose. Of course, in each *kairos* there must be a prophetic voice which reinterprets for his or her own time the supreme *kairos*—the fullness of time which came in Christ. This means that the kingdom of God which has come into history is continually being actualized in newer and deeper ways within the movement of historical existence. Every fresh *kairos* or period of opportunity involves a new manifestation of the kingdom of God.[135]

This *kairos* approach means that history is not a matter of steady progress. It is a mixed picture, with an opposition of good and evil.

There is some progress in science, technology, and medicine and in the humanizing of working conditions. The history of every field of human endeavor gives such evidence. These value potentials are inherent in God's creation and are actualized by his continuing creativity in providence and grace.

Yet evil and ugliness often grow, too; we see this in tyrannical governments, nuclear threats, repressive social systems, environmental pollution, rape of natural resources, decaying inner-city ghettos, discrimination, and every inhumanity of person to person. The explanation for such evil is human fallenness and irresponsible self-seeking. These are restrained by the providential activity of God in history, but they still pervert the potential of God's creation.

Of course, the biblical hope is that good will completely triumph over evil by God's intervention in history in the second coming of Christ. The resurrection of Christ from the dead is offered as a guarantee of his eventual triumph.

(2) The Important Place of Individuals and Groups in History. According to the biblical view, God works out his purpose in time and history through special individuals in a particular group. As we shall see, in the New Testament period this is the Christian church or churches, or the Christian community, or the Body of Christ.

God makes himself known not in the isolated, timeless, mystical experiences of unrelated individuals, but rather in the course of history through individuals and groups who are tied in to that redemptive history.[136]

(3) The Centrality of Jesus Christ in History. Jesus Christ—his life, death, and resurrection—is central in the New Testament view of history. He inaugurated a new era of history and will complete it.

Even before his death and resurrection, Jesus' message of the kingdom and his claim to act for God placed him in the center of the course of divine action. After the resurrection, his uniqueness, authority, and significance for God's redemptive work were still clearer. His death was then seen not as a tragic occurrence but as a positive part of the redemptive work of God.

Jesus preached that "the time is fulfilled" (Mark 1:15). He himself saw, in what God was doing and was about to do through him, the fulfillment of the Old Testament anticipation and the Israelite hope. The apostles from the first preached that in Christ this fulfillment had occurred.

In God's own intention and action, Christ is central and decisive. The true and full understanding of all stages and aspects of God's total work for humankind in history is to be gained by starting with Jesus Christ and relating everything to him.[137]

(4) Backward and Forward Emphasis in the Christian Era. For the Christian community there is both a backward and forward look. The life of the Christian does indeed have a constant tie with the contemporary Lord and Head of the church, but it also has a time framework in two quite notable respects.

The Christian view of history has a constant backward look. It has its basis and justification in God's central and decisive act in history through Jesus of Nazareth—his life, ministry, death, and resurrection. But the Christian perspective faces forward as well—anticipating the full realization of God's purposes at the end of the age.

This means that the Christian lives with a certain tension in regard to time. The era of the church is that in which God has begun his decisive redemption, but has not yet fully completed it. This time must move forward under the Lordship of Christ until the day when Christ comes to complete his work.[138]

This unique approach to life and history has been described as living between the *already* and the *not yet.* New Testament believers live in the last days, but the Last Day has not yet arrived. They are in the new age, but the final age is not yet here. Although they enjoy "the powers of the age to come," they are not yet free from sin, suffering, and death. Although they have the first fruits of the Spirit, they groan inwardly as they wait for their final redemption.

(5) The Probability of Suffering and Persecution for Christians. A standard aspect of the New Testament view of history is that Christians can expect suffering. An integral part of discipleship is that Christians be willing to witness, as Jesus did, with their lives.

The New Testament repeatedly stresses that the Christ who brings not peace, but the sword (Matt. 10:34), will repeatedly suffer persecution at the hands of the counterforces he himself called to life—and that applies to his followers, as well. Far from being an unexpected setback that upsets the outlook for the kingdom, such persecution is actually an unmistakable indication of the presence of God's kingdom on earth. That is why in the New Testament suffering is often spoken of in great soberness but with an undertone of great joy. In the Sermon on the Mount we read "Blessed are those who are persecuted for righteousness' sake, for theirs is the kingdom of heaven" (Matt. 5:10). James states "Count it all joy, my brethren, when you meet various trials" (James 1:2, LB).

It is not surprising, then, that the whole concept of being Christian is reviewed by Paul in this light. "And if children, then heirs, heirs of God and fellow heirs with Christ, provided we suffer with him in order that we may also be glorified with him" (Rom. 8:17). The church is to represent her Lord to the world through her suffering—and this applies both to individual Christians and to the corporate community.

(6) The Development of Apostasy and Competitive Doctrines of Salvation. In the study of the concepts of apostasy, Antichrist, and other aspects of eschatology (last things), Hendrikus Berkhof of the University of Leiden has become an internationally recognized scholar. Especially notable have been his books, *Christ, the Meaning of History, Christ and the Powers,* and *Well-Founded Hope.* In his writings, he points out that the idea of apostasy—the withdrawal from or rejection of the faith—is most often addressed in the New Testament in the form of competitive doctrines of salvation. In other words, rejection of biblical faith is usually coupled with accepting another religion or ideology that promises some form of salvation. False prophets are often mentioned in this connection.

This is appropriate because apostasy by itself cannot survive for long. It is a negative concept—the absence of faith or loyalty—and human beings cannot live on the absence of something. The inevitable result is that another form of faith —either religious or ideological—will step in to take its place.

Of course, apostasy from the gospel and the subsequent adoption of competitive offers can take place only where the gospel has taken root in one form or the other. According to the biblical worldview, we can expect both apostasy and competitive doctrines of salvation in places where the gospel has been established.

Berkhof suggests that if we translate this into cultural categories, the encounter between the gospel and the culture begins with the opposition of the old forces which characterize that particular culture. The anti-Christian revival of the great world religions which is now taking place after the initial period of missionary activity must also be seen in this light. (An example is the reaction of the exponents of the Hindu religion in India to missionary activity.)

Once the gospel has taken root in a culture and the old powers are more or less driven back, apostasy appears in the foreground. This has increasingly been the case in Europe during the last three centuries. The pressure of post-Christian indifference is part of the burden of suffering now placed upon the church.

Because human beings cannot long endure the absence of a faith, apostasy always carries with it the probability of a new competitive doctrine of salvation. This doctrine is often outwardly tolerant, although it is usually coupled with great inner pride, as is the case with a perspective that says it will take the best from the teachings of several religions (syncretism).

In times such as the present, when nihilism has undermined the faith of many people, a new type of competitive doctrine of salvation comes in. This is usually in the form of a totalitarian ideology such as National Socialism and Communism. The only possible attitude that these groups can take toward the church is that of persecution.

Berkhof sees Islam as a competitive doctrine of salvation that has put a significant stumbling block in the progress of God's kingdom in history. Muhammad began with the thought of bringing the Judeo-Christian revelation to his own pagan people. However, the idea of revelation underwent a fundamental change in the hands of Muhammad. The result is a fundamentally different doctrine of salvation which keeps millions of people from an encounter with Christ because they believe they possess the higher form of religion.

Islam, according to Berkhof, is a great apostasy and a competitive doctrine of salvation in one—it both rejects the gospel and offers an alternative route to salvation. Ethically and culturally, Islam is seen by Berkhof as an adversary of an authentic Christian gospel because it gives a person the illusion of being delivered from paganism without giving that person the freedom and power which come through the salvation offered in Christ.[140]

(7) The Work of the Antichrist. An important concept in the New Testament view of history—one closely related to the probability of persecution—is that of the Antichrist, who is described in 2 Thessalonians 2:8 as "the lawless one" and mentioned in 1 and 2 John as an opposer and denier of Christ. There is evidence that the Antichrist theme occupied a central place in the thinking of the early church, and its precise meaning and implication for history has been much debated in the church over the years.

The meaning of *anti* is "in the place of" and "against." The Antichrist is not separated from Christ. He is both Christ's competitor and caricature. Paul characterizes him as one who "takes his seat in the temple of God, proclaiming himself to be a God" (2 Thess. 2:4).

We should not seek to force biblical thought into Western thinking and try to decide whether the Antichrist is a person or a group, a tendency or a spirit of the age. Christ is a person, and at the same time he is the head of a Body who, with his Spirit, moved triumphantly through the world. The Antichrist is similar to this. The beast from the earth (Rev. 13:11–17) is placed beside the Antichrist (denoted as the "beast from the sea") in order to point out what a strange and far-reaching influence will be placed on the minds of "those who dwell on earth." This does not take away the fact that the center of all this is a person. The Antichrist is more than a group. He is the object of the worship of the groups who follow him, and the object of such worship can only be a person.

In 2 Thessalonians 2, it seems to be clear that Paul was not thinking of a contemporary, but was pointing to a future figure; every attempt to identify this figure with a historical person is expressly discouraged (vv. 3, 6, 8). The whole matter stands or falls with the certainty that Jesus cannot yet return because the Antichrist has not yet arrived.

In like manner, the Antichrist of Revelation is both Rome and not Rome. In other words, the implication is that Rome is partially the appearance of the future Antichrist. The Antichrist will repeat and increase what was done by Roman emperors such as Nero and Domitian.

It should also be noted that the Antichrist is characterized by the limited time allotted to his work and power. The Dragon knows that "his time is short" (Rev. 12:12). For a moment, the Antichrist appears on the stage, only to be chased away. He exists through an impotent power.

The background of all of this is that the Antichrist is only the shadow of Christ. Without Christ he can do nothing, and whatever he does is a witness to Christ's victory. The Antichrist is the union of the adversaries called to life by the coming of Christ. However, they are not able to overcome Christ. Against their own will, the Antichrist forces, through their negativity are a witness and affirmation of Christ's kingdom. They will eventually be permanently defeated by Christ.[141]

(8) The Importance of the Exhibition of the Fruits of Loyalty to Christ. An integral part of the New Testament view of history is that every member of the Christian community is to exhibit before the world the fruits of his or her loyalty to Christ. The nature of Christian influence toward outsiders is of great importance.

The Antichrist cannot be the last word regarding the Christian view of history. This is true since Christ not only suffered and was crucified but also arose and was glorified and now lives as the victor over all that opposes him. This is the positive side to living in the kingdom. Paul states that "we were buried therefore with him by baptism into death, so that as Christ was raised from the dead by the glory of the Father, we too might walk in newness of life" (Rom. 6:4).[142]

(9) Involvement in the World and Ambiguity in History. The tension described above between the "already" and the "not yet" implies that alongside the growth and development of the kingdom of God in the history of the world since the coming of Christ, we also see the growth and development of the "kingdom of evil." Accordingly, there are themes in both the Old and New Testament concerning withdrawal from the evil world. These themes have been picked up periodically over the course of history and stressed by certain groups, especially in times of persecution.

However, the idea of withdrawal from the world is not dominant in either the Old Testament or the New Testament. More characteristic is the prophetic emphasis of the Old Testament prophets and of Jesus and Paul. Their stress on engagement and confrontation indicates that for the Christian complete pessimism regarding the world, which releases the community from responsibility in order to withdraw, is not possible. God has not withdrawn himself, but is able to and will do "signs and wonders," for which we must diligently look and expectantly wait. Our responsibility is thus here in this life now; and there must be no evasion of it.[143]

Here again is the ambiguity of history as the biblical worldview sees it. History does not reveal a simple triumph of good over evil nor a total victory of evil over good. Rather, evil and good continue to exist side by side, and conflict between the two continues during the present age. However, since Christ has won the victory, the ultimate outcome of the conflict is never in doubt. The enemy is fighting a losing battle.

We should not be surprised that a Christless or even anti-Christian autonomy and ideology threatens to disintegrate life. On the contrary, we should marvel that these forces are repeatedly limited, held back, turned back, or converted by the positive signs of Christ's reign in the world. This tremendous fact should fill us constantly with gratitude and amazement, giving us power to enter the future without fear and with the expectation of seeing new signs.[144]

In the parable of the tares (Matt. 13:24–30, 36–43), Jesus taught that the tares (weeds), which stand for the sons of the evil one, will keep on growing until the time of harvest, when they will finally be separated from the wheat. In other words, Satan's kingdom will exist and grow as long as God's kingdom grows until the day of judgment.[145]

(10) The Importance of the Climax of History in the Second Coming of Christ. In the New Testament view, history and the consummation of history are closely connected. Forces of the kingdom of God which are already active in history will be loosed from the grip of sin and death in the consummation. In this respect, the consummation is a crowning moment of history. But this crowning moment is at the same time the glorification by which history is placed above the possibilities known to us.

In Jesus Christ, God "fulfilled time" for us. This "fulfilled time" was revealed in our midst particularly during the forty days between the resurrection and the ascension.

Fulfilled time means that past, future, and present are revealed anew in their unity without losing their differentiation. Fulfilled time is also the representation of God's time, which we call eternity, and in which past and future are connected in an eternal present.

Those individuals who share in Christ receive even now a small beginning of that fulfilled time. This is true because the atoning work of Christ has become their past, which moves along through time and determines their present. In addition, the kingdom of God becomes their future, which already has come near in the present.[146]

3. Implications of the Great Commission for the Meaning of History

(1) Definition. One aspect of the Christian responsibility in the world is related to the Great Commission, Christ's "marching orders" to his followers to go into the world and make disciples of all people. Since Christ has indeed inaugurated the kingdom of God and given us the Great Commission, the central task of the church is the mission effort to bring the gospel to every creature.

Christ himself said, "This gospel of the kingdom will be preached throughout the whole world, as a testimony to all nations; and then the end will come" (Matt. 24:14). According to 2 Peter 3:9, one reason Christ has not yet returned is that the Lord is patient with men, "not wishing that any should perish, but that all should reach repentance." These considerations all add up to one thing: The missionary activity of the church is to be the characteristic activity of this age between Christ's first and second coming.

(2) New Meaning for Freedom. Hendrikus Berkhof claims that the unique Christian philosophy of history is closely related to the missionary proclamation and the Great Commission. For example, freedom takes on a new meaning in relation to missionary proclamation. Missions signifies the possibility and call of individuals to direct themselves to God and to choose God. In this way, a person becomes a child of God when he or she accepts the revelation of God in Christ. And then follows the call for the Christian to share the good news with other men and women.

The call to proclaim the gospel neither forces us nor leaves us uninvolved. Instead, it makes a call and invites us to arise and walk a new way. This is how it respects our freedom.[147]

(3) New Idea of Being Human. The Lord who makes his entrance into the world through the missionary proclamation is the Redeemer who comes to seek and save that which is lost. He comes not to be served but to serve. He seeks the single sheep, and he has compassion for the poor. He also heals the sick and he forgives sinners.

This emphasis, which is rooted in the Old Testament, brings a new idea of being human into history. This is not the proud humanity of the Greeks, but the humanity of humility. The individual is recognized in his or her own significance. The human personality is respected. Particular attention is given by the gospel to the suffering and the oppressed.

All this means that the idea of social justice so well known to us was injected into history by the missionary proclamation. Without these ideas proclaimed by the gospel, democracy informed by Christianity (which is infinitely more democratic than Athens) and our social institutions would not have come into being.[148]

(4) An Undergirding of Marriage. The proclamation of the gospel also undergirds monogamy. Monogamy, which reflects the love of Christ for the church, presupposes that the wife is no longer seen as an object, but as subject in a relationship of mutual maturity (Eph. 5). Marriage is no longer only an institution; it is also a very personal encounter. Sexuality has a new dimension as the expression of personal love between man and wife.[149]

(5) New Significance for the State. In the biblical view, the powers of nature are desacralized. This even includes the power of the state, which was considered most sacred. The statement, "we must obey God rather than men" (Acts 5:29), dethroned the state. From the biblical perspective, the state has a purpose but it is not sacred. It is to fulfill a limited and functional purpose under God.

(6) New Meaning for Work. Since God who is working still, according to John 5:17, entered our lives through his actions and included us in his history through the call to proclaim the gospel, work has taken on new meaning. Hence comes the idea that not to work is a vice.

Furthermore, the missionary endeavor was the first fundamental worldwide work. The significance for the world of the spread of European culture can be understood only against this background. The existence of the United Nations is also rooted in this Christian concept.

It is true that some of these emphases—such as the uniqueness of man and justice—in greater or lesser degree were already anticipated by the Stoics. However, the Stoics remained only a small, intellectual "upper crust." Early Christian writers correctly pointed out that it was the Christian church which translated these ideas into forceful cultural factors.

Emphases such as freedom and respect for persons which are undergirded by the Christian gospel are appreciated when a person visits or lives in communist countries or in certain Islamic lands.[151]

(7) An Allowance for the Misuse of Freedom and the Demonic. Wherever missionary work has gone, a curious situation arises. A whole nation eats of the fruit of the missionary work, but only a minority of the people desire the tree which produces Christian fruit. Many people even try to forget or deny from which tree these Christian fruits are derived. Instead, they tend to make the fruit an end in itself; they concern themselves with the humanization of life as an end in itself.

Often, when the missionary proclamation has broken the power of naturalism and cleared the field of much of the pagan culture, the people want consistently and above all else to look to Greece. They become enamored with the view of the autonomy of humanity which was begun in Greece and which sooner or later is called into existence by the missionary proclamation.

However, a part of the missionary message is related to the story first told in the Garden of Eden. Whenever freedom is awakened in the fallen world, there will also be a misuse of freedom. As did Adam and Eve, people listen to the voice which tells them that they might just as well or better use their God-given freedom against God. Then they can be like God and determine for themselves what is good and what is evil. This means that the proclamation of the gospel can cause people to move in two directions. The prisoner of nature can become a child of God in Jesus Christ in his maturity, or he can take the role of a false god. It is a fact of history that the missionary endeavor calls into existence the greatest forces and counterforces. Sometimes the people enthrone Christ, and at other times they want their own autonomy.[153]

(8) An Allowance for the Possibility of Secular Nihilism. The Christian church on mission walks a narrow road. On the right there is the threat of slavery to the forces exhibited in nature worship, witchcraft, shamanism, magic, and distorted religion. On the left is the threat of the anarchy of autonomous secular life that too often steps in when the power of nature and pagan religious forces is broken. The risk of secular nihilism seems to be even greater than the risk of pagan naturalism, whose shackles have been broken in many places in the world since the missionary proclamation.[153]

Berkhof maintains that this development will end either in a destructive nihilism and secular humanism or in a conscious quest for Christ, who came to free and guide life in a fulfilling way. If there is to be any long-range benefit from the breaking of pagan naturalism in underdeveloped areas, then the proclamation of Christ must accompany technological aid and cultural importation. The missionary proclamation must be resumed with unmatched force by the young churches, missions and the mainline churches. Without the power and perspective of Christianity, technology and a lifestyle that is freed from pagan nature-worship can be harmful.[154]

(9) An Allowance for the Outworking of the Biblical Teachings. Those of us who understand the biblical teaching should not be surprised by the seemingly negative developments brought on by the spread of the gospel. In 2 Thessalonians 2:7, Paul states that the power of the Antichrist has come into operation together with the great mystery of Christ. The nature of the Antichristian power is human self-deification (2 Thess. 2:4) and blindness to the truth of God (2 Thess. 2:11). This power is still a hidden activity, masked by false appearances, and is often closely connected with the power of Christ.

Paul is aware of a double mystery—the work of Christ and the work of the Antichrist—because he is aware of the twofold influence of Christ on this world—both redeeming the world and stirring up the forces of opposition against him. The certainty wherewith Paul speaks about the mystery of history in 2 Thessalonians 2 and elsewhere rests on this fact.[155]

After the description of the Antichrist in this same important passage of 2 Thessalonians, we read about a "restrainer" or "suppressor" of the Antichrist's activity (v. 7). What is this power which suppresses Antichristian forces? According to the Swiss scholar Oscar Cullmann, the sixteenth-century reformer John Calvin, and Berkhof, this suppressor or restrainer is the proclamation of the gospel. This is not only Paul's theology of history; it is closely parallel with such expressions as "the gospel must first be preached to all nations" (Mark 13:10; see also Matt. 28:18; Acts 1:7) and with Paul's arguments in Romans 11:13–32.

This concept is that the preaching of the gospel, which is closely connected with Israel's rejection of it, precedes and to some degree postpones the second coming of Christ. It is also possible that the first figure from Revelation 6, the rider on the white horse, represents this same insight—the worldwide proclamation of the gospel restrains or holds back the developments of the Last Day.[156]

Christ's resurrection power was to the early church a tangible historical reality in a way we can hardly imagine now. They believed that although the gospel of Christ was already opposed and that opposition was bringing suffering and persecution, the adversary could not reach his objectives since Christ truly arose in this world. The early church believed that the enmity which Christ's work calls to life is suppressed with a powerful hand. This insight originates in faith in the resurrected Christ, but it is also affirmed by the work of the Holy Spirit in the church's growth and in the irreversible progress of the gospel proclamation.[157]

The apostle Paul also expected the salvation of Israel to occur before the final climax of history. According to Paul in Romans, the faithfulness and sovereignty of God are at stake. Israel, which he likens to olive branches broken off the tree so that wild branches (Gentiles) could be grafted on, must eventually come back to the tree where she originated (Rom. 9–11).

Israel's fall was a part of God's plan, insomuch as the Gentiles have been drawn to the light because the Jews did not accept Christ. Israel was also rejected through her own fault. But in Romans 11:11, Paul indicates that Israel cannot deny her calling in the end times, for she is still a link between the Messiah and the nations. In Romans 11:12, Paul states that one day the remnant which has accepted Christ will grow to include the whole of Israel. Thus Paul seems to be indicating that there will come a time, seemingly between the first and second comings of Christ, when God's faithfulness will triumph over the unfaithfulness of his people and Israel will realize her destiny.

It is not clear in what way Israel will fulfill her calling. According to Berkhof, it is enough to know that God's apparent humiliation at the hands of Israel will be changed into the triumph of God's faithfulness. His faithfulness has already in this age revealed itself in Christ's resurrection to be sufficiently powerful over all that may resist it.[158]

A number of evangelical scholars, myself included, maintain that John in the Book of Revelation expected that after the brief reign of the Antichrist and the return of Christ there will be a period on earth called the millennium. For advocates of this view, the underlying faith of Revelation 20 is the same as the faith of Paul as spelled out in Romans 9–11. In Romans it concerns God's faithfulness to Israel, and in Revelation 20 it is a further demonstration of Christ's power in this age before Christ turns over his kingdom to God's all-encompassing dominion in the age to come. According to this view, it is essential to the faith of the New Testament that we be able to expect great things to happen in history for the sake of God's faithfulness and God's honor. The millennium also guards the realism of the Christian hope against mystical world denial.[159]

4. Modern Evaluations of the Biblical View of History

Of the elements in the Christian understanding of history, some have more appeal for modern people than others. For example, belief that history is linear is in accordance with many modern assumptions, especially in the West. Even the idea of progress that has dominated so much modern thinking shares the Christian view of history as linear.

The teaching that history is moving toward a goal is less widely held. However, this is a necessary corollary of monotheism. A God who guides the course of history but who is opposed on the way will surely bring the process to a triumphant conclusion. This is a part of the Christian view of history which is shared with Judaism and Islam, the other monotheistic world religions. A monotheism with a purposive view of history's moving to a climax creates hope.

A note of hope retains its prominent place in the Christian view because it is based on confidence in the continuing divine control and activity in history and expectation of ultimate divine victory.

Serious objections to the biblical view of history usually concern particular interventions in judgment and the general doctrine of providence. They also concern themselves with the problem of suffering. Divine judgments oftentimes do cause suffering, and general providence permits suffering. In both cases God seems to be responsible. If God is all-powerful and loving, why should he not ensure that pain and trouble are excluded from a world that he controls?

There is another dimension to the problem. This is related to the seemingly unfair distribution of suffering. These and the other problems posed by providence and suffering will be dealt with in a later part of this study.

5. Representative Models Which Have Been Used to Implement the Biblical View of History

A brief survey of the historical models which have been used by those who profess to hold the Christian view will show that aspects of the biblical view have been overemphasized or neglected at certain points in history. However, bringing together the strengths of each of these views to complement each other should go a long way toward meeting the need for an adequate biblical view of history.

(1) Augustine and the City of God View. In the fifth century, Augustine wrote a classic book, *The City of God*, which helped to explicate one aspect of the Christian view of history. Augustine took biblical predictions that were normally taken to describe what would happen at the end of time and applied them to the period of the church. In this view, the new Jerusalem would not suddenly descend in the future, but has been coming down in the form of grace to create the church in this present age.

Augustine himself never relaxed his grip on the belief that the Christian hope is to be finally fulfilled in the world to come. Later interpreters of his teaching, however, shifted attention from future hope to present realization, and from last things to an emphasis on the present church. The institutionalization of the church over the centuries accentuated this tendency. The result was to decrease the awareness that history is moving toward a goal; the teleological or purposive dimension of Christian history was neglected. Little except the last judgment remained in man's future, and the medieval Christian worldview was thus remarkably static. This distortion of Augustine's view issued in the next example of the Christian approaches to history.[160]

(2) The Optimistic Church-Centered View. According to this view, the kingdom of God is realized in history primarily through the institutional church. The emphasis on last things (except for the beatific vision reserved for believers in heaven) is subordinated to the reality of an existing institution and a sacramental power available in the present. There is a visible historical realization in the traditional church, which is a hierarchical embodiment of the kingdom of God. The visible church bears the authority of the kingdom in the person of the Pope, who is Christ's viceregent on earth. Thomas Aquinas in the Middle Ages and Jacques Maritain in the nineteenth and early twentieth centuries can be seen as representative exponents of this view.

The real danger of this view is the identification of the kingdom in its fullness, its "last days" ultimacy, with the present church. This view deprives the eschatological kingdom of any future significance and removes the eschatological tension from the church's life. The Roman church asserts that the kingdom is already and fully actualized in concrete historical existence in the church. Its belief is that even though the church may have its imperfections and its individual members are subject to divine judgment, its head and its institutions are beyond judgment. According to the evangelical view this is simply not true. The church may be God's chosen means of working in the world, but it is still earthly; it is no more wholly white than the world is wholly black.[161]

(3) The "Last Days" Pessimistic and Transcendent View. According to this view, the kingdom of God is realized by direct catastrophic action in the second coming of Christ. Therefore, the course of human events is not of great significance, although the earthly history of mankind warns of the imminent end of the world. There is little emphasis on the church as the earthly city of God serving as a providential means for the redemption of mankind. Instead, there is an emphasis in this viewpoint on the otherness of God, the radical divine judgment upon sin, and the fragmentary character of the meaning of all human institutions.

Martin Luther was very aware that secular history was filled with demonic activities. He saw his own time as the reign of the Antichrist, whom he identified closely with the papacy. He felt that the end of the world was imminent. He thus tended toward a pessimism about historical existence and an emphasis that all will not be put right until the final consummation. In the meantime, he believed, history goes on its own rebellious path, but is held in some order by God, who in Luther's view rules the world as well as the church. (Luther described God's rule of the world as "the kingdom of God's left hand.")[162]

A more radical version of this view is the contemporary dispensational approach to history. This view sees the mainline churches as apostate and history as growing progressively worse. Those who take this approach hold that authentic Christians will soon be taken to heaven before the "great tribulation" on earth. The nation Israel will then play an important role in God's plan for history.

It is important that the kingdom not be relegated wholly to the future. We cannot rest on a purely futurist eschatology. The kingdom has come in Christ, is present in his church, and shall come in its fullness. Even Luther saw the kingdom as present in the preaching of the gospel, although he did differentiate between the present manifestation in history and the kingdom that shall be unveiled at the end of history.[163]

(4) The Dynamic-Realization View. The dynamic-realization view neither identifies the kingdom of God with a particular historical institution, like the church-centered view, nor separates it from historical institutions, like the radical eschatological view. Instead it seeks the realization of God's sovereignty within an entire historical community, small or large. The reformer John Calvin can be thought of in this connection.

Calvin retained the eschatological emphasis and was very aware of the tension between the gospel and secular history. But he also related the church positively to the world and spoke in terms of reformation. For Calvin, this era is to be more than a tension-filled waiting period prior to the final consummation.

According to Calvin's dynamic approach, the church is waging war to transform the realm of historical existence according to the likeness of the Father's will in Christ. God is building his kingdom in this world and through the history of this world, and all must not be left to the end.

Calvin had a rich understanding of Christian vocation as one in which the grace of Christ could be expressed dynamically in a person's vocation. He also emphasized a positive attitude toward the state as God's minister. For Calvin, the state is not merely the restrainer of evil, but may also promote welfare. Despite his belief in the fallen state of humanity, there is a strong measure of Christian humanism in Calvin's approach.[164]

(5) The Mediating Pessimistic-Optimistic View. This view seeks to combine the strong points of all three of the preceding views.

John Baillie, for example, in his book, *The Belief in Progress,* states that man can hope to move toward moral and spiritual progress in history in the interim between the present time and the coming of Christ. However, this does not mean that progress is inevitable, because man is sinful and free to choose evil.[165]

Reinhold Niebuhr in *Faith and History* represents another version of this view. Because of God's power and humankind's ability under God, there can be some development within finite limits—as in human cultural achievement and social institutions. The meaning of history is disclosed in Christ's life, death, and resurrection, through which God takes human sin upon himself.

However, our sin forbids us to claim moral perfection or the ability to solve history by the rational dogma of progress. Through Spirit-empowered love made actual in deeds, the Christian participates in the limited development of a Christian social order without expecting to make this a perfect order in history. That perfect order will come outside of history as the act of God, by which time is transfigured into eternity.[166]

Eric Rust, in his book, *Towards a Theological Understanding of History,* can be seen as another exponent of this mediating view, which in his mind includes five elements.

First, we must affirm the lordship of Christ over secular history as well as over his church. Second, it is the task of the church not to turn its back on secular history, but rather to bring contemporary culture within the influence of the redemptive power of the gospel. Third, both the church and its environment of secular history are subject to demonic pretensions. Fourth, the first advent of Christ has made humanity fully responsible in a historical sense.

Fifth, the church knows that it and secular culture can never be united except in the end by the second coming of Christ. Antichrists will continually appear until the end of historical existence. However, the church fights on, believing that in so doing it contributes to God's purpose for mankind.

The Christian knows that at the second coming of Christ the demonic will be finally defeated. Then the divine content in human cultural life and social existence will be gathered up and cleansed of the distortions and perversions which have marred its historical actualization.[167]

IX. How Can We Summarize a Statement of a Comprehensive and Balanced Biblical View of History?

If we can achieve the delicate balance of the biblical emphases, we will have a dynamic and realistic view of the meaning of history. Seen in its fullness, the biblical view meets the criteria for an adequate view of history. It is comprehensive, coherent, creative, and personally satisfying.

For example, the biblical view is comprehensive. Neither the cyclical, inevitable progress, or the historicist views of history fit the facts of history as well as the biblical approach does. Because of sin, the biblical worldview holds that there can be no final or complete solution by human effort. However, that is not a reason for despairing pessimism, because God is active in history through his Spirit. With God's help, human beings can seek to integrate the secondary economic, social, and other material facts of history into God's purpose.

Eschatological linear action rather than cyclical motion or an indefinite spiral of progress characterizes the biblical approach to history. The glory of God in the present by the life of the Christian and at the end of history by the triumph of Christ is paramount.

The biblical view combines a "this-worldliness" and "other-worldliness." Therefore, a philosophy of history which is true to the Bible will include a "this-worldliness" which is concerned with bread, social order, justice, political freedom, and personal regeneration. But it will also contain an "other-worldliness" which affirms that history is moving toward its consummation in the second coming of Christ, and that the fullness of God's kingdom for the individual and the group lies beyond the incompleteness of history and time.

The biblical view insists that God controls history and on the other hand it defends human responsibility. The Christian outlook on history recognizes the fundamental tension between divine sovereignty and human responsibility.[168]

Thus history studied in the light of such a biblical interpretation becomes a revelation of the working in time of the eternal God of whom, through whom, and to whom are all things.

3

The Question of the Meaning of Religious and Biblical Language

I. What Is the Nature and Extent of the Attack on Religious and Biblical Language?

The question of the meaning of religious and biblical language is an ultimate question because it is closely related to the question of authority. Authority means the right to command belief and action. Evangelical Christians believe God has expressed his authority by creating through inspired authors a book, the Bible. Thus, for the evangelical, authority means biblical authority—the total truthfulness of the Scripture—for thought and life (2 Tim. 3:15–17). However, biblical authority cannot proceed very far without considering the validity and meaning of biblical language.

An interpretation or application of the Bible has authority only to the extent that it coheres with the Bible's intended or original meaning. Before we can say what the Bible means for today, we must know what it meant when it was originally written down. This involves understanding the genre or type of literature used in the Bible and the reasons for the seeming diversity in the biblical literature. There is a propositional or deep structure core at the heart of the Bible, but the form or surface structure by which the Bible was expressed differed according to the culture of the times when different parts of it were written down. The Bible is both literary and historical. These two features must be blended or linked in order to get to the meaning of the Bible and biblical language for the biblical period and for today.

Biblical language in particular and religious language in general have been under far more serious attack during the past century than many people realize. The defense against this attack is a crucial matter for those who accept the authority of the Bible.

1. The Attack of Hume and the Logical Positivists

An important forerunner of those who have made more recent attacks was David Hume, who summarized his view some two hundred years ago in a critical essay entitled, *An Enquiry Concerning Human Understanding*. In this essay, he contended that to be meaningful any statement must be either rational (logically self-evident, as in mathematics) or subject to the control of the five physical senses. If a religious book such as the Bible cannot meet these tests, he argued, then commit it to the flames.[1]

In more recent years, beginning soon after 1920, a group of European scientific thinkers called the "Vienna Circle" followed Hume's precedent in rigorously criticizing all religious and theological statements. Ernst Mach, an important man in the movement, advocated a unification of science and other forms of intellectual life through the elimination of consideration of metaphysical and religious statements.[2]

The Vienna Circle insisted that theological statements were meaningless, since they could not be brought under the control of the physically observable. The terms *logical positivism* and *logical empiricism* were coined about 1930 in reference to the Vienna Circle and its viewpoint. Later, the term was extended to refer to other Continental scholars and to some British philosophers, such as A. J. Ayer.[3]

Logical positivism is thus an attempt to set up a definite standard of meaning by which all language is to be measured. On the basis of this standard, the only meaningful uses of language are the mathematical type, or tautological language, and the scientific type, which meets the verifiability principle.[4] Statements about God's nature and will, man's spiritual nature and destiny, and all other theological pronouncements, are simply dismissed as empty rhetoric void of both rational validity and intelligibility.[5]

2. The Attack of Linguistic Analysis and the "Early" Wittgenstein

The movement called "linguistic analysis" had its historical origin in G. E. Moore's essay, "The Refutation of Idealism," which appeared in 1903. Moore, a prominent Cambridge University philosopher, attacked the leaders of neo-idealism, a philosophical movement which was strong in England at the time, and some religious writers because they tended to sacrifice clarity and preciseness. Moore set forth the view that the philosopher's primary business is the analysis of language.[6]

The most important exponent of linguistic analysis was Ludwig Wittgenstein. A native of Austria, Wittgenstein came to England to study and eventually became professor of philosophy at Cambridge, succeeding Moore. Wittgenstein's important early work, *Tractatus Logico-Philosophicus* (1921), contended that philosophy should primarily be a "critique of language" or "the logical clarification of thoughts."

According to the "early" Wittgenstein, consideration of religious or ultimate questions is irrelevant and meaningless. Religious language does not actually describe or denote anything, but only expresses the feelings of the speaker or writer. While such propositions may have the grammatical form and hence appearance of assertions, they are actually expressing the feelings, mood, and attitudes of the speaker. Like "Wow!" "Hurrah!" "Ouch!" and similar expressions, they are not susceptible to verification and falsification, and hence do not qualify as meaningful language. Since a person cannot speak of God in logical terms or in a way that can be proven by the senses, asserted Wittgenstein, it is best to be silent![7]

A reaction to this rigorous criticism of the validity of the Bible and of theological statements has developed in more recent years. Although the logical positivists carefully analyzed scientific and logical statements, they had a strange blindness to ethical, aesthetic, and religious statements—writing such statements off as "emotive" and therefore meaningless. Eventually, however, the absurdity of so dismissing a large number of concepts regularly employed in human speech came to be evident.

II. How Would You Describe the Defense of Religious and Biblical Language by the "Later" Wittgenstein and "Ordinary Language" Advocates?

It is especially notable that the same Wittgenstein who had earlier affirmed the meaninglessness of theological statements was the one to prepare the way for a new understanding of the purpose and function of religious language.

One day Wittgenstein was walking on the Cambridge University campus thinking about the various field games played in England—rugby, soccer, and tennis. It came to him that, just as rugby and tennis were not played according to the same rules, but were both valid games, perhaps religious and scientific language were just two activities following different rules. Perhaps, he thought, religious language did have value after all. This pattern of thinking opened up an entirely new trend of thought in Wittgenstein's life, and subsequently opened the door for people to begin rethinking the significance of religious language.

1. The "Language Game" Concept

Wittgenstein used the term *language game* to point up the fact that language is an activity. The problem with the verifiability principle laid down by the linguistic analysts does not lie in the criteria it sets for the empirical or scientific type of sentence. The problem consists in its failure to recognize other forms of language as legitimate and meaningful.[8]

This new development was described in the later work of Wittgenstein, *Philosophical Investigations,* which was published in 1953, after his death in 1951. This work shifts the emphasis from the *meaning* of words to their *function.* In this later emphasis, the British philosopher affirmed that the situation or context of language is important, because one understands the meaning of words only if you can locate them in the situation in which they are used. This situation or context is what Wittgenstein calls a "language game."[9]

Guided by the thought of Wittgenstein, linguistic analysis moved to another stage—from "verificational analysis" to "functional analysis." Whereas verificational analysis attempted to *prescribe* how language should be used, functional analysis attempted to *describe* how language actually is used.

To the functional analyst, it is apparent that the different language games each have their own rules. Problems arise either when these rules are violated, or when one slips from one "game" to another without realizing it, or tries to apply the rules of one game to another. A basketball player attempting to punt a basketball or a football team attempting a fast break down the field with a series of forward passes is making an illicit transfer from one game to another. The same would be true of, say, using the language of logic when declaring love to one's spouse.[10]

According to this line of reasoning, religious language is a unique language, and cannot be thrown under the "game rules" of any other "language game" and be fairly judged. This means that the criteria for judging the adequacy of the Bible and of religious language must take into account their unique purpose and function.

For example, treating the biblical account of creation as a statement about the empirical or scientific origin of the universe is a switch from one language game to another—from theological language to empirical language. Mixing the uses of language in one game with those of another is called a category transgression. It leads to confusion and constitutes a misuse of language.[11]

2. The Ordinary Language Approach

Since World War II, the center of language analysis has remained in England, but has shifted from Cambridge University to Oxford University. The Oxford School is a continuation of the development of Wittgenstein's thought and has been characterized as the school of "ordinary language."

Influential leaders of the ordinary language approach are Gilbert Ryle and John Austin. For them, every kind of statement has its own peculiar logic and hence its own verification. Words carry meanings in different ways, and the meaning of a word is relative to the context in which it is used. This approach is more adequate than verification analysis. It opens up the possibility for religious language to receive proper recognition and analysis.[12]

III. How Would You Describe the Defense of Religious and Biblical Language by Recent Christian Thinkers?

1. The Work of Ian Ramsey

An important result of the work of the individuals who tried to eliminate religious language was the stimulation it gave to Christian thinkers. The Anglo-American response to the denial of the knowledge value of religious language was especially noteworthy. One of the pioneers in seeking to establish the validity of religious language was Ian T. Ramsey.

As a professor at Oxford, Ramsey lived and worked in the center of linguistic analysis study. However, he agreed with the "later" Wittgenstein that the Bible (as well as religious language in general) was not meant to give technical, scientific insights, because science has a different purpose and tends to change in every generation. He came to believe that the biblical language has a unique purpose.[13]

For Ramsey, religious language is not a set of labels for a group of hard, objective facts whose complete meaning can be immediately perceived by passive observers. There are in fact two levels of meaning for religious language. One level is the empirical reference which lies on the surface and is quickly understood. The other level involves a deeper meaning which is also objectively there, but must be drawn out. Religious language breaks open the enclosed nature of our awareness about ourselves, others, and the world around us, and sets these phenomena in transcendent light.[14]

In the eighteenth century, Joseph Butler's *Analogy of Religion* was directed against an early empiricism or emphasis on the physical senses alone. From Butler, Ramsey draws two categories of awareness or activity, which he calls "discernment" and "commitment," to describe the purposes of religious language.[15]

(1) The Idea of Discernment. According to Ramsey, to bring discernment or disclosure is an important part of the Bible's purpose. Ramsey seeks to illustrate discernment situations by calling forth various examples from life experience—situations in which a second level of meaning becomes apparent as one's perspective changes.

For example, at certain times a situation becomes alive and personal to the degree that it discloses something hitherto unseen. Picture a cold courtroom. Here is a judge who usually employs legal, technical, and impersonal language. Then an old college friend is brought before him, and the impersonal situation suddenly becomes alive. The "light dawns," and there is discernment.

In the Christian context, in addition to the effect of language framed in a special way, the discernment of which Ramsey speaks is aided by the illuminating work of the Holy Spirit.[16]

Discernment as Ramsey describes it can be related to the Christian teaching about the necessity of the experience of conviction for sin and a sense of need or lostness in relation to God and his purpose. When such a conviction comes as a result of the Holy Spirit's using biblical language and teachings, the result is discernment.[17]

(2) The Concept of Commitment. According to Ramsey's model, religious language also calls for commitment. Important discernments and times of crisis call for the response of involvement—putting oneself on the line in the service of the truth or insight gained through discernment.

Discernment and commitment must go hand in hand. Total commitment without any discernment whatever would be bigotry and idolatry. On the other hand, to have the discernment without an appropriate commitment would result in the worst of all religious vices—insincerity and hypocrisy.

Commitment is parallel to repentance, faith, surrender, and dedication to God's provision for salvation and the Christian life through Christ. Biblical language is not merely informative. True Christianity is present only when commitment is present—and a total commitment at that. The process of discernment is a necessary means to that end.[18]

(3) The Place of "Odd" Language and Analogy. According to Ramsey, the Bible, in order to fulfill its purposes of bringing discernment and exacting commitment, uses language in a way that is peculiar or odd when compared to scientific or technical language.

Biblical language is an object language which has been given special qualifications so that it is logically peculiar. Taking words from common speech, a biblical disclosure situation uses words for an uncommon purpose. Words and phrases that in their ordinary usage refer to the everyday world are qualified in a way which "stretches" them and makes the supernatural dimension transparent through them. For example, the word *father* is qualified by the adjective *almighty* and thereby transposed onto another plane of meaning.[19]

What all of this suggests is that religious language will be based upon empirical referents, but will employ odd methods to bring the readers or hearers to an understanding of the full meaning. It will commit whatever "category" transgressions are necessary to convey the meaning that cannot simply be unpacked by an exegesis of the literal meaning. It must be emphasized that this is not subjectivism—the fuller meaning is always objectively present, even if not obviously so. When the odd use of language accomplishes its purposes, the result is an opening of the eyes, a sense of "Aha, I get it!"—or, as Ramsey likes to put it, "The penny drops; the light dawns."

Ramsey has given us a helpful new slant on the ancient language tool of analogy, which is a way the language of this world can be made the vehicle of meaning beyond this world. For Ramsey, it is through the method of analogy that the empiricist or scientific challenge can best be countered. Analogy makes it possible to take account of the difference between the world of ordinary perception and the world of God without falling over into the conclusion that talk about God must be lacking in cognitive or knowledge justification and content. By using dramatic and colorful metaphors, contrasts, and picture language, the Bible speaks to the emotions and the will, as well as to the intellect.[20]

The Bible, for example, uses metaphors in profusion. It often talks of God in human terms, describing him as Father, King, Lord, and Husband. The apostle Paul uses a variety of metaphors in describing the atonement—stating, for example, that Christ delivered us from the slave market of sin and that Christ declares us free as in a law court (Rom. 6:17–18; 8:4).

Frederick Ferre, the American philosopher, undergirds the work of Ramsey. He also emphasizes that the Bible represents the nature of ultimate reality through vivid stories and dramatic images. The keystone of the biblical scheme is the concept of God. The reality of God is constantly revealed to man in terms of vivid personal models and dramatic historical events.[21]

2. Jerry Gill and the Importance of the Metaphoric Mode

Jerry Gill, a prolific American writer on philosophy of religion, has developed some further and significant ramifications of this revolution in the philosophy of language in his emphasis on the "metaphoric mode." According to Gill, it is possible to make a case for the primordial nature of metaphoric speech, including analogy and parable, in relation to so-called "literal" speech.

It is fairly easy to show that the words and statements we now regard as literal were actually once metaphoric in character. In other words, there are only two kinds of speech—"live" metaphors and "dead" ones. (Even the term *literal* is a dead metaphor, as a quick check with a good dictionary will indicate.) Since so-called literal expressions were once metaphoric, it follows that the metaphoric mode is more basic to language.[22]

Language arises out of our primordial interaction with the world, both physical and social. At this level, the connection between the world, speech, and ourselves is more integral than our more precise and articulated speech would lead us to believe. Religion itself can be seen to arise from this more primordial level of human existence. This means that God-talk has its deepest grounding in the metaphoric mode.[23]

The standard objection to this way of thinking is to claim that since increased precision brings increased understanding, it follows that nonmetaphoric speech is preferable to metaphoric, especially in theology. The difficulty with this approach, as Wittgenstein has shown, is that precision is neither possible nor necessary as an ideal for communication.

The reason that precision is not *possible* is that no matter how many refinements we make, contexts will always arise or be imagined in which further precision is advisable. There is no such thing as absolute precision, only significant precision in keeping with the context and purposes at hand.[24]

That precision is not *necessary* to meaningful communication can be seen from the fact that, if it were, no one would ever be able to learn a language. Precision moves by degrees from less to more, but one must start where one is, with what communication can be established, and become more precise as is needed. In fact, we must be able to understand one another at a basic level before we can effect greater precision. Not every word or statement can be explained in terms of others, or we would never get started.[25]

When this understanding of the nature of language is related to the question of the meaning of religious and theological discourse, the results are exciting and astounding. We come to realize that in the realm of God-talk, our chief aim is not just to convey abstract knowledge about God. Rather, as Ramsey affirms, we are seeking to bring people to conviction and faith and a personal relation to Christ. To achieve this purpose we use dramatic, vivid, and metaphoric language.[26]

It is significant that Jesus' primary means of speaking about God, the kingdom, and faith was the metaphoric mode. Basically, Jesus was a storyteller. When speaking of the kingdom and of our relation to it, Jesus's consistent use of analogies and parables can be said to be one of the most characteristic features of his entire ministry. The Incarnation occurred through a person who lived and spoke in concrete terms. In this manner he mediated spiritual reality and truth.[27]

Gill points out that there is a twofold advantage to the metaphoric mode's "open texture" for understanding the function of religious language. On the one hand, metaphoric religious language creates a space or an "existential arena" where the hearer can encounter the truth without being "force-fed." This space preserves and respects the hearer's freedom and dignity. On the other hand, the double-edged quality of metaphor invites and encourages the hearer to step into the space it creates, if he or she is sincerely seeking the truth. Thus it emphasizes and urges individual responsibility and commitment.[28]

Often we see Jesus creating this space between himself and the persons he meets by answering a question with yet another question or by telling a parable. His metaphorical activity always engages them at the concrete level where they live and encourages them to see or walk forward to a richer understanding and commitment.[29]

3. The Importance of Language Immersion

George Lindbeck of Yale University and Stanley Hauerwas of Duke University both emphasize that there has been an enormous growth in the sciences of linguistics and cultural anthropology over the last quarter of the century. They draw on some developments in these fields to set forth some fundamental ideas about how religious language relates to religious life in general.

As the linguists and cultural anthropologists point out, there is a very intimate connection between the language of a culture and its worldview, the way it perceives things. There is some truth in linguist Benjamin Whorf's famous thesis that all our thinking is shaped, determined, governed, and limited by the language we use.

Lindbeck asserts that a religion can also be viewed as a kind of cultural and linguistic framework or medium that shapes the entirety of one's life and thought. Being a Christian (or, for that matter, being anything more than merely an individual) is much like learning a language. We learn certain words, grammar, and syntax that enable us to say certain things and not say others. The enculturation that this language provides gives us a new perspective on life and forms us into particular persons.

This means that the proclamation of the gospel, as a Christian would put it, is first of all the telling of the story—the sharing of a linguistic framework. This proclamation gains power and meaning insofar as it is embodied in the totality of community life and action.

The fact of language enculturation also means that the first task of Christian educators is to induct a person into the faith community and to give him the skills, insights, words, stories, and rituals that he or she needs to live this faith in a world that neither knows nor follows the One who is the basis of the faith.[30]

Religion, therefore, is not primarily a set of presuppositions to be believed or disbelieved, but a set of skills to be employed in living. Such skills are acquired by immersion in biblical language—learning the stories of Israel and Jesus well enough not only to interpret the world, but to do so in specifically Christian terms.[31]

Excursus: The Bible as a Unique Combination of the Historical and Literary

Before we leave the discussion of the metaphoric nature of biblical language, let us digress and reemphasize the historical nature of the Bible. The Christian faith is based upon objective events which are behind the biblical narratives. If there is not an essential historicity in the biblical accounts, as the apostle Paul said, "our . . . faith is in vain. . . . We are of all men most to be pitied" (1 Cor. 15:12–19).

For the Christian, salvation comes through what God *did* in Christ in reconciling man to himself rather than just through what Christ *said* or what was said about him. If the Incarnation of God did not occur in the historical events of the life, death, and resurrection of Jesus Christ, then the Christian gospel dissolves into just another myth about the recurrent cycles of renewal. The Sermon on the Mount may be true regardless of whether Christ lived, but the Christian drama of human salvation is inextricably dependent upon time, place, and personality. If God did not act in history in Jesus Christ, it may still be true that men are sinful and that this is a bad thing, but in the distinctively, uniquely Christian sense there will be no escape or salvation in that fact.

In addition to being historical, however, the Bible is also a dramatic, literary, and metaphoric book. In fact, it is surely a part of God's wisdom that he raised up people who recorded and preserved the story of our glorious religion in a way "sufficiently dramatic to attract a crowd." More is involved in our Bible than a set of archives and a scholarly chronicle of the events. Technical reports would have attracted but little attention beyond a restricted circle of specialists. If, as Christians believe, certain historical events and certain historical understandings are relevant and necessary for all men, then these must be conveyed in a manner which can reach and affect all sorts and conditions of men. Our Bible, therefore, like any great literary work, must accomplish a twofold objective. First, it must be basically faithful to the events treated. Second, it must be dramatic, so that it can reach a wide audience and convey an indelible impression.[32]

The biblical writers effectively employed certain standard literary devices for communication purposes—parables, epics, poems, and so on. This was done in order that the history of God's redemptive purpose should be made lastingly and meaningfully relevant to audiences removed in space and time and cultural identity from the original happenings.

IV. How Would You Describe the Particular Emphases and Methods of Biblical Language?

The emphasis of the scholars considered so far have given attention to general religious language as well as explicitly biblical language. The next group of persons to be considered are more specifically interested in biblical language. A scholar who had a particular interest in establishing the meaningfulness of biblical language was J. V. Langmead Casserley, the late professor of philosophy of religion at Seabury-Western Seminary.

1. The Biblical Emphasis on the Singular

According to Casserley, genuine knowledge or experience cannot always be fully expressed in human language. This tension between language and thought is not peculiar to metaphysics and religion. Whenever unique personages or events—for example, the first trips of the astronauts—are discussed, language is pressed almost to its limits.

The special problem of metaphysics and the Bible alike is the problem of talking about the Absolute Singular—God. This problem is seen also in the writing of history and dramatic literature and even in everyday speech.

Casserley's main emphasis and contribution is his insight into the fact that it was Christianity which first forced the problem of the singular upon philosophers. In contrast, the Greeks saw individuals primarily as representative of a class. Recognition by the Bible of the singularity of the transcendent creator led to the perception of a similar singularity in each historical individual.[33]

In general, language tends to fall short when an attempt is made to do justice to a unique or singular individual. This can be seen in the vivid and somewhat ambiguous language often used to describe a human love relationship. When a person's experience involves the Absolute Singular (God), language finds even more difficulty. Pascal used the words, "Fire, Fire, Fire" to describe his experience with Christ. Although the kind of language which refers to experiences with persons is difficult and oftentimes fails, it does not fail entirely.

2. Methods of Conveying the Revelation of the Singular God

Casserley's contribution is found in his exploration of the logic of the singular. He outlines three principal linguistic conceptions which are important in any discussion of unique entities. These conceptions are negation, analogy, and paradox.[35] It may be helpful to look briefly at each of these three conceptions.

(1) The Way of Negation. Although it is impossible to say all one wants to say about the singular in a positive way, it is always possible to say what the singular is not. This is the way of negation. In describing God, for instance, words fail in describing what he is, but we can describe what he isn't. We can say, for instance, that God does not have a physical body, that he is not confined and does not have limits.[34]

(2) The Way of Analogy. According to Casserley, analogy or likeness is not an argument, but a way of giving meaning to pure concepts. Certain realities such as God and religious experience may be hard to conceptualize, but through analogy they can be shown to be not altogether foreign to human experience. Analogy can impart a certain human and earthly touch to a pure concept.

Following the approach of Augustine, Casserley contends that the knowledge of the existence of God is given to man in self-consciousness. Assuming this is true, the Christian draws his analogies of God from the drama of his own self-conscious and personal existence, from human history, and from the inward life of humankind. Any speech about singulars must be carried on in a richly analogical way.[35]

In speaking of a particular person who is very fat, for instance, you might call that person a "butterball." Naturally, this does not mean that the person is a literal ball of butter! But the analogy says something useful and descriptive about the person's shape and general appearance. Through analogy, therefore, we can bring a human and earthly touch to an abstract concept. This is the method of the Bible.

For example, God is like a father. This, of course, does not mean that in the human sense God has marital relations with a woman and helps to procreate children. However, there is some analogy between the way I relate to my sons if I am a good father and the way the heavenly father relates to the Christian. There is a parallel here that all can see. Similarly, when the Bible states that God is the rock of our salvation, it is showing that as a rock has stability, so has God. The statement that God has arms indicates that as arms have power, so God has power.

In Exodus 33 it is written that God wears a skirt, and that as God walks by, he pulls up his skirt and allows Moses to see the back side of his leg. This analogy would have been especially meaningful in the Victorian era, when women wore long skirts and pulled them up slightly to give men a small glimpse of their charms. The metaphor in Exodus 33 means that God is holy and is far beyond us, but that on this occasion God allowed Moses to catch a glimpse of his glory.

In Isaiah 6, the prophet wrote, "I saw the Lord sitting upon a throne, high and lifted up." John Calvin, commenting on this passage, once remarked that behind this passage is the biblical concept of the transcendence or otherness of God. In order to communicate this to Isaiah and to us, Isaiah was given the vision recorded in Isaiah 6. But this does not mean that God is literally sitting on a throne a few thousand feet up in the sky. It means that this was an appropriate way to convey to an inspired prophet in the eighth century B.C. that God is high and mighty and qualitatively different from human beings.[36]

The Song of Songs (4:4) furnishes us with another example of the Hebrew use of analogy. It describes a young lady whose neck is like the tower of David. If one were to take this description literally, the picture of such a girl would be ridiculous. But the writer here was using a picturesque, Hebraic analogy to describes the girl's chastity. As the tower of David was beyond the reach of an army, so this girl was beyond being reached for immoral purposes.

The book of Revelation is rich in analogous language. Take, for example, the description in Revelation 19:11–15 of Jesus' appearing on a white horse with a sword protruding from his mouth and blood running down his side. Again, a literal interpretation of this description would be grotesque, but as an analogy it is a dramatic picture of power in first-century terms. Since the Roman Empire was supreme at that time, and since the ultimate symbol of power in Rome was a ruler who rides a chariot pulled by white horses, Christ is described in those terms. This does not mean that he literally will come on a white horse with a sword in his mouth, but there is reality behind the analogy. In a similar way, Revelation 20:11, which describes God as seated on a white throne, symbolizes God's majesty.

(3) The Way of Paradox. A third way in which the Bible communicates is paradox, the use of seemingly contradictory statements or images to make a point. But it is important to emphasize that in cases of biblical paradox there is no contradiction from God's perspective. For example, the Bible portrays Jesus as completely human and completely divine. Sören Kierkegaard, the eminent Danish philosopher, pointed out that by the traditional laws of logic this idea is contradictory; Jesus must be either human or divine, but not both. But we know by revelation that both ideas are true, so we must live with the paradox of Jesus' full divinity and full humanity.[37]

The apostle Paul clearly indicates in his various epistles that people are both free and determined. Here is another contradiction from a human perspective. But Paul insists on both elements, and those people who have insight into their own personalities and experience will affirm how accurate Paul is in this regard. We are both free and at the same time determined by heredity, environment, genetics, and other factors.

Since God exists neither wholly in time nor wholly in eternity, unusual combinations of expressions must be used to affirm his uniqueness. It is easy to see the importance of paradox in describing such qualities as love and wrath and mercy and justice. It should be noted, however, that paradox is not limited to religious language; it is essential to all references to singularity and personality. In history, drama, and personal conversation, paradox is important. The singular demands singular expression, and negation, analogy, and paradox can help to achieve genuine singularity of expression.

3. The Importance of Event-Symbols in the Bible

Since, for Casserley, God is a singular being, "event-symbols" are especially important in talking about him. The Bible points out certain events as self-revelatory acts of the living God. In these cases, the event-symbols do not portray something universal in the human condition, but something specific and proper to the divine existence.[38]

The Hebrews saw the events of their history to be unique. God is involved in all of human history. However, it is God's acts in and through certain events—those unfolding throughout the biblical drama—which illuminate all of history from a redemptive perspective. Thus the unity of theme which knits the Old Testament (and the New Testament also) into a continuity is God's special revelation through a people specifically chosen and called, and the working out of his purpose of redemption in a series of unique events.[39]

(1) The Exodus, Creation, and the Fall. For example, the Old Testament is built around a central event, a great happening called the Exodus. This event occurred at a time when God's people were hapless slaves in Egypt. Through the

miracles of the plagues and the opening of the Red Sea, God delivered his people from the hands of the mightiest power in the ancient world.

Because of the great significance of this event, the Old Testament story of the Creation is related to the Exodus story. Obviously, nobody was around when God created the world out of nothing, nor was anyone around to record the story of the Fall. Christians believe that God worked through inspiration, showing the Hebrews that as it was God's power which had delivered them from bondage in Egypt, so it was God's power which had created the world *ex nihilo*, out of nothing.

It is no wonder that Moses and the great Old Testament prophets, who encountered Yahweh as the Lord of history, the ruler of the destinies of the nations, should conclude that the world of nature, which is the theater and stage of history, was under the sovereign control of the same Lord. And since God is the Lord of history, it was considered inevitable that he created the world by the word of his mouth.

In the New Testament, the encounter with the creative Word of God in history (Jesus Christ) served to deepen for the apostolic church the knowledge of God as creator. The apostles had seen God by the power of his incarnate Word bringing into being a new creation.[40]

The story of the Fall is also related to the Exodus experience—especially to the events surrounding the giving of the Law at Mt. Sinai. When Moses came down from the mountain with the stone tablets, he was shocked to find that the people had begun constructing a golden calf. How could this people who had been delivered and sustained by Yahweh suddenly do an about-face and behave in such an idolatrous way?

To account for such actions, the Hebrews were brought to the understanding that God had created people in his own image and had limited himself in giving them freedom. However, Adam and Eve, the first persons created in God's image, rebelled against God. Consequently, a proclivity toward evil entered into the bloodstream of the human race. Nobody other than Adam and Eve witnessed such an event. However, the record of the beginning of evil, as well as the revelation of the happenings at the end times, were given by revelation to God's chosen spiritual leaders. The Fall, especially, was correlated with and confirmed by the actual historical experience of human rebellion and sin.[41]

(2) The Cross, the Resurrection, the Last Judgment, and the New Age. After the coming of Christ, his followers believed that the original covenant between God and Israel had been replaced by a new covenant—a new agreement established in power and love through the life, death, resurrection, and continuing presence of this unique person, Jesus Christ. The Christians believed God had now acted decisively in human history through a unique event or series of events in which, through their own commitment of faith, they themselves shared. To them, this was the event which illuminates all other events, and in which the very significance of human existence in relation to God stood disclosed.[42]

In the New Testament, the Cross was experienced as the demonstration of God's love in allowing his only Son to die for humanity's sins. The Resurrection was also experienced by Jesus' followers. In 1 Corinthians, Paul mentions that more than five hundred people then living had actually seen the resurrected Jesus (15:1, 3–6). These events meant that Christ's person was experienced in holiness and love in Palestine.[43]

Because of these historical events and experiences, Christ's followers had no difficulty in believing the later revelation about the Last Judgment, because they had personally experienced the reality behind these accounts. Peter, in a confrontation with Jesus in Galilee, cried out, "Depart from me, for I am a sinful man" (Luke 5:8). He had faced the holiness of Christ in person and had seen the power of God in his raising Jesus from the grave. It was not hard for him to believe that one day he would have to face this same Jesus at the Last Judgment.

The center of the Christian idea of the Day of Judgment is most simply stated in Paul's words, "We must all appear before the judgment seat of Christ" (2 Cor. 5:10; see also Rom. 14:10). As Christ moved among men and women, displaying pure goodness in all his words and actions, they found themselves judged. This judgment became most acute when he went to his death, because there the glory of the divine goodness was most completely disclosed. And this is what gives meaning to the expression "the judgment seat of Christ."

Behind the doomsday symbolism of Revelation (often fantastic to our minds) there is the truth that the verdict upon history, and upon all the actors in it, is pronounced simply by confrontation with the Word of God, made flesh in Christ. Those who had stood under his judgment in history and acknowledged its finality knew that he must be the judge of the quick and the dead. As the account of the Creation and the Fall was confirmed by the experience of Israel in history, so the account of the Last Judgment is confirmed by the experience of those who had found themselves judged by Christ.[44]

According to the New Testament, the final judgment is to be followed by the "new heavens and new earth." This event involves a realm very far removed from our known order of space and time. Yet even here humankind's experience of God's ways in history through Christ in his glorious resurrection gives us an understanding of what lies beyond.[45]

(3) Historical Events and the Confirmation of the Ministry of the Prophets and the Apostles. The historical and event-centered nature of the Bible indicates the public and coherent nature of the personalities who received key biblical truths —the Old Testament prophets and the New Testament apostles.

The prophet was a "public man." His encounter with God was not a private experience withdrawn from contact with workaday things, like that of the mystics and sages of many religions. The pressure of public movements and events upon his spirit was the occasion of the encounters with God which brought compulsion upon him. Furthermore, the inspired truth which the encounter forced upon his mind was public property.

It is true that the encounter with God is often described in terms of what we call "religious experiences." These experiences were sometimes abnormal or at least unusual—such as seeing visions and hearing voices. This fact sometimes causes difficulty to readers in the modern world. And it is certainly true that visions and voices may be no more than illusions. Yet to infer (as some have done) that the biblical accounts of such experiences are illusory—that Isaiah's vision had to be due to hysteria or Paul's conversion due to an epileptic seizure—is clearly illegitimate. Most of the prophets were embarrassed by the presence of "false prophets" whose mental processes were not distinguishable psychologically from their own. However, they remained totally convinced that God really had spoken to them.[46]

Two things seem important to note about the validity of the prophetic experience. First, when the prophets said, "I saw the Lord," or "The Lord said unto me," or "The Spirit of the Lord came upon me," we can see that the experience to which they refer was an element in a total experience of life which was rational and coherent, forming a logical unity in itself. We can see this quite clearly in prophets such as Isaiah and Jeremiah, whose biographies are in large measure open to us. Their visions and auditions were not aberrations, unrelated to their experience of life as a whole. These were clearly the kind of men of whom it is credible that they did meet with God, whatever psychological form the meeting may have taken.[47]

Second, the personal experience of the prophets was also organically related to the course of the history in which they played a part; it enabled them to give an interpretation of the situation which could stand up to the facts. Also note that the effects which flowed from the prophets' intervention in history were in keeping with its alleged origin in an encounter with God. It should be noted that the prophets made a momentous impact for righteousness upon their time, affecting the whole subsequent history of humankind. It is therefore unlikely that the experience which impelled them to speak and act as they did was a delusion, whatever the form in which it may have been embodied. The prophetic experience is related to the empirical stuff of history itself, inasmuch as its consequences are seen in history.[48]

The coherence and public nature of the experiences of the Old Testament prophets is somewhat similar to the experiences of the New Testament leaders. For example, note the experiences which determined the New Testament interpretation of events: the appearances of the risen Christ to his followers.

Here again we have strictly firsthand witnesses. For example, the apostle Paul expressly claims to have had an encounter with the risen Christ, and he appeals for corroboration to a large number of other witnesses, whose testimony in a number of cases is indirectly reported in the Gospels and the Acts. When, therefore, Paul speaks of his meeting with Christ, he is not speaking of some private, incommunicable experience, but of an experience which he shared with others—an experience of "public" facts.

It seems clear that the New Testament experience of an encounter with the risen Christ was similar to the prophetic experience in terms of its effect in history. If we question the validity of a reported encounter with the risen Christ, the same tests may be applied. Paul's meeting with Christ is of a piece with his total experience of life. It is no aberration. We know Paul very intimately from his letters; they reveal a singularly coherent personality. And this coherence depends to a marked degree upon the reality of what we call his conversion.

Paul says he was "arrested" by Christ. Well, he was certainly arrested by something, to great effect. It is noteworthy that the effects of the "arrest" in the whole of his career were in keeping with their alleged cause. Moreover, the remoter effects in history were in keeping with that which the apostles declared to be the starting point of it all. Note the rise of the church—the highly original character of its community life, its astonishing early expansion, and its no less astonishing spiritual and intellectual achievements. The originating event was the apostle's meeting with the risen Christ, in whom he saw the glory and salvation of God. It is unlikely, even from a secular perspective, that all of this was based upon a delusion.[49]

(4) The Virgin Birth as an Event-Symbol. In order to further illustrate the idea of an event-symbol, Casserley discusses the doctrine of the virgin birth. If the story of the virgin birth were meant to be a universal myth, as many claim it to be, it must symbolize something universal in the human condition. The obvious meaning would be that there is a radical incompatibility between sexuality and spirituality.

Casserley rejects this Manichean interpretation, which despises sexuality. Instead, he affirms that the virgin birth narrative is not a myth-symbol, but an event-symbol with a quite specific reference to an utterly singular character. The virgin birth as an event-symbol signifies that the Son of God "enters into" the world process and does not "emerge out" of it; it is an entirely novel act of God similar to the creation of the world. For Casserley, it is only as an event-symbol that the virgin birth is capable of bearing a Christian meaning.[50]

(5) Historical Events and the Revelation of Truth. The distinction between myth-symbols and event-symbols is even clearer in connection with the resurrection narrative. For Casserley, the apostolic witness to the resurrection is not primarily a truth of faith. In other words, a Christian does not believe in the resurrection event because he has Christian faith. Actually the opposite is true —a person has Christian faith because he believes in the resurrection event. The New Testament testimony to the resurrection is not a faith-truth, but a historical truth. This historical truth is that which arouses or even causes faith in the minds of those people who find themselves confronted by it.

For Casserley, historical truth precedes faith in logic and in time. Faith is a trust in God, by whom the event was initiated and of whom it is a sign. In this light, the resurrection narrative is seen to be an event-symbol which reveals the one living God in action, and not a myth-symbol which suggests a generality such as the regeneration of nature. This is an important distinction, for if an event-symbol is translated into a myth-symbol, the meaning is altered.[51]

According to Casserley, man made religion and it is therefore mythic. On the other hand, God gave the gospel, which is therefore event-centered or historic. Myth, in many cases, is existentially valid and insightful, but only events are theologically revealing. Only from an event can we derive any knowledge of the God who is and who acts—the living God who presents himself in the biblical testimony.[52]

We should remember that a particular event may reveal truth even though it does not give rational or demonstrated proof. Proof or demonstration is a process which classical metaphysics took over from mathematics, with some ambiguous results, such as the statement that an "eternal truth" can only be proved by demonstrative metaphysics. Certainly the moment of revelation, the incident which provokes the mind to the perception or conception of a hitherto unrecognized truth, does not provide rational proof in an empirical or metaphysical sense. Both rational proof and empirical verification are clearly subsequent to the moment in which a religious, metaphysical, or scientific possibility or hypothesis is communicated to or created in the mind as the result of the stimulating pressure of events. It can never be validly claimed that truth is proved or demonstrated by particular events.[53]

However, it should be noted that a particular event may suddenly reveal or betray an abiding but unsuspected truth. This is not a process peculiar to religious revelation. According to popular legend, it was an apple falling upon his head which revealed to Newton the hypothesis of gravity, whose subsequent verification gave him undying fame. In the detective novel, it is usually one particular incident which evokes the flash of insight in which the master detective suddenly sees the light and his jumble of clues composes itself into an unexpected pattern.

We have all enjoyed similar experiences of the revealing occasion. But such moments, although they often communicate to us a subjective certainty which may strengthen us to wait patiently for the final verification, never supply anything like rational proof. Revealing and proving are two different things. Revelation insists that if God is singular, it is appropriate that he reveal himself initially in the singular event and in singular fashion. What is revealed is not a universal truth, as that term is understood in rationalist metaphysics, but a singular reality. Biblical philosophy is rooted in the singular.[54]

(6) Historical Events and Non-Christian Myths. Critics often respond to the biblical accounts of events by pointing out that many cultures, such as the Babylonian, had their own creation stories. It is true that other cultures have stories about a fall, and about a messianic or hero figure. Some of the mystery religions have stories of gods who die and rise again. These religions also have blood rituals which in some ways are similar to the atonement.

According to Amos Wilder, it is important to remember that since we are made in the image of God, it is only natural that all cultures have the same longings. All cultures have felt that there must have been a creation and a fall, and they long for a messianic figure to deliver them from their guilt. It is the Christian contention, however, that God answered these distorted interpretations of longings and partial revelations by coming to humankind with an inspired and saving revelation—first through the Hebrews and then finally in Jesus Christ.[55]

V. How Would You Describe the Uniqueness of Biblical Language?

From an evangelical perspective, it is important to emphasize that biblical language is not only meaningful but unique. In a singular and unique manner, God has chosen to accommodate himself to our human finitude within the forms of time and history; indeed, history supplies both the arena and mode of God's revelation to us. A realization of this uniqueness is important in order to have a proper appreciation of the nature of the Bible.

1. The Contrast of the Bible with Prelogical and Deductive-Logical Thinking

The well-known French psychologist, Lucian Levy-Bruhl, wrote in 1906 that there are two primary forms of thinking: prelogical and logical. By prelogical thought, Levy-Bruhl meant the thinking process typical of cultures which lack any clear conception of deductive or logical thinking. People who are prelogical, both ancient and modern, do not think in terms of cause and effect. Their epistemology, or doctrine of knowledge, operates on hasty associations. Many primitive cultures, for example, have associated human sexuality with fertility of the soil, and therefore human sexual rites developed as ways of improving agricultural yields.[56]

The formalization of logical thought, according to Levy-Bruhl, began with the ancient Greek rationalists. For these Greeks, reality consisted of universal logical forms and could only be approached by rational means. Their preferred mode of reasoning was deduction, which is a mode of moving accurately from given assumptions to a conclusion. Deduction uses the laws of identity and contradiction. Identity states that a term must have the same meaning throughout an argument. Contradiction states that one cannot both assert and deny the same concept; for example, a person cannot be very wise and at the same time foolish about money.

In essence, the Greeks believed that if an assertion can be proved by means of logical or deductive categories, it is true. If it cannot be so proved, it is false. This logical approach has persisted and prevailed in scholarly circles since the times of the ancient Greeks and especially since the Enlightenment. It has been perfected and even computerized in modern times.[57]

2. The Bible and the Empirical-Logical Approach

In the 1930s, William Foxwell Albright of Johns Hopkins University began to formulate a clear objection to Levy-Bruhl's classification of human thinking. Albright contended that there was a third category of thinking, which he called empirical-logical thinking. Empirical logic came into clearest focus with its masterpiece, the Old Testament, but it has continued wherever men seek to learn from experience.[58]

(1) The Inductive Approach and Modern Science. Albright points out that modern science did not begin until the fifteenth century, when the inductive approach to logic was formalized and utilized in science. At that time, thinkers learned to use not only the approach of *deduction*, including the laws of identity and contradiction, but also the approach of *induction*.

Inductive reasoning had been discovered in antiquity but, according to historians of philosophy, was not set out systematically until Francis Bacon in the sixteenth and John Stuart Mill in the nineteenth century. Mill developed rules by which it is possible to distinguish between superficial and untrustworthy judgments about the actual world and more penetrating and dependable judgments.

The idea of induction is that truth can be found out by observing many examples of particular objects or occurrences. After making these dozens of observations, a person can derive from them some general laws or principles. This allows for a tentative hypothesis, which is the working basis for further testing.

(2) The Inductive Approach of the Bible. According to Albright, the Hebrews were using the inductive or empirical-logical method in the area of religion more than twenty-five hundred years before it was used systematically in the development of modern science. Hebrew empirical logic brought to light a discovery which has had great impact upon our understanding of the nature of the Bible and biblical language. This insight is based on the idea that experience in history yields religious knowledge.

For Albright this means that the Old Testament has a strength and soundness which cannot be found in classical philosophical structures. The classical structures start with more or less elaborate sets of assumptions, but their basic postulates are seldom carefully analyzed. In fact, good logic sometimes carries unsound premises to dangerous conclusions. In contrast, the Bible is rooted in the rough-and-tumble of events which forced a certain, inevitable interpretation of themselves upon their witnesses. These witnesses, according to the biblical worldview, were inspired by God to leave behind a record of these events and their interpretations in spoken and written language.[59]

(3) The Revelation of God in Relation to Historical Events. G. Ernest Wright, a student of Albright, agrees that it was the history of Israel which caused her thinking to be empirical. God had broken into Israel's history in specific events, and Israel sought to explain that experience under divine guidance.[60]

How, for example, did the Israelites come to their knowledge of the nature of God? Surely nobody went out under a tree, meditated for a period of time, and then came up with an idea out of the blue.

No, the Hebrews were slaves, and they came to know God's *power* in an existential, concrete experience—being delivered out of Egypt. They came to know his *love* because God cared for them when nobody else did. That is why they were later to put such emphasis on caring for orphans, widows, and children. And they came to know his *holiness* through being punished for their sins. For even though the Hebrews were God's chosen people, when they broke the covenant he raised up first the Assyrians and then the Babylonians to carry them into captivity. From all these particular experiences, as interpreted by the prophets, the Hebrews induced or learned the nature of God.

This same type of history-oriented knowledge was acquired in New Testament times. Through the Cross, people learned of God's love. Through the Resurrection, they learned of God's power. Through the presence of Jesus, they learned of God's holiness. This empirical confrontation in history is one reason why the Bible is unique among religious documents of the ancient world; it is rooted in concrete events and in divinely interpreted experience.

Thus we have a Bible which is the result of special revelation rooted in history. That is, human minds were illuminated by God's Spirit as they wrestled with the problem of interpreting God's will in the concrete historical situation of their own day.

It was in the midst of the upheavals and crises of Israel's history that the Old Testament prophets gave us their teachings about the fact that God is righteous and merciful. In the same way, the apostolic bearers of the Christian gospel found in the concrete teaching and work of Jesus Christ the source of their own teaching. From Hebrew history they learned of God's judgment upon the disobedient Jewish people—and therefore by implication upon the sin of the whole world. They also learned of God's purpose of restoration and forgiveness for mankind in the setting up of the New Israel, the church of Jesus Christ.

According to Wright, the biblical Word of God is not to be conceived primarily as a truth or proposition given to God's people apart from events. Rather, it is in relationship to the events of daily life that they received divine revelation. The culminating event was Jesus Christ, who formed a powerful creative image which restructured many lives in history to conform to him. The images found in the Old and New Testaments are coherent, particular, and structured, although great variety is seen in biblical history.[61]

Until Albright's writing in this area, it was commonly assumed that the Old Testament was prelogical because it antedated Greek rationalism. Using the same reasoning, many New Testament scholars sought to force the New Testament into a formally logical mold because of its date and the fact that it was written in the Greek language. But despite the emphasis of James Barr and others on the diverse nature of the Old Testament, substantial biblical scholarship stresses that Israel's testimonies are based on a unified underlying framework. In fact, there is a fundamental unity of the Old and New Testaments. This unity is based primarily on Hebraic thinking, which in turn is characterized by empirical logic.[62]

3. The Importance of the Concreteness of Biblical Language in Achieving Its Purpose

The biblical worldview is not reasoned out in a treatise, the manner in which the Greeks worked out their perspective on philosophy. The Hebrews did not deal with the timeless issues of being and becoming, matter and form, definition and demonstrations, but rather with specific persons, places, and events in history. For someone accustomed to the Greek type of thinking, it is rather strange to be thrown into a book which talks about widows and orphans and about the corruption of judges and affairs in the marketplace.

It is this very concreteness of biblical language, however, that enables the person who accepts the Bible as a guide to apprehend the reality about which the Bible speaks. In contrast, the abstract terminology of Greek philosophy limits reality to the world of abstract concepts.

Even the imagery of the Bible is concrete—it relates spiritual things to down-to-earth, specific objects and activities. It must be remembered, however, that the Bible almost never limits itself to just one concrete image when describing a spiritual truth; rather, it uses multiple images to convey the full biblical truth about that reality. Jesus, as well as Paul and other biblical writers used many parables and images to point to one truth. God, for example, is depicted as a father, a king, a lord, and a husband. Some images prove more effective than others and thus are used more often in the Bible. And sometimes one image is used to portray several different realities. A shepherd may be used to portray an image of God as a source of guidance and comfort (Psalm 23), or he may portray an image of one who is suffering God's wrath (Jer. 25:34). This points up the importance of context.[63]

The primary purpose in studying the Bible, therefore, must be to gain an experience of the realities it describes. The Bible, as such, is not a technical textbook of science and philosophy. Although the Bible is concrete, it is not inconsistent in its overall structure. It simply prefers the concreteness of imagery to the abstractness of scientific or technical terminology.[64]

4. Biblical Language and the Biblical Worldview

Claude Tresmontant defends the uniqueness of biblical language and bases it on the uniqueness of the biblical worldview. To properly understand the biblical language, he suggests, a person must first understand this worldview.[65]

Tresmontant concedes, however, that the biblical worldview is implicit or semi-hidden rather than explicit, and he seeks to construct, from this implicit metaphysic, a clearly portrayed view. (It is well to remember that any literature which expresses a way of life and a viewpoint on reality implies a metaphysic or worldview of some sort—even though that metaphysic may be incorrect or inconsistent.)[66]

According to Tresmontant, there is an organic interrelatedness and coherence to the biblical approach to reality. He maintains (and in this he is supported by Cherbonnier) that there are three primary categories in the biblical worldview: creation, incarnation, and history.

(1) The Category of Creation. The biblical concept of creation avoids either metaphysical dualism (the eternal tension of two coequal forces) or metaphysical monism (the concept that all reality is one—as in an idealistic or materialistic type of pantheism). The Bible affirms that there is a personal, spiritual power behind the universe. That power has created this world to be good and real. This means that the created world is not to be despised, nor is it to be worshiped.

(2) The Category of Incarnation. The biblical metaphysic is also characterized by the concept of incarnation. The Incarnation implies a special type of personalism—one in which personal relationships between man and God are meaningful. The Bible contends that God's primary concern in the world is to restore that part of the universe which is made in God's image—humanity. We have rebelled against our Creator. But since he loves us, he created a plan whereby, without destroying human freedom, he could help us. God sent his own Son in the form of a person, Jesus, to be the second Adam, to give us the model, the plan, the help that we need in order to be restored.

The Incarnation also implies that the knowledge of universals is subordinate to the knowledge of persons. It further implies that, within certain limitations, anthropomorphisms (talking about God in human terms) are legitimate, because God is conceived as a person.

(3) The Category of History. As argued in the last chapter, the biblical worldview is also characterized by a historical view of reality. God is known in history. Knowledge of God does not come primarily through a mystical experience withdrawn from history, but through interpreted events. God is known through such events as the Exodus and the life, death, resurrection, and teachings of Jesus Christ, and through inspired teachings related to these events.

As an historically oriented book, the Bible is unique among primary religious writings. It is not just a poetic or symbolic book, even though it contains many symbols. The difference is that the Bible is tied to particular events in history.[67]

Similarly, the Bible is not a technical, scientific book—even though modern men and women persist in trying to evaluate its contents according to technical standards. This was true even in John Calvin's time, when some people took issue with the Bible's statement that the moon sheds light (Gen. 1:15–16). By Calvin's time, with the advent of the Copernican revolution, people realized that the moon did not shed light, but only reflected light from the sun. So a certain group decided that the Bible was unscientific and therefore inaccurate. Calvin insisted that Moses could not have cared less about the technical details of astronomy and the moon. He stressed that the important thing was the Bible's revelation of the primacy of restored relations between God and his creatures, as well as among the people themselves.[68]

Understanding biblical language in the context of the categories of the biblical worldview clearly shows that its purpose and function are not primarily poetic or scientific in a technical sense. Rather the aim of biblical language is knowledge of the truth concerning God's revelation. But as was shown in chapter one, these concepts, "knowledge" and "the truth," must also be understood within the biblical worldview. For in the Bible, knowledge primarily means knowledge of a Person, not just knowledge through sense experience and logic.[69]

5. The Importance of Language from the Biblical Perspective

It should be noted that, according to the biblical view, language is possible because of humanity's God-given endowment of rationality and the imprint of the image of God. These endowments precondition our ability to think and speak. Since every mind is lighted by the *logos* or reason of God, thought stands behind and underlies language. The Bible portrays human beings as specially equipped by God for the express purpose of knowing God's rational-verbal revelation. Humans can communicate with God in praise and prayer and discourse with their fellow humans about God and his will. Language is therefore a vehicle used by the chosen writers of the Bible to convey divine revelation.[70]

God utilized the human symbol systems of the Hebrew and Greek languages to address human beings concerning the meaning of his acts in history, his character and will, and the human predicament and destiny. Religious language in the Bible, as elsewhere, has many functions, but a basic function is to teach definitive Truth about God's nature and purpose for men.[71]

Historical events are revelatory only when they are accompanied by the revelatory word. It should be noted that God sometimes reveals himself by words alone through inspired biblical writers.[72]

VI. What Are Appropriate Concluding Emphases Concerning Religious and Biblical Language?

1. Summary Review

The emphasis on the empirical-logical worldview of the biblical writers and the unique categories of creation, incarnation, and history is significant for an understanding of the dynamic, concrete, and descriptive nature of biblical language. Fortunately, a number of devout scholars, some of whose writings we have noted, have helped to establish the meaningfulness, significance for knowledge, and uniqueness of biblical language.

2. The Stimulus of the Criticism of Biblical Language

In many ways, the biblical worldview owes a debt to its critics in the logical positivism and linguistic analysis movements of the past two centuries. This is because the criticisms suggested by these movements have helped to stimulate a restudy of the nature and purpose of religious and biblical language.

All language, including the scientific, is written from a particular perspective. Competent scholars trained in linguistic analysis have pointed out that religious and biblical languages are meaningful if restricted to their own unique purposes, and others have built on that base to build a strong case for metaphysical and religious reality. As linguistic studies have developed, a narrow empiricism or scientific orientation has been revealed as inadequate in the evaluation of biblical language. At the same time, the biblical model has been reexamined and has been shown to have much relevance; distinctive biblical categories have been shown to create a language of tremendous moral and spiritual power. As will be shown in the chapters on science and religion, both biblical literalism and "demythologizing" are inadequate approaches to biblical language. New developments in philosophy have shown that, in light of the realism of historical developments, traditional idealism is also inadequate as a structure for biblical language.

From a more positive perspective, the radical criticism of biblical language has given us a new appreciation of the vivid, story-type, concrete, and dynamic language of the Bible—and of the comprehensive, coherent biblical worldview this language presents.

The purpose of the Bible, as we have seen, is not to provide us with technical, scientific information. Rather, the purpose of the Bible is primarily personal and redemptive. It aims first to lead us to the discernment (conviction) that our basic problem is a wrong relationship with our loving Creator God. Next, the biblical purpose is to lead us to commitment to Jesus Christ, whom God has provided to restore us by his vicarious death and renew us by his risen power. And this commitment carries its own means of verification. In John 15:1–11, Jesus Christ points out the relationship between obedience and discipleship and intimate knowledge of God and spiritual fruitfulness.

The language of the Bible, which to Hume and the logical positivists looked foolish and meaningless, is now seen to constitute a unique and powerful Book. It is one of God's great instruments for his redemptive purpose. As Christians, we should be proud to be called "the people of the Book."

4

The Question of Science and the Biblical Worldview—with Special Emphasis on the Origin and Development of the Earth and the Human Race

I. How Would You Describe the Conflict between Science and the Biblical Worldview in Relation to Origins and Development?

1. The Biblical View on the Defensive

A few years ago in New York, my wife and I attended Jerome Lawrence's well-known play, *Inherit the Wind.* It is based on an actual incident in American history, the famous Scopes "monkey" trial of 1925. A young high-school science teacher in Dayton, Tennessee, allowed himself to become the focus of a challenge to the state law which banned the teaching of evolution in Tennessee public schools. Clarence Darrow, the well-known lawyer and iconoclast from Baltimore, defended the young teacher, while the famous orator William Jennings Bryan defended the law and what he called "the orthodox view" of the Bible.

In the play, Darrow is the evident and obvious hero, while William Jennings Bryan is made to look like a fool. That night in New York, the Broadway crowd screamed in delight as the play made fun of the Bible and Bryan's attempts to interpret and defend it.

Unfortunately, *Inherit the Wind* and the reaction of that Broadway crowd typify the common conception of the biblical worldview in terms of the origin and development of the world and the human race. Since the seventeenth century, when Galileo Galilei was tried by the church for challenging the accepted view of the structure of the universe, there has been tension between the claims of science and the claims of religion.

Increasingly, since the time of Galileo in the seventeenth century, science has tended to replace theology on the throne of Western thought. It has won this position through many conflicts in which biblical Christianity found itself on the defensive—caricatured and ridiculed by those who hold absolute faith in science as the only dependable explainer of the earth's past and present. All too often, as in Jerome Lawrence's play, the biblical view of man's beginning, uniqueness, and development has been laughed out of court, and biblical Christianity has been characterized as closed-minded, obscurantist, and hostile to free inquiry and scientific progress. (In fact, Galileo's condemnation by the Roman Catholic Church has been held up over the centuries as a prime example of this attitude.)[1]

Don Cupitt, for example, in a recent BBC television program, asserted that science-based culture is activist and progressive; it promotes and requires analytical and critical habits of mind. In contrast, he asserted, religion is obscurantist, morally backward, and resistant to change; it promotes an acquiescent and noncritical temper of mind.[2]

For several years I taught at Rice University, a well-known scientifically oriented school. Here I met a number of competent scientists who were also devout Christians. And yet I also encountered a widespread doubt that a person can be a competent, honest scientist and at the same time an evangelical Christian who accepts the biblical stories of the creation of the world and of human origin and development.

Is the ongoing conflict over the origin and development of the earth and humankind really a conflict between authentic science and authentic biblical religion? In Galileo's case, an academic conflict originating within the university grew into a theological issue for the church. Ambition, envy, prejudice, and special interests also entered into the conflict. And unfortunately, this is often true of today's conflict as well.[3]

2. The Focus of the Contemporary Conflict: "Creation-Science" versus Evolution

There are many areas where science and the biblical religion have run into conflict in the past century. For example, in the area of psychology, the teachings of Sigmund Freud reduce religion to wish fulfillment and God to a father "projection." B. F. Skinner, with his view of psychological determinism, and neurophysiology, with its disturbing research into the interrelationship between mind and body, also raise issues that have been problematic in terms of the biblical worldview.

But in no area has there been more emotional controversy in schools, churches, homes, and the courts than in the area of the origin and development of the earth and the human race. In particular, the conflict has centered on the differences between the biblical accounts of creation and the Darwinian concept of the evolution of the human race.

Interestingly enough, in the United States, there has been strong opposition in the past few decades to the dominant scientific view in this area. The New York audience may have derided William Jennings Bryan's position in *Inherit the Wind*, but in recent years proponents of similar views have made strong political and social inroads across the country.

In the public schools, the teaching of what has been called "scientific creationism" or "creation-science" has become a matter of much debate. Scientific creationism affirms that it can correlate scientific data about origins with a literal reading of the Genesis creation account. Most proponents hold to six twenty-four-hour days of creation, a "young earth" method of dating, and a worldwide "flood geology."

In 1969, the California State Board of Education was petitioned to recognize "creationism" as a scientifically valid doctrine deserving equal status with other scientific explanations of origins. Subsequently, local school boards, state boards of education, and state legislatures across the country came under pressure to mandate the teaching of "scientific creationism" in the public schools.

The celebrated trials over this issue in Arkansas and Louisiana, which continued over several years, rudely awakened public consciousness to a phenomenon more widespread and tenacious than most had imagined. In fact, creationist bills demanding equal time for a "creation model" of origins have been submitted to legislatures in more than thirty states. State boards of education, including those in Texas and California, have been pressured to accept textbooks that include creationist materials. Local boards of education have also been targeted by creationists for grassroots action as a means of achieving their goals regardless of legislatures and state boards.[4]

Publishers of science textbooks have also come under pressure. In order to have their books accepted as texts, a number of publishers have accommodated creationist demands in various ways. They have reduced the space given to discussion of evolution and referred to evolution as "only a theory." They have included creationist materials and placed references to evolution in a final chapter which the teacher can conveniently omit. In fact, some new biology texts have managed to avoid the word *evolution* altogether.[5]

By now the fully revived controversy over various views of biblical creation and biological evolution has produced hundreds of articles and dozens of books. Currently in print are more than three hundred and fifty books challenging evolutionary science and advocating creation-science. A well-financed effort has been made to flood the Christian bookstore and mail-order markets with similar literature.[6]

There are now nearly fifty creationist organizations in the United States, another dozen in Canada, and more in other countries ranging from England to Australia and from Germany to India and Brazil. Many of these organizations have their own newspapers, magazines, pamphlets, tracts, study programs, graded materials, cassettes, films, and books, as well as field workers and speakers' bureaus. The combined circulation of creationist periodical literature is in the millions. And cultic magazines such as *The Plain Truth*, with its seven-million monthly circulation, also frequently contain creationist essays.[7]

There is also a growing network of fundamentalist private schools dedicated to an antievolutionist and biblically literal creationist position. The American Association of Christian Schools, with more than a thousand member institutions, makes acceptance of the statement, "We believe in creation, not evolution," a condition of affiliation. The creationist position is taught not only in the AACS science textbooks, but also in texts for history, geography, social science, and literature. "Equal time" is given to evolutionary materials only in the sense that the concept of evolution is repeatedly dismissed as evil. No room is made for alternative approaches, not even alternative approaches to biblical interpretation. According to the AACS, literal creationism is right; all other positions are wrong.[8]

In a way, the current focus on creation-science and evolution is surprising, since the most radical changes in twentieth-century science have occurred not in biology, but in astronomy and physics. The theories of special and general relativity, an expanding universe, and a new physics at the subatomic level have taken the place of the more static Newtonian universe characterized by permanence and balance. For the average person, however, the realm of biology presents the most urgent need to relate the biblical and scientific views since the theory of evolution has again sparked such widespread controversy.[9]

Many people ask why creation-science has found such a response at this particular time. Evidently it meets some deep inner concerns and anxieties on the part of those who hunger for certainty, dignity, meaning, and significance and who feel that the dominant belief in naturalistic evolution has undermined these values. Many Christians with a simple faith and little knowledge of science have long been suspicious of scientists as a group, fearing that many scientists are proclaiming atheism in intellectual garb. For a long time, such Christians saw their alternatives as being either faith or belief in science. Then came the new generation of scientific-creationists who affirmed that the Bible had been right all along, and that science itself points to creation rather than evolution. For many pressured and discouraged Christians, creation-science has become a symbol and a case to help them stand firm and attain dignity and meaning.

The new activism of creationists in the United States means that they are no longer dismissed lightly by their opponents. In fact, the creationist pressures on public education and policy have become so strong that a group of evolutionary scientists have founded a new journal (*Creation/Evolution*), a "Committee of Correspondence," and a *Creation/Evolution Newsletter* aimed at defending evolutionary science and dismantling creationist arguments. The American Civil Liberties Union, the National Education Association, lawyers, legislators, and judges have been similarly forced to deal with the issue because of the numerous bills and civil suits demanding equal time for creationism.[10]

The conflict between the Bible and evolution has immediate implications for classrooms and courts, pulpits and churches. What is needed is a clear understanding of the issue that does justice to both perspectives. Regrettably, however, the developments in the creationist-evolutionist dispute have tended to be confrontational, with each side dedicated to defeating the opponent rather than to exploring the possibility of some agreements. The result is an increasing tendency toward polarization of the positions of "scientific naturalism" and "scientific creationism." Neither extreme seriously looks for or imagines a mediating position.

It is a classic confrontation of antagonists bent on mutual destruction, each unwilling to see an accommodation with the other as anything but an act of disloyalty to the cause.[11]

3. A Method for Approaching the Issue: Four Basic Questions

In the midst of all the debate is the average Christian, who is usually a layperson in both science and religion, and who finds the situation confusing. Most have only a Sunday school knowledge of the Bible and perhaps a high-school understanding of science. And even those who are more versed either in science or theology have a hard time sorting out the issues.

How can Christians react to the ongoing debate concerning the origins of the world and of the human race? Do responsible and clear-headed people have to shift their minds into neutral on Sunday when they go to church and read the Book of Genesis? Are the biblical accounts just an exercise in nostalgia—like Santa Claus, fairy tales, and the Easter rabbit?

Or, on the other hand, must committed Christians ignore the claims of science and close our eyes to the scientific advances of three centuries? In order to remain true to the biblical worldview, must we close our eyes and ears to realities that seem self-evident to scientifically minded people around the world?

Or is there not an alternative approach? Many of us believe that both science and the biblical religion are important ways to understand reality. We believe that these approaches to reality should complement each other. In fact, many of us believe that, apart from their partnership, the fullness of God's truth for man cannot be known.

In looking at the conflict between the Bible and science, with special focus on the origin and development of the earth and the human race, it is helpful to think in terms of four basic questions, which can serve as a framework for further discussion:

- First, what is modern science, and what are its primary purposes and limitations?
- Second, what is the biblical religion, and what are its primary purposes and limitations?
- Third, what does modern science have to say about the origin and development of humankind?
- Fourth, what is the response of the Christian community to modern science and its teachings about the origin and development of the earth and the human race?

II. What Is Modern Science, and What Are Its Primary Purposes and Limitations?

1. The Development of Modern Science

Science as we know it today is a direct result of the rise of experimental science in the sixteenth and seventeenth centuries, when a revolution in the human approach to the natural world took place. This involved a rejection of the Aristotelian view, which had dominated Western science for more than fifteen hundred years.

Aristotle's philosophy held that the human mind, in seeking to understand the world, operates with an antecedent set of ideas and concepts that have little basis in experimental observation and testing. An early attack on Aristotle's system of thought was made by Nicolaus Copernicus in 1543, with the publication of *On the Revolutions of the Heavenly Spheres.*[12] Next came Johann Kepler (1571–1630), Galileo (1564–1642), and Sir Isaac Newton (1642–1727). The discoveries of these four men in astronomy and physics—and especially their method of investigation—established a new kind of science based on a foundation of mathematics and experimentation rather than preset ideas and principles. This approach to the natural world led to the development of modern chemistry in the eighteenth century and modern geology and biology in the nineteenth, then to a second revolution in astronomy and physics in the twentieth century.[13]

2. The Nature of Scientific Inquiry

Scientific inquiry, as it has developed since the sixteenth and seventeenth centuries, involves an adoption of the view that the human mind can understand the world only through ideas and concepts that it derives from the world itself through empirical contact. It is thus the task of science to devise experiments in which appropriate questions may be put to nature in order to encourage the disclosure of its coherent patterns of behavior (which could not otherwise be known). In the light of what is discovered in this way, explanatory theories can be formulated.[14]

Most scientists agree on the following presuppositions:

- First, nature has an underlying order, shown in patterns and regularities that can be discovered. The fact that the results of experiments can be reproduced presupposes that the universe is neither chaotic nor precarious.
- Second, the forces of nature are uniform throughout space and time. What happens in the United States in one laboratory also occurs in other labs in other countries around the world (both past and present) under the same conditions.
- Third, reliable data can be obtained through the human senses.
- Fourth, if more than one theory or explanation fits the data, the simpler one is to be preferred.[15]

3. Definition of the Scientific Method

The scientific method is not easy to define, but the general components are clear. The first step is usually an observation of some phenomenon in nature. The scientist reflects upon what has been detected by the senses and constructs a hypothesis that might explain what has been observed. The hypothesis is then tested by additional observations and, if possible, by experimentation.

If the hypothesis appears to be supported by this investigation, it may come to be regarded as a theory. A theory is subject to continued scrutiny over a long period of time and by many investigators. Refinements and modifications are usually made. The accumulation of evidence may necessitate that a theory be abandoned—or may lead to its general acceptance. In some cases, a theory may gain the status of a law—as in the case of the law of gravity.[16]

Central to the scientific method is a willingness to consider new data and to modify or abandon a view if new evidence justifies such action. The work of a scientist is never finished. Even what are thought to be the most secure concepts are always subject to revision.[17]

4. Moral and Social Requirements of the Scientific Enterprise

Even though modern science claims not to make value judgments or moral pronouncements, nevertheless, there are certain moral and social principles which are presupposed in order for science to proceed as a community enterprise.

One of these principles is moral responsibility. All scientists are expected to report honestly the results of their experiments so that others can have confidence in their data and use those results in their own research.

The other principle is consensus of acceptance. Scientists around the world engage in research in the same discipline and use similar procedures and equipment. They test research results, thereby ensuring (or at least increasing) the objectivity of their results. Acceptance is based on the agreed competence of persons who are known to be trained, skilled observers.[18]

5. The Subjective and Social-Context Approach to Science

In recent years, philosophers of science have questioned the scientific presuppositions and methods outlined above. Scholars such as Karl Popper and Thomas Kuhn have pointed out that "scientific observations" are not themselves free from dependence on theories, which themselves are often leaps of creative imagination. Kuhn's *The Structure of Scientific Revolutions* contends that the theory or conceptual framework which the scientist brings to his research determines the standards or guidelines for his work. Scientific revolutions occur when one theory is replaced by another, which may accommodate more information and be more satisfying psychologically. An example of this would be the switch in this century from Newtonian physics to the approach of Einstein.[19]

Other scholars, including some Marxists, have pointed out that social conditions and the social context—not just objective observation—help to determine scientific theory. There is evidence that social goals and political aspirations directly influence scientific work. Science is even used by religious unbelievers and believers alike to justify their own worldview. One notorious example is the Nazi use of science to prove racial superiority (Germanic) and inferiority (Jews).[20]

The classic presuppositions of modern scientific enquiry are not without their defenders, however. William Newton-Smith, the British philosopher of science, claims that the views of Kuhn and the social context group are too relativistic. Newton-Smith grants that theories are always provisional; however, he claims that the history of science is a record of increasing approximation to the truth. Furthermore, science has had great success and has shown amazing predictive powers. This indicates that scientific statements are close to physical reality.[21]

Christian scholars are varied in their views of the reliability of the scientific method. Some Christians agree that even scientists filter their work through tinted glasses. Other Christian scholars, such as Donald McKay of Keele University in England, maintain that exact natural sciences come close to value-free knowledge.

David Livingston, research officer at Queen's University of Belfast, believes that Christian doctrine explains both viewpoints. The Creator's world is intelligible, but defects in knowledge arise from the fall of man. This biblical view accounts for the many achievements of science, but also helps explain its mistakes, conflicts, and misuse. Science is an ever-changing, finite endeavor. For this reason, it can be a helpful servant, but is a bad master.[22]

As we have already indicated, the Christian doctrine of the Fall teaches us that the image of God in humankind is defaced, scarred, and distorted through rebellion. All humans have a congenital bias to revolt against what is good and true and right. Scientists fall within this universal "reign of sin." Thus the biblical view of the Fall reminds us that no particular brand of scientific knowledge is immune from the taint of sin. Christian scientists, of course, are also tainted, but because of Christian understanding they should be in the vanguard of scientific self-criticism.[23]

6. The Role of the Biblical Worldview in the Development of Modern Science

Studies in the origin and development of modern science have led historians to ask why the brilliant intellectual powers of the ancient Chinese, Indians, Egyptians, and Greeks, in spite of their achievements both in observation and in pure speculation, never brought forth the dynamic science of the modern era. It has been very plausibly argued that the decisive factor is to be found in the biblical vision of the world as both rational (capable of being comprehended by the mind) and contingent (finite, limited, and filled with mystery).

On the one hand, the enterprise of science would be impossible if there were no principle of rationality in the universe. Without a passionate faith in the ultimate rationality of the world, science would falter, stagnate, and die. However, faith in the rationality of the universe would not sustain science without the concurrent belief that there is a certain contingent or surprise quality in the universe.[24]

Indian metaphysics has been totally committed to the rationality of the universe, but has understood it as necessary being, that is, a part of the eternal cycle of evolution and involution. The universe and man are the emanations of the Hindu concept of an ultimately impersonal god, not the creation of a personal God. The ultimate secrets of the universe are therefore to be discovered within the recesses of the human soul, where it makes direct contact with the cosmic soul, not through empirical observation and experiment. Therefore, science in the sense in which it has developed in our culture is not impossible, but it is unnecessary.[25]

Scientific thought in Greek circles was controlled by the idea of perfect numbers and perfect circles, or by the concept of the purposeful organism. In other words, it was controlled by the idea of a completely immanent rationality. Once again, there was no need for observation and experiment. And the same was true of the great cultures of ancient China and Egypt. Consequently, in spite of the brilliant intellectual powers which these great civilizations manifested, science in the modern sense did not develop.[26]

Such lines of evidence show that Christianity was more of a senior partner of the new science than its enemy. The biblical revelation portrays a God who is consistent in character and orderly in creative activity. Furthermore, the important concept of the contingency of nature has a biblical source (Isa. 42:5–7; 51:9–11).

The concept of contingent intelligibility, based on the biblical doctrine of creation, became the foundation on which the empirical sciences rest. In other words, nature is not understood through inherent, self-explanatory principles, but by observation and experiment. The world is what it is, not what we think it must be. The universe is what God has made it to be—a contingent, open-structured order reaching beyond what we can grasp or define within the limitations of our propositions or equations. Hence, the universe has a surprising or contingent character. Unexpected twists and turns take place in the course of scientific research.[27]

It should be noted that the Protestant Reformation made an important contribution to the new science. On the continent of Europe, the Reformers had a generally positive view of science as they knew it in its beginning stage. John Calvin, for example, saw astronomy as useful and as an art that unfolded the wisdom of God. The doctrinal thought-forms of the Reformers, such as the love of nature, the glory of God, the welfare of humanity, and the priesthood of all believers, were congenial as a background for experimental science. Nevertheless, both Calvin and Martin Luther were concerned that concentration on science might divert attention from the Creator and give people the impression that natural processes are outside God's control.[28]

In seventeenth-century England, science and religion interacted with each other in an even more positive way. Puritans took the lead in establishing Newtonian science and were active in the Royal Society of Science. Because of the biblical tradition's high regard for manual work performed for the glory of God, the mechanical arts and experimentation were fostered.[29]

III. What Is the Biblical Religion, and What Are Its Primary Purposes and Limitations?

1. The Biblical Focus on Revelation in History through Act and Word

To some people, the Bible seems outdated. However, when properly understood, the biblical message has special relevance for our scientific and technological culture. It provides answers to urgent contemporary questions of meaning, values, and purpose in life—questions which are outside the purpose of modern physical science.[30]

It is important to understand that the focus of the Bible is different from that of science. As we have seen, modern science focuses on elements of the natural world that can be observed, measured, and explained empirically and mathematically. In contrast, although the Bible has some significant teachings about the natural order, its primary concern is in the arena of human history, within which God reveals himself and his purposes.[30]

(1) Revelation in History. As we have seen in earlier chapters, the Bible presents a linear durative view of human history with a purpose and a goal—a series of unique, decisive events fulfilling a purpose.

Approximately 60 percent of the Old Testament is historical narrative. It is a record of events in the lives of individuals, families, tribes and nations. The Gospels and Acts, also primarily historical narratives, comprise about the same proportion of the New Testament; while the other New Testament books contain considerable theological interpretation of history through letters to specific individuals or churches. God reveals his character and purpose for humanity primarily in and through the medium of history. In that arena, archaeology and historical research have consistently demonstrated the reliability of the biblical records.[31]

And the natural world, under God's providential management, also has a history and a future. It is neither an eternal, unchanging reality nor a cyclical system of recurring states. Rather, the natural world is dynamic, purposeful, and developing. It participates in the drama of salvation, for it too will be transformed in the final consummation.[32]

(2) Revelation in Act and Word. In the Old Testament, the key person was not a scientist, but a prophet. Through the prophets, God took the initiative to reveal himself and his purposes in the world he created. The key term in this revelatory action is *word,* which is a symbol of communication. The spoken Word of God is proclaimed and then committed to writing. The written Word, as Holy Scripture, is preserved and transmitted to future generations.[33]

However, God's revelation is not solely verbal. As the Lord and judge of human history, God also reveals himself in mighty acts of salvation, judgment, and mercy. And both *act* and *word*—events and their interpretation—constitute the biblical revelation, which is firmly grounded in history. The combination of *divine act* and *prophetic word* effectively communicates God's character and purpose. This gives us the *who* and *why* of the created order.[34]

There is a fundamental problem, however, with the meaningful revelation of God to his people. Jesus taught that "God is spirit, and his worshipers must worship in spirit and in truth" (John 4:24, NIV). And the apostle Paul wrote about a God "who alone is immortal and who lives in unapproachable light, whom no one has seen or can see" (1 Tim. 6:16, NIV). How can we comprehend someone who is spirit and cannot be seen or approached?

As we saw in the chapter on religious language, God uses the principle of analogy in making himself known. Analogy involves pointing out a partial resemblance, or similarity in certain respects, between things that otherwise are unlike. God also uses models, which are systematic sets of analogies drawn from familiar situations of life.[35]

In the biblical revelation, the central model for God is a person. The analogies that make up this model are called anthropomorphisms, since they picture God's activities as if he were human. For example, God is represented as having human emotions such as love, anger, and jealousy. This human model is sometimes seen as primitive and crude by modern scholars, but it has the vividness and dramatic power needed to reveal God to ordinary people in every culture and century.

Often the Bible describes God in terms of the roles people assume in society. Each of these descriptive models—ruler, judge, employer, and parent—is used to emphasize some characteristic of God. However, unlike scientific models (e.g., the "billiard-ball" model used to explain the kinetic theory of gases), biblical metaphors (e.g., "the Lord is my shepherd") have emotional overtones, and they influence attitudes and actions.[36]

Of course, there are dangers in using models for God, especially when a person employs a literalism that equates a metaphor with the reality it portrays. The prohibition against graven images in worship is more than a warning against idolatry; it is also a reminder that God is spiritual and cannot be captured in any sensory form—even the form of the models used to describe him. However, various facets of God's personality are portrayed to us in the metaphors of Ruler, Judge, and loving Father.[37]

The supreme model for God in the New Testament is Jesus Christ. He is the living Word who reveals the character and purposes of God. The focal point of the Gospels is the death, resurrection, and ascension of Christ. In his person and work, Christ is the climax of God's redemptive activity. The apostles proclaim those events and their meaning.[38]

God revealed his character and purpose in his message through the prophets, but he also guided its commitment to writing. In one of his letters, the apostle Paul wrote to Timothy, "From infancy you have known the holy Scriptures, which are able to make you wise for salvation through faith in Christ Jesus. All Scripture is God-breathed and is useful for teaching, rebuking, correcting and training in righteousness, so that the man of God may be thoroughly equipped for every good work" (2 Tim. 3:15–17, NIV). The Word of God is thus communicated in human words. These words accurately convey the intended ideas, just as composers' notes express their music and scientists' formulas embody their theories.[39]

2. The Purposes and Appropriate Uses of the Bible

There are two primary purposes for which the Bible is inspired. The first purpose is to provide understanding of the salvation which is provided through faith in Christ. The second purpose is equipping the faithful for a life of good works. The Bible embodies teaching (doctrine) designed to rebuke, correct, and train in righteousness. Historically, it has been accepted by Christians as final authority in matters of faith and conduct.

It is essential to remember that these characteristics relate to the primary purpose of Scripture. Today, unfortunately, as in Galileo's time, biblical authority and reliability are often mistakenly extended to the technical realm of scientific explanation.[40]

The Bible is not, as most will agree, a technical science book—it was never intended to be one. We should therefore not turn to the Bible as a textbook for the study of physics or biology. Nor should students learn their science at church, although this sometimes happens. The Bible is simply silent about most of the hows and whys that concern most scientists. There are, however, as we shall see, some very important statements in the Bible about the natural order which are quite definite and universally true. The Christian cannot surrender these realities to any scientific theory.[41]

3. The Basic Method of Understanding the Message of the Bible

A crucial question related to the Bible is the matter of interpretation. How can we understand the message we are supposed to trust?

A two-stage process is required:

- First, we try to discover what the message meant to its first hearers or readers.
- Second, we try to decide what it has to say to us.

The determination of the original meaning of a passage involves four steps. First, we must consider the *historical context*—what were the actual historical occurrences covered in the passage? Second, we must consider the *literary context*. It is important to take the literal parts literally and the figurative parts figuratively. This means that we should be aware that the biblical writers use a variety of literary forms to convey God's truth. Once the historical and literary contexts are understood, a third step is to consider the *content* of the passage. And finally, the fourth step is to *interpret Scripture by Scripture*—to consider how the passage or Book fits into the Bible as a whole. The whole process of linking historical and literary context with content and biblical context is often called the grammatico-historical-theological method.

The next task is to determine the contemporary relevance of the biblical message. How does the original meaning apply to our situation? Here, once again, we must guard against any tendency to read into a text a meaning quite different from that intended by the writer. Without this precaution, a passage can be read to mean whatever the reader wants it to mean.[42]

4. Application of the Basic Method of Interpretation to the Creation Passages in the Old Testament

(1) The Historical Context. We have noted that the basic method of interpretation affirms that what a biblical author meant in his own day should be the basis for determining what the message means now. This is a crucial principle for interpreting the Genesis creation narratives, which are the basis for much of the conflict between the scientific view and the biblical view of the origins of the earth and humankind.

The commonly held evangelical position accepts the fact that the Genesis creation narratives were given to the Israelites in the wilderness, after the Exodus from Egypt but before the conquest of Canaan. This view considers the Pentateuch to be a revelation from God. Most of it is seen to have come through the prophet Moses, who may have used earlier sources. Obviously some editing took place later.[43]

For more than four hundred years, the Hebrews had lived in Egypt, far from the land promised to Abraham. Those centuries took a spiritual as well as a physical toll. The people had no Scriptures, only a few oral traditions passed down from the time of the patriarchs. Devotion to the God of their forefather Joseph had largely been forsaken for the worship of the gods of other nations; in fact, the incident of the golden calf related in Exodus 32:1–6 suggests that fertility cults may have been part of Hebrew religious life in Egypt. Even though they were miraculously delivered from slavery and led toward Canaan, many of the people had a limited understanding of the God of Abraham, Isaac, and Jacob. When the Hebrews arrived at Mt. Horeb, their worldview and lifestyle differed little from that of the surrounding nations. Their culture was essentially pagan.[44]

Moses faced a difficult task. His people needed a radically different worldview as a basis for a proper understanding of God and his purposes. They also needed a new perspective to restructure their attitudes toward the created order.

In relation to creation concepts, the primary concern of the biblical texts was to affirm the radical difference between a polytheistic and a monotheistic cosmology. All the surrounding cosmologies identified the major regions of the cosmos with their various gods and goddesses. Genesis was radically opposed to this viewpoint, which it counters with a firm affirmation (1) that there is only one God; (2) that this God is not identified with or contained by any region of nature; (3) that the pagan gods and goddesses are not divinities at all, but rather creations of the one true God; and (4) that the worship of any of these false divinities is idolatry. This powerful affirmation—not a particular cosmological picture—is what the Genesis text teaches and celebrates.[45]

The pagan myths commonly pictured the origins of natural phenomena in terms of the marriages and births of various gods and goddesses. In Babylonian myth, the salt-water goddess (Tiamat) mated with the freshwater god (Apsu) and begat the gods and goddesses of silt and the horizon, who in turn begat heaven (Anu), who begat the earth (Enki). Genesis, on the other hand, portrays the One God as creating all those things which other cultures worship as the divinities of nature. The theological order of Genesis, therefore, is not a genealogy of the gods (theogony), but a relationship of creator and creature. "In the beginning God created the heavens and the earth." Thus the true opposite of the Genesis account of creation is not any scientific model of origins, evolutionary or otherwise, but the pagan procreation model of polytheistic myth.[46]

According to Conrad Hyers, professor of religion at Gustavus Adolphus College, the creation accounts of Genesis were not attempting to present a more cosmologically—let alone scientifically—correct way of representing physical relationships in space or time. In other words, Genesis is not setting forth a "creation model" that can be placed in competition with other physical models. In particular, it is not offering a "flat earth model" in competition with "round earth" models or a "geocentric model" in competition with astronomical models. To put Genesis on the level of a physical discussion of the natural order is to secularize it.[47]

(2) The Literary Context. The style of Genesis 1 is remarkable for its simplicity and its economy of language. Its literary genre can be called "semipoetic narrative." The prominence of repetition brings the writing close to poetry. Sometimes called a "hymn," it appears to be a unique blend of prose and poetry.

Despite its poetic elements, however, Genesis 1 is essentially a narrative of past events, an account of God's creative words and acts. The text does not have the earmarks of a parable, which is a short allegorical story designed to teach a truth or moral lesson. Genesis 1 is "historical" in the sense of relating events that actually occurred. The writing can be called historical narrative, or primeval history, to distinguish it from legend or myth, which are simply ideas couched in story form.[48]

An approach to Genesis 1 should not assume that the events narrated are necessarily related in strict chronological order. In both its overall structure and use of numbers, the writer paid as much attention to the form as to the content of the narrative. This suggests mature meditation and careful literary craftsmanship.

Essentially, the structure of this opening chapter of Genesis is that of two parallel groupings of three days. When this is understood, it is no longer a problem that the creation of the sun, necessary for an earth clothed with vegetation on the third day, should be linked with the fourth day. In view of the author's purpose the question is irrelevant. The account is not intended to follow a chronological sequence.

Another important aspect of the literary context of Genesis is the use of the word *day*. The meaning of this word must be determined (as in the case of any other word with several meanings) by the context and usage of the author. The context itself gives no indication of referring to eras or geological ages; creation is pictured as occurring in six familiar periods of morning and evening, followed by a seventh for rest—corresponding to the days of the week as Israel knew them.

The fact that the text speaks of twenty-four-hour days, however, does not require that they be considered the actual duration of God's creative activity. Preoccupation with how long it took God to create the world in days or epochs deflects attention from the main point of Genesis 1.

What was the intended meaning of the "days" for the ancient Hebrews? First, their significance does not lie in a one-to-one correlation with God's creative activity, but in an analogy that provides a model for human work. The normative pattern of six plus one, six work days plus rest on the seventh day, highlights the sabbath. The pattern also emphasizes the uniqueness of humanity. Made in the image of God, and given rule over the world, man and woman are the crown of creation. They rest from their labor on the sabbath, which is grounded in the creation (Gen. 2:2; Exod. 20:11). The fact that Genesis 1 speaks of "day" in its ordinary workaday meaning and does not refer to epics or ages makes possible the metaphor of God's creative activity as a model for human work of six days followed by sabbath rest.

The way in which God's creative activity is linked to days of the week also serves to fortify the purpose of countering the pagan view of nature. By stretching the creation events over the course of a series of days in a linear, historically oriented fashion, the biblical writers draw the sharpest possible line between this account and every form of mythical thinking. Genesis 1 contrasts sharply with the cyclical, recurring creations accepted by Israel's pagan neighbors, whose views were based primarily on nature's cycles.[49]

It is important to understand that looking at the historical and literary context of Genesis in no way lessens its total trustworthiness. On the contrary, it is an important safeguard against the tendency to read into biblical texts meaning that is not there or interpret the texts as saying what we want them to say. As with any other kind of literature, the meaning is best determined by recognized rules of interpretation respecting the author's purpose, historical context, literary forms, and usage of words.[50]

5. Basic Characteristics of Biblical Language About Nature

Even though their major concern is the arena of human history and God's redemptive purpose, both the Old and New Testaments abound with references to nature. In considering the conflict between science and religion, it should be helpful to look at several basic characteristics of the biblical language used in referring to nature.

For example, it is helpful to realize that the Hebrew measurement of time was imprecise by our standards. The ancients used physical organs such as the heart, liver, and bowels to represent psychological functions.

Biblical language concerning the natural world is clearly popular rather than technical. A scientist uses technical language to communicate with colleagues and to publish in professional journals, but in ordinary conversation that same individual uses everyday language. It is unreasonable to interpret the popular writing of the Bible as though its terminology were technical. It is equally irresponsible to find hidden references to modern science in the Bible. It seems obvious that the Holy Spirit never intended to communicate such things through the biblical writers.[51]

Christians have noted that statements in the Bible about the natural order are frequently observational in nature and do not claim to be otherwise. And clearly, absolute precision was not intended in many cases. Article XIII of *The Chicago Statement on Biblical Inerrancy,* formulated by leading evangelical Christians in 1978, states: "We further deny that inerrancy is negated by biblical phenomena such as a lack of modern technical precision, irregularities of grammar or spelling, observational descriptions of nature."[52]

John Calvin observed that the biblical writers describe natural events as they appear to the senses, not in scientific terms. For everyday communication, scientists, like others, use phenomenal or common-sense appearance terminology. For instance, few astronomers would object to using the phrase, "the sun rises," in conversation, although a modern astronomer would vehemently deny that the sun moves around the earth.

The biblical writers make no effort to describe the mechanism of natural events; they tend to ignore the immediate "how" and stress instead the "Who" and "why"—the Creator and his goals.

Modern scientific language is not a standard against which ancient Hebrew writing should be measured. Each literary form has its own characteristics and purposes. It is more appropriate to say that biblical language is "nonscientific" or "nontechnical" or "nontheoretical."

To summarize, biblical language regarding nature is cultural, popular, and nontheoretical. The third characteristic is especially significant to its relationship with science. Scientific theories are provisional and not permanent. They are subject to change or even replacement. If the Bible were supposed to be scientifically accurate in any generation, it would be outdated in the next generation. There would thus be a loss of confidence in its trustworthiness.[53]

6. The Basic Attitudes of the Bible toward Nature

Although the Bible offers no systematic explanation of the natural world, several basic attitudes are evident.

First, belief in the creation of the universe by God is central to all of the biblical text.

Second, biblical writers make it clear that nature is neither to be worshiped nor despised, but rather admired as God's work. Any form of nature worship is a forbidden idolatry.

Third, the biblical writers assume the regularity and predictability of nature, and they base this assumption on their understanding of God's character (Jer.

31:35–36). The same conviction of order in the world, the uniformity of natural forces, also undergirds the scientific enterprise, yet the biblical writers do not speculate about the mechanism of those regulating forces.

Fourth, a conviction of God's providence in maintaining the universe pervades the Old and New Testament. The biblical view opposes both pantheism and deism; God is neither just a part of the world nor is he locked out of its activity. Instead, he is constantly working within nature as well as in human history to achieve his purposes. The biblical writers attribute *all* events in nature, including both the recurring and the miraculous, the predictable and the unexpected, to the power of God.[54]

IV. What Does Modern Science Teach About the Origin and Development of the Earth and the Human Race?

1. The Theory of Evolution

(1) The Impact of the Life and Teachings of Darwin. Charles Darwin is one of the most influential and controversial men in history. He early aspired to be a medical doctor, but failed the qualifying examinations. Next he went to theological school, but made poor grades. Finally he did get a theological diploma, but it was obvious that he had no gifts for the Christian ministry.

Darwin then turned in other directions. In 1832 he went to sea on the survey ship *Beagle* as the ship's naturalist. A five-year voyage took him around the world. During his voyage, he made studies of slight variations among species, especially the finches in the remote Galapagos chain of islands. His observations formed the seeds of an idea that later would be formulated as his theory of natural selection.

Evidently, Darwin was greatly influenced by the comments of economist T. R. Malthus on the role of human population pressure and competition. In 1838 he found in Malthus's writings the clue for a theory to interpret his extensive data.

Darwin had his "survival of the fittest" theory essentially complete by 1844, but he took another fifteen years to mature it. In 1859 he published his landmark book, *On the Origin of Species by Means of Natural Selection*. By that time he had spent twenty-five years amassing an array of observations from a variety of biological species.

Although Darwin was not the first to suggest the *possibility* of the evolution of species, he presented a wealth of evidence to support a possible *mechanism* whereby evolution might take place—the concept of natural selection. His work illustrates the basic scientific method of interaction between observation and theory. No amount of data constitutes or produces a scientific theory unless this theory can be tested by observations and can provide a guide as additional data is collected.

Darwin's theory of the origin of species by natural selection combines several concepts. First, it postulates that there are random variations among the individual members of a species. Second, it assumes that there is a struggle for survival in which a slight variation gives an advantage in the intense competition for existence. Third, it concludes that the individuals with that advantage will become predominant because, on the average, they will live longer and have more progeny.[55]

In his first book, Darwin avoided a discussion of human origins. But in 1871 he presented a thorough treatment of this subject in *The Descent of Man*. He attempted to show how all human characteristics could be accounted for by a gradual modification of anthropoid ancestors through the process of natural selection. In his view, not only physical elements, but also human mental and moral faculties, differed only in degree, and not in kind, from the capacities of animals. Our own human existence thus came within the sphere of natural law, to be analyzed by the same methods used for other forms of life.

The publication of the *Origin of Species* and the subsequent *The Descent of Man* initiated a period of intense excitement. Although many secondary points such as the mechanism of natural selection had been debated for more than a century, the change in outlook associated with Darwin was a major shift in intellectual history.

Darwin's theory of evolution was to lead to three major changes in the generally accepted view of nature. First, the idea of the world was transformed from that of a fixed hierarchical order into a dynamic process. Second, nature came to be seen as a complex of forces interacting in organic interdependence; the relationship between man and his environment therefore assumed greater significance. Third, the idea of biological evolution as a natural law extended the concept of natural law into many other areas of nature. As a result, determinism, or the belief that all facts and events exemplify natural law, gained ground in the following decades.

Over the years since Darwin, *evolution* has become a term that conjures up a host of images and conceptual extrapolations. These images or concepts are widely recognized. They include such ideas as "nature red in tooth and claw," social Darwinism (the application of the "survival of the fittest" idea to human society), "robber barons" and *laissez-faire* capitalism, reductionist materialism, aggressive atheism, ethical relativism, human perfectibility, and a self-existent universe.[56]

(2) The Development of Evolutionism or Evolutionary Naturalism. Charles Darwin himself never claimed that natural selection was the exclusive mechanism of evolution. However, his name came to represent a rigorous naturalism which totally denied the role of any divine agency in directing the course of events in the world and especially denied that these events occurred according to a plan and purpose. This point of view became known as evolutionism or evolutionary naturalism.[57]

Evolutionism soon made extensive claims. A form of naturalism, evolutionism soon came to consider the natural world to be the whole of reality. It also came to see its method as the only valid approach to understanding reality. The biological evolutionary model was so influential that the evolutionary idea was applied to every field from astronomy to ethics. This historical and genetic approach viewed all ideas, institutions, religions, and cultures as following the evolutionary model.

In fact, evolution as a scientific theory became the springboard to a full-blown philosophy of evolutionary naturalism and even a religion of moral and ethical evolutionism. A method was made into a metaphysic, and a theory became a comprehensive worldview.[58]

Evolutionism views all of life as one grand development from lower to higher forms, leading to continuing human improvement as people now become conscious of evolution and seek to complete for themselves the age-long process. For some, evolutionism can become a pseudo-religion. It is seen as a faith system competing with Christianity for people's allegiance.[59]

In theory, of course, the scientific method precludes such metaphysical speculation. In reality, however, scientists over the years have succumbed to the temptation to venture outside the limits imposed by their method. And this became true for many of the evolutionists.[60]

David Livingston believes that some who claim to be neutral scientists have pushed evolution into biological determinism. The essence of biological determinism is the belief that all human thoughts and activities—even moral concepts and values—are rooted in biology rather than social or transcendent realities. The outworking of such a perspective has led to the excesses of behaviorist psychology and environmental determinism. An example is the grosser form of a brutally manipulative "scientific" racism.[61]

2. Microevolution and Macroevolution

In all fairness to science, attention should be given not only to evolutionism, but to two more precise definitions of evolution. Science, in general, differentiates between evolution as special theory (microevolution) and evolution as general theory (macroevolution).

Microevolution, or the special theory of evolution, can be defined as the proposition that many living animals can be observed over the course of time to undergo changes so that new species are formed. In certain cases, this type of evolution can be demonstrated by experiments. Therefore, in this limited sense it is possible to call evolution a fact. Current scientific literature shows that most biologists are giving their attention to microevolution. They can verify genetic changes in the laboratory and in nature at this limited level.

Macroevolution, or the general theory of evolution, is defined as the theory that all the living forms in the world have arisen from a single source, which itself came from an inorganic form. This is the classic evolution theory taught in textbooks and in courses in zoology.

The amount of time and space required for macroevolution precludes the possibility of its confirmation by laboratory experiment or observation of the entire process of nature. Therefore, evidence for this theory must come from such areas as comparative anatomy and physiology, embryology, zoogeography (the study of the geographical distribution of animals), biochemistry, and the fossil record. Sometimes such evidence—for example, the stages of fetal development or vestigial organs in animals—is taken as proof, when in reality it is simply an example of reasoning on the basis of assumptions and analogy. (An exception to this is the fossil record, which does provide fairly concrete evidence that different life forms existed long ago.) For example, it is assumed that because small changes occur in a brief time, large changes will take place over a longer time—but there is no actual proof that this is true. Like other scientific generalizations, macroevolution includes gaps and extrapolations.

At present, no one evolutionary sequence, with an explanation of its mechanism, is widely accepted. Leading biologists advance significantly different proposals. Nevertheless, macroevolution with its assumptions, like other scientific theories, is still used as a working hypothesis that attempts to correlate the data and guide further research. To be scientifically accurate, however, textbooks and lecturers should refrain from giving to the general theory of macroevolution the status of factuality enjoyed by the special theory, microevolution. Eric Rust, trained in both science and theology, sets forth in detail the strengths and weaknesses of macroevolution in his significant book, *Science and Faith.*

The distinction between microevolution and macroevolution is important to understand when considering the general concept of evolution. Most attacks on "the theory of evolution" are really concerned with macroevolution. Some scientists who are Christians accept microevolution based on empirical evidence but reject macroevolution. However, it is common for evolutionists to represent an attack on this general theory as an attack on the special theory (microevolution), for which more empirical evidence exists.[62]

V. What Has Been the Response of the Christian Community to Modern Science and Its Teachings About the Origin and Development of the Earth and the Human Race?

1. The "Middle Ground" Approach: Theistic Evolution

A widespread response to the modern scientific teachings about origins and development might be called the "middle ground," or theistic evolution, approach. It is called a "middle ground" approach, because it basically accepts the theory of evolution without accepting the atheistic or agnostic attitude that sometimes accompanies the theory. This view adds an adjective to negate any atheistic implications of the word *evolution*—theistic evolutionists see evolution as a mechanism God may have used in his task of creation.[63]

(1) Some Proponents of Theistic Evolution. An early theistic evolutionist was James McCosh, a theologian and president of what is now Princeton University. He suggested in 1871 that the scriptural and scientific views of nature could be reconciled as parallel revelations. McCosh believed that natural selection was only one of several means by which evolution took place, and that even that mechanism is consistent with divine design. For McCosh, supernatural design produced the process of natural selection. Understood in this light,

he said, evolution, is in no way inconsistent with Scripture; it is simply God's method of creation.

Another proponent of theistic evolution in the latter part of the nineteenth century was Asa Gray, professor of natural history at Harvard and one of the great botanists of his time. Gray claimed he could coordinate the theory of biological evolution with a vital Christian faith. He further contended that the Mosaic books were not handed down to us for our instruction in scientific knowledge. Rather, it is our duty to base our scientific beliefs upon observation and inference, unmixed with considerations of a different order.

Gray stated that the true issue regarding origins and development is not between creationism and Darwinism, but between design and chance, purpose and no intention. As a professing Christian, Gray was convinced that final causes—God's ultimate purposes—remained untouched by evolution.[64]

It is noteworthy that three conservative leaders of this same period—B. B. Warfield, George F. Wright, and James Orr—showed sympathy with the ideas of theistic evolution. Warfield, for example, acknowledged the possibility of evolution, although he cautioned that it "cannot act as a substitute for creation, but at best can supply only a theory of the method of the divine providence."[65]

Wright wrote in volume 4 of *The Fundamentals,* published by The Bible Institute of Los Angeles in 1917, that "the word evolution is in itself innocent enough, and has a large range of legitimate use. The Bible, indeed, teaches a system of evolution. The world was not made in an instant, or even in one day (whatever period day may signify) but in six days. Throughout the whole process there was an orderly progress from lower to higher forms of matter and life. In short there is an established order in all the Creator's work."[66]

James Orr, the eminent Scottish theologian, wrote in his book, *The Christian View of God and the World,* "On the general hypothesis of evolution, as applied to the organic world, I have nothing to say, except that, within certain limits, it seems to me extremely probable, and supported by a large body of evidence. This, however, only refers to the fact of a genetic relationship of some kind between the different species of plants and animals, and does not affect the means by which this development may be supposed to be brought about."[67]

(2) General Principles and Problems of Theistic Evolution. Modern-day advocates of theistic evolution emphasize God's continuing involvement in and with his creation. God began the biological process by bringing the first organism to life. He then continued by working immanently and internally toward his goal for creation. At some point, however, he also acted supernaturally, intervening to modify the process, but employing already existing materials. God created the first human being, but in so doing he utilized an existing creature. God created a human soul and infused it into one of the higher primates, thereby transforming this creature into the first human. Although God specially created the spiritual nature of Adam, humankind's physical nature is a product of the process of evolution.[68]

A recent advocate, David L. Dye, who is a respected scientist and a Christian leader, writes, "At some point in time, perhaps 20,000 years ago, perhaps earlier, one of the primate products of the God-designed biological processes had a body somewhat similar to the body of today. . . . God took this primate, and made a man of him."[69]

Theistic evolution has no great difficulty with the commonly accepted teachings of biological evolution, since it teaches that the physical dimension of the human race arose through evolution. This allows it to accommodate any amount of evidence that there is a biological continuity from the lower forms of life to the first humans. With respect to the biblical data, many proponents of theistic evolution hold to the belief in an actual primal pair, Adam and Eve. When this is the case, there is no difficulty reconciling theistic evolution with Paul's teaching regarding the sinfulness of the race.

In dealing with the opening chapters of Genesis, theistic evolutionists follow one of two strategies. Either they assert that Genesis says nothing specific about the manner of man's origin, or they regard the passage as symbolic. In the latter case, "dust" (2:7), for example, is not taken literally. Rather, it is interpreted as a symbolic reference to some already existing, subhuman creature.[70]

The theistic evolution view contends that the Bible does not sharply divide God's creative activity into theological and philosophical compartments of creation and providence, supernatural and natural, primary and secondary causes. The Bible writers were not concerned with scientific mechanisms. They ascribed everything in nature, from beginning through to the end, to God the Creator and Sustainer of the world, who is also the Lord and Judge of history, Israel's Redeemer and Preserver.

Since both creation and evolution have varied meanings, the theistic evolution approach sees it as a mistake to use the terms *creationist* and *evolutionist* as if each represented only one concept, or as if they were mutually exclusive positions. Many competent scholars accept both biblical creation and biological evolution. They claim to have full confidence in the reliability of the Genesis accounts of creation, and they also use macroevolution as a scientific theory to correlate known data and guide future research. This view is common among a number of evangelical Christians in science today. And both mainline Protestant and Roman Catholic scholars generally see evolution as God's *modus operandi*, at least for organisms below the human level.[71]

Some conservative and evangelical scholars, however, see problems or question areas in the approach of theistic evolution. Many of these center around Genesis 2:7, which states, "Then the Lord God formed man of dust from the ground, and breathed into his nostrils the breath of life; and man became a living being."

As we have seen, theistic evolution claims that the physical dimension of humankind developed from an earlier species, and that Genesis 2:7 refers to a moment when God infused a human soul into this already existing creature. It follows that this progenitor must necessarily *already* have been a living being. But this tenet of theistic evolution contradicts the statement in Genesis 2:7 that man became a living being when God formed him and breathed into him the breath of life.[72]

Carl F. H. Henry contends that, although the Genesis creation account does not rule out the existence of humanlike forms prior to God's creation of the first human, it provides no basis for postulating an animal lineage for humankind. Scripture does not identify the appearance of Genesis man, who is made in God's image, with earlier creatures whose anthropological distinction is that they walked upright or otherwise resembled humans. Skeletal resemblance is not necessary proof that pre-Adamic anthropoids were humans of the Adamic "kind."

Scripture declares humankind to be the bearer of the divine likeness—a distinct "kind" of being. In the Genesis account, the "dust" into which Yahweh breathes "the breath of life" (2:7) was clearly not a living animal. In fact, the Hebrew word translated "dust" can mean clay, mortar, rubbish, or ashes. The human chemical makeup consists simply of the 105 or so atomic elements that belong to inanimate creation. But into this dust God breathed the breath of life, even as he gave life to the beasts of the field, and to reptiles and birds (Gen. 1:30).

When the Bible deals with likeness in the context of creation, it does so not in terms of earthlike substance or of humanlike apes, but in terms of Godlike Adam. What especially distinguishes Genesis man from all the animals is his creation in the image of God (Gen. 1:26–26). In consequence of this uniqueness, humankind is assigned a special cosmic role and mission.[73]

2. The Fiat Creationist Approach of Protestant Fundamentalism

A second approach or response of the Christian community to the origins of the earth and the human race is usually called fiat creationism. This view, which is generally held by Protestant fundamentalism, sees evolution as undermining the basic biblical doctrine of creation and reducing human beings to products of blind chance. The fiat creationist view holds that God, by a direct act, instantaneously brought into being virtually everything that is.

There are three basic features of this view. One is the brevity of time involved —perhaps a calendar week or so—and hence the relative recency of what occurred at creation. While there were various stages of creation, one occurring after another, no substantial amount of time elapsed from the beginning to the end of the process.

A second feature of the fiat creationist view is the idea of direct divine working. God produced the world and everything in it, not by the use of any indirect means or biological mechanisms, but by direct action and contact. In each case, or at each stage, God did not employ previously existing material. New species did not arise as modifications of existing species; rather, they were fresh starts especially created by God. Each species was totally distinct from the others. Specifically, God made the first human in his entirety by a unique, direct creative act. This means that humankind did not derive from any previously existing organism.

A third feature of fiat creationism is that it reflects a strictly literal reading of the Genesis text. This is the way the account was understood for a long time in the history of the church. The statement that God brought forth each animal and plant after its kind has traditionally been interpreted as meaning that he created each species individually. It must be pointed out, however, that the Hebrew noun which is rendered "kind" in most translations is simply a general term of division. It may mean species, but there is not enough specificity about the word to conclude that it does. Therefore, we cannot claim that the Bible *requires* fiat creationism, although it clearly permits it.

It is at the point of scientific data such as geological formations and fossil records that fiat creationism encounters difficulty. For when the data are taken seriously, they appear to indicate a considerable amount of development, including what seem to be transitional forms between species. There are even some forms which appear to be ancestors of the human species.[74]

3. The Creation-Science Approach of Protestant Fundamentalism

(1) Definition and History. A widely held fundamentalist approach identifies itself as scientific creationism, or the creation-science approach. As shown at the beginning of this chapter, the proponents of this approach have attracted national attention in recent years through their political activities and courtroom controversies.

Creation-science has its roots in the late 1950s, when the launching of the Russian satellite Sputnik caused many Americans to feel that the United States was falling behind the Soviets in science and that American science education was inadequate. This fear led to a new emphasis on science in the public schools. Subsequently, in the early 1960s, the federally funded Biological Sciences Curriculum Study introduced a series of science texts that included teachings on the origin of life and evolution of major types of organisms. In 1968, the United States Supreme Court ruled a 1928 Arkansas anti-evolution law unconstitutional, and by 1970 the last of the state laws forbidding the teaching of evolution had been repealed. In many states, some form of evolutionary theory became the sole explanation given for origins and was usually taught in public schools as a "scientific fact."

A group of creationists in California reacted to these developments by petitioning the State Board of Education. Their statement contained two emphases. First, special divine creation is not just a theistic belief, but can also be explained as a scholarly and scientifically valid doctrine by the Creation Research Society. Therefore, it deserves equal status with other scientific explanations concerning the origin of man. Second, the current science framework presents an unbalanced philosophical approach, atheistic humanism, and such an unbalanced approach is prohibited by law.

The kind of creationism which was offered as an alternative to evolutionary theory taught that the universe is about ten thousand years old, and that the major species were created in six twenty-four-hour days. Proponents of this view hold that geological data can be explained by the worldwide flood of Noah, which lasted about a year. A detailed description of how the flood explains the geological data is given by two scientists, Henry Morris and John Whitcomb, Jr., in the widely circulated book, *The Genesis Flood.*

Instead of trying to outlaw evolution, as they had done in the 1920s, these fundamentalist Christians now attempted to gain equal time for their view of creation. Rather than appealing to the authority of the Bible, they downplayed the Genesis account in favor of what they now termed creation-science. And they turned their efforts toward gaining "equal time" for their views in public-school science classes.[75]

This effort was reflected in Arkansas Act 590, a "balanced treatment" act which became Arkansas law in 1981. Arkansas Act 590 defined creation-science as follows:

> "Creation-science" means the scientific evidences and related inferences that indicate: (1) Sudden creation of the universe, energy and life from nothing; (2) The insufficiency of mutation and natural selection in bringing about development of all living kinds from a single organism; (3) Changes only within fixed limits of originally created kinds of plants and animals; (4) Separate ancestry for man and apes; (5) Explanation of the earth's geology by catastrophism, including the occurrence of a worldwide flood; and (6) A relatively recent inception of the earth and living kinds.[76]

In 1982, Arkansas Act 590 was challenged in federal district court and ruled unconstitutional. Judge William Overton concluded that the law was an attempt by creationists to characterize as science an essentially religious statement. He pointed out that if creation-science were genuine science, it would offer mechanisms, propose problem-solving strategies, and test hypotheses without recourse to theology. Equally important, conclusions would be accepted on their scientific merits by many scholars of differing theological persuasions. He observed that such was not the case—that creation-science was essentially a religious view, and that religion should remain outside the schoolroom.[77]

In response, Norman Geisler, a widely published Christian apologist from Liberty University, contends that the creation-science view is not just a matter of biblical teaching. He points out that the Arkansas law did not mandate teaching the biblical view of creation. There was nothing in the law, for example, about the creation of Adam from dust or Eve from Adam's rib. There was nothing about six days of creation, nor was the time of creation specified. In fact, the law forbade teaching the biblical or any religious view of origins. The creation-science view, affirms Geisler, is not a religious teaching, but a credible scientific theory.[78]

Norman Geisler affirms, in addition, that the Arkansas decision shows a misunderstanding about this law and academic freedom. He points out that, in a way, the trial which overturned Arkansas Act 590 was a reversed "Scopes" trial. In 1925, the Tennessee judge pronounced it illegal to teach evolution. In 1982, the Arkansas judge pronounced it illegal to teach creation as prescribed by this law. According to Geisler, perhaps the best comment on both decisions is one made by Clarence Darrow in 1925, that it "is bigotry for public schools to teach only one theory of origins." In Geisler's view, this applies whether the bigots are "fundamentalists" or "humanists."[79]

According to Geisler, the Arkansas ruling, in effect, establishes the religion of "secular humanism," since it permits only its tenets to be taught in the science classroom. For Overton ruled that any reference to or implication of a Creator or any nonnaturalistic explanation of origins is a violation of the First Amendment. This means that the only views that can be expressed about origins must entail reference to (1) no God, (2) some kind of evolution, and (3) natural law explanations. And it just so happens, claims Geisler, that these are identical to the most fundamental beliefs of the self-avowed religion of secular humanism. So Geisler affirms that by favoring evolution, naturalism, and nontheistic explanations, the judge has in effect established the religion of secular humanism in violation of the Constitution.[80]

Charles E. Hummel, a Yale-trained scientist and Christian educational leader, disagrees with Geisler. He affirms Judge Overton's contention that creation-science is not a truly scientific view, but a theological one. And he charges that creation-science discovers its scientific explanation (in this case, a catastrophism linked with the fixity of species) in a certain view of biblical teaching, then expects empirical data to fit into this explanation. This theological basis of creation-science has been described by J. C. Whitcomb and H. M. Morris: "The real issue is not the correctness of the interpretation of various details of the geological data, but simply what God has revealed in His Word concerning these matters."[81]

Hummel further suggests that the creation-science legislation of Arkansas Act 590 offered a false choice between two packages, based on an oversimplification of "creation" versus "evolution." For example, many evangelical Christians hold one of the creation-science items listed in the act ("sudden creation of the universe, energy and life from nothing") and at the same time hold one of the evolution-science items ("explanation of the earth's geology and the evolutionary sequence by uniformitarianism"). The Arkansas law ignored such various possible combinations.[82]

Davis Young, professor of geology at Calvin College, also contends that scientific creationism should not be taught in our schools and that Judge Overton's decision should not be viewed as a setback for genuine biblical creationism. According to Young, the narrow creationism of the so-called "scientific creationism" movement ignores opposing views held by a great number of legitimate creationists. A careful examination of Scripture reveals that this narrow creationism ignores much biblical data and is no more biblical than several other views. (This is interesting in view of the fact that its proponents claim it is the only biblically legitimate view of creation.) Young identifies a number of Scripture passages which he contends contradict creation-science teachings (e.g., Psalm 104:3, 13 opposes the vapor-canopy idea of the flood). Finally, states Young, this narrow "scientific creationism" cannot be defended on scientific grounds.[83]

(2) Contributions of the Proponents of Creation-Science. As Conrad Hyers points out, the creation-science proponents have pointed to genuine problems in the teaching of science, which the scientific community would do well to acknowledge. For example, the theory of evolution has been presented in the context of an antitheistic, secular, or humanistic worldview. This leaves the implication that this worldview is truly supported by scientific evidence rather than being a faith perspective attached to evolutionary readings of the data. Evolution is often taught with the implication that it and the biblical account are necessarily mutually exclusive. In fact, evolution as taught in most public schools is largely weighted in the direction of a philosophical naturalism. Furthermore, the mechanism of evolution as presented implies materialism as a worldview.

Evolutionary theory is strongly influenced by reductionism, which explains the higher orders of things in terms of lower orders. This leads to a scheme which implies that the lowest forms ascended to the higher forms by a naturalistic internal force. First and final causes are eliminated from meaningful consideration. Instead, chance and accident are substituted as reasons for development. Religious truth is often dismissed as being emotive, valuational, and relative—hence not trustworthy. In summary, the researching and teaching of evolution has been carried on in a largely secular and anti-religious atmosphere.

It is hardly surprising in a scientifically dominated culture that the cumulative effect of such biases should be an increase in those who draw agnostic, if not "secular humanistic," conclusions from science in general and evolution in particular. The science of some scientists is in fact "scientism," and their teaching of evolution is "evolutionism." That is, science and evolution are given a quasi-religious status. They are converted into a metaphysical worldview which affirms that the naturalistic level of scientific investigation represents the whole of reality and the sum total of cognitive truth about reality.[84]

Unfortunately, the plea of William James at the turn of the century has often gone unheeded: "The universe . . . is a more many-sided affair than any sect, even the scientific sect, allows for. . . . Why, after all, may not the world be so complex as to consist of many interpenetrating spheres of reality, which we can thus approach in alternation by using different conceptions and assuming different attitudes?"[85]

Thus, Hyers concludes, the creationists have done the world a service in calling attention to the negative tendencies in science and evolutionary theory. At the point that secular scientists have transformed methodologically self-limited statements into an all-encompassing metaphysical judgments, they must be challenged.[86]

In keeping with the emphasis of some creation-science leaders, Davis Young maintains that we should counter the teaching of evolution in the schools and all the pro-evolutionary propaganda in the media. But it is vital that we distinguish between evolution as biological change and evolutionism as a philosophy. Biological evolution, especially microevolution, does not necessarily include evolutionism. The scientific theory cannot legitimately be used as proof of an evolutionistic worldview, even though some scientists have tried to do so. We should seek through proper legal channels to eliminate the teaching of evolutionism on the grounds that a religious worldview is being promoted by government. In other words, evolutionism must be challenged on a philosophical-religious level—just as creationism is so challenged.[87]

(3) Problems and Weaknesses of Creation-Science. However, as Hyers, Hummel, and Young have pointed out, the concept of creation-science has several problems and weaknesses. Rather than carefully distinguishing between the concept of development and evolutionism, and between science and scientism, the creationists concede everything from the start. "If you accept evolution," they argue, "even a well-meaning, theistic evolution, the result will eventually be pantheistic evolution, which in turn will become atheistic evolution." This is projected as a series of logical steps to inevitable conclusions. According to Hyers, no position could have been better calculated to support and strengthen the case for secular humanism.

In the creation-science view, continues Hyers, little attention is devoted to a careful study of the specific type of biblical literature being interpreted, or the ways this literature is different from technical scientific literature. Neither is time spent on the original issues that the creation texts were addressing and the original meanings of the words for those first using them.[88]

In fact, the fundamental mistake made by creationist-scientists is the same as that made by defenders of the spatial cosmology employed by the Bible (a flat-earth and earth-centered cosmos). Creation-scientists have simply shifted the argument to the temporal side of the cosmology the Bible uses. Most of us now, including the creation-scientists, accept the spatial cosmology as metaphoric, but the creation-scientists still insist on taking the temporal side literally.

A century ago John Hampden was defending "the clear and unmistakable flat-earth teaching of the Bible," and insisting that "no one can believe a single doctrine or dogma of modern astronomy and accept Scripture as divine revelation." Note the very similar words of creationist Henry Morris in defending six literal and recent days of creation: "The creation account is clear, definite, sequential and matter-of-fact, giving every appearance of straightforward historical narrative. . . . Belief in evolution leads usually and logically to rejection of the trustworthiness of the Bible."[89]

According to Hyers, if Christians and school boards must be eternally committed to preserving the temporal side of biblical cosmology, then consistency demands a return to preserving the spatial side as well. Some creationists have tried to avoid such consistency problems by arguing that the temporal aspects are of a different order than the spatial—that spatial relations within the universe are presently observable, whereas temporal relations in the matter of origins are not. So we are forced to take the spatial references poetically, they argue, but there is not enough evidence to force us to take the temporal references as anything but literal statements of scientific truth. It is clear from such an evasion, however, that the principles of biblical interpretation employed by the creation scientists derive from modern scientific issues rather than from the issues which led the biblical writers to use the particular cosmological form they did.[90]

Hyers points out that the creationists think of themselves as staunch conservatives. They engage in a loyal defense of biblical teaching. To some extent they are, inasmuch as they are seeking to preserve a doctrine of creation against secularism and scientism. In other respects, however, they are themselves very much influenced by secularism and scientism. They confuse what is being taught theologically with the cosmological garb in which the teaching is being presented. In other words, they are conserving the right things in the wrong ways. In so doing, they focus most of their attention on the technical physical issues of modern science—which were not the issues the Bible writers faced. Endless statements must be made on all scientific fronts—geology, biology, paleontology, astronomy, chemistry, physics, meteorology, genetics, sedimentology, radiometry, and the like —either to try to discredit evolution or to defend creation—without addressing the fundamental biblical concerns.[91]

The terminology favored by the creation-science movement is itself indicative of the degree to which modern scientific questions and secular modes of thought dominate their discussion of creation. They call their movement Bible science, creation-science, scientific creationism, creation research, or origins research. Not only do such terms dramatize the confusion between the biblical worldview and matters of physical cosmology; their use also becomes a species of secularism and modernism in itself. Many of the leaders of the movement are scientists and engineers, not theologians and biblical scholars. Apparently, it seems almost unthinkable to such people that the ancient Hebrew texts could have been written without a passionate interest in the technical physical relationships of space and time. It also seems unthinkable that divine revelation would not be concerned with the kinds of issues that preoccupy modern minds. Surely God would not stoop to employ the lowly earthbound categories of ancient cosmologies or descend to the language of common appearances![92]

And yet we have seen that God gave us his revelation in specific times and places and in historical terms. The Genesis creation narratives were given to oppose the pagan myth of that day. Properly interpreted, they can still expose and challenge evolutionism and secular humanism on the philosophical religious level.[93]

4. Representative Conservative Theories of Harmonizing the Bible with Science

Before 1750, it was generally accepted that God created the world in six twenty-four-hour days, although some early church fathers such as Augustine viewed the "days" allegorically. In the seventeenth century, the Irish theologian and scholar Archbishop James Ussher even calculated the date of creation as 4004 B.C. But as the science of geology matured in the 1800s, many were shocked to discover that, according to most scientific interpretations of the geological evidence, the earth was millions of years old. Since modern science had gained so much prestige, many interpreters strove to retain credibility for the Bible by attempting to demonstrate its scientific accuracy. Therefore, a variety of concordistic (harmonizing) views were proposed to correlate biblical teaching with current scientific theories.[94]

(1) Gap Theory. The "restitution" or "gap" theory was popularized by a Scottish clergyman, Thomas Chalmers, in 1804. According to this view a catastrophe occurred between Genesis 1:1 and 1:2 to allow the necessary time for the geological formations to develop. This view holds that Genesis 1:2 should properly be translated, "Now the earth *became* without form and void." The implication is that the original perfect creation, which lasted for an indefinite time, ended in a catastrophic ruin that rendered the planet formless and empty. The six days following verse 2 are ordinary days of reconstruction from the earth's state of ruin, rather than days of original creation. The earth is considered ancient, and the vast stretch of time required by the geological ages is accommodated by the indefinitely long "gap" between verses one and two.

The view could be compatible with a theory of biological evolution, although most gap theorists reject evolution. Some maintain that pre-Adamic human races were destroyed in the ruin-event of verse two, and that such a catastrophe might account for humanlike bones that are part of the fossil record.

The gap theory was held by Christian leaders such as William Buckland, Adam Sedgwick, Edward Hitchcock, Jay Kurtz, J. P. Smith, C. I. Scofield, and Arthur Custance, as well as Chalmers. It has been popularized in the widely circulated Scofield Bible.[95]

(2) Day-Age Theory. Although such a theory accounted for the time that science required, it could not explain the sequence of the geological record. The "day-age" interpretation attempted to address this problem by postulating that the Genesis "days" were metaphors for geological ages. This view was advocated by the influential North American geologists J. W. Dawson and James Dwight Dana, as well as by many theologians. The Genesis days were correlated with the sequence of events indicated by the geologic record, and the two more or less corresponded. (Another version of this view retained literal twenty-four-hour days of creative activity, but separated these days by geological epochs.)[96]

Most adherents of the "day-age" view would insist on the miraculous creation of Adam. It is generally maintained that the flood was relatively limited in its geological effects. Scholars such as Charles Hodge, A. A. Hodge, W. G. T. Shedd, A. H. Strong, J. O. Buswell, Jr., Herman Bavinck, J. P. Lange, F. J. Delitzsch, Orton Wiley, and Arnold Guyot were generally favorable to the day-age theory.[97]

(3) Framework Theory. Other views less tied to scientific developments have been advocated by conservative scholars. One is the framework theory, sometimes called the literary view of the six days. This view proposes that the main interest of Genesis 1 is topical rather than chronological. Because time is not of major concern to this view, belief in the antiquity of the earth and acceptance of biological evolution would be consistent with it. The main exponents of the framework theory have been Nicholas Ridderbos and Meredith

Kline. However, A. H. Strong, Bernard Ramm, and J. I. Packer also stress the topical aspects of Genesis 1.[98]

(4) Pictorial or Revelation-Day Theory. Still another view is the pictorial theory or revelation-day approach. Archaeologist P. J. Wiseman considers the six days as days in which the narrative about creation was revealed. For example, on the first day of the series, a seer may have received a vision from the Lord regarding the initial creation of light. On the third day, the seer would have a vision about the formation of dry land, and so forth. Wiseman notes a precedent for that literary form in other ancient literature. Whatever the merit of this view, it at least uses the historical background approach to focus on what the narrative could have meant to the first hearers. This approach is compatible with the antiquity of the earth and with evolution, although proponents have not generally supported evolution.[99]

5. The Mediating Approach of Progressive Creationism

Another viewpoint, a conciliatory approach, can be identified as "progressive creationism." This approach tries to make an interpretation of the biblical narrative harmonize with a developmental scientific theory. (The adjective *progressive* is added because the word *creationism* has picked up such a strong "young earth" connotation.)[100]

The progressive-creationist view sees the creative work of God as a combination of a series of *de novo* (created afresh) creative acts and an immanent or processive operation. God at several points, rather widely separated in time, created new life forms, not relying on previously existing ones. While God might have brought into being something quite similar to an already existing creation, there were a number of changes, and the product of his work was a completely new creature.

Between these special acts of creation, development took place immanently through the indwelling spirit and through the channels of evolution. For example, it is possible that God created the first member of the horse family, and the various species of the family then developed through evolution. This is "intrakind" development (microevolution), not "interkind" development (macroevolution).

With respect to the biblical statement that God made every creature after its kind it should be remembered that the Hebrew word is rather vague, so that it is not necessarily to be identified with biological species. It may be considerably broader than that. Moreover, considerable amounts of time are available for microevolution to have occurred, since the word translated "day" may also be much more freely rendered.

According to progressive creationism, when the time came for a human being to be brought into existence, God made him directly and completely. God did not make humans out of some lower creature; rather, both the physical and spiritual nature of humankind were specially created by God. The Bible tells us that God made man from the dust of the ground. According to the progressive-creationist view, however, this dust need not be actual physical soil. Dust may be some elementary pictorial representation which was intelligible to the first readers.

Progressive creationism agrees with fiat creationism in maintaining that the entirety of man's nature was specially created. It disagrees, however, in holding that there was a certain amount of development in creation after God's original direct act. It agrees with theistic evolution in seeing development within the creation, but insists that there were several *de novo* acts of creation within this overall process. Although it agrees with theistic evolution that man is the result of a special act of creation by God, progressive creationism goes beyond theistic evolution by insisting that this special creative act encompassed man's entire nature, both physical and spiritual.[101]

The progressive-creation view has been held by a number of committed, Bible-believing scholars, such as Bernard Ramm, Davis A. Young, Robert C. Newman, Herman J. Eckelmann, Jr., and Pattle P. Pun. They contend that the progressive creation view can assimilate or explain both the biblical and the empirical data. Millard J. Erickson, for example, contends that, although the progressive-creationist view is not without difficulties, it is nevertheless a more viable position than theistic evolution because it does a better job of explaining and integrating the biblical and scientific data.[102]

Conrad Hyers maintains, however, that Genesis 1 is not in the business of teaching progressive creation or any form of scientific approach to creation. It does not teach any of these views of science and natural history because it is not using language in that way or for that purpose.[103]

6. The "Two Realms" Approach of Neo-Orthodoxy

The "two realms" view sees theology and science as having radically different spheres, jurisdictions, or arenas. This approach has become a popular way to avoid the conflicts between science and religion by defining them as having absolutely nothing to do with each other. The one is said to deal with tangible, factual, and objective reality, while the other is claimed to treat intangible, valuational, and subjective reality.

Twentieth-century neo-orthodox theologians such as Emil Brunner and Karl Barth are exponents of the two-realms approach. Barth, for example, sees the Genesis texts (Gen. 1–3) as a product of the prescientific world with its prescientific cosmologies. These texts, however, do find the Word of God "in, with, and under" the cosmology. Revelation does not intend to teach science, and therefore the Word of God is independent of the cosmology. The theological teaching of the text does not compete with modern cosmological explanations of the universe. There is neither conflict nor harmony, for they are explanations of different orders.[104]

The two-realms model, in its various versions, has the advantage of avoiding the conflict between science and religion altogether. Yet it is unsatisfactory because it fails to do justice to the biblical revelation and its teaching about the natural world. These two emphases should not be assigned to unrelated realms.

Theology and science do live in the same world and observe some of the same phenomena. According to Jerry Gill, this neat dichotomy, promoted largely by existentialist thinkers, purchases cognitive or knowledge peace at too great a price. It is a sort of schizophrenic existence in which one's faith has absolutely nothing to do with one of the more important and indispensable dimensions of human experience. Thus, while it is not best to view science and religion as essentially doing the same thing, it seems every bit as disastrous to define them as entirely separate.[105]

7. The Complementary or Partial-View Approach to Science and Biblical Religion

(1) Definition of the Partial-View or Complementary Approach. As an alternative to other attempts at reconciling the scientific and biblical views of nature, scholars such as D. M. MacKay, T. F. Torrance, Richard Bube, and Charles Hummel suggest yet another approach, a partial-view model. In this model, the biblical and scientific descriptions are to be seen as complementary perspectives —different kinds of maps for the same terrain. Their respective limitations are not a matter of territory (as in the two-realm model), but of purpose and methodology. The self-imposed limitations are inherently required by the kind of description and the language used. Each partial view of nature serves its intended purpose and should be appreciated for the specific contribution it makes to our lives. According to Bube and Hummel, the biblical and scientific perspectives on nature can mutually benefit from interacting with each other as allies with complementary approaches.[106]

(2) The Partial-View Approach to the Origins of the Human Race. What does the partial-view approach have to say about the historicity of the account of the creation of Adam and Eve as founders of the human race? Two comments should be helpful.

First, the popular idea that modern science and evolutionary theory render such a belief untenable is erroneous. Even a thoroughgoing demonstration of the validity of macroevolution would not eliminate the possibility of that unique event, any more than our "scientific laws" of physiology rule out Jesus' miraculous conception or resurrection. Claims should not be dealt with on grounds which prejudice an acceptance before the total evidence is examined.

Second, the most accurate biological description of human development in accordance with evolutionary theory can neither account for nor discount the meaning of humans being made in the image of God, much less the facts about our origin. Evolutionists should be cautious in making an extrapolation from theories of biological evolution into a dogma which excludes other than biological dimensions.[107]

A prominent Christian scientist, V. Elving Anderson, uses the specific and often debated example of how human beings are related to the higher primates to describe the way scientific research and the Bible can complement each other rather than being in conflict. He points out that within the last decade a number of research developments have expanded our understanding of both human and primate ancestry and makeup. New hominoid (human or apelike) fossils have been discovered, leading to the revision of former ideas about relationships between humans and apes. Extensive field studies of primates in their natural environments have shown individual and social behavioral patterns to be more complex than previously thought. And results of genetic studies indicate that the total amount of genetic material is essentially alike for the human, chimpanzee, gorilla, and orangutan.[108]

Within the framework of belief in God as Creator, Anderson points out, this data raises two possible questions—each depending on a different interpretation of the creation story:

- If the human form was brought into being by God as a separate creative act, why did God use a plan so similar to that of other primates?
- If God used some preexisting animal form when he made humans in his image, how could a reshuffling of the genetic material result in the generally recognized uniqueness of the human species?

Anderson states that he cannot think of any kind of scientific methodology that would provide a conclusive, independent test to distinguish between these options. It is possible that we may never be able to determine when humans in the biblical sense first appeared.[109]

Fortunately, he points out, there are important guidelines from the sciences and the Bible alike that can be followed.

Some statements can be made from science:

- Humans have their own nature and not that of another species.
- Human behavior, taken as a whole, is unique. There are indications of tool making, tool using, communications, and other complex behaviors in other species, but the degree of development and overall combination found in humans are not paralleled elsewhere.
- Evolution is at best the description of a process, not a self-sufficient cause. It is not scientifically correct to state that evolution caused human beings to be formed.
- Humans occupy a significant place in the universe.
- The human body has inestimable value. The chemicals in the human body are worth little when reduced to ash. However, the complex chemicals organized into human cells and tissues could not be purchased at any price.
- The fact that humans have characteristics similar to other species has been beneficial to the human race in that these species have provided experimental animals with which to study human problems and test possibly toxic or otherwise harmful materials.[110]

Other statements can be made from the Bible:

- Human existence was planned by God and resulted from a deliberate creative act.
- All creatures are God's handiwork, but humans are in a unique relationship with him.
- Humans were created in God's image. The resulting human nature made the Incarnation possible.
- God's charge to Adam included the basis for science (to study, classify, and name) and for technology (to subdue). But both of these were to be carried out in the spirit of being answerable to God.

The above statements remind us that we need to insist on making the distinction between scientific methods on the one hand and scientism and evolution on the other. To obtain a total picture of humankind, we need both a proper science working within its limitations and the biblical view of humans as distinctive because they are created and sustained by God and given meaning and purpose by him.[111]

(3) The Partial-View or Complementary Approach to the Age of the Human Race. According to the partial-view approach, science and the biblical view can also be shown to complement each other in the area of the antiquity of the human race. In a basic sense, some evangelicals do not see that the issue is of great consequence. Either we cannot determine the age of the human race, or it would make no particular difference if we could. Benjamin Warfield, for instance, emphasized that the question of the antiquity of humankind has of itself no basic theological significance. It is to theology, as such, a matter of entire indifference how long man has existed on earth.[112]

However, both biblical scholars and scientists do seek to complement each other's insights in this area. For example, from a scientific point of view, there are several criteria used to determine what makes humankind human. Tool making is considered one important mark of humankind. The ability to conceive, fashion, and utilize tools is what distinguishes humans from subhuman creatures. If this is the criterion, then man's origin is to be dated quite early, perhaps five hundred thousand to two million years ago.

Other scientists point to burial of the dead as a practice that sets humans apart from other creatures. According to this criterion, the first human is to be identified with the so-called "Neanderthal man," whose remains were first unearthed in the Neanderthal valley in Germany, and who has been dated as living about fifty thousand years ago.

But more importantly, humankind can be distinguished by the presence and use of complex symbolism or, more specifically, of language. It is language which makes possible the type of relationship with God which would be experienced by a being created in the image of God and described in the Bible. On this basis, science can correlate the beginning of humankind in the full biblical sense with the evidence of a great cultural outburst about thirty thousand to forty thousand years ago. The first human in this sense is not to be identified with Neanderthal man, but somewhat later, probably with "Cro-Magnon man," which lived roughly ten to thirty thousand years ago.

According to Bertram S. Kraus and Millard J. Erickson, this last view seems to have the fewest difficulties from a biblical point of view. The growth in culture between thirty thousand and ten thousand years ago is best understood as the result of the beginning of language at that time. The biblical record appears to indicate that Adam and Eve possessed language from the very beginning. Communication with one another and with God presupposed possession of language.[113]

(4) How the Partial-View Approach Encourages Self-Imposed Limitations for Science and the Biblical Religion. Those who hold the partial-view approach stress that, in our scientific age, it is especially important that both science and religion recognize their limitations of purpose and method.

The Bible reveals the who and why of the universe, the Creator and his purposes for nature and for humanity. The biblical message, meant for all cultures and generations, is communicated in the everyday language of sense perception, not in the language of mathematics. which is the primary language with which science represents the how of natural events.[114]

Similarly, science needs to seek to free itself from positivistic philosophical presuppositions and acknowledge the limitations of its method. Lesslie Newbigin agrees that the methodological elimination of final causes from the study of nature by science has been immensely fruitful on certain levels and for limited purposes. However, the attempt to explain all that exists solely in terms of secondary causes is not appropriate from the standpoint of logic and the total evidence available concerning human nature and activity.

When the ultimate explanation of things is found in the creating, sustaining, judging, and redeeming work of a personal God, then science can be the servant of humanity, not its master. In turn, biblical studies, freed from futile attempts at *doing* science, can focus on the broader issues of using science (and technology) for the good of humanity and the environment.[115]

In the last analysis, says David Livingston, a Christian approach to science must be both confessional and critical. It must encourage us to confess our commitment both to the Bible and science, to the God of creation and to the creation itself. On the other hand, it must call for both philosophical theologians and scientists to be humble and self-critical before the Creator, his creation, and his inspired revelation to mankind.[116]

VI. What Is the Significance of the Biblical Worldview, the Doctrine of Creation, and Genesis for Today?

Beyond the area of conflict with science, the doctrine of creation and Genesis have great significance for contemporary life.

In the first place, the Bible in general and Genesis 1 in particular teach a radical and comprehensive affirmation of monotheism, rejecting every kind of false religion—including polytheism, idolatry, animism, pantheism, and syncretism. The biblical creation account also opposes superstition (astrology and magic), as well as naturalism and nihilism. This is a remarkable achievement for so short an account as Genesis 1 (about nine hundred words), written in everyday language and understood by people in a variety of cultures for more than three thousand years.

In addition, the Genesis creation account and the doctrine of creation contributes an important sense of meaning and creativity to human existence. By showing that humankind was created in God's image for a purpose, and that men and women were made in the image of a Creator God, it clearly shows both that human life has meaning and that human beings were made to create.

It should also be noted that both the Old and New Testaments connect God's creative power with his redeeming love. God the Creator of the universe is the Lord and Judge of history who comes in Jesus Christ to demonstrate his saving love and power. The doctrine of creation thus provides the basis for the Christian confidence in ultimate victory over all forms of evil. Creation is also closely connected with eschatology, the doctrine of the end times; the biblical worldview holds that it will be in the final days that God ultimately will vindicate his own creativity.

Yet another contribution of the biblical worldview and the Genesis creation account is a proper understanding of nature. By purging the cosmic order of all gods and goddesses, the Genesis creation account "de-divinized" nature. According to the biblical worldview as set forth in Genesis 1, the universe has no divine regions or beings who need to be feared or placated. Israel's intensely monotheistic faith thoroughly demythologized the natural world, and this in turn made way for a science that can probe and study every part of the universe without fearing either trespass or retribution.

That does not mean, however, that nature is secular and no longer sacred. It is still God's creation, declared to be good, preserved by his power and intended for his glory. The disappearance of mythical stories and polytheistic intrigues clears the stage for the great drama of redemption and the new creation in Christ. It does not, however, give humankind free reign to exploit the earth.

And this brings us to yet another contribution of the biblical doctrine of creation. As God's creation, set in place as stewards of the rest of God's creations, we have a responsibility to care for the earth. A fresh appreciation of this responsibility is especially needed in a day of increasing environmental concerns—when we are seeing the negative consequences of years of irresponsibility.

In the biblical view, the natural world was created by God and significant for his purposes. This means that Christians should be stewards of the earth. Environmental problems have scientific, technological, political, economic, social, and legal aspects. But there are important moral and ethical concerns to be derived from the biblical doctrines of creation and human responsibility for the earth. Christians should also emphasize both individual and social responsibility for the use of scientific knowledge.[117]

A final contribution of the biblical doctrine of creation is an understanding of humankind's unique dimensionality. Unlike the Greeks and the Hindus, who taught that there is a radical split between the human soul and body and that the physical aspect of life has no real meaning, the Bible teaches that humans are body-mind unities. We were made out of the dust, just as the animals were, but we were also brought to life by the breath of God. Our spiritual life is obviously closely related to our physical makeup. Interestingly enough, this is borne out by scientific studies showing the contributions of the endocrine glands, genes, and chromosomes to human personality.

The Bible is thus in keeping with a scientific view that sees men and women as complex, many-leveled unities. The highest of these levels, according to the biblical view, is that of the self in relation to God and other people. Human beings have levels of activity not found among other creatures. We have a capacity for abstract thought, symbolic language, self-conscious awareness, critical self-reflection and creative imagination. We search for truth, have a concern for moral values, and have a distinctive God-consciousness. The Genesis story points out this uniqueness in simple, beautiful language.[118]

VII. What Is an Important Concluding Observation?

Science is obviously quite significant in our world. Actually, Christianity and science are distinct and different responses to nature and human life. But they nevertheless share some vital components. Both are rooted in faith-commitments to a reality beyond ourselves. Both are community activities sharing respected traditions. They should be seen as allies rather than enemies because both have vital contributions to make to humankind.

In fact, religion and science have been allies in the lives of many through the centuries who have regarded science as their Christian vocation. An example is the distinguished scientist Blaise Pascal. Pascal, who lived and worked in the seventeenth century, was a mathematical and scientific genius and pioneer. In addition, he was a devout Christian whose books, *Provincial Letters* and *Pensées,* have had an increasing influence over the years. He integrated his biblical and scientific views of nature—along with his philosophy, inventions, and literary works—in a beautiful and constructive way.[119]

In the final analysis, science cannot solve our basic problem, which is egocentricity, pride, and rebellion against the Heavenly Father. A person who is in spiritual and social trouble reaches out for resources different from those found in buying a new machine or increasing skills. The Bible works at a deeper level than Freud or Marx or Darwin; it sees human problems as more than lust for economic goods or sexual self-interest or survival of the fittest. And the Bible further contends that in Jesus Christ the way has been opened for every man and woman to be delivered out of the bondage of corruption, self, and guilt into the glorious liberty of a child of God.

In the absence of moral direction and purpose, our scientific knowledge, power, and freedom may be misused to bring us to disaster. But if we can recover the dimensions of the biblical worldview, science, under such guidance and empowerment, can play even more constructively its God-ordained role in human development and the furtherance of God's purposes.

5

The Question of Science and the Biblical Worldview—with Special Emphasis on Miracles, Providence, and Intercessory Prayer

I. What Are the Scientific Developments Which Have Questioned the Validity of Miracles, Providence, and Intercessory Prayer?

1. Science and the Naturalistic Mindset

Recently I spoke at a university. During a discussion period, I was asked what was the difference between now and the "old days" (when I was in college). I could think of several things, but one that really stood out in my mind was the tremendous growth in science. Since the modern scientific method became dominant in the West in the seventeenth and eighteenth centuries, the effect of science on human lifestyles and modes of thought has been tremendous—and increasing. It is reported that there are more technical scientists living now than in all previous periods of history.

As shown in the previous chapter, science and the scientific method presuppose that this world is rational, orderly, and fundamentally uniform. This assumption has certainly proved true on an experimental level; unless there is a dependable pattern in the universe, the kind of research which led to the discovery of insulin to help the diabetic would have been impossible. And this basic assumption is essentially harmonious with the biblical worldview, which also affirms an orderly and understandable universe.

However, since the seventeenth century, a particular brand of scientific and philosophic thinking has increasingly conflicted with the biblical belief in the possibility of miracles and providence and the power of intercessory prayer. This so-called scientific way of thinking puts such tremendous emphasis upon order that it questions the possibility of any changes or exceptions to that order. This view sees the universe as operating according to incontrovertible natural laws—like a machine that operates according to a certain mechanism once it is set in motion. Consequently, it questions the validity of any occurrences that seem to be contrary to this "mechanical" order.

Such thinking was typical of the eighteenth-century philosopher David Hume, who defined miracle as a "transgression of a law of nature by a particular volition of the Deity, or by the interposition of some invisible agent." According to this definition, Hume concluded that most so-called miracles are based on deception or limited knowledge.[1]

Hume's definition of miracle is completely deistic. It assumes a universe in which the natural process goes on with invariable regularity, and in which God is allowed to operate only at certain points. Deism, which was influential in Hume's time, held that God created the world, then left it to run according to inexorable natural laws. Deism assumed that once creation was complete, God removed himself from it and is no longer personally active in the universe.[2]

Unfortunately, this way of thinking has been very influential in much scientific thinking. In many cases, it has evolved into naturalism, which assumes that the natural world is the whole of reality. In fact, the naturalistic mindset has penetrated the everyday thinking of contemporary men and women—Christians included. Missiologists, from their perspective of working in other lands, have alerted us to the possibility that many Christians have capitulated to the naturalistic and technological paradigms of modern Western culture. Consequently, many modern people have difficulty with those aspects of the biblical record and of Christian history which seem to involve exceptions to the natural law.

2. Questions About Miracles

Since Old Testament days, miracles have been an integral aspect of the biblical worldview. At key points in the history of the Hebrews, there were miracles or signs and wonders of unusual demonstrations of God's power. The life of Christ—his deeds, existence, and especially his resurrection—has been considered miraculous by countless millions, and the Bible records many miracles in the early days of the church. In addition, certain branches of Christianity maintain a continuing tradition of miracles through the centuries and up to the present day.

Actually, there is a core of historical evidence for Christ's resurrection which meets adequately the tests used in historical research. Alan Richardson, for example, points out that the apostolic witness can account for the "data" of the New Testament better than any other hypothesis available. But an increasing number of people find that they cannot believe such miraculous accounts—even the central miracle of the Christian faith, the Resurrection.[3]

So often today, the skeptical modern mind approaches the biblical records with a naturalistic turn of mind which has been engendered by the success of modern science (but which by no means is a necessary implication of modern science). This way of thinking has led many to deny the biblical records on what they call "scientific grounds" without ever investigating the evidence. The naturalistic view, for instance, would claim that the story of Jesus' feeding the five thousand was impossible, because the physical amount of food present in five loaves and two fishes could not be expanded to feed a large number of people.

Since the natural law perspective does not allow God's activity in miracles, many people feel the need to find some alternative explanation for the biblical miracles. One common explanation is that the biblical miracles are part of a first-century prescientific or primitive mindset or just a quaint way of conveying spiritual truth. Other people suggest that miracles are actually the manifestations of little-known or virtually unknown natural laws. If we fully knew and understood the laws of nature, they suggest, we would be able to understand and even predict these events.

People with this perspective suggest that some of the healings of Jesus could well have been psychosomatic healings, that is, cases in which the power of suggestion removed hysterical symptoms. Because many illnesses involving physical symptoms are functional rather than organic in origin and character, it seems reasonable, they say, to assume that Jesus simply utilized his extraordinary knowledge of psychosomatics to accomplish these healings.

There is much about this view that is appealing to modern men and women. However, from a biblical perspective, there are basic problems with adopting it as an all-inclusive or adequate explanation of miracles.[4]

3. Questions About Providence

For centuries, Christians have found comfort in the understanding that our lives are overshadowed with divine concern. We call this divine concern "providence" or "government." Providence means the continuing action of God, by which he preserves in existence the creation he has brought into being and guides it toward his intended purposes for it.

For those with a naturalistic mindset, however, the concept presents a problem, because they see providence as nothing but a continuing group of miracles in the life of either an individual or a people.[5] If a miracle is impossible, then a series of miracles is even more impossible.

From this point of view, the ancient Israelites must have been wrong in their crucial belief that God led them out of Egypt; they were merely lucky. And if the conception of natural law, which science seems to require, is the true conception, then the experience of those who feel the guiding hand of God in the events of their own lives is sheer self-delusion. Since the question of providence plays such a big role in a person or nation's understanding of their lives, then, the answer to the question of providence is one that cannot be neglected or answered lightly.

4. Questions About Intercessory Prayer

Ever since New Testament days, Christians have believed that God hears and acts upon our prayers. But modern, secular men and women, who see little place for God in this world, also see little place for intercessory prayer.

(In certain circles, the term *intercessory prayer* is often used to refer to prayer on behalf of someone else, as opposed to a prayer of personal petition for oneself.

However, I am using the term in its more general sense, referring to any prayer for God to act in the world to accomplish something that the pray-er cannot accomplish himself or herself.)

In earlier days, God was believed to be the solution to mysteries. He was behind everything that happened—the explanation of the existence of the universe and the complexity of creation. And he was considered the solver of problems, such as sickness and trouble.

Today, however, human beings have come to understand their universe scientifically. They trust in technology to find the answers to the many problems besetting humankind, such as illness or poverty. To them, prayers for help or healing seem ineffective or inappropriate.[6]

Even if they do pray for God's intervention, many contemporary men and women have difficulty praying with the full consent of all their faculties. So broad has been the influence of scientific and naturalistic thinking that even some believers have difficulties with the concept of intercessory prayer. People have long prayed for rain, for instance, but how can this be done by honest persons who know something of meteorology?

Here again, the naturalistic mindset works to cause many to doubt the possibility of God's working in an unusual way for a special purpose. Many feel that the situation is already fully determined by natural laws. If God is shackled to the impersonal uniformity of nature, how can he answer prayer?

The logical result of a naturalistic outlook is that prayer, if it is considered valid at all, must be confined within the realm of attitude and inner spiritual disposition. In other words, prayer in a mechanical order is reduced to mere autosuggestion—if not irrational superstition.[7]

II. What Is the Response of the Biblical Worldview to the Criticism of the Validity of Miracles, Providence, and Intercessory Prayer?

1. A Purposefully Ordered Universe

(1) Rejection of a Naturalistic or Superstitious View of the Universe. The biblical worldview clearly affirms the reality of God's intervention or continued action in the universe he created; therefore, it must reject the deistic or naturalistic view of a universe ordered on incontrovertible natural law.

This does not mean, however, that the biblical view of nature is not an ordered one. For the biblical worldview also clearly rejects the idea of a universe based on chance or the capricious intervention of various gods and goddesses who act in nature according to their whim.

It is typical of many ancient societies that people lived in fear of the caprice of their gods. The ancient Greeks, for instance, believed that if their chief god, Zeus, had a lost weekend of drunkenness and debauchery, he would have a headache on Monday and send a storm or a tornado.

According to Stephen Neill, 40 percent of the people of the world still live in a primitive world which fears such capricious intervention. A great deal of the belief in divine intervention has been on no higher level than this primitive view. But this is nothing other than naïve spiritualism which cannot honestly be defended. A capricious God would not be worthy of reverence. People who have worked in primitive societies, as Neill has, are especially quick to emphasize that rejecting a naturalistic, god-evacuated world does not have to mean accepting a spirit-populated world in which most things are brought about, whimsically and arbitrarily, by spirits who cause good and bad things to happen. The God who reveals himself through the Bible is certainly not such a being![8]

(2) Affirmation of a Purposive Order. The biblical view agrees with science that the universe is orderly and knowable and that the investigation of the world is a good pursuit to follow. In fact, as shown in the previous chapter, modern science has its foundation in the biblical beliefs that the creation is understandable, that it is basically good (since it was fashioned by a good God), and that dominion over nature is part of our mandate as children of God.

However, the biblical worldview is distinct from the commonly held scientific view in that it adds the dimension of purpose to the dimension of order. According to the biblical view, God is a God who continually holds the world in being (preservation) and is personally active in the universe for redemptive purposes (government).

The purposive order view, from the biblical perspective, can best account for the delicate combination of regularity and novelty which history, experience, and the Bible teach.[9] For while we often describe what God does in terms of processes and laws, these are simply modes of our description of God's activity, not limits on what he is able to do in order to fulfill his purposes.

To perform a miracle, God needs only to act in a manner different from his "regular" or "normal" action. He does not need to suspend natural law to do something "unnatural." The God of the Bible is not a Master Craftsman who adjusts a former creation that exists independently of him. Rather, he is the Creator and Sustainer who holds all things "in the palm of his hand."

(3) A Truly "Scientific" Outlook. Interestingly enough, newer developments in science seem to undergird or at least open the door for a consideration of the concept of purposive order. A more current view of nature and the universe underlines the fact that scientific laws and theories do not prescribe (legislate) what must have happened in the past or will happen in the future. Rather, they describe (explain in mathematical terms) some repeated events we have been able to observe so far. At best, scientific laws predict what will probably happen in the future—since we believe in the orderliness of God's creation. All they prescribe is our expectations, so that we can make predictions and act accordingly. Therefore, it makes no sense to complain about a miracle breaking the "laws" of nature. These laws, unlike criminal and civil law, do not prohibit the possibility of certain kinds of divine activity.[10]

According to the biblical view, therefore, it is inappropriate for science to declare that miracles are impossible. It would be closer to the truth for science to admit it has trouble with acknowledging miracles because the structure of a miracle is foreign to experience and improbable on the basis of normal empirical scientific theory. Actually, since miracles are unique historical events, science properly can say nothing about them at all, one way or the other. The only judgment that science can bring fairly is to say, "I would not expect one." But that, after all, is the very nature of a miracle and hardly constitutes an argument against their reality.

In the last analysis, the question of purposive order and miracles is primarily an issue for philosophy and history. Regrettably, scientists sometimes fail to remember this and make religious or philosophical pronouncements under the guise of scientific statements. For example, Carl Sagan's pronouncement "The cosmos is all there is, all there was, and all there ever will be" is likely to be taken by the public as a scientific truth. In reality, it is Sagan's philosophical assertion or his article of faith.[11]

It is important to remember, even when scientists forget, that a scientific theory offers only one perspective (among many) on the physical world. It provides a partial view of nature's forces through a mathematical lens that discovers nature's mechanisms.[12]

In fact, with regard to miracles, the biblical worldview is often more "scientific" than the view of the philosophical naturalist, in that it is open-minded about their possibility. For it is integral to the scientific method that a scientific theory or hypothesis is provisional—simply the best explanation we have to work with until a better one is discovered. Any theory, including the concept of natural law, is subject to revision or replacement as the reigning paradigm if the empirical evidence demands it.[13]

The dogmatic naturalist who refuses to consider the evidence for miracles is, ironically, more like a Greek philosopher than a modern scientist, since he or she is deciding the matter deductively, on the basis of first principles, rather than on the basis of evidence. Such an attitude resembles that of the professor at Pisa who refused to look through Galileo's telescope at the reported moons of Jupiter. His refusal was based on the fact that Aristotle had taught that such a phenomenon could not exist.[14] And he was not about to be swayed by evidence to the contrary.

2. Purposive Order and An Understanding of Miracles

(1) Constancy of Purpose and Variety of Procedure. The idea of the universe being ordered according to God's purpose rather than an unbreakable set of natural laws casts a different light on the concept of miracles. For in a universe that is so ordered, constancy of purpose may well call for variety of procedure.

The parenting task, frequently used in the Bible as an analogy for God's relationship with human beings, can also provide a helpful analogy for God's work in the universe. The responsible parent has the constant purpose of the advancement of the child's welfare. However, loyalty to this purpose often calls for a variety of behaviors at different times in the life of the child. The order which comes from purpose has, thus, a unity of aim and variety of method.[15]

According to the biblical drama, God limited himself and gave freedom to humankind, only to have them promptly rebel. Then, in order to restore humanity without destroying their freedom, God inaugurated a redemptive plan which called for him to work through a selected people. When that people repeatedly disobeyed him and broke the covenant he had established with them, God moved on with his redemptive plan, which led to the appearance of Jesus Christ in history. Over and over again in biblical history, God's constancy of purpose made necessary a conspicuous adjustment of means.

Miracles can thus those be seen as striking or unusual workings by which God intervenes supernaturally in the world to achieve his larger purpose. They are those special works of God's providence which are not explainable on the basis of the usual patterns of nature. God does not suspend the laws of nature, however. They continue to operate, but supernatural force is introduced, negating or adjusting the effect of what the secular world calls natural law. This view has the advantage of regarding miracles as being genuinely supernatural or extranatural, but without being antinatural.[16]

Over the centuries, miracles have been primarily associated with the preaching of God's Word, the spreading of the gospel of Jesus Christ, and the manifestation of God's witness in the world. When seen in this light, they clearly become distinguished from the world of magic and sorcery. From this redemptive purpose perspective, it becomes clear that miracles are not arbitrary violations of natural law to impress the people involved. Rather, they are appropriate evidences of God's free activity in making himself known.[17]

(2) Miracles as a Reasonable Feature of Purposive Order. The idea of purposive order makes miracles a reasonable feature of a world system. This is a distinct intellectual gain since there has long been evidence for the existence of miracles, but many have found themselves forced to reject the evidence *a priori* because of a belief in natural law which made belief in miracles seem impossible.

The notion of a purposive order can set minds free from the bondage of such dogmatism. Unless we have a superstitious reverence for natural law as an independent entity, we do not decide in advance the question of the actual occurrence of apparently miraculous events, such as the resurrection of Christ, but decide on the basis of the available evidence.[18]

For anyone willing to consider empirical evidence, miracles are essentially a question of history. The issue is one of historical record: Were reliable witnesses present? Have their reports been accurately preserved? Is there a better alternative explanation of the faith and achievement of the Christian church than the Resurrection? The criteria are the same as those for determining the historicity of any reported event. Professor von Compenhausen of Heidelberg University, after extensive study as a historian, concludes that Christ's resurrection and the empty tomb are to be regarded as real events in the light of a strictly historical assessment of the relevant evidence. Unfortunately, even the best evidence fails to convince those who choose not to believe.[19]

The importance of credibility has become intensified in recent years by the claims of miracles made by folk religions everywhere. New Age cults are also claiming miracles. These reported miracles are done in a spiritual context utterly different from and hostile to the biblical worldview. This means that there should be reliable and trustworthy testing. Furthermore, miracles are to be seen in the context of the larger vision of God's redemptive purpose. Health, for example, is not the highest or final goal. Thus Christians have a strong reluctance to make claims for miracles without being ready to submit them to objective testing and to theological interpretation.[20]

(3) The Meaning and Purpose of Biblical Miracles. The relationship between miracles and God's redemptive purpose can be clearly seen in the way miracles are presented in the Bible. Rather than being scattered throughout the Bible in a haphazard way, they are clustered around three key places or periods in biblical history: the Exodus and the wilderness wanderings; the crucial days of Elijah and Elisha, when the purity of Israel's worship was at stake; and the time of Christ and the apostles, with the introduction of the kingdom. Each of these crucial periods in God's redemptive drama lasted something less than one hundred years, but in each period there was a concentration of miracles. And each period of intervention was important to the accomplishment of God's long-term purposes for the Hebrew people, the Christian church, and the entire world.[21]

The first group of miracles is centered around the Exodus of God's people from Egypt and their entrance into Canaan. Moses (and later his successor, Joshua) was given the ability to do signs and wonders that were geared to convince the people that God was with them and speaking through them. Exodus 3–13, for instance, records how Moses was given power to bring the ten plagues upon Egypt and to force Pharaoh to let the Israelites go.[22] Such miracles confirmed to the Israelites that God was speaking to them, and that he had the power to lead them out of bondage and into the Promised Land. It was also during this general period that God introduced the law (the Ten Commandments), the new nation of Israel, the tabernacle, sacrifices, and the priesthood.[23]

The second group of miracles is related to the great ninth-century prophets, Elijah and Elisha, in their battles with the prophets of the pagan god Baal. Particularly dramatic evidence of God's power over nature can be seen in the case of Elijah, who effectively prophesied a three-and-a-half-year drought and then, at Mt. Carmel, was able to call down lightning from heaven.[24] The miracles of Elijah and Elisha were effective in convincing believers and unbelievers that what they spoke was the Word of God. A graphic illustration of this is found in 1 Kings 18, where Elijah defeated four hundred prophets of Baal before a large crowd of Israelites.[25]

It is significant to note, incidentally, that there is no such concentration of miracles surrounding the careers of the great king David or the significant prophet Jeremiah. In other words, the biblical story shows that supernatural intervention in history was only one method used by God at specific times for accomplishing his purposes. They are not by any means his only, or even his usual, mode of operating.

The third group of miracles in the Bible is centered around the incarnation, ministry, death, and resurrection of Jesus and the life and ministry of the early New Testament church. In fact, Jesus' power over nature was partly responsible for the disciples recognizing that he was God. Peter, speaking at Pentecost following Jesus' ascension, referred to this fact when he reminded the assembled crowd that Jesus the Nazarene was "a man attested to you by God with mighty works and wonders and signs, which God did through him in your midst" (Acts 2:22).

The wonders and signs performed by Jesus are well known to anyone familiar with the New Testament: turning water to wine at the wedding at Cana, feeding the five thousand, healing the sick, causing empty nets to be filled with fish. When he calmed a severe storm at sea by speaking the words, "Peace! Be still!" (Mark 4:39), his disciples asked themselves, "Who then is this, that he commands even wind and water, and they obey him?" (Luke 8:25).[26]

During the time of the early church, the same kind of power belonged to the apostles. The Book of Acts records many instances of healing and deliverance carried out by God's power through the apostles. On Paul's first missionary journey, he and Barnabas ministered in Iconium, "speaking boldly for the Lord, who bore witness to the word of his grace, granting signs and wonders to be done by their hands" (Acts 14:3).[27]

In all the biblical miracles—those connected with the Exodus, those involving Elijah and Elisha, and those centered around the life of Christ and the early church—at least three purposes can be distinguished. One purpose was to glorify God. The beneficiaries and observers of the biblical miracles generally responded with praise and worship. A second purpose of biblical miracles was to establish the supernatural basis of the revelation which often accompanied them. The Greek word translated "signs," which frequently occurs in the New Testament as a term for miracles, underscores this dimension. A third purpose of miracles, especially those in the New Testament, was to meet human needs. Christ's primary purpose in the world was to establish his Messiahship, not to heal the sick and feed the hungry. And yet Christ frequently is pictured in the Gospels as being moved with compassion for the hurting, needy people who came to him. He healed them to relieve the suffering caused by such maladies as blindness, leprosy, and hemorrhaging. He never performed miracles for the selfish purpose of putting on a display.[28] In fact, he was critical of people's hankering after signs and wonders (Matt. 12:39; 16:4; Luke 11:16; John 4:48).

3. Purposive Order and the Doctrine of Providence

(1) The Centrality and Specificity of Providence. In certain ways, providence is central to the conduct of the Christian life. The assurance that God is present and active in our lives, that we are in his care and that what happens to us is not by chance, is what enables us to face the future confidently. The biblical view sees the world as a God-permeated cosmos. The God above all things is present with

power in every dimension, material or mental, physical or spiritual, of the universe. He is in the regularity and predictability of the universe. He formed the world and keeps on forming it. Even after the Fall, the Creator is active in the universe to continue his special redemptive activity in Jesus Christ and further his redemptive purpose.[29]

It should be noted that the biblical view of providence is dramatically specific. This means that God works out his purposes not merely in life's generalities but in the details and minutiae of life as well. According to the biblical view, there is nothing in our lives that falls outside God's will and concern. Not just the mass of humanity, but each individual as well, is significant to God.[30]

Various pictures Jesus gives us of the Father indicate the personal dimension of his care. He cares about the one lost sheep (Luke 15:3–7) and searches until he finds it. The good shepherd knows his sheep and calls them by name (John 10:3–6, 14, 27). The Father knows the very hairs of the heads of those who are his (Matt. 10:30).[31]

Even sinful human actions can be a part of God's providential working. Probably the most notable instance of this is the crucifixion of Jesus. Peter attributes the crucifixion to both God and sinful men: "This Jesus, delivered up according to the definite plan and foreknowledge of God, you crucified and killed by the hands of lawless men" (Acts 2:23).[32]

(2) The Relevance of Providence in a Depersonalized World. The personal dimension of God's providence speaks significantly to the contemporary situation. With growing automation and computerization has also come increased depersonalization. Too often, individuals are seen only as cogs in the machinery, faceless robots, numbers on file, scratches on microchips, or entries on tape. The government of our nation seems increasingly distant and depersonalized. The doctrine of the providence of God assures us that his personal relationship to us is important. He knows each of us, and each one matters to him.[33]

The doctrine of providence also speaks to the feeling of anxiety and despair which tends to hang over contemporary life. Chaotic world events foster a sense of cosmic incoherence, and many see our world at the mercy of blind forces.[34] Yet the doctrine of providence assures us that God is in charge of the events in history and will see to the outworking of his purpose.

(3) Providence and the Nations. God's government also involves human history and the destiny of the nations. A particularly vivid expression of this is found in Daniel 2:21: "He changes times and seasons; he removes kings and sets up kings." And there is a dramatic illustration in Daniel 4:28–35, where King Nebuchadnezzar of Babylon was struck down at the pinnacle of his reign and then restored. Isaiah also gives an example of God's providence in history, when the Lord used Assyria to accomplish his purposes with Israel, then in turn brought destruction upon Assyria as well (Isa. 10:5–12).[35]

(4) The Multiple Dimensions of Providence. The naturalist will have his own interpretation of events which a Christian calls providential and will reject the Christian reading of those events' significance. That should not be surprising,

since all knowledge is personal knowledge, and our reasoning is determined by a prelogical commitment to some worldview which to us is self-evidential.

Yet the Christian holds that such faith and commitment is evoked in us by a divine self-disclosure which comes through the media of nature and history. Since our approach is through the biblical revelation, such self-disclosure reaches its climax at the personal level, so that the disclosures through nature and history are brought to a focus in the Incarnation of Jesus Christ.[36]

From the perspective of divine providence, the history of nature, like human history, takes on a directed meaning. Providential situations thus bring to a focus for faith an immanent and yet transcendent presence and activity that are present throughout nature and history, guiding and sustaining them. Chance and probability, randomness and indeterminacy are woven into the fabric of history by the divine designer.

The biblical worldview portrays human beings as having personal depth which cannot be discerned by scientific methods. Likewise, the processes of nature and history have a divine personal depth which science and historical positivism do not grasp. Creatures who do not have access to the depth dimension are limited to what has been called "Flatland." They will know the regularities, invariants, and scientific probabilities in a limited form and explain them in that way. They will be unaware of forces operative in the transcendent dimension which guide the ongoing dynamics of life and history. So the biblical person sees providential activity where the scientist as scientist sees none.

If that transcendent dimension is opened up to him in some way, maybe even through capacities for knowing which have been hitherto undeveloped, then a whole new way of understanding his world and a new attitude toward it becomes possible. The new attitude does not abrogate the old but embraces it.

Thus we see that, whereas science by its method is concerned with the impersonal, the personal form of reality becomes evident to faith as that is evoked in the primary disclosure of the Incarnation. The disclosure situations present in providential activity take their final coloring for the Christian from this initial and redemptive act. In describing this awakening to the personal dimension through divine disclosure, the biblical person uses the term *miraculous.*[37]

(5) Providence and Human Responsibility. Important as providence is in the biblical worldview, it is possible to misunderstand and misuse the concept of providence. It is not uncommon for the idea of providence to be used as an excuse for human irresponsibility.

In the first place, providence does not mean that human activity and divine activity are mutually exclusive. There is no basis for laxity, indifference, or resignation in the face of the fact that God is at work accomplishing his goals. The certainty that God will accomplish something in no way excuses us from giving ourselves diligently to bringing about its accomplishment. For while it is true that God accomplishes the ends he has in mind, it is also true that he does so by employing means (including human actions) to those ends.

For example, the normal and most fruitful way to combat the disordering effects of evil in nature is to cooperate with God's ordering processes against alien disorder. God's presence as the designing sustainer makes possible the work of medical science and the healing arts. There is the occasional demonstration of God's power in an unusual way for special purposes, but the chief emphasis in the Bible is on God's constant purpose and power working through humans who follow the way of working through ordered nature.

Furthermore, providence does not mean that we will always understand God's activity in the world. Thus, we need to avoid dictating to God what he should do to give us direction. We often fail to take into account the complexity of the universe and the large numbers of persons whom God must be concerned about. We know that everything does have a significance within God's plan. But we must be careful not to assume that the meaning of everything should be obvious or that we should be able to identify that meaning.

Finally, it is also important to be careful what we identify as God's providence. In a fallen world, there will continue to be events which, though redeemable by God, are essentially evil and not his work. A notable instance of a too-ready identification of historical events with God's will is the case of "German Christians" who in 1934 endorsed the action of Adolf Hitler as God's work in history.[38]

(6) Providence and the Battle of Wills. One aspect of the biblical worldview is to picture the events of the universe as an immense battle of the wills. The one will is the power of destruction, disorder, and apostasy—the empire of Satan. The other will, which opposes the powers of destruction, is the manifestation of the inbreaking, restorative dominion of God.

This immense and cosmic battle of wills has been going on since Satan's rebellion. And since the fall of man, it has asserted its claim to dominion and is holding in possession these sick and sinful people. The biblical view states that the one human society derived from Adam and Eve as a primal creation of God frustrates every utopian ambition because Satan, sin, and rebellion impinge on all its motivations and deeds. And although Christ has overcome Satan in his cross and resurrection, Satan will not be completely subdued until the second coming.

God's work as Sustainer and his work in what we know as miracles and providence combine to form God's activity against the power of disorder and chaos. God providentially preserves the fallen race from chaos through his sustaining immanence and supernatural interventions, as well as through the establishment of civil government to restrain disorder and injustice. However, his greatest act of power is through the moral renewal of penitent sinners through Jesus Christ and their restoration to fellowship with God in the church as the new society.[39]

4. Purposive Order and the Doctrine of Intercessory Prayer

As we have already noted, the Bible points out that God often works in a sort of partnership with man, accomplishing supernatural activity through human agents. For instance, in the Gospel of Matthew, we see Jesus healing a centurion's paralyzed servant, but only after the centurion sought him out, "beseeching him"

(8:5–13). He also healed the woman with the hemorrhage after she reached out to touch the hem of his garment (Matt. 9:18–22). These are illustrations of faith which, demonstrated in petition, resulted in God's working.

In the biblical worldview, this is the way prayer works. It does not change what God has purposed to do; rather, it is the *means* by which he accomplishes his end. For this reason, prayer is vital, for without it the desired result will not come to pass.[40]

The other side of this partnership, of course, is that God *does* act in response to prayer—either personal petitions or intercessions in behalf of others. This means that prayer is much more than just a method of creating a positive mental attitude in ourselves so that we are able to do what we have asked to have done. Rather, it is a way of working in partnership with God to accomplish his purposes. In other words, prayer not only "changes us"; it also "changes things."[41]

Any Christian knows, of course, that we do not always receive what we ask for in prayer. Jesus asked three times that he be spared from his impending death by crucifixion (Matt. 26:39–46). The apostle Paul prayed three times for the removal of his thorn in the flesh (2 Cor. 12:8–10). In each case, the Father granted instead something that was more needful—in Jesus' case, resurrection, and in Paul's case, assurance of the sufficiency of God's grace.

According to the biblical worldview, therefore, the believer can pray confidently, knowing that a wise and good God will give us not necessarily what we ask for, but what is best. Edwyn Bevan remarks that "no father who cared for his child with any intelligence would grant all its desires. He would care more for his child's character than for its pleasure."[42]

As in the case of miracles and providence, prayer depends on the concept of God's purposive order. Unless God does work beyond the laws of what humans see as the natural order to accomplish his purposes, our prayers are meaningless monologues. For logically we can pray to God for specific things only if we assume that everything has not been fixed and that the future is not unchangeably settled.[43]

III. What Are Representative Models Used by Christian Groups in Interpreting Miracles, Providence, and Intercessory Prayer?

The importance of this general subject can be seen in the fact that almost all Christian groups have recently been concerned with developing an approach to miracles, providence, and intercessory prayer, with special concentration on the nature and extent of miracles. It should be helpful, therefore, to survey six representative models. Lessons can be learned and excesses and weaknesses avoided as a result of such a study.

1. The Existentialist View

This Christian group attaches little importance to the objective reality of miracles described in the New Testament. They call for what they understand as a spiritual, not a physical emphasis.

For example, German theologian Rudolf Bultmann, who is known as a Christian existentialist, said that the miracle stories which gathered around Jesus are part of a Hellenistic tendency to adorn Christ with imaginary wonder stories. The content of the biblical gospel, according to Bultmann, is also related to the mythology of Jewish apocalyptic literature and to an early form of Gnosticism and is not credible for us today. In his view, we must strip away the mythological framework from the New Testament and get down to the existential power of the myths that offer us salvation through an encounter with God who "acted" in Christ.[44]

(In broad perspective, existential philosophers such as Karl Jaspers, Camus, or Heidegger and existential theologians such as Bultmann emphasize the ultimate significance of obtaining "authentic existence" as opposed to any objective, historical, or scientific basis for philosophical or religious truth. Such existential experiences cannot really be communicated from one person to another, nor can their validity or meaning be tested by objective or scientific criteria.[45])

2. The "Get the Gospel on the Track" View

The "get the gospel on the track" approach is the traditional mainline Reformed approach. It teaches that overt or spectacular miracles were real and important in biblical times, and that their primary value was to undergird the inauguration of Christianity or "get it on track" (see Acts 2:22; Acts 15; Heb. 2). But once that purpose was accomplished, they believe, there was no more need for overt or outwardly spectacular miracles; they do not continue in the present.

Among the representatives of this view was Benjamin B. Warfield, who set forth his basic ideas about miracles in the 1917–1918 Thomas Smyth Lectures at Columbia Theological Seminary, South Carolina. These lectures were published in 1918 under the title *Counterfeit Miracles* and were later retitled *Miracles: Yesterday and Today, True and False.*[46] In the generation after Warfield, E. J. Carnell adopted a similar stance in *An Introduction to Christian Apologetics* (1948). Other well-known proponents of this view were James Orr and A. H. Strong.

According to this view, tongues, healings, and outward physical miracles primarily served as signs to authenticate an era of new revelation. As the era of revelation came to a close, the overt signs ceased also. As Warfield pointed out,

> Miracles do not appear on the pages of Scripture vagrantly, here, there, and elsewhere indifferently, without assignable reason. They belong to revelation periods, and appear only when God is speaking to His people through accredited messengers, declaring His gracious purposes. Their abundant display in the Apostolic Church is the mark of the richness of the Apostolic age in revelation; and when this revelation period closed, the period of miracle-working had passed by also, as a mere matter of course.[47]

Those who hold to the "get on the track" view of miracles attest that, in the Bible, God always makes it clear when his messenger is bearing new revelation.

In addition, he verifies that revelation with wonders and signs. Look, for example, at Hebrews 2:3–4, which states that God confirmed the message of Christ and his followers with supernatural signs:

> How shall we escape if we neglect so great a salvation? It was declared at first by the Lord, and it was attested to us by those who heard him, while God also bore witness by signs and wonders and various miracles and by gifts of the Holy Spirit distributed according to His own will.

Here is a clear biblical word that the miracles, wonders, and sign gifts were given to the first-generation apostles to confirm that they were messengers of a new revelation. And the same thing happened in the time of Elijah and Elisha, as well as the time of Moses and Joshua.

Once again, this approach to miracles emphasizes that Christ was the climax of revelation. This means that overt or spectacular miracles do not continue after the apostolic era. (The word translated "attest" in the Hebrews passage is definitely in the past tense.)

In fact, Carnell even remarked at one time that "the doctrine that miracles no longer occur is one of those fundamental canons which separate Protestantism from Roman Catholicism." He went on to reiterate the traditional Reformed view that "Miracles are a seal and sign of special, covenantal revelation; but revelation has ceased. There cannot, therefore, be new miracles."[48]

3. The "God Keeps Them Coming" View

The Roman Catholic Church has long held that miracles not only occurred in New Testament times, but continue up to the present day. Perhaps the most impressive contemporary general study of miracles from a Roman Catholic standpoint is Louis Monden's *Signs and Wonders: A Study of the Miraculous Element in Religion* (1966), a work of massive learning, exhaustive research, and deep piety. It answers the question of whether miracles are possible by producing a documented account of the "major miracles in the Catholic church," notably the healings associated with the healing shrine of Lourdes in France. For Monden, miracles, like the church and the sacraments, have continued in an unbroken line which is "the normal prolongation of the Incarnation."[49]

This does not mean, however, that every reported supernatural happening is a true miracle. He stresses that the character of any alleged miracle has to be taken into account in any assessment of its factuality. Any alleged miracle associated with immorality, charlatanism, trickery, magic, illusion, sensuality, or mere sensationalism must be ruled out.[50] True miracles, on the other hand, testify to the human agent's character as being transformed by God's saving revelation. In addition, they testify to a divine mission, and they occur in the context of prayer and a divine message.[51]

According to Monden, the particular persuasive force of miracles is bound up with what he calls their "regular irregularity" through the ages. In asserting this view, Monden stands in marked contrast to Warfield and Carnell, who see miracles as divine confirmations that ceased with the apostolic age and the completion of the canon of Scripture. However, he is stating a traditional Roman Catholic view. For the Roman Catholic Church, both historically and today, has officially recognized certain miracles which have occurred since the apostolic era.[52]

For example, the Roman Catholic Church accepts certain medieval miracles, such as the ability of Joseph of Copertina and St. Teresa of Avila to levitate or rise in the air. (When in Naples, Italy, I was told that the Roman Catholic Church accepts the fact that the blood of a saint who died in A.D. 304, San Gennara, is liquefied in an annual miracle.) In the Middle Ages, attention was focused upon the relics of the martyrs as the instruments of healing. The Protestant Reformers rejected the manipulation of relics and shrines. They believed that preoccupation with miracles seduced believers from the heart of the gospel's spiritual message and moral mandate.

More recently, the church has recognized visions of Mary granted to young people. Examples are the visions of the Virgin given to Bernadette of Lourdes in France in 1855 and to three children at Fatima in Portugal in 1917. Roman Catholics encourage regular pilgrimages of sick people to Lourdes. Cures are claimed, but no cure is claimed as miraculous unless there is a detailed medical history of the case. The number of cures each year that are reckoned by the Roman Catholic investigators to be beyond the powers of nature to effect amount to between five and twelve.[53]

One of the recently approved miracles is the assumption of the body of the Virgin Mary to heaven. And of course, in the Catholic view, the greatest continuing miracle in the church is transubstantiation, the actual changing of bread into the body of Christ which Catholics believe takes place during the Eucharist or Mass.

Not surprisingly, the Roman Catholic view of miracles has its critics, especially among Protestants. B. B. Warfield, for example, is critical of many of the church-sanctioned miracles because of their extravagance and lack of evidence. Warfield also questions their positive or constructive relationship to God's redemptive mission in the world. In addition, John Henry Newman, in his early Protestant years, claimed that, on the whole, these ecclesiastical miracles differ in object, character, and purpose from those in the Bible.[54]

4. The "If You Have the Gift, You Can Do Them Now" View

Roman Catholics, of course, are not the only Christians to believe in contemporary miracles. Signs and wonders have long been a special concern of charismatic Christians. In addition, in recent years the charismatic groups are emphasizing that we are experiencing the "latter days." To them, this means that all nineteen spiritual gifts listed in the New Testament, including the gift of doing miracles, are being restored and are "now" gifts which are valid today.

David duPlessis, a prominent charismatic leader, contends that "the New Testament is not a record of what happened in one generation, but it is a blueprint of what should happen in every generation until Jesus comes." This is the view of the majority of the charismatics, who say that what happened during New Testament times was intended to be the norm throughout the church's history, especially in the "end times." According to this perspective, all Christians should be receiving revelations, visions, voices, tongues, the power to heal, and the ability to perform miracles.[55]

(1) Emphasis on Signs and Wonders in the Recent Charismatic Movement. It is important to distinguish between charismatics and Pentecostals. The modern Pentecostal movement began in the early 1900s and until 1960 was largely contained in denominations such as Assemblies of God, Foursquare, and United Pentecostal. But in the early 1960s, Pentecostalism spilled over denominational lines. The charismatic movement or "neo-Pentecostalism" spread into mainline denominations such as Episcopalian, Methodist, Presbyterian, Baptist, and Lutheran. One of the emphases of the charismatic movement is on continuing or contemporary "signs and wonders."[56]

The emphasis on present-day signs and wonders was brought to a crescendo in 1971 with the publication of Mel and Dudley Tari's book, *Like A Mighty Wind*, which described miraculous events among Christians in Indonesia, especially in the Timor area. The Taris reported that simple Indonesian Christians were raising the dead, walking on water across rivers a quarter of a mile wide and forty feet deep, and making wine out of water—in fact, repeating all the miracles of Exodus 14 and the Book of Acts.

Many of the reported spectacular miracles were discounted by further investigation. For instance, George Peters, a professor at Dallas Theological Seminary, visited Indonesia twice to investigate these alleged miracles, and he found them extremely difficult to evaluate. Peters found that the miracles were mostly reported by people of primitive mentality who were imaginative and intuitive. They do not think analytically, but rather live in a world of visions and dreams. Peters also found that most of the so-called resurrections were actually resuscitations of people who were not actually dead. And he was unable to verify the nature miracles such as walking on water and turning water to wine.[57]

But whether or not modern-day spectacular miracles can be verified, the fact remains that there is a deep and growing interest in healings and other kinds of external signs and wonders. John F. MacArthur, Jr., speculates that one reason for this is spiritual hunger. People hear that speaking in tongues and performing or witnessing spectacular miracles is the way to have a deeper spiritual experience. They want this "something more."

Another possible explanation is that the charismatic movement is a reaction to the secularized, mechanized, academic, cold, indifferent society in which we live—as well as to the cold, lifeless Christianity that is found in many churches. The person who joins the charismatic movement is one who is looking for action, excitement, warmth, and love. He or she wants to believe that God is really at work in his or her life in a tangible, observable way.[58]

(2) Some Criticisms of the Charismatic Emphasis on Signs and Wonders. Even though the appeal of the contemporary charismatic movement is understandable, there are some valid criticisms that can be leveled against their emphasis on modern-day signs and wonders. In the first place, as Peters showed as a result of his trips to Indonesia, many of the overt spectacular miracles are difficult to verify.

Furthermore, there is no guarantee that such spectacular miracles are helpful or in keeping with true biblical faith—or even that they are Christian. For signs and wonders are widely attributed to numerous gods, spirits, and healers in other faiths. There are testimonies to miracles performed by voodoo spirits in Latin America and by Tirupathi Venkateswara in South India. The interested reader will find a fund of material in such books as Sudhir Kakar's *Shamans, Mystics and Doctors: A Psychological Inquiry into India and Its Healing Traditions*, and *Magic, Faith and Healing: Studies in Primitive Psychiatry Today*, edited by Ari Kiev. The question of satanic wonders and signs will be addressed in a later chapter.[59]

If we think of the Christian gospel simply in terms of signs and wonders, then we are thinking on the wrong level and in the wrong way. For a right relationship with God does not result from external shows of power or magic displays, but upon God's saving grace. In fact, the authentic gospel of salvation by faith through God's grace is undermined if spiritual worth is judged by a person's ability to perform external signs and wonders.

Perhaps the most powerful criticism of the charismatic emphasis on signs and wonders is that it tends to foster an "easy out" mentality—an expectation that Christians should miraculously be exempted from discomfort, illness, and unhappiness. This is in direct contrast with the biblical witness. For the kind of "authentic spirituality" Paul talked about would not be popular with many who seek external signs and wonders. According to Paul, his life was weak and wretched and desperate and humble. He was in a constant state of stress, tension, fear, and even misery from the time he came to Christ until he was beheaded by a Roman executioner. The same story is told about the other apostles who knew something about suffering and true spirituality—notably Peter, James, and John.

Nowhere in Scripture can you find even a hint that Christians are to be exempt from the realities and struggles of life. In fact, Jesus predicted specifically that his followers would have trouble in the world. And external signs and wonders do not necessarily result in true spirituality. In fact, the search for such spectacular and external signs or proofs will probably lead a person down the wrong road from where true spirituality lies.[60]

This is especially true when it comes to the question of physical healing. Unlike some believers who feel that an admission of sickness is an admission of loss of faith and loss of face, Paul admitted frankly that he had a chronic "bodily ailment"—a "thorn in the flesh." We cannot be absolutely sure what this ailment was. But we do know that Paul prayed about it (2 Cor. 12:8–9) and that, although his prayer was answered, it was not answered in the way he had hoped. The weakness remained, but in it Paul experienced something greater.

He experienced the grace of God. Paul's response to the fact that God did not remove the affliction was not one of depression or bitterness, but exactly the opposite (2 Cor. 12:9–10).

In fact, Paul ended his letter to the Philippians with the assurance: "And my God will supply every need of yours according to his riches in glory in Christ Jesus" (Phil. 4:19). At this point, Paul was in prison, on trial for his life. He knew what it was to face plenty and to face hunger, abundance, and want. And yet he had learned, in whatever state he was, to be content. Paul had learned to depend on God to judge what his true needs were and how they were to be met. This is the kind of authentic spirituality the biblical worldview promotes—not the easy out of miraculous deliverance.[61]

(3) The Biblical Teachings on Signs and Wonders. Charismatics often cite biblical sources to support their contention that signs and wonders are as valid today as they were in biblical times. However, a careful analysis of these texts usually shows no specific biblical mandate for present-day signs and wonders.

For example, the Gospels tell us of two special missions in which Jesus gave his disciples authority to perform miraculous healing and cast out demons. On the first occasion Jesus sent out the Twelve (Matt. 10:1–42; Mark 6:7–13; cf. 3:15; Luke 9:1–6). The second mission is mentioned only in Luke. This time the Lord sent seventy (some texts read seventy-two) (Luke 10:1–20). But it is clear from the accounts that these were special missions with specific goals and that they had a definite ending point.

And when we turn to the Great Commission at the end of Matthew's Gospel, which contains Jesus' specific instructions to his disciples for the days to come after his resurrection, there is no mention of signs and wonders and healing (Matt. 28:19–20). The stress falls on preaching the gospel and on what is involved in being a disciple. Jesus' parting words as recorded in Luke 24:47 also make no mention of miracles. In John's account, the bestowal of the Spirit is linked with the authority to forgive and retain sins (John 20:22–23). In short, the church has no specific ongoing mandate from Jesus to perform the external signs and wonders that are recorded in authentic Scripture. (Mark 16:9–20, which deals with picking up poisonous snakes and the drinking of poison, is not in the two most reliable early manuscripts and is thus put in italics at the bottom of the page in recent translations such as the RSV).[62]

What then about Jesus' promise recorded in John's Gospel: "Truly, truly, I say to you, he who believes in me will also do the works that I do; and greater works than these will he do, because I go to the Father. Whatever you ask in my name, I will do it, that the Father may be glorified in the Son; if you ask anything in my name, I will do it" (14:12–14)? Does this mean, as many charismatics have taken it to mean, that we should all expect to be able to do miracles? Does it mean we are falling short as believers if we do not perform external signs and wonders?

If we follow through the thought of John 14:12 as it is worked out in the remainder of the Gospel, we see that the disciples are given the promise and mandate to bear fruit (John 15:16), which again is linked with an invitation to ask the Father in Jesus' name. The disciples are promised the Holy Spirit, who will convict the world of sin, righteousness, and judgment (John 16:7–11). Finally, the disciples are given the Holy Spirit and with him the authority to forgive and retain sins (John 20:22–23). In other words, neither the context of John nor the information we have from other places in the New Testament support the interpretation of this passage as a promise that Jesus' followers would or should be able to perform physical miracles. Physical miracles are, in fact, seen as lesser works when compared with those that have to do with the conviction of sin and forgiveness, judgment, salvation, and eternal life.

And we may well believe that the total scope of healing in all the medical and psychiatric hospitals, clinics, and other institutions that Christian believers have been enabled by the Spirit to build and operate all over the world have brought many more healings than Jesus Christ performed during his brief stay on earth. It may also be true that spiritually motivated movements of social reform have improved the living conditions of people to a quantitative degree far greater than the occasional physical healings that Jesus performed as testimonies to his messianic office. In these ways the believing community has done "greater works" than Jesus did.[63]

James 5:13–16, which describes anointing a sick person with oil, is often cited as the basis for modern healing miracles. As Colin Brown points out, however, in the context of the argument of the letter of James as a whole, this passage may be seen as a word of comfort to the dying. The rite is one of reconciliation involving the elders of the church, as those responsible for discipline and pastoral care, and the confession of sins. There is no suggestion that the elders or anyone else have a special gift of miraculous healing.[64] In any case, the rite is prescribed only for members of the church; no public invitation is given indiscriminately to the sick and afflicted of the world.

Brown goes on to reiterate that perfect health and miraculous healing are not things we have any right to expect just because we are Christians. They are not guaranteed to us as our birthright, any more than is material wealth and prosperity or total and instantaneous sanctification. Nor has anyone the right to hold out promises of them to people if only they will believe.[65]

This is not to say, of course, that there are no gifts of healing today inside the church—or outside it, for that matter. Physical healing is not the greatest or the most important gift of God. The healing of the body is of much less importance than the healing of the soul. God's greatest gifts are the forgiveness of sins, peace with God, and eternal life.

Furthermore, this is not to say that one should not pray for the miracle of healing. There are numerous encouragements in the Bible to pray and to trust God. They could be summed up in the exhortation that Paul wrote from prison to the Philippians: "Have no anxiety about anything, but in everything by prayer and supplication with thanksgiving let your requests be made known to God. And the peace of God, which passes all understanding, will keep your hearts and your minds in Christ Jesus" (Phil. 4:6–7). Paul encouraged the

Philippian Christians to pray. But he went on to say that he had learned, in whatever state he was, to be content.

Brown concludes that the miracles and external signs and wonders that we read about in the New Testament were bound up with the manifestation of Jesus as the Son of God and his decisive work in salvation history. They belong in the category of God's special saving acts, but they are not everyday occurrences. And there is no mention of such external signs in the ongoing mandate of Christ to the church.[66]

(4) A Balanced Approach to Signs and Wonders. H. L. Mencken once observed that for every complex problem there was always a simple solution—which was almost invariably wrong. The same could be said about external signs and wonders.

It is simplistic and dangerous to take biblical texts out of context and use them as pretexts for justifying our practices. The signs, wonders, and miracles mentioned in New Testament passages such as Hebrews 2:4 belong to the witness that God gave to the saving work of Christ, but these passages contain no suggestion that they will continue in this spectacular form for all time. The fact that Paul or the disciples performed such signs does not mean that we should be able to do the same. It is similarly poor interpretation to take prophecies like Isaiah 42:1–3 and 61:1–2, which applied specifically to Jesus, and to apply them to ourselves and our ministries.[67]

We should note that everything should have its proper place in life. In most cases, there is no need to resort to the supernatural in place of the natural. The natural remedies that the Good Samaritan used on the man by the wayside (Luke 10:34) and that Paul urged Timothy to take (1 Tim. 5:23) were the right remedies in those situations. When Luke became a Christian, he did not cease to be a physician. (Paul does not speak of him as "the ex-physician," but "the beloved physician," Col. 4:14). In view of Paul's "weaknesses," Luke doubtless cared for Paul not only as a Christian companion but also by drawing on his professional skill.[68]

It is true that God gives us many things—even sometimes the things that we want. But God can also turn even the things we dread into blessings. God's greatest gift is his love—not external signs and wonders. When all is said and done, God's promise "My grace is sufficient" is the best promise of all.[69]

5. The "It's a Possibility—But Watch Out" View

(1) The Approach of George Peters. George Peters of Dallas Seminary believes that miracles could well accompany gospel proclamation in pagan lands where people are under Satanic domination. In pioneer territories, he asserts, there could be a recapitulation of the Book of Acts.

Unlike Warfield, Peters does not believe that the New Testament necessarily declared an end to miracles, although it does not explicitly promise the continuation of such miracles, either. On the subject of continuing miracles, the Bible remains silent and open to the Holy Spirit's giving such gifts as he sees fit.

Peters stresses, however, that reports of such miracles should be carefully tested. Testing is not a sign of disbelief. Imagination—even religious imagination—has no bounds, and somehow, miracle stories seem to grow in their retelling. For this reason, it is important to be critical as well as open-minded when confronted with a contemporary report of a miracle.[70]

(2) The Approach of Fuller Seminary. A variation of this approach is the viewpoint set forth in a faculty publication of Fuller Theological Seminary in Pasadena, California. Their perspective is described in *Ministry and the Miraculous: A Case Study at Fuller Theological Seminary.* In his foreword, President David Hubbard applauds the document's approach, which he says lies "between the shoals of denying the possibility of miracles in our day and the rocks of presumption that demands miracles according to our need and schedule." He also points out, in particular, that scholarly treatment of the miraculous has not kept pace with reports of "signs and wonders" coming from Third World missionaries.[71]

Generally, however, the document downplays the importance of miracles, stating that "ordinary healings [resulting from medical science] are no less divine than miraculous healings." Furthermore, "healing of individual ailments is a very minor theme in Christian ministry compared to the deeper needs of God's people and God's world."[72]

The document stands firmly against some of the teachings that have emerged from charismatic circles. In a chapter on suffering, it asserts, "We reject any suggestion that believers have a blank check from God that offers them certain healing from sickness and handicaps if only their faith is strong enough."

In another chapter, the study concludes there is "reason to doubt that the temporary commission that Jesus gave his disciples in Matthew 10 [to heal the sick, cleanse lepers, cast out demons, and raise the dead] is a permanent mandate for the churches." While acknowledging that Jesus performed miracles, the authors point out that he "was critical of people's hankering after signs and wonders."[73]

Despite its careful approach and warning of possible abuses of belief in miracles, *Ministry and the Miraculous* does affirm that God works miraculously in the present. It warns against the temptation to accept "the secular hypothesis that all physical reality has only physical cause and thus to surrender all expectations of healing incursions of God's kingdom into our disease-ridden world. . . ." But it also notes that the presence of signs and wonders does not always indicate God is at work, pointing out that other religions also lay claim to the miraculous.

The document calls for credibility: "We must be transparently ready to submit our claims of healing to the most rigorous of empirical testing." And it urges caution, especially in cases of alleged discernment of the demonic in people: "It may be as important to protect people from exorcists as to protect them from demons."[74]

6. The "Tied to Redemption" View

(1) Miracles as Related to God's Redemptive Purpose. This view, which is held by many evangelicals such as Carl Henry and Millard Erickson, including E. Y. Mullins and W. T. Conner, who are no longer living, emphasizes that miracles are *real* but are closely related to God's redemptive purpose. According to this approach, miracles are not used in the Bible and should not be used now as "knock-down" arguments or proposed as incontrovertible proofs for non-Christians—with the exception of the Resurrection and the Exodus, which are critical to the formation of the biblical faith.

Those who hold the "tied to redemption" view point out that miracles are relatively scarce in the biblical narratives as a whole, especially when compared to the holy books of other religions. And they show clearly that miracles in the Bible are primarily associated with the preaching of God's word and the working out of God's redemptive purpose in the world. They are never capricious or fantastic. Thus, they are completely different from the signs and wonders of magic and sorcery.

(2) The "Tied to Redemption" Idea of Present-Day Miracles. The "tied to redemption" view holds that, because Jesus Christ was the historical climax and fulfillment of God's revelation, it should be obvious that God does not continue to reveal himself today in the same spectacular way as he did in the biblical period. (In fact, the Holy Spirit came to illuminate and make real the dynamic implications of the all-sufficient historical revelation in Jesus Christ.)

Nevertheless, God *is* actively at work today, just as he has been throughout Christian history. All around us we see evidence of God's marvelous work. There is the miracle of the new birth in the lives of millions around the world. There is also the healing of illness in answer to prayer and the matching of people and resources in providential circumstances to bring glory to God. That churches have survived ruthless persecution and attack through the centuries and continue to do so today is a miracle in itself.[75]

From this perspective, God is seen as working in the events of history but in a more subtle and indirect way than he did in the apostolic period. After the historic inauguration of Christianity, continued overt and spectacular demonstrations of power would tend to manipulate people, override their freedom, and forfeit their development in the image of Christ, claims W. T. Conner. In fact, according to E. Y. Mullins, miracles and outward wonders in themselves are never an adequate means of creating in men a full religious or spiritual response to God. Miracles can impress people without touching them in the depths of their lostness and moral corruption.[76]

Even in the last part of the biblical period, the preaching of the gospel, applied by the Holy Spirit in regenerating sinners and imparting moral power, was receiving more emphasis than spectacular miracles and external signs and wonders. This is especially noted in the Great Commission of Jesus in Matthew 28 and in the important Pauline Epistle of Romans.

What God does in us and through us today is different from what he did in the apostolic age. This is because he had a special purpose for the apostles, and that purpose was served. He also has a special purpose for us, and what he does in us and for us and through us will be marvelous because he is God and what he does is always marvelous.[77]

More specifically, when it comes to the question of healing, the evangelical view points out that the healings done by Jesus and his disciples were very different from the "healings" being offered today over television, on the radio, in direct mail gimmicks, and in some pulpits across the land. This is not to say that divine healing is not possible today, but it does suggest that it is very important rightly to understand God's Word about this area and to act responsibly, recognizing that God is capable of working through doctors and modern medicine as well as through direct intervention. To do anything else in such a crucial area as the healing of disease is to tamper with the physical, emotional, and spiritual well-being of thousands.[78]

(3) The Charismatic Influence and the Recovery of a Spiritual Emphasis. Under the influence of the recent charismatic movement, many evangelical Christians have reexamined the biblical teachings and recommitted themselves to spirituality and spiritual growth. In recognizing that spiritual hunger is one reason people are attracted to charismatic fellowships, evangelicals have been reminded that dead orthodoxy can never replace a warm and vital relationship with God. Similarly, knowledge cannot replace brotherly love. And while emotions must be kept under the control of biblical truth, truth must not suppress emotion.

Evangelicals are also rediscovering that Scripture is alive and active, and that when it is used as the sword of the Spirit, it still pierces the hearts of men. For all these reasons, Christians need to be aggressive with the proclamation of the gospel, participate fully in worship, and put greater demands on themselves in regard to commitment.[79]

(4) The Evangelical View of Providence. The evangelical view sees God's providence as working through the lives of individuals and larger events. This can especially be seen in hindsight. Paul, in Romans 8, saw God working in his own privations and sufferings as well as in his joys—seeking to make him into the likeness of Christ. Joseph looked back and was able to see his brothers' treachery and jealousy as God's plan to bring him to a place of supreme usefulness in Egypt.

The evangelical view affirms that there are many benefits for the believer in the doctrine of providence. These include the peace and confidence which stem from knowing that events are shaped not by chance, not by mechanical necessity, not by blind fate, not by Satan, but by the sovereign Creator and Preserver of all.[80]

(5) The Evangelical Approach to Prayer. Intercessory prayer is surely considered possible and necessary in the "tied to redemption" approach. According to this view, Christian prayer rises out of the heart of the Christian experience of reconciliation. Therefore, its supreme preoccupation, in accordance with its source in the experience of God's saving and reconciling work in

Christ, becomes the furtherance of God's kingdom and his saving and reconciling work in the world.

In prayer, according to this view, we seek to be on God's side—cooperating and dialoguing with him concerning the future of the world and his kingdom. Prayer involves praise, adoration, and personal petition, as well as petition on behalf of others.

The idea that prayer is primarily related to kingdom purposes clarifies the approach and objects of prayer that are undertaken in behalf of others. It indicates, for example, that such prayer, to be effective, must be more than the mere repetition of a formula. It must be an expression of a love which is cleansed and enhanced by its own experience of the divine love in Christ. It must also include that imaginative self-identification with the other person's situation which is the mark of all genuine love. There must be the deliberate effort to enter deeply into his or her need.

The concept of kingdom prayer also spells out the conditions which govern prayer for the success of the Christian's own enterprises in the world. Christians must bring to God all that engages their daily activity. Insofar as they can sincerely relate their prayer to those activities which are directly or indirectly a part of God's kingdom purposes, they are entitled to pray for the success of those activities.

According to this way of looking at prayer, for example, it would clearly be blasphemous to pray for the success of a business enterprise in which methods are determined and success measured purely in terms of dividends for the bank account. However, to pray for the success of the business because it is seen, even under the scrutiny of God, to be a service to mankind, and because there is bound up in it the well-being of countless men and women, is surely appropriate. Admittedly, the temptation to self-deception in this area is peculiarly great, but we must try.[81]

Prayer must follow divine insight and guidance as to the limits of the objects of prayer. In general, that decision must be left to the divinely illumined insight of individuals as they seek with all their best powers to serve the will of God in the immediate situation with which they are confronted.

There are certain kinds of petitions which God can never grant, inasmuch as to grant them would be to deny his nature and purpose. Some petitions, therefore, will inevitably disappear from the Christian's prayers as he or she enters more deeply into the life of fellowship with God. A Christian will know, with the insight of a love that is being more and more conformed to the image of Christ and the will of God, for what things he or she ought to pray.

Once again, it is the individual Christian's God-given insight that must determine what these limits of prayer are; it is not, for example, for science to say. Most Christians do, as a matter of fact, instinctively set certain limits to their prayers and have always done so, altogether apart from their knowledge of what science may be supposed to say about the matter.

Thus Christian people pray for recovery from pneumonia, but not for the growing of a new limb in place of one that has been amputated. They pray for rain, but not for the sudden upstanding of the crops when once they lie black and ruined on the parched earth. They pray for a loved one's safety, but not for his immediate resurrection from the dead when once he has been killed. They pray for courage to face failure, but not for the ability to write a play like *Hamlet* or a symphony like Beethoven's Fifth.

Yet, so far as abstract scientific theory has anything to say about the matter, all these things are equally possible or equally impossible. The source of these distinctions can only be found in the fact that a basic insight is given to humankind, especially to the person whose inner life is being cleansed and reconciled to God by Jesus Christ. This insight helps the Christian see into those limits which the divine love has itself set, at least for the time being, upon the open possibilities of this world in any situation.

Science may give us some discernment, which will keep us from lapsing into egotism or dabbling in magical ideas. Yet, the final decision is not with science itself as such. The decision is with the insight of the life of Christian devotion as it stands within its own historical situation and confronts the call of God to the service of his kingdom. It is of no great concern that different Christians will draw the limits in different places, so long as every decision is made in a positive endeavor to further God's purposes.[82]

Incidentally, according to this view, God is pledged to answer in a special way prayer voiced by believers "in Jesus' name." But this does not mean prayer which tags the phrase "in Jesus' name" by rote on the end of any prayer. Praying "in Jesus' name" means praying in accord with the revelation of God's character and purpose manifest in the Nazarene. It is that kind of prayer that the Father is pledged to answer (John 14:13).[83]

According to the "tied to redemption" view, the experience of prayer by Christians through the centuries calls for purposive order. And this brings us to one of the most important decisions human beings can make about their theory of reality. The essence of the mechanistic or naturalistic view is that it is totalitarian, seeking to embrace all of reality in a single system. However, such a view is undermined whenever we can point to experiences which cannot be understood or accounted for on the mechanical level. The experience of prayer is part of the evidence which shows the inadequacy of the closed system. We must finally decide between what is only a metaphysical prejudice and what is truly a living experience, confirmed by the testimony of countless persons whom there is reason to trust.[84]

IV. What Are Appropriate Concluding Observations?

Miracles, providence, and intercessory prayer are clearly of pivotal importance to biblical faith, regardless of how they are understood. Of particular importance are the great inaugurating miracles of the Bible—the Exodus and the life, death, and resurrection of Jesus Christ. And of all these, the resurrection of Jesus is the pivotal miracle, the climax of a sequence of inaugurating miracles. Without the resurrection, there would be no Christian faith, no New Testament, no Lord's Day, no New Testament, no way of explaining the New Testament church.

In addition, the biblical worldview holds that God continues to intervene in his world through continuing miracles, providence, and answers to prayer. Various Christian groups differ in their understanding of whether God's intervention takes overt form or occurs in more subtle and indirect ways.

But surely all who hold the biblical view would agree that the greatest continuing miracle is regeneration. A person who is a "closed system" spiritually, utterly inadequate and self-centered, suddenly becomes an "open system." His or her life is unified and centered on the omnipotent Creator through the power of Christ and the Holy Spirit. A life which was a chaos is now a cosmos with order and meaning and a goal. He is "born again"—a miracle of grace, a living testimony to the power of the God of creation, who also is the God of salvation.

It is also a continuing miracle when a person is progressively sanctified by God's power, and when he keeps his new life fresh by full obedience to God's plan for his life.

It is the prayer of evangelical Christians that we may see those miracles of regeneration and sanctification continue to happen—along with any other miracles that will lead men and women to Christ and enlist them in the furtherance of God's redemptive purpose.

6

The Question of Cosmic Evil, Satan, and the Demonic Powers

I. Why Is It Important to Reconsider the Question of Satan and the Demonic Powers in Our Time?

1. The Prevalence of Disbelief, Neglect, and Confusion concerning Satan and the Demonic Powers

Since biblical times, satanic influence and demonic activity have been cited by the Christian church as a vital part of the explanation for individual and corporate evil. In the past few centuries, however, as a naturalistic and scientific outlook has become more and more the norm in Western countries, belief in the reality of Satan and the demonic has waned.

Some years ago, for instance, I was asked to participate in a conference, sponsored by the Roman Catholics in Galveston, Texas, on the problem of Satan and the demonic forces. Many physicians were there, mostly psychiatrists. However, there was not one physician who would admit that he really believed in the reality of a personal Satan and demonic invasion. In confirmation of this experience, Scott Peck, a well-known psychiatrist and writer, states that in his earlier years, in common with 99 percent of the psychiatrists in the nation, he did not believe that Satan exists.[1]

As *Newsweek* magazine points out, Satan has been debunked by rationalists, exorcised by psychotherapists, and mythologized by theologians. Walter Wink, Professor of Biblical Interpretation at Auburn Theological Seminary, New York City, even suggests that if you try mentioning demons, or the devil, in sophisticated circles, you will be quickly appraised for signs of pathological violence and then quietly shunned.[2]

To substantiate their criticism, the materialists state that those who do teach the reality of the satanic and the demonic are often manipulative and tyrannical; they use the Satan image to excuse irresponsibility and terrify people into compliance to sectarian mores.[3]

Admittedly, in many Christian circles, the image of Satan has been used as a tool for enforcing specific belief systems and building personal theological empires. Too often, he has been whittled down to the stature of a petty being obsessed with undermining personal—especially sexual—morality, but unrelated to larger, corporate evil. As a result, these groups denounce such personal evils as sexual promiscuity, adolescent rebellion, crime, and substance abuse while ignoring or even condoning other evils that plunge and drive our times like a ship before an angry sea. (For example, certain television evangelists try to terrorize us with Satan and then speak favorably of South African apartheid.) Evil runs roughshod through corporate boardrooms and even churches, unnoticed and unnamed, while "Satan" is relegated to superego reinforcement and moralistic scare tactics.[4]

On the other hand, certain more liberal Christian groups have so reacted against the misuse of the Satan-image in fundamentalist circles that they have tended to throw out the notion of a personal Satan altogether. Unfortunately, however, the absence of any profound means of portraying radical evil has often left such Christians at the mercy of a shallow religious rationalism that is naïvely optimistic and self-deceiving.[5]

2. The Contemporary Renewal of Interest in the Satanic and the Demonic Powers

(1) Recent Concern of the Media, Psychiatrists, Theologians, and Academia. In spite of centuries of neglect and confusion, however, belief in Satan and demonic influence is not dead. Recently, in fact—perhaps in recognition of the continuing power of evil in society and human life—interest in the satanic has surged.

Some years ago, for example, in its eleventh edition, the *Encyclopedia Britannica* stated that "science has made so much progress in helping us understand our inner life that there is little room for an interest in Satan." Then, in the early 1970s, just when everyone thought demons were finished, William Peter Blatty's novel, *The Exorcist,* and the immensely popular movie based on that novel, brought them back into public view. The interest in the phenomenon of the satanic has increased. Other movies and books dealing with this subject have been consistently well-attended and widely discussed. *Hostage to the Devil,* a 1976 book by a former Jesuit priest, Malachi Martin, which described five cases of possession and successful exorcisms, became a Book-of-the-Month Club main selection.[6] In the late 1980s, talk-show host Geraldo Rivera featured Satanism on a controversial but widely viewed television special.

If the current interest in the satanic were only a matter of popular credulity and superstition—and it is that in part—reason might be the prescribed cure. In the view of many, however, "reasonable" and optimistic scientific views of progress have failed to account for escalating evil in our time. This seems to call for at least a second look at the biblical view. The Bible gives an explanation of the reason for the evils that are submerging our age into night, leaving us filled with a sense of helplessness and horror.[7] Can one adequately explain the genocidal campaigns of Adolf Hitler or Idi Amin, the murder sprees of Charles Manson or Ted Bundy, the suicide/murder of Jim Jones and his cult followers in Guyana, or the success of the "kiddie-porn" industry without at least considering the possibility of a personal power of evil in the universe?[8]

It is significant to note, moreover, that the revival of interest in satanic activity involves not just the popular press, but professional therapists and serious students of the human condition. In 1975, for instance, only a few years after the Galveston meeting at which I had spoken, the Christian Medical Society called for a conference on the demonic at the Notre Dame Conference Center. The participants included psychiatrists, anthropologists, psychologists, and theologians.

Basil Jackson, professor of psychiatry at the University of Wisconsin, opened the conference with this statement: "A sense of desperation has come upon some of us. We cannot cope with certain problems that we have been faced with clinically. The people with these problems make little response to our professional ingenuity. Perhaps we have missed something quite important both psychologically and spiritually because we have ignored the material in the Bible about Satan and the demonic."[9]

Jackson's words summarized a realization of many thoughtful men and women today that a naturalistic or materialistic outlook is insufficient in the face of the continued experience of evil. While materialism has served as an integrating agent for modern society, that integration has been bought at the cost of neglecting spiritual realities. The result is that the modern world now finds itself without an adequate vocabulary for dealing with powers even more real today than they were two thousand years ago.[10]

This is also the affirmation of Scott Peck, whose experience as a psychiatrist confirms the accuracy and depth of understanding of Malachi Martin's book on exorcism. Peck asserts that, before witnessing his first exorcism, he had been intrigued but not convinced by Martin's book. It was another matter after he had personally met Satan face-to-face. He wrote his book, *People of the Lie,* in the hope that, as a result of his experience and that of Martin, closed-minded readers will become more open-minded in relation to the reality of Satan.[11]

Walter Wink is an example of a serious theologian who has become convinced that the dominant materialistic worldview, which has absolutely no place for Satan and demons, is wrong. Wink has come to believe that the demonic forces should not be seen as relics of a superstitious past, but taken seriously as real powers at work in the world today. The views of Walter Wink are a part of his work in which he is restudying and reappraising the importance of the satanic and demonic. He has already published two volumes (*Naming the Powers,* 1984, and *Unmasking the Powers,* 1986) of a three-volume study of the demonic. This work is receiving widespread attention.

Finally, Jeffrey B. Russell, professor at the University of California at Santa Barbara and a specialist in historical studies about Satan and witchcraft, contends that a concept that does not correspond to human experience will die. But the concept of Satan is very much alive today, in spite of opposition from many theologians as well as those hostile to all metaphysics. Indeed, the idea of Satan is more alive now than it has been for many decades, because we are again aware of the nature of perversity in our own behavior that exceeds and transcends what could be expected in an individual human life. We also have a direct perception of evil manifesting itself in governments, in mobs, and in criminals. According to Russell, many people are reporting the additional experience that behind all this evil, and directing it, is a powerful, transhuman personality. This is Satan. He transcends the depth psychology arguments that the demonic only exists within the human mind, or collectively among human minds.[12]

(2) Evangelical Response to the Renewed Interest in the Satanic. Resurgence of interest in satanic activity in the media and medical circles has its counterpart in evangelical circles as well. Fuller Theological Seminary in California, for example, recently introduced a course on how to cope with the devil. Later it added a second course to help future pastors distinguish between mental illness and demonic possession.

In the late 1930s, many theological professors confessed to having difficulty with the doctrine of a personal Satan. And yet, since that time, prominent theologians, especially those coming out of Europe after the Holocaust, have affirmed that belief in Satan is an important part of any adequate understanding of theology. Otto Piper, a German theologian exiled by Hitler, is said to have brought the devil back to Princeton.

But in a more systematic way, how can evangelical Christians understand the almost contradictory and sometimes confusing developments relating to cosmic evil and the demonic? How do we approach this problem which is attracting so much attention on every hand today? Some people still regard belief in a personal Satan as part of humankind's nursery furniture—a concept to be discarded by mature, rational people. However, the concept of a personal Satan has remained a basic part of any view that claims to be biblical and evangelical.

Granted, the biblical teaching concerning Satan has been distorted both during the Middle Ages and in recent years. For example, in the Middle Ages the image of a horned, tailed, hoofed, and hairy Satan with bat wings became popular. At various points in Western history, some societies have sought to persecute the devil indirectly in the person of his followers, and the result has been the torture and murder of hundreds of admitted or alleged witches and sorcerers. In modern times there has been a tendency by some to identify almost all human ills as demon possession.[13]

The present-day student who accepts the biblical teaching about Satan need not be committed to such crude imagery and misguided interpretations. However, the medieval and modern distortions suggest that a careful consideration of the biblical teaching is especially needed.

After participating in discussions on this subject with numerous university, medical, and ministerial groups, I have come to see that the grounds of belief or disbelief in Satan and demons are subtle and profound. The question cannot be dealt with in isolation. What a person believes will depend on many factors. Is there meaning in assertions which cannot be reduced to a summary of physical observations? How valid are experiences which cannot be subjected to typical laboratory testing? How does a person's attitude toward the Bible influence his or her viewpoint?

In many ways, the satanic and the demonic are a scandal, a stumbling block, a bone in the throat of the modern, materialistic worldview. In fact, Wink suggests that the recovery of the concepts of the satanic and demonic and a sense of the experiences that they describe can play a crucial role in eroding the soil from beneath the foundations of materialism. These concepts can also provide a language for naming these experiences in the revitalized biblical worldview that is emerging.[14]

Accordingly, this study accepts the biblical revelation as a normative guide in the difficult and critical area of cosmic evil, Satanism, demonology, and the Christian deliverance from their power (exorcism). For this reason, we will look at the biblical sources before discussing the credibility of the demonic for the twentieth century.

II. What Are the Biblical Teachings about Satan and the Demonic Powers?

1. Old Testament Teachings

The Old Testament is especially relevant in light of the fact that its people lived in a world remarkably like our own in its preoccupation with the sensual, the occult, and the demonic. Israel knew well three other cultures—the Egyptian, the Assyro-Babylonian, and the Canaanite. In each culture, the demonic was an important factor. The Old Testament, however, strikes a surprising contrast to these surrounding cultures—a dramatically different approach to the satanic and the demonic.

(1) The Reality of Satan. The Old Testament does recognize Satan and the fallen powers of the demonic world, although the meaning of some Old Testament references is not crystal clear and capable of proof.

Some scholars, for instance, identify Satan with Lucifer, the "son of the morning" addressed in Isaiah 14:12–15: "How art thou fallen from heaven! . . . how art thou cut down to the ground, which didst weaken the nations! For thou hast said in thine heart, I will ascend into heaven, I will exalt my throne above the stars of God. . . . yet thou shalt be brought down to hell, to the sides of the pit" (KJV). Other scholars see this reference as primarily a poetic comparison of the king of Babylon to the morning star Venus, which is the last star to fade before the sun. However, it should be noted that the Isaiah reference is similar to Luke 10:18, where Jesus himself speaks of Satan as falling like lightning from heaven, and to Revelation 12:4, which states that a great dragon pulls down a third of the stars.

The Old Testament makes it clear that Satan and fallen angels—rebels against God—were on the scene from the very moment of the world's creation. Disguised as a serpent, he was the agent of temptation for the first man and woman (Gen. 3:10). And in most of his other Old Testament appearances he is cast as the adversary of God's people. He seeks to lead God's people into presumption (1 Chron. 21:1) or slanders them to God's face (Zech. 3:1).[15]

In the book of Job, we have a fuller account of Satan's activities. He is the great accuser of humans in their claim to a right standing before God. He accuses Job of selfish and insincere piety. However, he acts within the limits which God has fixed for him (Job 1:12; 2:6). Even though he is acting with God's permission, Satan finds joy in his antihuman ministry. He is tending to become a more malignant being.[16]

(2) The Created Nature and Limitations of Satan. The Old Testament emphasizes that the demonic forces are secondary to God and powerless when confronted by Yahweh's power. Satan was created; he was not, as the Persians or Zoroastrians later were to suggest, coequal with God. He could tempt but not force.

God alone, said the Hebrews, was to be feared. In fact, many people think that one reason there is so little about Satan in the Old Testament is that God wanted the Hebrews to concentrate on him. God wanted to lead his people to a dynamic practical monotheism. In the Old Testament, the primary emphasis is on the supremacy of and the power of the God of Abraham, Isaac and Jacob, who delivered the Hebrews from the slavery of Egypt.[17]

2. New Testament Teachings

(1) The Background Influence and Challenge of the Persian and Interbiblical Confrontations. In the New Testament, especially in the first three Gospels, references to Satan and the demonic are open and extensive. Some scholars believe this emphasis is due in part to the Zoroastrians in Persia. The Hebrews had been carried off in 586 B.C. by the Babylonians, and the Babylonians in turn had been conquered by the Persians in 536 B.C. Thus, the Hebrews lived under Persian dominance during a time when the teachings of the Persian prophet Zoroaster were popular. Zoroaster taught that there are two great personal forces in the world: Mazda, the god of light, and Satan or Ahriman, the force of evil, who existed with Mazda from the beginning. It has been suggested by some that the New Testament concept of Satan was derived from the Zoroastrian concept of Ahriman.

Other scholars contend that the New Testament profile of the devil owes its essential features to a diverse collection of apocryphal scriptures that appeared in Palestine between the second century before Christ and the second century after. Written mainly by apocalyptic Jews and early Christians, many of these books dramatized themes also found in the Dead Sea Scrolls. They told of a world fallen for a time under the dominion of a powerful opponent of God, and they prophesied that this evil eon would soon pass with the coming of a Messiah, who would vanquish God's opponent and inaugurate a new era of glory for Yahweh and his faithful remnant. Except for a few minor texts, none of these writings were ultimately accepted into the Jewish or Christian canons as the authoritative word of God. Nonetheless, they were widely circulated.[18]

An explanation more consistent with biblical teaching would affirm that the Hebrews were faced with the problem of Satan in a more dramatic way as they were living with these Persian people and as they read apocalyptic and apocryphal writings. For even though there are some similarities between the New Testament references to Satan and the teachings of the Zoroastrians and the apocryphal literature, there are also significant differences.

For example, in the New Testament we find no hint of the ultimate or absolute dualism suggested by the Zoroastrians. Satan is clearly set forth as subordinate to God and defeated by him, not as a coequal force.

The apocryphal and apocalyptic literature, most of which was written between the Old and New Testaments, despaired of history, feeling it was completely dominated by evil. This literature is dualistic, pessimistic, deterministic, and passive. In contrast, the New Testament saw God's kingdom as both present and future.[19]

(2) The Clear-Cut New Testament Teachings. By the time the New Testament books were written, God had led their authors to a clear-cut doctrine of Satan. This doctrine located an origin of evil in Satan which recognizes a reality of evil outside the will of men. The New Testament avoids identifying evil with the direct will of God. It also keeps it always and finally subordinate to God.

Matthew, Mark, and Luke clearly accept and teach a doctrine of a personal Satan and his agents, which are called fallen angels or demons (Mark 3:22). Matthew 4:1 tells of Jesus' being tempted by the devil in the wilderness. In Matthew 25:41, hell is described as being prepared for the devil and his angels. In Luke 13:16 and Matthew 17:5–18, Satan and demons are seen as able to inflict disease, and in Luke 22:3, Satan is said to have possessed Judas.

The apostle John also accepted the doctrine of a personal Satan. His Gospel describes Satan as the prince of this world who opposes Jesus and is defeated by him (John 12:31; 14:30; 16:11). The Epistle of 1 John depicts the whole world as being in the power of the wicked one (1 John 5:19).[20]

The apostle Paul's worldview teaches that Satan is the god of this age. According to Paul, the cosmos or unredeemed world is now under Satan's power, who is the "commander of the spiritual powers of the air" (Eph. 2:2, NEB) and leads "the superhuman forces of evil in the heavens" (Eph. 6:12, NEB).[21]

The writers of the general New Testament epistles, such as 1 and 2 Peter and James, give graphic descriptions of Satan's activities. Second Peter 2:4 speaks of the "angels" who "sinned" and Jude 6 of the "angels that did not keep their own position but left their proper dwelling." The constant use of violence and deceit by Satan requires that believers manifest courage and extreme vigilance (1 Peter 5:8–9), but Satan nevertheless can be successfully resisted (James 4:7).[22]

Revelation 12 portrays a vision of the powers that operate in the spiritual world behind the scenes of human history. The red dragon, or Satan, is seen as seeking to destroy the woman (a representation of the ideal and historic church) in an age-long battle. In verses 4–5, Satan's effort to destroy the Messiah is frustrated. Instead, Satan himself is cut down from his place of power as the result of a spiritual conflict (7–8). Because of his defeat, Satan is even more infuriated and seeks to destroy the woman. This conflict between the dragon and the woman would help to explain the evil which the church has experienced throughout its history (12:11). This evil can be seen as beginning at the hands of the Roman Empire and being culminated in the final Antichrist.

In Revelation 12:4, John states that the tail of the dragon draws a third of the stars of heaven and casts them to the earth. This is usually seen as referring to the primeval war in heaven, since stars are familiar symbols of fallen angels. In Revelation 20, a dramatic portrayal finds the dragon, or Satan, being bound and shut up in the bottomless pit for a thousand years. At the end of the thousand years, he is released and entices men to rebel against Christ and the saints. Finally, he is cast into the lake of fire, along with the Beast and the False Prophet (20:10).

Revelation also depicts Satan's activities as involving not only individuals but communities. Political forces can become servants of the devil (Rev. 12, 13). Revelation 2:13 even speaks of a throne of Satan.

(3) The Centrality of the Satanic and Demonic in the New Testament. A number of contemporary scholars, including G. K. Barrett, James Kallas, and George Ladd, see the basic message of both Jesus and Paul as closely related to both satanology and eschatology. In other words, they see the work of Christ primarily in terms of the battle with Satan. According to this view, evil is radical and rooted in the personal—not the abstract. It is greater than humankind and is personal—much more than mere mythology.

Other conservative theologians, such as James Denney, see Christ's work as primarily related to guilt and forgiveness. They do not emphasize the work of Christ in overcoming demonic powers.

There is abundant biblical evidence for both views. The established or classical principles of biblical interpretation, however, demand that if one view is primary in the Bible, it should be determinative and the other secondary. The first group of scholars mentioned above contend that the demonology-eschatology motif is dominant, constituting some three-fourths of the material in the first three Gospels and Paul's Epistles. This means the New Testament teaches that satanic forces have a measure of real control in the world.[23]

Even those who hold that the satanic and demonic emphasis is central in the New Testament also stress that there is less of this emphasis after the Resurrection. Once Christ won the victory over Satan through the Cross and the Resurrection, the emphasis was less on driving out demons and more on preaching, teaching, and baptizing. In the Book of Romans, for example, Paul gives no specific teachings about demon possession and exorcism. Rather, he talks of the law of the spirit of life in Christ Jesus which has enabled us to be free from the law of sin and death (Rom. 8:2).

The New Testament portrayal of evil in a personal form, as in the fallen angel story, avoids the dual pitfalls of monism (the metaphysical teaching that there is only one reality) and dualism (the concept of an eternal struggle between equal forces of good and evil). It does not place too much emphasis on the power of the demonic, but preserves man's responsibility for his sin. Even though humans permit the demonization of their creative works and sometimes pass under bondage to the demonic, their life and their world remain in the hands of God. They can never be ascribed to the absolute sphere of satanic influence. The category of Satan and the demonic thus provides the necessary theological tool for understanding the almost overwhelming power of sin and human distortion in historical existence.[24]

Several evangelical scholars suggest that God allowed us to see the satanic world in its fullness only in the presence of Jesus Christ—hence the greater emphasis on Satan in the New Testament. With Christ present, the power of Satan to entice and enchant and deceive is diminished. In fact, Os Guinness affirms in his well-known book, *Dust of Death*, that it is only with the loss of the presence of Christ in the twentieth century that Satan and the demonic forces have been able to move into our culture. He suggests that the central fire of Christ's presence has burned so low that the jungle creatures symbolizing the satanic forces are moving in closer.[25]

III. What Are Guidelines for Evaluating Current Discussions of Satan and the Demonic Powers?

D. L. Moody once stated that he had two reasons for believing in the existence of Satan. One was that the Bible says that Satan exists. The second reason was that "I have encountered him. I have done business with him."

After extensive experience as a Christian psychiatrist, Scott Peck agrees with Moody. He states, "I now know Satan is real. I have met him."[26]

From the Bible and from the experience of those who have encountered Satan, we are able to establish four broad guidelines to help us evaluate the current discussions of Satan and the demonic.

1. Satan's Personal Nature and Plural Manifestation

First, Satan is personal in his nature and plural in his manifestation and his work. Christ's ministry, as we read in Matthew 4:1, began with his confronting Satan on the Mount of Temptation. Christ, of course, was sinless. Temptation, therefore, did not arise from within him, but came through the personal suggestion of Satan. This is also true in our experience. We do not encounter evil, Satan, and the demonic as an impersonal fate or a biological deficiency.

William Hendricks, professor of theology at Southern Baptist Seminary, affirms the biblical view that evil is personal. He states that if we have lived long enough, read Scripture often enough, and reflected deeply on the destroyed patterns of life, there are four things we would want to affirm: (a) The Bible speaks of evil in personal terms even as it does of God. We cannot have a Hebrew (personal) God and a Greek (impersonal) devil. (b) Personhood is the highest and lowest category by which we can think of good and evil. (c) The personification we give to both good and evil, God and the devil, are expressions of function (what they do), not descriptions of existence (how they look). (d) We all have had "help" in doing the good and in undoing the good with the bad.[27]

A related question concerns the existence of lesser demons. There is evidence in the Bible that they work as manifestations of Satan's power. However, there is apparently less freedom in the world of demons than in the world of human beings. By virtue of their cowardice and terror and belief in their own lies, lesser demons act in such strict obedience to their superiors that they tend to lack individuality as we ordinarily think of it.[28]

2. Satan's Created and Limited Nature

According to the biblical view, Satan is not coequal with God. In contrast to Zoroastrian philosophy, the biblical message is no dualistic story of two equal powers in eternal, unresolved conflict. Rather, the Bible clearly shows that Satan is a creature of God. Furthermore, Satan has limits. His leash may be long, but he nevertheless is on a leash.

The decisive battle in the war between good and evil was fought and won by Christ in the crucifixion and resurrection. Satan has been defeated, and although he continues to fight on desperately, his fate has long since been sealed. All that remains is for the final chapters of history to unfold and Satan's downfall to be completed.[29]

3. Satan's Impotence

Satan's power over an individual is also limited. He can tempt, deceive, accuse, and attack us, but he cannot force us to do something against our wills. We cannot truthfully say, "The devil made me do it."

Today, as in every century, people tend to concretize their fears. They want a scapegoat to deliver them from responsibility. But the fact that Satan is active in the universe, tempting and deceiving humankind, does not release us from responsibility. Satan and the demonic forces cannot dominate or possess us except by our own consent. The believer will not be tempted beyond his power of resistance (1 Cor. 10:13), because Satan acts only within the limits set by divine sovereignty. In fact, as Hendricks points out, we cannot blame our problems and disclaim our responsibilities solely because of God, either. Because God has given us freedom, both good and evil human actions are joint ventures between God and the self and the evil one and the self.[30]

4. Satan's Sure Defeat

The positive emphasis of the New Testament is that Satan and the demonic forces have been overcome by the life, death, and resurrection of Jesus Christ. In fact, Jesus came into the world to "destroy the works of the devil" (1 John 3:8). The Cross and the Resurrection constitute a decisive victory over Satan and Satan's host (Col. 2:15). This victory insured that countless numbers would be delivered from the dominion of darkness and transferred to the kingdom of Christ (Col. 1:13).

Through the Cross and Resurrection, the defeat of evil is utterly assured. The crucial victory occurred almost two thousand years ago. Necessary and even dangerous and devastating though our own personal battles may be, they are but mopping-up operations against a retreating enemy who has long since lost the war.[31]

Furthermore, we are offered invincible protection in these battles. In Ephesians 6:11–18, Paul describes the armor of God which protects us if we but put it on. This armor, constituted of the biblical gospel, integrity, peace through Christ, faith in Christ, and prayer, furnishes spiritual security to the believer.

The recent fascination with Satan and demons is in reaction to an earlier disbelief. Christians should beware of excessive gullibility as well as extreme oversimplification. Knowledge about Satan and evil angels alerts Christians to the danger and subtlety of satanic temptation, but we should not become too preoccupied with the satanic. We must remember that the main thrust of Christianity is on the availability of God's power and love in Jesus Christ and the Holy Spirit.

IV. What Are Some Representative Controversial Models or Methods for Understanding Satan and the Demonic Powers?

With the help of the Bible and the guidelines outlined above, we are prepared to evaluate critically and to learn from some of the representative controversial models or approaches to evil, Satan, and the demonic powers which are being presented in the latter part of the twentieth century.

These various approaches begin from one of several standpoints. Some are primarily concerned with interpreting the biblical witness, particularly Jesus' comments and actions concerning the satanic or demonic. Others attempt to explain experiential evil in the form of personal pathology, sickness, or alienation—the *symptoms* attributed to demonic influence in the Bible. Appropriately, those that attempt to explain experiential evil also suggest means whereby that evil can be eliminated.

1. The "Speaking Down" or Accommodation Model

This view, which is held by some intellectuals, teaches that there are no demons, and that Jesus knew this. In referring to demons, he was simply speaking down to the people, communicating with them in terms of the popular ideas of that day.

C. H. Dodd, for instance, suggests that Christ had to adapt his language to communicate to the prescientific mind.[32] Other scholars have presented similar ideas. It has even been suggested that Jesus used exorcism of demons as a "magic show" to draw a crowd and create a dynamic image of his own personality.

2. The "Child of the Times" Model

Another view of the demonic in the Bible also holds that there are no demons, but that Jesus did not know this. Edward Langton, for instance, believes that, as a corollary of his incarnation, Jesus was limited in his knowledge about the reality of demons. He did not deliberately teach a false theory of demons; he simply accepted the dominant worldview. According to Langton, we know today that there are no such things as demons. There are no supernatural evil influences; simply our own evil impulses.[33]

The most radical yet straightforward attempt to deal with New Testament demonology is that of Rudolf Bultmann, the well-known German biblical scholar. He frankly admits that demonology (and eschatology) are central in the thought of Jesus and Paul. For modern man, however, Bultmann contends that demonology is irrelevant and invalid. He suggests that the modern mindset sees personal pathology, distress, and alienation not as a theological problem (as in demon possession), but as a *medical* one.

In Bultmann's view, therefore, Christians should give up being hypocrites and/or idiots. We must "demythologize" the Bible, including references to the demonic. When we do this, according to Bultmann, we will see that demons are our own evil impulses, not personal external forces.[34]

In speaking of demythologization, Bultmann claims he wants to alter only the *form* of the gospel—not its *content*. However, Kallas and other biblical scholars contend that Bultmann alters both the form and the essential content of the gospel. Moreover, if one says that man is not open to evil personal and external powers, then, to be consistent, one must go on to say that man is not open to good personal and external powers, such as Jesus Christ and the Holy Spirit.[35]

3. The "Structures of Power" Model

This view attempts to explain personal pathology, distress, and alienation in terms of capitulation to oppressive power structures. Such a perspective is held by some liberation theologians, Marxists, and a wide spectrum of social theorists. According to those who ascribe to this viewpoint, personal evil is rooted in structures and society. This means that people who display "demonic" symptoms are held in submission to alienating structures and ideologies. They cannot be liberated by personal insight, unless that insight includes the ways in which their inner demons are the internalized product of brute institutional power. Help is to be found in social struggle, reform, or revolution.[36]

4. The Psychological Model

(1) A Definition and Variations of the Psychological View. This view, held by the majority of people in the Western world, concerns itself primarily with personal manifestations of evil. This model maintains that the symptoms once attributed to satanic influence and demons are actually the consequence of personal developmental malfunctions. Help is to be found in personal analysis, behavioral modification, or lifestyle changes.[37]

The psychological viewpoint holds that the demons described in the Bible are what we would call today psychoses and neuroses. In other words, demons are primitive approximations of mental illnesses now more exactly named. Accordingly, Christ performed psychological cures when he cast out demons. This is the view of Vernon McCasland, professor of religion at the University of Virginia, as set forth in his book *By the Finger of God.*[38]

The originator of the psychological view was Sigmund Freud, the father of modern psychoanalysis. Freud postulated that both Satan and God are mental projections. Freud speculated, for example, that our despair at seeing our fathers grow older and die leads us to "project" a heavenly father to compensate for our loss. According to Freud in regard to Satan, the same thing happens. We project and create in our own minds the idea of a Satan.

From another psychological perspective, Carl Jung states that our complexes split off from consciousness and lead a separate existence in the unconscious. The anima (one of the archetypes of the unconscious) is the chaotic life or demonic urge.[39]

(2) The "Mutual Appreciation" Approach of Christian Psychologists and Psychiatrists. Most of the psychological views described above rule out theological interpretations of human pathology. However, there are also those who hold that supernatural and psychological interpretations of evil are not mutually exclusive. In response to those who would reduce the explanation of the demonic to psychological categories, for example, Wayne Oates, a professor at the University of Louisville Medical School, concurs with British psychologist Victor White that "Psychology, properly utilized, has value within limits. The theological and psychological approaches are not mutually exclusive."[40]

In fact, there is a movement in psychology today which seeks to consider transhuman or supernatural forces, both good and evil, as explanations for human behavior. According to this view, two approaches to the human personality are valid—the empirical and the observational (psychology) and the theological (Christian).[41]

Psychiatrist Scott Peck states that the differences between the two approaches fall into two categories: conceptual frames of reference and the use of power. These frames of reference need not be mutually exclusive. Peck has been combining them in various mixtures in ordinary psychotherapy for some years with many patients and apparently with considerable success. Increasing numbers of other therapists have been doing likewise. In fact, Peck states that his most requested speech among professional therapists is entitled "The Use of Religious Concepts in Psychotherapy."[42]

William Wilson, an evangelical Christian and professor of psychiatry at Duke University Medical School, also combines a psychological and a Christian approach to experiential evil. He states that clinical data compels him to conclude that instances of the inner control of humans by evil spirits do occur. In such cases, the evil spirit is a counterpart of the Holy Spirit and can control and guide human actions.[43]

5. The "Ritualistic" Model

The ritualistic approach holds that Satan and demons are real and can be driven out by formal rituals of exorcism. This view emerged in the third and fourth centuries A.D. and was widely followed in the medieval Roman Catholic Church as well as in other liturgical churches. It is still practiced to some extent, especially by Catholics. Some Roman Catholic leaders, however, question some aspects of medieval exorcism rituals. And as we will see, some Protestants practice exorcism but seek to emphasize the spiritual dynamics and downplay formal rituals, which they suggest can come close to magic. Some charismatic and Pentecostal groups utilize an informal exorcism ritual, but it is different in approach from the more formal Catholic rituals.[44]

(1) The Historical Excesses and Problems of the Ritualistic Approach. In the Middle Ages, many people were said to be dominated by Satan or were acting as instruments of Satan. In some cases, persons who protested against traditional views of society were said to be serving Satan and were branded as witches. A number of suppressed or repressed groups did in fact turn to witchcraft or Satan worship.

One example of this concerns women in particular. Wink points out that women in the Middle Ages had many grievances. Some were denied access to power, especially ordination to the priesthood. Others were unwilling to suppress their sexuality or were rebellious against male authority. Some hated God for a particular evil suffered ostensibly at God's hands or were angry at the church. There were those who were frustrated at the inability to use their talents except at "women's" work, or greedy to the point of selling their souls to the devil in return for success. Still others wanted revenge over a rival or a love potion for a lover.

For some of these women, witchcraft and Satan worship represented a gesture of defiance to a patriarchal God and to a male-dominated society. They also provided a means of seizing power against men. In addition, much of what was called witchcraft was the underground continuation of ancient fertility cults, now shaped and colored in reaction to the dominant Christian religion.[45]

(In some ways there is a similar situation today. At least a part of the appeal of contemporary Satanist cults and witchcraft derives from a reaction against the "God" of Christendom. Satanists do not doubt God; they *hate* God. In reaction to Christianity, Satanism is a kind of adolescent rebellion. It is a product of a type of repressive Christianity.[46])

In response to the fact that the church in the Middle Ages had identified so many dissidents (men as well as women) as Satan-dominated, ritual exorcism became widespread—so prevalent, in fact, that the Roman Catholic Church had to take decisive steps to control it. The *Roman Ritual,* issued in 1614 under Pope Paul V, offered strict rules for exorcism. Later, exorcism was restricted to priests who had gained official church permission.[47]

In more recent years, especially since the 1960s, there has been a mixed reaction in Catholic circles toward the satanic itself and the exorcism ritual in particular. For instance, some mainline Roman Catholic clergy have been disinclined toward any kind of exorcist ritual. There was a reaction against an emphasis on Satan. In response, in 1972, Pope Paul VI called for all orthodox Roman Catholics to affirm once again the reality of Satan and the demonic.

The eminent Roman Catholic theologian, Karl Rahner, holds that in rare cases a person can be possessed by Satan or demons, although in his opinion it is very difficult to distinguish between mental illness, parapsychological faculties, and demon possession. He therefore grants that there is a place for the exorcism ritual, perhaps in conjunction with psychological help. Rahner stresses, however, that exorcism must be conducted by people of strong emotional, intellectual, and spiritual powers.[48]

(2) The Historic Development of Exorcism. The elaborate exorcism ritual which the Roman church uses in relationship to people who are alleged to be possessed by demons developed as early as A.D. 200, according to Eusebius. The person who performed the exorcism ritual later became one of the minor officials in the church.

At one time, there was a relationship between the function of exorcism, the development of infant baptism, and the developing dogma of original sin.[49] According to Grillot De Givry, in those early centuries it was taught that a child entered the world under the auspices of a demon. A voluntary renunciation of the devil was therefore required of a candidate for baptism. When infants were baptized, the renunciation was undertaken by sponsors on their behalf. (This aspect of the baptismal service has been retained by some liturgical churches.) The prebaptismal exorcism ceremony included a command, "Come out of him, thou unclean spirit!"

Over the years, the exorcism ritual took more elaborate form and became separated from baptism. The type of ritual portrayed in the movie, *The Exorcist*, with its abjurations addressed to the demon, the sprinklings with holy water, the stole passed around the patient's neck, the repeated signs of the cross, and so forth, developed over time. Books are available giving the exorcism sentences used by such notables as Ambrose and Cyprian.[50]

(3) Critiques of the Ritualistic Approach. Most evangelicals have difficulties with the ritual approach to Satan and the demonic, because they find it difficult to think of any ritual sacrament or ordinance as being meaningful apart from personal faith on the part of the participant. In addition, evangelicals find no developed exorcist ritual in the New Testament. They believe that close examination will show that most of the elaborate rituals of exorcism have been developed subsequent to the New Testament period.

Actually, the elaborate, *Exorcist*-style ritual is deplored by many sensitive Roman Catholic scholars as well as by Protestants. Karl Rahner, for instance, is opposed to exorcism as a theatrical ritual in which demons as well as God are addressed. In his view, this sort of demonstration can of itself induce possession-like symptoms in a psyche that is already weak.[51]

The debate continues in Catholic circles on the advisability of performing exorcist rituals. Church leaders admit that the practice of exorcism can be dangerous and that in the past it has caused many medical precautions and treatments to be neglected. Many mainline Catholics, however, urge continuation of exorcism if the demands of the *Roman Ritual* in verifying the demoniac nature of the affliction are met.[52]

6. The Charismatic or Pentecostal Model

A widely held view of the satanic is the "charismatic" approach—sometimes known as the "Pentecostal" approach. The more extreme form of this approach might also be described as the "demons everywhere" approach.

This view, in keeping with the general charismatic view of the miraculous and the supernatural, holds that the signs and wonders carried out during the apostolic era should be normative for the life of the church today. This applies also to the gift of distinguishing between the spirits, mentioned in 1 Corinthians 12, and casting out demons as Christ and the apostles did.

The charismatic model has both extreme and more moderate exponents. Because of the widespread acquaintance with the extreme model through the world and for the purpose of contrast, we will describe and evaluate the extreme view in this section.

(1) The Extreme Charismatic View. The more extreme form of the charismatic approach might be described as the "demons everywhere" approach, because proponents of this view see demons behind every negative experience. While giving lectures at a prominent university I met some students who were caught up in this approach. They explained that it was necessary for them to perform an exorcism ritual for every professor and every classroom before they would enter the class on any particular day.

Charismatic authors Frank and Ida Mae Hammond, in their book, *Pigs in the Parlor*, maintain that the charismatic movement has restored both the gift of discerning evil spirits and the gift of exorcism. The Hammonds claim to have found several hundred types of demons extant, and they have classified them into fifty-three major groups. Examples are extensive. Cancer is caused by a demon. Schizophrenia is a demon. Tobacco is a demon. Asthma is a demon.[53]

The Hammonds believe that the gifts of discerning and exorcising demons are among the gifts listed in 1 Corinthians 12. They also believe they are "now" gifts, available to contemporary Christians. In *Pigs in the Parlor*, the Hammonds include numerous "how-to" charts showing how to discern and exorcise demons. (A number of other charismatic writers do this also.)

For example, the Hammonds state that a person who is demon-infested will have snake-like eyes. He or she will often hiss like a serpent, since serpents are portrayed in the Bible as instruments of Satan. The Hammonds contend that cancer demons have an especially bad odor. One way to recognize the demon of pride is to note if a person has folded arms held together in a proud manner. The dancing demon causes a woman to sway at the hips.[54]

The Hammonds go on to discuss some methods for casting out demons. For instance, they believe it is important to have a person who is being exorcised sit on a chair and bend over slightly. This helps because, according to the Hammonds, demons have bodies which come out through the mouth or the nose. It takes some time for the residue of the bodies of the demons to be regurgitated. Often there is vomit, gagging, and foam in the mouth as the remnants of these demon bodies are expelled.[55]

(2) Criticism of the Extreme View. Not everyone who is sympathetic to the charismatic view holds the "demons everywhere" approach, however. A more moderate view would hold that, while the gift of distinguishing between the spirits is potentially available to all Christians, in practice its exercise is limited to a small number of Christians who use the gift reluctantly when occasion demands and who follow biblical restraints. (The need for such discretion is mentioned in 1 Timothy 4:1.)[56]

Furthermore, this group would hold that, while demons are real and can indeed take control of a human personality, not every personality dysfunction is attributable to demons. For example, as a Christian psychiatrist, Scott Peck has difficulty with the charismatic's so-called "deliverance ministry." Deliverance is a sort of "mini-exorcism" frequently conducted to treat people suffering from "oppression." This is defined as a sort of halfway state between demonic temptation—which the charismatics would say we all undergo—and frank possession.[57]

There is much controversy over these matters of "oppression" and deliverance. Many charismatics practice deliverance in cases in which others would find no evidence of demonic involvement. Indeed, some will attempt to cast out such things as the "spirit of alcoholism," "spirit of depression," or "spirit of revenge." They report many instances of dramatic success. Yet Peck wonders how long-lasting such "cures" are. He speculates that there are probably many failed cases which go unreported. And he warns that many of these almost casual and generally untrained interventions may actually be harmful. There is no way of knowing, he says, until the work of deliverance practitioners can be scientifically evaluated.[58]

Wink shares Peck's caution about seeing demons as the cause of every form of human distress. He goes on to stress the importance of distinguishing between what he calls "outer personal possession" and "the inner personal demonic."

By outer personal possession, Wink means the possession of an individual by something that is alien and extrinsic to the self. By the inner personal demonic, he means a split-off or unintegrated aspect of the self which is not alien, but intrinsic to the personality. In his view, such a split-off part of the self does not need to be exorcised, but rather to be owned, embraced, loved, and transformed as part of the struggle for wholeness.[59]

According to Wink, the biblical reference point for inner personal demons is not the stories of exorcisms, but Jesus' instruction concerning inner evil in Mark 7:14–15, 21–23. Jesus does not subscribe to the opinion that our emotions or habits can or should be cast out by exorcism. To attempt to cast out something essential to the self is like performing castration to deal with lust. In Wink's opinion, great harm is done by well-intended, self-appointed "exorcists," largely in charismatic or Pentecostal circles, who attempt to exorcise people who are not genuinely possessed by outer personal demons.[60]

As an example, Wink tells of taking a depressed friend to a charismatic prayer meeting where the leader offered to pray for her. In doing so he "cast out" her spirit of depression. But this woman's depression, as Wink later learned, was caused by frustration and repressed anger over the lack of opportunities for creative expression in the new community to which she had moved. In her case, "casting out" her depression merely drove the reasons for her depression deeper into her unconscious and denied her the opportunity of gaining insight into her problem. In addition, it added another layer of guilt for not getting better.[61]

Wink contends that it is imperative that any person dealing with the demonic learn to discern between inner and outer demons. Inner demons are usually not intrinsically evil, but are rendered grotesque from suppression, paralyzed from disuse, or wounded from rejection. They are the part of us regarded as socially unacceptable. Such inner personal demons rob us of our self-esteem. They undermine our ego's strategies for gaining respect by an outer show of competence or virtue. They are not worthy of fear, but they can be a terror to the person who has not entered upon the death of the ego and rebirth to a positive life in Christ. With the power of the indwelling Christ taking a central position in a person's life, progress and ultimate victory are possible. In the case of such inner personal demons, psychotherapy can prove invaluable.[62]

Beginning with the New Testament, it has been traditional, according to Wink, to speak of the distinction between inner personal and outer personal demons by contrasting "losing one's soul" and "being freed from a spirit." "Losing one's soul" referred to the danger of being deprived of some essential aspect of personal identity (Matt. 16:26). To this they contrasted being freed from a "spirit"—an alien invader that has seized the personality and holds it captive (Luke 4:31–37; 8:26–38). It is therefore a loss to "lose one's soul," but a relief to lose a "spirit."[63]

V. What Is the Classical Orthodox or Evangelical Model and Its Practical Implications?

In general, the evangelical approach has heeded the advice of C. S. Lewis, who once stated that there are two dangers in dealing with the satanic and the demonic. One danger is to disbelieve or underestimate their reality and power. The other danger is to have an excessive interest in or obsession with the satanic and demonic.[64]

1. The Source of Our Knowledge About Demonic Activity

In the evangelical view, the essence of our knowledge about the work of Satan and demons rests on the authority of revelation. The Bible shows us that demons are continually at war against God and humanity. They haunt and exploit the material world and those who inhabit it. They are strong and cunning, yet devoid of true wisdom and powerless against the Cross. Theology can seek to draw out the implications of what is said in the Bible.[65]

In addition to the biblical revelation, there are two experiential sources of knowledge about fallen angels and their methods. One source is a kind of direct, nonsensory spiritual awareness. The other source of knowledge is observation of the effects of their deliberate actions. Humans can perceive in themselves and others the effects of demonic activity and so draw conclusions about them. Experience shows us, for example, that although demons cannot act directly upon the will, they can and do act upon the imagination, thoughts, emotions, and desires. Where they find a passion alive and active in us, they can play upon this passion and so intensify it. Bodily sensations, too, evidently can be awakened by the same agency.[66]

There are, however, difficulties in relation to these experiential sources. One is that it is too easy to accept an event uncritically as a product of demonic agency without adequately considering other causes which may also be at work. This is especially true where there is a strong imaginative and emotional interest in the idea of the demonic and a comparatively slight knowledge of the ways of the world and of the human soul. For this reason, discrimination is certainly needed when it comes to discerning the work of the demonic in this world—and the biblical witness should always be the primary source.[67]

The Fuller Theological Seminary Task Force which studied discernment of spirits and exorcism pointed out that the gift of discerning the presence of evil spirits in people, above all other gifts, must be exercised with great care and reserve. Within any Christian community, the power accompanying discernment must be used only with humble submission to the community's open critique. The danger is perhaps greatest when a child is involved.[68]

2. The Evangelical View of Satan's Methods

(1) Satan the Deceiver. Satan works as a spirit. A person may say truthfully that he or she has met Satan, but not in the sense that we meet another human being. For Satan is not tangible in the way that matter is tangible. In particular, he no more has horns, hooves, and a forked tail than God has a long white beard. (John A. Sanford suggests that the horned image of Satan was derived from a horned male god of the pre-Christian era in England.)[69]

Like God, Satan can manifest himself in and through material beings, even though he himself is not material. Peck tells of one case in which Satan manifested himself in a patient through the patient's writhing serpentine body, biting teeth, scratching nails, and hooded reptilian eyes. But there were no fangs, no scales. Satan was, through the use of the patient's body, extraordinarily and dramatically and even supernaturally snakelike. But he is not himself a snake. He is spirit. His power was exercised through the patient's body.[70]

Although there is a certain mystery in the way Satan works, his chief means of operation is clear: He is a liar and a deceiver. He began his evil work with a lie in the Garden, convincing Eve that eating the forbidden fruit would be good for her. And he continues his work in the world today through lies and misrepresentation.

Paul said that Satan often disguises himself as an angel of light, and that his servants disguise themselves as servants of righteousness (2 Cor. 11:14–15). Even worse, he has "blinded the minds of the unbelievers, to keep them from seeing the light of the gospel of the glory of Christ, who is the likeness of God" (2 Cor. 4:4). Satan's use of deception is also mentioned in Revelation 12:9 and 20:8, 10, where he is depicted as deceiving the entire world.

Scott Peck tells of two patients who became possessed because they bought Satan's false seductive promise of "friendship." Possession was maintained because they believed his threats that they would die without him. And the possession was ended when both chose to believe his lies no longer, but instead to transcend their fear by trust in the resurrected Christ and to pray to the God of Truth for deliverance. For these patients, the process of exorcism was actually the process of confronting Satan's lies. And each exorcism was concluded successfully by a change of faith or value system. Peck states that he now knows what Jesus meant when he so frequently said, "By your faith you have been healed."[71]

Satan's deceitful nature is important to remember in view of the recent flare-up of interest in the phenomenon of demon possession. Some Christians have come to regard highly emotional and dramatic cases of possession as the primary manifestation of the forces of evil. In actuality, Satan, the great deceiver, may be encouraging interest in outwardly dramatic cases in hopes that Christians will become careless about other more subtle forms of influence by the powers of evil.[72]

Satan is subtle, and he works by making evil attractive. It is only after we have been enslaved by him that we see the ugly, destructive, devastating side of Satan. From the outside, evil is attractive, luring, enticing, promising much. Adam looked at the fruit on the tree and it looked ripe and luscious—not poisonous and decayed. If it had not been beautiful, would he have been tempted to eat it?[73]

Satan and the evil he promotes have always been attractive, never ugly. That is why he entices so many. Surely the modern drug addict with glazed eyes, hollow hopes, and a dashed future did not at the outset intend to prostitute his potential and shatter his life! No addicted youngster would become involved if at the beginning he could foresee the result. No, at first, drugs did not appear ugly at all to the future addict. Instead, they held out the hope of an expanded mind, an exhilarating vision of goodness, or at very least a release from pain and alienation. It was only after the pact had been made that the savagery of drugs exploded, carrying away all hope in the tidal wave of dehumanization.[74]

(2) Personal Evil and Structural or Collective Evil. Satan's work in the lives of individuals is widely recognized. But it is important to understand that Satan also works through groups of people and organizational structures—political, social, even religious. In fact, one of the problems with the *The Exorcist* is that it depicts the devil and the demonic as primarily concerned with individual sexual aberration. But the New Testament reveals that in Jesus' day it was not so much the harlots as the respectable Pharisees and the religious and political systems who were the chief agents of Satan.

Now, this is not to say that Satan does not work in individuals or that he has nothing to do with sexual aberration. From the perspective of the inbreaking new order of God brought by Jesus, both the personal and the structural views are correct, but only in tension with each other. The notion that people are solely the victims of Satan as he works through outer oppressive structures is too limited. The view that Satan works exclusively through the individual isolates people from the social context and thus ignores a vital aspect of human experience.[75]

A truer understanding of persons sees them as the network of relationships in which they are embedded. This means that the individual can never be considered in isolation from the political, economic, and social conditions into which he or she was born and by which, to a significant degree, he or she has been formed.

Increasing numbers of therapists and theologians are recognizing that personal healing is impossible to attain if it ignores the political, economic, and social conditions that helped produce the problems in the first place. On the other hand, some liberation theologians are recognizing that long-term struggles for justice require more than tools of political analysis and a praxis or strategy for social transformation. Also needed are therapies capable of removing "all the flaming darts of the evil one" (Eph. 6:16) that have carried the poisons of self-doubt, fatalism, and personal sin directly into the bloodstream of oppressed individuals.[76]

Today, evangelicals tend to see Satan as working at both the individual and the corporate level. But he is seen as especially powerful when incarnated in social institutions. In fact, Wink suggests that there is an actual inner spirit in dehumanizing institutions and social systems. The social demonic is the spirit exuded by a corporate structure that has turned its back on its divine vocation as a creature of God and has made its own goals the highest good—exploiting its workers and paying little heed to the needs of the surrounding community. The demonic is the spirit that enters itself into "the system" that dehumanizes all it touches. It is the spirit that inhabits today's drug culture and social patterns of adult culture such as excessive drinking, racial hatred, materialism, and greed. Satan rules from within by the consent of those involved, but the evil that results is greater than the sum of the evil in the hearts of the individuals.[77]

The personal darkness and evil in the depths of the human soul are attracted to the collective expressions in society. They can even erupt into a frenzy of violence in the permissive context of a riot, revolution, or war. Feelings of inferiority can be played on by dictators to produce monsters who compensate for their low self-esteem by seeking revenge on those whom they blame for having caused it. An evil ego like Hitler would get nowhere if he were not riding the cresting wave of resentment from millions of would-be evil egos longing to be released from the restraints of truth and civility. Together the institution and the individual form a united front of hostility to the redeeming purposes of God.[78]

Sören Kierkegaard once stated that diabolical possession in modern times happens en masse. It is for this reason that people gather into flocks—in order that natural, animal hysteria should take hold of them; in order to feel themselves stimulated, inflamed, and beside themselves. Wink points out that we puzzle over what it was in an individual that caused him to become insane. As members of a society which is ravishing the environment and arming itself to oblivion, we are perplexed at the high rate of suicides. The early church had already to some degree anticipated our situation. It regarded everyone prior to conversion as possessed, by virtue of belonging to a world that is in rebellion against God.[79]

Today, even the inoculation of conversion and baptism has not prevented our being sucked up into mass possession. Our century has known some of the most bizarre and horrifying examples of collective possession in human history. Charles Manson, Jim Jones, and Adolf Hitler tapped a deep longing in their followers to belong to a movement that gave their lives significance and to surrender themselves to the all-wise power of a "godlike" ruler. Collective demonism is the abdication of human answerability to God and the investment of final judgment in some kind of divinized mortal being—either an individual or a system. And those who are thus possessed seldom know it until too late.[80]

Martin Luther King, Jr., declared in 1967 that the United States is the greatest purveyor of violence in the world. But we do not feel possessed. Wink maintains that we do not see that the demonic has been installed at the heart of national policy. The nation (administration, Congress, armed forces, CIA) carries out for us the dirty work required to maintain American political and economic dominance in the world. Most of us would rather not know the bloody tale of deeds performed on our behalf. According to Ernest Becker, when evil is socialized, the public is relieved of guilt and rendered morally exempt in what is in fact a condition of group sadism.[81]

(3) Observed Techniques of Demonic Operation. Several different interpretations have been presented by evangelicals as to how the demonic actually operates. British theologian J. Stafford Wright contends that the place of possession by an evil spirit is the human spirit, which is the gateway to the spiritual world. In this view, the human spirit is the "control center" for the whole of a person's being. If a person's spirit is empty, he will be either unorganized or organized around some inadequate center. Unhealthy complexes may develop as a natural consequence, producing mental and physical symptoms. Possession by a demon may intensify these symptoms and may also produce a flood of supernormal effects. The demon may seize on unpleasant personality groupings that are already forming and emerge as a new personality in the person. If the case is genuine demon possession, the casting out of the demon in the name of Jesus Christ will enable the normal personality to function again and the symptoms to disappear.[82]

Scott Peck sees the process of possession as a gradual one. Peck states that he very much doubts that somebody can go walking down the street one day and have a demon jump out from behind a bush and penetrate him. According to his observation, possession happens over a period of time, in which the possessed person repeatedly sells out for one reason or another. One primary reason people sell out to Satan seems to be loneliness. But there are other possible reasons—reasons that Peck suspects might be primary in other cases.[83]

Donald G. Bloesch states that too often demon possession as a state of spiritual bondage is dismissed by modern thinkers because of its association with primitive mythological religion. Thus he suggests that, in contrast to primitive conceptions, the names of demons should be understood as representing desires implanted in the heart by Satan, such as death, lust, and hatred. The voices of the demons, which are regarded as so significant in primitive religious circles, should generally be interpreted as the voices of the other self, the alter-ego, although the content of what is said may very well be directed by the devil. At the same time, a "split personality" or "multiple personality" does not always indicate possession; it could signify incomplete possession, since there are still aspects of the personality not under the control of Satan.[84]

(4) The Progressive Steps of Demonic Enslavement. In the work of Satan, there are several levels of progressive influence—only the last of which is actual possession. First, there is the level of temptation. Then there is the second level of oppression or obsession. At this stage a person still has some freedom in his or her personality, but is on the way to becoming a slave of sin (Rom. 6). Someone who is oppressed by Satan is oftentimes depressed, discouraged, and disillusioned. There may also be a nonreceptivity to divine things, deep doubt, continued compulsions, and chronic fears.[85]

The third and final stage is possession. It is quite rare. The authentic marks of demon possession are very extreme and seldom seen. They are easily recognized as pathological, even if their true nature is unrecognized. (Distinguishing between possession and mental illness will be discussed in a later part of this chapter.) Scott Peck and Malachi Martin agree that most of the cases we call possession should more properly be termed "partial," "incomplete," or "imperfect" possession.[86]

Bloesch suggests that we should distinguish between being a prisoner of Satan, which is possession, and being the servant of Satan, which is subjection. All servants of sin are in one sense servants of Satan, in that sin is the will of the devil and not the will of God. Yet to be a prisoner of Satan in the full sense means that one must choose just as the devil chooses. Sinners as such still have the freedom to choose between greater and lesser evils. Some say this should be seen as a distinction between oppression by the devil and possession by the devil. All people, including Christians, are tempted by the devil, but only a few people become wholly possessed.[87]

The Roman Catholic Church claims to have found only nineteen or twenty cases in the twentieth century that they believe are authentic cases of demon possession. This underlines the evangelical conviction that actual possession is quite rare. It most likely occurs after considerable and persistent moral decay has taken place. Recurrent temptations are common to all Christians and these should be dealt with through repentance and cleansing by the atonement of Christ. Demonic oppression requires the same remedy, and may also be helped by careful counseling to deal with the effects of the oppression (such as depression). Insanity is in no way synonymous with demon possession.

3. The Evangelical View of the Relation of Occult Activities and the Demonic

In general, evangelicals follow the traditional church view that there is a direct connection between involvement in the occult and demonic influence. Scott Peck, for instance, tells of a case in which the demonic enslavement process seemed to have begun with involvement in the occult at the age of twelve. It seems clear from the literature on possession that the majority of cases have had involvement with the occult—a frequency far greater than might be expected in the general population. This does not mean to imply that all people who involve themselves with the occult will become possessed. However, any relation to the occult does seem to increase the chances of demonic possession or at least demonic influence.[88]

The traditional churches have spoken of the danger of the occult as far back as their literature goes. From its earliest beginnings, the church has recognized the reality that certain human beings could have extraordinary powers, such as prophetic ability. It labeled such powers "charisms," or gifts. By this word, *gift*, the church implied that such powers could be given to humans by God at a time and for a purpose of God's own choosing. However, when one involves oneself in the occult, wittingly or unwittingly, one is attempting to obtain, maintain, or enhance such power for one's own purposes. This the church calls magic and denounces as contrary to God's purposes.

Practitioners of the occult often also refer to it as magic, but they distinguish between white magic and black magic. White magicians decry black magicians for practicing their art for evil motives. However, they feel comfortable with their own practice because they are convinced of their loving motives. But it is very easy to be self-deceptive about one's motives as well as to predict the outcome of one's actions. So, as far as the church is concerned, magic is magic, and all of it is black or potentially so.[89]

4. The Relationship between the Demonic and Human Sickness

(1) The Relationship between Demonic Powers and Illness in General. Evangelicals generally believe, with Colin Brown, that it is wrongheaded to attribute all sickness to demonic powers and to treat healing as if it were basically a matter of exorcism. The two are not identical, and Jesus did not treat them in the same way.[90]

There is nothing in the New Testament to suggest that all illness is attributable to demonic activity; possession is clearly distinguished from physical illness. Furthermore, contrary to the assertions of some charismatics, there is no suggestion in the New Testament or anywhere in the Bible that different parts of the human body are subject to different demons. Again, we do not find any warrant in the New Testament for cursing particular diseases, as do some charismatics. This was not the practice of Jesus.[91]

(2) Distinctions between Demonic Activity and Mental Illness. The same principle, in general, applies to mental illness. Just as Christians are prone to physical

illness, so they may fall victim to mental illness. Nothing can be more harmful to those who are distressed psychologically than to be told they are possessed or to be "treated" by exorcism.[92]

The distinction between demonic activity and mental illness is more difficult to make, however, because the symptoms of the two can be quite similar. In addition, the two may occur simultaneously, and possession may cause or worsen mental illness.

Donald Bloesch makes a helpful distinction in pointing out that, while mental illness is a disorder of the mind, demon possession is the bondage of the will to radical evil. And it is possible for mental illness to be a symptom and manifestation of such spiritual slavery. Bloesch also points out that the insights and methods of psychology are not fully adequate to deal with some cases, which represent the bondage of the will rather than disorders of the mind.[93]

Scott Peck believes that there has to be a significant emotional or mental disorder for the possession to occur in the first place, and that once the possession has taken place, it will both aggravate the original problem and create new ones. According to Peck, the proper question is not: "Is the patient possessed or is he or she mentally ill?" but rather: "Is the patient just mentally ill, or is he or she mentally ill *and* possessed?"[94]

In one case, Peck had a patient who had originally gone to another psychiatrist to be treated for an actual complaint of possession. The psychiatrist—an unusually skilled, open-minded, and caring individual—did not believe this self-diagnosis and repeatedly attempted to treat the case with drugs and psychotherapy, without any success. This patient was aware from the beginning not only of the self-destructive part of himself, but also of the fact that this part had a distinct and alien personality. In many ways, the secondary personality seemed like a personified resistance, although it was not reported as being frankly evil. However, in the therapy that eventually resulted in exorcism, the secondary personality was revealed to be blatantly evil.[95]

Wink agrees with Peck that exorcism should be utilized only as a last resort, after every other avenue of help has been exhausted. Even for the most experienced exorcists, discernment can be a tricky business.[96]

The Fuller Seminary Task Force agrees that we must be sensitive to life's mysterious vulnerability to destructive demonic forces. However, we must be equally sensitive to the need for responsibility in any actual diagnosis of demons as the cause for mental illness. The need for controls is intensified if the discerner of the demonic also claims the power to exorcise.[97]

5. Considerations in Treating Demonic Possession on a Personal Level

(1) The Criteria and Symptoms of Demonic Possession. There are some generally accepted criteria and symptoms of demonic possession. Wink lists four:

First, the exorcist discerns an evil presence or personality that is alien to that of the individual being exorcised. The presence of demonic "personalities" in stricken people has been reliably documented, and it is hair-raising. Many examples of possession are given in T. K. Oesterreich's classic study on demon possession. But here again we must discover whether the phenomenon in question is personal or collective—and, if it is personal, whether it is an inner or outer demon. If the problem arises from the personal subconscious, it must be accepted, owned, loved, and integrated. Otherwise exorcism becomes the amputation of a part of the self, not a healing. Only if the "demon" is genuinely outer and alien should it be "cast out."[98]

Second, the possessed person speaks in voices distinctly other than his or her own, or even in foreign languages unknown to the victim. According to the New Testament, demons are able to speak, presumably using the vocal equipment of the person possessed (e.g., Matt. 8:29, 31; Mark 1:24, 26, 34; 5:7, 9–10; Luke 4:41; 8:28, 30). It is extremely difficult to tell whether the "voice" emanating from a person is his or her own, cast in a different range, or an alien "demonic being" speaking through the person. Its presence in conjunction with other symptoms of possession is significant, but not sufficient of itself to indicate the need for exorcism.[99]

Third, the possessed person utters blasphemies against God and everything sacred. Often this appears in total contrast to the person's usual demeanor. He also resists any divine influence. What usually comes out is an inversion of the values that the person holds. Again, however, it is difficult to know whether the blasphemies are repressed feelings of the person or genuine diabolical tirades.

Fourth, the possessed person displays "impossible" physical contortions and undergoes convulsions. Contortions and convulsions may attend demonic possession, but they are not adequate criteria for identifying a phenomenon as demonic.[100]

(2) The Need for Corporate Wisdom. Wink is not enthusiastic about retrogressing to a world obsessed with the fear of demons and a paranoid tendency to find evil anywhere but within. He believes that the majority of cases of pathological behavior are probably due to inner personal demons—those alienated aspects of the self that need to be embraced, not exorcised. But Wink insists that in cases of genuine outer personal possession, it is important to build a team to counter the evil, and that team should include a skilled theologian and a cooperative psychiatrist. In Wink's opinion, we have let ourselves grow too unfamiliar with such things; therefore, corporate wisdom is required.[101]

Once again, however, it is important not to become obsessed with the workings of the demonic. It must be remembered that the early church freed people from fear of demons, not so much by grim combat, but by a triumphant mocking of their importance in the face of the risen Christ. Athanasius, an early church father, said that the Christians chased the demons away and mocked at the devil. In other words, Jesus and his first followers focused on the *new reality*, not on the darkness. And successful confrontation with the powers of darkness today require that same kind of focus on Christ's assured victory. Christian exorcists have learned by experience to ask no questions of the alleged indwelling demons, but to emphasize that Christ is sovereign over them.[102]

(3) The Nature of Psychic Disintegration. Donald Jacobs suggests that much psychiatric work is little more than an exercise of description. Ultimately the question remains: Why do people have a tendency toward pathological disintegration? At least a partial answer to this question is to be found in the area of the will, where a person makes either positive or negative decisions about the business of living. If the questions about why a person should love or live are not answered, then the demons can move in and produce a variety of symptoms ranging from schizophrenia to suicidal compulsion.[103]

In fact, Scott Peck has defined mental health as an ongoing process of dedication to reality at all costs. Satan is utterly dedicated to opposing that process. Accordingly, the best definition for Satan is that he is a real spirit of unreality. It is important to stress that word *real,* however. There are systems of thought these days, such as Christian Science, which define evil as unreality. But this is only a half-truth. For although the spirit of evil is one of unreality, the evil one himself is real.[104]

Satan's personality cannot be characterized simply by an absence, a nothingness. It is true that there is an absence of love in his personality. But his personality is also pervaded by the active presence of hate. Quite simply, Satan really exists, and he wants to destroy us. To think otherwise is to be misled. Indeed, as several have commented, perhaps Satan's best deception is his general success in concealing his own reality from the human mind.[105]

(4) Importance of the Dynamic Power of Christ and Love in Addressing Personality Disorders. When people reach the low stage of disintegration, society moves in and tries to help reintegrate them. In most cases, the person is placed in the hands of the modern shaman, the psychiatrist. The psychiatrist is supposed to lead them to self-understanding and convince them that there is purpose in life. If this does not become clear, more powerful techniques, such as drug therapy or electronic shock therapy may follow, and in some cases, conditioning techniques are used.[106]

But as Scott Peck points out, traditional psychotherapy—whether it be psychoanalytically oriented or not—deliberately makes little or no use whatsoever of power. It is conducted in an atmosphere of total freedom. The patient is free to quit therapy at any time. Indeed, he or she is free to leave even in the middle of a session. Except for the threat of refusing to see the patient anymore, the therapist has no weapons with which to push for change beyond the persuasive power of his or her own wits, understanding, and love.[107]

Exorcism is another matter. Here the healer calls upon every power that is legitimately, lovingly available in the battle against the patient's sickness. First of all, as Wink pointed out, exorcism is usually conducted by a team of at least three or more. In a sense, this team "gangs up" on the patient. Unlike traditional therapy, which is a matter of one "against" one, in exorcism the patient is outnumbered.[108]

In ordinary psychotherapy, the session is no more than an hour, and the patient knows this. If they want to, patients can evade almost any issue for an hour. But exorcism sessions may last three, five, even ten or twelve hours—as long as the team feels is required to confront the issue.

Finally—and most importantly—the exorcism team, through prayer and claiming the victory of Christ over the demonic world, invokes the power of God in the healing process. The nonbeliever would deem this an ineffective measure or else explain its effectiveness in terms of the mere power of suggestion. But the Christian exorcist believes that God—not the exorcist—completes the process and does the healing. The whole purpose of the prayer and claim of the Christian resources is to bring the power of God into the fray.

(5) Requirements for Effective Exorcism. As a trained physician, Peck contends that exorcism is not a magical procedure. As in psychotherapy, it makes use of analysis, of careful discernment, of interpretation, of encouragement, and of loving confrontation.[109]

Exorcism also calls for intuitive insight, spiritual discernment, deep understanding of theology, thorough knowledge of psychiatry, and great experience with prayer. No one person can possess all these skills. In exorcisms of a serious nature, while the exorcist is the coordinator in charge, a true team approach is necessary. The Fuller Seminary Task Force emphasizes that the Christian community should insist that the team include people trained and skilled in diagnosis and therapy. All involved should be spiritually mature and responsible.[110]

Perhaps the most important tool the exorcism team must bring to bear is love. Peck suggests that Satan's intelligence is afflicted with a basic blind spot. By virtue of his extreme self-centeredness, he has no real understanding of the phenomenon of love. He recognizes love as a reality to be fought and even to be imitated. But because he himself is utterly lacking in love, he does not understand it in the least.[111] For this reason, love is an effective weapon against him.

(6) Dangers and Safeguards in Exorcism. Because it not only condones but insists on the use of power, exorcism is a dangerous procedure for both the patient and the people who undertake the exorcism.[112] For this reason, it is not to be undertaken lightly or casually.

In fact, the New Testament seems to suggest that a confrontation with Satan should be avoided whenever possible. It is significant that in the ministry of Paul we read only once of his casting out an evil spirit, and this he did apparently reluctantly after being bothered for many days by the girl who was possessed (Acts 16:16–18).

Some Christian leaders, especially during the counterculture revolution and occult craze in California, have similarly been forced by circumstances into exorcism. As a result, they suffered extreme mental, physical, and emotional exhaustion. And while they have rejoiced in the victory which has been accomplished in the name of Christ, they nonetheless shrink from any further direct confrontation with Satan unless it is absolutely necessary. This attitude is strikingly different from that of some Christians who are seeking spirits everywhere to cast out. It underlines the conviction that a confrontation with Satan is not something to be sought out unless there is no other choice.[113]

According to Scott Peck, most trained Christian psychiatrists would agree that there is real psychological danger to the exorcist and the other team members. Even though team members are carefully chosen for their psychological strength as well as their love, the procedures are stressful for everyone. In addition, because power is always subject to misuse, there is a certain danger to the patient as well.[114]

For these reasons, Peck believes exorcism should be used only in cases of personality disturbance so severe that regular varieties of psychotherapy are doomed to failure. Moreover, he believes it should be regarded as an experimental procedure until it has been scientifically investigated.

Furthermore, Peck believes that what prevents exorcism from being true brainwashing is that, as with surgery, the individual consents to the procedure. Therefore, as a safeguard against the misuse of power in exorcism, he stresses the issue of informed consent. Peck believes that before the procedure of exorcism, persons should sign not simple but elaborate authorization forms. They should know exactly what they are letting themselves in for. And if a patient is clearly incapable of such awareness, a guardian should be enlisted to make a reasoned decision for him or her. Careful records should be kept.[115]

Peck goes on to say that the greatest safeguard in the process of exorcism is—once again—love. Only with love can exorcists discern between interventions that are "fair" and necessary and those that are manipulative or truly violating. The healing of serious cases requires more than knowledge and skill; only love can heal.[116]

6. Dealing with Collective or Mass Demonic Possession

Up to this point, we have talked primarily about the process of confronting or driving out the outer personal demons. But collective or mass possession by the demonic also calls for a kind of exorcism, modeled after Jesus' act of cleansing the temple (Mark 11:11, 15–19).

This act is pictured as the climax of Jesus' ministry and the central focus of his journey to Jerusalem. It was the final provocation of his arrest and execution: "And the chief priests heard it and sought a way to destroy him" (v. 19).

The act of cleansing the temple stands in the line of the great symbolic acts of the prophets as exorcisms of collective evil. The fact that the buyers and traders were back in their stalls soon after in no way invalidates the efficacy of Jesus' act. In fact, the destruction of the temple in 70 A.D. confirms it. But the point of collective exorcism is not primarily reform, but revelation. There must be the unveiling of unsuspected evil in high places.[117]

It is important to remember that the success of an attempted collective exorcism has no bearing on its immediate results. It is an act of obedience, performed in the name of the inbreaking new order in Jesus Christ. Its truth may not be acknowledged by the targeted evil power or by the public at large. However, the act is efficacious if it bears witness to the truth in a climate of lies.[118]

One important task of the church in the face of collective possession is therefore consciousness-raising. Whenever people "love not their lives even unto death" (see Rev. 12:11), they become free from Satan's final threat and Satan is cast down. The witness of the martyrs does not end Satan's power; rather, it drives him to desperation, "because he knows that his time is short" (v. 12). None of this negates the value of the martyr's witness. For through what they tell about what they see, they make it possible for people to continue to take their stand against evil.[119]

The act of collective exorcism can unveil a system dominated by Satan. It reveals an entire network of injustices that the kingdom of Satan maintains for those who benefit from evil. Exorcism is also radical. It speaks to the problem of ideological blindness. To a much greater extent than we are aware, we are possessed by the values and powers of our sinful order. It is not enough then simply to repent of the ways in which we have consciously chosen to cooperate with evil. We must be freed from our unconscious involvement as well by being confronted by the total biblical revelation.[120]

This understanding of exorcising collective evil can reconcile the institutional, social, and individual views of evil. We must realize that the person possessed must see that he is a part of the sickness of our culture. On the other hand, the collective possession of our culture feeds on the unredeemed darkness of individuals. The demonic confronts us as a single realm, personal and collective and inner and outer.[121]

Once again, the resources to confront and combat both personal and collective evil are in the biblical revelation. There we find the cause of evil and the biblical presentation of the deliverance from evil in Jesus Christ.

7. The Central Evangelical Thrust Regarding the Demonic

The main thrust of the New Testament and, hence, the evangelical approach, is the positive emphasis on Christian resources. I have already indicated that both the Old Testament and the New Testament are practical and redemptive. They are also triumphant; as Colossians 2:15 says, Christ has overcome the demonic forces.

Both Luther and Wesley, following the New Testament, reacted against the elaborate exorcist rites that had been developed by the Medieval church. Both Reformers said that there should be less emphasis on the power of Satan and more emphasis on the positive proclamation of the Christian gospel and prayer.

In a similar vein, Donald Bloesch contends that we are freed from the demonic powers not by incantations and magic, but by the proclamation of the gospel and the prayers of the church. Although Bloesch admits that there may be a place for a liturgy of exorcism, he stresses that the church must be aware of a pseudoexorcism which is actually magic. Our reliance must not be on psychic dynamics and drama, but on the word of the Cross, which alone is able to expel the demons.[122]

When it comes to facing evil and the reality of satanic power, it is important to remember that in Christ's resurrection and ascension and in the coming of the Holy Spirit, the powers of Christ are available to us today wherever we live. Since Christ has this power, we do not have to struggle by ourselves. As the apostle Paul said, "I will all the more gladly boast of my weaknesses, that the power of Christ may rest upon me . . . for when I am weak, then I am strong" (2 Cor. 12:9–10).

This, of course, does not mean that the Christian life is easy. Satan keeps us under attack. This is what we call demon influence. Even when we have had our shining hour, when we think that our personal victory has been won, Satan still pursues us. He pursues the church and the denominations. Alexander Whyte, the famous Scottish preacher, said that the bloodhounds of Satan will follow us all of the days of our lives and leave their bloody slaver on the gates of heaven as we go in.

But even as Satan pursues us, Christ upholds us. This, of course, points up the importance of prayer, fellowship, and worship in growing closer to the Source of our strength. We also grow stronger as we try to help other people and channel our resources in redemptive channels.

Centuries ago, John Bunyan portrayed the powers of darkness as lions chained on a short leash on either side of the road which leads to the celestial city. The lions can maul travelers who wander from the middle of the path. But they cannot touch those who walk precisely in the center. In our struggle, then, we must remember that the satanic forces are chained by the victory of Christ. Their attacks can simply force us back to reliance on Christ's redemptive work.

VI. What Are Some Summary Concluding Emphases?

In today's troubled times, there are those, such as writer Hal Lindsey, who claim that these are the last days and that Satan has literally taken over our culture. However, Richard Lovelace, a historian of Christianity from Gordon-Conwell Seminary, cautions us about making such assumptions in a dogmatic manner. No crisis era in history has been without those who claimed they were living literally in the very last days.

But Lovelace introduces another possibility. The revival of the demonic in our days may be a sign not of Satan's triumph, but of a renewed Christian offensive. It is possible that revived and reformed Christianity could regain some of its power over the conscience of the Western world and reach out in a new way to all nations of the world with the Christian message of redemption.[123]

Gustave Flaubert, the well-known French writer, once described the village church of his boyhood experience. During stormy days, two kinds of beings used to flee into the churches for refuge. First were the birds, who would come in to protect themselves from the storm. Then the villagers, the peasants, would come seeking help from the demonic forces that they felt were unchained and were about to overcome them. Let us pray that in the midst of the demonic forces besetting us that many people will once again come fleeing to Christ and his church for deliverance.

Our task as Christians today is not to reinforce or simply echo secular society's morbid preoccupation with satanic power. Rather, it is important for us, who know the victory over Satan and the demonic that is available in Christ, to share our vision and victory with a renewed urgency. We should stride forward vigorously into the mainstream of our time with the transforming shout of victory, the good news of the gospel, which is the announcement that Jesus Christ is stronger than sin, death, and the devil.[124]

7

The Question of Evil and Personal Suffering

I. What Is the Background of the Urgency and Extent of the Question of Evil and Personal Suffering?

The problem of evil and personal suffering has always been a human concern. Through the centuries, men and women have experienced pain and sorrow and groaned, "Why?" Today, when every newscast seems to bring a new tale of woe—starving children, mass murders, political oppression, incurable disease—the question is an especially crucial one. The anxiety we feel about the problem of evil and suffering—especially the suffering of innocents—is in fact reflected in modern art, literature, drama, and films.

1. Representative Modern Expressions of Evil and Suffering as a Crucial Issue

(1) The Writings of Camus. For example, Albert Camus, one of the most widely read novelists of the twentieth century and the winner of the 1957 Nobel Prize for literature, was almost overwhelmed by the problem of evil and suffering. Note the titles of his major works: *The Stranger, The Plague, The Fall,* and *The Rebel.*[1]

Camus's preoccupation with the problem of evil is mostly rooted in his own unhappy childhood. He was born in Algeria during the days when it was controlled by France. His father was killed in war when he was a baby. His mother was deaf, had a speech impediment, and could neither read nor write. She worked as a cleaning woman to support her family. Living with them in their two-room apartment were a grandmother who was dying of cancer and a paralyzed uncle. At the age of seventeen, Camus looked death in the face through an acute attack of tuberculosis.

Following his mother's example, Camus rejected with contempt the religion of the poor around them, who quietly accepted their suffering. His master's thesis, in fact, was on early Christianity, Augustine, and the problem of evil. His subsequent fiction also centered around the themes of evil and suffering. For example, in *The Rebel,* published in 1951, he estimated that seventy million human beings had been uprooted, enslaved, or killed in the twentieth century alone. In his mind, suffering of such dimensions could not be explained by anything but an absurd, purposeless universe.[2]

Even though Camus considered that the fact that the world is without purpose and existence is a guarantee of suffering, he did not call for escape or suicide. Rather, he suggested that we should assume the burden of existence and rebel continuously. By such "metaphysical rebellion," as he called it, he did not mean simply a disbelief in God, but a profound protest against the way things are. "The rebel defies more than he denies," asserted Camus, and so the rebel commits himself to the desperate effort to build up human values and a tolerable human existence in the midst of a world which threatens him constantly with suffering and death. But Camus believed that, in the end, even rebellion is hopeless and no less absurd than the absurdity against which it protests.

Camus's concerns and ideas were shared by several other influential writers of his day—most of whom are classified with him as existentialists. Franz Kafka, Eugene O'Neill, and Jean Paul Sartre all in their own way saw life as alienation and absurdity, yet also insisted that people should continue to strive after what little meaning and dignity is possible.[3]

(2) The Holocaust. In a larger context, the paradigm evil event of the twentieth century is the Holocaust—the murder of six million Jews by the Nazis during World War II. Through tales told by survivors and through the grim witness of photographs and newsreels, the names of death camps such as those at Auschwitz and Dachau have become etched in our collective minds as symbols of evil on an unprecedented scale.

In a sense, the Holocaust changed forever the way modern men and women think about the human capacity for evil, because it rendered all our previous explanations of suffering either obsolete or insufficient. Not only does the Holocaust evoke new questions about suffering; it does so on a public scale which has a traumatic impact on our souls. In the face of this event, how can human beings claim to be created "in the image of God"? How can they claim any dignity and decency? Does not the Holocaust, as many have asked, proclaim the utter bankruptcy of human nature—even the death of Western Christian culture?[4]

In an earlier time, the paradigm natural evil event was the terrible Lisbon earthquake of 1 November 1755. Followed by fires and even a flood of the Tagus River, the disaster destroyed the city and killed tens of thousands of people. An equally powerful example of natural evil occurred in December of 1988, when Soviet Armenia suffered the most devastating earthquake of recent history. It claimed approximately sixty thousand lives and left five hundred thousand people homeless.

The Lisbon and Armenian earthquakes are examples of natural evil; the Holocaust, of moral evil. Although the earthquakes are important symbols of human suffering, it is perhaps fitting that the Holocaust has replaced such natural evil events as earthquakes in our minds as *the* evil event of history. Twentieth-century people, because of the advances in technology, have seen the rise of mass organization and totalitarian political ideologies. This means that we are acutely conscious of the tremendous power human beings have to inflict suffering on each other.[5]

(3) Recent Intensification of the Problem of Evil and Suffering. The modern era does not have a special corner on suffering, of course. In contrast to former times, however, modern technology and the media bring world events and their attendant suffering directly into our homes. Such proximity to world events is a new feature of our time. It is also a cause of much stress and anxiety, not only because the reality of far-off events overwhelms us psychologically, but also because our new awareness of our interdependent world reminds us that any event anywhere may affect us directly.

Our exposure to suffering is a daily and global reality. Indeed, it seems to hit us from every direction and from every corner of the earth: repressed blacks and terrified whites in South Africa, struggling laborers in Poland, beleaguered Jews and Arabs in the Holy Land, starving children in Africa, refugees in camps around the world. And these random samples do not even include the plight of the homeless in our streets, or conditions in the Bronx or Brownsville, or the breakdown of farm life in the Midwest.[6]

The suffering in our time is not helped—indeed is often made worse—by the proliferation of technology, and the impersonal nature of modern society. The wide acceptance of computers and other "high-tech" machinery has aggravated a highly bureaucratic and impersonal way of behaving; the result is a culture that too often treats people as items in a statistical column and can only worsen the personal needs of people in distress. Moreover, modern society is so structured that in a way it acts like human machinery—everyone "passes the buck," and no one seems personally accountable.

The response of many modern people when confronted with such widespread suffering is to surrender to cynical resignation or hopeless despair. Others adopt the attitude that history is just "one more damn day after the other" and settle for just "hanging in there" with the help of private survival techniques such as psychotherapy, drugs or alcohol, or simple denial. In our apocalyptic time, the hopeful optimism of former days, which enabled us to see ourselves through times of suffering or to give those times a positive meaning, does not seem to work any more.[7] The scope and intensity of global and private suffering call for an answer of depth and realism and cosmic scope.

2. The Facts of Experience Which Create the Problem of Evil and Suffering

As already indicated in this chapter, the fact of evil in the world is almost inescapable. Our everyday experience and the experience of those we hear about impress on us the reality of evil and suffering. In general, almost every experience of evil and suffering falls into one of two categories: natural (or physical) evil and moral evil.

(1) Natural or Physical Evil. Natural evil has its origin in natural events independent of human action, ranging from earthquakes and tidal waves to cancer.

The wholesale destructiveness of floods and typhoons and the ruthless process of disease and decay give an almost irresistible impression of a ruthless indifference on the part of the universe toward human life and works.[8]

The amount of sheer physical suffering at any given moment, even in the human family, is staggering to contemplate. Thousands each day die of cancer, and other thousands are permanently incapacitated by disease. Although in a profound sense the Declaration of Independence is right that all men (and women) are created equal, in nearly all the less profound senses we are created strikingly unequal. Many begin life with frail bodies or in such grinding poverty that the odds are against their ever leading what we think of as a "normal" life. And, of course, many who are born with more advantages are struck down in their later encounters with the natural evils of existence.[9]

(2) Moral evil. Moral evil has its source in human actions. The range of moral evil is from the physical violence of war and tyranny to the blighting psychological effect of crime and injustice. At times, moreover, it seems that wickedness does its work unchecked. All too often in this world, the wicked prosper and the innocent suffer. These facts seem to take their place alongside the earthquakes in lending to the whole world the appearance of brazen indifference.

3. Concern Over the Problem as Evidence for the Existence of a God of Love and Power

In a sense, the problem of evil does not exist for the unbeliever. This does not mean that unbelievers are *unaware* or *unconcerned* about evil and suffering. But to one who does not believe that the world is ruled by a loving and powerful God, the existence of pain in nature and the cruelty of human to human do not constitute a philosophical problem. In a godless universe, pain and suffering are not the least surprising!

The affirmation of the Christian, however, is that God is good and loving and powerful. Evil and suffering, therefore, are real problems for the Christian. The obvious question that comes to mind is: How can a loving and powerful God allow such suffering in the world?

Since the problem of evil cannot exist, logically, for the unbeliever, the widespread concern over the problem of evil and suffering is actually an impressive piece of evidence. The fact that the demand for an adequate explanation of evil and suffering is so nearly universal is one of our best indications of how widespread the belief in God really is. This evidence is made far more impressive by reason of the fact that it is largely unconscious and indirect.[10]

It is also important to note that the human race survives and wants to survive in spite of all the sufferings which afflict it. Humanity wants the experiment of life to continue, however distressing some aspects of it may be. If suffering were utterly massive and intolerable, then mass suicide or at least the loss of the will to live would be the appropriate response for the human race to make. But despite the extent and depth of human suffering, people still seem to believe that life has some purpose and meaning—or at least they want to keep on living. This implies that they believe—at least subconsciously—that there is a God of purpose at the heart of the universe.[11]

4. Theoretical and Practical Aspects of the Problem of Evil and Suffering

The challenge of evil to religious conviction seems to have been felt in the early Christian centuries and in the medieval period as acutely as it is today. In the fifth century, Augustine was intensely concerned with the problem and worked out a systematic Christian response that has proved very influential. (Even today we speak of the "Augustinian type" of solution to the problem of evil.) And in the thirteenth century, Thomas Aquinas listed the reality of evil as one of the chief intellectual obstacles to Christian theism. Indeed, the problem of evil for the Christian has been equally challenging and unavoidable in all historical periods.[12]

In approaching the problem of evil and suffering from a Christian viewpoint, it is important first to bear in mind the Christian understanding of God. For the problem of evil arises only for a religion which insists that the object of its worship is at once perfectly good and unlimitedly powerful. The challenge is thus inescapable for Christianity.[13]

The accepted name for the whole subject comprising the problem of evil and its attempted resolution is theodicy. This word is a kind of technical shorthand term used to describe the defense of the justice and righteousness of God in face of the fact of evil.[14]

(1) The Theoretical Problem. The theoretical problem of evil may be stated as follows: If God is both almighty and good, why should there be evil? This raises two horns of a dilemma: Either (a) God wills to remove the evil and is not able or (b) God does not will to remove the evil.

If we accept the first horn of this dilemma, God cannot be considered omnipotent (all-powerful). Thus there is doubt as to whether we have a genuine monotheism, for if God is not all-powerful, there must be other powers equal to God or superior to him. Thus, the first alternative is unacceptable from a biblical point of view.

However, if we accept the second alternative, we have a different problem. A God who is able to remove evil but does not care to do so is no longer worthy of our love and trust. He would, indeed, be morally inferior to some of his creatures, a situation which is hardly acceptable.[15]

Just giving up on the problem does not provide an acceptable answer from a biblical viewpoint, either. This would mean a retreat to naturalism, which of course is unsatisfactory. This view would leave unsolved the formidable problem of accounting for the presence of good in the world. To overcome a difficulty about the meaning of the world by adopting a hypothesis according to which nothing has meaning is a bold step, but a logical follow-up on the implications of this view reveals its own difficulties.[16]

(2) The Practical Problem. While the theoretical problem may concern philosophers of religion or laypersons in more reflective moments, it is the practical side of the problem that more often occupies the attention of most people.

Simply stated, it is this: In view of the presence of evil, how can I be saved from distortion and evil and death? How can I achieve victory in the midst of pain and suffering and evil?

II. What Are Representative Nonevangelical Approaches to the Problem of Evil and Suffering?

1. The "Evil As Illusion" Approach

A number of non-Christian philosophic approaches have been developed to deal with the problem of evil. One of these systems solves the problem of evil by denying its existence. In this system, evil ceases to be a philosophic problem because all of material reality—rocks and trees, as well as pain and suffering—is considered to be illusory. The "evil as illusion" approach is the basis for a number of religions and philosophies in both the East and the West.[17]

(1) Hinduism. As shown in earlier chapters, Hindus believe the physical world to be basically or ultimately unreal—their word for this unreal quality is *maya.* To believe in the reality of the physical is to put faith in an illusion. Such a belief also is a kind of enslavement, for it separates humans from Brahman, the ultimate or supreme reality.[18]

According to the Hindu view, a person may "seem" to experience the world as being perverse and evil, but such perceptions are false. The famous ninth-century Hindu thinker, Sankara, argued that Brahman is the sole reality. The external world only appears to be real, in the same way a rope appears to be a serpent until we get closer. Brahman "causes" the world to appear diverse and evil only in the sense that the rope "causes" the serpent to appear.[19] The truth, however, becomes apparent upon a closer look.

The Hindu law of moral retribution, karma, demands that people be continually reborn until, through patient suffering, they have been purged of their illusion. At such a time, a person will at last be absorbed into Brahman and attain nirvana, the state where all self-consciousness is forever lost and a person no longer exists as an individualized soul.[20]

(2) Christian Science. There are Western versions or adaptations of the view that evil is unreal. Such an approach insists that what appears to be sin and suffering is but an illusion of the mortal mind. All such apparent evil has no existence for the divine mind—the Infinite Being. The ultimate basis of such a theory is pantheism, which identifies God with the universe and the universe with God.

Christian Science is a contemporary example, insisting that God is good, God is mind; hence all is of the character of mind and is good. Matter, therefore, is unreal and, accordingly, disease, sin, and evil are also unreal. In addition, the senses are the source of error and ultimately, therefore, the source of evil.[21]

What is true of evil in general is also true of one of the most serious of natural evils, disease. Christian Science holds that disease is an illusion; it has no reality. What is experienced as disease is caused by wrong belief, failure to recognize the unreality of disease.[22]

Christian Scientists believe that the senses are deceptive in the area of disease as well as in other areas. Accordingly, the cure for sickness is not to be achieved through the medical means most persons mistakenly utilize, but through the knowledge of the truth. In other words, the cure for disease is for the person to recognize the imaginary nature of the pain he or she feels. Once sickness and pain are acknowledged to be unreal, they will no longer afflict the individual. Death is also considered by Christian Science to be illusory. Death is considered but another phase of the dream that existence is material. In fact, Mary Baker Eddy, the founder of Christian Science, never prepared an official funeral ceremony. If death occurs, it is considered an indication that people do not fully practice the truth of Christian Science.[23]

According to Christian Science teaching, Jesus came to seek and to save those who will accept the reality of the divine mind. His whole ministry was to free people from the false belief in the reality of matter, including disease and evil.

Obviously Christian Science has points of appeal. It recognizes the power of thought over matter, or mind over body. It magnifies the idea of God and proposes to bring him near. ("God is all and in all" is often repeated in *Science and Health,* the basic source of Christian Science teaching.)

But two weaknesses of the Christian Scientist view of evil are easily apparent. (Christian Science as a faith can be shown to have other weaknesses, also, but outlining them is beyond the scope of this book.) First, it simply does not work! If the Christian Science claim that correct understanding will dispel evil, including disease and death, were true, Christian Scientists would be uniformly free of disease and would live forever. But Christian Scientists do become ill and die, and there is no evidence of a total absence of other evils in Christian Scientist circles. Second, if evil is an illusion, why do all people experience it from the moment of birth? Does the illusion originate at birth, or is it passed down to each generation? If all is God and God is all, where does the illusion of evil come from?[24]

2. The "Evil Is Basic to Human Existence" Approach

(1) Buddhism. To a Buddhist, there is a basic alienation between humankind and the universe. At its very best, the cosmos is no more than a merciless and impersonal cause-effect sequence; at its worst, it is almost malignantly evil. This fact calls for immediate detachment from all sensual satisfactions. The Buddhist solution of the "problem" of evil, moreover, is a completely individual and existential one. It consists in the individual's willed escape from all fetters that bind him or her to present individualized existence, for it is individualized existence as such that is the root evil.[25]

(2) Schopenhauer. The "Evil is Basic" approach is represented in Western thought by the ideas of Arthur Schopenhauer, an early nineteenth-century European thinker. Although strains of pessimism can be found in earlier thought, Schopenhauer was the first Western philosopher to state systematically

that suffering and evil are intrinsic to human existence. His chief work, for our purposes, was *The World as Will and Idea.*[26]

For Schopenhauer, ultimate reality is the irrational will to live, which pushes us blindly ahead. This will to live is evil because it created our bodies and endowed them with desires that cannot be satisfied. Suffering, then, is caused by this ceaseless desire, which forever seeks, yet never attains, satisfaction. Pain and illusion are not unfortunate incidents in human life. They are inevitable. Man is essentially a creature of pain. The greatest tragedy of man is that he was ever born.[27]

Schopenhauer held that a temporary solution to the problem of evil and suffering was to be found in art. His view of art was that it implied pure contemplation, pure detachment, and was therefore a calmer of the passions. However, Schopenhauer believed that the only final solution to the problem of suffering is to eradicate the will. The only way to avoid suffering is to kill desire and cease to want happiness: "Our goal should be to sink back into the blind center of all being. With abolition of the will, the world can pass away, and we can come face to face with empty nothingness."

Interestingly enough, Schopenhauer's actual life was inconsistent with his philosophy. While professing that the will to live should be eradicated, he continued an active life into his seventies and even gathered disciples in his later years. While deploring praise from the world, he basked in it when fame finally came to him.[28]

Schopenhauer's pessimism and professed desire to escape life is clearly opposed to the Christian faith, which has the gaining of life as a central theme. Philosophical pessimism holds that the only solution to human suffering and the problem of evil is to escape from existence. Such a view, which denies any basic significance to human life and history, will inevitably clash with the biblical worldview, which holds that history is meaningful and purposeful.

3. The "Matter Is Evil" Approach

In this approach, evil is attributed to the material world, as contrasted with the "real" world of ideal form or spirit. This view is necessarily connected with the concept of finitude, the idea that the "real" spirit is limited or sullied by being mixed with matter. Therefore, the only way to overcome evil, according to this view, is to "unmix the mixture" and allow the spirit to rise out of its bodily prison to eternity.[29]

Matter goes under various labels in this philosophical tradition; it is variously called "nonbeing" (because real "being" is spiritual), "chaos," (as opposed to the order of pure form), "the receptacle" (of the spirit in the world), "nothingness," and the "void." Matter is that which is deficient in being. Thus evil is viewed in terms of privation and deprivation.[30]

Plato is probably the key figure in the tradition of cosmic dualism, at least in the West. For him, evil stems from the resistance of chaotic matter to ideas and form and structure. Evil lies in recalcitrance and deficiency, not in aggressive rebellion. The philosophy of Gnosticism, which constantly threatened the early church, stems partly from Platonism. Gnosticism, an amalgamation of Hellenic and Oriental philosophical speculation, conceives of the phenomenal world as basically evil.[31]

Among the great philosophers who stand more or less in this tradition are Plato, Aristotle, Plotinus, Hegel, Heidegger, Jaspers, and Whitehead.[32] In the modern era, Hegel in particular shows the influence of the Platonic approach to evil. For the most part, he attributed evil to the "raw material" of the world that has not yet become spirit.[33]

4. The "Coequal-Power" Approach

Another perspective which has enjoyed quite a following over the years is that which explains evil in terms of a supernatural creative will other than God. Such a will is equal to and opposed to the will of God.

(1) Zoroastrianism. The religion of ancient Persia, often called Zoroastrianism, is the classical example of a dualistic approach to the problem of evil. Zoroaster and his followers believed that at the beginning of the universe there existed two ultimate and coequal spirits or principles, one representing evil or darkness and one representing good or light. The evil power is generally thought of as uncreated, simply a force that has always been present. There is therefore a struggle between God and this evil power, with no certainty as to the ultimate outcome. God is attempting to overcome evil, and would if he could, but he is simply unable to do so because he is equally matched by the power of darkness.[34]

(2) Manicheism. Another classic form of cosmic dualism is Manicheism, the philosophical system developed by the Persian prophet Mani in the third century A.D. The chief characteristic of this system is that it rejects any possibility of tracing the origins of good and evil to one and the same source; evil must exist as a separate and completely independent principle from good. Manicheism contends that two primal principles of light and darkness have existed coeternally but independently, each dwelling in its own realm.[35]

For a period of about nine years, Augustine was strongly attracted to Manicheism and even attained the status of an auditor, or layman, in the Manichean sect. When Augustine became a Christian, therefore, he addressed many of his arguments for Christianity against Manicheism. He was especially convinced that the Manichean conception of God was utterly and dangerously mistaken, because it pictured God as less than absolute, and as but one of two coequal, warring powers. Against this view, Augustine upheld vigorously the integrity of God's goodness and the universality of his rule. Indeed the reality and perfection of God both as the ultimate of being and power and as infinite in goodness and beauty lay close to the heart of Augustine's theodicy.[36]

5. The Deterministic or "Sovereignty of God" Approach

A widely held approach to the problem of evil begins with the absolute sovereignty of God. It defines that sovereignty in terms of complete power. Such reasoning proceeds from this starting point to the conclusion that every event is directly caused or determined by God. If this is not so, it is argued, then God, in that particular event, would not be all powerful.

(1) Islam. The religion of Islam is a classic example of a deterministic outlook concerning man's relationship with God. In Islam, the will of Allah is considered to be "certain, arbitrary, irresistible and inevitable" before any event transpires.[37]

The essential doctrine of Islam is that of the supremacy of God. The practical effect of this view is a tendency toward fatalism. Most Muslims deny all free-agency in humankind; they say that all humans are necessarily constrained by the force of God's eternal and immutable decree to act as he wills them to do. God wills both good and evil, and there is no escaping from the determinism of his decree. Thus, religion for many becomes resignation to Allah's determined will. In some instances, this is seen to hinder human initiative and creativity.

(2) Extreme Calvinism. Christianity has by no means remained free of this fatalistic or deterministic emphasis. It has appeared at various times in Christian history, most notably as an extreme form of the Augustinian or Calvinist emphasis on predestination. It is sometimes called "double-edged predestinarianism," because it alleges in general that God is the source of both good and evil and argues specifically that God has decided before creation that some human beings will be saved and some will be damned.[38]

There is considerable theological debate over the extent and implications of the doctrine of predestination, especially as upheld by Calvin and some of his followers. John Hick contends, for example, that the double predestination doctrine, the concept that some are predestined for heaven and some to hell, bulks large in Calvin's writings and has been taken up in the thoughts of most of Calvin's successors and followers.[39]

German theologian Dorothee Soelle also locates the doctrine of "double predestination" in the thought of Calvin, and she strongly objects to this emphasis, which she calls "Christian masochism." Soelle especially derides what she sees as the logical consequence of this approach, which is passivity in the face of suffering—especially suffering to which humans could put an end by taking action against its root causes. If believers finally see themselves obliged to speak of God's "inscrutable decrees," she says, they are admitting that all that is left to them as a last possible consolation and source of pleasure in their suffering is an unconditional submission.[40]

Some Calvin scholars maintain that Calvin himself is not as extreme in his doctrine of predestination as some of his followers. For example, E. A. Dowey of Princeton suggests that behind Calvin's doctrine there is a profound religious concern that has exercised a strong attraction upon many deeply Christian minds. It accentuates the wonder of the free divine grace which we have found, and which has found us, in Jesus Christ. Dowey points out that within the structure of Calvin's *Institutes,* predestination is attached to the doctrine of salvation. It is offered as a means of appreciating the wonder of God's redeeming grace and does not indicate determinism in regard to evil and suffering.[41]

Bernard Ramm further suggests that Calvin's doctrine of predestination is best understood in the context of his broader view of the glory of God. All that is done in this world is done for the glory of God. Evil is not something that slipped unexpectedly into the universe posing an unexpected problem for God. God has decreed this whole world order to reveal and promote his glory and also his love and compassion for man. Hence, evil functions strictly instrumentally and is never out of God's control. Evil is therefore restricted, limited, and relative. In the total scheme of things, including the course of human history, evil does promote good.[42]

According to Ramm's understanding of Calvin's view, evil is instrumental in revealing God's glory, his power, his wisdom, and his love. In the case of those very baffling cases of evil that seem utterly to defy any attempt to show that they can promote good, Calvin takes refuge in the secret counsels of God. If we knew those counsels, the situation would cease to baffle us. Therefore, we must retain our faith in God's love and sovereignty in even the blackest of nights.[43]

Without attempting to solve the dispute among Calvin scholars, it can be said that the double predestination doctrine, which tends toward determinism in regard to evil, is prevalent in some parts of Calvin's systematic writings such as the *Institutes*. This emphasis has been carried to an unbiblical extreme by some of his successors and followers.

6. The "Finite-God" Approach

In contrast to the deterministic view, which views God as the source of both good and evil, there is the view that God is finite or limited. This is the attitude behind Rabbi Harold Kushner's bestselling book, *When Bad Things Happen to Good People*. Before the untimely and unfortunate death of his fourteen-year-old son, Rabbi Harold Kushner had held the traditional view of God as all powerful and also the source of all good. But after his son's painful and protracted death, he found that theologically he could no longer hold both concepts. He came to the conclusion that if he had to choose between an all-powerful God who would let a boy suffer and die or a limited God who was good and full of compassion for those who suffer, he would choose the limited God of love.[44]

The view of the late Professor Edgar S. Brightman of Boston University is also typical of the finite-God idea. Brightman arrives at this position through rejecting other possible solutions. He is unwilling to assert any type of metaphysical dualism, and yet he is disturbed by unexplained suffering. He says that it is wrong to ascribe all of the darkness of creation to human will, but he finds no satisfaction in the idea of a personal Satan. To explain the existence of evil, therefore, he has postulated that the universe contains something God did not create and which is an obstacle to his will. This limitation is inherent in the eternal nature of God—in the very warp and woof of his consciousness—and is not the product of his will or choice. This limitation Brightman calls the "Given."[45]

Brightman's God is a personal consciousness, of eternal duration and an eternally active will, who must work with the "Given." The "Given" consists in part of the eternal, uncreated laws of reason—logic, mathematical relations, and the Platonic Ideas. The "Given" also consists of "equally eternal and uncreated processes of nonrational consciousness." These processes exhibit all of the ultimate qualities of sense objects, including disorderly impulses and desires. All constituent elements of the "Given" are distinguished by two characteristics: (1) they are eternal within the experience of God; (2) they are not a product of will or creative activity.

Brightman uses the term "surd evil" to refer to "an evil that is not expressible in terms of good, no matter what operations are performed on it." There is something which in effect places a limitation upon what God is able to will. Brightman says that "all theistic finitists agree that there is something in the universe not created by God and not a result of voluntary self-limitation, which God finds as an obstacle to his will."[46]

Brightman's answer to the problem of evil, then, is to affirm that God is limited by a "given" quality within God's own nature, against which he struggles. Evil is the result of this quality which God cannot control. In this view, as in Rabbi Kushner's view, God is perfect in will and love, but not in achievement and power. In effect, however, Brightman's finite-God concept also casts a question mark upon God's goodness. If the "Given"—with which God struggles and which is the source of evil—is a part of God's own nature, how can God be referred to as good?[47]

What about the future of the struggle between God and the "Given"? Brightman's view is that "God can make an increasingly better conquest of it throughout eternity without ever wholly eliminating it."[48]

7. Practical and Scientific Approaches

(1) Confucianism. The major explanation of evil in Confucianism is related to a person's activities in society. In the Confucian view, a person who disregards any of the basic five social relationships is swimming against the current of social reality and will come to grief. Confucius was convinced that much of the social disarray of his own time was due precisely to ignorance and disregard of these five great structural forms of human life and that a society composed of such uncultured and immoral persons was bound to suffer shipwreck. But he did not find in human nature itself any deep-lying evil that proper education and family discipline could not rectify. In his view, human nature, properly treated, would rectify itself and work intelligently to overcome the social evils of its generation.[49]

Mencius, the foremost disciple of Confucius, also held that human nature was innately good. In his view, the fundamental evil is social impropriety. Accordingly, one can overcome evil simply by observing the rules of reciprocal social propriety. Salvation is found simply in good manners, good example, and good government. In the light of historical developments, of course, this view can easily be seen as overly optimistic.

(2) Modern Scientific Humanism. The Western equivalent of Confucianism is scientific humanism. This is a common-sense, this-worldly, eminently practical

way of approaching human life and the problem of evil. In the scientific humanist view, evil is whatever seems to interfere with maximum satisfaction of human desires and needs. In addition, life is seen to be the product of natural causes without purpose or direction.

For contemporary philosophical humanism, the goal is much the same as with communism, although (and quite importantly) the means thereto are different. Scientific humanism holds that abundant living, both material and cultural, is to be achieved by educational and scientific means rather than through violent seizure of political power. But here, as in communism, the good life on earth is seen as the only and ultimate goal.[50]

The eighteenth-century French philosopher Jean Jacques Rousseau was one of the forerunners of this view. He asserted that humankind was intrinsically good, and that evil can be ascribed to the corrupting influence of society. Karl Marx traces the conflict in the world to the class struggle. The perfect brotherhood of man will finally become a reality when inequity is overcome. Erich Fromm, a twentieth-century psychoanalyst, views alienation and crime as being rooted in the social matrix. This means that the alienated person accurately mirrors the alienated condition of his or her society.[51]

A naturalistic philosophy like this invariably fails to see that the source of evil is in the realm of spirit rather than nature. It cannot account for the fact that when man's bodily and even social needs are satisfied, crime and delinquency and suffering still prevail. It does not see that behind poverty and inequity lies unbelief, a broken relationship between God and man. The position held by Marxists and various scientific or secular humanists that human beings can be changed by altering their social environment contains some truth, but it does not do justice to all the facts of experience. The modern welfare states such as Sweden, whose social systems are largely based on the perspective of scientific humanism, are presently plagued by mounting alcoholism, suicide, and crime, which are all signs of a disorder within humanity itself.[52]

Most of the philosophical and religious approaches which we have considered in this section are at heart either dualistic or monistic in their attempts to solve the problem of evil. For the dualists, evil is reducible to some given reality, such as matter, which is opposed to spirit or to God. For the monist, evil is only appearance and illusion. Sometimes it is held that the world itself or even human existence is evil. Other views say evil is found in inadequate ideas or the delusion of mortal mind. According to the biblical worldview, however, these approaches fail to account for the real evil in the world, and most of all within humankind itself. For the evangelical Christian, evil is perversion and corruption and is rooted in personal and collective rebellion against a holy and loving God.[53]

III. What Are the Revealed Principles of the Biblical Approach to Evil and Suffering?

In examining the biblical approach to evil and suffering, it is important to include the teaching of both the Old Testament and the New Testament. In the area of suffering, the principles of the Old Testament are especially important as the foundation for the New Testament teachings. The Old Testament principles, which are given their fulfillment and finalization in the New Testament, enrich, complement, and correct each other. They afford a coherent scriptural framework which provides us with the normative pattern for the Christian understanding of evil and suffering.[54]

It should also be noted that the faith of Israel and the New Testament church was directed toward a divine being who was personal and active, who had created the world and its inhabitants and who guided them in accordance with a persistent purpose. Over the centuries of the very diverse history of Israel, there emerged certain great principles for interpreting human suffering. All of these principles have some permanent value for our guidance, provided we take them in due proportion. The very fact that there are at least eight of these principles serves to remind us of the complexity of the data and warns us against too simple an interpretation of them. Suffering is one of the universal conditions of life, and our interpretation of suffering must be broad and deep and as varied as life itself.[55]

1. The Punitive or Retributive Principle

The retributive solution to suffering is basic to all others in the Bible. Stated simply, it attributes suffering to God's judgment on people's sins. If the government of the world is administered by the one and only God, who is a God of righteousness, then, sooner or later, human righteousness will be rewarded and human unrighteousness punished.[56]

The Book of Deuteronomy gives eloquent expression to this principle. This can be seen especially in the closing exhortation of chapter 30, which begins, "See, I have set before you this day life and good, death and evil" (v. 15), then goes on to spell out the consequences of choosing disobedience and sin.

Isaiah also speaks often of the retributive principle. This may be seen in the statement: "Woe to the wicked! It shall be ill with him, for what his hands have done shall be done to him" (Isaiah 3:11). Although many of the prophets utilize other principles, they maintain the association of sin with suffering and the entire retributive position as a basic concept.

The punitive principle is also fundamental for much of the Wisdom teaching. Its most striking literary expression is found in the Book of Job, where the three friends apply it rigorously to the sufferings of Job. This was the orthodox doctrine of Israel. (Job himself developed another principle, which is discussed below.)

The retributive principle is carried over, with necessary limitations and modifications, into the New Testament (cf. Matt. 7:24–26). We should be careful to note, however, that Jesus rejected the view that retribution is the *only* solution to suffering (John 9:13; Luke 13:1–5). Furthermore, he refused to identify prosperity with righteousness (Luke 16:19–23), which is the opposite side of the retribution coin.

The apostle Paul, notwithstanding his emphasis on the doctrine of grace, also does not hesitate to say, "We must all appear before the judgment-seat of Christ, so that each one may receive good or evil, according to what he has done in the body" (2 Cor. 5:10). Paul gives a classic exposition of the wrath of God and its effect upon humankind in Romans 1:18–32, which will be discussed in more detail later in this chapter.[57]

It is a mistake, then, to dismiss the principle of retribution as an Old Testament concept that is completely superseded by the doctrine of divine grace. For the New Testament as well as the Old makes it clear that while divine retribution is not the only explanation of suffering, it is a legitimate explanation of much suffering. For while it is not true that all suffering is the result of sin, it *is* true that all sin brings suffering.[58]

The notion of retributive justice is an integral component of a rational and harmonious view of the world, one in which all parts work together to contribute to an orderly cosmos. There is a direct correlation between sowing and harvesting, cause and effect; actions determine people's destinies and produce their own fateful and unalterable consequences.[59]

When this moral conception of world order is lifted into the religious sphere, God becomes the guarantor and executor of this moral law. At times, Israel's prophets expressed the hope that God's retributive justice and judgment would not be his last word and that his mercy would prevail over his judgment. This motif manifests itself in the recurring theme that Israel had not been punished as harshly for its sins as it deserved (Amos 5:14–15; Isa. 1:16–20). Nevertheless, Israel never abandoned its view of God as a retributive judge who punishes evil and rewards good, because it needed to safeguard both the moral order and the intelligibility of God's creation.[60]

The concept of retributive justice is directly related to our hope for the future. It views suffering not as an irrational blow of fate, but a deserved and necessary punishment for evil and injustice. Therefore, retribution preserves the moral order and guarantees a more stable future. It imposes suffering with the expectation that its punishment will lead to repentance or at least to a cessation of evil acts.[61]

2. The Disciplinary or Educational Principle

This solution is associated with the covenant idea in the Old Testament and with the New Testament description of God as a heavenly Father. Like the retribution principle, it considers affliction as a visitation from God, but for a reason other than vindication or punishment. God disciplines his people, collectively and individually, that they may be brought closer to him. The purpose of God's discipline is often to teach a lesson, to train and to mature his children through suffering.

There are many evidences of the disciplinary and educational view of suffering in the Bible. In a basic passage, Proverbs 3:11–12, the chastening of God is compared to the discipline of a father for his beloved son. Jeremiah 18:1–10 compares God's disciplinary action to the work of a potter who breaks a vessel and remolds it after his own design. Other prophets also illustrate the disciplinary view. Even a limited examination of the New Testament evidence must include the experience of the Prodigal Son (Luke 15:16–22), as well as Hebrews 2:10; 5:8–9; and 12:5–11.[62]

3. The Probational or Evidential Principle

A third biblical view on suffering is that pain is probational and evidential. Three major ideas are included in this approach: (1) Since the world is evil and often in the control of wickedness, the godly must wait for the disposition of wickedness and righteousness which is sure to come. (2) In this probational period, the depth of a person's faith is submitted to a rigid test, the result of which reveals the true character of his or her faith. (3) In the New Testament, especially, this struggle is seen as inevitable for the Christian life, and hence is evidence in itself that one is a Christian.

Examples of the probational and evidential approach to understanding suffering are abundant. It finds one of its classic expressions in the prophecy of Habakkuk. The problem of this Book is threatened destruction of the nation by the Chaldeans. How God can honor a wicked nation above a divinely appointed one is the question in the prophet's mind as he comes to argue with God's justice. The answer which he receives declares that the problem is temporary only. Retribution is promised against the enemy. The people are to be patient and to rejoice in God. The prologue of Job also is clearly expressive of this view.[63]

The author of Hebrews faces a similar situation in Hebrews 10:32–39. His problem is the suffering of Christians. (Even though God has made a promise, a promise is something future, and suffering is all too present.) At this point, the author of Hebrews gives Habakkuk an added interpretation. For the answer given is a vision not just of coming justice, but of the "coming one"—Jesus Christ (v. 37). The implication is that when the Lord comes, he will avenge and reward the faithful Christian, and that the persecutors, the ones who are cruel to God's dear children, will receive their just punishment. Faith in this context—in those times when God seems silent, when the righteous are cruelly treated, when wickedness seems unchecked—becomes a matter of holding on to the belief that God will resolve the problem of evil.[64]

4. The Revelational Principle

The view that suffering is revelational refers to physical evil as the occasion of humankind's entry into the fuller knowledge of God. This view is implicit in many passages of Scripture, and is often seen in connection with other biblical solutions to suffering. The fact that many have found the true glory of God in times of great suffering confirms the truth of the biblical implication.

The classic illustration of the revelational view is found in Hosea. Through a series of domestic sorrows, Hosea finds a new insight into God, into his own mission, and into the message which he is to deliver. So advanced an idea of God would be inconceivable at that stage of the history were it not for the context of Hosea's personal experience, through which God was revealed to him.[65] Jeremiah also gained new insight into God through personal suffering, as did the apostle Paul (Rom. 8:28–38).

It is obvious, of course, that suffering does not drive all people to God. Thus, whether or not suffering is revelational depends upon the attitude of the sufferer.[66]

5. The Redemptive Principle

The term "redemptive principle" actual refers to two closely related but distinct theories. Physical evil may be redemptive in the sense that it is suffered for others or instead of others. Physical evil also may be redemptive for the sufferer in the sense that God can achieve victory in spite of, and even through, suffering.

The Old Testament, confronting the problem of the suffering of the innocent, reaches what is known as "its deepest solution" in this conception. The suffering of the innocent, so often inflicted through others, may also be endured *for* others. The Suffering Servant passages in Isaiah, particularly Isaiah 40–55, form the primary illustration of this view.[67]

That the sufferings of Christ are vicarious (undergone in the place of others) may be clearly seen in the New Testament. The late H. Wheeler Robinson, an Old Testament scholar at Oxford, further contends that such passages as Colossians 1:24, Philippians 3:10, and 2 Corinthians 12:7 are indicative of the possibility of the Christian's bearing suffering for others in the spirit of Christ. Thus, the sacrificial view of suffering becomes applicable to Christians as well as to their Lord. They may bear voluntary and involuntary suffering in the faith that God's redemptive purpose for others may be at work through their own pain.[68]

The second theory of the redemptive view—that physical evil may be redemptive for the sufferer as he or she wins a victory over it—is also closely related to the death of Christ. Evidence for the practical application of the victory theory to human suffering is presented in Romans 8:28–30. This is a typical expression of a major tenet of the redemptive view of suffering—that God can turn suffering from defeat to redemption. Paul's own personal experience of this truth, as recorded in 2 Corinthians 12:7–10, gave him firm ground for his faith.[69]

6. The Mystery Principle

The Bible often confesses the mystery of suffering. It is not strange that such is the case, for in many ways the problem of evil is beyond theoretical explanation. The Book of Job furnishes the Old Testament's classic illustration of the view that suffering is mysterious. In this book, Job's chief struggle is to arrive at an assurance that he is in fellowship with God in spite of the calamities which his friends interpret as retributive.

In Job 42:1–6 Job himself points out that the ways of God are necessarily a mystery to the human mind—before which we are to have a trustful humility.[70] The problem of evil is not solved for Job, but he learns how to live with it. He learns that he may well trust God in the mysteries of evil, for he has learned to trust God and his goodness and wisdom in the clarities of creation.[71]

This approach makes a twofold contribution. First, it goes beyond a theory that is not applicable in some situations and so opens the way for an alternative and perhaps more adequate solution. Second, by its own grandeur it makes us feel the vastness and mystery of the universe, as well as the need for humility and patience and faith in our quest for a solution to evil and suffering.

The view that suffering is mysterious is also verified in the New Testament. W. T. Conner, who was professor of theology for many years at Southwestern Baptist Theological Seminary, identifies it as the basic solution to suffering offered by Jesus. According to Conner, Jesus, by his clinging to God in the darkness of the Cross, gave an example to his disciples of a faith which perseveres in spite of circumstances.[72]

7. The Eschatological Principle

The eschatological solution to suffering sees the answer to the problem of evil and suffering as existing beyond the present conflict. This view is expressed in a faith that in the time of greatest darkness and fear, God will suddenly burst into history to reveal himself, to triumph over evil, and to redeem and to reward his own.[73]

The eschatological response to Israel's crisis of faith refuses to surrender the world as God's creation and to render the suffering of the righteous meaningless. The crisis of faith is embraced within a structure of hope. Although the eschatological writers still often view suffering as deserved punishment or as a form of divine testing and instruction, they attribute suffering basically to the activity of hostile powers and view it in large measure as undeserved.

Nevertheless, even undeserved suffering is endurable for eschatological writers, because they believe that God will vindicate their suffering and will soon achieve a final and complete triumph over the hostile powers that thwart God's redemptive purpose for Israel. They have been granted insight into the mysteries of God's wisdom and thus know their God to be a God of justice and faithfulness who "for his own sake" will soon break into history, abolish the suffering of the righteous, establish his kingdom of justice, and right the present wrongs of undeserved suffering. This view is clearly expressed in the writings of Daniel, especially in Daniel 9:7–19.[74]

The eschatological view of suffering, so begun in the Old Testament, comes to its maturity in the New. The eschatological response is the predominant framework of thought for New Testament reflections on suffering and hope in the light of the death and resurrection of Jesus Christ. For example, Revelation is primarily directed toward the imminent coming of a "new heaven and new earth" (Rev. 21:1), the time of the last judgment which will destroy the evil powers of this world and reward the oppressed followers of the Lamb (14:4).[75]

The resolution anticipated in the New Testament is eschatological in its assertion that all human sin and suffering, agony and death, blood and tears, will be erased in the New Jerusalem and remembered no more; righteousness, peace, and joy will reign forever. Whatever the mystery of evil is, therefore, whatever its human or Satanic origin and whatever harm it has done, its career is doomed to end. God stands in absolute clarity as the ultimate Victor; his love and goodness and holiness and wisdom no longer stand under a shadow.[76]

8. The Satanic Temptation Principle

An outline of the principles of the Hebrew-Christian solution should surely include reference to the biblical emphasis on the extrahuman world as a source of temptation and perversion. This is more than a simple question of biblical exegesis. We who live in this world must face the ultimate question of the origin of evil, both moral and cosmic. Evangelical scholars affirm that no satisfactory solution to evil and suffering can be formed without belief in an evil personal force, such as is described in the New Testament as the devil or Satan.

As shown in chapter 6 of this book, both the Old and New Testaments affirm the real existence of a personal devil. According to the biblical witness, Satan cannot be made to stand simply for collective evil. In addition, human experience in every generation suggests that there are wicked spiritual agencies which tempt and seek to get control of men.

Satan is revealed as a personal tempter in the account of Adam's fall. The narrative of our Lord's temptation, found in the first three Gospels, also clearly reveals Satan as a personal power. For even though human beings are a mixture of good and evil motives, we cannot say that Jesus was such a mixture without admitting the sinfulness of Jesus. A person can be tempted by a power outside of himself and still be sinless. If the evil arose within Jesus himself, would he still be sinless?[77]

Well-known evangelical philosopher Alvin Plantinga appeals to an often neglected aspect of Christian tradition which was also used by Augustine in his writings on the problem of evil. This emphasis sees Satan or Lucifer as the cause of natural evil (Rom. 8:19–21). He is viewed as a mighty nonhuman spirit who, along with many other angels, was created long before God created man. Unlike most of his colleagues, Satan and a third of the angels rebelled against God and have been wreaking whatever havoc they can. Therefore, much of the natural evil we find in the world is attributable to the free actions of nonhuman spirits.[78]

In holding the doctrine of a personal Satan, we must keep certain underlying principles in mind. First, we need not be committed to all of the crude imagery which has sprung up around belief in the devil. Second, we have to beware of ascribing to Satan any other kind of existence than that of a created being. Third, we must remember that the main concern of the Bible is not with the devil, but with God and the gospel of his grace—the redemption from evil. Fourth, we must never lose sight of the fact that, whatever emphasis the New Testament places on the devil as tempter, it never loses sight of the fact that man is responsible for his own sin—he is guilty before God.

IV. How Would You Formulate a Systematic Approach to the Theoretical Problem of Natural Evil?

Each of the eight principles listed above was attained by revelation in the struggle with evil. Taken together, they provide us with the groundwork for a way to interpret the great riddle of evil and suffering. These eight principles form the basis for a biblically based theodicy—an explanation and justification of the ways of God with man. Our systematic solution to the problem of evil and suffering will be based on these eight revealed principles.[79]

First of all, the following observations could be made regarding the problem of natural, or physical evil:

1. Moral Evil as Responsible for Much Natural Evil

In the first place, there can be an intimate connection between natural and moral evils. Even though events of natural evil are sometimes referred to legally as "acts of God," the fact is that occurrences of flood, famine, and pestilence are often caused by human selfishness. For example, floods are frequently the result of the irresponsible policy of the lumbering industry which takes away from the hills their natural means of holding back rainwater.

It is a sad fact that human sin, more than any other factor, has been responsible for sowing discord in the world of nature. The human rape of the earth is a hideous and frightening story. Instead of living in partnership with the rest of creation as we were intended, instead of humbly learning God's laws and obeying them, we humans arrogantly set out to exploit the world and our fellow humans. We are only now understanding what terrible and irreversible forces we have set in motion. Centuries of our wars have hastened the dissemination of microorganisms from one area to another, decimating and enfeebling whole populations. By cutting down forests and overusing farmland, we have brought famine to larger and larger areas of the world. Not content with creating deserts and wastelands, we have poured our garbage into the seas, which seem now to be slowly but surely dying.[80]

Taking into consideration the evils caused by human folly, sin, and vice explains many of the problems related to natural evil. Romans 8:19–20 and Genesis 3:17–18 imply that the whole created order has been cursed by human sin and satanic influence.[81]

2. Natural Evil as a Possible Judgment upon Sin

Natural evil is not only attributable to moral evil, however. The Bible also clearly shows that physical evils have been used by God for the punishment of individual and national wickedness. The Noahic flood, the destruction of Sodom and Gomorrah, and the fall of Jerusalem are examples. This does not mean, however, that all physical evils are the punishment of physical or moral sins.

3. The Redemptive Possibilities of Suffering Related to Natural Evil

A basic purpose of human existence on earth is to develop Christian character and prepare and discipline us for eternity. In the biblical view, natural evil can play a part in this purpose by disciplining us and shattering our false sense of self-sufficiency. It is or can be redemptive. With the poet John Keats, we can call this world a "vale of soul-making." Or with Canon Streeter, we could call it a "school of manhood."

Can character come without the tumult, the pain, the endless struggle? That we do not know, but we can see from experience that the emergence of character is an end that often justifies the struggle.[82]

John Macquarrie affirms that if human lives were completely protected from beginning to end, untroubled by pain, anxiety, guilt, and deprivation, living would be like curling up in a cocoon, insulated from all danger, and not really engaging the realities of existence. Indeed, to be delivered from every suffering and inconvenience would be like returning to the womb, where all needs are satisfied but the possibility for growth past a certain point is limited.[83]

Acknowledging the redemptive possibilities in suffering does not encourage us to condone or tolerate evil or suffering, but it does allow us to see some purpose and rationality in the tragedy of human life. Even cases of unrelieved insanity, which obviously cannot discipline the individual concerned, are a constant warning to others of the temporal limits which are afforded man to establish his spiritual roots.[84]

4. The Future Vindication of Righteousness

It is only in the life to come that the biblical tradition looks for the complete vindication of the righteousness of God. The Christian gospel sees our earthly life as incomplete and unintelligible in itself; it has meaning and rationality only by virtue of its relation to a wider purpose, which can be realized only in eternity. Christian faith is meaningless apart from belief in a future life: "If for this life only we have hope in Christ, we are of all men most to be pitied" (1 Cor. 15:19).[85]

This promise of life beyond death is more than an escape from the problem of evil and suffering. It is not to be regarded just as compensation for the suffering we encounter in the present phase of our experience. Rather, it is the fulfillment of spiritual capacities which could not have been brought into being without the earthly life and the suffering it often entails.

In this light, it is important to affirm that the God of Scripture hates suffering in his good creation. Although he is capable of using human suffering for his redemptive purposes, suffering remains fundamentally alien to his coming kingdom. Accordingly, Christians are to celebrate God's coming kingdom as that domain where physical suffering will be no more (Rev. 21:3–4).[86]

5. The Need for a Stable Environment

In a sense, natural evil can be attributed to the regularity of God's creation. Natural events—even those that result in human misery, such as earthquakes, volcanoes, and storms—occur as the result of certain God-ordained natural laws. The storm that destroys a harvest and brings famine is as much the regular product of meteorological law as the harvest it destroys is the product of agricultural law. Volcano eruptions occur because the pressures which form in the heated interior of the earth are law-abiding. When the pressure is sufficiently great, the crust is broken and the lava flows on the earth's surface. If people live near the danger areas, they suffer accordingly.

At creation, God chose to limit himself by creating a world system that operated on such regular principles. Some natural evil, therefore, can be attributed to the necessary operation of natural uniformities, and those uniformities cannot be disrupted without disturbing the stable and dependable environment necessary for personal life to develop. Like freedom, this regularity of nature is an important factor in developing human personality—a necessary ingredient of fundamental moral and mental life. To the discipline of natural law, we owe our power to think rationally, to calculate and foresee, to draw analogies and to reason from cause to effect.[87]

C. S. Lewis stresses that God's preservation of a stable order is what permits rational deliberation and action. Sporadic miraculous interruptions could only diminish or destroy the context for meaningful choice.[88]

The laws, we must remember, can be generally dependable without being absolutely inflexible or mechanical. The crucial point is that providing we are to have such a stable setting for our personal development, not all situations can be equally agreeable to all persons.[89]

The rigid laws of God's universe may hit us sorely sometimes. However, if that is the price we have to pay for being delivered from the terrifying alternative, every soul of us would say "It's worth the price!" Robert Browning knew what he was talking about when he cried, "All's love yet all's law!"[90]

6. Physical Suffering as Part of the Balance of Nature

The cycle of nature is an amazing thing, and the relationship of life to life sets up a magnificent balance in nature. Unless a very large number of certain forms of life are consumed, such as insects and fish, the earth would be shortly overpopulated with them. Some fish lay eggs into the millions and if all such eggs hatched the ocean would shortly be all fish. Carnivorous animals and fish keep the balance of nature.[91]

In addition, it appears that plants and animals die so that humans may live. One life form is sacrificed for another life form in order to provide food energy for the survival of the higher form. Since we live in a physical world governed by physical laws of energy flow, which Christians believe was established by a sovereign God, we are able to see the forms of physical suffering mentioned above as part of the balance of nature.[92]

7. The Exaggeration of Sufferings in the Animal World

Some people regard the pain suffered in the animal kingdom beneath the human level as the most baffling aspect of the problem of evil, for the explanations often advanced for suffering—discipline, learning, redemption, just retribution—simply do not seem to apply to the animal world. What can be the purpose, therefore, in allowing animals to suffer pain, hunger, and other physical evils?

The subject of pain in animals must, of course, remain largely a field for speculation and theoretical interpretation. We cannot enter into the consciousness of the lower species or even prove that they have consciousness. There is, however, sufficient evidence for the presence of some degree of consciousness and some kind of experience of pain, at least throughout the vertebrate kingdom, to prohibit us from denying altogether that animals suffer.[93]

According to Hick, a realistic response to the problem of animal pain is to see it as part of the general organic survival system. This means that pain is a response of an animal's nervous system which steers the individual animal away from danger. The human nervous system, of course, functions the same way, and physical pain serves the purpose of alerting us to the possibility of physical danger.[94]

There are, however, respects in which the animal's experience of pain and suffering differs from that of a human. The chief of these appears to be the awareness of the future and the passage of time. The animal's experience does not seem to be shadowed by any anticipation of death or by any sense of its awesome finality. The animal also seems to be unaware of the dangers and pains that may lie between the present moment and its inevitable termination. To an animal, good and evil appear to be exclusively involved with the present moment; in general, it lives from instant to instant. Thus the picture of animal life as a dark ocean of agonizing fear and pain is incorrect and arises from the mistake of projecting our distinctively human quality of experience into creatures of a much lower and simpler order.[95]

According to British evangelical leader John Wenham, however, demonstrable suffering on the part of animals is at its worst when animals are in closest touch with man. An increased capacity for suffering seems to be developed by animals that are integrated into a human community. The anxieties felt by captive animals when approached by a cruel master, for instance, are simply not paralleled in nature. Animals in their natural habitat experience fear, but it is a wholesome sort of fear related to survival of the species.[96]

It is important to remember that the Bible in general and Jesus in particular regard the natural and animal world in an optimistic way. There is often a dwelling on its brightness and beauty, the care providence exerts over the creatures, and their happy freedom. This is in striking contrast to the morbid brooding over the struggle in nature found in some modern treatises.

V. How Would You Describe a Systematic Approach to the Theoretical Problem of Moral Evil?

For most people, moral evil is more problematic than natural evil. Suffering that results from human cruelty and callousness seems harder to take than suffering that results from impersonal events such as earthquakes or disease. The biblical worldview also has some basic observations regarding suffering that results from human agency.

1. God's Self-Limitation in the Name of Freedom

(1) The Free-Will Defense of Evil. What were God's aims in creating the universe? The biblical revelation implies that he wanted two things. First, he wanted to create the best universe possible. Second, he wanted to create a world in which created rational agents would decide freely to love and obey him. Accordingly, he created a world in which there originally existed no moral or natural evil, and he created angels and human beings with the facility of free moral choice.[97]

Obviously, in making angels and humans free, God ran the risk that they would choose evil rather than good. The possibility of freely doing evil is the inevitable companion of the possibility of freely doing good. The nonexistence of evil was quite possible; the angels and humans could have chosen to obey God. Sadly, some of the angels and the first humans chose differently. Alvin Plantinga contends that while a world containing moral good but not moral evil may be logically possible, it is in fact not divinely possible so long as free will is preserved.[98]

Human beings are not cosmic slaves, in complete subjection to the reigning powers of the natural world, as the ancient Mesopotamians believed. Furthermore, humankind is not placed, as the early Egyptians believed, in a preordained station in a static universe. Rather, humankind is endowed with freedom. Freedom is God's gift to men and women to enable them to accept and fulfill their divinely given task. It is not a natural or absolute condition in itself. It is the ground of human dignity, given in order that human beings may serve.[99]

Thus we see that God purposed the existence of free persons who would freely return the love he gave them. Accordingly, he invites us to fellowship with him; he does not compel. Robots might respond in an automatically correct way in every situation, but they would be machines, not persons, and not even God can love machines in the sense that persons can be loved.

This does not mean that God is not all-powerful. Rather, it means that we must not be childish when we think about his power. God made man capable of saying no, even to God. Limitation is inherent in God's own choice and character, rather than in some force outside God's power. The suffering of the innocent is part of the price that must be paid if we are to be really personal beings. We must have the power of choice, and persons who make bad choices are bound to harm others. In spite of the horrible suffering choice can involve, most of us would prefer such a world to its alternative.[100]

(2) Attacks on the Free-Will Defense. Since 1950, analytic philosophers such as J. L. Mackie and Anthony Flew have made a major attack on the free-will defense of evil as outlined above. These critics grant that God intended to create genuinely free persons and not mere puppets. However, they ask, could not God nevertheless have so made humans in such a way that humans would always freely do what is right?[101]

Ninian Smart, a professor at the University of California at Santa Barbara, has characterized the proposition that humans could have been created wholly good as "the Utopia thesis." To counter it, he asserts that the notion of goodness would be emptied of content if there were no such experience as temptation and therefore no occasion to choose good as distinct from evil. A creature not subject to temptation—or to fear, lust, envy, panic, anxiety, or any other demoralizing condition—would no doubt be innocent, but could not justifiably be praised as being morally good.[102]

John Hick further points out that, according to the Bible, God created humans free not only so they would act rightly toward one another, but also so they could enter into a personal relationship with him. Even if we grant that God could make humans so that they would always act rightly toward each other of their own free will, we must go on to ask whether it is logically possible for God to make human beings so they would always freely respond to him in love and trust and faith.[103]

There might, indeed, be great value in a world of created beings who respond to God in freely given love and trust and worship which he himself instilled in them by his initial formation of their nature. But if human analogies entitle us to speak about God at all, we must insist that such a universe could be only a poor second-best to one in which created beings without "fixed" responses come freely to love, trust, and worship God. God has not chosen to constitute humans so that they would be guaranteed to respond to himself in authentic faith and love and worship. Instead, the freedom of humankind has been respected.[104]

In response to recent critics of the idea that Adam and Eve had real freedom, John Wenham gives his answer by making a study of the narratives and portrayals in Genesis. These stories indicate that God did not create free, rational, and perfectly good beings who had immediate access to his unveiled presence. Instead, he gave them a probationary period in which there would be a time of real testing in a situation where his glory was not fully revealed. (The mention of fallen and unfallen angels suggests that they also had a time of probation.) If humans were placed in the full light of the unveiled majesty of God, it is hardly conceivable that they would have any freedom to choose sin. So humankind was put in a world where God is not fully seen in his total glory, but in which his glorious handiwork is seen and his voice is at times heard. This situation provided a period for real choice and freedom.[105]

The story of the Garden of Eden seems perfectly to describe the required situation—humans not overwhelmed by the presence of God, yet perfectly aware of right and wrong and left free to go either their own way or God's way.[106]

2. Human Misuse of Freedom

Sin is not natural, normal, or necessary, nor is evil grounded in the original constitution of the world. Evil cannot be explained as being part of the original human nature or attributed primarily to animal inheritance or to the demons of the flesh. Actually, in fact, most of the moral evil concerned with animal appetites is comparatively superficial. In contrast, that evil concerned with self-centeredness is both profound and far-reaching in its effects. The center of our trouble is not primarily the turbulent appetites, but the personality as a whole.[107]

In essence, moral evil stems from human misuse of the freedom God gave humanity. Moral evil exists because human beings freely chose evil in the beginning—and continue to choose evil today. We cannot blame Adam for our sin, since we ourselves voluntarily assent to temptation. An individual is always personally responsible for his or her sin, even though he or she may be inwardly propelled in a downward direction.[108]

Thus we see that the evangelical Christian sees evil as more than a defect. It does not signify a deficiency of being, as Plato and those who hold similar views would say, but the perversion and corruption of being. Rather, in the evangelical view, the seat of evil is in humanity itself—in the heart, the center of the human personality. Evil consists in the struggle of the soul against God, not in the dichotomy between soul and body. The human problem, as the Bible understands it, is not between spirit and nature, nor is it between knowledge and ignorance. Rather it is between the holy God and sinful, rebellious humanity. The conflict lies in will against will.[109]

It should be emphasized that sin has its source in the perversion of the will, not in a lack of rational capability or understanding. We must not suppose that sin resides just in the passions or just in reason, for the driving power of sin engulfs the whole person, including the passions and the rational faculties. Sin is irrational in that it turns reason from its divinely ordained end, which is the knowledge and service of God. Sin perverts and misuses reason, but does not abandon reason. Sinful reasoning, however, is characterized more by blindness than by wisdom and more by scheming than by disinterested inquiry.[110]

Sin came from the free act of humans annulling their original relation to God. This implies a pure point of beginning in the history of the race. Humanity fell from an original state of purity. Human beings wanted to obey and live in communion with God. Yet, on the other hand, they desired to be like God.

This emphasis on rebellion and disobedience is not the arbitrary invention of some philosopher or theologian. Rather, it emerges from the biblical story of the moral freedom of God's creatures and of the contingent entry of evil into the world as described in Genesis 2 and 3.[111]

Essentially, the question of the origin of evil is inextricably entwined with that of the origin of the human race. And as chapter 4 of this book points out, the question of human origin is one of immense complexity and much debate among theologians, philosophers, and natural scientists. John Wenham contends, however, that we must hold to an irreducible minimum of Christian belief in this area.

It is essential, for instance, to hold that there is an absolute spiritual difference between human and animal—humans alone are made in the image of God—and that, therefore, there must have been some initial creative act that made the first humans, whether by a new creation or by the breathing of the breath of life into an already existing creature. Christian doctrine therefore demands an Adam and Eve of some sort. But if there was an initial creative act by a wholly good being, then it makes more sense to regard the first man as created sinless than as created sinful. (The obvious historical parallel is Jesus himself, the last Adam, whose humanity, apart from its sinlessness, was precisely like ours.) Further, since it is undeniable that humankind is no longer sinless, a fall of some sort must have occurred at some point.[112]

These two basic biblical events, Creation and Fall, have far-reaching implications, for they imply that the development of the world cannot be understood in terms of a purely naturalistic evolution. If these two key events, which fall outside any naturalistic scheme, actually happened, then the twentieth-century Christian is justified in taking the narrative of Genesis with all seriousness, picturing Adam and Eve as unique historical figures who started in fellowship with God but then disobeyed him out of their own free choice and brought death upon themselves and their descendants.[113]

3. Satan's Role in the Human Revolt

The fact that humankind was tempted reveals the fact that there was a tempter. Freedom and anxiety are preconditions of human sin, but biblical revelation also recognizes an outside factor—Satan. The Bible tells that an angelic rebellion preceded and prepared the way for the rupture in the human relationship with God (2 Pet. 2:4, Jude 6).[114]

Sin in Satan has no explanation; it is an irrational surd. Such sheer sin is not subject to salvation. (Apostasy is the only human sin in this category.) Satan was evidently perfect in the original state; pride seems to have been the cause of his fall (1 Tim. 3:6).

Why God permitted the angels to fall and why humanity yields to their enticements cannot be completely comprehended by reason. But Satan is a real objective and dynamic power with purpose and direction, not an irrational chaos or negative reality shorn of power. The devil is to be understood not as a nonbeing, but as a spiritual antidivine being.

Furthermore, the devil still has tempting power in the world even after the Cross. Therefore, we are not to treat the devil lightly, but always to be on watch for him (cf. 1 Pet. 5:8–9).[115]

4. God's Continuing Redemption

Because human beings are sinful creatures in moral revolt against a holy God, the just penalty of death—of divine displeasure issuing in eternal separation from God and all things good—should be humanity's only proper expectation. However, another factor enters the picture—the grace of God. Only the holy love of God as Redeemer can meet the challenge of his wisdom and goodness as the Creator of humankind. God not only created humans as free to sin; he has also preserved humankind in spite of its sinfulness. The most extraordinary thing in history is not simply the evil and alienation of the world, but rather the work of God the Redeemer to reconcile the world to himself.[116]

5. God's Methods in Dealing with Evil

According to the biblical message, God deals with moral evil in any of several ways:

(1) Judgment and Divine Retribution. The biblical emphasis on divine punishment and the painful consequences of sin is found in countless places, from God's first warnings to Adam to the final vivid descriptions of the Apocalypse. Through his judgment on sin, which often results in human suffering, God has made the way of the transgressor hard. But behind God's judgment is the ultimate purpose of mercy, not vengeance. God's wrath is motivated by his passionate love for his people. As the old preachers would say, God's painful judgments in this life are part of his "blockade of the road to hell," part of his "trumpet call to the unconverted." They are warnings lest men and women allow themselves to be destroyed in the Last Judgment.[117]

The apostle Paul gives a classic interpretation of God's judgment in Romans 1:18–32, which implies that the basic sin is idolatry—the rejection of God's self-revelation and rebellion against God's sovereignty (cf. also Rom. 9:19–21). This idolatry creates a chain reaction: It provokes God's wrath; God's wrath causes immorality and injustice (Rom. 3:10–18); and immorality and injustice result in human suffering. In other words, God's wrath permits people to be what they desire to be in accordance with their idolatrous intent. Divine retribution, then, is portrayed here as a paradoxical form of punishment: God's judgment increases the evil of his rebellious world rather than putting an end to it.[118]

Romans 1:18–32 argues that idolatry affects the whole range of human experience—intrapersonal, social, and ecological. It suggests that, once a person's relation to God is perverted, his or her relation to the created order becomes chaotic and perverted.[119] (Although Paul does not specifically refer here to the consequences of idolatry for our environment, it is not difficult to draw the ecological consequences from his portrayal of the wrath of God. Once humankind ceases to be the guardian of God's created order as God intended, creation becomes a mute object for human greed and technological manipulation, and the result is immense suffering in our world.)[120]

In this connection, John Wenham contends that it is good that the results of sin are not confined to the doer, for it is in the cumulative effects of sin in society that the true horror of evil in the human heart can be seen. Our human tendency is to hush up sin, but God shows forth his glory and goodness by exposing sin and bringing it into the light. We want to turn our eyes away from the horrors of the Inquisition, the slave trade, the industrial revolution, the gas chambers, the atom bomb; but God forces us to look. The movements of the individual human heart, seemingly as insignificant as a tiny strip of film, are by the brilliant light of the corporate principle cast in all their terror upon the screen of human history.[121]

The principle of judgment upon and annulment of evil can be discerned at work in history and even in individual lives, as well as in the Bible, but this principle rarely works in the precise and immediate detail we might desire.

Sometimes, in fact, it seems that God's judgment on sinful humanity must be incomplete or in suspension—how else would the continuing prevalence of sin in the world be explained? The essential freedom of persons doubtless requires that wickedness should have some rope. But, we ask, must it have quite so much rope as it appears always to have had—not least in this present time of unspeakable brutality and anguish?[122]

But this delay of divine judgment is to be expected if the world is, as the Christian faith maintains, a training ground for personality. Men and women must learn to love righteousness and hate evil for their own sakes, not for their immediate consequences in terms of reward or punishment. A world in which every sin was instantly penalized would not be a suitable place for character to grow.[123]

Wenham emphasizes that it is actually good that sin is linked with suffering as retribution—and not just as a deterrent to further sin. More important in the long run is the fact that a retributory system is essential to the welfare of mankind. As pointed out earlier, human nature demands justice. In fact, the human conscience, until deadened by sophistication, warmly responds to just retribution. A child prefers to live in a world where the rules are kept and where in ordinary circumstances punishments are swiftly and fairly administered.[124]

Just law is an expression of God's character, and so it is that the theme of God's judgment permeates the Bible. God professes to treat humans as responsible beings, according to their deserts. If the effects of original sin were allowed to work themselves out unchecked, man's inhumanity to man would know no bounds. Such elements of stability, freedom, mercy, and goodness as we enjoy, we owe to the operation of God's righteous judgments among us.[125]

According to the Bible, the supreme retribution is death; and death, both physical death and eternal spiritual death, is what sin deserves. To go against the will of God—that is, to reject the likeness and the love of Christ—is death. This is not only basic to the teaching of the Bible, it is also sober, logical sense. If God exists, and if humankind is made for the very purpose of enjoying God's love, the rejection of that love can mean only ultimate disaster.[126]

To sin means ultimately to forfeit heaven, and this is the greatest possible punishment anyone can ever receive—the punishment which sin deserves. Compared with this, all other punishments, however terrible, are relatively insignificant. Furthermore, because sin deserves death and we are all sinners, it means that all our mercies are undeserved mercies. None of us will ever receive harsher judgment than we deserve. In the New Testament, God's undeserved grace is the unending theme. In the biblical view, the marvel is not that men die for their sins, but that we remain alive in spite of them.[127]

(2) The Incarnation, the Cross, the Resurrection, the Holy Spirit, and the Church. The heart of the biblical message is that God has done more in the face of moral evil than just judge humankind. Rather, God took specific initiative in history—in the incarnation, crucifixion, and resurrection of Jesus Christ and his continued presence through the Holy Spirit and the church. Christ showed us that God is not only a God of law; he is also a God of

creative love, struggling with us to bring us a new life. Through Christ, God brought us forgiveness and restoration in the face of our evil choices.

The victory of Christ is the center of historical redemption. It is a temporal event, but it is also part of the eternal reality which the gospel proclaims. So far as history means anything at all to God, this is actually and positively his central victory within it.

The Christian faith affirms that God is able by his grace to transform all evil into good, whether past, present, or future. Christians see God as doing this on the Cross and in the Resurrection. Christians also see God as transforming the evil in their own hearts, and they trust God to do the same on the vast scale of his universe.[128]

It is important to note that Paul does not leave unanswered his bleak description of human idolatry, divine wrath, and human suffering in Rom. 1:18–32. Indeed, his whole discourse on divine wrath is given in the context of God's saving righteousness in Christ (1:16–17), which proclaims that God has intervened in his perverted world and has created a new one, where the power of idolatry with its attendant suffering has been overcome. The reversal of idolatrous worship brings about a new relation of the self to itself, to other selves, and by implication to God's creation. And the vanguard of this new order is the church, which in Paul's view is the vanguard of God's new creation, inserted into the idolatrous old creation by God's grace in order to exhibit a new form of life.[129]

The church is for Paul the place where authentic hope is made possible because the suffering of human injustice is here overcome. Its new language of family intimacy calls the almighty God "our Father" and so bonds members together as brothers and sisters. In this context, suffering and joy are shared together (1 Cor. 12:26). Moreover, the body of Christ seeks ways to enflesh its new hope into the world by drawing people out of the idolatrous structures of the world and their attendant suffering in order to incorporate them into its new world of hope—the first fruits of the coming kingdom of God.[130]

6. God's Promise for a Suffering-Free Future

God promises final victory over evil and suffering in the new heaven and the new earth. This ultimate solution emerges from the account of God's final triumph over all the forces of sin, disorder, and death as described in the Epistles of Paul and in the Book of Revelation. The Bible repeatedly looks beyond the present in order to interpret the problem of evil in an eschatological context. In terms of scriptural justification of God's ways, Scripture portrays sin in the framework of God's almighty end-time vindication of the good as it was and is anticipated by the resurrection of Jesus.

Any effort to picture the biblical view merely as a speculative theodicy breaks down in the light of Paul's declaration that "the creation waits in eager expectation . . ." (Rom. 8:19, NIV). This promise sets the biblical view of the universal subordination of evil in the dimension of hope. Even in the Book of Revelation, innocent suffering cries out for eschatological righteousness (Rev. 6:10, 18:1ff.).

Biblical eschatology projects a regenerate universe delivered from natural disasters, from human abuse of nature, and from man's inhumanity to man. It insists also on heaven and hell as final and fixed states of contrasting personal destiny.[131]

The biblical promise for the ultimate future of the earth and humankind is important, for it casts evil and suffering in a completely different perspective, allowing us to see it in the context of the meaning of the whole. (This "big picture" solution to the problem of evil, called sometimes the aesthetic theme, goes back to Augustine.)[132]

In the biblical description, God's regenerate world is pictured as the place where God will wipe away every tear from our eyes (Rev. 7:17). Moreover, the saints that have suffered are depicted as wearing white robes, suggesting that evil and injustice will find their compensation in God's final settlement. In addition, Revelation pictures God's people praising throughout all eternity the Lamb that was slain, that is, the ransom paid for moral evil. The crucifixion, an obvious result of evil and injustice, will not have been passed over and overcome; it will actually be featured—an object of eternal devotion and wonder.

The context of the final reconciliation also deserves notice, for in the renewed and restored order natural evil will be completely overcome. It will be a perfect environment for the new moral order. Thus, the final purpose of God signifies a perfection and realization of the purposes we glimpse only imperfectly now.[133]

And so the biblical vision offers a promissory word in the face of suffering due to the power of death. That promise instills in us the hope of God's triumph in the face of the agonizing burden of suffering which so many of us carry. Although the awesome "not yet" of God's final triumph over suffering and death all too often fills us with agony and despair, the promise of the gospel continues to evoke in us the prayerful cry, "Come, Lord Jesus" (Rev. 22:20).[134]

VI. How Would You Describe a Systematic Approach to the Practical Problem of Achieving Victory in and through Evil and Suffering?

1. The Importance of the Practical Approach

Intellectually or theoretically, I think we have shown that the evangelical view offers a meaningful and helpful approach to evil and suffering based on biblical principles. But its genius is in its practical or experiential ability to help us to constructively live with evil and suffering and attain victory in and through Christ. The distinguished British theologian P. T. Forsyth contends that the final answer to the problem of evil and suffering is in no discovered system, no revealed plan, but in an effectual redemption. It is not really an answer to a riddle, but a victory in a battle. And we do not see the answer; instead, we trust the Answerer.[135]

A Christian may not find the complete answer to the theoretical question, why, but he or she can know the practical answer to the questions how, and who. For the Christian, the ultimate solution is a practical solution which proceeds from and shares in the life of the Incarnate Son of God. Christians have no guarantee against suffering, but they can have victory over or in suffering. Victory, however, is not found in an escape from life but in the transformation of life. Our chief concern in this section, therefore, is not to lay down an explanation or theory of evil and suffering, but to show how we can lay hold of the power which can transform us.[136]

(It should be noted, however, that a practical answer must be rooted in the broad theological framework of the biblical worldview. In his widely acclaimed book, *When Bad Things Happen to Good People,* Rabbi Harold Kushner also adopts a very pragmatic approach. But as pointed out earlier in this chapter, his view is weakened by an inadequate view of the sovereignty of God, as well as a lack of understanding of the future orientation of Scripture.)[137] For help in the practical approach we turn to the apostle Paul. The extent and plurality of the letters of Paul not only give us easy access to his thought, but also show us the depth of his reflections on evil and suffering. In fact, the depth of Paul's thought can provide, for a person engaged in reflection about suffering and hope, a catalyst for further reflection.[138]

2. The Practical or Experiential Approach of the Apostle Paul

The apostle Paul has given us a classic study of the practical Christian approach to suffering in Philippians, 2 Corinthians, Colossians 1, and Romans 8. Romans 8:35–37 states that even in "tribulation, or distress, or persecution, or famine, or nakedness, or peril, or sword. . . . we are more than conquerors through him who loved us." The original language points to one great factor—the Cross—as being the great instance of his love. So the apostle Paul could be interpreted as saying, "In all these things we are more than conquerors through the Cross."

(1) God's Actualized Sympathy for Our Sufferings. We can trust God because of his actualized sympathy. The God who is the world-Creator and the world-Redeemer has voluntarily limited himself to the creation of cosmos out of chaos, to a redemption of rebels by grace instead of a forceful annihilation of them. God has accepted the burden of the whole process of redemption in time, with all that its sin must mean to his holiness. He has become involved at the cost of much suffering on his part.[139]

In the first place, the Bible and the Cross tell us that *God suffered for us.* We live in a moral universe that demands payment for sin—and God, through Christ, paid the price for our sin. Though Christ was rich, he became poor for our sakes. Jesus, the incarnate Son of God, endured the agony of the Cross, suffered the punishment of divine wrath, and satisfied the demands of the moral order in order to free us from the eternal penalty of our sins (Phil. 2:8).

The Father's love sent forth the Son; the Son's love drew him to earth to become human, so that he might save humankind. God himself bears our sins. "God was in Christ reconciling the world to himself" (2 Cor. 5:19). Forgiveness does not remove the penalties of sin. Rather, the one who forgives bears the effects of the other's sin himself and thus takes the sinner's place. Christ was the sinner's Substitute, the one who bore the sinner's punishment. The price was fully paid.[140]

We sense something of the price of this suffering in Christ's fourth word from the cross: "My God, my God, why hast thou forsaken me?" (Matt. 27:46). His sixth word was: "It is finished" (John 19:30). The experience of Christ on the cross reminds us that the Christian faith grounds its knowledge of God's relationship to evil and suffering in the central events of salvation history—the cross and the resurrection of Jesus.

Suffering is not extraneous or accidental to the redeeming actions of God. God in Christ suffers for us. Indeed, a close examination not only of the last events in Jesus' ministry, but also of his entire life tells us that from first to last his life was one of suffering. Yet Jesus found within his sufferings a meaning for himself and for us, as he transformed the tragedy of suffering into the glory of the Cross and the victory of the Resurrection.[141]

A second part of God's actualized sympathy is that *God suffers with us.* This, too, is the clear message of the Bible and the Cross.

During World War II, the father of a Marine who had been killed demanded of a pastor, "Where was God when my son was killed in the war?" Like this father, some people think of God as standing outside the sufferings of this world—as apart and uninterested, abiding in the untroubled peace of heaven.

But stop a minute and look at the cross. Who is suffering there? It is not just another martyr dying for his faith; it is God in human flesh. When we see this, we begin to see that the idea of God's abiding apart from the sufferings of the world is the wrong idea.

Look at the cross and remember the words of Christ: "He who has seen me has seen the Father" (John 14:9). Then we must affirm that God is not outside the tears and tragedy of life. In every pain and sorrow that tears a human heart, God has a share. And in every dark valley of trouble and suffering, God is always present.[142]

The pastor was right when he answered the bereaved father with another question: "Where was God when his own Son was crucified at Calvary?" God was there. Because of God's character, it is not possible for evil and suffering to be the concern of humanity alone. God shares in the tragedies of the world he has created.

It is important to remember that the Cross is not an explanation of the existence of evil or a philosophical resolution to the problem of evil, but the answer to the question of evil. Times of personal tragedy tend to call into question the love and goodness of God, and that justifiable question is definitively answered in Christ and his cross, where God's goodness and love are apparent. Therefore, in those tragedies where God seems silent or absent, the Christian's foundation is not destroyed, even though he may have his spasms of perplexity and doubt. The love and goodness of the Cross is a greater assurance of God's love than any conceivable tragedy can be a denial of that love and goodness.[143]

Karl Barth has followed this very approach in his own theodicy. For Barth, the Cross is the clearest revelation of God's love, goodness, and wisdom. Therefore, when tragedy happens in any of its forms, from the mildest to the most shocking, the Christian finds comfort by looking once again to the cross of Christ. Here there is no shadow present, but only the bright light of divine truth that tells us of the unspeakable love of God.[144]

The Cross gives the Christian the ability and strength to tolerate evil, to live with confusion, to endure ambiguity, and to suffer through great evils. No event of evil can be so terrible that it can undermine the love of God as revealed at the Cross.[145]

As a loving companion who dwells with us, God changes the actual events of life and history into interpreted events or transformed facts of experience. In this way, God gives us a perspective on suffering and new strength in our suffering.[146]

A friend of mine was going across the western part of the United States in an airplane. Across from him sat a prominent New York attorney who was going to the West Coast to bury his only sister—his last close relative. He was bolstering himself up against the tragedy by soaking himself with liquor. In a supreme crisis, he had no resources on the inside or from above, and so he was trying to take in some from a bottle. It was a pathetic performance for a distinguished lawyer.

Contrast that with George Matheson, the great Scottish Christian. Torn by grief when he became blind and his sweetheart refused to marry him, he nevertheless found strength and help in his Christian faith. And he in turn has strengthened Christians ever since with his well-known hymn: "O Love that will not let me go,/I rest my weary soul in Thee. . . ."

Think what God's burden of suffering must be when the pains of all his children are in his heart! A person who sees this will never again cry out against God as not caring, but will instead keep silence before the love and agony of God.

A final or third aspect of God's actualized sympathy is that *God suffers in us*. The relationship of the Holy Spirit to evil and suffering is best expressed by the preposition *in*. The Scriptures speak of the indwelling of the Spirit in terms expressive of suffering. The Bible uses such terms as "grieved," "vexed," "helping," and "taking our infirmities."[147] It is not just that God knows and sympathizes with us in our troubles, as any close friend might do. He is much closer than the closest friend, because as the Holy Spirit he lives within us. Therefore, our sufferings are his sufferings; our sorrows are his sorrows.

The suffering and evil in our individual and collective lives, whether past, present, or future, are materials waiting to be transformed by the Holy Spirit in us. God is indeed a Comforter, for his suffering in us lifts our suffering and our evil to a new level and gives them a new meaning.

(2) God's Use of Our Sufferings to Help Others. In mystical union with Christ, all of our sufferings can become helpful as we become creative fellow workers with God in the continuation of that redemptive work which was initiated at Calvary. This is called the transformation approach to suffering.

The transformation approach accepts the fact that suffering is inevitable in the human condition. However, at the same time it seeks to transform suffering and integrate it into human life in such a way that we come to see that life would be poorer without it. The Cross is the preeminent Christian symbol, at once an instrument of torture and acute suffering and the promise of wholeness and salvation.[148]

This does not mean that our sufferings are vicarious or substitutionary in the way that Christ's sufferings were vicarious. The work of Christ on the cross was adequate and unique; our suffering is not required to complete it. However, suffering, when it comes to us or when we undergo it for the cause of Christ, affords us an opportunity to cooperate with Christ in his transformation and redemptive work. Colossians 1:24 says that we are to "fill up" the sufferings of Christ (KJV). By taking our personal griefs and troubles and sacrifices and offering them up on the altar alongside the sacrifice of Jesus, we can share in the eternal passion of God by which humanity is to find healing. It is as though God says, in our day of darkness, "Here, my child, is your little share in the burden which I have been carrying since the foundation of the world. Here is your part with me in the agelong cross I must bear."[149]

Such a fellowship of suffering with Christ and with all who belong to his mystical body surely lifts all suffering potentially to a new plane. Looking at suffering this way can give suffering a new meaning. For if God is "in it with you," sharing your suffering, you are also "in it with him," sharing his redemptive activity and his victory.[150]

What does this mean in practical terms? In a universe of complex interrelationships and a world of law, suffering often comes to Christians. Through these sufferings often comes the opportunity to share, to identify, and to help. In almost every case of suffering there is a Christian who has had a similar experience and who can witness and share out of his or her experience. In almost every situation there will be a Christian who can go to one who has cancer or to those who have a retarded child or to those whose son has been killed and say, "I have been in a similar situation, and I know what Christ can mean in such a situation."

The death of Jesus, a historical event, is transformed by God into the fact of the resurrected Christ. The meaning of any historical event is the transformed event, that is, what is done with the event. For Christians, evil and suffering never appear as bare happenings. Rather, God as Father suffers with us; God as Son suffers for us; God as Spirit suffers in us; and, accordingly, we in our suffering can share in his redemptive activity. With the help of the triune God, suffering and pain, human tragedy and loss, can become transformed events and even be used to help others.

In the New Testament there is still another dimension to God's use of the Christian's suffering. The suffering of Christians and the church is to be marked not only by passive endurance and transformation, but also by aggressive redemptive action. The church is called to endure the hostility of the world's oppressive powers, a suffering which Paul characterizes as "sharing in Christ's suffering" (2 Cor. 1:5; Phil. 3:10) or as "suffering with Christ" (Rom. 8:17; cf. also "becoming like him in his death," Phil. 3:10).[151]

The church, the new creation of God in the midst of the old creation, is called not only to endure suffering, but also to engage suffering. Therefore, the church is not allowed to interpret its suffering as tragic and meaningless or just as a form of divine discipline or punishment.[152]

The Book of 1 Peter, which describes the suffering of the Christian churches of Asia Minor toward the end of the first century A.D., underscores both the intensity and scope of their experienced suffering (4:12–16). The opening to the Book greets the Christians of Asia Minor as "the exiles of the Dispersion," implying that they suffer the lot of outcasts and displaced persons in the very towns and cities where they live. This suffering is not necessarily caused by official state persecution (as suffered later by the Christians under the emperor Domitian) or by a statewide pogrom authorized by the central government, but rather by a hostile social system.[153]

In spite of these difficulties, the author of 1 Peter believes that there are some "missionary" possibilities for Christian faith in the midst of oppression. Christians can show its attractiveness to outsiders, gaining their respect and hopefully converting them. First Peter's interpretation of suffering in the world is not purely passive, but has redemptive and "hopeful" features (2:9, 12, 15; 3:15–16).[154]

(3) Personal Victory and a Developed Christian Character Through Suffering. Think once more of Christ on the cross. At first glance, the crucifixion looks like defeat—as if suffering and sorrow have blotted out our hopes forever. But if you look again, you will make a marvelous discovery. This time you will see that it is not Christ that is defeated. Christ is the Victor! The Cross signaled the defeat of suffering and the mystery of evil and all the dark powers of evil (Phil. 2:8, 9).

But, you ask, how does that relate to us? Christ may have conquered, but I still have my troubles and my battles, and others around me have it even worse. If evil at its worst has been met and conquered by Christ, then surely, on the lesser scale of your own life, victory can come to you and through you by union with Christ through faith. In Romans 8:37, the apostle Paul is speaking as one who has been through some of the worst tragedies of life. He has suffered, therefore he has a right to speak. And his powerful assertion is that in all those heartbreaking things which happen to human beings—physical pains, mental agonies, and spiritual midnights—we can become more than conquerors, not through our own strength but through Christ who loved us.[155]

This does not mean all things that happen to Christians are good. But the promise is that in everything—good or evil—God can and will work to bring good to those who love him and are in submission to him, seeking his will. The good that God works is the good of making us conformed to the image of his Son. Even Christ was perfected through sufferings (Heb. 2:10). The Holy

Spirit is able to make persons more like Christ if they offer up their sufferings in love. Furthermore, there is a special experience of intimacy and understanding with Christ when this is done.

Christians whose attitudes have been transformed and taught by the Holy Spirit will find that all sufferings—including tragedies and even the mistakes and hates of others, can be turned to make us more conformed to Christ in our lives.

A similar view was developed in a systematic way by the great church father Irenaeus, who lived in the second century A.D. Irenaeus understood this present world as the context for gradual spiritual growth, and he believed that in the contrasting (and often painful) experience of good and evil, a person is taught to love one and despise the other. In other words, Irenaeus viewed evil as a pedagogic tool to lead people to maturity. Such a view, sometimes called the purposeful or "soul-making" view of evil, has been especially popular in Eastern Orthodox Christianity.[156]

One does not have to agree with all the theological implications of Irenaeus's view to see it as a promising approach. Granted the presence and pervasiveness of evil, can God use it to accomplish his purpose in people's lives? Experiences of hardship often do produce character and discipline in individual lives. This is pointed to by experience and specifically stated in the epistles of Peter and Paul. (Peter's writings contain the theme that suffering purifies the church, and Paul pictures suffering as equipping the people of God for ministry.) If evil can be used in a higher purpose, if suffering produces character, then it is possible that God's unwillingness to create a world in which evil is impossible reflects neither on his goodness nor on his power, but flows from his eternal and unchanging purposes.[157]

(4) The Possibility of Rejoicing in Suffering. The apostle Paul, especially in Philippians 1:29, states that we are to rejoice in our suffering. There is joy in a willingness to even go to the point of death for the sake of the gospel. This joy does not take away the reality of pain, of course. Rather, joy comes from our ability to witness and fulfill our Christian calling through our pain and suffering. Paul suffered in a jail. The Philippians suffered. Christ suffered. They shared a mutual fellowship of suffering. There is an indication in this emphasis that the world will probably see the power of Christ only as Christians suffer and even become martyrs. Here is the beginning of a martyr theology: "The blood of martyrs is the seed of the Church."

Martin Luther saw suffering as a sign of God's grace, proof that we are God's children, and he emphasized the importance of the discipline of suffering as part of becoming like the Master.[158] Dietrich Bonhoeffer, the modern German theologian who was martyred by the Nazis, carried this Lutheran emphasis into the twentieth century.[159]

Bonhoeffer resurrected a term from the early church, the "secret discipline" by which the faithful lived in a culture that overwhelmed them. He believed it was an appropriate term for the present, seemingly God-forsaken age. The secret discipline of suffering makes no claims of heroism, nobility, honor, or splendor—as it would necessarily in the case of Greek tragic heroes. Linked with Christ, this participation is instead simply an unavoidable reality.[160]

However, such suffering can be positive because it provides an active opening to the world. It permits resistance to evil—as shown clearly by Bonhoeffer's courageous opposition to Hitler. It does not involve whimpering, and it does not make believers passive in the face of pain. One of its most important aspects is sympathy and support; it involves the church's sharing of the burdens of the diseased or despairing in their midst.[161]

Despite the witness of Bonhoeffer and others like him, the biblical idea of joy in suffering has been deeply misunderstood in the last two centuries and has come under attack from several directions. The Marxist tradition, for example, accuses Paul of being an escapist because he told people to bear with suffering and not seek to change conditions. Others, such as Edmund Bergler, have postulated that Paul was a masochist. Quoting 2 Corinthians 12:10, they say that Paul delighted in pain.[162]

The biblical worldview, however, holds that Paul was neither a masochist nor an escapist, but a Christian realist. In suggesting a way to handle suffering, he was giving the Philippians a practical strategy for confronting the problem of evil. Paul viewed suffering on the one hand as an *evil* which will be undone when God's kingdom is established on earth, and on the other hand as a *redemptive necessity* to be suffered by Christians because of and against the world's idolatrous schemes.[163]

In 1 Peter 1:8, the early Christians were said to have demonstrated joy in suffering. They, too, were neither escapists nor masochists. Their joy amidst suffering was possible because their life and thought was anchored in a tightly knit support group, the house-church, that gave social and spiritual cohesion to their lives, yielded comfort in the midst of oppression, and enabled them to devise some strategies of hope.[164]

Notice that in 1 Peter 4:14 the admonition to rejoice in suffering does not romanticize or glorify suffering for its own sake. Only that suffering which "shares in Christ's sufferings" or which is "suffering as a Christian in the name of Christ" is a cause for joy and blessing (4:13–16). The joy comes not from the suffering itself, but from the fact that suffering means "following in Christ's steps" (2:22), the innocent Suffering Servant of God (2:21–25).[165]

Joy in suffering also comes from the hope of future joy at the coming of Christ. In the light of this hope, suffering can both be endured and realistically assessed. There is no need to repress it or to elevate it "spiritually."[166] It is important to understand that 1 Peter shares with most New Testament writings an apocalyptic perspective. Thus 1 Peter does not view the suffering of Christians as their final destiny, but as only a penultimate reality. Yet the otherworldliness of the hope is not divorced from "hopeful" possibilities in the present time.[167]

It should be noted, finally, that the hope which inspires joy in suffering is not simply otherworldly hope or simply passive endurance. Rather, hope in the imminent coming of God's definitive victory and glory motivates Christians to devise strategies of hope amidst their daily experience of suffering. It is not only a manifestation of what Kierkegaard calls "being in the truth," of living one's life in accord with God's will and holiness (1:15–17), but also a demonstration to a hostile world of the civic loyalty and "good works" of Christians in its midst.[168]

VII. What Are Some Concluding Summary Statements About the Christian Approach to Evil and Suffering?

After all the solutions are considered, we must plainly acknowledge that the problem of evil and suffering is still not completely solved. At the level of reflection and theory, all that the Christian can fairly ask is that the Christian view be compared, in its strength and weakness, with other major approaches.

The Christian, as a finite creature and not the Creator, recognizes that his or her understanding is limited. There are such things as mysteries; not all theological questions can be answered. There is a point at which Christians can do nothing but trust in God in the face of evil and suffering, trusting that some day they will know the answers as God now knows them: "For now we see in a mirror dimly, but then face to face. Now I know in part; then I shall understand fully" (1 Cor. 13:12).

Christians believe, however, that the situation changes, and more help is given, when the point of view shifts from reflection to action, from theory to practice. As Frederick von Huegel has written, "The greatest theoretic difficulty against all Theism lies in the terrible reality of Evil; and yet the deepest adequacy, in the actual toil and trouble of life, of this same Theism, especially of Christianity, consists in its practical attitude towards, and success against, this most real Evil."[169]

An important part of any faith or worldview consists of the illumination, stimulus, and power it provides its followers for facing the evils and tragedies of daily existence. The biblical worldview holds that evil and suffering may actually be met and overcome by the Christian faith. As we have seen, the meaning of the doctrines of the Cross and the Resurrection are central in the Christian approach to evil and suffering. Christianity is a religion of both cosmic and personal salvation and victory rather than cosmic and personal resignation or pessimism. On this basis, it rests its case regarding the problem of evil and suffering.[170]

8

The Question of Death and the Life Beyond

I. What Are Some Background Considerations Related to Death and the Life Beyond?

1. The Importance of the Question of Death and the Life Beyond

(1) The Inevitability and Universality of Death. All of us, without exception, must face death and the end of our own lives. In spite of recent advances in medical science, death continues to be an absolutely universal experience.

Of course, there are many types of death. Those people who have "checked out" psychologically or withdrawn from the world because they cannot cope with reality are "dead" in a sense, even though they continue with the basic physical life functions. It is possible to be spiritually dead, yet physically and psychologically vibrant. In this chapter, however, we will be speaking of the end of physical life.[1]

However "spiritual" we may become, and whatever dominance we acquire over nature, human beings remain embodied. The physical basis of human life is closely related to the dynamic interflow of natural forces. Furthermore, there is a limit to the duration of physical life. Under favorable conditions, the body might function for eighty years, more or less, but eventually it wears out. Although better medical care keeps most people going longer nowadays than would once have been the case, the extent to which human life can be extended is very limited. Every human being reaches an end when consciousness is extinguished, the life processes cease, and the organism disintegrates. No account of humanity, therefore, can be complete if it does not ask about the significance of death and the question of the life beyond.[2] In a sense, it is one of the most ultimate of life's ultimate questions.

In recent years, psychologists, philosophers, and social scientists have given unprecedented attention to the subject of death. While some writers emphasize that certain lower animals have a vague presentiment of their approaching extinction, few scholars challenge the view that only human beings have a clear awareness of death.[3]

It is true that young people tend not to think much about death. Everyone knows that death will eventually come, but death is a general truth with as yet little personal significance for young people. In youth, death seems something far off. In middle age, however, the situation changes. One's parents die, and when that happens a familiar, reliable presence is withdrawn from the world. For many people it is this event that brings a personal, nonabstract awareness of the radical finitude and transience of human life. Then other things begin to happen that make death seem more real and immediate. One's older friends die, and the time comes when one's contemporaries begin to die too. Life no longer seems to stretch endlessly in front, as it does in youth. We begin to realize that the future is limited. At age fifty or soon after, most people must face the reality that one's main achievements are already over and that soon a contraction of activities will begin to take place. Death then begins to assume a personal reality that it did not have before.[4]

Related to the fact of death are many questions: When we die, what happens? Do we black out forever? Do we experience joy and reunion with others? Do we see God, or do we move inexorably to higher dimensions, to more subtle planes of consciousness? What about rewards, punishments, and personal accountability?[5]

Since death and dying are universal and very personal concerns, Christians in every generation must deal with these questions in the light of new issues and challenges.

(2) The Threat of Global Annihilation. In addition to the universality and inevitability of personal death, the threat of planetary death also confronts those of us who live in the atomic age. Since the advent of nuclear weapons, the entire human race has been faced with the threat of imminent extinction on a global scale.

Many people—including young people—have the awareness of this unprecedented death threat constantly lurking at the edge of their consciousness. It is ironic that in a time when the traditional churches are saying little on the subject of last things, we are experiencing the rise of what could be called "secular apocalypticism." The reservations that often accompany projections into the future today are "*If* humanity is still around," "*If* there is a year 2000."[6]

For the first time, without the spur of religious teaching, men and women are living with the conscious or unconscious realization that at any moment, in the words of Shakespeare's Prospero, "the great globe itself, yea all which it inherit shall dissolve." Life goes on, more or less as usual, but underneath there is the sense of mortal danger, an awareness that the end is no longer a poetic or theological concept, but a reality hovering near. The new apocalyptic mentality broods over our art, politics, literature, and science. It surfaces in casual conversation. It sets a question mark on all plans and projects.[7] And it makes an understanding of death and dying an even more crucial question than it has always been.

(3) The Relationship Between an Adequate View of the Question of Death and the Life Beyond and the Ability to Live Meaningfully. Still another reason why it is important to face the question of death and the life beyond is that a person's

understanding of these realities is directly related to his or her understanding of this present life. Without an adequate and hopeful concept of what comes after death, life usually seems meaningless and untrustworthy.

Most humans at heart have a sense that we were not made to die. Our brief span of life seems to argue that all our achievements are less than worthwhile in an eternal sense. Although we belong to the lower creation physically, we yet transcend it in spirit. Thus, we are not satisfied with that death to which all nature is subject. Questions dawn on our consciousness, yearning for some fulfillment beyond the reach of decay.[8]

The loss of purpose and hope that comes from a belief that life is meaningless and death the end of it all can help explain self-induced death or suicide. And we are seeing an alarming increase in the rate of suicide today, especially among younger persons. Today suicide is the third highest cause of death among college students. And children in their teens and even younger are committing suicide in disturbing numbers.[9]

Another consequence of the loss of meaning in life and hope in eternal life is that human beings become depersonalized. This prepares the way for nihilism and totalitarianism. When the transcendent ground of responsible personality is withdrawn, there is no longer any limit to the expression of a self-centered assertiveness. The will to power tends to make itself absolute and unleash itself in boundless ferocity.[10]

Ernest Becker, in his well-known book, *The Denial of Death,* even suggests that the failure to come to terms with the reality of death is at the core of most neuroses. (In this he directly contradicts Freud, who saw the sexual impulse as the root of neurosis.) Becker argues that the fear of death is intrinsic to human nature and that all sickness of the soul is rooted in the denial and repression of this reality. Becker shows that the reality of death reaches into every nook and cranny of life. It casts a shadow over the cheerful play of the child as well as the optimistic and idealistic dreams of youth.[11]

Becker also suggests, however, that faith in God is the most viable way to live with this fear of death and so achieve mental health. According to Becker, the way out is to have faith in a transcendent being who is able to sustain the human person in a continual state of reality. Even though Becker's conception of God is rather vague from an evangelical perspective—a kind of supracosmic power to which one attaches oneself, rather than the personal and saving God of the Bible[12] —he does show effectively the human need to come to terms both with death and God in order to lead a meaningful life. Quoting psychoanalyst Otto Rank, who claimed that man was a "theological being—not a biological one," Becker argues that religion and psychology come together in this analysis of the self.[13]

(4) The Continuing Interest in Death and the Life Beyond. It is interesting that in the twentieth century, which is by far the most "scientific" age humankind has seen, there is a continuing interest in death and the life beyond. Ray Anderson, Professor of Theology and Mission at Fuller Theological Seminary, points out that in the nineteenth century, in reaction to the skepticism of

science, there was a revived interest in the human personality and in the rich experiences of life not capable of being accounted for through scientific and philosophical rationalism. In a similar way, the contemporary mind, despite the pervasive nature of scientific empiricism and secular materialism, continues to be preoccupied with the question of what lies beyond the physical world—including what lies beyond the end of physical life.[14]

A part of the appeal of many cultic and occult groups is the detailed teaching of these groups about the nature of death and the life beyond. This is further evidence of desire for information about life beyond death. When churches in the classical Christian tradition fail to speak clearly about death and the life beyond, many people turn pathetically to the innumerable sects which thrive on promises of occult glimpses into the future, with little biblical base or relevance to present earthly tasks.

It is noteworthy, moreover, that in universities nationwide there has been a proliferation of courses on subjects related to death and dying. One author has stated that he has reviewed over eight hundred books on death and dying, and has more than two thousands articles in his files on the same subject![15]

It is not just scholars and writers who are interested in the subject of death and the life beyond. James Kidd, an Arizona copper miner, left in his estate a generous bequest to stimulate research which would provide, in the words of his will, "some scientific proof of a soul of the human body." Following Kidd's death, the money was placed with the American Society for Psychical Research. This organization has used the money to conduct out-of-body experiments and cross-cultural studies of deathbed experiences. They have also experimented with Kirlian photography, a technique developed by Russian engineer Semyon Kirlian which supposedly portrays the subtle psychic essence, or aura, which emanates from a person.[16]

Traditional non-Western cultures have, by and large, eschewed a materialistic or scientific view of death and retained interest in the cosmologies, religious systems, and philosophies in which physical death is not seen as the absolute end of human existence. These systems range from concepts of the afterlife which teach an eventual absorption into impersonal consciousness to images of other-world existence which resemble earthly forms. Nevertheless, they hold in common the belief that death is transitional and a bridge to a further stage.[17]

Since there continues to be a need and interest on the part of Christians and non-Christians both in the United States and around the world, it is especially important to present a balanced biblical view about death and the life beyond.

2. Reasons for Avoiding, Suppressing, or Neglecting the Question of Death and the Life Beyond

Despite the evidence of a widespread and continuing interest in death and the life beyond, there is a parallel trend in our culture to avoid or suppress the subject. As mentioned earlier, some see this neglect as rooted in psychological repression—a surface denial of underlying interest. Various other reasons are given—some of which contain a germ of truth which needs to be heeded in presenting a balanced Christian perspective.

(1) Reaction Against Unreasonable Assertions. Avoidance of the question of death and the life beyond is sometimes a reaction against the distorted and nonscriptural teachings of some churches or cultic groups who are preoccupied with details of life after death. (Jehovah's Witnesses, for example, present teachings which are almost fantastic in their speculations.)

(2) The Prevailing Naturalistic Mode of Thought. This is a generation for whom Christian teachings about the life beyond are being undercut by the relentless onslaught of scientific materialism and secular humanism. Many who accept intellectually the traditional Christian teachings are nonetheless anything but secure in their faith—particularly when it comes to the issue of death and dying.[18]

The typical Western view of death has become more pragmatic and dissociated from religious or philosophical worldviews. Aging and dying are seen as reminders of our limited ability to control nature, despite technological and scientific achievements in this regard. The educated Westerner therefore tends to regard belief in consciousness after death as a manifestation of primitive fears and relics of religion.[19]

Several factors have been cited as contributing to this situation. Some have attributed the origin of the modern "death-denying" culture to the rise of secular humanism. British philosopher John Hick suggests, for example, that the sources of the contemporary situation are rooted in the materialism which resulted from "Western, science-oriented humanism." The world and human beings, says Hick, are now considered to be no more than a part of the phenomenon of nature. Human life is seen as a product of biological evolution, where individuals perish absolutely at death like all other organisms of the species.[20]

(3) Belief That Interest in Death and the Life Beyond Will Lead to Neglect of Present Concerns. Some contend that hope for a glorious fulfillment in the life beyond makes people insensitive to the concerns of the present life. Karl Marx suggested, for example, that in drooling over the mansions in heaven, we neglect the plight of the poor and show no interest in social justice here on earth.

(While on a tour of Russia several years ago, we requested our Soviet guide to take our study group to a church in Moscow. Afterwards, I asked her what she thought of the church service. Trained in Marxist propaganda, she immediately answered, "Marx was right. Religion is escapism. These poor people spend their energies in worship and talk about heaven and neglect concern for the new economic society we are building.")

There is some truth in this criticism of an overemphasis on the life beyond. For example, the humanists of the Renaissance period suggested that a preoccupation with the next world weakened the vital powers of the present life. This led to the attempt by some eighteenth-century philosophers to deny the immortality of the soul as the "priestly lie." They said that this "lie" had to be unmasked and destroyed in order to secure a better life and freedom in the here and now.[21]

Improperly understood, the doctrine of heaven or details about the second coming of Christ can lead us away from an interest in this present life. However, as we will note later in the chapter, such a hope should lead to a dynamic sense of stewardship and ethical concern and action in this life.

(4) Belief That Concern about Death Is Too Morbid and Self-Centered. Some people claim that the life beyond is a needless notion and that belief in it is a mere symptom of human arrogance. And admittedly, there have been times when at least some people have surrounded themselves with reminders of death's inevitable approach. These were times when the threats to life from social disorder and widespread epidemics were more numerous than they are now. It was also a time when the Day of Judgment weighed heavily upon people.

Today, many people consider this preoccupation with death as morbid. This modern sense reflects the greatly increased perception of security in life and the decline of belief in a Day of Judgment. However, as we have already noted, new threats of life, such as nuclear destruction and AIDS, are beginning to wear away at the modern sense of security.[22]

(5) Unwillingness to Face the Reality of Death. Many people find the idea of death very unpleasant and therefore avoid the subject. While they may intellectually acknowledge the reality and the certainty of death, they do all they can to avoid facing the inevitability of their own death.

In a way, this attitude is characteristic of our entire culture. The very word *death* is suppressed. A study of sympathy cards, for example, shows that only 3 percent mention the forbidden word. "Leave-taking" or "called upstairs" are among the many verbal fig leaves used to cover the four-letter word *dead.* In contrast to the weather, dying is what everyone does and no one talks about. In fact, "Never say die" is one of our most common sayings. Like superstitious primitives, contemporary Americans seem to believe that something that is never mentioned will eventually disappear.[23]

David Hendin labels death as "un-American" and says, "Its inevitability is an affront to our inalienable rights of 'life, liberty, and the pursuit of happiness.'"[24] In *The Immortalist,* Alan Harrington defiantly asserts, "Death is an imposition on the human race, and no longer acceptable."[25]

So we see within our society numerous attempts to avoid thinking of death. The embalmer's cosmetic art is highly developed and apparently aimed at concealing the appearance of death. We no longer have graveyards; instead we have "memorial parks." Many people put off making a will because they are so uneasy over the thought of death.[26] Jessica Mitford, in her widely read book, *The American Way of Death,* describes in detail the many other ways in which Americans avoid or cover up the ugly fact of death.[27]

Charles Jackson comments on the disappearance in America of the rural cemetery in favor of modern parklike settings where "perpetual care" is offered without need for any more personal thought or concern. In a grotesque caricature of Jesus' aphorism, we leave the dead to think about the dead.[28]

To the existentialist, this unwillingness to come to grips with the reality of death is a prime example of "inauthentic existence." Death is one of the harsh realities of life: Every individual is going to grow old and die—that is our inevitable end. Life, if it is to be lived properly, must include acceptance of the fact of death and its implications.[29]

While a growing number of moderns may suppress fear of death, at least outwardly, they do not completely succeed in eliminating vexing anxieties concerning death. More than one person removed to a hospital's terminal ward has declared the approaching sense of becoming "nobody" to be the worst and least endurable of all human experiences.[30]

(6) Death As the Final Taboo. Some people suppress a concern with death because it to them represents the "final taboo." According to Helmut Thielicke, Professor Emeritus of Theology at the University of Hamburg, death holds a deep mystery and even a quasioccultic power which must be masked off from our direct observation and encounter. Human beings have always clothed their deepest mysteries in taboos.[31]

William May, a professor at Southern Methodist University, holds that there is a "sacral power" in death. Despite the prevailing secularism of the contemporary mind, says May, this silence and avoidance of death is evidence of the very sacred event with which death unavoidably confronts us.[32]

There is an immensity about death which goes beyond the biological event. The rituals of evasion which surround the contemporary avoidance of death do not stem from a sense that it is trivial or incidental. Rather, people in our culture feel an inner sense of bankruptcy before this sacred, and impenetrable immensity. Thus, says May, "The attempts at evasion and concealment are pathetic rather than casual."[33]

II. What Are Some Representative Subpersonal or Impersonal Views of Immortality?

1. Biological Immortality

Tennessee Williams, in his play, *Cat on a Hot Tin Roof*, has the character, "Big Daddy," demand that his son and daughter-in-law furnish him what he called "seed" or grandchildren. He was actually demanding what is called biological immortality.

Biological immortality is rooted in reproduction. If one raises a family, one's genes are transmitted to one's offspring and, eventually, to subsequent generations of offspring. In a way of speaking, then, elements of an individual continue to "live" in generations to come—almost forever.

The universal appeal of this type of immortality can be found in an African saying: "An ancestor lives on as long as there are children who remember." This emphasis is also prominent in Confucianism, which holds that a cultural as well as a physical inheritance is implanted in one's progeny. Living on through children and grandchildren is still a prominent reason for human procreation.[34]

Gilbert Ogutu, a lecturer at the University of Nairobi in Kenya, believes that the desire for biological immortality is the reason behind the deeply entrenched practice of polygamy in Africa. The idea is not just to raise a large family, but to ensure that a man is survived by one or more sons when he dies. The high mortality rate among infants makes it necessary for parents to raise as many children as they can in the hope that at least some will survive. This often leads a man to marry more than one wife or causes the woman to fetch another wife for her husband from among her kin.[35]

Interestingly enough, biological immortality is the only kind of immortality acknowledged by naturalistic and scientific humanists, who hold this natural order of space and time to be the whole of reality. In a naturalistic system, the only immortality possibility is that inherent in the biological continuity of the human race.

2. Social Immortality

Another kind of immortality people seek is the social influence of what they do, say, and achieve. According to this view, immortality is to be attained through the influence of gifts, charities, books, good deeds, and living on in the memories of our friends. The idea is that a person who does something which has social impact will live on. For example, Abraham Lincoln and other national heroes are said to be "alive" today because they live in the hearts of United States citizenry. The revolutionary ideas of Thomas Jefferson, Susan B. Anthony, Martin Luther King, Jr., and other famous people affect us even as they did their contemporaries—perhaps even more.[36]

A similar view is related to biological immortality. It affirms that we live on through the memory of our descendants, who keep us alive by keeping us and our deeds in mind. This perspective is shared by such diverse groups as modern Judaism and traditional Chinese religion.[37]

It is ironic that those who insist that "when a person's dead, he's dead," and that "death brings nothingness," often seek to leave a desirable impression on the lives of others. They seek to gain an "immortality of influence" by some contribution to society, some artistic achievement—even a financial contribution to some cause.[38]

Social immortality has interested the irreligious at least as much as the religious. Friedrich Engels concluded his funeral speech for Karl Marx with this prophecy: "His name will live through the centuries and so will his work."[39] At the center of the capital of China is a memorial to the Communist Revolution. On it is inscribed a slogan of Mao Zedong: "The people's heroes are immortal."

3. Impersonal Immortality

Still another kind of immortality involves the loss of personal consciousness and unification with some sort of larger reality. Hindus, for example, talk of being taken up into a universal spirit or Brahman. This view, which takes varying forms, affirms that we as individuals or our souls are swallowed up again into the universe, the realm of eternal being or the "world soul," from which we originally came. This position sometimes takes the form of pantheism, in which the one reality—God or the universe—receives the individual person to itself as the drop of water is lost in the vast ocean.

4. Subjective Immortality

Modern process theologians often refer to being remembered in the mind of God. Whitehead, for example, states that individuals are "objectively immortalized" in the mind of God. This means that Whitehead did not advocate a form of personal immortality involving the existence of real persons after death. In his conception, millions of people will become "occasions" in a never-ending process of becoming, but will only survive in God's memory.[40]

From the biblical perspective, subpersonal or impersonal views of the afterlife are inadequate. The New Testament clearly shows that, for believers, the individual personality will be retained in a transformed state as part of a new heaven and a new earth. In this study, accordingly, we will primarily be concerned with objective personal immortality in a new creation. This means living on as a unique individual beyond death in a corporate community with a spiritual body.

III. What Are the General Arguments for Immortality Taught by Philosophers, Religionists, and Poets?

The attempt to provide a rational demonstration of the possibility of a future life usually takes the form of three arguments for personal immortality. First, there are the arguments which proceed from man's belief and desire. Second, there are those arguments which are based on human nature. The third approach is constituted by those arguments which are derived from belief in the nature and power of God. In this section we will survey the arguments from human belief and desire. The third approach is the distinctive biblical approach and will be developed at length in a later section.

1. "The Widespread Hope and Desire for Immortality"—
The Historical Argument

Popular belief among all nations and ages shows that the idea of immortality is natural to the human mind. A hope that reaches beyond death is extremely ancient—as old, in fact, as the human race. While sophisticated modern philosophers may say that death removes all meaning from life, the majority of humankind has never been willing to accept so bleak a conclusion.

In ancient times, beginning long before human thoughts were written down, societies showed through their burial practices that they were thinking about death and were already entertaining hopes that reached beyond death. The bodies of the dead were buried with the greatest care. In many cases implements or ornaments that they had used in life were buried with them, as if they might still have need of them. Sometimes the bones were daubed with red ocher. Anthropologists suggest that the red symbolizes blood and therefore life.[41] The

Etruscans carved pictures of the rising sun on the urns that held the ashes of their dead. The Indians of the Americas placed arrows in the resting place of their braves, presumably to arm them for the life beyond. All this bears testimony to an as yet inarticulate hope for the dead.

The practice of ancestor worship in ancient cultures also attests to an innate desire for personal immortality. This worship involves such practices as holding periodic festivals at family tombs; the dead were supposed to be present in a nonsensory manner during these celebrations. These practices still go on in various parts of the world today.

The great civilization of ancient Egypt seems to have been fascinated to an extraordinary degree with death and what comes after death. Egyptian burial practices included the mummification of bodies and the provision of the necessities of daily life for the deceased within the tomb. The ancient Egyptians also believed in a final judgment and speculated on the transformation of the mode of human existence.[42]

In Central America, the Olmec, Toltec, Mayan, and Aztec cultures developed a ball game which was linked to their belief in immortality. This game was regarded as an initiation into the eschatological destiny prefigured by the heavenly sun and corn gods.[43]

Many of the traditional beliefs about the dead would be judged by us today to be mere superstition. Yet there is something impressive in the persistent belief that a human life is not annihilated by death. In all the myths and ceremonies, some very deep conviction of men and women about themselves is trying to find expression. They sought the recognition that every human being has a unique worth and should not simply perish when the biological mechanism is worn out.[44]

In a sense, instincts are prophecies. They express the most primary and fundamental needs of the organism and sustain the life of the individual and of the race. Human beings are creatures of instinct, born with our natures packed full of them. Out of this great deep of the human soul comes the instinct of immortality. This is an impulse and desire looking toward a future life which is as old and wide as the human race.

There are other instincts in our earth: that, for instance, by which the homing pigeon traces his path. These other instincts do not prove false. It would not seem possible for a desire to endure, becoming purified age after age, if there were not reality to satisfy it. The hope itself is its own argument.

Carl F. H. Henry contends that, despite human sin, general divine revelation continues to function universally in nature, history, and human conscience. It penetrates even today to the mind of every individual. If man bears God's image and was intended by creation for fellowship with him, the question of an afterlife is a concern of all human beings.[45]

Despite the influence of science and materialistic teachings, a number of anthropologists and sociologists see humans as strange restless creatures who are never quite at home in this seen and temporal world. We are dissatisfied with our own frustrations and imperfections. We are conscious of powers within ourselves requiring a different climate and a wider horizon for our full development and fruition.

From the Christian perspective, this type of argument is but a tenuous beginning, for biblical faith is much more robust than this. But at any rate, we have an indication of the force of the question concerning man's ultimate destiny, asked by countless men and women in age after age. To such a persistent impulse it seems reasonable to suppose that there is an answering reality and that man's hope and expectation are not in vain.

2. "Life Seems Incomplete without a Life Beyond"— The Teleological Argument

Our days on earth are full of loose ends: tasks begun but not finished, dreams unrealized, powers wasted, opportunities lost beyond recall. We do not feel this just for ourselves, but also for those we have learned to love and respect. Our deepest dread is that their individuality will be lost. We hope that those who have gone on before us will be able somehow to keep on enriching the universe, in which we all live together, according to their special abilities.

All of this means that life as we know it appears incomplete—a fact which leaves us stubbornly unreconciled with death. Death almost always seems untimely—even among the elderly. The decay of physical power, which is death's foretaste, thwarts older people just when the wisdom of experience and skill gained of practice have made them most useful to their neighbors. As the great French novelist Victor Hugo wrote at age seventy, "Winter is on my head, but spring is in my heart. . . . I have not said one thousandth part of what is in me."

3. "Life Is Irrational without a Hereafter"—The Rational Argument

Closely akin to the teleological argument is the rational approach. It seems irrational that life has brought this marvelous thing called personality into being, with all its splendid powers of love and heroism and nobility, only to annihilate it in the end. It is hard to believe that the universe, having toiled and travailed and agonized to produce its crowning creation, proceeds then to throw it out on the scrap-heap of death. It is hard to believe that souls which have shone with the radiance of faith and hope and love and honor and valor and self-sacrifice can be finished irrevocably and forever by a microbe, a piece of shrapnel, or a careless driver's twist of the wheel.

One cannot contemplate the destruction of high character in the universe without asking serious questions about the whole meaning of existence. If the evidence should overwhelmingly (or even clearly) favor the arbitrary denial of the ripest fruit of life, we might well reconsider our whole hypothesis about the nature of the universe.

G. H. Palmer summarized this attitude succinctly after gazing upon the dead body of his wife, an outstanding woman of her time who had been killed by a drunk driver. He said, "Who can contemplate the fact of her death and not call the world irrational, if out of deference to a few particles of disordered matter, it excludes so fair a spirit?"[46]

4. "Immortality Is Needed to Undergird Justice"—The Ethical Argument

According to this view, human beings are not adequately punished in this world for their evil deeds. Our sense of justice leads us to believe that God's moral administration will be vindicated in a life to come. Mere extinction of being would not be a sufficient penalty, nor would it permit degrees of punishment corresponding to degrees of guilt. This is therefore an argument from God's justice to the immortality of the wicked. The guilty conscience demands some form of afterlife for the purpose of justice. The evil that men do, as well as the good, lives with them.

Socrates, for instance, used this argument when he contended that the psyche's (soul's) immortality is implied by the nature of justice. Justice is recognized as a divine quality basic to government. However, many evil people go to their graves unpunished, and many innocent people are punished. If psyches are extinguished rather than extended at death, there is no way to avoid concluding that life is unfair and that we do not live in a moral universe.[47]

Immanuel Kant, the father of modern philosophy, agreed that complete justice requires the existence of an immortal soul and an infinite afterlife. Kant then concluded that only a divine being could create these conditions for the reward of the righteous and the punishment of the wicked.[48]

Excursus on Extrasensory Perception (ESP)

A specific body of researchers who call themselves psychical researchers believe they have found evidence that the mind does have an extrasensory way of perceiving and that the senses are not the only channels of cognition. Researchers in this field are firmly convinced that these tests offer empirical evidence of the mind's independence of the body and, accordingly, survival after death. The tests that have been made deal with three basic areas: thought transference or telepathy; clairvoyance, or the ability to see objects not normally perceptible; and psychokinesis, or the direct influence of mind over matter.[49]

1. History of Psychical Research

The Society for Psychical Research (SPR) was founded in England in 1882. Henry Sedgwich, a prominent philosopher at Cambridge, was instrumental in gathering influential people into this society. The membership included such men as former Prime Minister William Gladstone; future Prime Minister Arthur Balfour; Poet Laureate Alfred Lord Tennyson; authors Lewis Carroll and Sir Arthur Conan Doyle (the creator of Sherlock Holmes); and philosopher C. D. Broad.[50]

The SPR investigated occult experiences in a scientific manner. They exposed fraudulent cases and sought to establish claims which were valid. In investigating over 17,000 cases, they dismissed all but 1,684. But through the cases they validated, they sought to provide evidence that humans did indeed survive death and did exist as conscious persons who could communicate with persons who were still physically alive.[51]

One important outcome of this movement is represented in the work of Joseph Banks Rhine. Becoming involved with the SPR while a faculty member at Harvard University, Rhine, along with William McDougall, later developed a department of psychic studies at Duke University.

It was Rhine who coined the term *ESP*—which stands for "extrasensory perception." Other terms such as *paranormal psychology* and *parapsychology* were also developed out of this new research. Rhine's work led to serious study of the phenomenon of human consciousness as existing "outside" of or beyond the limits of the material body.[52]

Rhine believed that everyone had ESP to some degree. It was out of this conviction that he began to experiment with such things as playing cards to demonstrate the existence of ESP. His research seemed to pay off in the 1950s. The scientific community's interest was aroused when Rhine published results which seemed to reveal that some people had the ability to know what card was next in the deck or was being held in the hand. By the 1960s, excitement over ESP had begun to snowball, and before another decade had passed it had attained "fad" status on college campuses. By the beginning of the 1980s, the mass media were featuring parapsychological experiments on TV and radio and in popular magazines such as *Reader's Digest.*[53]

Public interest was also stirred when the Soviets released their findings on psychic research. These findings were popularized in *Psychic Discoveries Behind the Iron Curtain,* published by Prentice-Hall in 1970. To admit that "mind over matter" is possible means that the "mind" cannot be viewed as being solely influenced by a material object such as the brain. Therefore, the fact that some Soviet atheistic materialists were willing to accept parapsychology or ESP encouraged the secular humanists in the West to accept it as well.[54]

2. Evaluation of Psychical Research

It is very difficult rightly to evaluate the evidence offered by psychical research. One problem is its relationship to spiritualism, séances, and the like. A certain amount of evidence has been gained from more credible research techniques—enough to attract a number of adherents. However, the objective observer must be careful about overrating even this evidence. Many exaggerated claims have been made on the basis of scant findings. There is not enough evidence to state that psychic research provides serious "hope" of scientifically establishing the fact of immortality.

A telling criticism of psychic phenomenon as proof of immortality is the type of immortality it professes to offer. As philosopher William James once wrote, "The Spirit-hypothesis exhibits a vacancy, triviality, and incoherence of mind painful to think of as the state of the departed." The messages purportedly received from the dead are vague and broken, and it would be a difficult task to prove they are from any particular deceased person. On any showing psychic researchers do not prove more than a limited survival of the soul after death. The evidence, even when rated at its highest, cannot carry us further than a conviction that the souls of the departed linger on in a kind of attenuated existence.[55]

It should be noted that the contemporary preoccupation with evidences for conscious life outside of the body and even beyond death is not dependent upon religious belief. In fact, in many cases, the research is conducted by atheists. They say that belief in God is not necessary to support belief in life after death as a personal and conscious existence of the same person.[56]

IV. How Would You Describe Representative Approaches to Death and the Life Beyond?

The general arguments for an afterlife that have been described above—the historical, the teleological, and the ethical—have a broad appeal and have been used throughout the centuries. However, most scholars agree that it is more realistic and comprehensive to arrange discussion of the life hereafter according to four models or approaches.

1. The Naturalistic Approach—"When You Are Dead, You Are Dead"

In ancient times, Epicurus held this view. He taught that all that is above as well as below the neck in humans is reducible to matter in motion. The view of Epicurus, described in modern terms, would affirm that what we call psychic activity is actually the rapid movement in the skull of atomic particles too small to be seen. Epicurus argued that the existence of rational process and spiritual awareness is totally dependent on the life of the physical body. Epicurean ideas were later taught in Roman culture by a poet named Lucretius. "When the body has died," he argued, "we must admit that the soul has perished." Both Epicurus and Lucretius believed that the conscious self cannot survive when physical processes terminate.[57]

In the eighteenth century, the English philosopher David Hume made a serious attack on belief in the survival of life after death. Stressing the empirical reality of what is perceived through the five senses, Hume regarded concepts of human life as impossible apart from a structure of sensory experience.[58]

Ernst Haeckel carried the naturalistic viewpoint toward life after death to an extreme. Haeckel, a noted nineteenth-century scientist, assumed that anything real has mass. Hence, he reasoned, if there were a soul, it should be a gas which can be caught in a test tube when it is "breathed out" at the moment of death. Then, by lowering the temperature of the gaseous stuff, "soul snow" crystals should precipitate. After trying such an experiment with negative results, obtaining no results, Haeckel concluded that there is no such thing as an immortal soul.[59]

A person who subscribes to a naturalistic worldview regards the scientific method as the only true way of knowledge and the world described by the natural sciences as the only real world. If this assumption is correct, then life is only a physiological process and its spiritual aspects—including an afterlife—are illusory.

Advocates of this approach claim that the process of death is clear and verifiable. Human beings die when the functions which characterize a living organism come to an end. The lifeless body begins to decompose. It is attacked by lower forms of life—worms, molds, and bacteria—which break down its cells and tissues back into its original inorganic constituents. These are made available to other organisms, and thus the cycle of life goes on. But the human individual has ceased to exist. His or her death means no more and no less than the death of other animals. It is as natural as birth and should be accepted without any illusions.[60] This view of death is thoroughly consistent with the view of life with which it starts, and it honestly accepts the reality of death without fanciful speculation.

As William Hendricks effectively points out in *A Theology for Aging*, the naturalistic view of death is one that some people lapse into as they grow older. They see loved ones and friends "going down the valley one by one," and they never see anyone return. A theology based solely on such experience might well conclude that the dead are dead, and that is the end of the story—"They are nowhere. They cease to exist." We all know people who believe this—young as well as old. Often this view is born of depression, despair, long observation, or even an intense courage that dares to face nonbeing.[61]

Currently the most popular variety of the naturalistic or materialistic approach is the mind-body identity theory. This theory does not deny that humans have both mental and physical attributes, but affirms that both are attributes of the same thing—namely, the living human organism. A human being *is* his body, and the body is the person.[62]

This view makes much of the idea that the human personality is totally brain dependent, that a human being is alive only when his or her brain cells are alive. Artificial parts can replace other decaying segments of the body, but once the brain cells die, the person dies.[63]

Excursus on the Mind-Body Relationship

1. The Problem

The mind-body relationship is one of humankind's persistent problems. In the modern era, beginning with Descartes in the seventeenth century, this has been an issue of the first importance to all those who are concerned about what it means to be human.

How is it that a human being, compounded out of ordinary chemicals, is yet able to transcend physical limitations and to live a life of the mind? Or, to come at the mystery from the opposite direction, how does it happen that a rational mind, capable of speculating about truth, beauty, and goodness and of worshiping a supreme being, nevertheless finds itself embedded—some would say, imprisoned—in a body consisting of flesh and bone, blood and muscle?

However one states the problem, it remains a deep and perplexing mystery. How are we to explain the fact—or what seems to be the fact—that the very same entities, human beings, are characterized both by physical properties and by mental properties?[64] Is the mind merely an activity of the brain cells, a product of nerve stimulation, as some thinkers would suggest? Or on the other hand, does the mind dominate the body, using the physical organism as its instrument of expression?

The question of the mind-body relationship is important to the question of life after death because the answer that one gives to this question will generally determine one's attitude toward survival beyond death. In fact, the most powerful objection being voiced today to the concept of human immortality is the dependence of the mind on the body and the apparent dissolution of both at death. Humanist philosopher Corliss Lamont, for instance, builds his entire case against immortality on a psychological monism which implies the indissoluble union of soul and body.[65]

Other interpretations of the relationship between the mind and body range all the way from a rather complete denial of the existence of the mind to the assertion that mind is the only fundamental reality. These extremes, however, have been avoided by most thinkers, who generally acknowledge the reality and the interrelatedness of both mind and body.

2. The Search for a Solution

What is the solution to the problem? Is it true that personality is nothing but an organic function? Does the dissolution of the body pose an insurmountable barrier to the logic of immortality? Novelist Aldous Huxley suggests: "It is impossible in the present state of knowledge to arrive at a rigorous proof for any theory of the relation of mind to matter." This admission opens the door to some suggestions that allow a place for belief in immortality or a personal existence beyond death. The simple fact is that no modern theory of body and mind—scientific or otherwise—enjoys anything like universal recognition.[66]

According to the biblical teaching, humans are closely akin to the animals, but they are much more than what some have designated as "rational animals" with large, complex, highly developed brains. B. F. Skinner's psychological works on pigeons and rats tell us something about humans, but they cannot tell us everything. There is something unique about the human race.[67] Humans are made in the image of God.

Strictly speaking, science is incapable of giving any comprehensive verdict on the mind-body question. Its method is primarily descriptive and limited to its distinctive purpose. As we noted in earlier chapters, there are two approaches to human personality—the scientific and the theological. They both have their appropriate tasks, methods, and resources.

3. Factors Underlying a Solution

In order to provide a comprehensive approach to the solution of the mind-body problem, there are three factors which must be taken into consideration:

First, it is important to realize that the body does play a significant part in the life of the mind. In the complex being that we call a human, we can get rid neither of the materiality of the body nor of the transcendent characteristics of the soul or mind, and we cannot absorb either into the other. They exist in synthesis.[68]

Second, one must remember that the mind is not confined exclusively to sensory stimulation. In this life man has many experiences and values which are not directly related to sensory experience or spatial orientation.

Third, any theory that takes into account all the facts must realize the unity of the human organism. An organism asserts itself against its environment as a unity; it acts as a whole. Its actions are selective and chosen in the interest of the whole. This coherent unity is well attested in experience.

4. The Importance of Psychosomatic Unity

This last factor is especially important, because life itself seems to demand a central unifying principle which is not a product of material forces. John Macquarrie sets forth an approach which he believes is comprehensive and helpful. He suggests that we agree to say that the human being is a psychosomatic unity of a unique variety that we call personal. This view offers an approach to the subject of the embodiedness of human existence that is not obviously biased toward idealism or toward materialism. This approach has the advantage of beginning not with two hypothetical entities, mind and matter, that have to be put together, but with unitary human beings as we know them.[69]

The understanding of the human being as a single reality of which the mental and the physical are two aspects or poles has considerable empirical evidence in its favor. Although a mental event—a conscious thought or feeling—is of an entirely different order from a physical experience, the two seem to be intimately correlated in human life. If someone is hit over the head, for example, he or she may lose consciousness altogether. If certain parts of the brain are artificially stimulated, this again will affect the person's consciousness. On the other hand, there seem to be states of mind that have effects on the body. Deep-seated anxieties can inhibit the use of limbs or other faculties, so that the removal of the anxieties results in an apparent miracle of healing. Long-term stress can cause ulcers or other physical dysfunctions, as well as lead to mental or emotional disorders. And, conversely, a settled serene disposition often goes along with good physical health.

For the biblical worldview, the problem is not so acute as it is for philosophy. While modern thought tends to support the view that a human person is a psychosomatic unity, this has been from ancient times the teaching of the biblical tradition.[70]

From the biblical perspective, the human creature is an indivisible whole. Human existence is wholly dependent on God, and the significance of death is derived solely from man's relation to God. When we die there is nothing in natural man's own power that is capable of resisting the destructive power of death. The Christian hope, however, is that when our bodies cease to function, we do not fall into the hands of nothingness, but into the hands of God.

There are still problems related to the mind-body relationship. However, the Christian believes that the answer to survival beyond death is found in the power of the God who raised Jesus Christ from the dead and offers that same resurrection of body and mind and spirit to those related to the crucified and risen Christ in faith and love.

2. The Community-in-History Approach (Contemporary Judaism)

For the contemporary Jew, the continuity of history itself through the projection of corporate Judaism constitutes the primary "redemption from death." Death may be the end of the individual person, but the corporate Jewish personality continues.[71] Differences related to the possibility of a personal life beyond death are found among the modern Reformed, Conservative, and Orthodox divisions of Judaism. (Later in this chapter the Old Testament view will be discussed.)

The Jewish theology of death builds upon foundations that are unique to the beginnings of Israel as a historical community. There is a relative indifference in the Old Testament Scriptures to the length of life. The fact that Adam lived "930 years; and he died," suggests nothing more than the fact that Adam satisfied his commitment to history, then passed from the scene, his task completed (Gen. 5:5).

For the Jew, death does not have an arbitrary power to break continuity of life, because life is related to the continuity of God's purpose in history. It is precisely for this reason that the Holocaust is of such consequence for the modern Jew. The horror of the Holocaust lies not only in the fact that over six million Jews died, but also in the fact that the event was a deliberate attempt to annihilate the history of the Jewish people on earth. If God is understood to be the guarantor of a people's history, and if that history then comes to an end, the logical conclusion is that something is deeply wrong.[72] "If the Exodus led to Sinai, then where does Auschwitz lead?" asks Jewish writer Joseph Neusner.[73]

In the face of the Holocaust, some contemporary Jews such as Richard Rubinstein, the outspoken liberal Jewish leader, conclude that realities such as Auschwitz point toward the death of God. However, there are other Jewish leaders who protest against such an interpretation of the Holocaust. Emil Fackenheim, a more conservative Jewish leader, for example, argues that Hitler must not be given a "posthumous victory" by allowing the history of the Jew to perish. "A Jew may not respond to Hitler's attempt to destroy Judaism by himself cooperating in its destruction."[74]

Ray Anderson points out that death is a threat whenever it has the power to effect a discontinuity which robs life of meaning. The modern liberal Jew's understanding of the meaning of death lies with the affirmation that death marks an absolute end of personal existence on earth. Continuity does not consist, therefore, in a theory of individual immortality which extends a person's life beyond physical death. Rather, the hope of the modern Jew is in the assurance of a future in which there is continuing conversation and relationship between God and his people. Death cannot destroy the Jew, in this view, as long as there are Jews to die.[75]

This contemporary Jewish view, of course, is in sharp contrast to the Christian perspective, which is not based on the continuity of a racial or community presence in temporal history. Rather, our hope is based on the continuity of God and our continuing conversation and relation with him beyond life in temporal history into the period of the "new heaven and the new earth."[76]

For Christians, fellowship with God is restored within history through the incarnation of Jesus Christ. The resurrection of Jesus Christ enables the Christian to continue personal life beyond death into a new time and history. Unlike the modern Jew, then, the Christian believes that the existence of the church within history cannot provide the continuity needed to sustain a person's future identity. The continuity of history must be related to the resurrection history of the risen and exalted Christ.[77]

3. The Dualist, Idealist, or Innate-Immortality Approach ("Make It on Your Own in the Life Beyond")

This approach teaches that humans possess a soul or spirit that is separate from the body and is innately immortal; it survives after the death of the physical body. Because it emphasizes a body-soul separation, it is often called dualism.

In the West, this view was first developed as a philosophical theory by some of the Greek philosophers, notably Plato. It had significant influence in the period of the early church fathers. As a result, there existed in the medieval church a strong belief in the natural immortality of the soul. The doctrine of the immortality of the soul was declared official dogma by the Roman Catholic Lateran Council of 1512 and was accepted in principle by the Protestant Reformers.[78]

In recent times this view has been seriously questioned by biblical scholars, but it continues to be the working viewpoint of large numbers of people and as such demands serious consideration.[79]

(1) The Development of the Innate Immortality View by the Greeks. In ancient Greece, by the sixth century B.C., the problem of life after death was a matter of deep concern. The Orphic mystery religion, which was developed by those who accepted the truth of the writings of Orpheus, held that the body was the source of evil, while the soul was of like substance with the gods. A human being's sole duty, therefore, was to free himself from the chains of a sinful body. This could be accomplished by union with the god Dionysus. The initiation ceremonies developed by the Orphic religion were intended for the purpose of breaking the ties of earth.[80]

At best, the Orphic confidence in the immortality of the soul rested only on intuition; it was simply an emotional belief. The followers of the Orphic religion, however, claimed that this belief could be confirmed in a personal ecstatic vision.[81]

Plato brought the religious intuition of the mystery religions into the realm of philosophy. For Plato, a concern for immortality became a specific object of philosophical contemplation and construction. In his thought immortality attained its most elaborate philosophical exposition and defense.[82]

Plato argued for an immortality complete with reward and punishment and predicated soul survival on the supposed intrinsic "divinity" of the psyche. To be sure, he spoke rather loosely of this divinity and did not specifically claim that the human soul is a part of God. Plato distinguishes the soul sharply from the demiurge, the agent of creation, who fashioned it from the nous, or world of ideas, to which or to whom the demiurge was subject. Yet he depicts the soul as having within itself the basis for its immortality.[83]

Plato was impressed with the power of the human mind to rise above bodily desires and passions to the contemplation of eternal ideas. This view led him to teach that what is real in any human being is an immaterial, indestructible, immortal soul.[84]

According to Platonic philosophy, one's soul is one's divine and immortal essence. The body is its prison and is mortal. The soul, however, is independent of both the birth and the death of your body. The soul preexists, and it does not die when the body does. Accordingly, in the most important sense, death is not real. One's essential self, the soul, does not die at all.

The soul has within it the power to leap out of the grave into another form of existence. Just as the body has all along eliminated useless waste products, so the soul eventually casts the whole body aside as so much waste.[85]

In the *Timaeus,* Plato spoke figuratively of the Supreme Creator's having fashioned the human soul out of the same cup from which he made the World-soul. The body and the mortal part of humans were made by the created gods. The soul, therefore, was the divine element in a human, while the body was the mortal element.[86]

Plato offered four specific proofs of life after death. These proofs of the natural immortality of the human soul are elaborated in his dialogue called the *Phaedo,* which movingly depicts the final hours of Plato's mentor, Socrates, as well as elaborating on the meaning and significance of death.

The first principle is that of an endless cycle from life to death and from death to life. The second proof is based on recollection. Here he argues that if properly questioned a person will recall a previous existence.[87]

(This idea of the pre-existence of the soul has continued throughout history. It was prominent in the work of nineteenth-century writers, notably the poets Wordsworth and Tennyson, and often finds its way into funeral orations. William Wordsworth's "Ode: Intimations of Immortality from Recollections of

Early Childhood" is permeated with Plato's outlook on the soul. This kinship is evident in the following lines:

> Our birth is but a sleep and a forgetting:
> The Soul that rises with us, our life's Star,
> Hath had elsewhere its setting,
> And cometh from afar:
> Not in entire forgetfulness,
> And not in utter nakedness,
> But trailing clouds of glory do we come
> From God, who is our home.
> Heaven lies about us in our infancy!
> Shades of the prison-house begin to close
> Upon the growing Boy,
> But he beholds the light, and whence it flows,
> He sees it in his joy.[88]

Plato's third argument is that the human soul is "simple" and so it is unable to fall apart into complexity. This belief in the natural immortality of the "simple soul" was related to the concept that the human being is a spark of the divine soul, and medieval mysticism made much of that idea.[89]

The fourth argument teaches that the soul participates in a life-giving power that does not admit of death. In the light of this argument, the soul cannot die; a "dead soul" would be a contradiction in terms.[90]

As the *Phaedo* draws to a close, Socrates is depicted by Plato as not being the least perturbed over the fact of his own approaching departure from earthly existence. In the Platonic view, when the curtain closes on the final act (death), the real drama continues unhindered by the unsubstantial forms of bodily and earthly existence. Continuity is achieved through the soul's own immortal relation to the eternal truths. Death is dissolved of its power to destroy the self. Life in its bodily form is viewed as only of passing significance; death is considered only a passing away of that which is unnecessary to the true personality of the soul.[91]

As we shall see in more detail when we look at the biblical view, there are many difficulties with the Platonic view from the biblical perspective. For example, in the biblical view, there is no natural or innate power of the soul to continue through the dissolution of the body in death. The continuity resides in the continued power of God, who created the human person in his own image and likeness and who upholds that person in a relationship which guarantees life, even in the face of being mortal by nature.[92]

The continuity of life beyond death, in the biblical view, retains the essential unity of body and soul. In other words, the biblical view rejects any dualistic perspective. In fact, if one could imagine a soul that exists apart from the body, it is hard to see how such a soul could relate to a world or to other people or have any content to its experience. It is through the body that we relate to that which is other than ourselves. Thus, there could be no worthwhile human existence without relatedness. So, even if there were an independently existing soul, it would still be doubtful if it could sustain in any significant way the hope of a life beyond death.[93]

The biblical view teaches that human persons are in no way created to be or to become immortal by their nature. Rather, persons created in the image and likeness of God live within the limits of a human nature bounded by mortality and dependent upon God for the gift of immortal life through resurrection from the dead. (The promise of immortality is defined in the New Testament as personal and bodily resurrection from the dead.)[94]

The New Testament explicitly teaches that God alone, as Lord, has the power of life and death. It portrays the death and resurrection of Jesus Christ as a demonstration of the power of God, who is bringing in the new age of redemption and restoration. In this new period, death will be swallowed up in victory. Mortals who accept Christ as Savior will be transformed into the image of Christ and share the immortality of God through the divine Sonship and resurrected humanity of Jesus Christ.[95]

Thus we see that the Greek idea of the innate immortality of the soul is alien to the teaching of the Bible, even though such ideas have become mixed in with Christian doctrine at various times in the centuries since Plato. The idea of the emancipation of an immortal soul from a mortal body is unthinkable to the biblical mind. However akin we may be to the Supreme Person, we are nevertheless dependent beings. In the last analysis, our future rests with Him.

Since Neoplatonism, which was based on a combination of Platonic philosophy and Eastern mysticism, was the prevailing spiritual philosophy during the formative period of Christian theology, it is not surprising that many of the church fathers identified the Christian doctrine of eternal life with the Platonic view of innate immortality. Among the Moslem and Jewish philosophers of the medieval period, the Platonic view also was in great vogue. In the seventeenth and eighteenth centuries, this Greek approach to the life beyond was employed by Descartes, Baruch Spinoza, Leibniz, and George Berkeley. It also appeared in the philosophical writings of the psychical researchers in the nineteenth century and early twentieth centuries. (The British physicist and author Sir Oliver Lodge was especially fond of this argument.) It has even been included by some fundamentalist Christians as a "scriptural proof" of survival beyond death.[96]

(2) The Hindu Version of the Innate-Immortality Approach. For the Hindu, continuity of life is not connected with concrete personal, historical existence as such. Hope for continuity is found in the concept of "being," which is contrasted with both life and death. Life and death are a form of existence,which is not real in the sense that being is real. Life, with all its pleasures and pain, is not real according to Hindu belief; it is an illusion. Death, therefore, is seen as merely the end of the illusion of life, not as the loss of being. For the Hindu, that which *is* can never cease to *be.*[97]

The Hindu view is difficult for the Western mind to comprehend. It is important to grasp that for the Hindu it is only the atman or soul that is real and thus has continuity. Even selfhood as personal existence is seen as an illusion. Thus, death is not a power which threatens the real, for being can neither begin nor cease to exist.[98]

This means that the Hindu sees unenlightened life as a state of separation, imprisonment, and delusion. On the other hand, death is seen as reunion, spiritual liberation, and awakening. Death represents an opportunity for the individual self or soul to break away from worldly illusion (maya) and experience its divine nature (Brahman).[99] In order to achieve this final reunion or merging of the atman with Brahman, however, many reincarnations are necessary to work off the bad karma surrounding or enveloping the soul. Thus the doctrine of reincarnation is central in Hindu thought.

Like the Platonic view, the Hindu concept of death involves a fundamental dualism with regard to the reality of the "otherworldly" and the unreality of this present temporal existence. Hinduism is representative of all dualistic views of reality in which the historical and temporal are not taken seriously as real expressions of personal identity. Clearly, such a definition of death undermines the reality of life as defined in terms of temporal and historical existence.[100]

In contrast, the biblical view takes seriously the reality of temporal, historical existence as the embodiment of personal being. It views the human self as created and subject to the conditions of mortal existence. It seeks continuity of personal existence through a relationship to God in both life and death. In fact, it is Jesus Christ who carries the continuity of all believers from Adam onward through death into eternal life. If death came through the first man (Adam) and death reigned as a result of sin in all humans, so, says Paul, in the second man (Jesus Christ), has death been destroyed and eternal life granted to all humans who are related to God in Christ (Rom. 5:18–21).[101]

(3) The Buddhist View of Immortality. In the discussion of the Buddhist view, we will refer to the teaching of the original type of Buddhism, which developed primarily in the southern part of Asia and is called Southern Hinayana, or Theravada Buddhism. Its teachings differ considerably from the complex views of a later form of Buddhism, which developed in China, Korea, and Japan and is designated as Northern or Mahayana Buddhism. A detailed statement of these differences will be developed in chapter 9.

For the Hinayana Buddhist, as for the Hindu, all temporal existence is transient. Everything that comes to be passes away. To be born is already to have begun to die. And even the most apparently solid and enduring realities are secretly in the process of dissolution. The Buddha taught—a common theme in Indian thought—that such brief, contingent, and unstable patterns of flow and swirl cannot be ultimately real or finally valuable.[102]

A second Buddhist teaching is that the empirical self, like every other aspect of existence, is a process and not a timeless unchanging entity. Throughout life, from womb to worm, a person's body is undergoing processes of growth, decay, and repair. His stream of consciousness is a flux, changing moment by moment. And the set of behavioral dispositions which constitutes his character is likewise in process of continuous modification. There is no empirical self or person, and no psycho-physical organism, outside this ceaseless flow of change.[103]

As we have seen, the Hindu view teaches that an individual soul is an individual "spark of divinity" whose being, in its hidden identity with Brahman, or God, is eternal and unchanging. This notion of an immutable soul or atman, which has no beginning nor end and is the basis of our individual being, is explicitly rejected by the Buddha's *anatta* or "no-soul" doctrine.

According to the Buddha's doctrine of no-soul, the empirical self—the conscious, responsible, remembering ego—is not a self-existent substance. It exists only in time as an ever-changing process of consciousness, and there is no self outside this ceaseless temporal flow.[104]

Hinayana Buddhism holds that the goal of life is to escape from individualized existence. The self must progressively strip itself of egoism, self-centered desire, and clinging, including the basic clinging to its own separate ego-history. This can be done through following the activities outlined in what Buddhists call the "Eightfold Noble Path."[105]

At death, according to Hinayana Buddhist thought, the elements which constitute human nature disintegrate and the psycho-physical individual which they have formed ceases to exist. The individual does not survive death, and he or she is not reborn to live again. That particular conjunction of elements which had held together for, say, seventy years is no more. But an aspect of the individual does continue—not indeed eternally, but until it has finally expended itself out at the end of many lives.

That which thus continues through eons of time, playing a part in the formation of individual after individual, consists of a system of character dispositions or traits, the karmic deposit of former lives. (Each person leaves behind bad or good influences, which automatically flow into future human lives.) These influences are animated and propelled onward by the power of craving or desire (for power, material goods, sensual activities, and so forth—in Buddhist teaching the basic cause of human trouble). They survive physical death and by entering the womb help in the development of a new individual.

This life-craving system of dispositions which goes forward to give its basic character to a new embryo is not a conscious self, but a formation of nonconscious psychic elements. It is in this area of the unconscious and subconscious that the continuant from life to life is to be found. The first thought of the new life stream or mental life of the new individual is thought to be the immediate successor to the last thought of the dying individual; thus, it is sometimes called the "relinking consciousness." However, that which "rebecomes" is not actually consciousness as such, but something more like the unconscious dispositional state which constitutes the karmic deposit of the past.[106]

Moreover, this immediate rebirth or rebecoming is not necessarily into our earthly world; indeed, only a minority of births are into human life. Rebecoming may occur in any of many "worlds"—the sense worlds, including our earth and purgatory; the worlds of visible form, though not of sense, which include the "further Brahma" and "supra-Brahma" spheres; and the incorporeal worlds of thought.[107]

For the Buddhist, then, death means a rebecoming into a possible variety of worlds until the elements from an individual's life are expended or blown out. Life, accordingly, is to be seen as a spiritual pilgrimage, with the ultimate goal of extinguishing the fire of (physical) life and freeing the individual from the wheel of death and rebirth.[108] This, once again, is in direct contrast with the biblical view, which sees the empirical self as a conscious, responsible, and remembering ego that after death is held in existence in heaven or hell by the active will of the Creator God.

(4) The Innate Immortality View of Transcendentalism. One of the most influential American expressions of the innate immortality view is the philosophy of transcendentalism, which was developed principally by the nineteenth-century poet and essayist Ralph Waldo Emerson. For Emerson and his contemporaries Margaret Fuller, Henry David Thoreau, and Walt Whitman, transcendentalism offered a new kind of spiritual freedom and updated the older view of the innate immortality view of the soul.[109]

The transcendentalists borrowed from the Eastern scriptures, molding them to fit American standards of autonomy and individual determination. In so doing, they set the stage for New Age leaders to take the spotlight more than a hundred years later.[110]

For Emerson, both soul and nature are ultimately divine. Nature is filled by an immanent divinity. (This explanation of nature's purpose is quite different from that of biblical Christianity.) The purpose of divinized or spirit-filled nature, he proposed, is to lead individual souls to the knowledge of their essential divinity.

The underpinnings of transcendentalism were evident as early as 1838, when Emerson delivered an address to Harvard's senior divinity class. Throughout this address, Emerson gave expression to a new theory he believed would eventually prevail—a theory which he called "compensation." The theory stresses deeds, not faith, as the ground for spiritual salvation. The fact that the theory of compensation judges and rewards every act at performance made the Christian conception of an ultimate Day of Judgment unnecessary.[111]

Emerson's new theory of compensation did more than repudiate the idea of a final Judgment. It also freed Emerson to reject the doctrine of salvation through faith in the atonement of Christ. From Indian philosophy Emerson derived the idea that the universe is ultimately reducible to Absolute Spirit. Physical reality, then, is conditional. It is unreal in the sense that all of the particulars of experience have no meaning in themselves; they are really nothing but manifestations of the Absolute Spirit. However, it is real to the extent that the basis of all experience is the ultimate reality of Absolute Spirit. [112]

By 1844 Emerson had been further influenced by the Indian classics to reject the Christian belief in one lifetime in favor of the theory of transmigration or reincarnation. The Indian classics teach that the goal of human existence is mystical identification of the soul with Brahman or God. When such a mystical experience occurs, the soul is freed from the cycle of birth, life, death, and rebirth. Emerson came to agree.

According to Emerson, the goal of human life is to grow in knowledge of one's immanent divinity until one reaches the achievement of complete mystical absorption. He taught that the soul evolves upward through all of the lower orders of nature. When the soul finally achieves mystical experience, it no longer needs to pass through further incarnation. Merged with the All, it loses its particularity.

Emerson's adaptation of the Greek and Hindu views of innate immortality led him to renounce the Bible. We grow in God through experience, he said, not through reading the Bible. Furthermore, since human beings are ultimately divine, they do not need a mediator between themselves and God. Rather, they need a teacher to instruct them in how to achieve their own innate divinity.

Transcendentalism, then, assumes the essential divinity of the soul, repudiating recourse to divine intervention. Instead of depending on God's goodness, it postulates, we grow in the knowledge of our immanent divinity by performing virtuous acts. Transcendentalists also reject Christianity's linear view of history. Terrestrial existence will not be terminated by God's intervention, they hold; rather, its future will be one of open-ended progress. The nature of divinity becomes progressively manifested in this upward evolutionary spiral.[113]

This updating of the innate immortality view by the transcendentalists and the merging of the classical Greek and Hindu views have been widely accepted and very influential in the twentieth century. In fact, the so-called "Age of Aquarius" concept that was popular in the 1960s and early 1970s was a modern expression of basic transcendentalist ideas. According to this view, our solar system was moving from the Piscean age in the great zodiac into the next age—the Aquarian—and would henceforth encounter new physical, mental, and spiritual conditions, which would be made explicit through the teaching of the spiritual master for the age. Christ's message had summed up the conditions for the Piscean age, but with the dawning of the Aquarian age, a new message would be needed.[114]

Another twentieth-century heir of transcendentalism is the "human potential movement," which includes many forms of modern popular psychology and is based on the transcending impulse for self-realization first formulated by the transcendentalists. Denominations such as the Divine Science Church, the Church of Religious Science, and the Unity School of Christianity, as well as Christian Science, have their roots in "New Thought," a collection of ideas influenced by Hindu Vedanta wisdom as well as Emersonian philosophy. Also closely related is theosophy and the teachings of Madame Blavatsky. These groups are important precursors of present New Age groups, which have co-opted the language and trappings of the traditional Christian churches, thereby making newcomers feel more comfortable in their transition to these nonbiblical forms of belief and practice.[115]

(5) The Innate Immortality View of Spiritualism. Closely related in many ways to the idealist or innate immortality view is spiritualism. For the spiritualists, as for the others who hold the innate immortality view, the human soul is naturally immortal. You do not need God's power to live on beyond death.

The initial interest in what was later to be developed into a more formal group was ignited by the Fox sisters, who lived in Hydesdale, New York. On 31 March 1848, these sisters conducted a séance in which the spirit of a murdered man was supposedly contacted. He informed them that his corpse could be found in the basement. This proved to be true; a body was found. The "spirit" of the dead person was thought to make its presence known through a "rapping" sound on the table. This led to the fad of "table rapping" séances which became fashionable, almost as a parlor game.[116]

The French word *séance*, meaning "session," came to be used to refer to a meeting with spirits of the dead which is presided over by a psychic, also called spiritualist or medium. The psychic goes into a self-hypnotic trance in an attempt to establish contact with people presumed to be in the spirit realm and to obtain from them messages or assurances for clients.[117]

Earlier this century, a renowned medium named Arthur Ford lived in Philadelphia. Episcopal Bishop James Pike, distressed over the suicide of his son, made an appointment with Ford in hopes of getting in touch with his son's departed spirit. Pike left the séance satisfied that he had obtained messages from his son. After consultations with other psychics, Pike wrote a book, entitled *The Other Side*, about his experiences. That book, coupled with a television program in 1967 based on Ford's séance with Pike, attracted wide attention.[118]

Modern Western spiritualist literature contains extensive descriptions of the experiences of those who have recently died as related through trance mediumship.[119] There is debate, however, as to the origin of these communications. Some contend, for instance, that most of them are consciously invented by the medium.

(Shortly after Ford's death in 1971, his biographer disclosed that the psychic engaged in careful research before conducting a séance. He learned numerous tidbits of information on his famous clients from newspapers and from *Who's Who*. Then, at the séance, he duped them into believing that personal information extracted from library resources was descending from his contact person in the spirit world.)[120]

The basic belief of the spiritualists is that there is a psychic double of the body, an astral or etheric body, which detaches itself at death from the physical corpse. The astral body then either sleeps or remains in a confused half-conscious state, sometimes called "hades" in the spiritualist literature. This state may last for a longer or shorter time, said to average three or four days. The soul or astral being then wakes up into the next phase, which is usually a dream world or sphere of illusion that reflects the individual's own expectations and desires. For many people this existence may be so like that on earth that they do not at first realize they have died.[121]

In the spiritualist literature, the realm where most people go is called Summerland, the memory-world, or the plane of illusion. For some it can be an experience of delightful wish-fulfillment. In this happy state, illnesses are shed and bodily deformities disappear; and "if we are getting on in years we can return to that period in life known as the prime and there we can stay."[122] But for others it may be a purgatorial experience.

The plane of illusion or Summerland, however, represents only a phase in what is intended to be the upward movement of the soul. There are said to be seven planes. The lowest plane is that of physical matter; the next, the plane of "hades," described as a confused borderland between earthly life and the next world; then the plane of illusion or Summerland, in which most souls spend a considerable time. Beyond Summerland is a plane of "color," a plane of "flame," and a plane of "light." Finally there is a plane beyond time in which souls become one with God.[123]

As indicated above, the basic technique of spiritualism is the séance, where the medium sits down and goes into a sleeplike trance. In this state, the medium claims, his or her own consciousness is suspended and replaced by the consciousness of someone who has died and who wishes to communicate with those still on earth. In spiritualist terminology, the supposed communicators are known as spirits, and the living persons who attend the mediumistic séance are called sitters.

Spiritualists claim that the same spirit (called the medium's control) uses the medium's speech organs at a number of different séances and relays messages from other spirits, whom he often speaks of as standing around him and with whom he apparently converses as well as with the sitters. The sitters claim that they are indeed in this way in communication with deceased relatives and friends, whom they can identify both by the content and by the manner of their utterances. The mediums claim that the spirits are able to give information which was not known to the medium and even some information which was not at the time known to the sitters. If this interpretation is accepted, spiritualists maintain that we are in possession of good evidence for the fact of human survival after bodily death and also of a description of the actual conditions of life beyond the grave.[124]

A contemporary expression of spiritualism is known as "channeling." Like more traditional trance mediumship, channeling is a form of voluntary possession in which spirit-beings communicate to the living. They operate through humans by temporarily assuming control of a human body during a trance. People who subject themselves to such entrancement and control are called channelers or simply channels. The controlling spirit or entity will lecture, counsel, teach, or otherwise advise its human audience through these channelers.

Channeling, a New Age phenomenon, was widely publicized during the 1980s. Celebrities endorsed it, and stars of stage, screen, and television gave public testimonies about their spirit guides. Actress and New Age leader Shirley MacLaine has been especially vocal about her experiences in consulting Ramtha, who is described as a thirty-five-thousand-year-old ascended master. Ramtha was once a barbarian warrior king, later a Hindu god, and is now beyond even deity itself. Now he is channeled by J. Z. Knight, a Washington State housewife and breeder of Arabian horses.

Ramtha and others like him have no physical existence, that is, they are spirits or spirit-beings. They are mainly interested in dispensing their philosophy of life to human beings. For example, Ramtha/Knight once appeared on the Merv Griffin television show. In answer to Griffin's question, "What is your most important message that you want everyone on this planet to hear?" Ramtha replied, "God is within your being. That which is called Christ is within your being, and when you know you are God, you will find joy." These entities deny death and repeat the primal lie that humans are gods and that salvation and power are achieved primarily through knowledge of self.

Some critics say that these spiritual entities are real and lying to us. Others say the entities are a mental dysfunction and should be recognized as such. Others say that the entities are a conscious fraud for purpose of gain.[125]

Related to the practice of channeling is the assertion that people in the remote past had contact with extraterrestrial beings which taught them to live in harmony with nature. According to this view, there are remnants of these great civilizations in Atlantis, Stonehenge, the pyramids of Egypt, and in South America, but, because of pride and misuse of their powers, they fell. Shirley MacLaine claims to have experienced contact with these extraterrestrial entities on the site of certain South American ruins. She claims that these extraterrestrial advisers promised to help restore our declining planet through mystic encounters and occult practices.[126]

The Christian response to those who hold spiritualist views is varied. Some evangelicals see some reported communications with the other world as frauds. Other communications are seen as examples of extrasensory perception or demonic confusion. Whatever the specific instance, the response of the biblical worldview to spiritualist practices is uniformly negative. The Bible forbids rather than encourages attempts to communicate with our loved ones or others through mediums (Deut. 18:10ff.) or necromancers (talkers with the dead).

In 1 Thessalonians 4:13–18, Paul discusses the problem of those Christians who had died and urged those left behind not to sorrow like those who have no hope. Here a spiritualist would have added, "Come to the service on Sunday and comfort yourselves by speaking to them." Instead, Paul urged his readers to wait patiently until the reunion at the second coming of the Lord.[127]

Finally, in answer to spiritualism, the biblical worldview claims that a person's greatest need is to come into right relationship with God. Merely moving on to another existence does not meet this need. God in the Gospel promises infinitely more than life "on another plane." Eternal life in the risen Christ is something that begins now. If the Bible is correct, to depart, for the Christian, is to be "with Christ" (Phil. 1:23), which means an existence in a spiritual body in a restored community in the "new heaven and the new earth."[128]

Excursus on Reincarnation

1. The Extent of Belief in Reincarnation

As we have seen, in most Eastern cultures and groups influenced by the Greeks, the theory of reincarnation has been the predominant mode of conceiving life after death. Of the global population today, approximately a billion people believe in reincarnation. These groups hold in common the belief that the soul, as the conscious character- and memory-bearing self, can assume one or more bodies in succession. Thus, death is a "transmigration of the soul" from a body which is perishing to another body which can sustain the life of the self. The degree to which personal identity can be said to be sustained, however, is dependent upon the form of the reincarnation theory.[129]

Until well into this century, reincarnation was not popular in either Europe or the United States. But now, according to several surveys including a 1982 Gallup Poll, about one-fourth of all Americans believe in some form of reincarnation. The proportion rises to 30 percent among persons under age thirty. The wide U.S. acceptance of the concept of reincarnation has received a major assist from screen and entertainment celebrities as well as New Age personalities.[130]

2. Origins of the Reincarnation View

The idea of reincarnation originated in northern India around 1000–800 B.C. This ancient theory of transmigration of souls holds that the soul may be incarnated not only in human bodies but also in the bodies of animals and plants. The Western version of this theory, however, has been redefined to limit cyclic rebirths to human form only.[131]

The Hindu viewpoint can best be seen in its most treasured scripture, the Bhagavad-Gita. That epic tells of the dilemma of Arjuna, a warrior at the time of a civil war. He is unable to attack another human being on the battlefield until he can justify killing as beneficial. The god Krishna reveals to Arjuna that the essential self is unkillable, so slaughtering bodies with the sword does not damage the victims' inmost personalities. Having resolved his qualms of conscience, Arjuna charges forth to separate souls from bodies. Hindus often chant at funerals this passage from the Bhagavad-Gita: "Even as a person casts off worn-out clothes and puts on others that are new, so the embodied self casts off worn-out bodies and enters into others that are new. Therefore, knowing it to be so, you should not grieve."[132]

Closely associated with the notion of reincarnation cycles is the concept of karma, which asserts that the evil deeds of past lives relate to the present life and that one's present actions have implications for future lives. Essentially karma is the law of cause and effect, of action followed by reaction.[133]

Hindu scripture describes how people reap what they sow: "Those whose conduct here has been good will quickly attain a good womb. . . . But those whose conduct here has been evil will attain an evil womb—the womb of a dog, a pig, or [an outcast]." Involved here is a cosmic bookkeeping system. For example, a lower-caste person who dutifully performs what has been traditionally expected of those in that status can reasonably hope to become a prince or a priest of one of the higher castes in the next incarnation. Or again, a glutton's punishment might be assignment to the body of a buzzard in the next enfleshment.[134]

3. Implications of Reincarnation

In the Orient, the belief in karma has resulted in a basically pessimistic view of life. Human existence is often seen as a dreary, endless cycle of pain, suffering, and rebirth. Karmic reincarnation does not resolve the problem of evil. It requires self-salvation leading to ultimate liberation from the wheel of rebirth. The concepts of divine forgiveness and mercy are absent.[135]

The doctrine of reincarnation is viewed as an explanation of the inequalities of life. It recognizes the fact that individuals start out in life in unequal circumstances with respect to intellectual potential, physical health and resilience, economic wealth, and political freedom. If reincarnation is true, then persons need not blame God for their having been born in situations which make success unlikely. Also, believers in reincarnation have a moral imperative as they look to the future. If they regulate their lives by high principles, their self-development will be enhanced in future lives.[136]

Critics point out, however, that Hindu priests have used the doctrine of reincarnation to preserve the status quo. Brahmans have designated themselves as the highest caste. They can more easily keep their subjects in subjection if rewards in an afterlife are promised to the compliant and horrible punishments are threatened for the noncompliant. Also, the priests can rationalize that they deserve their exalted position as a payoff for goodness in past lives. Likewise, mistreatment of the lowest caste, the "untouchables," is justified by the belief that they are receiving what they deserve because of viciousness in past lives.[137]

4. Western Developments Related to Reincarnation

Plato, the most influential of the ancient Western philosophers, taught the concept of reincarnation. In his myth of Er, recounted both in the *Republic* and *Phaedrus*, Plato depicts the psyche or soul in the act of selecting the role it wants to play during its next incarnation on earth. What it decides to become is dependent on the character formed in the previous life.[138]

The modern Western expression of reincarnation emerged during the Enlightenment of the eighteenth century, and it was revived by such nineteenth-century occultic movements as theosophy, founded by the influential Madame H. P. Blavatsky, and Alice Bailey's Arcane School, a theosophy offshoot.[139]

John Hick, a prominent British philosopher and religion professor, has attempted to combine reincarnation and Christian teachings about the life beyond. Hick argues for a third possibility—an alternative to eternal heaven or hell or repeated earthly reincarnations. He calls for a series of lives, each bounded by something analogous to birth and death, lived in other worlds in spaces other than that in which we now are.[140] Through this third model, Hick seeks to provide a "global theology of death" which will provide a synthesis between the traditional doctrine of resurrection to an individual personal life and the eastern concepts of reincarnation.

Hick pictures a continued series of "births and deaths" following physical death, leading to the goal of a personal existence in the form of the atman. This appears to be quite similar to the eastern concept of undifferentiated consciousness, although Hick has not abandoned differentiation in the life beyond altogether. In evaluating Hick's theories, however, Ray S. Anderson concludes that the form of differentiation by which personal identity is maintained beyond death in Hick's view is more of a logical distinction than a material one. One is still not assured that the individual has a distinct personal identity in the state after death.[141]

5. The Biblical Evaluation of Reincarnation

As we will see in our later discussions, reincarnation in its various versions is distinctly different from the biblical teaching. The ultimate objective of reincarnation is to fuse with "ultimate reality," to merge with God or to become God. Reincarnation teachings are largely based on a monistic, mystical-occult worldview that promotes the essential divinity of humanity. They deny the notion of a sovereign personal God, which of course is the foundation of the biblical worldview, and they offer the promise of esoteric wisdom. The Christian's disavowal of reincarnation is anchored in the biblical assertion that "man is destined to die once, and after that to face judgment" (Heb. 9:27).[142]

Excursus on Near-Death, Out-of-Body Experiences (Thanatology)

1. Widespread Interest in Thanatology

In recent years, extensive publicity has surrounded a quasiscientific discipline called thanatology (from the Greek word *thanatos,* meaning death). The work of Swiss-born American psychiatrist Elisabeth Kübler-Ross has been especially influential in this area. Kübler-Ross's pioneering book, *On Death and Dying,* which appeared in 1969, stimulated much interest in life-after-death possibilities, and this interest was heightened with the publication in 1974 of *Questions and Answers on Death and Dying.* Raymond Moody, the author of *Life After Life* and *Reflections on Life After Life* has also been instrumental in bringing thanatology to the public's attention.[143]

The teaching of Kübler-Ross, Moody, and other contemporary death researchers is that death is the final phase in the glorious evolution of each individual. In their view, rewards, happiness, fulfillment, and reunion await almost everyone after death regardless of their beliefs and behavior on earth.

The assertions of these thanatologists are based largely on reported out-of-body experiences of patients who were clinically "dead" and later revived. Moody, who coined the term "near death, out of body experiences" (NDOBE), presents these experiences in his books as afterlife "samples," and he contends that they are spiritual "peeks over the fence" into the eternal spirit world.[144]

2. The Reported Patterns in NDOBE

Although variations exist in the accounts of NDOBEs, they follow a strikingly similar pattern. Most involve: (a) the experience of leaving the body, often as if floating above it and able to look down upon it; (b) passage through some kind of dark tunnel, sometimes accompanied by a life-review or evaluation of one's entire life; (c) emergence from the tunnel into light, harmony, and peace on the other side; (d) communication with another being or beings (often a previously deceased relative or personally significant religious figure) and either being told to return to life and finish uncompleted work or being given a choice, although urged to return to life; (e) return to the embodied existence.[145]

Many of those who report NDOBEs describe them as highly positive experiences, and most say that their greatest desire was to press onward into the experience of death. They regret the loss of the experience and report returning to life with reluctance. People having had such experiences typically report that upon their return, their fear of death is entirely gone.[146]

In contrast to these positive experiences, however, other individuals report negative experiences; they describe traveling to a "hell" rather than to a "heaven." In fact, cardiologist Maurice Rawlings, who has been involved in many resuscitations and interviewed patients immediately after their experiences, claims that up to half of the cases of NDOBE he has encountered contained "hellish" elements. Rawlings contends that most researchers interview their subjects too late, after the negative dimensions of their near-death encounter have all been suppressed.[147]

(Kenneth Ring answers Rawlings's observations by pointing out that Rawlings is writing from a conservative Christian standpoint and that he is intent on demonstrating that the negative experiences are the result of not turning to Christ. Ring further points out that cultural studies, containing many non-Christians, did not report signs of judgment or damnation.)[148]

3. Some General Evaluations of NDOBE

In all fairness to the work of Kübler-Ross, the acknowledged leader in NDOBE study, it must be pointed out that her work has had a number of positive results. She can be credited with the development of the recent emphasis on open communication with dying persons. She effectively showed how, with the help of counseling, the dying can be helped to unload their feelings of fright, loneliness, inadequacy, and embarrassment. Kübler-Ross's approach has also been personally helpful to many nondying persons whom she has directly or indirectly instructed, enabling them to face situations involving death with honesty and compassion.[149] Another related result of her efforts is a dramatic change in physicians' attitudes about informing terminal patients of their condition.[150]

As to the NDOBEs themselves, numerous questions and criticisms have been raised—both positive and negative—and various attempts have been made to give medical and psychological explanations for these experiences.

Some say, for instance, that NDOBE can be explained by the makeup of the human brain. Under the traumatic conditions of physical death, the brain tends to produce a common type of hallucination which is colored with the particulars of one's own life experiences.[151]

Others suggest that such phenomena can be explained by pointing to the latent potentialities of the neurological network and the complex physiology of the brain, which can be triggered in stress situations. Psychologists have drawn numerous parallels between the thanatologists' findings and subconscious wish fulfillment. Fantasies are routinely set in action by a brush with death. There is also the ever-present possibility of intellectually dishonest research, with facts manipulated or rearranged to agree with the researcher's presuppositions.[152]

Still other critics point out that NDOBEs refer to "*near*-death experience, and that being near death does not necessarily mean one has actually entered the state of death and then returned. There appears to be such a yearning for evidence of an afterlife, however, that testimonies are often believed by the tellers and the hearers—including Moody—as proof of life beyond death.[153]

4. Some Evangelical Evaluations of NDOBE

In addition to these more general criticisms, evangelicals are specifically concerned with the open connection between the discipline of contemporary thanatology and occult and Eastern-mystical beliefs. Scholars point out that contemporary accounts of near-death experiences are especially similar to the views of two ancient religious traditions—Zoroastrianism and Tibetan Buddhism.[154]

Thanatology also has a relationship to necromancy, demonism, and apostasy. For example, the occult or spiritualist traditions have long boasted of out-of-the-body experiences as one of the standard skills of the occult elite. The theosophists call it "astral travel," a separation of soul and body, usually during sleep. A colleague of Raymond Moody's is Robert Monroe, the author of *Journey Out of the Body*. Monroe runs an organization called M-5000 that purports to help its clients learn the techniques of leaving their bodies. According to the Spiritual Counterfeits Project, a Christian organization for the study of cults, Kübler-Ross has served on the board of advisers for M-5000 and has referred patients to Monroe.[155]

In addition, Kübler-Ross has testified that her encounters with out-of-body experiences have led her to believe that immortality and reincarnation are scientifically true. She has come to believe that people "are reborn again in order to complete the tasks they have not been willing or able to complete in this life." In fact, she claims that one of her soul's previous incarnations was in a woman named Isabel who taught Jesus.[156]

The connections between thanatology and Eastern religions or the occult have led some evangelical leaders to be concerned over the popularity of NDOBE narratives. For example, Vernon Grounds, president emeritus of Denver Conservative Baptist Theological Seminary, has noted that thanatology may be related to telepathy, extrasensory perception, and other areas of psychical research. Grounds further suggests that thanatology has the potential for being a serious block to the Christian faith.[157]

Mark Albrecht and Brooks Alexander of the Spiritual Counterfeits Project contend, moreover, that the teachings of thanatologists such as Raymond Moody are almost totally amoral. These teachings relegate the concepts of sin, repentance, accountability, and divine judgment to the medieval trash heap of useless and antiquated beliefs. Moody's surrogate "good news" is that all people, regardless of belief or behavior, will "make it" after death, provided they have not committed heinous evils. A "being of light," usually associated with God, receives their sins with understanding, humor, and compassion, pointing out that such shortcomings are part of the evolutionary learning process.[158]

Jesus Christ tells us plainly in Luke 16:19–31 that life is not peaceful and pleasant for everyone, regardless of their relationship to Jesus Christ, after death. Moody and Kübler-Ross seem to imply a view that is open-ended, relativistic, and not based on a God of standards and wholeness. The impression they leave is that we just ooze into an eternal growth laboratory of moral lessons.

Many evangelicals believe that Satan has used such ideas as the natural immortality of the human soul and life after life to deaden and anesthetize the mind against the piercing reality of death as curse and judgment and thus seal people off from God and the Gospel of Christ. In other words, they believe that in movements such as thanatology Satan appears as an "angel of light" (2 Cor. 11:14) to deceive people about the true nature of death. The Bible presents death not as normal and happy, but as something alien and abnormal—an enemy (1 Cor. 15:26). Thanatologists, however, present death as essentially pleasant. Since in their view there is no need for redemption and repentance before God, the work of Christ is unnecessary. As we shall see, Christians say that it is only through the death and resurrection of Christ that death can be transformed with a means of deliverance from death's guilt, finality, and power.[159]

Finally, for the Christian, the issue of thanatology and NDOBEs is an issue of authority. The central question is: On whose authority do we accept the reality of life after death? The historic Christian answer is: On the authority of the risen Christ and of those who were with him for forty days after his resurrection as this is described and interpreted in the New Testament.

4. The Existentialist Approach to the Relationship between Death and Authentic Living

Most of the approaches to death we have considered up to this point have been the classic religious and philosophical views. To a large extent, these views have in common an assumption that there is a purpose or meaning that is given to life and death by a divine being or reality. In the twentieth century, however, there has developed in Western culture an attempt to explain death in terms that usually avoid any reference to a transcendent being or reality beyond death. In this attempt, death itself is defined as a limiting concept which can be seen to be a positive factor in giving life meaning and reality. This is the tack taken by the existentialists.[160]

(1) The Importance of Death for the Existentialists. The seriousness with which many secular existential philosophers and psychologists have treated the subject of death stands in marked contrast to the embarrassed silence about death in our popular culture and equally embarrassed speech from many of the theologians.[161] In fact, Peter Koestenbaum, Professor of Philosophy at San Jose State University, argues that the current interest in death originated with the existentialist philosophers, especially Kierkegaard and Nietzsche; with the novelists Dostoevski and Tolstoy; and with their successors in existentialist thought, Heidegger and Sartre. The topic has been extended by existential psychologists such as C. G. Jung, Viktor E. Frankl, and Rollo May.

The basic philosophical point made by these existentialists is that our certain death is the key to understanding our human nature. Death not only helps us define human nature; it also puts us in touch with our deepest feelings—anxieties and hopes, needs and opportunities—as existent human beings.[162]

From a psychological perspective, Koestenbaum suggests the following themes that flow from the existentialist approach to death: We need death in order to savor life. Death puts us in touch with the sense of real, individual existence. Death gives us the strength to make major decisions. Death shows us the path to self-esteem. It gives us the capacity to do something important. Once an individual has recognized death, he or she is on the way to becoming decisive. By remembering death, human beings concentrate on essentials. To accept death means to take charge of one's life. The thought of death helps one to assume a total plan for life.[163]

(2) Heidegger's View of the Significance of Death. The twentieth-century German philosopher Martin Heidegger was a central figure in framing the existential approach to death. In his seminal work, *Being and Time*, Heidegger characterized everyday existence as "inauthentic." He observed that human beings find themselves thrown into their world, their mental universe, without preparation or forethought. As a result, we give our attention to the pressing experience of everyday cares and events, and genuine being remains undiscovered. Each human becomes merely a member of the crowd, hidden in the rat race of crises and moods.

Heidegger believed that facing death is a basic way to break loose from the trivial, disordered concerns of experience and attain genuine self-knowledge. Death comes to each of us as an individual; in facing death, therefore, we cannot lose ourselves in the crowd. Also, our life develops a unity as we focus on its ending.[164]

While Heidegger was not a theologian, he expressed a deep religious concern in his writings. First, there is his constant focusing on our finitude and death and the related belief that an awareness of death leads to authentic existence. Second, Heidegger's basic criticism of the contemporary world—that we are too concerned with factual details and not concerned enough with true being—is essentially religious in nature. Third, Heidegger directly attacked Christianity for contributing to this self-betrayal by making truth a matter of propositions rather than of existence. Fourth, Heidegger gave central importance to language, seeking to reorient theological and philosophical talk away from the modern scientific ideal. He saw language as crucial to understanding the human "life world," which eludes the grasp of scientific analysis.[165]

Heidegger taught that it is precisely death that allows human life to have meaning. If human beings were immortal and life went on forever, it would have no unifying pattern; it would simply be a meaningless progression of one event after another. In Heidegger's view, human life can have meaning and unity only if it looks toward an end—a boundary that gives a perspective within which priorities can be set and various events and possibilities seen as parts of a sense-giving whole. Death is a basic constitutive factor in finite human existence, and this existence is even called by Heidegger a "being towards death." Heidegger thus calls for us to live in the realistic anticipation of death. This realization allows us to see life as a limited whole and so to live with a measure of purpose and energy in the face of the end. It is an eschatological understanding of life.[166]

To use the word *eschatological* to describe Heidegger's understanding of life in the face of the end suggests a comparison with the first generation of Christians who lived in expectation of an imminent end of the age. Because they lived in this expectation, they were perhaps the most dynamic generation of human beings that has ever existed. One may contrast this with the modern evasion of death and concern for longevity. But a life that went on for even a hundred years and was mostly taken up with trivialities would be infinitely poorer than a life which had with zest and intensity realized some meaningful pattern, however brief its duration.[167]

(3) An Evaluation of the Existentialist View of Death. Philosophers such as Glenn Gray of Colorado College affirm that the existential approach to death is not so much wrong as inadequate. Gray agrees that we should heed the existentialists' warning that we should be ready to die at any moment and hence should try to make sense of life, independent of its duration. The awareness of death may well be, for many of us, a deep fountain of possibility, stirring us into full realization of the preciousness of living. But as an untimely occurrence, it can be also an unmitigated calamity, defying all efforts at understanding.[168]

Gray contends that there must be a place for religious faith in the life beyond death. Though belief in the life beyond should not tempt us, as it did Spinoza, to deny the reality of death or to avoid facing its great threat, still we need a deep-seated faith that we are not suspended over an abyss. We must hold on to our conviction that death as an occurrence also holds the promise of a greater fulfillment in the life beyond.[169]

For Christians, what is believed about death cannot be based on some "inner meaning" which death has for us as a philosophical concept. As Christians, if we are to speak about death at all, then there must be a word which comes to us from beyond death. The Christian faith claims that it has heard this word—spoken through the life, death, and resurrection of Jesus Christ.

Christians do not see their principal task as attempting to draw implications for life out of the limitations of death. The answers are to be found not in the so-called limiting situations such as death, but in Jesus Christ, who meets us in the center of life. In other words, the answer as to the nature and meaning of human life must precede the question as to the nature and meaning of death.[170]

V. What Is the Biblical Approach to Death and the Life Beyond?

We have seen that most humans seem to have an intuitive belief in some sort of an afterlife—or at least a quasireligious hope that their life's work will survive and that "eggs are not hatched in vain." We have noted that there is a certain attraction in the West to the Eastern concept of reincarnation, which at least offers a promise of continuity, though not at the level of personal identity.

It should also be noted, however, that the biblical view has not yet surrendered its psychic hold on the contemporary consciousness. Multitudes still expect to hear a Christian answer to Job's ancient question: "If a man die shall he live again?" (Job 14:14).[171]

The Christian answer brings distinctive elements to this age-long question, such as the doctrines of bodily resurrection and judgment confirmed and evidenced by works. The biblical view declares that human destiny is dependent upon a decision of personal faith in the crucified and risen Redeemer and is related to the power of God shown in Christ's resurrection. These and related teachings bring a precision to the biblical view that lift it above the intuitive and philosophical views.[172]

1. The Biblical View of Death

(1) The Old Testament View. The Old Testament assumes that when a person dies, he or she continues to exist before God and by God's power. This continuing existence or life force is not a power one has as a natural endowment, but one that is itself derived out of a relationship to God.[173]

In the Old Testament view, however, this life beyond death is weak. Persons continue to "exist" in the underworld, or Sheol, as shadows of the real self. There is no praise of God in Sheol, and the dead have no memory of the living (cf. Ps. 6:5).[174]

There is some expectation of redemption from death in the Old Testament; however, it is an expectation based solely on the promise and power of God not to forget those he has elected to be his own. The chief difficulty with death expressed by persons of faith in the Old Testament was that it separated them from life with God. Consequently, it was natural that those who believed in God's love and care would come to believe that God would eventually remove the separation (cf. Ps. 139:8)—that God in life would guide them with his counsel and afterward receive them with glory (Ps. 73:24). An illustration of what was meant by being received in glory can be found in the cases of Enoch and Elijah, neither of whom suffered death, and both of whom were taken directly to God's heavenly abode (Gen. 5:24; 2 Kings 2:11).[175]

The strongest statement to this effect is Daniel 12:2: "And many of those who sleep in the dust of the earth shall awake, some to everlasting life, and some to shame and everlasting contempt." This verse hints at a possible resurrection from the dead, though we are not told the precise form of this life after death. Thus we see in the Old Testament that the hope of the dying is in God who has power to keep the life of the one who has died. This belief in the resurrection of the dead hinted at in Daniel became widespread in the intertestamental period, though there continued to be those who retained the position of the earlier Old Testament literature and disbelieved the resurrection (cf. Eccles. 3:20–21; and the Sadducees of the New Testament time, described in Matt. 22:23). Yet for the majority of the Jews, the faith in God's redemptive power had finally won its victory over death.[176]

(2) The New Testament View. In the New Testament, the basic orientation toward death is in continuity with that of the Old Testament. The limited amount said about death as a physical event is because it has been "marginalized" and given a lower status of a "background extra on the stage of life." This is because of the triumph of Jesus through the resurrection.[177]

The key issue in the New Testament is not whether human beings have an essence that survives death (natural immortality), but whether the God in whom they believe has the power and moral integrity to "make good," beyond death and into eternity, on the lives he himself has called into a salvation existence through Jesus Christ. This new salvation is eternal life shared in fellowship with God through the resurrection of both body and soul.[178]

The doctrine of creation in Christian theology includes the belief that human individuals bear the image and likeness of God. This is based on the creation story: "Let us make man in our image, after our likeness. . . . So God created man in his own image, in the image of God he created him; male and female he created them" (Gen. 1:26–27). As biological creatures, humans are part of the continuum of natural life. This means that they share with animals the prospect of biological death. However, according to the biblical view, humans are under a different determination than animals—they are made to share in fellowship with God a destiny and life which transcends mortal and finite conditions. In other words, human life experienced as a personal relation with God does not share the same fate as the natural life of other creatures.[179]

For nonhuman creatures, natural life is fatalistic and deterministic; there is no escape from biological nature. Humans, however, are oriented toward life with God and with one another, which is a mark of the image and likeness of God. Human personhood has the possibility of continued life based on the promise and power of God. Thus we are free from natural determinism and the fate of biological nature.[180]

This potential for the life beyond is not the same as the possession of an immortal soul. The New Testament does not once mention the "immortal soul." The word *immortal* occurs only three times in the New Testament, and even then the immortality is not attributed to the soul, but to the risen Christ and the embodied person in the new age (cf. 1 Cor. 15:53ff.; 1 Tim. 6:16).[181]

2. The Human Prospect of Immortality before the Fall

(1) The View of Karl Barth. According to Barth, our human finitude is part of our original God-given nature, and is not the result of sin. The experience of physical death, then, is also intrinsic to our created human nature. In Barth's view, whatever corruption and susceptibility to death occurs in nature, including disease, were present in the world before there was sin. However, this empirical reality of human nature had no absolute power over Adam and Eve, because they were upheld in their human nature by the sovereign power of God as Creator and Lord of life and death.[182]

In other words, according to Barth, sin did not cause human nature to become finite and mortal. The biological organism was given its own temporal and finite lifespan in both the human and nonhuman natural form. What sin did was cause a separation between humankind and the life-sustaining promise and gift of immortality which issues from God alone. This separation is the "death" which the New Testament says entered into the human race as a consequence of sin (1 Cor. 15:21).[183]

Ray Anderson believes this approach relieves us of having to postulate a somewhat grotesque notion of a prefallen human nature to which none of the biological laws as we presently know them apply. It allows us to face honestly the empirical fact of biological death, while also accepting the New Testament view that death is a consequence of sin. For all creatures but the human, biological death is itself a natural "fate." In addition, the spiritual death that is caused by sin strikes directly at the human person by threatening him or her with loss of a relation to God and to the community in which one's personal identity is bound up.[184]

This spiritual death, then, is thus seen as serious, as an effect of sin, and as a judgment of God upon the human person. It is this spiritual death which to the human person is a terrible evil, and which is concealed in our dying as a mortal human individual.[185]

According to Barth, humans as originally created by God are not immortal, either actually or conditionally. However, as persons created in God's image and likeness, they are called by God to receive the gift of immortality, which is experienced as transformation of our mortal human nature into the immortality which is actually achieved through the resurrection of Jesus from the dead (cf. 1 Cor. 15:35–58).[186]

(2) The Traditional Evangelical View. Evangelical theology has generally held that death was not a condition to which Adam was subject prior to the fall. In this view, physical death entered human experience only as a consequence of Adam's transgression.

This view takes the creation and fall as a portrayal of the historical origin of humanity. According to Millard J. Erickson, if humans had not sinned, they could have partaken of the Tree of Life and thus have received everlasting life. Humans were originally mortal in the sense of being potentially capable of dying. When they sinned, that potential or possibility became a reality. We might say, then, that humans were created with contingent or conditional immortality. They could have lived forever, but it was not certain that they would. Upon sinning, they lost that status.[187]

According to the evangelical view, a human being does not differ from the animals in terms of having a naturally immortal soul that cannot die. The difference between human and animal lies in human beings' having been created in the image of God to have their existence in the fellowship and love of God. The tragedy of human life, therefore, is that because of sin humanity no longer exists in that love and fellowship. Humans are sinners and must die. It is awareness of this broken personal fellowship with God that makes death more terrifying to humans than to other creatures.[188]

The resurrection of Christ, of course, changes this condition of separateness and sin and death for those who believe in him. But then the question arises as to why a believer is still required to experience death at all. If death, physical as well as spiritual and eternal, is the penalty for sin, then when we are delivered from sin and its ultimate consequence (eternal death), why should we not also be spared from the symbol of that condemnation—physical death?[189]

It is necessary to distinguish here between the temporal and the eternal consequences of sin. The eternal consequences of our own individual sins are nullified when we are forgiven by Christ. However, the temporal consequences, or at least some of them, may linger on.

This approach to the consequences of sin is not a denial of the fact of justification, but merely an evidence that God does not reverse the course of history. What is true of our individual sins is also true of God's treatment of Adam's sin or the sin of the race as well. All judgment upon sin and all guilt because of original and individual sin are removed through Christ, so that spiritual and eternal death are canceled. As Christians, we will not experience the second death. Nonetheless, we must experience physical death simply because it has become one of the conditions of human existence.

One day, when the new heaven and new earth are established, every consequence of sin will be removed for the Christian, but that day has not yet arrived. The Bible, in its realism, does not deny the fact of universal physical death. However, it insists that death has different significance for the believer than for the unbeliever.[190]

3. The Biblical View of Hope for Life Beyond Death

(1) The Different Nature of Christian Death. We know from the accounts in the Book of Acts that death—even violent death—was well known to the early Christian community. During the very early days of the church, for example, Stephen died as a martyr at the hands of the Jewish authorities, who charged him with heresy. James, the brother of John, one of the original disciples, was beheaded by Herod (Acts 12:1–2).

Such deaths understandably raised anxiety among the early Christians. In what is perhaps the first letter to one of the early churches, the church at Thessalonica, Paul had to write and give assurance in the face of the death of some of their own number. "But we would not have you ignorant, brethren, concerning those who are asleep, that you may not grieve as others do who have no hope" (1 Thess. 4:13).[191]

In this passage, Paul recognizes the reality of death, even for Christians. But he also asserts here, as he does in other passages, that the death of Christians is qualitatively different from the death of those who do not belong to Christ. Christians who die are even spoken of as having "fallen asleep in Christ." They are not merely dead, they are "dead in Christ" and will be raised to meet Christ (1 Thess. 4:16–17).

(2) The Meaning of Christ's Death and Resurrection. The New Testament states that Christ's resurrection was not just an event that would mark the end of the age, but an event that occurred within history. In addition, the resurrection of Christ was not viewed as taking place outside of or beyond the historical continuum on which other events occur. It is itself an eschatological reality which occurs within the space-time continuum and which merges with the continuum of the life and death of others.[192]

This is most noticeable in the remarkable forty-day period following the Resurrection, when Jesus was present with the disciples prior to his ascension into heaven. Although not limited to the same boundaries during these forty days as in his preresurrection human existence, Jesus nonetheless stayed within these boundaries for the most part. He was not seen as a ghost nor as a phenomenon of psychic experience, but as a personal presence—as the Lord of this community of believers.

During these forty days, the disciples' encounter with Jesus "corrected" their understanding of his history with them prior to the resurrection. The resurrection put all that had taken place earlier in an entirely new light. Events and ideas began to fall into place and steadily to take on a depth of meaning and consistency that had been impossible before. Following his resurrection, Jesus showed the two disciples on the road to Emmaus the "inner necessity" of the events of crucifixion and resurrection: "Was it not necessary that the Christ should suffer these things and enter into his glory? And beginning with Moses and all the prophets, he interpreted to them in all the scriptures the things concerning himself" (Luke 24:26–27).[193]

It should be noted that the resurrection of Jesus did not destroy the natural order of time and space. The time and history of the disciples continued to take place within its limitations—it was still a history of death. However, this history had now been radically reoriented to the new creation, which already had impinged upon the old. This new creation assured the disciples that the resurrection of Jesus was part of the unbroken continuum which was constituted by his birth, life, and death.

It should also be noted that the death from which Jesus was raised was his own personal death, properly belonging to him through his assumption of humanity at birth, not merely death as an abstract concept. There is a connection between the resurrection of Christ and this death. In a sense, it involved the death of a "sinner," because the very flesh Jesus assumed was a human existence under "sentence of death" due to the sin of Adam.[194]

All of this means that the entire event of the birth, life, and death of Jesus of Nazareth is reconstituted through resurrection and given an entirely new cast. The continuum of created time and space on which human persons exist has been opened up to include a new reality. With the ascension of Christ, this new creation is hidden from us in such a way that we relate to it through faith and not by sight. Nonetheless, the truth remains that in the risen Christ our human nature in its temporal and historical dimension is now also redeemed from the power of death.[195]

In his resurrection, Jesus resumed and completed the redeeming work begun through his incarnation. In order for Jesus to overcome death through resurrection, he had to be "able to die." In order for God, as the eternal Son, to redeem humanity from death, he had to become human and so to "share in flesh and blood," so that "through death he might destroy him who has the power of death, that is, the devil, and deliver all those who through fear of death were subject to lifelong bondage" (Heb. 2:14–15).

Christ, himself sinless, endured death. Unlike the Greek philosopher, Socrates, who faced his demise with a smile, Jesus wept and trembled as he faced death. He cried out, "My God, my God, why hast thou forsaken me?" Christ could conquer death only by actually dying. He cried out again, "It is finished." By taking himself into the sphere of death, the destroyer of life—the sphere of abandonment by God—Christ conquered death. (In 1 Cor. 15:26, Paul calls death the last enemy of God.) Furthermore, if life is to issue out of so genuine a death as this, a new divine act of creation is necessary. Death must be conquered by the resurrection.

So Jesus overcame death by extending human time and history through death. This was done in the sphere of time and space, so that death itself is not removed. Instead, what has been radically altered is death's power to end the personal time and history of human beings. Time is transformed in such a way that it extends through physical death into resurrection.

In his resurrection, Jesus was the "first fruits" of all others who will be raised at his coming (1 Cor. 15:23). The death and resurrection of Jesus of Nazareth includes the death and resurrection of all persons who are united to this Jesus through a common humanity and through a shared experience in his resurrection life.[196]

(3) Reorientation of the Christian Pilgrimage. For the apostle Paul, the entire pilgrimage of human life, from birth to death, has been radically reoriented because of the resurrection of Jesus and his transformation of time and history. Death no longer looms as the final point on the continuum of life. Instead, the cosmos itself has undergone a transformation and is no longer subject to the bondage into which it fell with the entrance of sin into the world (cf. Rom. 8:18–25). We have received the "down payment" on this redemption through the Holy Spirit, who is the Spirit of the resurrected Lord himself (cf. Eph. 1:13, 14). Yet we also "long" for our redemption, even though it be through death.[197]

This does not mean that Christians are exempt from the experience of death, nor that the death of Christians can ordinarily be expected to be any less traumatic and painful physically than the death of any human being. However, the resurrection of Christ changes, for the human who believes in him, the trajectory through the passageway of death. Death is no longer the final word and the mortal end to the time and history of each individual.

The death and resurrection of Jesus Christ affects our life and death by placing us within the context of that new history of life and death which extends through death to eternal life with God. It is Jesus of Nazareth who anchors us within that eternal life by giving us his own Spirit and life (Rom. 8:11). To die in Christ is to have one's entire life upheld by the life of the one who was born, who died, and who continues to live beyond the power of death.[198]

Excursus on the Historical and Experiential Evidence for the Historical Resurrection of Jesus Christ

1. Representative Critical Theories Concerning the Resurrection

The resurrection of Christ is clearly the pivotal event of the Christian faith, and it is especially pivotal to the Christian understanding of death and the life beyond. At the same time, its clearly supernatural nature has made it a stumbling block for many through the centuries. Accordingly, there have been many attempts on the part of scholars to account for the Resurrection.

In the first place, there have been attempts to explain the Resurrection as a natural occurrence. Some have suggested that Jesus did not actually die, but fell into a kind of deep swoon, from which he recovered in the tomb. Others have postulated that the appearances of the resurrected Christ were merely hallucinations on the part of the severely stressed disciples, or that the stories of the Resurrection were simply legends that sprang up years after Jesus' death.

Those scholars that reject the naturalistic theories take varying approaches to the Resurrection accounts. Some, such as Temple University professor Paul van Buren, assert that the nature of the original eyewitnesses' experiences cannot be known. Van Buren believes, for example, that "something happened" which changed the disciples' outlook from discouragement to faith. Although these experiences were more than subjective and were expressed in terms of actual appearances of Jesus, we still cannot know their true nature.[199]

Other scholars, such as Karl Barth, state that the Resurrection can be known only by faith, completely apart from any verification. Barth believed that Jesus actually appeared to his disciples, but that this event occurred in a different sphere of history.

There are also those who hold that the Resurrection is an actual historical event, but that it cannot be demonstrated by historical methodology. Jürgen Moltmann, for example, believes that the disciples were the recipients of appearances of the risen Jesus which involved spoken messages and commissioned the hearers to service in the world. These events, however, are not strictly verifiable by present historical methods, although they are subject to future verification.

Still another view of the Resurrection, one which is closer to the evangelical view, is that available historical evidence demonstrates the probability that Jesus was literally raised from the dead. The well-known German theologian Wolfhart Pannenberg, for example, argues against naturalistic theories and concludes that the historical facts support the empty tomb and the literal appearances of Jesus. And yet Pannenberg argues against a corporeal resurrection body; in his view, Jesus' appearances were described in terms of a spiritual body which was recognized as Jesus by his followers.[200]

2. Representative Evangelical Approaches to the Historicity of the Resurrection

It should be noted that the fact that Jesus Christ died and afterward rose from the dead is both the central doctrine of Christian theology and the major fact in a defense of its teachings. This was true in the earliest church and remains so today. It is thus important to suggest various methods of undergirding belief in the resurrection of Jesus Christ.

(1) The Documentary and Eyewitness Evidence. The earliest documentary evidence for the Resurrection is that of Paul as recorded in 1 Corinthians 15, especially statements in verses 3–9. Here Paul records material which he had "received" from others and then "delivered" to his listeners. It is agreed by virtually all contemporary theologians that this material contains an ancient creed that is actually much earlier than the book in which it is recorded:

"For I delivered to you as of first importance what I also received, that Christ died for our sins in accordance with the scriptures, that he was buried, that he was raised on the third day in accordance with the scriptures, and that he appeared to Cephas, then to the twelve. Then he appeared to more than five hundred brethren at one time, most of whom are still alive. . . . Then he appeared to James, then to all the apostles. Last of all, as to one untimely born, he appeared also to me. For I am the least of the apostles, unfit to be called an apostle, because I persecuted the church of God. But by the grace of God I am what I am, and his grace toward me was not in vain."

The early date of this tradition is indicated by Paul's rather technical terms for receiving and passing on tradition. There is also the somewhat stylized content, the non-Pauline words, the specific names of Peter and James (cf. Gal. 1:18–19), and the possible Semitic idioms used.[201]

These facts have accounted for the critical agreement as to the early origin of this material. In fact, New Testament scholars R. H. Fuller and A. M. Hunter, along with Wolfhart Pannenberg, date Paul's receiving of this creed from three to eight years after the crucifixion itself. These data are quite significant in that they further indicate that both Paul and the other eyewitnesses proclaimed the death and resurrection of Jesus (1 Cor. 15:11) immediately after the events themselves. This anchors their report firmly in early eyewitness testimony and not in legendary reports arising later.[202]

(2) The Evidence of Known Historical Facts. In addition to the evidence for the Resurrection found in these eyewitness accounts, there is the evidence of known historical facts. At least five facts related to the Resurrection period are admitted by virtually all scholars as knowable history. These include the death of Jesus by crucifixion, the subsequent despair of the disciples, their experiences which they believed to involve appearances of the risen Jesus, their corresponding transformations, and the conversion of Paul due to a similar experience. These facts are capable both of arguing decisively against each of the naturalistic alternative theories and of providing some strong evidences for the literal appearances of the risen Jesus as reported by the eyewitnesses.[203]

The apostle Paul is a witness of special directness and weight. He was a man of genius and scholarship. He was also, before his conversion, a bitter opponent of the early Christians and especially of the doctrine of the Resurrection. After his vision of the resurrected Christ and his conversion, however, the totality of his life was redirected into a pattern of Christian discipleship and service based on the death and resurrection of Christ. His own experience was confirmed by those who had been eyewitnesses of Christ's resurrection (1 Cor. 15:3–11).

(3) The Evidence of the Existence of the Early Church. Still another major piece of evidence for the Resurrection is the existence of the church. Had the crucifixion ended the disciples' fellowship with Jesus, it is hard to see how the church could have come into existence and lasted until now.

The events of Good Friday left the disciples in a state of sadness, disillusionment, and disorganization. Had nothing further happened, faith in Christ surely would have collapsed. No church would have arisen, and the story of Jesus would have merged into the darkness of the world history as an unimportant episode of Jewish sectarian history. The message of the early church depended on the reality of the appearances of Jesus after his resurrection, just as it does today.[204]

(4) The Evidence of the Existence of the New Testament. In addition to the evidence of the church, there is the evidence of the New Testament. If Jesus had died as a crucified revolutionary, surely no follower would have bothered to have written the New Testament documents. Every written record of him was put down by men who were firmly convinced of his resurrection.

It is not this or that in the New Testament—not the story of the empty tomb or of the appearing of Jesus in Jerusalem or in Galilee—which is the primary evidence for the resurrection; it is the New Testament itself. The life that throbs in it from beginning to end, the life that always fills us again with wonder through its pages, is the life which the risen Savior has quickened in Christian souls.[205]

(5) The Evidence of the Existence of the Lord's Day. The very existence of Sunday as a day of worship is impressive evidence of the Resurrection. The Jews were very conservative and held the seventh-day Sabbath tenaciously and even fanatically. The Christian Jews would never have abandoned it without sufficient cause. No Jew or Christian would have dared change the sacred Sabbath to the first day of the week unless that day had a crucial meaning—most likely the fact that Christ was raised from the dead on the first day of the week.[206]

(6) The Evidence of Reported Encounters with the Risen Christ. There are many today who have never read a book demonstrating the truth of the Resurrection, but who believe he is alive, having experienced his redeeming presence. The historical and empirical evidence only bear witness to the assurance of man's inner experience.[207]

(7) A Summary Conclusion of the Evidences for the Resurrection of Jesus Christ. Even with a negative prejudice, it is a difficult task to refute the documentary evidence. It can be granted that an element of faith is needed to accept Jesus Christ as the divine-human redeemer and risen Lord. However, it is not a faith that lacks historical evidence. To remove all references to the Resurrection in the New Testament would entail its complete annihilation. Further, to set aside the evidence of Christian experience would require a denial of almost all of church history from Clement of Rome to the present.

4. The Biblical View of Personal Identity Beyond Death and the Resurrection Body

(1) The Biblical View Which Is Rooted in the Old Testament. The resurrection to life is the Christian answer to the threat of death. If there is to be full life beyond death the whole person will need to be redeemed—including the body.[208] According to the biblical view, the human body, being a part of God's

good creation, is essentially good, not evil. It is no prison in which he is confined as a prisoner and from which he may escape at death. Rather, the body is part of man's essential existence and subject to God's redemptive activity.

The Christian hope of resurrection of the body, however, is not merely a question of resuscitating a corpse or an urn of ashes containing the remains of a cremated person. Rather, our hope is that God will recreate or reconstitute us as an individual with an appropriate spiritual body.

As we have already noted, the early part of the Old Testament portrays life after death (in Sheol) as only a shadow of historical existence. The later New Testament writings, however, speak of resurrection, and the contrast between the dread and despair that gripped human souls at the prospect of Sheol and the hope aroused by the prospect of resurrection is striking. Passages such as Isaiah 26:19 and Daniel 12:2 affirm that God would abolish death in the new age so that redeemed men and women need never be separated from him—and this would be true even for those who died before the new age arrived. This doctrine of the resurrection of the dead, which is in keeping with the unitary view of humankind, was the perspective which would be carried over to the New Testament.[209]

(2) The Importance of Christ's Resurrection Body. The fact that the resurrected Christ was seen and recognized in bodily form by many of his followers has special significance in terms of personal identity after death and the resurrection of the body. This was clear to the writers of the Gospels, who found it of significant concern that the resurrected Jesus who appeared to the disciples was indeed the same Jesus they had seen crucified. Luke, especially, takes pains to show that the disciples needed to be convinced it was truly Jesus whom they met, not some glorious apparition from another sphere. In Luke's Gospel, Jesus is quoted as saying to the disciples, "Why are you troubled, and why do questionings rise in your hearts? See my hands and my feet, that it is I myself; handle me, and see; for a spirit has not flesh and bones as you see that I have" (Luke 24:38–39). Then he said to them, "These are my words which I spoke to you, while I was still with you" (24:44).[210]

Christian theology holds that there must be some form of personal identity between the Jesus who died and the Jesus who confronted the early witnesses after his resurrection. If the early disciples were convinced that it was the same Jesus, then they were able to hold as a confession of their own Christian hope that there would be the same kind of identity for each of them in the resurrection.

The answer to the question of the survival of personal identity through death is a question that has been answered in the death and resurrection of Jesus Christ. Our personal identity is not a predication we can make based on our creaturely nature. Rather, it is predicated upon the initiative of God, who addresses us and upholds us as the persons we are before him and with each other. Though the continuity of our time and history is broken with death, as Paul indicates (1 Cor. 15:42ff.), our personal identity continues to exist because it is grounded in our time and history with God.

There is an answer to the question: "Will I exist as the person that I now am, and as I am known by others, in the resurrection from the dead?" It comes when we answer the question: "Do we believe, along with his disciples, that the same Jesus of Nazareth whom they knew before his death appeared to them in his resurrection body?"[211]

(3) Paul's Answer to the Gnostics' Denial of the Importance of the Body. The belief that the body as essential to man's true selfhood is to be redeemed has both ethical and eschatological significance. This view is one of the major differences between the Greek and the biblical views of humankind.

The gulf between the two views is vividly illustrated in the conflict between the apostle Paul and a group of Gnostics over immorality in the church of Corinth (1 Cor. 6:12–20). The Gnostics, whose ideas were partly derived from Platonism, tried to justify the most sordid type of sexual behavior with the slogan, "all things are lawful for me" (6:12). They assumed that the acts of the body had no effect on the human spirit, so that one could be joined to a prostitute with his body while being joined to the Lord with his spirit.

Paul, looking on human beings as psychosomatic unities, was horrified by these rationalizations. He stated firmly that not only do those who are united to the Lord become one in spirit with him, but their very "bodies are members of Christ" (1 Cor. 6:15). Men and women are to glorify God in both body and spirit, not only because they are a unity, but also because both body and spirit are to be redeemed. The ethical realism of Paul was rooted deeply in his view of last things. Man is to glorify God in his body because the body is to be glorified.[212]

(4) Paul's Answer to the Question of the Nature of the Resurrection Body. We can now understand why the apostle Paul affirms that there is no true afterlife without a body. But Paul also points out that in God's economy there are various kinds of bodies—earthly and heavenly, perishable and imperishable, psychic and spiritual (1 Cor. 15:35–44).

Paul disavows the Jewish view, developed in the intertestamental period and written down in the Book of Baruch in the Apocrypha, that every particle of the physical body will be raised. (In modern times, some have raised the problem of how one's body can be reconstituted from molecules which may have become part of another person's body. Cannibalism presents the most extreme example of this problem. Human bodies serving to fertilize fields where crops are grown and the scattering of human ashes over a river from which drinking water is drawn are other cases in point—not to mention the transplanting of body parts!)

Paul insists that our postdeath survival is not simply a physical resuscitation. There is a utilization of the old body, but also a transformation of it in the process. Some sort of metamorphosis occurs, so that a new body arises. This new body has some connection or point of identity with the old one, but is differently constituted. Paul speaks of it as a spiritual body (1 Cor. 15:44), but does not elaborate. He uses the analogy of a seed and the plant that springs from it (1 Cor. 15:37). What sprouts from the ground is not merely that which is planted, although it grows out of that original seed.[213]

The Corinthian Christians to whom Paul wrote at length about the resurrection of the dead were familiar with the idea of immortality, but the presentation of their final destiny in terms of a resurrection body was strange to them. He therefore expected one of them to ask: "How are the dead raised? With what kind of body do they come?" (1 Cor. 15:35). And the apostle's reaction to such anticipated questions is, "You foolish man!" Such would doubtless be his answer to many of the questions which we are inclined to ask: "Will the one who died as a baby rise as a baby and the old man as an old man?" "Will the person with red hair or blue eyes still have these traits?" And "How is it possible that the molecules which once constituted my body and then in the cycle of nature passed over into the body of someone else can still belong to me?" The Word of God discourages idle and flippant speculation about "what no eye has seen, nor ear heard, nor the heart of man conceived." But, as we have seen, it does not leave us without some indication of a way to answer major questions.[214]

(5) The Basis of Our Identity. The broader philosophical problem concerning resurrection, of course, relates to the basis of identity. What is it that marks each of us as the same individual at birth, as an adult, and after resurrection? Certainly not the cells of the body, for we know that there is a complete change of cells within a person's body once every seven years. If biological cells were the basis of identity, adults would not be the persons they were at birth. There is evidently a continuity of identity, however, despite all the changes. The adult is the same person as the child, even if substitutions have been made for every cell in the body. Similarly, despite the transformation which will occur at resurrection, we know from Paul that we will still be the same person.[215]

Your body will reflect your uniqueness—like a good portrait condenses what you have become through the experiences and decisions of the life process. According to John Hick, it is conceivable that in the resurrection world we shall have bodies which are the outward reflection of our inner nature but which reflect it in ways quite different from that in which our present bodies reflect our personality.[216]

(6) The Relation of Our Resurrection Body to the Resurrection Body of Jesus. It is often assumed that our new bodies will be just like that of Jesus in the period immediately following his resurrection. His body apparently bore the physical marks of his crucifixion and could be seen and touched (John 20:27). Although the Scripture does not explicitly say that Jesus ate, we draw that inference from Luke 24:28–31 and John 21:9–15.

It should be borne in mind, however, that there were more steps remaining in Jesus' exaltation. The ascension, involving a transition from this space-time universe to the spiritual realm of heaven, may well have produced yet another transformation.

The change which will occur in our bodies at the resurrection occurred in two stages in his case. Our resurrection body will be like Jesus' present body, not necessarily like the body he had between his resurrection and ascension. We will not have those characteristics of Jesus' postresurrection earthly body which appear inconsistent with our resurrection bodies, which the apostle Paul calls "spiritual bodies" (1 Cor. 15:44). The characteristics we will need will not necessarily include physical tangibility and the need to eat.[217]

In conclusion, the Bible teaches that there will be a bodily reality of some type in the resurrection. An analogy is the petrification of a log or a stump. While the contour of the original object is retained, the composition is entirely different. We have difficulty in understanding because we do not know the exact nature of the resurrection body. It does appear, however, that our new body will retain and at the same time glorify the human form. We will be free of the imperfections and needs which we had on earth.[218]

5. The Biblical Teaching about the "Intermediate State"

(1) Practical Concern of the Issue. The question concerning the condition of human beings between their death and the resurrection is of great practical concern. Many pastors and parents have been asked at a graveside, "Where is Grandmother now? What is she doing? Is she with Jesus already? Are she and Grandfather back together? Does she know what we are doing?" These questions are not the product of idle speculation or curiosity; they are of crucial importance to the individual posing them. An opportunity to offer comfort and encouragement is available to the Christian who is informed on biblical teaching.[219]

(2) The Limits of the Biblical Teaching on the "Intermediate State." There is no extensive discussion of this question in the Bible. The early church evidently expected the period between Jesus' departure and his return to be relatively brief. This meant that the period between any human being's death and resurrection would be relatively brief as well. Furthermore, the intermediate state is merely temporary and, accordingly, did not concern the early believers as much as did the final states of heaven and hell.[220]

Nevertheless, there are a considerable number of scriptural references concerning the existence of an intermediate condition between the death of an individual and the general resurrection of the dead. And there is the important New Testament teaching that the new creation has already begun and provides the believer with an unbreakable union with Christ.[221]

(3) The Biblical Teachings about a Two-Part Intermediate State. The two-part view concerning an intermediate condition is based on a number of teachings. The word "paradise" in the saying of Jesus, "Today, you will be with me in Paradise" (Luke 23:43) is understood to refer to this intermediate condition rather than to the eternity that will follow the day of judgment. Similarly, the reference to Lazarus' being transported into Abraham's bosom (Luke 16:22) is understood as having reference to this intermediate state. Paul, too, seems to teach an interim existence when he shudders at the "nakedness" of being without a body before being clothed with the new resurrection body (2 Cor. 12:2–3).[222]

The German New Testament scholar Joachim Jeremias points out that the New Testament distinguishes between Gehenna and Hades. Hades receives the unrighteous for the period between death and resurrection, whereas Gehenna is the place of punishment assigned permanently at the last judgment. The torment of Gehenna is eternal (Mark 9:43, 48). On the basis of these biblical considerations, we can conclude that upon death believers go immediately to a place and condition of blessedness, and unbelievers to an experience of misery, torment, and punishment.[223]

Once again, the Bible gives few details concerning the conditions of the dead in the intermediate state. For example, the New Testament says nothing about a preliminary judgment for each individual when he dies, aside from the judgment that already took place when he was confronted with the gospel. Nor does the Bible speak about a preliminary resurrection of the dead.[224]

(4) The Positive Biblical Teachings about the Intermediate State. From a positive perspective, the New Testament does give us some general truths. Those who are in Christ continue to be in Christ; death cannot bring about a separation. Whether we live or die, we are his. The blessed dead are with Christ, and after the removal of earthly limitations, closer to him than before.[225]

The Holy Spirit, the resurrection power of Christ, continues to work in the blessed dead, to bind them to Christ and to transform them into Christlikeness. The Spirit also serves as the "earnest" or down payment of the final resurrection with Christ (2 Cor. 5:1–3).[226]

The imperfection of the interim before Christ's return is indicated by the images of nakedness, sleep, and waiting (Matt. 27:52–53; Rev. 6:9–11; Heb. 11:40; 1 Thess. 4:14–15). Paul, writing to the Corinthians, urged them not to lose heart, even though death might overtake them, for "while we are at home in the body we are away from the Lord," but "we would rather be away from the body and at home with the Lord" (2 Cor. 5:6, 8). Yet, as he pictures this transition, Paul appears to shrink from the idea that, being without the body, he would "be found naked." In verses 3 and 4, he states that the Christian's desire is not to be "unclothed" (i.e., disembodied), but "further clothed" (5:3, 4). Certainly Paul finds no encouragement in the prospect of a disembodied, conscious state between death and resurrection. In spite of these images of imperfection, however, the Bible still projects an assurance to God's people that they are experiencing a foretaste of the awaited perfection in their nearness to Christ.[227]

(5) Soul Sleeping and Soul Extinction. Some denominations and groups such as the Seventh Day Adventists and the Jehovah's Witnesses, hold the doctrine of "soul sleep." Of these groups, some hold to the annihilation of the wicked during the period of sleep, with the righteous being raised and given a resurrection body. Others hold that both the saved and the lost sleep during the interim period and both are raised for either eternal life in heaven or eternal torment in hell.[228]

James Packer responds to these teachings by pointing out that no biblical text unambiguously asserts annihilation, and many texts deny it. Annihilationists cannot warrantably squeeze the idea of annihilation out of the New Testament's fire and destruction imagery. Furthermore, the theological argument of the Annihilationists—that preserving the lost in endless punishment rather than annihilating them during the time of soul sleep is needless cruelty on God's part, since his glory does not require it—fails in two ways: (a) On that view, preserving the lost till the day of judgment is *already* needless cruelty on God's part; and (b) demonstration of God's retributive justice *is* praised in Scripture as a truth integral to his glory (Rev. 19:1–5). What is certain is that any speculation diminishing the awfulness of the prospect of a lost eternity for those who reject Christ frustrates the purpose of the New Testament imagery.[229]

In answer to the general concept of soul sleep, it should once again be noted that there are several biblical references to personal, conscious existence between death and resurrection. The most extended is the parable of the rich man and Lazarus (Luke 16:19–31).[230]

(6) The Concept of Purgatory. A fundamental doctrine of the Roman Catholic church is a belief in purgatory. Purgatory is described as an interim period after death set aside for the forgiveness of venial sins (less serious sins, as contrasted with the more serious mortal sins) for those who, although in a state of grace, are not yet spiritually perfect.[231]

According to Roman Catholic teaching, the forgiveness of venial sins can be accomplished in three different ways: by unconditional forgiveness on God's part, by suffering and the performance of penitential works, and by contrition. Although God can forgive unconditionally, he has chosen to require contrition and works as conditions of forgiveness in this life. Therefore, according to the Roman Catholic interpretation, it seems likely that he does not forgive venial sins unconditionally in purgatory either.

Since the soul in purgatory is not able to perform positive or active works of satisfaction such as making restitution, it can atone only by passive suffering. But there are also three means by which the souls in purgatory can be assisted in their progress toward heaven by the faithful still on earth—the mass, prayers, and good works. These three means reduce the period of time necessary for purgatorial suffering to have its full effect. When the soul arrives at spiritual perfection, with no venial sin remaining, it is released and passes into heaven.[232]

The major points in the rejection of the concept of purgatory are points which distinguish Catholicism and Protestantism in general. First, the major texts supporting purgatory are found in the Apocrypha, which Protestants do not accept as canonical Scripture. Further, the concept of purgatory implies a salvation by works. Humans are thought to atone, at least in part, for their own sins. This idea, however, is contrary to many clear scriptural teachings, including Galatians 3:1–14 and Ephesians 2:8–9.[233] Thus the doctrine of purgatory or any view which posits a period of probation and atonement following death is rejected by evangelicals.[234]

(7) The Importance of the Relationship with Christ Through Death. It should be noted that the New Testament is not concerned for a "state" which exists between death and resurrection, but for a "relation" which exists between the person and Christ through death. The state of those who have died is not described in terms of those who continue to live in the flow of temporality, but

in terms of the relationship of that person to Christ. This relation is one of immediacy, with no time interval projected into it at all.[235]

Looked at from the perspective of the new creation, there is no gap between the death of the believer and the second coming of Christ. However, looked at from the perspective of time that decays and crumbles away, there is a lapse of time between them. Thus we cannot "think" these two spheres of reality together; we cannot "synchronize the clock" of eternal time with our temporal time. It is the attempt to do this which has led to the speculation and unfortunate controversies over the so-called intermediate state.[236]

Anderson suggests that we affirm, along with Paul, that we will not be found "naked" or "unclothed" after our death, but that we will be "further clothed," so that our personal identity will be sustained as an embodied self with the same continuity with which Christ himself moved through his death and resurrection. After all, the "three days" during which he was said to be dead and buried were the result of a perspective from the time and history of death itself. Jesus certainly did not have to spend three days in a disembodied state awaiting a resurrection body. Having been raised by God in the power of the immediate relation which suffered no discontinuity through death, Jesus met the disciples after *their* three days were over.[237]

6. The Biblical Teaching about the Importance of the Second Coming of Christ and Last Things

(1) The Historical Development of Concern about "Last Things." For the first nineteen Christian centuries, personal eschatology was central in Christian thinking. The "four last things" (death, judgment, heaven, hell) occupied most believers' attention, and not much thought was given to the Second Coming. In the twentieth century, however, global eschatology has become central, as evangelicals have placed more emphasis on the second coming of Christ and the millennium. There is also the fact that nuclear and ecological concerns have caused the future of the world and the human race to be debated both in secular and Christian ecumenical contexts.[238]

(2) The Balanced Biblical Approach to "Last Things." The New Testament describes the entire sweep of human existence in terms of "this age" and "the age to come." It affirms that in the first coming of Christ, the blessings of the future age have been made available for human enjoyment. However, the present age continues to experience negative developments because Satan is still active and powerful. The Bible repeatedly says that the fullness of redemptive blessings awaits the glorious appearing of the age to come. The main emphasis of the Bible, therefore, is that the age to come is always an object of hope and expectation.[239]

In general, eschatology and the Second Coming have suffered from two attitudes in the church: neglect and overemphasis. In established, stable churches and theological systems, formal belief in end-time events has usually been retained, but these events have often been delegated to the heavenly stratosphere or the distant future. They have lost any direct influence on present conduct and thought. However, smaller groups outside the mainstream, especially in unstable times, have stressed little but eschatology. Concern over the exact details and timing of coming events has often been their major preoccupation.

Since both approaches have separated eschatology from the core of church life and teaching, eschatological hopes have often been taken over and secularized by other groups. For example, as shown in earlier chapters, the intense biblical desire for a final age of universal justice, fellowship, and peace has become an important root of many humanistic, socialistic, and communistic movements.[240]

In the Bible, however, eschatology is not merely a set of beliefs which may be pushed aside when certain events are delayed or which push aside everything else when the events are thought to be near. Although the Bible does not specify exactly when the consummating events will occur, it insists that the last times are already here. The eschatological atmosphere of the "already/not yet" pervades every action and thought.

Ultimately, from a biblical perspective, it does not matter whether the consummation of time is near or far off. In either case, the hope of Christ's return puts all things in a new perspective. If Jesus has already conquered the powers of evil and if he will surely return to consummate all of God's plans, then no situation of evil, tragedy, or despair can be as threatening as it looks. It must pass away. If the final evil, death, has already been conquered, and if the power of the resurrection now lives within us (cf. Eph. 1:19–21), then nothing, not even death, can defeat the life and love which now flow through us.

In short, the eschatological expectation of the first Christians gave them a unique vantage point from which to view every dimension of reality—as well as a unique impulsion to act in light of this hope. The eschatology of the early church was not merely a set of beliefs concerning future events, but also the attitude or atmosphere aroused by these events.[241]

Eschatology, including the second coming of Christ, is thus not one element of Christianity, but is the basic perspective of Christian faith. It is the glow that suffused everything here and now in the dawn of an expected new day. Therefore, the eschatological outlook should be characteristic of all Christian proclamation, of every Christian existence, and of the whole Church.[242]

7. The Biblical Teaching about Hell and the Last Judgment

(1) Humankind's Intuitive Sense of Judgment As a Background for the Biblical Teaching. It should be noted that fear of divine retribution following death is not a fear introduced into the human experience through the biblical literature alone. In his important book *The Judgment of the Dead,* S. G. F. Brandon documents the fact that many cultures portray death as an evil which results from defilement of life. They often speak in lurid language about torment and judgment following death.

Thus, not only in the New Testament, but also in the literature of ancient India, China, and Japan, under the influence of Hinduism and Buddhism, references to punishment after death are to be found. One thousand years before the time of Moses, inscriptions on the tombs of Egyptian kings reveal expectations of avoiding future punishment beyond death by means of good deeds performed during life.[243]

(2) The Biblical Teaching about the Consequences of the Rejection of God and His Righteousness. The righteousness of God, conceived in ethical terms, carries with it the theological cargo of consequences for actions done in this life. To allow death to annihilate the existence of sinners and so release them from these consequences would be to grant death a power over God's moral judgment. Thus, punishment of the wicked after death was a logical extension of the belief that the righteous would not be forgotten by a holy and just God. The teaching of Jesus and the early Christian community that sin had consequences extending through physical death and warranting punishment and judgment in the life to come rested upon a doctrine of God that was consistent with Israel's knowledge of Yahweh.[244]

Some have mistakenly assumed that it is the Old Testament which pictures negative consequences after death, while the New Testament is positive and more "human." Actually, the reverse is true. It is the New Testament which fills out the contours of the vague Old Testament teaching about Sheol and populates it with real, substantive human beings. Here we read of Dives, who in the realm of the dead is in "anguish in this flame" (Luke 16:24). It is in the New Testament that we first hear of people being cast into outer darkness where they will "weep and gnash their teeth" (Matt. 22:13). It is also in the New Testament where we first read of the place where "their worm does not die, and the fire is not quenched" (Mark 9:48). It is here that we read the terrible description of Revelation 14: "And the smoke of their torment goes up for ever and ever; and they have no rest, day or night" (v. 11).[245]

It is against this backdrop that we see Jesus himself expressing a strong warning against breaking the divine law and entering hell (Matt. 5:29; 18:9). It is God who is to be feared, and not man, because he has the power to "cast into hell" (Luke 12:5). In coming under God's judgment in his death, Jesus himself is placed in the condition of the sinner who is under the curse of the law.

On the basis of Christ's death for sinners, the apostle Paul argued that death, which spread to all people through the sin of Adam, has now been overcome through the death of the one man, Jesus Christ (Rom. 5:12, 15, 16). Christ's saving death contains a universal offer of salvation which must be appropriated through individual repentance and faith in Christ.[246]

(3) The Biblical Teaching about the Last Judgment. *Krisis,* the word which the New Testament uses for judgment, basically means "separation" or "division" (2 Cor. 5:10). The judge on the last day is not to be thought of as a courtroom judge who decides the fate of the accused. Rather, he is like the judge of an art exhibit or an oratorical contest who discriminates between a good performance and a poor one. The decision of an individual's fate has already taken place before the final judgment; the act of judgment is one of inclusion or exclusion.

The Last Judgment, which will come at the end of the age, will clearly specify those who have responded inwardly and truly to Jesus Christ. The New Testament stresses that the basis for the final differentiation is a "quality of life" as expressed in a person's deeds (Matt. 25:31ff.).

Now, at first glance, there may seem to be a conflict between this kind of judgment and justification by faith through grace. But there is no actual contradiction in saying that a person is saved by grace, yet judged by works. Grace is a creative power by which the new life in the spirit is generated. Works are the fruits of the new life. When the grace of God is received in living faith, it produces the works of love. In our Lord's own description of the Last Judgment (Matt. 25:30–46), it is the judge who enumerates the works performed by the righteous. They themselves have kept no record of them, for they ask, "When did we do these things?" They performed righteous and loving acts not in order to be saved, but because they had been saved by that perfect love which casts out both fear and calculation and gives true hope on the day of judgment.[247]

The gospel always presents people's deeds as indications of the total quality of their life as determined by their relation to God. Unless the faith which appropriates God's forgiveness manifests itself as a forgiving disposition toward other human beings, it is not a true faith.

The Bible does seem to indicate that there will be degrees of judgment, depending on the "amount of light" or degree of enlightenment people have received. An example is those who have not heard of the historic Christ. Clearly, such people cannot be expected to have placed their faith in a story they have not heard. However, as Paul asserts in Romans 1, even people who have never heard the gospel have a revelation of the cosmic Christ in their conscience and nature. Paul sadly states that, for the most part, they have not accepted even this amount of light and followed it. Therefore they, too, have rejected Christ.

But even among believers on the judgment day there are different degrees of development in the attitude of self-forgetting love. A relevant passage is found in 1 Corinthians 3:11–15, which describes a process whereby each person's works are tested "as through fire." The Christian who has sought personal glory and demonstrated vain pretensions unlike the mind of Christ has in effect built a personality edifice of wood, hay, and stubble, which the fire of judgment will destroy. In other words, such believers will not be allowed to enter their final destiny with a false estimate of themselves. Although their guilt will thus be made manifest, the forgiveness of sins in Christ will still hold, and such persons will be saved. Thus, the end is a life everlasting, with true humility and with a consciousness of his need for further growth in Christ.

The New Testament describes the Last Judgment as the time when the final destiny of every human being will be sealed. The determiner of this destiny is none other than the Son of Man, who is also the Son of God. As we have seen, there is nothing arbitrary about this judgment, for it is only the unveiling of the basic orientation and quality which each life has already assumed.

The sifting process of judgment goes on whenever men and women are confronted with the gospel. God's offer of grace may be accepted or rejected. Judgment thus hinges upon each person's decision regarding the gospel, and the final division only makes clear the choice already made. In the words of Jesus, "He who believes in him is not condemned; he who does not believe is condemned already. . . . And this is the judgment, that the light has come into the world, and men loved darkness rather than light, because their deeds were evil" (John 3:18–19).[248]

(4) The Biblical Teaching about Eternal Hell. Most Christians shudder at the idea of anyone's having to experience eternal hell. And yet the plain situation is that not all of our acquaintances and loved ones die in the Lord. When one combines this grim reality with the larger-than-life preaching of some who seem to be spiritual sadists in their descriptions of hell, the situation is emotionally and psychologically intolerable for many people.[249]

Yet we must be careful not to set up our own meager conceptions of love and justice as standards for God or to manipulate his Word to suit our desires. We may revolt at the crude imagery with which hell is so often pictured by the theology of other days, but we cannot dismiss the urgency the biblical message places on individual decision.[250]

The fact God offers salvation in Christ to all people does not mean that this offer will be universally accepted. Scripture sets forth both God's sovereign love and human responsibility. The message of the gospel is not, "God so loved the world that anybody, whether or not he or she believes, will have eternal life." The dark thought of "perishing" is present even when God's love is described as embracing the whole world.

The human will is capable of becoming so hardened in its rebellion against God that the individual will reject God's grace and involve himself or herself in ruin. That is why our Lord spoke in such dead earnest about the peril of losing one's life or forfeiting one's life.[251]

It is Christ himself who stated that "it is better to enter the kingdom of God with one eye than with two eyes to be thrown into hell, where their worm does not die, and the fire is not quenched" (Mark 9:47–48). And when he declares, "And they will go away into eternal punishment, but the righteous into eternal life" (Matt. 25:46), he uses the same word, *aionios* (eternal), to describe both damnation and blessedness. Thus if the one is not eternal, neither is the other. In the light of this clear teaching of the Lord himself, we cannot accept the view that all human beings will eventually be saved.[252]

This teaching of Christ about hell is also reflected in the Book of Revelation, which describes the wicked as being "tormented with fire and brimstone . . . for ever and ever" (14:10–11).

(5) The Characteristics of Hell. The physical torments described in the preceding passages are indeed fearful, but they are only symptomatic of the true torment of hell. For hell is characterized most of all by the absence of fellowship

with God or banishment from his presence. It is thus an experience of intense anguish, whether it involves physical suffering or mental distress or both.[253]

There are other tragic aspects of hell. There is the hopelessness of realizing that this separation is permanent, and that the condition of one's moral and spiritual self is similarly permanent. Whatever one is at the end of life will continue for all eternity.[254]

(6) Biblical Teachings about Universalism. The New Testament clearly teaches that at the end of the age there will be a curtailment and cessation of active opposition to God's will and a complete subjugation of the powers of evil. In that sense, the Bible does teach that there will be a final universal acknowledgment of the lordship of Christ (Eph. 1:10; Phil. 2:9–11; 1 Cor. 15:24ff.). The sovereignty of the righteous merciful God thus guarantees that the universe in its final condition will be undisturbed by sin. The impenitent agents of evil will be excluded from Christ's kingdom and subordinated to the will and purpose of God.

However, to translate the emphasis on a final acknowledgment of the lordship of Christ into a "universal homecoming," as some so-called "universalists" have done, is unjustified by the biblical data. When universalists say that the universal homage described in Philippians 2 ("Every knee should bow. . . . and . . . every tongue should confess that Jesus Christ is Lord," Phil. 2:10–11, KJV) implies that all humanity will be redeemed, they merely conform the text to an advance assumption. Paul was speaking about a universal acknowledgment of Christ's lordship, not a universal saving confession of Christ.[255]

The universalist appeal to Colossians 1:19–20 ("God was pleased . . . through him to reconcile to himself all things, whether on earth or in heaven, making peace by the blood of his cross") is similarly inconclusive. Paul's term *reconciliation* here has a cosmic sense, one that suggests restoration of an original harmony long disrupted by sin. The forces of evil are stripped of their power by the victory of divine righteousness (Col. 2:15).[256]

In contradiction of the universalist position, the Bible explicitly connects salvation with personal faith (John 3:16; Rom. 3:28ff., 4:5; etc.) and teaches that unbelief excludes salvation (John 3:18, 8:24; Rom. 2:5ff.; etc.).[257] In particular, James Packer contends that three questions seem fatal to the universalist speculation:

- Does not universalism fly in the face of the biblical stress on the decisiveness of this life's decisions? (Cf. Matt. 12:32, 25:41, 46, 26:24; Luke 16:26; John 8:21; 2 Cor. 5:10; Gal. 6:7.)
- On the universalist hypothesis, was the preaching of hell for unbelievers by Jesus and the apostles inept ignorance or immoral bluff? (It was the former if they did not know universalism was true, and the latter if they did.)
- Is not universalism contrary to each person's own conscience? Charity may prompt it, but "I dare not say to myself that if I forfeit the opportunity this life affords I shall ever have another; and therefore I dare not say so to another man" (James Denney). What is certain is that there is no salvation without faith, essentially because of what salvation is.[258]

The view which is clearly in harmony with the whole of divine revelation and has therefore had predominance in the church through the centuries is the doctrine that the ultimate fate of humankind is twofold: heaven and hell, eternal life and eternal damnation. It is unmistakably stated in the words of Christ himself: "Then the King will say to those at his right hand, 'Come, O blessed of my Father, inherit the kingdom prepared for you from the foundation of the world.' . . . Then he will say to those at his left hand, 'Depart from me, you cursed, into the eternal fire prepared for the devil and his angels'" (Matt. 25:34, 41). This teaching is related to the portrayal of the Last Judgment, and it indicates that heaven and hell obtain their true meaning only after that judgment has taken place.[259]

8. The Biblical Teaching about the New Heaven and the New Earth (Heaven)

The final destiny of Christians beyond physical death is described in the New Testament by the utilization of various metaphors which are largely synonymous. The most frequently used terms include heaven, new heaven and new earth, heavenly Jerusalem, and new Jerusalem.

(1) The Biblical Language Used to Portray Heaven and the Future. The biblical language used to describe the future is pictorial, evocative, and evaluative rather than prosaically informative. The Bible is a Near-Eastern Book written several thousand years ago, and accordingly it communicates the reality of the future according to the method of thinking peculiar to that period and place. Those of us in the modern West see this language as quasipoetic prose. Oriental imagination expresses thoughts in "visuals" that are often incompatible in themselves and decorated with further "visuals" to indicate importance rather than to add to our precise knowledge.

An example is Revelation 7:14 where the saints "have washed their robes and made them white in the blood of the Lamb." Here John is expressing a theological thought and not a precise bit of information. If the statement is taken literally it would be contradictory.[260]

(2) The Rationale for the Doctrines of the Millennium and the New Heaven and the New Earth. As shown in a previous chapter, the Bible states that at the end of the age, God will establish a new heaven and a new earth. Many scholars also interpret the biblical record as predicting that before this there will be a thousand-year reign of Christ's kingdom on earth, either before or after the tribulations of the end time.

The resurrection of the body implies that the richness of social relationship and cultural creativity cannot be done away with and that even the order of nature must also share in the glorious liberty of the sons of God. Just as the body expresses the range of the human personality, cultural life expresses humanity's creative relationships, and the natural environment provides a setting for all the rich gifts with which the Creator has endowed the human race. Those Christians who look for a millennium kingdom within time and at the end of history are expressing the belief that the cultural structures of historical life and the world of nature must in some way participate in the ultimate consummation.[261]

Both the doctrines of the millennium and the new heaven and the new earth teach that when the limitations of this order are done away, the whole structure of historical existence and cultural life within its natural setting will in some way be purified, fulfilled, and glorified. In the end, secular history and nature will not be totally annihilated, but will be resurrected to provide the setting for the perfected fellowship of the redeemed community. The Bible insists that the world is not merely instrumental to the fashioning of personalities, after which it will pass into nothingness. Rather, the world will be taken up in a transfigured form into the realized purpose of God.[262]

George Ladd, a leading exponent of historical or moderate millennialism, suggests that the kingdom of the future will be realized in two stages. First, there will be an interim millennial kingdom after the Second Coming. Then there will be the final consummation, which will introduce a redeemed order.[263]

Scripture describes all creation as groaning under the curse of evil and death, earnestly waiting for God to bring his work to completion. When this takes place, the curse will be lifted, the groaning will be silenced, the restless striving of the imperfect toward the perfect will cease, and every defect will be purged away. A new heaven and a new earth will reflect in every aspect the justice and the love of God. Churches will be unnecessary, for all of life will worship in the direct presence of God himself. "I saw no temple in the city," says the sacred writer of Revelation, "for its temple is the Lord God the Almighty and the Lamb" (Rev. 21:22).[264]

(3) The Question of Heaven. Transcending all images which describe it, heaven is the final fulfillment of our personal relationship to God. To be in Christ is to be bound with close ties to our loved ones, to all of God's redeemed children, and to a renewed earth.

Like hell, many images have surrounded heaven—some biblical and some developed over the centuries. Gates of pearl and harps of gold are images of the "glory that is to be revealed." The highest bliss of heaven is contained in our Lord's word, "I go and prepare a place for you, I . . . will take you to myself, that where I am you may be also" (John 14:3).[265]

Despite these images—or perhaps because of them—many people have a hard time imagining what heaven will be like. For instance, many people ask whether in heaven there will be any memory of life on earth. There are enough hints in the Bible to understand that heaven is not just an endless time of dull amnesia. It will surely involve some memory. There will be recognition. In fact, we will know each other more thoroughly than now, for there will be no possibility of camouflage.

Life in the age to come will certainly involve continuing activities and relationships that will contribute to the glory of the holy city throughout eternity. There will be no blurring of uniqueness or memory or relationships, but rather the fulfillment of the ways we have been originally created and the ways we have lived out our created individuality. And the surprise is that the uniqueness does not isolate us from each other.[266]

Revelation 21:2–4 describes the New Jerusalem as a city with life, activity, interest, and people—a community. That is the picture given in John's vision—a city coming down, God dwelling with his people on earth, a covenant of full fellowship inaugurated. Revelation 21:24–26 presents a remarkable picture of "the nations" and "the kings of the earth" entering the holy city and bringing their splendor into it. In this vision, the nations of the world are honored and set free from the old competitions and fears.[267]

Revelation 21:24–26 also indicates that there will be purposeful activity in heaven. Carl F. H. Henry affirms that eternity will be no haven of inactivity where inhabitants draw unemployment benefits. The spiritual rest that heaven offers the redeemed is not a life of indolence. In contrast, redeemed humanity will bear fully God's image as Worker. The creation model of work-week and sabbath-rest is a pattern turned by the fall into burden and hardship. For the Christian in heaven, this model will be turned into a fulfilling rhythm of work and rest. Our time in heaven will be a time of life and growth.[268]

Another disputed question regarding heaven is whether it is a place or a state. While placelessness may make sense if we accept the Greek idea of a formless soul, the biblical teaching concerning the resurrection of the body seems to require place. However, because we are discussing another dimension of reality, it is difficult to know what features of this world apply to the world to come and exactly what the term *place* means in relation to last things.[269]

Yet another issue concerns the question of physical pleasures and sexuality. Jesus indicated that in the resurrection—and so presumably in the life hereafter—there would be no marrying or giving in marriage (Matt. 22:30; Mark 12:25; Luke 20:35).[270] Hendricks suggests that we will be sexual beings in the sense of being intrinsically male and female—how else could we know one another? On the other hand, we will not exercise physical sexuality, for we will not be physical in our present sense.[271]

It should be understood that the experiences of heaven will far surpass anything experienced here. Paul said, quoting Isaiah, "'What no eye has seen, nor ear heard, nor the heart of man conceived, what God has prepared for those who love him, God has revealed to us through the Spirit" (1 Cor. 2:9–10). It is likely that heaven's experiences should be thought of as, for example, suprasexual or transsexual, transcending the experience of sexual union with the special individual with whom one has chosen to make a permanent and exclusive commitment.[272]

Some raise the issue which relates to the question of perfection. John Baillie speaks of "development *in* fruition" as opposed to "development *toward* fruition."[273] In other words, Christians have a new status in Christ in heaven which in one sense is complete and perfect. However, we will need to develop the implications of this new status.

As intimated earlier, there is some evidence that there will be varying rewards in heaven. This probability is seen in, for example, the parable of the pounds

(Luke 19:11–27). It is also indicated by 1 Corinthians 3:14–15, which contrasts the way two kinds of believers will enter heaven ("If the work which any man has built on the foundations survives, he will receive a reward. If any man's work is burned up, he will suffer loss, though he himself will be saved, but only as through fire").

Erickson suggests that the difference in the rewards will not be in the external or objective circumstances, but in the subjective awareness or appreciation of those circumstances. Thus, all would engage in the same activity—for example, worship—but some would enjoy it much more than others. An analogy here is the varying degrees of pleasure which different people derive from a concert. The same sound waves fall on everyone's ears, but the reactions may range from boredom (or worse) to ecstasy. A similar situation may well hold with respect to the joys of heaven, although the range of reactions will presumably be narrower.[274]

Finally, there is the question of time and space in heaven. Thomas Finger, a professor at Northern Baptist Seminary, suggests that heaven will likely bring so many new dimensions to our experience that our present ways of reckoning temporal sequence will seem highly inadequate. Yet its final coming and continuance will at least be identifiable on our present chronological scale. Perhaps length, width, and depth will seem artificial abstractions from the far more complex reality of things, yet such spatial coordinates will not be entirely meaningless. This view is in keeping with the idea the "eye hath not seen" the surprises which will be revealed to us in heaven.[275]

Excursus on Practical Problems Related to the Biblical Approach to Dying, Death, and the Life Beyond

1. The Issue of Death with Dignity

(1) The Question of Extending Life Through Medical Technology. In recent years, modern medical technology has raised a serious question that in a way is unique to our time: What is death? In many ways, life-support systems for seriously ill people are a blessing; they assist in basic life functions such as heartbeat and respiration until the sick person recovers enough to function on his or her own. But these very systems raise some difficult issues because they are capable of sustaining physical life—often at great expense—in cases where the ill person has almost no chance of recovery. In instances of medically irreversible comas, for example, or instances of brain death, are life-sustaining devices helpful or harmful?

A Christian perspective on this issue is grounded in the tension that must be maintained between affirming life and, at the same time, allowing death when human life is itself in danger of becoming grotesque and even monstrous. "We are forbidden to hamper the Lord of life and death by medical gadgetry that can also lead to madness," writes Helmut Thielicke.[276]

Determining the point where this "madness" occurs, of course, is the critical issue. It certainly is not a theological decision alone. But the context in which this decision is made must include, in addition to scientific expertise, a theological perspective on human life. This perspective includes a point of view in which life and death are viewed as already held fast within God's actions in Jesus Christ.[277]

Actually, there are two distinct issues, or perhaps three, included in the overall issue of extending life through medical technology: "active" euthanasia, which means deliberately bringing about death by "pulling the plug," administering fatal drugs, and so on; "passive" euthanasia, which means simply not taking certain steps to prolong life—such as deciding to "no code" a patient or not take unusual measures in the case of a crisis. And a side issue is whether or not this is done at the patient's request.

Although the issues are complex, many people recognize that forestalling an inevitable death in order to perpetuate an existing familiar form in a vegetating state is not necessarily "caring" for the person. To allow the decision to extend biological life and to permit the definition of clinical death to be made primarily in terms of scientific or technological criteria may itself be an act of irresponsibility, humanly and theologically speaking. Many Christians, in fact, reject the concept of an absolute right to extend biological life through extraordinary means. This concept violates the fundamental coresponsibility which upholds the integrity and sanctity of life.[278]

Quite a few thoughtful people, such as William Hendricks, suggest that when severe brain damage or brain death has occurred, when the possibility of active life is not present, and when one's limited financial resources are used up and loved ones may be obliged to pay exorbitant medical costs for an indefinite period, it might be better to permit death with dignity than to continue it through unusual means.[279]

In a similar emphasis, Carl F. H. Henry affirms that where the terminally ill person continues to live beyond all medical prognostication under his or her own amazing resources, the Christian family may with good reason hesitate to approve deliberate life-suppressing measures. This approach would demonstrate the compassion for the weak that distinguishes the Christian from the pagan community. This view would trust that the sovereign God who preserves life may intervene by way of special providence. But one is surely not called upon to sustain life artificially in the hope that science may suddenly find a cure. We are only responsible for what we know or could have known and not for what we cannot know, even in our relationships with loved ones. The unbeliever can least afford to make a mistake in the matter of responsibility for taking a fellow unbeliever's life. The Christian, in contrast, knows the God who forgives the failures of the contrite, and he also knows that at death a fellow believer passes to a better world and reward.[280]

This, of course, brings up a central concept that can inform the Christian's view of any of the practical problems concerned with death and dying. For Christians, death can be a blessing, not only because it means the end of suffering, but also because it is a way home—to the Father's house.[281]

Thus our approach to problems related to terminal illness are rooted in the Christian belief that human life and death are bracketed under the determination of God. We have shown that the life, death, and resurrection of Jesus Christ has enfolded the life and death of human persons within that future time and history which the resurrection of Jesus Christ reveals.[282] Our decisions about extending life through medical technology need always to be made in the light of the saving work of Jesus Christ.

(2) The Question of Providing Hospice and Home Care. Closely related to this issue is the movement to "humanize" the event of dying through providing a more domestic and familial type of caring environment. This concern for relatedness in dying has found expression in the hospice movement. The word *hospice* connotes an interaction between human persons, not merely a physical environment or a "place to stay." Seeking to retrieve what has been most humane and sensible in the tradition of healing and ministry to the dying, the hospice seeks to establish a new standard for care of the dying without diminishing the effective resources of medical science. The key word for the hospice is "community." At the center of the hospice community is the concept of a body coexisting with a belief. The body is the dying patient, and the belief is that the patient is something more than a body.[283]

The hospice movement recognizes that specialized care is necessary for dying persons, and that the home and family unit cannot always provide that. It also recognizes, however, that in many cases the isolating and dehumanizing aspects of hospital or nursing home care can be even worse for the dying person than the experience of dying itself.

This is true because, like nature, a human life has an *ecology*—a delicate balance of forces that helps sustain our sense of purpose and dignity. In a person's last days, this ecology is upset. Little by little, the dying person loses control of his or her body or private space; this loss of control is at some point permanent. However, when this is marked by the transfer of our body out of the familiar space of our own domestic and familial life, we are bound to experience ecological shock. The fact that this is meant for our good, and that the body can now receive care that will ensure its survival for a longer period of time, is often taken as both necessary and good. However, under the dehumanizing or impersonal conditions of medical care as experienced in many modern hospitals, the ecological system which is necessary for the upholding of our human dignity can be broken.[284]

An argument can be made, then, for the presence of the human and Christian network which upholds the dignity and humanity of the person even through that ambiguous point of death.[285] And that is the whole purpose of the hospice movement, which aims at providing a network of caring human beings as the environment of the dying person. This is provided through the hospice staff and through trained staff and volunteers who regularly visit dying people in their own home environment. The emphasis is usually on controlling pain through medication and helping the dying person make whatever arrangements are necessary for him or her to die in peace.

The hospice movement stresses that it is also important to uphold the truthfulness of death through the process of dying. This means that the ultimate betrayal of personhood is to deceive another about his or her death. Rather than the truth of dying constituting a shock to the person, it can actually be a therapeutic gain and a resource of courage and hope.[286]

(3) The Question of Prayer in Relation to Sickness and Death. The ecology of death leads us to acknowledge a many-faceted network of relations to which the dying person is connected—not least of which is the relation of the person to God. The Christian community is concerned with a coresponsibility for upholding one another in death. We uphold the humanity of the other when that person no longer has control of his or her own human environment.[287] We can also uphold the faith of a person who is dying.

The Christian perspective is not easy to sustain. Under the stress of illness and impending death, some lose sight of the promises altogether and sink into the present reality with a fatalism and despair which concedes all hope to the inevitable victory of sickness and death. Others grasp at the promises with spiritual and emotional fanaticism, living on the precarious edge of the miraculous and the fantastic. Thus part of the responsibility of upholding one another in death is keeping the dying person oriented toward the saving perspective of the Christian faith.

Prayer for the one who is sick and dying has a definite purpose. It is not a desperate and fanatical act to gain a supernatural intervention as an advantage over life, with its sickness and death. Rather, it is the appropriation of one's life into the ultimate healing event, which takes place through death and resurrection.

This perspective casts a different light on the question of healing itself. Where there are evidently manifestations of immediate healing as an answer to prayer, these healings are to be viewed as a foretaste of the resurrection and a sign to the entire community that the promise of ultimate healing is true. Therefore, the healing of one person is not a "truth" which condemns others who are not healed. The healing of the one is a foretaste of that truth which holds good for all. Healing is a gift of God to the community for the purpose of sustaining the faith of the members of the community.[288]

Interestingly enough, prayer itself has been shown to have a therapeutic effect. Experiments in pain control have shown that injections accompanied by prayer and the touching of the person's body are more effective than when performed as a routine medical procedure. This simply highlights the fact that we as Christians are called to have the last look, the last touch, and the last word with those who are dying—to minister to them and uphold them.[289]

2. The Issue of Suicide

(1) The Definition of Suicide. Suicide is generally defined as a fatal act of self-destruction undertaken with conscious intent. This means that a man who dies in a hurricane because he did not heed a radio warning is not a suicide victim, nor is someone who carelessly consumes an overdose of barbiturates and dies. A

woman who kills herself by jumping from a burning building has not committed suicide, nor has a child who is killed by a train while exploring a railway tunnel. A motorcyclist who dies from head injuries because he or she did not wear a helmet would not be reported as a suicide. None of these examples involves voluntary extinction of life.[290]

It is often difficult to determine absolutely if a death was intentionally self-inflicted. And because suicide is taboo in our culture, the official record reflects that the benefit of a doubt has often been given in order to avoid stigmatizing the family name or voiding a life insurance policy. Even though the most tragic suicides may be among the young, the greatest number of suicides continues now, as in the past, to be among those of the senior generation.[291]

(2) The Views of Different Religions and Denominations Toward Suicide. Religion is a statistically significant factor worldwide in the suicide rate. For example, the suicide rate in Egypt is one-sixtieth that of the United States. The Egyptian outlook on life has been heavily impacted by the Muslim condemnation of suicide.[292]

In traditional Asian cultures, on the other hand, altruistic suicide has been deemed a meritorious way of fulfilling social expectations, and suicide is therefore more common. One example of this is the Japanese custom of *hara-kari* in situations of disgrace or dishonor. Another example is the centuries-old Indian practice of *suttee*, which involves a widow's voluntarily throwing herself on her husband's funeral pyre. The British outlawed this practice in the nineteenth century, but a few women still express total devotion to their dead spouses in this way.[293]

It should be noted that there are "right to die" movements that are strong in the United Kingdom and some European countries, such as Belgium, and have also been influential in the United States. These societies have even issued handbooks of instruction on how to commit suicide. The plays, *Whose Life Is It, Anyway?* and *'Night, Mother* (both made into films) reflect the "right to die" idea.

Countries with a predominantly Roman Catholic population—such as Ireland—generally have a lower suicide rate than Protestant countries. For many centuries, the Roman Catholic Church has condemned suicide.[294] In fact, Catholic doctrine teaches that one who takes his or her own life is not permitted to be buried in holy ground because that person has died in sin—not having lived to ask forgiveness through the church.[295]

(3) Reasons for Suicide. Since suicide is usually a secretive and private act, it is difficult to discover reasons why people take their own lives. One main cause is depression caused by the shattering loss of someone or something highly valued. The death of love drives some to a love of death. Some who are separated by death from those they love imagine that suicide affords a means for quick reunion. Losing out to others in the upward mobility race—whether real or imagined—is one of the multiple factors that intensify the risk of suicide.[296]

The issue of suicide is also closely tied to the concept of death with dignity. It is not uncommon for those who face the prospect of increasing physical or mental disability and eventual death to seek to hasten that death. Several years ago, for example, the Protestant Christian community was shocked by the suicide of Elizabeth and Pitney Van Dusen. Pitney, aged seventy-seven, was the former president of New York's Union Theological Seminary and a distinguished Presbyterian minister. Before they both took an overdose of sleeping pills, his eighty-year-old wife, Elizabeth, wrote:

> We have both had very full and satisfying lives. . . . But since Pitney had his stroke five years ago, we have not been able to do any of the things we want to do . . . and my arthritis is much worse. There are too many helpless old people who without modern medicinal care would have died, and we feel God would have allowed them to die when their time had come.
>
> Nowadays it is difficult to die. We feel that this way we are taking will become more usual and acceptable as the years pass. . . . We are both increasingly weak and unwell, and who would want to die in a Nursing Home . . . ?
>
> "O Lamb of God, that takest away the sins of the world, Grant us thy peace."[297]

(4) Conflicting Christian Views of Suicide. Unlike the Roman Catholic Church, which over the centuries has unequivocally condemned suicide, the Protestant church has been divided in its reaction to suicide.

After the deaths of the Van Dusens for example, a committee of the Presbytery of New York City concluded that "for some Christians, as a last resort in the gravest of situations, suicide may be an act of their Christian conscience."[298]

The Lutheran theologian Dietrich Bonhoeffer held a quite different view, however. While this leader of German resistance to Hitler was being persecuted, but before his imprisonment and execution by the Nazis, he affirmed: "God has reserved to Himself the right to determine the end of life, because He alone knows the goal to which it is His will to lead it. . . . Even if a person's earthly life has become a torment for him, he must commit it intact into God's hand, from which it came."[299]

Congregational pastor Charles Luckey agreed with Bonhoeffer. A month before his death in 1974, he dictated this letter to his friends:

> What . . . does the Christian do when he stands over the abyss of his own death and the doctors have told him that disease is ravaging his brain and that his whole personality may be warped, twisted, changed? Then does the Christian have any right to self-destruction, especially when he knows that the changed personality may bring out some horrible beast in himself? Well, after 48 hours of self-searching and study, it comes to me that ultimately and finally the Christian has to always view life as a gift from God, and every precious drop of life was not earned but was a grace, lovingly bestowed upon him by his Creator, and it is not his to pick up and smash.

> And so I find the position of suicide untenable, not because I lack the courage to blow out my brains, but rather because of my deep abiding faith in the Creator who put the brains there in the first place. And now the result is that I lie here blind on my bed and trust in the sustaining, loving power of that great Creator who knew and loved me before I was fashioned in my mother's womb. But I do not think it is wrong to pray for an early release from this diseased, ravaged carcass.[300]

(3) An Evangelical Perspective on Suicide. Another perspective is that held by William Hendricks, who looks at the issue as a member of an evangelical church. Hendricks believes suicide is wrong, but it is not the unpardonable sin. In his view, the Roman Catholic argument that suicide rules out the possibility of repentance and therefore of forgiveness is invalid. Pointing out that many Christians have died without repenting of their sins, he holds that making an absolute judgment against suicide on this account is setting too much store by the last moment of life.[301]

Ray Anderson, another evangelical, suggests that the originating cause of suicide is the freedom of the human person to act in self-justification over and against God. Despair becomes the occasion for this act of self-justification to take place.

It should be noted that it was precisely because of the arrogance of self-justification that human beings became sinners and came under the power of death. This self-justification, which denies that our life is dependent upon God for its sustenance and survival, is produced by sin. According to the apostle Paul (cf. Rom. 5:12–21), it is present as the form of human life and has afflicted all since Adam.[302]

The incarnation of God in Jesus Christ, taking this form of death upon himself, turned the self-justification of the sinner into the obedience of the Son and, through death, restored life to the disobedient. The death of one who commits suicide is therefore *unnecessary* as a final desperate act of self-justification. This is the tragedy in all such cases of self-destruction.

For Anderson, there are no theological grounds to deny a Christian who commits suicide the effects of the death and resurrection of Jesus *for sinners.* And yet, we cannot encourage or condone suicide in principle. We cannot ignore suicide as a serious social and human problem. There *is* something terribly wrong when self-inflicted death is a better solution than life for so many people.[303]

The Bible teaches that human persons as created in the image and likeness of God have dignity and value in terms of relatedness to God and to each other. In an absolute sense, therefore, the claim to have a right over one's own life is a denial of this dignity and value as constituted by our being created in God's image. The theological case against suicide must be a case for the integrity of human life as coresponsibility. The one who commits suicide tears something from the fabric of human life itself when he departs. And this is not even to mention the trauma suicide brings to family and friends.[304]

3. The Issues of Mutilation and Cremation

As indicated in previous discussion, the concept of bodily resurrection does not simply affirm the resuscitation of a corpse, but a bringing of the total being into a new type of life. Resurrection is a new creation. This means that our chemical components are not required to be kept intact in order for us to have resurrection. The mutilation, amputation, and disintegration of our human chemicals will in no way affect the resurrection of ourselves. For he who holds us in life does not need these specific ashes and dust to reconstitute us anew for his time and space.

This understanding can be encouraging to those who have lost loved ones in disastrous ways and have concern about the future of those whose physical bodies were mangled or destroyed. It can also be reassuring to those who have concerns about the practice of cremation, which ecologically and economically may become the predominant form of burial. However, some may continue to prefer traditional burial as a purely formal way of symbolizing their affirmation of the resurrection of the body.[305]

4. A Concluding Word about the Importance of the Biblical View of "Last Things"

It is the conviction of evangelicals that no worldview can be comprehensive and adequate unless it deals with the direction of history and the goal of the universe. An adequate worldview must also deal with the matter of the ultimate destiny of humankind and the problem of death and the life beyond.[306]

Most secular worldviews lack a doctrine of last things. Many religions reveal but a casual or partial interest in both the end of individuals and of the entire human race. They usually deal only with either personal individual destiny or with the comprehensive goal of the cosmos, but not with both themes. The cyclical view of history espoused by the Greek thinkers taught no final historical goal. Plato saw no purpose in history as a whole; however, he stressed that man's soul is naturally immortal. In modern times Marx, on the other hand, denies personal immortality but taught a purpose in the whole span of history. In contrast, the Bible teaches that all history—both personal and communal—has a purpose and goal, that history is unrepeatable, and that it moves toward the final triumph of the good.[307]

The Bible teaching on last things differs from the secular perspective not only in its insistence on purpose, but also in its specific emphasis on bodily resurrection. It is the resurrection of the crucified Christ, affirms the New Testament, that inaugurates at the time of its occurrence the "last days" or final historical epoch. Embraced in God's final goal is the perfection of his initial creation and the comprehensive salvation of repentant mankind from the dread consequences of sin.[308]

Some would say that the biblical hope is escapist or morbid. A larger perspective, however, shows that it is positive. Facing the life beyond in the right way teaches us how to live. It teaches us to see life as a whole. The hope of the life beyond is a fulfillment of our experience and work in this life. In fact, our positive and creative acts in this life add something to the eternal kingdom of God. Even nature is to share in the renewed creation.

George Beasley-Murray points out that the biblical hope undergirds an intense and constructive present. It provides us with a sense of purpose and a personal dynamic. This expectant attitude, in turn, provides a solid sense of responsibility. Paul says in 1 Corinthians 15:58 that in light of our hope in Christ we are to be steadfast, unmovable, always abounding in the work of the Lord.[309]

As evangelical Christians, we cannot embrace the naturalist, Greek, Hindu and spiritualistic beliefs. We can, however, offer the world, from our own Christian resources, a dynamic and superior alternative.

We believe that only the Word of the living God has the resources to fill the vacuum in our national and personal lives. There is hope for us now and hereafter in Christ. It is the responsibility and privilege of each of us to appropriate and share this hope.

9

The Question of Religion and World Religions

I. How Would You Define Religion?

Religion is a much discussed subject in the United States and in the world—and a very elusive, intriguing, and difficult subject at that. Recently in a health club "bull session," I heard a loud-mouthed iconoclast describe religion as the sum of the scruples which impede the free exercise of human faculties. Another would-be philosopher joined in to render his opinion that religion is the device of priests and religious flunkies to keep themselves in bread, butter, and jewelry.

This is just the beginning! The definitions of religion, positive and negative, abound. In fact, one researcher has listed fifty different definitions of religion. These many definitions of religion have been proposed, criticized, and rejected or recast. Many scholars resignedly conclude that, although we all know what we mean by religion, it is impossible to give a satisfying definition.

Still, what we know can be expressed in the general description of religion as the human attitude toward a world beyond. This attitude finds its expression in a body of myth, rite, and individual and social behavior.[1]

The word *religion* can be used both in an objective sense and a subjective sense. When we say, for instance, that "Islam is a monotheistic religion," we are using the term *religion* objectively. The noun *Islam* signifies an objective reality, a specific body of beliefs followed by a group of people. Most objective religions have a creed, a code, a ceremony, and a community.

On the other hand, when we say, "Religion is characteristic of humankind everywhere," we are using the term *religion* in a subjective sense, as something which can be attributed to the human personality. In this subjective sense, religion is not a complex of doctrines, worship, organizations, laws, temples, sacrifices, and the like, but a fact of the human consciousness.[2]

II. What Is the Evidence for the Universality of Religion?

1. The Evidence of General Observation

Social scientists generally agree that all societies have had religion in one form or another. (At a time when it is difficult to find professional agreements in many areas, that bare statement of itself may be something of an accomplishment!) Missionaries and anthropologists also report that religion, in some form, is universal among humankind at the present day.[3]

For hundreds of years religion was of supreme importance. It dominated and colored all other interests. Even today, religion remains important. However, in modern times, the phenomenon of the so-called religionless or secular humanity has appeared. Undeniably, religion and religious observance have declined in many parts of the world.

Some see this decline as indicating that religion does not belong to the essence of humanity, that it is simply a characteristic of what will come to be seen as the childhood of the race. Yet there are many considerations that point in a different direction. Many times over the centuries, for example, when a religion seemed to have exhausted itself and to be on the verge of expiring, it has revived and launched out on a new and more vigorous chapter in its history.

We should also note that those who outwardly renounce more normative religions often find some kind of substitute for religion in their lives. Unfortunately, many of these are dangerous substitutes such as mass ideologies and perverted cults. Even if particular forms of religion grow old in the course of time and are no longer able to hold their place, the religious spirit itself endures and seeks new forms, because it has deep roots in our human nature.[4]

2. The Evidence of Phenomenology

In recent years, philosophy of religion has turned to the phenomenology or careful observation of the human person in seeking to establish the universality of religion.

(1) Schleiermacher and Humanity's Absolute Dependence. The phenomenological approach had its first great advocate in Friedrich Schleiermacher, the prominent eighteenth-century German theologian. He contended that all human beings have a sense of the infinite and a feeling of absolute dependence.[5]

For Schleiermacher, the irreducible religious core in humanity involves what may be called our elemental human self-awareness. When we discover that we are selves among others, we discern our relative dependence. Then, when we discover ourselves as fragments of a cosmic whole, we register an absolute dependence. This second discovery is crucial, for the feeling of absolute dependence is by definition unique. It is in this sense of absolute dependence that the secure and unique home of religion is to be found. Once we have recognized absolute dependence, said Schleiermacher, there is no necessity to resort to the rational arguments for God's existence.[6]

In his later years, Schleiermacher sought to avoid the impression of making religion an entirely subjective affair. He did this by affirming that the feeling of absolute dependence is at the same time "a coexistence of God in the self-consciousness." Unfortunately, in spite of Schleiermacher's own intentions, his appeal to feeling and inner experience does lead to the subjectivizing of religion. His new approach was purchased at the price of surrendering the claim to be making any objective assertions about a transhuman reality or God.[7]

(2) Otto and the Experience of the Holy. German scholar Rudolf Otto, writing in the early twentieth century, contended that the essence of religion is the human experience of the holy. Otto was influenced by the rise of a science which was new since Schleiermacher's time—anthropology. In particular, he was helped by the investigations of anthropology into primitive religion. He was particularly impressed by the work of R. R. Marett, who claimed that religion consisted of a feeling of awe.[8]

The most valuable part of Otto's work is his careful phenomenological or observational analysis of the experience of the holy. (He used the term *numinous*, which means supernatural or surpassing comprehension, to refer to the Holy One, or God.) Otto's analysis is summarized in the three-part Latin expression, *mysterium tremendum et fascinans*.

The first element of this term, *mysterium* (mystery), emphasizes the "otherness" of the holy—its different and distinct nature: "That which is mysterious is the 'wholly other.'"

The next element, *tremendum* (mighty or great), refers to the quality in the holy which evokes a response of awe. (This is not the same as fear.) Otto uses the expression "creature-feeling" for the self-awareness of the finite in the presence of the numinous being, or God.

The third element in Otto's analysis is *fascinans* (captivating, spellbinding). In Otto's words, "Besides that in the mystery which bewilders and confounds, he finds something which captivates and transports him." The *fascinans* side of God contains his love, mercy, pity, and comfort. In his later writing, Otto went on to claim that the human mind has a special faculty for responding to God.[9]

(3) Eliade and the Universality of Religious Myths and Rites. In more recent years, Mircea Eliade of the University of Chicago has sought to establish the universality of religion. Starting with the myths and rituals, the symbols and sacred objects of Hindu folk religion, he began to uncover the rich cultural subsoil of prehistoric religions. In a lifelong quest unparalleled in modern scholarship, Eliade went on to research unexplored areas of archaic religion. He also sought to demonstrate how ancient perceptions about humanity and the cosmos persist in modern beliefs.[10]

For Eliade, humanity is essentially *homo religiosus*—the being who craves the transcendent. This inherent craving is most evident in the elaborate myths and rites of initiation through which archaic people understood and organized their world. Ordinary objects such as a mountain, a stone, water, or a tree were assigned a sacramental character which revealed the sacred. This was done without erasing or downplaying their profane or secular identities.

For Eliade, the history of religion is the study of the sacred and its manifold manifestations. According to Martin Marty, it was primarily the influence of Eliade's distinctive approach to religion that made it possible for hundreds of publicly funded universities in the United States to add religious-studies programs without violating the separation of church and state.

In Eliade's view, the sacred is not simply a primitive stage in human consciousness, but a permanent "structural element" of the mind. Even in our own desacralized societies, he argues, the sacred is present, but camouflaged within the profane or secular. For example, Eliade finds elements of the archaic religious outlook in the prevalence of astrology, New Year observances, and the occult in popular culture. Unfortunately, according to Eliade, these traces of transcendence are culturally impotent. They do not furnish an overpowering presence of the sacred or give meaning and informal direction to the whole of life.

Despite the complaints of some theologians that he is subtly counseling a return to pre-Christian forms of religion, Eliade sees his lifework as a demonstration of human solidarity, with spirituality at the source. Future generations, he believes, will break out in new forms of religious expression. "Spirit is very strange," he says. "It has an obligation to create."[11]

(4) William James and Universal Themes in Religious Experience. It was in the United States that the field known as psychology of religion arose as a formal discipline. This discipline was pioneered in *The Varieties of Religious Experience* by the American philosopher and psychologist, William James (1842–1910). In this book, which is a classic in its field, James investigates the manifold forms of religious experience from an empirical and psychological standpoint. He states that psychology can go far toward explaining in natural terms many features of the religious life which have in the past been deemed supernatural. However, he also contends that the observable effects of religious experience in regenerating human nature and in influencing conduct provide empirical confirmation for the religious hypothesis that our lives are continuous with a larger spiritual world from which help comes to us.

III. What Are the Reductionistic (Naturalistic) Explanations and Criticisms of Religion?

As we have seen, the religious interpretation of life affirms a reality beyond the subjective religious experience. In other words, these experiences are described as the presence of God or a word from God or the grace of God or as a sign of God's judgment—all references to the objective reality of God.

In opposition to this view, in modern times there has come into being a whole group of human sciences which interpret subjective religious experiences in purely naturalistic terms.[12] It should be noted that the ever-present danger of such views is reductionism, the tendency to explain the higher orders of existence according to the lower ones. For example, if we see the influence of conditioning on our behavior, we might conclude that no behavior can be "free." But we need not make these conclusions, and in fact many scientists themselves refuse to do so.[13]

1. The Psychological View of Freud

One of the most widely known criticisms of religion is that of Sigmund Freud, the father of modern psychoanalysis. Freud's short 1927 work on religion indicates his attitude by its title: *The Future of An Illusion.*

Religion, Freud contends, is a human construct, a psychological projection of a lost father figure. We invent a father-god in order to feel more secure and at home in an alien, indifferent, even hostile universe. But according to Freud, this projection of a father-figure represents repression of our true feelings and a failing to come to grips with reality. It thus presents fertile ground for the growth of neurosis and psychosis. If humanity is to become more healthy psychologically, religion has to go.[14]

In other words, said Freud, the time has come for us to remove the repression that religion brings about and to replace it with the rational operation of the intellect. People ought not to go on being children, Freud insists. Rather, they need to be educated to reality.[15]

Two comments can be made here about Freud's claim that Christians project their desires onto God. First, it is true that Christians believe that God is the Creator and that there is therefore an analogy between God and humanity as created in his image. Therefore, it is not surprising that there are resemblances between the human person and the divine Father. In fact, Freud may have discovered one of the mechanisms that God uses for creating the idea of himself in the human mind. From the experience of a human father we gain some limited perception of a heavenly Father. However, the Bible reminds us that the real source of our idea of fatherhood is from God and not from our earthly father.

Second, it is understandable that people would invest their religious heroes with characteristics like themselves. But Christianity claims that what is most important about God is that he is *unlike* us. He is not only the loving Father and protecting Mother, but he is also a righteous Judge and holy Savior.[16]

2. The "Conditioning" View of Skinner

In the 1970s, behaviorist psychological views captured the popular imagination with the publication of B. F. Skinner's book *Beyond Freedom and Dignity.* Skinner's thesis was that everything in human behavior can be accounted for by environmental conditioning, that there is no "ego" unlinked to stimulus and response. In his view, the idea of some essential "human nature" or some enduring self blinds us to the real causes of behavior. (When we claim an action is "free," for instance, we simply do not see its real causes.) Therefore, said Skinner, we must abolish such conceptions and concentrate instead on controlling the environment to achieve positive conditioning. In his novel, *Walden Two,* he sketched the utopian community he believes could result from this kind of conditioning.[17]

From a Christian point of view, Skinner's views are essentially heretical. What we call sin is written off as merely habit deriving from a history of reinforcement. God is dismissed as an explanatory fiction. Heaven and hell are seen as the final positive and negative reinforcements, effective through their constant invocation in human behavior but having no objective reality. Although human beings are considered more than animals, like animals they are within the range of scientific analysis.[18]

In response to the views of Skinner and his followers, Christians do recognize that chemical, physiological, and environmental processes influence human behavior. But we do not agree that these things are the ultimate determinative factors in human personality. At stake here is the view of the person as a responsible agent responding to and creatively informing his or her environment. Human ability to choose is a basic component of the biblical worldview. It is graphically portrayed, for example, in the New Testament parable of the talents (Matt. 25:14–30).[19]

3. The "Social Forces" View of Durkheim

While naturalistic psychologists such as Freud and Skinner attribute religious faith to influences upon the individual, naturalistic sociologists tend to see religion as a product of social forces. The father of this perspective on religion was Émile Durkheim, who in 1915 published his classic study on *The Elementary Forms of the Religious Life*. It was Durkheim's conviction that the final reference in religion is not God (or gods) but society.[20]

Durkheim maintained that every culture develops its religion in keeping with its distinctive needs and concerns and in order to maintain and shape itself. Thus, both religious practices and religious beliefs are valuable and viable. Their value, however, lies not in the fact that they reflect some truth about God in relation to human life, but rather in the fact that they serve a useful sociological function.

A positive aspect of Durkheim's analysis of religion is that it reminds us that religious belief, whatever else it should be and do, should also make a contribution to the character and development of our society. There is a definite sense in which religious faith ought to serve a functional role in society.[21]

However, society's role in shaping religious faith may be freely admitted without reducing religion to a projection of society's structure. Durkheim fails to account for the universal reach of Christian convictions. Society may influence me to love my tribe or my race, but how can it impress upon me the view that God loves all people and that each person is obligated to love everyone he or she encounters? Neither can Durkheim account for Christianity's prophetic conscience: Can social structure explain Jeremiah or John the Baptist? In addition, Durkheim's view may describe a closed, static society, but how does it account for ethical innovation and change? Finally, an entirely naturalistic interpretation of Christianity such as Durkheim's has a difficult time explaining signs of supernatural direction.[22]

4. The "Opiate" View of Marx

In some ways the view of Karl Marx about religion is related to Durkheim's theory. Marx held that religion is part of a society's ideology; in his famous expression, it is the "opiate of the people." By this Marx meant that religion buttresses the economic status quo by "drugging" people into accepting the established order. The preacher is seen as a tool of the factory owner and the landlord, using the promises of religion to keep people contented with the bad condition in which they find themselves.

Marx further judged that as the population-at-large began to acquire the good things of the earth (through revolution), the need for religion would diminish. This would mean that the reality and practice of religion would eventually wither away.

Since, on Marxist assumptions, religion will die a natural death, Marx held that the state in principle may be tolerant of faith. In practice, however, Marxist governments have sometimes thought it necessary to attack religion because of its supposed alliance with capitalist or oppressive forces. In other situations, such as Poland or Latin America, overt Marxist opposition to religion has by necessity been largely given up.[23]

Whether the Marxist critique of Christianity is essential to Marxism as a method of sociological analysis has been the subject of much debate. In particular, some Christians in Latin America believe it is possible to separate Marxist social analysis from its philosophical and antireligious underpinnings. In some Latin American countries there has been a kind of alliance formed between Marxism and Christianity, with the goal of social change. But it is difficult to see how Marxist materialist and therefore atheistic assumptions can be so easily dismissed as secondary. Marx himself claimed that the criticism of religion is the premise for all other criticism of society.[24]

Religious scholars have reacted to Marx primarily in two ways. In the first place, they agree that religion has, in fact, often been used as a negative force in society. But a good thing can be badly used. And religion also has been a force for the enhancing of human life and the achievement of social justice.

In the second place, thoughtful scholars point out that Marx's theory of religion's inevitable decline does not seem to be validated by recent history. It has been noted that in the industrialized countries, as workers gain more security, their religious needs do not wither, but often increase. Relieved from the sheer struggle for survival and the meeting of basic needs, workers begin to seek out a meaning for the human enterprise in a more fundamental religious sense. This has been apparent in both the Soviet Union and in China. (There has also been a collapse of secular optimism in western Europe. Terms used are "Europessimism" and "the disappearance of hope." Young people speak of themselves as the "no-future generation." Such concerns have given rise to new eccentric faiths.)[25]

From a biblical perspective, a part of the Marxist fallacy lies in the myth of the "sinlessness" of the working class. This myth involves the illusion that if exploitation by the upper classes were brought to an end, then discord, crime, and evil would disappear, and the golden age would dawn. This of course is in direct contradiction to the Christian doctrine of sin and evil.

A second weakness of the Marxist fallacy from the biblical perspective is its assumption that every problem has an economic solution. Christianity holds that not only does society need a change in its economic structure, the individual also needs a radical spiritual transformation. And this is something the gospel of Marx cannot effect.[26]

5. Response of the Biblical View to the Reductionist Views

In broad perspective, we now see that the explanations of religion by Freud, Skinner, Durkheim, and Marx are inadequate because of the limited or reductionistic worldviews upon which they are built. It is the contention of a number of scholars of religion that reports of religious experience such as those described by William James in *The Varieties of Religious Experience* describe a relationship to a transcendent power or God. This explanation, it is believed, best explains the history of religion.

This explanation is also in agreement with an evangelical Christian perspective. Evangelicals see the universality of religion as a response to God's revelation of himself in nature, conscience, and history. Because of sin and rebellion, this response is perverted or confused except as it is corrected by Jesus Christ and the biblical revelation.

The biblical view that a religious experience flows from a relationship to a transhuman God does not mean that other explanations do not have some validity. Many evangelicals would agree that a human person can be seen from various points of view as a physico-chemical system or as a biological organism and may certainly be influenced by family dynamics or the conditioning of the environment. However, evangelicals also hold that the human person is a unique being with a sense and taste for the infinite—the one who has relations with a transcendent God. In the evangelical view, humanity sums up in itself many levels of being. However, religion has a basic claim to be considered as an essential element in any fully developed humanity. And religious answers certainly have the right to be considered as explanations for religious experience![27]

For example, there have been many attempts to explain Martin Luther's salvation experience in connection with his discovery of the Pauline teaching on justification by faith in the early decades of the sixteenth century. This was a crucial event not only in the life of Luther, but also in the history of Western Christendom. The Marxists emphasize the socioeconomic influences in the entire process of Luther's change. The Freudian approach is utilized in Erik Erikson's well-known study, *Young Man Luther* (1958), which suggests (among other things) that Luther's awakening was the resolution of an "Oedipal struggle" in Luther's family of origin. Social and political historians have offered still other explanations for Luther's experience.

There may be elements of truth in all of these explanations. However, as Daniel L. Pals, professor of religion at the University of Miami, argues, the alternative explanations should be subordinate to the "religious" explanation of Luther's experience because the experience itself was of a religious nature. Pals contends that in religion, as in other fields of inquiry, the interpreter has the right to insist that phenomena are best explained by appealing to factors which lie within their zone, as opposed to those which lie outside it. In Luther's case, for instance, his religious experience is best explained by appealing to religious factors. These include his conception of a righteous God, his certainty that in

God's justice sin must be punished, his dissatisfaction with the late-medieval system of penance, and his faith in the Christian gospel of grace.[28]

Using the same logic, the life of John Wesley is best grasped as expressing an ideal of holiness rather than as a repression of a sexual instinct. The motives of an Ignatius Loyola should be understood in the light of his faith rather than as the shadow of his frustrations. Stated generally, the best approach should consist of the interpreter's right to press for religious explanations when presented with religious data.[29]

To put it in another way, the phenomenology or careful observation of religion can be seen as part of the wider pattern of a phenomenology of human experience in general. This wider pattern calls for the recognition that the human being has spiritual as well as natural properties and therefore must be understood in theological as well as in psychological or sociological terms. In Ninian Smart's words, "we can be sure that no total picture of the nature of man can be complete unless it contains a theory of religion."[30]

All of this means that, according to the biblical worldview, the universality of religion is best accounted for on the presupposition that human beings are created in the image of God and are in constant relationship (positive or negative) with a transhuman power. Evangelicals further hold that the social sciences need this larger framework to undergird their theories and activities.[31]

IV. What Is the Significance of the New Situation in Regard to a Unitary World Culture and a Revival of World Religions?

1. The Religious and Cultural Situation in Earlier Times

Since ancient times, the migrations of peoples and the adventurous voyages of traders have led to the dissemination of religious and other ideas far beyond their native regions. But in general, for most of human history, it can be said that humankind was divided into fairly homogeneous cultural and religious blocs, each tending to concentrate in a particular region of the earth's surface.[32]

It should be noted, however, that two of the greatest religions of the world have in fact almost disappeared from their original cultural settings and, instead, have established themselves in what were once for them alien cultures. Buddhism virtually died out in India, where it originated, but took roots and flourished in China, Japan, and Southeast Asia. And Christianity began as a Jewish sect, but expanded largely among the Gentile peoples.

The spread of Christianity and Buddhism into remote cultural regions was due to missionary effort. But there are other instances of religions and philosophical systems influencing one another apart from any missionary activity. The European Renaissance, for example, was accompanied by a great renewal of interest in Greco-Roman philosophy, especially Stoicism, and this revival in turn greatly affected the expression given to Christianity. Then in the eighteenth century, Enlightenment philosophy, which had assumed the form of a rationalistic deism, found its pure prototype in the Chinese religion of Confucius, which emphasized practical wisdom.

These contacts and reciprocal influences remind us that there never was a complete isolation of religions and philosophies. Nevertheless, the general structure of separate religious and cultural blocs remained, until recent years.[33]

2. The New Situation in the World

Today, for the first time in history, we have a unitary world history. The primary cause of this unity is the impact of modern technology. From the West, technology has reached out into all the world. No tribe of human beings, however remote in the forests of Brazil or the uplands of New Guinea, has escaped from being drawn into the common stream of this new unitary history. There are radios and television sets almost everywhere. Peoples, languages, dress, eating habits, and religions are being intermingled all over the world. Planet Earth has become, according to media analyst Marshall McLuhan, a global village.[34]

Global exchanges, mobility, migration, international politics, and problems of world ecology and world economy demand that we interact with one another and that we repudiate assumptions of self-sufficiency. It is no longer possible to be physically or culturally self-enclosed.[35]

3. The Moral and Religious Implications of the New Technology

Theoretically, technology itself should be neutral, with either good or bad applications. In several ways, however, the rapid rise of technology has been harmful in moral and spiritual terms.

One unfortunate consequence of the rise of technology is that Western technology seems to be inseparable from an acquisitive mentality, even a spirit of greed. Since the planet's resources for satisfying the ever-rising level of demand are limited, acquisitiveness tends to lead to competition and then to aggression. No one yet has found a way to break the technology-acquisitiveness-aggression cycle perpetuated by the spread of Western culture.

In addition, certain forms of technology have predisposed the contemporary Western mind against religion by its assumption that all problems can be solved by the magic of techniques. (An example is the dominance of computers in all areas of life.) There are those who believe that techniques can even solve the spiritual problems of man.

This emphasis on the negative spiritual and moral effects of technology does not mean that we should do away with it. Indeed, we can no longer live without technology. The very physical survival of vast numbers of people now living on the planet depends upon the smooth functioning of the gigantic technological apparatus that we have brought into existence. (For example, population increase demands scientific agricultural methods and modern methods of transportation.)

We also should note that many problems, including those that bear on man's mental and spiritual life, have to some extent been helped by technical solutions. Modern communications have assisted in spreading the gospel around the world and teaching Christian truths to millions. Modern medical techniques that save lives have also opened doors for missionaries bringing Good News.[36]

We must realize, however, that we need more than technology to run the world and lead our lives. The determination of goals, the decision about what is most real and most valuable, and the direction of technology itself are not problems to be solved by techniques. They require moral and spiritual standards.

Similarly, although a reasonable standard of living can protect people from the dehumanizing ravages of deprivation, squalor, malnutrition, and disease, a reasonable standard of living is not enough to insure quality of life. Quality of life cannot be measured in terms of production and consumption. It has to do not with material productivity, but with spiritual renewal and development.

It is the Christian contention that only an authentic biblical religion has the spiritual dynamic needed for a radical change in human nature and human attitudes. Unfortunately, technology and secularism are already entrenched in the first phase of the emerging unitary world history. A result is that it has become a matter of great difficulty in certain areas to open up the dimension of the moral and spiritual.[37]

4. New Vitality of the Ancient World Religions and Communism as a Pseudo-Religion

In general, the twentieth century has seen the reversal of a four-century trend of Western colonial imperialism. Historians tell us that the decline of Asia during those centuries was caused initially by an internal cultural and intellectual erosion. This vacuum encouraged commercial, political, and cultural encroachment by the West. In turn, the Asian peoples' historic confidence in the autonomy and superiority of their cultures was shattered by the technologically superior Western civilization.

The end of World War II, however, marked the end of Western colonial imperialism. One result of this was a resurgence of traditional religions. Ancient faiths such as Hinduism and Islam took on new forms and a new vibrancy. Along with a general national revitalization after World War II, there was a movement toward a heightening of religious group consciousness. After the war, many religious leaders cooperated with political leaders in rebuilding a spiritual fabric for a new Asia and Middle East. They came to a firm conviction that their cultural and religious traditions had resources that were no less remarkable than those of the West.

During the immediate postwar era, leaders of Eastern and Middle Eastern religions expressed a new-found optimism that their faiths were the way of the future. Pakistan, for example, was created in order to enable Muslims "to order their lives in the individual and collective spheres in accord with the teachings and requirements of Islam."

In some areas, however, the pseudo-religion of communism has taken root instead of revitalized traditional religions. Communism tends to find acceptance where the impact of the technological West has undermined old religions and family and village loyalties and has robbed life of its spiritual comfort and purpose. People then seek a new code, a new certainty, a new religious substitute, and some of them turn to communism. In fact, the common weakness of Eastern religions thus far seems to be their failure to articulate to today's Asians the vision of their religion as helping in the area of economics and politics, and the encroachment of communism seems to be a likely result.[38]

5. Growth of the Eastern Religions in the West

Adding complexity to the encounter of religions in our time is the rapid growth of Eastern and Middle Eastern religions in the West over the past three decades. For the most part, this growth falls into three distinct types: ethnic-cultural, intellectual, and cultic.

The ethnic-cultural type of growth is easy to see. For economic and other reasons, large groups of Asian and Middle-Eastern residents are moving to Europe and the United States. It is hardly surprising that many of them practice and share their ancestral religious traditions. What is more striking today, however, is the phenomenal rise in the second and third groups.

Intellectual interest in Eastern religions is illustrated by a recent survey that lists 1,653 professors who teach Asian religious traditions in colleges and universities in Canada and the United States. In addition, a wide variety of cultic groups related to Hinduism, Buddhism, Islam, and primitive religions are now present in the West. These include not only the established groups such as Vedanta and Zen, but a whole series of newer groups such as the International Society for Krishna Consciousness (Hare Krishna), Transcendental Meditation, Nichiren Shoshu, and the Unification Church (known as the Moonies). I describe many of these new groups in my book, *Christ and the New Consciousness.*[39]

Unfortunately, the interest in Eastern religions and cultic groups may well be a symptom of a spiritual hunger on the part of many Americans—a reaction against the increasing vulgarity, skepticism, and hedonism of Western society. This possibility is pointed out by Eastern religious leaders themselves. Islam leaders point out that Christianity has somehow failed to discipline and retain its allegiance even in its own civilization. And Buddhist leaders see our Western difficulties as merely demonstrating the mistaken reading of human existence which Christianity teaches.[40]

6. Effects of the Proliferation of Religious Options

In a way unprecedented in human history, the new situation of global interchange and cross-reference has forced the question of religious options on many people. Traditionally, religious groups have had discussions primarily within the confines of their own faith. The new situation, however, is forcing people to face questions raised by those outside their faith. The multiplicity of faiths suggests a certain optionality, and people are realizing that in many cases the accident of birth largely determines a person's religious convictions. The growing sense that faith has many faces has resulted in insecurity of soul as well as bewilderment of thought.

Of course, for vast numbers there is no real optionality. Relatively few can take private initiative in the matter of changing belief. Illiteracy, cultural determinism, and poverty reduce the opportunity for change. In addition, optionality may have no conscious consequence for many who are secure in their religious identities and pay little attention to other possibilities.

However, an increasing number of people throughout the world are becoming conscious of new religious options. In particular, secular education has served to make many aware of the world outside their own cultural and religious tradition. In some cases such education has brought liberation from the tyranny of oppressive beliefs or apathetic traditions. For others, secular education induces fear and bewilderment as it erodes spiritual loyalties.

Of course, some persons who discover there are other claims to salvation become confirmed in their faith and eager to share it. But others resort to doubt and feel themselves threatened by the possibility of religious alternatives.[41] And those who do feel threatened may react in various ways.

Some people whose doubts are raised by religious alternatives gradually drift into irreligion and secularity. Some leave their original faith and take refuge in another religion. Others, determined to resist dislodgment when faced by factors that threaten to question their faith or render it marginal or obsolete, resort like Saul of Tarsus to vehement assertion. They adopt a siege mentality. Out of fear for the loss of religious identity, they bolster authority, even to the point of rigidity and dogmatism and even persecution of those with different beliefs.[42] This is the origin of many kinds of militant "fundamentalism."

7. Representative Approaches to Religion in Light of the New Religious Pluralism

As we have noted, religious pluralism is a fact of modern life. No religious group can remain private or domestic to itself, as many religions have for centuries. Two general responses to religious pluralism—apart from the biblical response—are common:

(1) The Neutral Approach. The neutral approach is sometimes called the historical and classification method. The idea behind it is that one simply describes religions and gives some account of their character and value without being committed to any one religion. This avoidance of commitment or connection as a matter of basic principle results from two perspectives. Some call for a neutral approach because they advocate an absence of belief in any one religion. Others see a neutral approach as the "scientific" method which safeguards academic integrity, objectivity, and freedom from prejudice.

It is true that "neutrality" has been helpful in accumulating religious data. It is important to develop an objective understanding of the content of other religions and how they have evolved. It is also helpful to comprehend each religion so far as is possible from the standpoint of its own aims and premises.

However, when we turn to the question of the truth and value of various religions, the shortcomings of the "scientific" neutrality principle become apparent. The reason for this is contained within the principle itself. It excludes the idea of any standard or criterion—and without that one can say nothing about the truth and value of a religion at all.[43]

(2) The Approach of Syncretism. One of the most widely held approaches to world religions is known as syncretism or inclusivism. According to this view, all religions (at least the major ones) are essentially equal in value. Each religion represents a different way of reaching God.[44]

This view is based on the presupposition that all organized religions are only reflections of a universal original religion and show, therefore, only limited differences. Thus, the syncretic approach is that there is no unique revelation of God in history. Rather, there are many different ways to reach the divine reality. Moreover, all these formulations of religious truth or experience are by their very nature inadequate expressions of that truth. This means that it is necessary to harmonize as much as possible all religious ideas and experiences so as to create one universal religion for humankind.

Actually, syncretism is not a new phenomenon. It was found in ancient Israel, where it was vehemently denounced by the prophets. It was characteristic of Hellenism and Gnosticism and was widespread in the Roman Empire. In fact, the Roman Emperor Alexander Severus had in his private chapel not only the statues of the deified emperors, but also those of the miracle worker Appolonius of Tyana, of Christ, of Abraham, and of Orpheus.[45]

In our time, in the West, syncretism has had two notable exponents: William Ernest Hocking and Arnold Toynbee. Hocking, who for many years was the Alford Professor of Philosophy at Harvard, served as the chairman for the Laymen's Inquiry concerning modern missions in 1931. The report was formulated into a volume, *Re-Thinking Missions,* in 1932. A later work by Hocking, *Living Religions and A World Faith,* was published in 1939. His approach to world religion, which I call the "add on and help" approach, can be summarized from these two works.

In Hocking's view, Christianity is merely one of the living religions of the world which seeks to help man with his quest of the eternal. Other religions also help in finding the righteous way of life and the transformation of human society through an evolutionary process.[46] Therefore, it is not the duty of the Christian missionary to attack the non-Christian systems of religion, but rather to present in positive form his convictions and let them speak for themselves. Christians must regard themselves as co-workers with the forces within each such religious system that are making for righteousness.[47]

According to Hocking, Christians should not seek to win converts from any other religion in the world. We should instead see all other religions as allies against secularism and irreligion. We should add our insights to theirs and help them whenever we go into various countries to fight secularism and irreligion.[48]

The other major modern exponent of syncretism was Arnold Toynbee, one of the most distinguished historians of Western civilization. He holds what I call the "purge and join" approach to world religions.

According to Toynbee, the religious world can be divided into two basic circles whose centers are at Benares in the Ganges Valley (Buddhism, Hinduism) and at Jerusalem (Christianity, Judaism, Islam).[49]

In Toynbee's view, Christianity should purge itself of any idea that it is the only exclusive religion. The basic human problem is selfishness or egocentricity, and the two religions which best address this problem are Christianity and Buddhism. This means that Christians should purge themselves of the idea that they have the exclusive truth and should join Buddhists in a great, joint religion which would seek to help deal with the problem of humanity's selfishness.[50]

Syncretism is a widespread phenomenon which has even been advocated by literary figures. One of its comparatively recent apostles was D. H. Lawrence. A certain syncretic spirit can be noted in his best-known novel, *Lady Chatterley's Lover*, which seeks to resuscitate the spirit of the ancient fertility cults. But the apex of Lawrence's syncretism is to be found in a lesser-known work, *The Man Who Died*, in which he goes so far as to portray the risen Christ as discovering true life when he embraces the priestess of the temple of Isis. Christ says, "This is the great atonement, the being in touch. The gray sea and the rain, the wet narcissus and the woman I wait for, the invisible Isis and the unseen sun are all in touch and at one."[51]

Orthodox Christianity has long held that syncretism and the biblical worldview are mutually exclusive. According to W. A. Visser 't Hooft, a prominent leader in ecumenical programs, syncretism is essentially a revolt against the uniqueness of God's revelation in history. True universality, it claims, can only be gained if the pretension that God has actually made himself definitely known in a particular person and event at a particular time is given up.

Syncretism conceives of religion as a system of insights and concepts rather than as a dialogical and saving relation between a personal God and his creature. Accordingly, in the syncretic view, religions seek to realize salvation rather than to receive it. However, by this teaching syncretism contradicts its own claim to universality, for it in fact excludes those religions—including Christianity—for which the revelation of a personal God is the central category.[52]

8. Representative Approaches to Christianity As a World Religion

In the present "global village," the task of presenting Christianity as a world religion has become both important and controversial. Christian scholars have developed at least three basic approaches to this problem:

(1) The "Highest Rung on the Ladder" or "Fulfillment" Approach. According to the "fulfillment" approach, the non-Christian religions are good as far as they go. However, they are incomplete and cannot fully satisfy human needs. Christianity, it is said, provides something extra which is needed to make them complete. Non-Christian religions are regarded as the stones in an arch, which is incomplete until the keystone of Christianity is put in place at the top of the arch. People who hold this view are impressed by the elements of truth that can

be found in most, if not all, other religions, and by the devotion and virtue of some of their adherents.[53]

Some who take this view would explain the elements of truth in other religions in terms of an original revelation which has never been wholly lost or forgotten. Others would discern in these religions the work of Christ himself as the eternal Logos and the "true light that enlightens every man" (John 1:9). It is he, they would say, who bears witness to and makes manifest the eternal truth which is written on the human heart.[54]

This view was held by Justin Martyr and the Christian philosophers of Alexandria in the second and third centuries. A modern exponent is Elton Trueblood, the well-known Quaker philosopher and theologian. Trueblood agrees with Paul Tillich's idea that world religions are a sort of universal preparatory revelation of Christ. In this view, there is a latent Christ living in everyone. Lay witnesses, therefore, should go to the peoples of the world and attempt to make manifest the latent Christ in adherents of all world religions.[55]

Others who hold this view in an even more extreme form include W. Cantwell Smith of Harvard and Raymond Panikkar of the University of California at Santa Barbara. After studying various religions and after fellowship with some of their adherents, Smith says that we have to recognize that these religious traditions are "channels through which God Himself comes into touch with these His children."[56] (I well remember a dialogue with Professor Smith which followed an evangelical missionary address I delivered in the Harvard Memorial Church. Professor Smith challenged my strong evangelical emphasis on Christ as the only way to a saving relationship with God.)

Panikkar, in accordance with Smith, affirms that the "good and bona fide Hindu is saved by Christ and not by Hinduism, but it is through the sacraments of Hinduism, through the message of morality and the good life, through the mysterion that comes down to him through Hinduism, that Christ saves the Hindu normally."[57]

Even more radical is the view of John Hick, a colleague of Panikkar's at the University of California at Santa Barbara. Hick suggests that Christians move from a Jesus-centered theology that shuts people out to a God-centered theology that welcomes them all in. By such a move, Hick hopes to remove the major hindrances to dialogue and cooperation among the religions and thus contribute to a more unified and peaceful world.

Hick is well aware that biblical christology stands directly in the path of such a proposal. Therefore, he has devoted considerable energy to reinterpreting the Incarnation in mythic terms so that it can remain as a Christian symbol without being a universal truth-claim. His interpretation is that in Jesus we see the love of God in action, but that we are not obliged to believe in the preexistence of the Son or the divine-human union in the more orthodox sense. The language of the Bible is simply the manner in which the first Christians liked to express themselves, but belongs more to the medium than to the essence of the message. One might think of it as a "language of love" defining a meaningful personal relationship, rather than as a truth-claim others have to reject.[58]

(2) The "Saving Balance" Approach. The "saving balance" approach is advocated by prominent Cambridge University scholar Herbert Farmer in his book, *Revelation and Religion*. Farmer affirms that to be a saving religion, a religion must present a delicate balance between God's transcendence (his holiness or otherness) and God's immanence in coming to man in grace and help. Farmer claims that most of the world's religions are inadequate in one or more of these areas. For example, he says, Islam teaches God's transcendence, but it does not have an adequate sense of God's grace. On the other hand, the bhakti discipline of Hinduism (which will be explained later in this chapter) has a tremendous sense of grace, succor, and help, but it does not have a sense of a unitary God who is a creator and above us.

Farmer believes that only Christianity has the delicate saving balance between transcendence and immanence. This is especially seen in the doctrine of the Trinity, which presents the complementary aspects of God as Father, Son, and Holy Spirit. Farmer points out that even Christianity as it has developed historically has had distortions and heresies. However, built into its very heart is the renewal work which is fostered by the indwelling Holy Spirit. Thus there is a sort of self-corrective process built into the Christian faith.[59]

(3) The "Yes and No" Approach. This view is presented by Hendrik Kraemer in his important book, *Religion and the Christian Faith*. He states that outside the realm of God's self-disclosure in the Law, the prophets, Jesus Christ, and the apostles, evidence indicates both a positive and a negative to God's manifestation of his everlasting power and divinity in nature and conscience (cf. Rom. 1:19–23).

According to the Bible, says Kraemer, the religious world outside God's special revelation is not exclusively a world of apostasy and rebellion. It is the world where man exhibits deep longings and gropings toward God.

Paul gives helpful elaborations of this perspective in the book of Acts. In Acts 14:8–18, for example, Paul states that the non-Christian religious way of life is in error, but that God goes on revealing himself to the peoples of this way whether they acknowledge it or not. Thus, they are both God-forsaken and also not God-forsaken. In Acts 17:16–34, Paul again affirms that all peoples have gone astray in their religion and imaginings. And yet, in the midst of this ignorance and its concrete embodiment in religious practices and ideas, they are dimly aware of God.

Romans 1:18–32 is a key passage in the biblical portrayal. In this passage, Paul writes that God has revealed and continues to reveal himself perennially. People can know him, but in fact, as is witnessed by their religions, they do not know him.

Looked at from the divine side, this religious situation is seen as both an expression of God's love and God's saving wrath (cf. Rom. 1:18–20). Looked at from the human side, religious expression is both humanity's rebellion against and attempt to escape from God and also humanity's search for righteousness and groping for truth. Another factor in this divine-human drama is the activity of Satan and his special ability to pervert the best into the worst.

According to the biblical insights, then, says Kraemer, all religious and cultural expressions apart from God's special revelation are responses to God that are both more or less positive and more or less negative. The good and the bad lie side by side, confused and interlocked. The only way out of this confused situation is for Almighty God to act in some unique way. He must take an action which will involve both judgment and fulfillment in regard to the self-contradictory aspirations and intuitions expressed in all philosophical, religious, and cultural striving. This situation calls for a Savior God. And, of course, states Kraemer, that is the God of Bible.[60]

V. What Are the Biblical Guidelines for Evaluating Religious Life?

The concern of this section is to evaluate the great human fact, religion, in the light of the biblical revelation, particularly in the light of Jesus Christ, whom biblical faith affirms as the Way, the Truth, and the Life. It is the conviction of evangelical Christians that this distinctive biblical approach provides greater depth and adequacy of interpretation to the riddle of human religious consciousness than any other approach.[61]

1. The Old Testament Guidelines

(1) A Uniquely Event-Centered Faith. The assumption of many Old Testament scholars during the first part of the twentieth century was that the most significant thing about Israel's faith was its evolutionary development from very primitive beginnings to the "ethical monotheism" of the prophets. But our present knowledge suggests that the clue to Israel's achievement is not to be found in such a development. It must rather be affirmed that the faith of Israel, even in the earliest days of the nation's history in Palestine, was radically different from its environment. It can only be interpreted as a new creation, a mutation. And its uniqueness lies in the fact that the religious life of Israel was founded on historical events and not on the pagan idea of harmony with the divine forces of nature.[62]

When the historical period of Israel began about 2000 B.C., Egypt, Mesopotamia, and presumably Palestine-Syria engaged in a highly developed and complex form of polytheism (the worship of many gods). In general, these polytheistic peoples saw the problem of their lives against the powers of nature, which they could not control, but on which they were utterly dependent. They were almost overwhelmed by the awesome power of a great thunderstorm, the majestic expanse and depth of the heavens, the mysterious brilliance of the moon and the stars, the wonderful blessing of the sun's warmth, the miraculous fertility of the earth, and the terrible reality of death.[63]

These polytheists did not distinguish between reality and the force in or behind it. In the storm they met the storm god. To them, nature was alive, and its powers were distinguished as personal because human beings had directly experienced them. There was no such thing as the inanimate. A human being lived in the realm of a throbbing, personal nature—the kingdom of the holy gods—and was caught in the interplay of gigantic forces into which he must integrate his or her life. The gods were known to an individual because he or she experienced them, not as objects, but as personalities so much greater in power that of necessity they must be worshiped and served.

In Mesopotamia, for example, the number of gods identified was in the thousands. The gods were believed to have organized the universe into a cosmic state in which each power had a specific role to play. Executive force was wielded originally by the storm god, Enlil, who had been selected as king of the gods. Decisions were made by the cosmic assembly, and it was the duty of the king to carry them out. In Canaan there existed a similar arrangement. The authoritarian head of the pantheon was El, but the chief executive, the king, was the personified storm, Hadad, the Baal or Lord of the gods and men. Each god had his goddess, and their children were likewise members of the cosmic order.

Law and order was the function of one or more gods. Sin was not considered a violation of the gracious will of God, as in the Bible, but anything that destroyed the harmony of affairs. So polytheism encouraged the status quo. There was never any positive emphasis on dynamic change.[64]

For Israel, on the other hand, nature was subordinate to Yahweh and used by him to further his redemptive work. Life, for the Hebrews, was seen as related to the will and purpose of Yahweh, who had chosen or elected this one people as his redemptive instrument. This election of the Hebrew people was not based upon merit, but upon Yahweh's mysterious grace. The reality of election was confirmed by the great saving acts of this God in history, particularly as expressed in the redemption from Egyptian bondage and in the gift of an inheritance.

Whereas biblical scholars once tried to identify the God of the early Hebrews with a mountain god, a fertility god, and a war god, from which the "ethical monotheism" of the prophets gradually evolved, it is now recognized that such identifications are figments of scholarly presuppositions and imagination. It is impossible on any empirical grounds to understand how the God of Israel could have evolved out of polytheism. He is unique and utterly different.[65]

It is true that the revelation to Moses on Mount Sinai traditionally was of such a character that Yahweh's appearances were frequently described in the categories of the storm (Exod. 19; Judg. 5; Hab. 3; etc.), together with many expressions which once were used of Baal in Canaan (e.g., Deut. 33:26; Ps. 68:4, 33). It is also true that Yahweh was seen as the power behind nature's fertility and as the dispenser of her good things, even as was Baal (e.g., Gen. 49:25; Deut. 33:13–17; Ps. 29:9). Yet such language was used only to exalt God's cosmic power; it was not the basic language of the biblical faith. In other words, the basic language of the Bible and of the Christian religion is a language drawn from the categories of history, personality, and community, rather than nature.[66]

(2) Emphasis on Radical Monotheism and the Jealousy or Exclusiveness of God. The polytheistic religions that surrounded the Hebrews were tolerant in their

very nature, as were the philosophies of mysticism which later developed out of it. Canaanite travelers and sojourners who traveled into Egypt, for example, found it comparatively easy to identify the chief gods of their homeland with new ones in the new land.[67]

In contrast, one of the most important aspects of the Hebrew religion was the jealousy or exclusiveness of its God. To him alone belonged all authority and power. No other deity was associated with him in his great acts (cf. Deut. 32:12). No other deity was to be compared to him; no other being was on his level. Nothing in the universe was worthy to be worshiped except him and him alone.

The Hebrew God would not put up with religious syncretism, but insisted on his people's exclusive and undivided loyalty to him. As time passed these assertions were made more explicit. The gods of the nations were ridiculed as "no gods." Isaiah forthrightly exclaimed that before Yahweh there was no god and that neither would there be any after him (Isa. 43:10–13).

When seen in the light of the entire Middle Eastern culture of the day, such claims for the exclusive prerogative of one deity are unique and astonishing. In all the vast sea of a tolerant polytheism, this jealousy or exclusiveness of Yahweh was a new and startling conception. In fact, many of the common people of Israel repeatedly sought to compromise this view, and numerous kings sought to qualify it.[68]

2. The New Testament Guidelines

(1) Rejection of Polytheism. The New Testament continued the Old Testament tradition of militant monotheism and specifically rejected the polytheism of the prevalent culture of its day. We moderns tend to speak with reverence of "the glory that was Greece and the grandeur that was Rome,"[69] but the truth is that, spiritually speaking, the Gentile world of the New Testament was spiritually confused and impotent. Her public life was permeated with polytheism, and her tolerant love of beauty sadly needed the backbone of a moral integrity derived from one great life-controlling faith. Athens, Rome, and the other cities had their gods. The guilds had theirs. The governments had theirs, and in many cases even claimed that their rulers were divine. In government, religion, business, amusement, labor, and social clubs, the pagan world was built on the pattern of a god for every interest and attitude.

The attitude of apostolic Christianity toward the polytheistic world was one of relentless opposition. Against the "gods many and lords many" of that outside world (cf. Gal. 4:8), Paul and his fellow-Christians set the "one God, the Father, and one Lord," (cf. Rom. 1:23). They were to serve the living and true God (1 Thess. 1:9).[70]

The most lenient New Testament treatment of polytheism and idolatry is that found in Acts 17:16–34 (cf. 14:15–16). Yet here, as always, a clean break with the polytheistic past is demanded. In addressing the crowd gathered in the Areopagus in Athens, the apostle Paul laid bare the idolatry and ignorance that persists in the human race, in spite of God's perennial nearness and the fact that human beings are inescapably related to him. Paul granted that in the midst of their ignorance and its concrete embodiment in religious practices and ideas, the Athenians were dimly aware of God. Yet he also said that without God's energetic initiative to break down this prevailing ignorance, humanity would remain in its self-willed and self-wrought imprisonment. Human "ignorance" is a perverted reaction to God's workings in and around him in history and nature.[71]

In Romans 1:18–32, Paul reiterates the fact that God has never been inactive in regard to humanity; he has never concealed himself. He has revealed and manifested himself to men, and his eternal power and divinity are plain and knowable. But nevertheless, as is witnessed by their religions, people do not know him. For the most part, the human response to God's revelation has been not faith but its opposite.

The consequence of this distorted attitude is humankind's entanglement in its own foolishness. People remain in darkness because of their uncomprehending hearts. They pervert everything, particularly in regard to worship and the objects of worship. Human beings who were created in the image and likeness of God persist in inventing gods in their own likeness and the likeness of animals. This is a mysterious reversal. And yet, even in the face of this demonic perversion, the ineffaceable relatedness of humans to God still shines through. Even in this abyss, God asserts his concern with humankind.[72]

(2) Stress on the Fallen Condition of Humankind. The New Testament teaches that the human condition is fallen, and that we cannot know God in a saving way in our own power. John 1:1–4 has been used to indicate that the cosmic Christ or Word is similar to the Stoic doctrine of the divine spark in the human soul, but there is a crucial difference between John's concept and the Stoic one. John indicates that natural humans cannot know the Logos or Word (his sole light and life) in their own power and thus they live in darkness.

John's prologue (John 1:1–18) states in an uncompromising, unmistakable way that the human condition is such that we are unable to know God as he really is—or ourselves as we really are—by our own powers. This knowledge can only happen through divine self-disclosure, faith, and the work of the Holy Spirit. The prologue, in essence, agrees with Paul that the Cross is a stumbling block to Jews, sheer folly to Gentiles, but the power and wisdom of God to those who believe (1 Cor. 1:18–25).[73]

(3) Stress on the Human Need for Transforming Power. The New Testament further teaches that the basic human problem is not ignorance, but rebellion and sin, and that humankind is in need of a transforming power. This directly contradicts the incipient Gnosticism of the New Testament period, which contained the idea that a revealed knowledge could save and that such knowledge was available to those who were "spiritual."

In the New Testament view, sinful humanity needs more than merely knowing the right answers and techniques. Rather, humans need a radical change of nature and attitudes, so that they are free from the grip of evil and are willingly led by the Spirit of God, whose power and guidance will keep them safe.[74]

(4) New Testament Opposition to an Emphasis on Mystical Absorption in God. The New Testament is also opposed to an emphasis on mystical absorption in God. The goal of some Gentiles of the New Testament program was to lose one's own consciousness and self, at least for a time, in the divine or God. Such a goal is totally different from both the Christian view of heaven and the Christian experience of worship. The human center of consciousness continues active and distinct in Christian worship and in the final, divinely established order. Personality is not lost or minimized, but rather preserved and enriched and given everlasting security. The New Testament offers no foothold for the idea of mystical absorption into God.

It is true that Paul once said that "Christ lives in me" (Gal. 2:20). But he went on to say in the same verse that he himself lived in the flesh at the same time that Christ lived in him. This indicates that Christ's living in him did not mean a cancellation of his personal consciousness. Paul's letters indicate that his Christian life was one of responsible personal existence. Led by the Spirit, he was still an individual man, not an absorbed portion of the divine. Moreover, he had absolutely no sense that by his own spiritual exercises he could lift himself into communion or identification with the divine.

Of his Christian life and privilege, Paul said that "all this is from God" (2 Cor. 5:18). He confessed that even his faith was the gift of God (Eph. 2:8), and that his worship, even his prayers, were the utterance of the Spirit (Rom. 8:26). Paul also saw his acts as the fruit of the Spirit. But nevertheless he continued to exist as an individual, infinitely indebted to God and ever led by the Spirit in the service of Christ his Lord.[75]

It is significant to note that none of the great "calls" or conversions recorded in the Bible involved mystical absorption in the divine. True, they were highly personal experiences. However, with the possible exception of Saul's conversion, they were not focused upon the experience as such, but instead upon commitment to a specific historical vocation. By these calls the powers of the individual for responsible action were given focus.[76]

3. Significance of the Biblical Approach

The kind of approach to and evaluation of nonbiblical religions and other spiritual worlds which we meet in both the Old and the New Testaments is quite different from the modern phenomenological, sociological, and psychological kind of approaches. The biblical approach is the theological approach, in strict orientation toward the living God in Christ. The other approaches are not necessarily discredited by the biblical, nor vice versa, provided each keeps in its due place.

The biblical-theological approach is exclusively concerned with understanding human spiritual expressions, not in terms of its cultural, psychological, or sociological value, but in terms of what happens in the depth between God, the Creator and Redeemer, and human beings, his creatures. In other words, the biblical-theological approach is concerned with ultimate and normative truth.[77]

The God of the Bible, moreover, is an utterly different deity from the gods of all natural, cultural, or philosophical religions. He is no immanent power in nature nor in the natural process of being and becoming.[78] Rather, the nature of his being and will is revealed in his historical acts. He thus transcends nature, as he transcends history; and, consequently, he destroys the whole basis of pagan religion. No force or power in the world is more characteristic of him than any other.

The real nature of the biblical faith is based on a confessional proclamation of the sovereignty of this God and on his saving acts in behalf of humankind. This is a proclamation which demands of its hearers that they make a decision as to where they stand in relation to God's sovereignty. God is not to be known in the first instance as the power in nature's rhythmic cycle, nor as the absolute of metaphysical speculation. Rather he is to be known as the "Lord" who "chose" Israel for himself and as the "Father" of our "Lord" Jesus Christ.[79]

VI. How Would You Describe a Systematic Approach to Religion and Religions Which Is Based on the Biblical Guidelines?

Commitment to the biblical worldview both requires us to define and assists us in defining a systematic method or procedure for studying and approaching non-Christian religious groups. The following is a presentation of the general steps involved in making a study of religions from the viewpoint of the biblical perspective. In later sections of this chapter we will look more specifically at the Christian approach to a number of major world religions.

1. Step One: Acknowledging Our Involvement

For Christians, the first step in studying religions from the biblical perspective is to acknowledge our involvement in the biblical faith. Our commitment to Christ and his gospel implies certain presuppositions in our approach to other religions.

(1) Impossibility of Neutral Observation. As Christians, we cannot be neutral observers in the area of religion. The gospel of Jesus Christ comes to us with a built-in prejudgment of all other faiths; when we accept Christ we accept him as the only way of salvation. For this reason, we know in advance of our study what we must ultimately conclude about them. This blanket judgment is not derived from an investigation of the religions themselves, but is given by the structure and content of the Christian faith itself.

For many Americans, this approach seems to go against the values of tolerance and openmindedness which have been widely taught. Americans have learned in the crucible of religious and political persecution the importance of religious liberty—the freedom for each religion to proclaim its teachings with zeal and persuasion but without attempting to use political or social pressure to enforce its view. But this does not change the inherent exclusiveness of biblical religion—the worship of a "jealous God" and of a Savior who clearly states, "I am the way, the truth, and the life; no one comes to the Father, but by me" (John 14:6).

(2) A Missionary Approach and a Confessional Stance. The specific charge of the Great Commission is to go into the world and make disciples of all nations,

including those of other faiths (Matt. 28:19). It follows, then, that a Christian's primary purpose in studying other religions is to convert their followers to the gospel of Jesus Christ. The gospel cannot be preached to humankind en masse, but only to this or that person or group in the context of the peculiarities of their existence. Knowledge of a person's or a people's religion is therefore necessary in order to assist our communication of the gospel to them.[80]

(3) Need for Objective Study. The Christian need to bring the gospel to each person in the context of his or her life requires an accurate and fair representation of each religion. This is the primary purpose of studying other religions. In other words, while the objective and impartial study of religions does not contribute to the redemptive content of the gospel, it is integral to the missionary proclamation of the gospel.[81]

2. Step Two: Evaluating Each Religion Separately

The second step in evaluating religions from the biblical perspective is to look at each religion as a specific religion instead of looking at religion in general.

This was not originally the emphasis of the modern study of religions. The objective of the study of comparative religion both in the eighteenth century and in its nineteenth-century maturity was to establish a scale of development by which to measure or evaluate the various religions. In other words, in these early studies, religion was religion writ large, and in some religions it was written larger than in others.

Discerning students eventually recognized, however, that each religion has its own categories for understanding itself and that the categories of one may not be applied to another without doing violence to that other. For instance, the ten avatars or incarnations of Lord Vishnu in the Hindu religion are something altogether different than the Word become flesh (incarnation) in Jesus Christ. Comparing the two would be like comparing apples and oranges.[82]

Accordingly, in the study of religions, each religion is to be considered as a self-contained unity or system organized around a faith-evoking center distinct from that of all other religions. The first concern in studying a religion is to determine what this center is—what in the religion calls forth a faith-response from its adherents and suggests to them a reason for being.

3. Step Three: Realizing That All Religions (except Judaism) Are Equidistant from God

The third step in a biblical approach is to realize that all nonbiblical religions belong to one and the same biblical category—sin. Speaking christologically, that is, in terms of a relationship to Jesus Christ, there are no degrees of proximity; thus, the several religions cannot be classified according to such categories as "higher" and "lower." Except in the case of Judaism, outside of faith in Jesus Christ, all men and religions are an equal distance from him. Christologically no one is better off or worse off than any other. Either we are Christ's or we are not.[83]

And yet, because every religion is different, every religion occupies a unique place in relation to Christ. In other words, the nature of its separation from Christ is unique.

This understanding of the christological position of nonbiblical religion means that each religion must be understood and described in two ways. First, there is its own self-understanding. Second, there must be an interpretation of its self-understanding in terms of its unique separation from the gospel. This means that there must be a gospel interpretation of Judaism, of Islam, Hinduism, of Buddhism, and other religions. This is more important than an attempt to give a Christian interpretation of religion in general.[84]

4. Step Four: Realizing That the Proclamation of the Christian Gospel to the World's Peoples Is a Precondition for the Final Stage of Christ's Kingdom

According to the New Testament, the final stage of God's purpose cannot be revealed until all nations have heard the Good News. Eric Rust, Joachim Jeremias, Johannes Munck, and Oscar Cullmann make this point very forcibly. The kingdom is already being realized in history. However, the full realization waits on the accomplishment of the world mission.[85]

(1) The emphasis of Mark and Paul. This emphasis is the theme of Paul in Romans 9–11, which in many ways is a commentary on Mark 13:10: "The gospel must first be preached to all nations." In Romans 10, Paul contends that God is following an exact plan. There must be offered to all an opportunity to hear the gospel (Rom. 10:14). The Jews have already heard it, but not all have received it. Therefore the call now goes to the Gentiles (although in the end, when the "full number" of Gentiles have entered the kingdom, all Israel will be saved).

For Paul, this is all in God's purpose. The full plan is surrounded with mystery, but he clearly sees his own calling as apostle to the Gentiles (Rom. 11:13) as an element in the working out of the mystery and thus in the furthering of the final consummation. So, therefore, Paul feels compelled to preach the gospel (1 Cor. 9:16) and declares that he is a prisoner of Christ for the Gentiles (Eph. 3:1). Paul and his fellows are ambassadors for Christ. They are pleading with people so that they can be reconciled to God (2 Cor. 5:20), for the full number of the Gentiles must be made up (Rom. 11).[86]

Oscar Cullmann supports the idea that the Second Coming waits upon the preaching to the nations. "You shall be witnesses" is an imperative, not an indicative—a command, not an observation—in the writings of Mark and Paul. God takes the initiative in the Cross and the Resurrection, and through his messengers he now offers his gospel to the world before the end.[87]

The church's missionary task is thus a crucial part of the final fulfillment. Its preaching is God's act through the testimony of his people. Through the church, the nations are now being invited to the eschatological feast by God's gracious activity in Christ and in the Spirit. This "now," this "end time," is the period of grace for the nations. The church by its preaching has the last word to the sons of frail humanity. Men and women are judged or saved by their attitude to this proclamation.[88]

(2) The Emphasis of the Book of Revelation. In the Book of Revelation, Cullmann finds another reference to his suggested approach. When the First Seal is broken, the three horsemen representing war, famine, and death are accompanied by a fourth whose identity is not so clear (Rev. 6:1–11). He comes on a white horse, and his figure is not sinister like those of the other three. Rather he is luminous and crowned, suggesting a beneficent power. He comes forth conquering and to conquer, and Cullmann suggests that he is representative of divine activity. Hence this scholar would identify the figure on the white horse with the preaching of the gospel to the world. This may be supported by the later vision of the angel who appears with the eternal gospel and issues a final call to repentance to the pagan nations (Rev. 14:6–7). Once more we are reminded that the preaching of the gospel is a necessary precondition of the end.[89]

VII. What Is the Biblical Approach to the Primitive or Tribal Religions?

1. Definition of Primitive Religions

"Primitive religions" is a designation which needs some clarification in its use. In this instance, the use of the term *primitive* does not refer to time, but to a type of culture. Usually, the followers of primitive religions cannot read or write. Their tools are simple, their livelihood usually that of hunting or agriculture, and their social organization usually tribal. (In fact, Edmund Soper, a well-known scholar in the field of non-Christian religions, prefers the designation "tribal religion" to "primitive religion.")[90] In general, their way of life has changed little over the centuries, although they have adopted certain aspects of modern civilization.[91]

Although sometimes primitive society may seem very exotic and remote to those of us in Western society, William Howells suggests that primitive devotees are essentially like us and are engaged with precisely the same kind of religious needs and yearnings as the more civilized. They are what we might be doing ourselves—and indeed what most of our ancestors were doing—three thousand years ago.[92] However, this picture is changing rapidly with the encroachment of Western civilization upon primitive societies, which in many cases is breaking up old tribal loyalties and bringing primitive religions into the cities along with its practitioners.

2. The Importance of Studying Primitive Religions

Stephen Neill, an Anglican who has served as a professor at the University of Nairobi in Kenya and a bishop in India, suggests that because of their numbers and influence primitive religions demand attention in the study of the world's religions. At least 40 percent of the world's population today still live under primitive conditions. Usually the outward conditions of their lives are reflected in their religious ideas and practices.

The prevalence of large numbers of primitives tends to be concealed, since a great many of those who can correctly be classed as "primitive" are usually included in the statistics for the greater religions. It is, for instance, taken for granted that everyone in India who is not a Muslim, a Christian, a Sikh, a Jain, or a Parsi is a Hindu, and the figures are given accordingly. On the basis of such statistics, it may be held that the "primitives" make up only a small part of the human race and are to be found mainly in Africa and in the South Seas. But, in fact, the religion of the inhabitants of most South Indian villages bears very little relation to classical Hinduism and much greater relationship to primitive religion.

Similarly, everyone has heard of the existence in Haiti and other Caribbean countries of the voodoo cults. These are nominally Christian countries, yet primitive Africa is very much alive in them.[93]

It should also be noted that many traces of primitive religions have survived in our modern societies, even among Christians. As we shall see, superstitious beliefs in ghosts, "luck," and other spirit manifestations survive from the primitive origins of our own society. But the presence of primitive religion in modern culture is not always just a cultural remnant. In recent years, primitive religious concepts have been deliberately reintroduced into the American culture by Black and Native American groups eager to recover a sense of cultural identity and by New Age practitioners eager for "spiritual" experiences. A psychological reaction against the intellectual and formal has led to a renewed emphasis on primitive dances and music. (For example, I have attended an annual festival in Gallup, New Mexico, where more than one thousand Indians meet to reenact snake, eagle, and other traditional dances.) In addition, for several decades there has been renewed emphasis on primitive concepts such as mana, tabu, black magic, divination, fate, and astrology.

3. The Presuppositions of Primitive Religions

(1) Animism. Animism is often called nature worship or spiritism. It is the belief that nature and all the objects of nature are peopled with, and possessed by, living spirits.

Generally speaking, the spirits are feared in primitive religions. They are believed to have power over human beings, and practicers of primitive religions are not sure exactly how to get the spirits to exercise good rather than evil powers. Much of the ritual that has grown up in tribal religion is an effort to control the spirits. The power held by the shaman or priest is due to belief by others that he has unusual or secret ability in this regard.[94]

Spiritism is becoming increasingly prevalent in certain parts of Latin America, notably in Brazil and the Caribbean. In fact, spiritism could well become Christianity's most ominous purely religious rival in areas of Latin America. It is also a rapidly growing phenomenon in the United States.

Closely related is the fear of ghosts, especially in the proximity of cemeteries (the departed spirits of the dead are supposed to hover around the locale of their dead bodies). This is a primitive fear that grips many an educated and "Christian" person in the United States.[95]

(2) Mana. Another basic concept of primitive religions is the belief in mana. Neill believes that mana, which he refers to as "force" or "power," is the key to understanding the logic of the primitive.

Howells affirms that mana is an important concept, and he adds that it can be compared to electricity. This comparison is helpful because both electricity and mana are impersonal but powerful. They flow from one thing to another and can be made to do a variety of things.[96]

Mana is believed to act either for the benefit or for the harm of humankind. It thus becomes of utmost importance for human beings to possess and control mana, and therefore its pursuit is the chief ingredient in the tribal religions. The effort to control mana is the basis of superstition, magic, faith in charms, amulets, and talismans. Because they claim to control mana, shamans or medicine men are revered and have controlling power among peoples who practice primitive religion.

The power of belief in mana is inconceivably great and is almost impossible to wipe out. Witness the many superstitions by which even Christian people in today's enlightened society are dominated. We see a carry-over of mana in a belief in or fear of an impersonal power which can influence and control human life—whether a black cat, a lucky pocket piece, or some more "religious" object. Such a belief is a rejection, in practice, of the Christian faith. And every such carry-over of primitive religion undermines the distinctiveness of the Christian faith; in fact, it is a rejection, however unwitting, of Christianity. In addition, these primitive practices can also be seen to undercut the validity and power of the Christian mission.[97]

The confrontation of Christianity and the primitive religions, therefore, must include a thorough re-examination of our own traditional heritage. We must have the courage to eliminate or overcome those elements in this heritage which are pagan survivals contrary to the Christian faith.[98]

(3) Ancestor Worship. For the primitive, the inevitability of death does not dissolve the continuity of personal existence. He simply expects to leave his body and take on another body which is less inhibiting than the one he had. Then he expects to live on in this new existence through the rites and ceremonies performed by the living, and it is believed he can have a direct effect on their lives through his spiritual influence.[99]

The primitive fears his ancestors and does everything possible to appease them. Much of the evil and suffering he experiences is attributed to unhappiness on the part of one of his ancestors with his conduct or some aspect of his life.

(4) High God. In the contemporary world, the study of primitive religions seems to have established that everywhere—even among the most remote and primitive tribes—there is a concept of one High God or supreme being.

German anthropologist W. Schmidt has given more elaborate study to this line of research than any other scholar. He found that among the Pygmies of Central Africa there is a clear sense of the existence of one supreme being to whom all other existences, natural or supernatural, are subject.[100]

But it is equally clear that this High God is given remarkably little thought, prominence, or attention in the rites and observances of most primitive religions. Instead, men and women are absorbed by the need to propitiate and placate a multitude of far more immanent spirits or gods.

The primitives seem either to have abandoned in practice a monotheism they once knew and still vaguely remember or to be fighting against this God. W. Schmidt himself regards this High-God concept as evidence of the survival, in part, of a primitive revelation of God which has become obscured and overladen by magic, animism, polytheism, and delusion. This is in keeping with Paul's teaching in Romans 1:19–23 that human beings suppress or stifle the truth that they really know.[101]

4. Primitive Religions and the Problem of Evil and Suffering

(1) Magic. Because spirits and mana are thought to be the sources of evil and suffering in primitive religions, the solutions to these problems are thought to lie in influencing or addressing spirits or mana. Primitive religions seek to do this through various kinds of magic.

Magic is based on the principle that there is sympathy between persons, things, and events. Such sympathy is of two types. One comes from the idea that like produces like; this is called homeopathic magic. Here the practitioner of magic acts on the assumption that he or she can produce a desired effect by imitating it. For example, it was once believed that burning an image of a person would cause the person himself really to be destroyed. This idea survives now in the practice of burning a person in effigy.[102]

The other type of sympathy is that of contact. Here the belief is that things once in contact remain in a kind of direct association, even though physically separated. This is known as contagious magic. Thus, for example, by injuring a piece of clothing, one seeks to induce injury to the person who has at some time worn that clothing.

In addition, magic itself can be of two types—white magic, or magical power used for purposes of good; and black magic, or magic used for evil purposes. A variation of magic is divination, wherein the seer foretells future events. Astrology is a form of divination which is very prevalent even in scientific societies. Unfortunately, it has a remarkable and growing grip upon quite a few Americans and Europeans.[103]

The practice of magic is still prevalent in all societies, whether primitive or civilized. Its appeal and, even more important, the fear of its consequences, are extremely difficult to eradicate.

(2) Shamanism. Primitives believe that addressing the spirits requires great knowledge of the spirit world and much time. For this reason, specialists or

professionals are employed in the use of magic and rituals meant to influence events. In general, there are two principal types of religious functionaries in primitive religions: priests and shamans.[104]

Priests are officials who serve in the temples and officiate at sacrifices. Not every person can be a priest. He must demonstrate his ability to hold spiritual intercourse with the gods. This he does by conduct which to the Western mind is clearly the product of intoxication or ecstasy or seizures, but which to the primitive clearly indicates possession by some spirit other than his own. The primitive mind stands in awe of what it considers to be the position of the unusual and the unexplainable. Therefore, the ability to go into trances or other hysterical symptoms are believed to be definite evidence that the person is able consciously to lift himself to the spirit level. And in that state, the person is thought to be able to establish control over spirits and to employ the mysterious powers of mana and magic.[105]

(The continued association of religion with the ability to induce frenzy, trance, and visions may be seen in the highly revivalistic expression of American Protestantism. An example is the frontier camp meeting, which is a part of the history and heritage of several denominations but is now largely found among the extreme Pentecostal sects. The phenomenon of speaking in tongues is another form of shamanistic tribal religion. This is a form of religious expression which has been controversial since the days of the apostle Paul.)

The shaman has a much wider practice than the priest and employs many more techniques to achieve his purposes. In most primitive societies the shaman is more important than the priest in that he has a closer association with the people; he is often employed in individual situations for specific purposes, particularly those involving healing. He believes he has received his power from the gods and claims a great perceptiveness in understanding and communication with the gods.

Certain faith healers in our day may be said to be shamans functioning within the context of the Christian faith. The most tragic part of the cult of such persons is the power and appeal of a survival of primitive or pagan religion. However, their misuse of faith healing should not be allowed to cloud the truth and usefulness of spiritual healing. Healing, done within biblical guidelines, is fully in accord with the Christian and biblical faith. In fact, the church's general rejection of this legitimate aspect of the Christian faith may have opened the door to the shamans of twentieth-century America.[106]

(3) Offerings and Sacrifices. Offerings are always given to procure the favor of the gods and never as an expression of love or gratitude. The objects brought as sacrifices are those things necessary to the nourishment, comfort, and pleasure of men. Since the spirits are thought to be anthropomorphic (humanlike) in their appetites and wills, it is assumed that their desires are similar to those of humans.

(4) The Absence of Morality. Morality as we know it is frequently unknown in tribal society. Primitive people may be both fanatically religious and grossly immoral (from our point of view) and sense no incongruity in this situation.

Unfortunately, a tribal or primitive view of the nonrelationship of religion and morality is coming to be prevalent throughout much of the United States. This way of thinking is directly opposed to the biblical view, which sees evil and suffering as directly related to the violation of God's revealed moral law.

5. The Importance of Sharing the Christian Gospel with the Primitives

It is evident from extensive study that many primitive peoples are losing their old faith but are not finding any adequate belief to take its place. Soper focuses vividly on this challenge. He contends that animistic religion is doomed, whatever we as Christians may do or not do. Military occupation and commercial and industrial enterprise tend to be soulless and have little concern for the moral and religious interests of the native peoples. They disrupt the life which the tribal people have been living from time immemorial and offer no new patterns by which they can develop a satisfying form of existence. Consequently, the primitives are left in a worse state than before. "Primitive people are in dire need of something, even though they may not know what that something is. They are separated from their past, which is beyond recall, and they can see little or no hope in the future."[107]

6. An Appropriate Method for Presenting the Christian Gospel to Members of Primitive Religions

Stephen Neill suggests that the Christian gospel should be presented to practicers of primitive religion as the message of the Trinity: the Father, and the Son, and of the Holy Ghost. There is much to commend this approach if it is properly spelled out.[108]

(1) Presentation of God the Father. As mentioned above, most primitives already possess some faint knowledge of a High God, but this supreme being is remote and faint in their consciousness. This means that they are not very much interested in the High God and therefore do not suppose the High God is very much interested in them.

But the primitive does respond to the preaching that the High God, whom he dimly discerns, is deeply concerned about his primitive children. There is in their minds something already prepared to respond to this emphasis in Christian preaching.

Next it must be made plain to them that the High God is interested in them only because he is equally interested in all other peoples as well. This is a shattering blow to the idea of the self-sufficiency of the tribe within its own world of humans and ancestors and gods. God can be known as Father only if he is understood to be the universal Father. It is precisely this that many African converts have identified as the new thing that came to them through Christian preaching.

Once the primitive inquirer has apprehended the idea that the High God is a living, near, and caring reality, the next thing he or she must be taught is that this God can never be controlled or influenced. This is quite a change from primitive religion, whose primary aim is to influence or control the spirits. The concept to be conveyed is that there is a world order which has been broken by sin, but which they themselves can do nothing to restore; the movement must be in the other direction. There is a covenant between God and humanity, but it depends solely on the will and mercy of God and not on any human initiative or influence. The first outlines of the doctrines of election and of grace are thus taught.

(2) Presentation of Christ the Son. At first, primitives will find themselves more at home in the Old Testament than the New and will find special appeal in the sublime stories of the early chapters of Genesis. This is as it should be. Unless the doctrine of creation has been well and truly understood, it will not be easy to build on it a genuinely Christian doctrine of redemption.

The danger is that the new convert may hear the message of the Old Testament and may fail to pass beyond it. But this Old Testament message itself will never make him a Christian. He must pass on from the doctrine of the Father to the doctrine of the Son.

The salvation which Jesus offers translates itself for the primitive primarily into the message of salvation from fear. Jesus is the conqueror of the demons. To the one who lives in constant fear of spirits and mana, this conqueror Jesus offers hope and liberation.

The problem, of course, is that primitive converts easily lapse back into their pagan fears and rituals. The members are sincerely Christian in that their intention is to follow the new way. At the same time, a deep feeling persists that it may be helpful to keep on good terms with the old gods. New Christians from primitive backgrounds, therefore, often revert to the use of charms and incantations and often take recourse to witchcraft and divination.

It is easy to see why this happens. Primitive superstitions run deep, and sheer numbers often make it difficult to give adequate teaching to converts. Conversion sometimes fails to lead the new converts to face in a radical way what the New Testament demands in terms of deep change. The new person in Christ is not the old person patched up.

It is true that God can use all that is good in the old, but this means *transforming* the old, not simply refurbishing it. Christ is the Savior of all that can be saved from the old way of life, and from the traditions of tribe and people. But he can be Savior only if he has first been Destroyer. Reconstruction can begin only if the sovereignty of the old life has been totally extinguished and the people have really made their exodus from the dominion of the ancient spirit world.[109]

It was by reaction against this danger that the German missionaries in New Guinea were led to adopt a very different approach to the problem of conversion. They were dealing with small isolated tribes, often of not more than six or seven hundred members. Their method was to go on with patient instruction until the whole tribe was prepared to declare itself ready to break with the past and with the old evil ways. Until this declaration had been made, no one in the tribe would be baptized. Thus the solidarity of the tribe was maintained, and the convert was saved from the dangers of isolation from the corporate life, on whose support the individual is so deeply dependent.[110]

(3) Presentation of God the Holy Spirit. We have seen the significance of the preaching of the Father and the Son in work among primitives. The logic of the situation drives us on to see the necessary place of the doctrine of the Holy Spirit in Christian work among primitives.

The application of this doctrine is especially helpful when it comes to matters of tribal affiliation and community. Although tribal existence, which is the rule for most practicers of primitive religion, has much to offer in terms of belonging and community, it also involves hampering limitations on the expansion of human powers and the restriction of the individual to traditional paths. The moment the Holy Spirit, the Lord and Giver of life, enters in, human beings are set free from their environment to be themselves. This results, to a certain extent, in the breakdown of the tribal order.[111]

This breakdown can be devastating to a tribal people unless the church, the community of the Holy Spirit, is ready to help in the transition. The tribe is the natural community. The church is the willed community brought into being by the will of the Father. Primitive people need to find on a new and higher level all that was of value in the closely corporate life of the family and the clan.

Unfortunately, in many Christian communities the quality of fellowship is very poor. Where all have come recently from the same background, something of the old corporate quality of life seems to survive. But where this quality of fellowship is most needed, namely in the cities where detribalized people feel their loneliness and isolation in all its bitterness, there are few churches where strangers can be quite certain they will be welcome. There are also few churches which provide such quality of life that draw in the primitive with the feeling of belonging and being at home.[112]

The obvious challenge, then, to those who organize and develop churches in primitive areas and in urban centers is to emphasize qualitative caring and Christian community. The radical individualism of the West needs to be complemented by the corporate or body emphasis stressed by the apostle Paul in 1 Corinthians and Ephesians.

VIII. What Is the Biblical Approach to Judaism?

1. The Unique Relationship of Christianity to Judaism

Among the non-Christian religions, Judaism holds an absolutely unique relationship to the gospel and the church of Jesus Christ. As the only two religions of biblical faith, Judaism and Christianity are bound together in an utterly incomparable and inseparable relationship. The very existence of Judaism is a strong witness to the reality and purpose of the God whom Christians worship, serve, and proclaim.[113]

Judaism and Christianity are radically united at the point of their mutual dependence upon the Old Testament and its interpretation of the unique series of events it records to be revelatory of the Living God. A Christian who studies Judaism would quickly see that Christianity would lose its distinctiveness if it separated itself from the peculiarity and particularity of the Old Testament and rooted itself in an alien philosophy. Similarly, the Jew who really bothers to study the Christian faith cannot fail to be impressed with how much of Jewish faith and tradition is carried on and into the world by Christianity.

Judaism, with no less zeal than Christianity, affirms the Old Testament declaration that God called Abraham out from among "the peoples" in order to create in history a new kind of peoplehood—his people Israel. Both religions understand this to be God's twofold act of judgment upon and redemption for humankind.[114]

The messianic hope, in its Jewish context, is emphatically a confidence in the sovereignty of God—his fidelity and power. Jew and Christian are one in their belief in the coming of a Messiah or messianic age within a theology of creation, covenant, and history. They differ in whether and where that hope is realized and fulfilled.[115]

It is important to keep in mind that the New Testament never finally rejects the Jews. Its authors, with the exception of Luke, were Jews themselves—as, of course, was Jesus himself. And although at times there was deep tension between the Pharisees and the New Testament church regarding the Christian claim that Jesus was the Messiah, Paul and other New Testament writers clearly expected the eventual redemption of Israel.

The sharp denunciations recorded in Jesus' preaching, as for example in Matthew 23, have to do with moral and spiritual problems to which all establishments are liable. The statements of Jesus are not against the Jews ethnically or racially. Indeed their tone is very much in the tradition of the Hebrew prophets and they take issue not with Torah as such but with its abuse. It was as custodians and not as a people that Jesus criticized the Jews.

It should also be noted that in the intense pastoral preoccupation of the apostles, as mirrored in the Epistles, there is a concern to reproduce in Gentile life and culture those qualities of integrity and discipline taught in the Torah. These are the qualities which Jews feared would be jeopardized by Gentile fellowship.

It would be wrong to read in Paul's Gentile priority in mission any final repudiation of his own people. The offering raised for Jerusalem, which took Paul into imprisonment, is the clearest index to a continual bond with his fellow Jews.[116]

Only recently, through the work of men like Johannes Munck, have we begun to see more clearly how Paul was positively related to Judaism even in his sharpest arguments in favor of the inclusion of the Gentiles among the people of God. And Paul's doctrine of a justification by faith without the works of the law was primarily a scriptural argument, according to the exegetical principles of Judaism, in defense of his mission to the Gentiles.[117]

2. The Background of the Separation of Judaism and Christianity

The religion of the Old Testament is both gracious and redemptive. The most spiritual of the people of Israel always realized this gracious-redemptive character of the Old Testament religion. But over the centuries, there have been forces and tendencies at work in Judaism to change it or reinterpret it in the direction of a nonredemptive religion of human merit.[118]

In the intertestamental period, for instance, there grew up a group of Jews, known as the Pharisees, who were especially zealous for the defense of the law of Moses. They believed that in the moral and ceremonial stipulations of the Torah God had supplied all the nation needed for the guidance of its life and the fulfillment of his will. Hence they sought to build up an earthly manifestation of the divine kingdom through obedience to the divinely given law. Where the law was too general or obscure, they compiled a system of interpretation which applied its general stipulations to the changing conditions of life. This body of unwritten law or tradition consisted of the rulings of the great rabbis and slowly became more authoritative than the law itself.

The Pharisees were attempting to establish themselves as a holy and separated people—the community of those who ordered their lives by God's law and meditated upon it day and night. In so doing, however, they became so tied up in the jots and tittles of the law that they lost the spirit which had moved them in their early days. The Pharisees came to believe that they could save themselves by their own efforts, put themselves right with God by their own striving, and share in the coming age by virtue of their own righteousness. The result was a spiritual bankruptcy clearly evident in the Pharisees of Jesus' day.

Despite the blind legalism of the Pharisees, however, there were still faithful souls among the Jews who continued to look and hope for God to act in history as he had promised. Grace remained operative in the lives of the faithful remnant who treasured the promise in their hearts.[119]

(1) The Differences in New Testament Times. As we open the pages of the New Testament, we find the religious leadership of the Jewish people sharply divided between two sects or parties—the Pharisees and the Sadducees. The Sadducees doubted or denied many teachings of the Scriptures, including the doctrine of bodily resurrection that had developed in the times of the prophets. The Pharisees, as we have seen, were scriptural and traditional literalists who clung tenaciously to everything Jewish against everything Gentile. The Pharisees also placed great emphasis on works of righteousness. The apostle Paul, before his conversion to Christ on the Damascus road, was an adherent of this sect of the religion of Israel.[120]

The New Testament is dominated by the conviction that what Israel hoped and longed for has been fulfilled in Jesus of Nazareth. We have seen how a remnant of pious and faithful Jews kept alive the covenant faith and cherished the promise in their hearts.[121] When the fullness of time came, however, it came in disguise, like a thief in the night. It was a hidden revelation.

It seems highly probable that during the early part of Jesus' ministry, many Jews did wonder if he were the Messiah. The question of John the Baptist ("Are you he who is to come, or shall we look for another?" Matt. 11:3) may well voice popular feeling. But when the Jews remained in political bondage to

Rome and Jesus died on the cross refusing to use violence or political measures to establish his kingdom, most Jews assumed the Messiah was yet to come.

Christians believe, of course, that the story did not end at the cross—and that the coming kingdom was far greater than any political entity. Out of Jesus' sacrificial death and triumphant resurrection there sprang a faith which affirmed, beyond a shadow of doubt, that he was the Messiah of God and that he would come again on the clouds of heaven to judge the earth. In both cruder and more refined forms, this faith dominates the New Testament writings. In Jesus of Nazareth, Israel's destiny was fulfilled, and the people of God were reconstituted on the basis of a new covenant, so that it might include those of all nations and actualize God's purpose in the world.[122]

(2) The Differences Related to Authoritative Documents. After A.D. 70, the Jews were dispersed by the Romans. As Judaism developed, it added much in the way of traditions and interpretations. Among these additions are the Mishnah, created in the second century after Christ. This was a list of four thousand rabbinic precepts calculated to adapt the Torah (law of Moses) to the conditions existing in the second century.

Learned Jewish scholars in Babylonia carried this elaboration and codification of the details of Jewish religion even further, bringing together all the previously unrecorded traditions into an immense book called the Gemara. Then the Gemara was combined with the Mishnah to form the enormous work known as the Talmud. One edition of the Talmud was produced in Palestine around A.D. 400, and another, more important, edition was completed in Babylonia about A.D. 500. Jewish devotion to the Talmud further separated Jews and Christians.

The Talmud in its Babylonian and Palestinian forms is an important authority for present-day Judaism, which bases its religion in the conception of law as enshrined in the Talmud and expressed by the holy words, deeds, way of living, and principles of faith. The word *Torah,* often used to refer to the Books of the Law, is also an all-encompassing term used to refer to this totality of Jewish faith.[123]

Torah, in fact, can be said to be the central concept of classical Judaism. Jews believe that the ancient Scriptures constituted divine revelation—but only a part of divine revelation. At Sinai, God was believed to have handed down a dual revelation: the written part known to one and all, but also the oral part preserved by the great scriptural heroes, passed on by the prophets to various ancestors in the obscure past, and finally handed down to the rabbis who created the Palestinian and Babylonian Talmuds. The "whole Torah" thus consisted of both written and oral parts. The rabbis taught that the "whole Torah" was studied by David, augmented by Ezekiel, legislated by Ezra, and embodied in the schools and by the sages of every period in Israelite history from Moses to the present. It is a singular, linear conception of a revelation, preserved only by the few but pertaining to the many, and in time capable of bringing salvation to all.[124]

The myth of the Torah is multidimensional. God and the angels are said to study the Torah just as rabbis do on earth. God dons phylacteries like a Jew. He prays in the rabbinic mode. He carries out the acts of compassion called for by Judaic ethics. He guides the affairs of the world according to the rules of the Torah, just as does the rabbi in his court.

A striking detail of the Torah myth is that whatever the most recent rabbi is destined to discover through proper exegesis of the tradition is considered as much a part of the way revealed to Moses as is a sentence of Scripture itself. It therefore is possible to participate even in the giving of the law by appropriate, logical inquiry into the law. God himself, studying and living by Torah, is believed to subject himself to these same rules of logical inquiry.[125]

In light of the Torah myth, the faithful Jew constitutes the projection of the divine on earth. Honor is due to the learned rabbi more than to the scroll of the Torah, for through his learning and logic he may alter the very content of Mosaic revelation. He is Torah, not merely because he lives by it, but because at his best he forms as compelling an embodiment of the heavenly model as does a Torah scroll itself. Learning thus finds a central place in the classical Judaic tradition.

The final element in the rabbinic Torah myth concerns salvation, which is thought to take many forms. One salvific teaching holds that had Israel not sinned—that is, disobeyed the Torah—the Scriptures would have closed with the story of the conquest of Palestine. From that eschatological time, the sacred community would have lived in eternal peace under the divine law. Keeping the Torah is therefore the veritable guarantee of salvation. When Israel makes itself worthy through its embodiment of Torah, that is, through its perfect replication of the heavenly way of living, then the end will come.[126]

(3) The Differences Related to the Messiah. The division between New Testament Christians and Jews over the Messiahship of Jesus has continued into the present. There are many kinds of modern Jews, but only those who have been converted to Christianity—the "Completed Jews" or "Hebrew Christians" —accept Jesus as the Messiah.

Modern Zionism, the movement to establish a Jewish state in Palestine, represented a peculiar marriage of Western romantic nationalism and Eastern Jewish piety. Zionism is a modernized, if not wholly secularized, Messianism. So far as Zionism aspired to create a state like other states and to "normalize" the existence of the Jews, it represented a massive movement toward assimilation. In creating the largest Jewish neighborhood in the world, where Jews lose a sense of being different, it refocused the center of Judaic existence out of its parochial mold and placed the Jews within the mainstream of international life.[127]

The result is that a considerable portion of the Jewish population of the Republic of Israel is secular. From one perspective, the Zionist movement which advocated return of the Jews to Palestine can thus be seen as primarily a secular, social-political or nationalistic movement rather than primarily an expression of religious faith. Accordingly, their interest is more in the future of Israel as a nation than in the expectation of a religious Messiah.

Religious Jews of today are divided into various branches or denominations, with the primary divisions known as Orthodox, Conservative, and Reformed.

Reformed Judaism, as its name implies, began as an effort to effect a reformation of the classical tradition. These were not Jews who would choose the road of assimilation; they chose to remain Jews and retain Judaism. One might say, however, that they wanted to be Jews without being too "Jewish." They founded their reformation upon the concept that "essential Judaism" in its pure form required none of the measures that separated the Jew from other enlightened people, but consisted rather of rational beliefs that were destined in time to convince all humankind and of ethics that were universal. Reformed Jews see themselves as bearers of a mission to mankind: God's kingdom would be realized only through Judaism, "that most rational and ethical of all religions."[128] The Reformed Jews do not expect a personal Messiah. For them, the Jewish faith is not regarded as a fixed or closed system, but as something capable of development in varying conditions.[129]

Jewish orthodoxy, with its two divisions—Orthodox and Conservative—sets forth a different ideal for modern Judaism. They adhere very closely to the historic documents of Judaism, especially the Talmud. Orthodoxy stands for tradition first, last, and always; it has accepted, but only grudgingly affirmed, the conditions of modern life. In the orthodox view, modernism is to be judged by the criterion of Torah, not the Torah by modernism. Orthodox Jews claim that they represent the true and authentic Judaism.[130] Some of them hope for the coming of a personal Messiah who will make Israel free and great again. Others have given up the expectation of a personal Messiah and hold that Israel collectively is the Lord's anointed with a mission to the world.[131]

(4) The Development of Persecution and Ostracism. Soon after the New Testament era, Christians became increasingly hostile to Jews. In the third century A.D., Bishop Melito of Sardis began the practice of accusing the Jews of deicide—the murder of God. Tertullian and others joined the attack against Jews as the enemies of Christ.

After Christianity was officially accepted in the Roman Empire by the Edict of Milan (A.D. 313), problems multiplied for Jews. Augustine developed a theology which excluded Jews from the people of God. John Chrysostom in the fourth century and others of his time and afterward engaged in passionate polemic against the Jews.[132]

Christian witness today constantly faces the sad fact of the church's long history of persecuting Jews. The Crusades and the Inquisition stand out in Jewish minds as extreme examples. And the Nazi Holocaust, while not carried out specifically by the church, was accomplished with relatively little protest from the church and with the complicity of many who claimed to be Christians.

3. The Basic Differences between Judaism and Christianity

(1) Differences Concerning the Messiah. Although Orthodox Jews and Christians look for a Messiah, they differ in whether and where that hope is realized and fulfilled. Some Jewish leaders, such as Martin Buber, declare that Jews will never recognize Jesus as the Messiah come, for this would contradict the deepest

meaning of their messianic passion. He also indicates that the basic difference between the Jewish messianic hope and the Christian faith is that the Jews know the world to be as yet unredeemed—in contrast to Christians, who speak as if the world has already been redeemed.[133]

This Jewish view of the Messiah was pressed upon me vividly at a Jewish-Christian dialogue in Cincinnati, Ohio. After I had presented my understanding of the Christian teaching about the Messiah, a prominent rabbi stood and asked, "How can you say the Messiah has come when you look upon the horrors of the world, including the Nazi destruction of six million Jews?"

In the broad Judaic view, the affirmation of Christ as the Messiah can only be read as Christian romanticism. Christians must be romantics who have failed to see, or refused to contemplate, the desperate wrongness of the world. After the Holocaust, especially, the Jews are all-too conscious of the evil in the world. They say that Christians should not wrap a legend of victorious love around the gross and chronic evil that is history and pretend that "God has reconciled the world." For the Jews, the Christian claim that the Messiah has come must be scorned as a cruel confidence trick unworthy of "the God of Israel." From the Jewish perspective, the evidence, including the Jewish agony in history, is witness to the conviction that there is no realized Messiahship—at least not yet, perhaps never.[134]

The Christian faith, in contrast, believes that the redeeming grace of the sovereign God has already been liberated into present history through the death and resurrection of Jesus. All appearances to the contrary, the redemptive power of God is active in our world. Yet Christians from the New Testament times have always known that the present world is not yet the kingdom of God and of his Christ in the fullest sense possible. How could they think this in the face of the Cross, not to mention the New Testament insistence that the kingdom in its totality is still to come at the second coming of the risen Jesus?[135]

For the Christian, the Messiah's task is interpreted in terms of suffering, death, and resurrection rather than in terms of what the world regards as kingly glory. The Old Testament image of the Suffering Servant (Isa. 53), which sees Israel suffering on behalf of others, becomes central in the interpretation of the messianic mission. If the age to come is to be one in which people are given a new spirit and their sin is remembered no more, God makes this possible through the sacrifice of Jesus. The sacrificial system of Israel is seen by Christians as a prediction and type of the crucifixion of Jesus for the sins of humankind.[136]

Finally, Christians consider the church to be the New Israel, the heir to God's promises made to Israel and the remnant through which the divine act of redemption in Jesus would be made effective for all nations. It was not only Israel that was to be redeemed in the sufferings of the Messiah; the Messiah was sent to be light and salvation to the Gentiles and all humankind. Jew and Greek alike could find their hopes fulfilled and their needs met in the Anointed One of Israel. A New Israel is built not on racial blood, but on the outpoured blood of the Redeemer, whose deliverance is effective for all human beings.[137]

The Jews, in response, point out that the setting in which Jesus lived and moved, from Galilee to Jerusalem, was alive with every form of messianic rumor or surmise. Expectations, even those of disciples, which could only be fulfilled in being first transformed, beset Jesus on every hand. This fact perhaps explains his frequent avoidance of the term *Messiah* and his preference for the more enigmatic "Son of Man."

In other words, Jewish scholars say, the evidence concerning Jesus as the Messiah is tangled and inconclusive. What decision(s) Jesus himself made and whether they could be said to be "messianic," perceptive historians must refuse to say. The thread of the story cannot be unraveled to the satisfaction of the Jews.[138]

Orthodox Christianity contends that there was indeed a messianic decision by Jesus. Furthermore, Christ's decision and understanding was sustained in filial communion with God and by the light of prophetic precedent. The Messiahship of Jesus was accepted by the disciples and the early church because he had taught and demonstrated his Messiahship. The faith in him as Messiah followed the fact.[139]

The Jewish refusal to accept Jesus as the Messiah rests on a variety of concerns. Given what we have described, within the New Testament, as a fact-faith situation, the Jewish response was, and is, to disallow the "fact" dimension. They will agree that the early Christians had faith in Jesus as the Messiah. However, the Jews say that the Christian faith was wrong because the Christian criteria for what constitutes the Messiah are wrong. Christians, on the other hand, hold that the early church had the true criteria when it acknowledged Jesus as the Messiah.[140]

(2) The Disagreement Over the Universality of Mission. Another difference between Jews and Christians concerns the question of whether the Messiah which the early church recognized in Jesus had a built-in destiny as the Savior of the world. The New Testament moves from its understanding of the Cross into a joyful relegation to the past of the essentials of the discrimination between Jew and Gentile. "Not for our sins only, but also for the sins of the whole world" (1 John 2:2) was the conviction of the Jewish leaders of the early church as to the relevance of the Cross.

There is no doubt that the Jewish establishment of Jesus' day read any such enlargement as a threat and a treachery. In their mind, the expansion of the Messiah's mission to include all humankind is contrary to the authentic continuity of everything Judaic and thus a threat and a treachery. Thus they disclaimed the Messiahship of Jesus.[141]

(3) The Disagreement Over Entrance into Faith of the Religious Community. Another difference of note between Jews and Christians is the fact that Judaism is "a life" and "faith" which one possesses by birth. The theme of being Jewish from the womb, of being born to be God's, found powerful expression in the writing of Franz Rosenzweig, the controversial German thinker of the early twentieth century. Rosenzweig had felt deeply the fascination of Christian faith but, in an intense experience in a Berlin synagogue, renewed his Jewish loyalty.

Emphasizing that "Christianity must proselytize," because one cannot be born Christian, he saw the Jew by contrast as "the product of a reproduction" who attests his belief by continuing to procreate the Jewish people. A position similar to that of Rosenzweig was maintained by Will Herberg of Drew University.[142]

In contrast, New Testament Christianity holds that there is a necessary "becoming" which involves a personal exercise of faith before belonging is authentic. Family may be an important factor, but does not of itself constitute membership and discipleship.[143]

This necessity of coming by faith into Christ explicitly suspended the old priority of birth. The "becoming" of which it spoke was accessible to all and was not "of natural descent" (John 1:13, NIV). It was also nonterritorial; it was not tied to a certain land, as was the Judaic. There was a sense, further, in which Christ became what the Temple had been in the old dispensation. "The temple of his body" meant the living organism of those, of any race and color, who came to be "in Christ" by faith.[144]

This is a dramatic departure from the Jewish tradition, which understood being the people of God as existing "in full physical reality" through history. It involves being born into a covenant community completely distinct from all other nations.[145]

The first-century Jews' aloofness from the new Christian option turned on interior convictions which persist into the exchanges of today. They saw the church as disqualified by its deliberate forfeiture of the very categories which "made" Jewry. It had no ground in "seed" and "organic peoplehood." It had no territorial home. On both counts the very founding principle of Israel was impugned.[146]

In the Jewish mind, the Christian community is either romantic, pretentious, or both to think that community for God could be constituted without the indispensables of the Hebraic heritage. These indispensables already existed before Jesus and were never to be paralleled or superseded. By its faith in covenant and election, Judaism evaluated all else. To accept Christ, with all that such acceptance implies, would mean to call in question the very stuff of Jewish self-awareness. Israel's election was God's experiment, and, as such, must be pursued intact.[147]

4. The "Two Covenants" Approach to the Relationship between Jews and Christians

From the Jewish side the two-covenants view was developed by Franz Rosenzweig. It suggests that Christianity should be seen as the extension of God's grace to Gentiles. Jews are not within the "new covenant" because they are already covenanted with God. It is possible for Jews, according to this view, to recognize and approve all that the church believed itself to be on the condition that it is seen as noninclusive of the Judaic peoplehood. Jews are "people of God" by birth and do not have to "become the children of God" by being "born again" as Gentiles do. Because they already belong in God, the gospel cannot involve them.[148]

Rosenzweig believed that the *de facto* reality of Jesus as the Messiah in the sense of Christian conviction is a fact of the human situation. It has been responsible for an amazing mediation to the world of things Judaic—psalms, ethics, and norms. Jews can acknowledge this actuality as an admissible form of monotheism for non-Jews. In this generous way, Jews could approve Christianity without Judaic compromise.[149]

As Kenneth Cragg, a British scholar in the field of world religions, points out, the problem with the two-covenants theory is that it totally alters the New Testament perspective. It amounts to a rewriting of "God so loved the world" so that it reads: "God so loved the Gentiles." It makes havoc of the dictum, "In Christ there is neither Jew nor Greek." It is still saying to the Jews, "You are not included." According to Cragg, this theory is contrary to the meaning and openness of Christ.[150]

5. Special Considerations for Christians in Approaching Jews

(1) The Emphasis of Grief. In approaching a Jew with the message of the gospel, it is appropriate for a Christian to express grief for the tragic legacy of the centuries created by the distortion at Christian hands of things Judaic. They should regret the teaching that the Jewish dispersion by the Romans was a punishment for "deicide." Christians should likewise grieve over the prolonged disparagement and active persecution of the Jewish people.[151]

(2) The Emphasis of Appreciation. Christians should express appreciation for the validity of the Jewish past as historical preparation for Christ. This validity need not be thought of as forfeited because Jewry withheld recognition of such fulfillment. The debt remains, and over the centuries Christianity has witnessed to this debt by its devotion to the Old Testament as an essential part of the Christian canon.[152]

(3) The Emphasis of Uniqueness. Christians should affirm that our dependence upon the Old Testament and our kinship with Judaism as the continuing people of the Old Testament are related to our dependence on Jesus Christ. It is true that insofar as Jesus Christ is a one-man Israel, we Gentiles through faith in him become members of Israel and heirs of God's promises. However, Jesus Christ is at the same time the sole cause of the separation between Jews and Christians in history. Faith in Jesus Christ does not make us Israelites primarily, but Christians.[153]

Jesus Christ, Christians affirm, is the fulfillment of God's promise to Israel and to the nations. In his people, the church, therefore, the distinction of Jew and Gentile is eradicated. This does not mean that the Gentile becomes a Jew or an Israelite. Rather, as Paul indicates in Ephesians 2:14–22, Christ leads Jews out of Judaism into the church and calls Gentiles out of the peoples into the church.[154]

Salvation through Christ is from the Jews, but it is also *for* the Jews, because it is really from God. In Christ and his church, Israel's history entered into its fullness.[155]

We Christians have no basis for pride in the New Testament teaching that the church is a development out of Israel which God intends to supersede Israel. But neither should we have any occasion for embarrassment in this faith. The apostle Paul has expressed the authentic Christian conviction on this matter: "I am not ashamed of the gospel: it is the power of God for salvation to everyone who has faith, to the Jew first and also to the Greek" (Rom. 1:16). The Jew is entitled to be the first to follow Christ into the church, for Judaism is and remains the community of preparation for the church, which is the community of fulfillment.[156]

The survival of Judaism in history, like the creation of the church to supersede Judaism, is an act of God. We cannot escape that conclusion. But the authentic biblical understanding is that the survival of Israel is not required in God's program of redemption.

Christians believe that only God's faithfulness to Israel accounts for the survival of Judaism. However, this does not subtract from the Christian claim that Jesus Christ and his church are the fulfillment, the full consummation of Israel. It therefore does not take away the responsibility upon each Jew to follow Christ out of Israel into the church. And it therefore does not reduce the responsibility of the Christian to take the initiative in bearing witness to the Jew at the right time and in the proper way.[157]

IX. What Is the Biblical Approach to Islam?

1. The Unique Relationship of Islam to Christianity

Islam, the religion of the followers of Muhammad (A.D. 570–632) is unique among the non-Christian religions in her relationship to Christianity. Because Islam began in the Middle East subsequent to Christianity, Islam has always been dealing with Christianity and has never been without some sort of reference to Christianity. Islam's holy book, the Koran, preserves and maintains this reference to Christianity, speaking specifically of Jesus and the Christian religion.

This does not mean, however, that Islam or the Koran is dependent upon Christian sources or that Islam is continuous with the historical communities of Judaism and/or Christianity. Quite the contrary. Early in its formation, Islam developed an "independent self-consciousness." Kenneth Cragg points this out in his book, *The Call of the Minaret*, where he writes, "The biblical narratives reproduced in the Koran differ considerably and suggest oral, not direct, acquaintance. There is an almost complete absence of what could be claimed as direct quotation from either Testament."[158]

In fact, all that can be said with certainty about the relationship between Islam and Christianity is that Muhammad was aware of Jews and Christians and knew something of their history. In the sixth and seventh centuries, the Jews were numerous around Medina, where Muhammad was first accepted as the supreme prophet of God (Allah), and they were present in Mecca, Muhammad's birthplace and the geographical center of the Islamic faith. Christians were strong across the Red Sea in Ethiopia and had a checkered, declining role in Southern Arabia. Both Muslims and Christians agree, however, that the Christianity represented in Arabia at the time did not present Muhammad with an authentic picture of Christ and the church.[159]

Muhammad claimed to be a biological heir of Abraham through Ishmael. It is through this tie with Abraham that Muhammad sees himself as the establisher of the true religion of the one God in Arabia. However, Muhammad claimed, the true religion which Abraham bequeathed to the Arabs became corrupt, even as Judaism adulterated her legacy. Therefore it was not biology but revelation which linked him and his message to original Judaism and original Christianity. Because he believed his revelation was identical in content with the original revelations to Abraham, to Moses, and to Jesus, Muhammad considered himself to be in direct succession with the Old and New Testament prophets.[160]

2. The Importance of Islam in History and in the World Today

(1) The Spread of Islam. It is generally agreed that in the history of religion, Islam stands out in regard to its founding and phenomenal growth. Within the span of a single decade, A.D. 622–632, the founder of this religion united the nomadic tribes of the Arabian peninsula into a single cohesive nation. Furthermore, he gave them a monotheistic religion in place of their tribal religion, organized a powerful society and state, and launched a religious and political movement which was to expand into a religious and cultural empire.[161]

Within a century after the death of Muhammad, the Islamic empire stretched from Arabia west through North Africa to Southern France and Spain. The movement also spread north of Arabia through the Middle East and east throughout Central Asia, right up to the borders of China. In the process of this expansion, much of the oldest and strongest Christian territory was lost to this new religion of Islam.

Islam has dominated the Middle East for the last twelve centuries and was a constant threat to Europe during much of that time, from Spain in the southwest to the Balkans in the southeast. Today it extends from the Atlantic to the Philippines. It includes such diverse peoples as primitive African and Philippines tribes and highly cultured groups in India. Egypt, Saudi Arabia, Yemen, Jordan, Syria, Iran, Iraq, Afghanistan, Pakistan, and Malaysia are Islamic states. Indonesia is principally Islamic in culture. There are many adherents of Islam in Lebanon, Albania, Yugoslavia, the Balkans, the U.S.S.R., India, and North Africa. In Africa south of the Sahara Desert, Islam is currently making tremendous advances, far outstripping Christian expansion.

(2) Militant Islam and Worldwide Religious Freedom. It should be noted, moreover, that almost every appraisal of resurgent Islam notes both the Muslim religion's militant character and the fact that it has yet to experience the scientific revolution and to multiply amid religious freedom in a pluralistic society.[162]

In recent years, Islamic fundamentalism, in countries such as Iran and Libya, has had harmful effects on world stability. Radical terrorist groups which often claim to represent Muslim religious organizations have threatened international air travel.

The secular, pluralist West has a difficult time understanding the extremes of some Muslim groups. But the West should remember that Islamic society has not gone through a critical Enlightenment that questions all traditions.

An example of Muslim attitudes was seen in the furor over a novel by Salman Rushdie, *The Satanic Verses*, published in 1989, which contains a satirical dream sequence about a Muhammad-like prophet whose human weaknesses call into question his reliability as a messenger from God. As we shall see in this chapter, for any Muslim to revile the Koran or the prophet Muhammad is an attack on the very foundations of their religion, because Muhammad, although not divine, is seen by the Muslims to be the special instrument of Islamic revelation. Rushdie was born into a Muslim family in India and so is subject to the Islamic principle that makes blasphemy a form of apostasy, a capital crime under Islamic law. And because he lived and wrote in London, he inflamed the widespread conviction of Muslims that Islamic society is under attack from the West. It is thus understandable why the book sparked riots and deaths in Pakistan and India, huge demonstrations in Iran, and the pronouncement of a death sentence on its author.

Before pointing fingers at the Muslims for this act of intolerance, however, Western Christians should remember the history of religious persecution in the West. The logic of the Ayatollah Ruhollah Khomeini—who made the death threat—is similar to that of St. Augustine: Better a heretic should die than allow false teachings or ridicule to lead others to eternal damnation.

In 1611, the first code of law for the colony of Virginia prescribed death for blaspheming Christianity or the Trinity, and even today many states retain antiblasphemy statutes. No one was ever sentenced to death for the crime in the colonies or the United States, although some individuals did suffer floggings, fines, or imprisonment. Even in recent history, accusations of blasphemy are made in the United States and Europe. In 1988, for example, fundamentalist and evangelical Christians demanded that the film, *The Last Temptation of Christ*, be withdrawn from distribution, and a theater showing it was burned in Paris.

Still, the movie met no legal obstacles in the United States. And unlike Rushdie, the director, Martin Scorsese, did not have to go into hiding.[163]

The potential of religious fanaticism of any sort in a pluralistic "global village" calls for the development of worldwide religious liberty. This view allows religious sharing and propagation and witnessing in a context of religious freedom and the separation of church and state. The United Nations charter favors such religious freedom. Such an approach means there should be neither government persecution of religion nor direct governmental help for a given religion. Each religion can proclaim its teachings with zeal in the right spirit, but each religion must be humble, realizing that human beings are finite and capable of being wrong. We must not force our view on others or use a wrong type of mind-control. We must not claim official validity or official monopoly or privilege for our religion.[164]

(3) Islam in the United States. The Islamic crusade in the United States began in a definite way in 1931 among the Blacks in Harlem. Since that time, a steady trickle of homegrown converts has joined a flood of immigrants to create a sizable American Islamic community. The number of Muslims among those entering the United States has doubled in the past two decades, and in recent

years they have constituted some 15 percent of immigrants. Recent estimates indicate more than four and one-half million Muslims live in the United States with the largest concentration in California. There are more than six hundred Islamic centers across the U.S. With these trends and their high birthrate, U.S. Muslims are expected to surpass Jews in number in less than thirty years and become the country's second largest religious community (after Christians).[165]

It should be noted, however, that there is no unified Islamic movement in America. American Muslims have difficulty obeying the traditional practices and moral tenets of Islam in a society that is both non-Islamic and highly permissive. Perhaps the most difficult practice to maintain is the prescribed five daily periods of prayer and prostrations conducted while facing Mecca.[166]

However, some Muslim leaders see an invigorating sort of challenge in the highly secular and sometimes hostile American environment. Many immigrants and "sojourners"—students who come for several years—are nominal Muslims who arrive knowing little about the faith. The freedoms of American society lead them to reflect on their beliefs, and many return to their homelands as leaders. The U.S. has thus become not only a melting pot for Muslims from all nations, but also an important "incubator for Islamic ideas."[167]

(4) Offshoots of Islam. Although on the whole, Islam is remarkable for its worldwide coherence and unity, it does have a few offshoots or derivatives. The most noteworthy of these is Baha'ism, which originally developed from a revival movement among Shi'ite Muslims in Iran about 1850. Baha'ism is a mystical messianism with political overtones. This group holds that Baha'ullah, who lived in the nineteenth century and was a Muslim prophet, is really the revelation of the "glory of God" (as his name suggests) in whom all the world's major religious faiths find their consummation.

No genuine Muslim would now claim Baha'ism as Islamic. However, it has its roots in a version of Islam which has an esoteric, mystical character. The Baha'ists have built a beautiful temple in Wilmette, Illinois, comparable in splendor to the one in Haifa, Israel, which serves as their world headquarters. Baha'i does not keep statistics on the number of its believers, lest this would limit their faith to being merely one more of the world's religions instead of the ultimate expression they believe it to be. In fact, Baha'ism considers all believers in the nine major religions, which they believe are antecedents to Baha'ism, to be at least potential Baha'ists.[168]

After the advent of Khomeini in Iran, militant Muslims began persecuting the Baha'ists, who can be classed as the nation's largest religious minority. The Baha'ists, who are said to number four hundred fifty thousand in Iran, are the only major non-Muslim group not recognized or protected by the Islamic constitution under Khomeini.[169]

Another offshoot of Islam is a mystical or New Consciousness emphasis known in the West as Sufism. (Its followers are called Sufis.) They claim to worship the same God as the one described in the Koran and Islamic tradition. There are two groups within Sufism, each with a different emphasis. One group says that they are only seeking to cultivate immediate communion with Allah. Another group moves closer to pantheistic forms of mystical absorption.[170]

3. Historical Developments Which Have Influenced the Attitudes and Doctrines of Islam

(1) The Idolatry of Mecca and Muhammad's Absolute Monotheism. An important influence on Islamic faith was the religious climate of the Arabian peninsula in Muhammad's day, particularly that of his birthplace, Mecca. Scholarship has given us considerable knowledge of the pre-Islamic Meccan world. From this knowledge, we can discern certain factors which influenced Muhammad and his views. Among the paramount factors were his encounter with religious pluralism, idolatry, and division among Arabs. It is likely that the three belonged together. Militant monotheism and the liberation from idols is a central motif of Muhammad's story. The outsider can certainly trace in some of the teachings of Islamic theology the problem of idolatry in Meccan/Arab life.[171]

When Islam arose in the seventh century of the Christian era, the people of Arabia worshiped a superabundance of divine beings. Several religions were active in the Arabian area. The religious life involved gross idolatry on the part of the various tribes, including the worship of the seven planets, the moon, and the stars. Many worshiped family household gods and various angels and intelligences. Others were involved in fire worship contributed by the Magians from Persia. In addition, there was a corrupt form of Judaism among some of the Arab tribes, and several Christian heresies were also represented.[172]

Because of Muhammad's hatred of idols, he placed an immense emphasis on the unity and transcendence of God. He exalted God far above the world and everything that human beings can understand. This unity was absolute in Muhammad's theology. The worst of sins, therefore, was the sin of saying that God has a partner. Accordingly, Islam is opposed not only to the Christian claim that Jesus is the Son of God, but to any suggestion that God could in any way relate himself to anything outside himself. Islamic theology holds that God is too highly exalted to enter into any kind of relationship. He makes no revelation of himself to humanity; he reveals only his will. Even in paradise, people will not know God as he is.[173]

(2) Political/Moral Chaos and the Alliance of the Political and the Religious. The Arabian peninsula in Muhammad's day was characterized not only by religious pluralism and idolatry, but by tribal warfare, brutality, and promiscuity. This context of chaos, added to the Islamic revelation of God as Lord led to Islam's emphasis on divine control and its later opposition to religious liberty and separation of church and state.

In Islamic thought, since Allah is Lord, he must be Lord of all. Hence there is a necessary alliance of the religious with the political. Prophetic revelation—at least the final one—must become operative and victorious through a state regime, divinely sanctioned and divinely established. Human beings have to be under enforceable command and prohibition both in terms of social evils and religious attitudes and actions. The revelation of the Koran is understood as the religious authority in and through all law: civil, criminal, constitutional, and moral. Personal autonomy is wholly controlled by Islamic law.[174]

Islam considers itself a civilization, not merely a religion—a way of life for all people in a society with reference to all aspects of their personal and corporate life. In other words, Islam strives for a complete unity between religion and the everyday world. The means to this end is a religious-ethical system that does not attempt to reach an ideal which good people ought to achieve, but rather emphasizes what people could and might fairly easily be expected to achieve in the light of their drives and human limitations.

Islam attempts to provide the answers to every conceivable detail of both belief and daily conduct under every circumstance. Furthermore, it gives to these answers the authority of the literal word of God himself.

This detailed guidance is provided through three sources, all of which are directly related to Muhammad. One of these is the Muslim Scripture itself, the Koran, whose name means "that which is recited or uttered." The second source of detailed guidance is the Hadith, or collection of the "sayings" of Muhammad. (These are apart from those he specifically declared to be revelation.) The third source of guidance in Islam is the Sunna, the record of the personal customs of Muhammad or the customs and laws practiced by his community in the earliest times of Islam.[175]

(3) Religious Chaos and Islam's Emphasis on Simplicity. Compared to other world religions, Islam is comparatively simple. And this simplicity is a major factor both in the appeal of Islam and in the grip it comes to hold over its adherents. At various times and places—including medieval Spain, nineteenth-century India, and Al Azhar University in Cairo, Egypt, today—more complex philosophical systems have been constructed for Islam, with Greek thought playing a major role. But these philosophies have not exerted any significant influence upon the Islamic religion in general.[176]

In the religious simplicity of Islam there is only one central idea: that there is but one God, who is Maker and Absolute Controller of all things and people. This concept is helpful to primitive or untutored minds. A central and understandable idea gives them relief from the competing interests of the many spirits and gods in tribal religion and from the complicated theology of the other culture religions.

This very simplicity was influenced by the necessity of bringing order and clarity to the chaos of tribal and animist religions in the Arabian peninsula. The desert Bedouins of the Arab world were mainly animists, worshiping springs, wells, stones, trees, and wild animals, all of which were conceived to be inhabited by jinn (demons). However, they also had a concept of High Gods, of whom there were three in their case.

Chief among the three High Gods was Allah, known from earliest times in Arabia, as attested by numerous ancient inscriptions. Allah—the term itself is simply Arabic for "The God"—seems to have held a place of especially high esteem in Mecca, where he was worshiped in the Kaaba, along with many other deities. (The Kaaba had been built to house a black stone which the people of Mecca believed had fallen from heaven in the days of Adam. It also gave lodgement to the gods associated with the stone by the pilgrims. Images of local and distant deities were placed in the dark interior. The Meccans also declared that the great patriarch Abraham, while on a visit to his son Ishmael, had built the Kaaba and imbedded the black stone in it.)

Muhammad selected the one deity, Allah, the best one among those known to the Arabs of his day, and declared him to be the only God. Or rather, he claimed to have been selected by Allah, to have received the foundations for the new religion through divine revelation.

In addition to acceptance of the fact of one God, there are only a few simple religious duties enjoined upon the believer. These duties, known collectively as the Five Pillars of Islam, include: (1) repetition of the brief creed, "There is no God but Allah, and Muhammad is his Prophet"; (2) prayer with directed motions, five times a day, facing toward Mecca; (3) almsgiving; (4) fasting during the month of Ramadan; and (5) pilgrimage, if possible, to Mecca at least once during one's lifetime. In addition, as occasion arises, jihad (holy war) can be declared the unequivocal religious duty of the Muslim man.[177]

(4) Historical Conflicts and Distrust and Hatred Between Christians and Muslims. Partly by conquest and partly by influence and persuasion, Muhammad gained both political and religious supremacy throughout Arabia. He died in A.D. 632, and was succeeded by Abu Bekr, who was called the "caliph." Under the caliph's reign, and afterward, Islam continued to spread, being promoted by extensive military campaigns. Jerusalem fell to the Muslims in 638, Egypt three years later, Iraq or Mesopotamia in 637, Persia in 649, and most of Asia Minor by 652. In these conflicts, the weary Byzantine Empire lost once-Christian Egypt, Palestine, Syria and part of Asia Minor. Later, Islam was carried by military force as far afield as India and beyond. In less than a hundred years after the death of Muhammad, all of North Africa and part of Spain were Muslim.

The spread of Islam in western Europe was finally checked by Charles Martel at the Battle of Tours (France) in A.D. 732—exactly a century after the death of Muhammad. Spain was later reclaimed for Christianity, but a wide belt of territory from Morocco to Pakistan and Indonesia has remained Muslim to this day.[178]

In the meantime, a series of Crusades were conducted from A.D. 1095 to 1291 as an expression of medieval European Christianity and chivalry. The Christian mission to Muslims, hard enough at best, was made immeasurably more difficult by the bitter enmities which the Crusades engendered between adherents of Islam and Christianity.

Although they ruthlessly suppressed paganism in the areas they conquered, the Muslims usually tolerated Christians and Jews as "people of the Book"—people who had a revelation related, though inferior—to that of Muslims.

Nevertheless, various regulations were imposed upon Christians in Muslim lands. One of the most devastating was the law against a Christian's converting a Muslim—accompanied by an absolute prohibition against the Muslim's accepting Christianity.[179]

Thus we see that the political threat of Islam to the "Christian states" of Europe, the reaction of these states in the form of the Crusades, and the regulations imposed by Christians in Muslim lands have created deep-seated hostilities and misunderstandings that seem almost insurmountable.[180]

4. Basic Differences Between Islam and Christianity

(1) God's Radical Transcendence versus the Sonship of Christ. As indicated earlier, the fundamental doctrine of Islam is God's monopoly on being God—his radical transcendence. God has no associates and will not share his Godhood with any other being of any rank. Being God is solely his prerogative. Therefore, all so-called "Companions of God" must be recognized for the nonentities they are and discarded. Hence Muhammad proclaimed, "There is no God but God . . . therefore worship Him alone."[181]

This radical exclusion is extended not only to idols and consorts, but to Christ as the incarnate Son of God. While the Muslims respect and revere Jesus, the confession of their faith precludes any association of Jesus with God. In their view, Jesus was God's messenger, not his Son. Islamic leader Abdullah Yusuf Ali has expressed what it means to a Muslim in our own day to hear Christians speak of Christ as God's Son: "It is a derogation from the glory of God—in fact it is blasphemy—to say that God begets sons, like a man or an animal. The Christian doctrine is here emphatically repudiated."[182]

In the view of the Muslim, with his compelling Allah-consciousness, Christian worship and theology fall short of radical transcendence. For the Muslim, the concept of "God in Christ" represents a compromise of divine exaltedness and the Incarnation represents a forfeiture of God's sovereignty. It is thought that the imperative of the divine will is somehow diminished by what Christianity affirms as divine condescension toward humankind.[183]

Christian theology embraces, indeed requires, christology; Islamic theology forbids it. Islam encloses Jesus strictly within the dimension of prophethood. The very idea of an incarnation of the deity is therefore anathema, or simple blasphemy, to orthodox Muslims. To them, Muhammad was God's inspired prophet, and they have come to regard him as impeccable and infallible, but not in any sense divine. It is partly for this reason that they commonly object to being called "Muhammadans"; they think this term implies that they regard Muhammad in much the same way as Christians regard Christ.[184]

(2) The Muslim View of the Koran versus the Christian View of the Bible. There are several crucial differences between Christianity and Islam concerning the nature and purpose of God's revelation, especially as concerns the nature and purpose of the holy books, the Koran and the Bible.

In the Muslim view, while Allah was the exclusive source of the revelation to

Muhammad, Allah himself is not the content of the revelation. In other words, Muslims view the Koran as a revelation not of personality, but of information. God the Revealer remains hidden; he is always God-above-revelation and God-beyond-revelation. Through the Koran he provides guidance for mankind in the form of information concerning how he expects men to relate their lives to him. The revealed will of God is something for man to believe and to do.[185]

In the Islamic view, moreover, the Koran has existed from all eternity with God in the Arabic language. The Koran is in every particular the utterance of God himself. There is no human element in it at all. Thus Muslims claim for the Koran something that Christians have never claimed for the Bible. Even the most conservative Christian admits some human element in the Bible. If that is so, says the Muslim, how can the Bible be the word of God?[186]

Thus we see that the Koran firmly understands itself in strictly verbal terms and excludes any incarnational dimension as either proper or necessary to prophetic revelation. As Scripture, the Koran has been understood by Islam as the final revelation. It was given to Muhammad in a form that is clear, mandatory, and explicit. It has an inalienable unity of form and meaning. By these qualities it can be seen as foolproof.[187]

Christians, on the other hand, believe that the manner as well as the goal of revelation should leave room for the responsive freedom of the human factor and invite active participation of mind and personality. The Bible does this. Moreover, Christians see the Bible as much more than a source of information and rules to follow; it is God's revelation of himself to his people. This revelation was given to a large number of people over a long period of time. And it was completed in God's revelation of himself through his Son, Jesus Christ. The Bible, therefore, is important and authoritative to Christians, but it is secondary to and dependent on God's revelation of himself through incarnation.

From the Christian perspective, moreover, the Muslim view of the Koran as arbitrary dictation from above is self-contradictory. If the Koran is a universal revelation, it would need to employ a universal language, and no such universal language exists. Any language used to record revelation must surely be susceptible of translation within a multilingual humanity. Such a language would need to be viable and capable of obedience within all the exigencies of human grammars and cultures.[188]

In the Christian view, revelation, by its very nature as a communication from God to human, is bound to have a particularity of place and point in time. The translation for other points of time and places will always have to be from its "there-and-then" to some other "here-and-now." Even the most strictly "literal" language must proceed by metaphor and allusion, and these are in the flux of the changing world. Faced with these facts, the Christian contends that we cannot conceive of the Bible in a static way. This is in conflict with any authentic understanding of the vitality of meaning within language.[189]

In summary, it is incontestable that the place and purpose of revelation are one thing for Islam and quite another for Christianity. For Islam, the revelation is the book of the revelation, the Koran. The Koran came straight from heaven and its sole author is Allah himself. In Christianity, however, the basic and primary revelation is the Person of Jesus Christ. The Bible is crucial, but its focus is to point to Jesus Christ and guide the Christian in following him as God's final revelation.

This distinction between the Koran and the Bible is radical. And the gap between the two is widened by the fact that the Koran specifically condemns Judaism and Christianity as corruptions. It denies, for example, the central Christian teaching about the crucifixion of Christ and rejects the Christian teaching about God the Father, God the Son, and God the Holy Spirit.[190]

(3) The Muslim View of Muhammad versus the Christian View of Jesus Christ. As the seal of the prophets, Muhammad repudiates the Christian teaching about the work and the finality of Jesus Christ.

The Muslim confession states, "I testify that there is no god but Allah and that Muhammad is the messenger of Allah." Uttering this two-tenet confession—called the Shahada—with intention is the very essence of what it means to be a Muslim. From the time that Muhammad's devoted wife, Khadija, uttered it and became the prophet's first convert, to the present, the Shahada has been the personal confession of faith of every Muslim. The Arabic word *Shahada* means, literally, "testimony."[191]

From what has already been said about the first element of the Shahada, it is evident that there is not and cannot be in Islam a doctrine of the divinity of Muhammad. On the contrary, there is unequivocal insistence on his humanity.

The Muslim points out that it is important to understand what it means to say that Muhammad is the messenger or prophet of God. Prophecy did not begin with Muhammad. At diverse times before Muhammad, God called or chose certain men to be his messengers to reclaim mankind from apostasy and superstition. The total number of these messengers is 313. Twenty-five of these must be remembered by every Muslim, so that if asked about any one of them he can confess his belief that this man was a messenger of God.[192]

Islamic faith holds, however, that there is a new element in the revelation to Muhammad. In the previous books which God had given to mankind, such as the Old and New Testaments, he promised a Coming One. But in the Koran there is no promise of another. On the contrary, there is an assurance that Muhammad is the "seal of the prophets," the final one in the succession. Muslims believe, therefore, not only that Muhammad is the latest in the succession of messengers, but that there will be no other.

Muhammad addressed his message particularly to the Jews and Christians, whom he hoped would recognize him to be a genuine prophet. He wanted them to accept his prophetic claims and declare the revelation he had received to be the confirmation of their own faith up to this time.

Muhammad gave the Jews and Christians what he considered ample time to consider, repent, and accept Islam. He then condemned their refusal of his summons as disloyalty to their own faith and pronounced judgment upon them and invoked the curse of God upon them. Thus, in the Muslim view, Christians and Jews are, if possible, worse off than the idolaters who have never known any better! Yet Muhammad never ceased to feel great disappointment over the refusal of the true faith by the Christians. He esteemed them in spite of the necessity of rebuking them.[193]

Muhammad freely acknowledged that Jesus was a prophet and a messenger of God—one of the important twenty-five. However, he flatly denied that Jesus was ever crucified. In his view, God could not allow crucifixion to happen to his chosen messenger, mere man though he was. Therefore, when the Jewish leaders approached Jesus with the intention of crucifying him, God took Jesus up to heaven to deliver him out of their hands, then cast the likeness of Jesus on someone else, who was crucified by mistake in his place.[194]

There has been much scholarly speculation as to how Muhammad came to hold such a view, and a Gnostic source has sometimes been suggested. But Kenneth Cragg is probably right when he says that the most natural explanation is that Muhammad here carried to its logical conclusion the instinctive reaction of Simon Peter at Caesarea Philippi. Peter exclaimed that it was no part of the messianic office to suffer and die, but rather to triumph and prevail. Similarly, according to Muhammad, God would not abandon his chosen messenger to death, for this would be a defeat and humiliation for the Almighty. The Muslim, therefore, feels that he is giving greater honor to Jesus and greater glory to God by denying the very possibility of the crucifixion.[195]

From the Christian perspective, of course, Muhammad failed to understand at this point not only the person of Christ, but the very nature of God himself. God did not abandon his Servant on the Cross. Rather, it was God himself who was there "in Christ reconciling the world to himself." Jesus was God manifest in the flesh. And this means that not only was Jesus just like God, but also the necessary corollary, that God is just like Jesus. Jesus is a God who comes to men "not to be served but to serve," not to take but to give, and not to remain aloof but to be involved, to suffer and to love.[196]

Also involved in this crucial difference regarding the role of Jesus and the nature of the Cross is a differing view of human nature. The Islamic view ignores the dark areas of human tragedy and perversity which are not subject to political or legal correction. The Christian faith, however, has always identified a much more deep-seated human wrong—pointing out through the prophets and apostles that human need and human depravity goes far beyond what exhortation or laws can correct.[197]

Accordingly, the Christian faith has always identified the crucifixion of Jesus at the hands of human beings as an expression of this evil propensity. "Behold," it has said, "the sin of the world"—there, in the cross of Jesus. It is this profound dimension of the work of Jesus which forbids Christians to limit his relevance to his teaching and his ethics and rather, requires us to enlarge his ministry to involve his substitutionary death and resurrection. Such a view of Jesus deepens his revelation from things said to revelation by things suffered.[198]

5. Special Considerations for Christians in Approaching Muslims

Christian-Muslim relations have benefited from the broadened knowledge, intercultural contacts, and the general spirit of religious tolerance in our day. However, there is still a great gulf between the two, made all the more pronounced by the greater similarities and more common heritage than is the case with other living religions, save for Judaism.

Nevertheless, Christians need to witness to Muslims. Islam is undergoing a vital revival and exerting a dynamic missionary outreach. How can the Christian meet this challenge? Here are some basic requirements:[199]

(1) The Approach of Acknowledging Basic Similarities. Christians and Muslims alike hold to one God, the "God of Abraham." Islam rejects all worship of other gods and all idolatry—more so even than Christianity has done in practice. Muslims as a group have been intensely faithful in heeding the first and second commandments of the Decalogue.

Furthermore, even a cursory reading of the prayer a Muslim is required to voice five times a day suggests to the Christian that Islam and the gospel are concerned about some of the same things. They are concerned about the reality, the oneness, and the sovereignty of God. They talk about the revelation and mercy of God. They emphasize human responsibility and are concerned about eternal life and destiny. They tell about God's call to submission and obedience and the need for decision on the part of human beings.[200]

(2) The Approach of Presenting the Radical Claims of Jesus in the Proper Spirit. As we have seen, though Islam is a religion of the biblical God and contains much of the same emphases as Christianity, it is in essence a totally different religion from the Christian faith. To ignore this fact is not a service to either Christianity or Islam, much less to the truth.

Acknowledging this fact of total difference gives no place for attitudes of superiority, of conquest, of condemnation, or of belligerence. The loving-kindness and compassionate concern of Jesus Christ must always mark the Christian in his relationship with the Muslim. Nevertheless, a presentation of the claims of Christ to a Muslim must include a clear recognition that the Muslim cannot be both Muslim and Christian. In spite of the common heritage and the areas where the two religions parallel one another, the two mutually displace one another.[201]

The Bible makes it abundantly clear that, when confronted by Jesus Christ, there are but two possibilities. On the one hand, there is the possibility of faith, of personal surrender. On the other hand, there is the possibility of rejecting him or passing him by—and this second possibility can take the form of respectful disinclination as well as ridicule or unconcern.[202]

(3) The Approach of a New Interpretation of the "Secular." There are those in contemporary Islam who call for a complete "de-Westernization" or desecularization in all areas of education. They call for the teaching of an Islamic sociology, psychology, political science, as well as an Islamic physics, chemistry, and technology. They believe that this will preserve all Muslims, and the educated young especially, from secular contagion.

A helpful Christian counter to this attitude is suggested by Kenneth Cragg, who contends that we do not understand the "secular" if we think of it in a static way over against the "sacred," and that we do not properly appreciate the "sacred" if we suppose that it should be insulated from the "secular." All so-called secular things are potentiality sacramental in meaning and usage, although of course the secular without the sacred penetration and perspective can be harmful.[203]

The proper use of the secular under divine guidelines cannot be coerced. We have to do with a God whose very being, in the sense of human recognition, is left to our consent. God and coercion do not belong together. The more any truth or right is coercive, the less it is religious. Divine being has such a character as to await the human will to love.

It is the Christian contention that the revelation of God in Jesus is the revelation of divine disposition. It is the disclosure of a loving, forbearing, forgiving, fulfilling, and charitable disposition. It is the Christian conviction that the experience of the perfectly loving disposition of God in Jesus Christ is the door to human fulfillment.[204]

(4) The Approach of a Loving Witness to the Practical Significance of the Trinity. Laurence Browne, former missionary to the Muslims and now retired after many years of teaching the history of religions in British universities, has declared, "The greatest difference between Christianity and Islam is seen in the Christian belief in the indwelling of the Holy Spirit in the hearts of men." The indwelling of the Holy Spirit is the experience of intercommunion between man and God. This presence of God in the human soul (but personally distinct from the human soul) is unique in Christianity. No other religion has a concept or belief which even approximates this Christian understanding of the Spirit.[205]

Back of the possibility of the indwelling Holy Spirit, however, is the necessity for the Son. Christ both reveals God and redeems and reconciles man to God, so that the fellowship of the Holy Spirit (God) may be possible. Here is a crucial element of difference between Christianity and Islam.

The Koran represents revelation from God, but not of God, for Allah is not a self-disclosing God. Central to the conviction of Jesus, however, was the sense that his mission was to reveal the Father, and that in his own person that revelation was made (cf. such passages as John 8:12–20 and 14:6–11). Thus one comes back to the essential fact that for Christianity the doctrine of the Trinity is both necessary and fundamental to all else.

Only witness, in love, should be made in any kind of confrontation with Islam. This witness emphasizes that not only is there one God, but that he loves humans personally and desires their companionship in return. Hence God has, in Jesus Christ, provided for humankind's forgiveness and reconciliation, and he has sent the Holy Spirit to dwell in his people. Herbert Jackson contends that this emphasis on the practical significance of the nature and meaning of the Christian faith about God, rather than discussion of theological problems involved in trinitarianism, is the approach to be pursued.[206]

(5) The Approach of a New Perspective on Morality. This approach also should be used in the realm of morals, with reference to the spirit of morality and to specific conduct. Christians do not seek to live godly lives on the highest plane of moral integrity because of some dictum or commandment laid down centuries ago in a radically different age and society. Rather, they constantly endeavor to know the will of the living, personal God for their individual situation and to obey that will out of gratitude to God for their salvation in Christ. This leads to a desire to do the Father's will and to grow and reflect God's character in godly living. This approach casts the entire realm of ethics onto a different plane from anything the Muslim knows. It puts into moral living a motivation which the Muslim cannot experience, precisely because of his different concept of God.

The people of Islam, if truly confronted by Christian faith, will discover in it a higher principle of conduct and a new basis for interpersonal relations (agape, or God-derived, love rather than duty). And, more important, they will find available a power, through Christ, to enable them to live by this new standard and spirit of morality.[207]

X. What Is the Biblical Approach to Hinduism?

Despite their differences, Christianity, Judaism, and Islam are related to each other as monotheistic religions related directly or indirectly to the biblical God. As indicated in earlier chapters, however, the religion of Hinduism has a completely different character and outlook and developed independently of Christian influence until relatively recently.

1. The Importance of Hinduism in History and in the World Today

(1) The Development of the Influence of Hinduism. Hinduism, which is centered in India, is a great cultural religion which in the early centuries of its development was largely ethnic in character. Through the centuries, however, it has developed the most complex and extensive philosophy ever known. This philosophy is not a consistent whole, but has numerous fundamental premises, often quite different from one another and even self-contradictory. Over time, great systems of thought have been constructed on each of these many premises.

Although the religion of Hinduism has ancient origins, most of its philosophical foundations are found in the Upanishads, a collection of treatises based on about three hundred years (800–500 B.C.) of religious reflection by various sages. These thinkers were obviously reacting to the extremely priestly and ritualistic character into which Hinduism had fallen.

Under the influence of the Upanishads, philosophy became paramount in Hinduism. The principle underlying the Upanishads is that humanity's spiritual problem is resolved neither by religious practices such as worship, nor by social service, but by the knowledge of what is actual reality or truth.[208]

The first important contact between Christianity and Hinduism came in the late eighteenth and early nineteenth centuries. Christian missionaries courageously took the initiative in advocating a number of social reforms to liberate the downtrodden in India from the oppressive Hindu social order.[209]

In all fairness, it should also be remembered that British imperialism brought political dominance and economic exploitation. Political and business representatives of so-called "Christian" Great Britain did not always reflect the highest Christian values in India.

However, it is also true that Hinduism and Hindu society, even by the admission of present-day Hindus, had become stagnant and degraded and was steeped in idolatry and superstition. Then came the flood of Western influences which inundated India—and most of the East—during the modern period. One result of that influence—especially the Christian influence—was that reform was provoked within Hinduism.[210] The outgrowth of that reform was Neo-Hinduism, which represents a revival of ancient or classical Hindu teaching, broadened extensively to fit the modern era of scientific insights and rapid social change.[211]

Until this time of reform, Hinduism had made little attempt to present itself as a religion for all humankind. It was Swami Vivekananda (1863–1902), an advocate of reformed Hinduism, who first presented Hinduism as a relevant and universal religion through his dramatic appearance at the Parliament of Religions in Chicago in 1893. From this time on, the Hindu polemic was not to be limited to a defense of the Hinduism of priests, temples, and castes in India. Instead, Hindus were stating their case especially for Christians and seeking to alter Christianity's monopolistic claims.[212]

(2) The Contemporary Influence of Hinduism. As detailed in earlier chapters, Hinduism has exerted great influence on Western thought and religion in the past two centuries. In order to better understand these influences, in the 1960s I traveled to the Hindu pilgrimage city of Benares, India. My visit there was an unforgettable time of study and consultation. Since that time I have returned to India several times with study groups seeking to understand the Hindu mind, its influence on Western society, and its relationship to the biblical worldview. At the same time, I have seen in my own country the flowering of many new groups whose roots are in ancient India.

The Hindu idea of reincarnation is basic to a number of philosophical and cultic systems that have originated in the West in the nineteenth and twentieth centuries. Baha'ism, which is basically rooted in Islam, nevertheless echoes Hinduism's emphasis on tolerance and the worth of all religions. The concept of personalized Nature in the transcendentalism of Ralph Waldo Emerson suggests Hinduism's Brahman. And Darwin's theory of the upward creep of creaturehood and his vague demarcation between humanity and animality indicate kinship with Hindu thought.

Theosophy, spiritism, the "I Am" cult, the Order of the Cross, and a host of so-called "New Age" systems are related to Hinduism. There are significant differences in organization and practices among Hindu-related New Age groups. The root worldview, however, which underlies most Hindu-related groups is the philosophy of Vedanta, or pantheistic monism. This view also undergirds the thought of Transcendental Meditation.[213]

In the Unity School of Christianity, in New Thought, and in Rosicrucianism, philosophical meditation similar to Hinduism is uppermost. Christian Science's stress on the nothingness of matter and the all-importance of mind exhibits close cousinhood with Hinduism.

2. The Basic Concepts of Hinduism

Earlier chapters have touched on certain aspects of Hindu thought, but for the sake of clarity we will outline them here as well:

(1) Atman, or the Self. To understand Hinduism, the place to begin is with the atman, or the self, because this is the reality that is immediately experienced and also because Hindus believe self-knowledge is the highest form of knowledge. However, Hindus do not think of the self in the same individualistic terms as we in the West do. According to Hindu thought, our desires and emotions may produce the impression that we are isolated and individual, but this comes from ignorance and is not the ideal or primary experience of the self. When we lose this false sense of individuality, we see that our pure consciousness expresses the unity of self with all reality.

(2) Brahman, or the One. The awareness of unity brings us to the second major idea, which is that all reality is ultimately one. There is one single indestructible reality in which all things participate, and that is Brahman—or the One, or God. The goal of existence is not to understand this so much as to experience it and to direct one's life in its light.[214] The supreme achievement of the Upanishads, in fact, is their insistence that to properly experience atman is to know Brahman.

Exactly how Brahman is to be described, and how much reality the individual self is to have, is much debated in Hinduism. Basically the Brahman is described in two ways. The first way, called the all-cosmic, emphasizes that the One is full of good qualities and refers to "him" in almost personal categories. The second way, called the acosmic, believes the One is without qualities and is indeterminate —the impersonal absolute which can be described only in a negative way. From this point of view, the world and the self are unreal—mere appearance.

(3) Maya, or Illusion. Ordinarily, according to Hindu thought, we are misled by our experience. This leads us to the third major conception in the Hindu religion: maya, or illusion. Because the One appears in an infinite number of forms or effects, we live among a surface-play of pulsating appearances that is not far from illusion. Much like Plato in the West, Hindu teachers explain that we are deluded by this semi-illusory world of shadows and partial truths, enchained by deceptive appearance, and thus distracted from experiencing the unity of all reality.[215]

(4) Karma, or the Law of Judgment. Karma is a fourth concept of Hinduism. It is in essence the moral law of retribution which requires each person to be continually reincarnated until he or she can attain release or liberation. The constantly changing forms of energy in which consciousness is diffused change according to this definite, inexorable law, which essentially determines that our immediately previous life is the sole cause of the nature and disposition with which we began this present life.[216]

(5) Moksha, or Liberation. The fifth major concept of Hindu religion relates to the goal of true philosophy: moksha or release. Spiritual liberation is the final and supreme aim of Hinduism.

The highest state for a human is a waking trance in which the self is disciplined to such an extent that the world is not experienced and awareness of the One is complete. But even this experience is a foretaste of a still higher form of existence, when a person is released from the cycle of birth and rebirth and has immediate awareness of bliss.[217]

(6) Three Disciplines, or Yogas. A person may strive after this final experience by means of rigorous disciplines, or yogas (English "yoke"). At any level of spiritual competence and in relation to any chosen deity, one of three basic yogas may be observed.[218] No one of these disciplines is considered superior to the other two. Depending upon the individual's needs and tendencies, one type of discipline will be best suited and preferable.

Energetic activists will follow the course of *karma yoga.* They will seek union with Spirit by yoking themselves to their chosen deity through disinterested good will and service. This means that all their deeds, whether manual, ritual, or ethical, will for them be holy deeds, acts of worship.

The second discipline is *bhakti yoga,* which is union through love with the chosen deity. Those who are strongly affectionate and need a recipient of their devotion shower their affection upon their chosen deity. Those who feel unloved and unlovable offer themselves to the gods of outpouring love who make them feel wanted, understood, accepted, and secure.

The intellectual type of personality pursues *jnana yoga.* This is yoking with the chosen deity and ultimately with Brahman by means of knowledge.

According to the Hindus, the Beatific Insight, or union with Brahman, can and has come from pursuit of each of these three paths. Some come to know the Truth by doing the truths; some come to know the Truth by loving the truths; others come to know the Truth by knowing the truths.[219]

(7) Avatar, or Manifestation. The bhakti yoga, or way of devotion to God, uses words familiar to Christians: *love, faith,* and even *mercy.* The conception of Brahman as clouded in mystery gives rise to a belief in avatar, or the manifestation of God in human form. The One or Brahman finds expression in certain holy men.[220]

(8) Contrasting Emphases. Thus we see that the religion of India has taken two approaches. One is impersonal and the other side is personal. The two sides are represented by two great classical philosophers of India, Shankara and Ramanuja.[221]

The thought of Shankara represents the predominant trend of Vedanta, which is monistic and impersonal. According to Shankara, who lived and taught in the ninth century A.D., human souls are parts of the Absolute, though sin may blind us to this truth. There is nothing real besides the Absolute; even the world of nature is maya, or semi-illusory. The Absolute is impersonal, though perhaps one could say that it is spiritual, and through retribution and rebirth it exercises a moral government. Salvation is achieved by realizing one's unity with the Absolute. In all this, one can see resemblances to Plotinus, Eckhart, and other Western thinkers. However, Shankara's doctrine is far more monistic than any of the Western teachings.

Ramanuja in the twelfth century was dissatisfied with this impersonal monism and taught the relative independence of nature and of the human soul. This allowed sufficient space between the souls and God for the possibility of avatars and personal devotion (bhakti).

In the sixteenth century, a Hindu religious leader, Chaitanya Mahaprabha, taught that direct love of Lord Krishna was the way to burn off ignorance, overcome bad karma (or retribution), and attain bliss. Since that time, Chaitanya's sect of Krishnaism has continued in India. In the 1960s, its teaching was brought to the United States and developed into the International Society for Krishna Consciousness, known popularly as Hare Krishna.[222] Thus we see that through Hare Krishna and other groups, popular Hinduism has given a prominent place to devotion to avatars.

Krishna is considered to have been an incarnation or descent (avatar) of the high god Vishnu. However, although he is Vishnu in human form, something of the impersonal and numinous otherness of the Brahman remains in the background.[223]

3. Basic Differences Between Hinduism and Christianity

(1) The difference between Brahman and the Biblical God. The Hindu conception of God maintains that an impersonal Brahman is always beyond any personal manifestation in an avatar. This is a major emphasis, even though according to certain branches of Hindu philosophy, Brahman can appear in personal form and may be said to have personal qualities. Personhood is finally only a part of the semi-illusory world of appearance.[224] This, of course, is in contrast to the biblical God, who is personal even though he is ultimate.

(2) The Difference between the Hindu World of Illusion and the Biblical View of Creation. Because the visible order is thought to belong to the realm of shadow and appearance, it is impossible in Hindu thought for the visible world to have any final value. Experience is finally illusory and usually serves to distract humans from the true nature of reality.

In contrast, the Bible insists that God is the source and end of all that is, and that his presence pervades creation, upholds it, and causes it to reflect his character. Rather than giving the world a shadowy or ephemeral character, God's presence gives creation substance and value.[225]

(3) The Difference between the Hindu Doctrine of Karma and the Biblical View of the Incarnation. Because the world has no intrinsic value in Hindu thought, the law of karma finally reaches a dead end; it cannot be creative. Since people are punished in a future life *by* their sins, they cannot be punished *for* them. Redemption, forgiveness, and genuine release are not possible since the law of cause and effect is irreversible.

This is in contrast to the Christian doctrine of incarnation. Christ claimed to be much more than an appearance or a revelation of God. He did not come to show us something about God. He came as God incarnate to do something about this fallen created order. God is personal and loving, and the world is good and ordered (though fallen). Therefore, God could intervene and change the created order and his relation to it. Newness and forgiveness have become permanent characteristics of this world and potentially the experience of every creature in it.[226]

(4) The Difference between Hindu Liberation and Christian Salvation. The Christian view of salvation has nothing in common with the Hindu view of release or liberation. Christianity involves personal communion with a loving God. Hinduism teaches timeless superpersonal union that is achieved through knowledge and eventually, in its ultimate form, by the end of personal existence. But Christianity claims that knowledge of the good is not enough for salvation, that one must be taken in hand by the transcendent personal God and transformed into his likeness. In the Christian view, nothing less than this is salvation. And for the Christian, salvation means a heightened, more meaningful personal existence, not the end of personal existence.

The contrast between Hindu and Christian views of human involvement in the world is likewise striking. Hinduism calls for intense mental concentration in an attempt to harness all human powers in the spiritual quest. Ideally, the latter part of a person's life is spent largely in meditation. In contrast, the biblical emphasis is on expression of spiritual illumination in a life of activity directed toward fulfilling God's purposes in history.[227]

4. Special Considerations for Christians in Approaching Hindus

(1) Understanding the Hindu View of Tolerance. There is a long Hindu tradition of absorption of other religions, of nondistinction between faiths, and of revering reverence per se—that is, of tolerating everything but intolerance. This leads to the fact that Hinduism is willing to embrace all other religious doctrines. However, this acceptance does not mean Hinduism is prepared to give up its fundamental doctrines. Rather, the Hindu seeks to embrace all other doctrines in order ultimately to modify them in accord with Hindu views.[228]

Hinduism can be sharply exclusive about its nonexclusivity. It is the Hindu instinct both to welcome Jesus and to detach him from the Christian context of his biblical meaning.[229] Thus, in approaching a Hindu with the claims of the Christian faith, it is important not to mistake this inclusive acceptance for true conversion.

(2) Emphasizing and Clarifying the Historical Nature of Christ and Christianity. An important distinction that should be made for the Hindu is the historical nature of the Christian faith. This is apt to be a foreign concept for the Hindu; as shown in chapter 2, the Hindu religion and culture have a limited sense of history and historical importance. Therefore, to make the distinction between Hinduism and Christianity clear to the Hindu, the Christian must stress

the crucial historical fact of Jesus the Christ and the validity of the knowledge of God (Ultimate Reality) found in him.

Hinduism is an eclectic, universalistic religion of experience. That is another reason for stressing the historical facts of Christianity. If a Christian's appeal to experience is made merely on the basis of an inner sense or inner experience, the Hindu will also claim validity and authority for his or her inner experience, whatever it may be.[230]

Christians must not leave history behind and emphasize mystical experience apart from the historical Christ. Untethered to the historical event of Christ, such an emphasis might be likened to a New Testament preaching detached from what happened as events and reoriented instead toward personal feelings and experience. All sincere experience could, in that sense, be claimed as Christian, if it chose to use the name.

That way, of course, is the emphasis of Gnosticism against which the New Testament and the apostolic church set themselves so firmly. The early Christians insisted that Jesus was "come in the flesh" and that he was "crucified, dead, and buried." Their theology affirmed the historical actuality of the living Jesus—born, serving, resolving, dying, and alive forevermore.[231] An authentic and effective approach to Hinduism—or to anyone—must also stress that historical actuality.

(3) The Approach of Emphasizing Quality of Life. Finally, the Christian appeal is to an experience rooted in the biblical witness to Jesus Christ. This experience can be observed in a new style and ethical quality of life which is created by Jesus Christ in each person and in the community of believers.

Edmund Perry states that Christians must demonstrate the insufficiency of the Hindu mentality by manifesting the adequacy of the Christian understanding of God and the world. This calls for Christians, both Indians and others, who can incarnate the gospel and at the same time show that the Hindu worldview must die if Christ is to be accepted and salvation and fulfillment—both in this world and the next—is to be realized.[232]

XI. What Is the Biblical Approach to Buddhism?

1. The Importance of Buddhism in History and in the World Today

(1) The Size and Extent of Buddhism. Buddhism is one of the most universal of the world's religions. Today there are over three hundred million who profess to be Buddhists of one tradition or another. In Sri Lanka, Burma, Thailand, Cambodia, and Laos, the population is almost exclusively made up of Buddhists who follow the oldest (Hinayana, Southern, or Theravada) tradition. The entire population of Tibet and Mongolia is, for all practical purposes, exclusively Buddhist of a form peculiar to that region alone, though continuous with other forms. In China, Vietnam, Korea, and Japan, Buddhism of the Mahayana tradition claims a high percentage of the populations. (It should be noted, however, that in these countries many Buddhists give allegiance to other faiths also, thus making an accurate differentiation impossible.)[233]

Scarcely a country in the world is any longer without some significant, though often numerically small, Buddhist representation. But in the countries mentioned, Buddhism has influenced the total culture. It has largely dominated the literature, art, ethics, and philosophy, as well as the social, political, and "religious" institutions.

It should be noted that in recent decades Buddhism has been undergoing a dramatic revival, reaching out in missionary activity as it has not done in many centuries. Of particular import for Americans is the fact that Buddhism is the dominant religion of the fiftieth state, Hawaii. This is the first time that any religion outside of the Judeo-Christian tradition has predominated in any state of the Union.[234]

(2) The Appeal and Importance of Buddhism. The appeal of Buddhism in the Far East is probably related to the fact that it addresses itself to a very real and universal human problem—the problem of pain or suffering. It provides a kind of peace and calm to distressed minds and hearts. The suffering and anguish of the millions of Asia is almost beyond comprehension for people who have lived all their life in Europe or America. The strength of Buddhism is in its promise of relief from endless misery.[235]

In the West, Buddhism (especially the Theravada variety) has both influenced and appealed to those interested in the scientific method and in psychoanalysis. Many in the West see Buddhism as the most modern and up-to-date of the religions. In a true sense, they say, it is the only religion compatible with current existentialist philosophy.[236]

In ways similar to Buddhism, existentialists are concerned with the human being in crisis. This crisis may involve human pride, the inability to come to terms with human finitude, as described by Nietzsche. It may be the futility, boredom, and vacuity of sensual living, as addressed by Sartre, or the complacent hypocrisies of religion, as pointed out by Kierkegaard. In a different idiom, it may be the social estrangements of an exploitative economic order, as portrayed by Marx. Or, as Camus vividly depicted, it may be an oppressive sense of absurdity which demands that human beings defiantly affirm their own will.[237]

Herbert C. Jackson, professor of religion at Michigan State University, contends that Buddhist psychology is the most detailed and profound ever developed. Modern depth psychology is heavily indebted to Buddhist psychology, although Western experimental psychology thus far has not begun to penetrate to the depths found in Buddhist insights.[238]

All of this means that Buddhism is both important and influential in the world today. Perhaps this explains why Buddhists are now engaged in their own "foreign missions" program. The two major divisions of Buddhism, Theravada and Mahayana, united into the World Fellowship of Buddhists in 1950. The Buddhists of Sri Lanka have developed a Missionary Training College where Buddhist monks spend five years in training for missionary work among the English-speaking and Hindu-oriented peoples of the world. In Sri Lanka, funds are publicly solicited for the spread of Buddhism among "the heathen of

Europe." And the Shin sect of Japan alone already maintains one hundred thirty missionaries on the American continent.[239]

2. The Historical Roots of Buddhism

(1) The Early Life of Gautama. The life of the founder of Buddhism before his enlightenment is surrounded by a multitude of legends, some of them quite fanciful. But a few pivotal facts seem fairly well established. The traditional date for the birth of Siddhartha Gautama, now accepted by most scholars, is 563 B.C. The place of his birth was a village in southern Nepal. He was the son of a petty rajah (chieftain). At sixteen, he was married to the most beautiful girl available and surrounded by all the luxury and sensuous pleasures which wealth and position could provide. This was an apparent effort to forestall the religious leanings Gautama had displayed from boyhood.[240]

In the twenty-ninth year of his life, shortly after the birth of his son, Siddhartha reached a crisis point in his life. According to tradition, he became aware of the tragedy of the human condition when he saw, for the first time in his life, the four signs of man's lot in this world: a sick person, a frail old man, a corpse, and a recluse. From these Gautama realized that suffering, disease, decay, death, and separation from true social fellowship are inherent in every life.

At this point, Gautama despaired so utterly about the meaninglessness of his life among royalty that he renounced it. He declared that family and friends, riches, power, and honor are meaningful only if one has within himself or herself something that gives meaning to them.[241] And so, having fulfilled his first duty to his family and to his kingdom by begetting a male heir to preserve the family name, Gautama left his luxurious surroundings and lived the life of a wandering seeker for some six years.

He first tried the philosophic intellectualism of the Hindu metaphysic. Next, he adopted the life of an ascetic and practiced extreme self-mortification until he became a mere skeleton. But in neither way of life did he find the answers he was seeking.[242]

(2) The Enlightenment of Gautama. Finally, Gautama admitted to himself that he was a defeated man. In this moment, he later claimed, there came to him an illumination concerning both the cause and the cure of the misery of existence. This illumination was what later caused him to be called the Buddha, "the Enlightened One."[243]

After his enlightenment, Gautama had the "great temptation" simply to remain in his state of nirvana, or deliverance, until death, after which he would never be reborn again. After some struggle, however, he made a missionary decision. He would not retain his insights merely for his own salvation. Rather, he would devote himself to teaching others so that they, too, might find deliverance from human suffering. It is this decision which has made Buddhism basically missionary in character.

Seven weeks of reflection and preparation followed. (This period of preparation reminds us of the apostle Paul going into Arabia after his experience on the Damascus Road.) Then Gautama made his way to Sarnath, near Benares, the sacred city of the Hindus. There he preached his first sermon and began a career of preaching and of gathering and teaching disciples that was to last until his death in 483 B.C.[244]

3. The Basic Concepts of Buddhism in Its Original or Hinayana Form

The Buddha stated his message in the framework of Indian thought, although this framework is not to be understood as definitive of the content of his message. Furthermore, the Indian framework is not the only one within which the teaching can be understood. Its translation into Chinese, Korean, and Japanese, and more recently into the Western languages, shows its universality. But general truths are always developed in the particular, so the Buddha originally framed his preaching for the Indian context. In so doing, he denounced Hindu asceticism, mysticism, and speculative philosophy.[245]

Gautama's teachings, recorded in the Buddhist scriptures, are known collectively as the Doctrine of the Middle Path. This designation implies a middle course between extreme mental development and extreme physical denial. Essentially, the Doctrine of the Middle Path consists of the Three Basic Principles, the Four Noble Truths, and the Eightfold Noble Path. It is the heart of Buddhism in its original form, known variously as Hinayana Buddhism, Southern Buddhism, or Theravada.[246]

(1) The Three Basic Principles. Buddha's teaching begins by defining the Three Basic Principles, the three basic characteristics of all existence. The *first principle* is that nothing is permanent, including human personality. Everything is in a perpetual or eternal state of constant change. The world has only relative, or semi-illusory, or seeming existence. Separate, individual existence of personality, therefore, is an illusion.

The *second principle* is that sorrow is implicit in all seeming individuality. The source of sorrow is considered to be the innate quality of clinging to the illusion of individual existence and to the sensory experiences associated with existence. Human beings cannot gain what they want, and they cannot escape what they dislike. This condition produces inner frustration and external conflict with others, and these in turn produce misery.

The *third principle,* the doctrine of "no soul," is the focal concept of Buddhism. Briefly stated, this doctrine maintains that there is no such entity as the personality or soul. Although humans cling to the illusion of individual and eternal existence, they are actually made up of five aggregates, or skandas, of which one is material and four are mental. These five aggregates—physical body, sensations, perception (abstract ideas), consciousness, and thought—are held together by an intangible "thread of life" which is never quite identified in Buddhism. In the experience called death, the five aggregates separate one from the other. They never come together again in the same combination, although each individual skanda will unite with four other skandas to constitute a new human life. Thus

Buddhism rejects all ideas of a unique entity that might be designated a soul dwelling in a body.

Buddhism, therefore, also rejects the concept of reincarnation that is so fundamental to Hinduism and many other religions. In Buddhism there is rebirth of skandas in ever-differing combinations, but no migration of a soul-entity from one body to another. On the basis of this doctrine of no-soul, in Buddhism the final salvation comes at the point when none of the component skandas ever again unites with others to constitute a new life.[247]

Thus Hinayana Buddhists do not speak of nirvana or salvation as a place to which a "person" or self goes. Nirvana is an event, something that happens to the psycho-physical process so that its cause-effect chain reaction is terminated. It is sufficient for the Buddhist to say that nirvana is perfect rest. This means that there is a final cessation of formation and reformation.

Buddhists claim that in their denial of the existence of a self they provide the only rational basis of compassion or fellow-feeling. The Buddhist claims not only to know that other humans suffer, but also to know why they suffer. Because Buddhists know that in their service to fellow-sufferers they are not storing up merit in heaven nor winning approval of a god, they can wish and work for the well-being of others and do this with disinterested good will. Buddhist compassion seeks nothing in return.[248]

(2) The Four Noble Truths. Buddhism also teaches Four Noble Truths. The *first truth* is that suffering is inevitable. All existence involves conflict, both within oneself and between oneself and others. This conflict leads inescapably to suffering of all kinds, including mental anguish and physical injury.

The *second truth* is that the origin of suffering is desire and craving—especially the desire for separate, individual, everlasting existence.

The *third truth* affirms that the extinction of suffering is achieved through the elimination of all desire.

The *fourth truth* describes the way to the destruction of all desire, namely, the Eightfold Noble Path.

(3) The Eightfold Noble Path. The Eightfold Noble Path, often simply called the Eightfold Path, falls into three categories. The first two paths that will lead to enlightenment and nirvana (salvation) are in the nature of higher wisdom, which involves right understanding and right thoughts. The next three paths are the ethical disciplines of right speech, action, and livelihood. The last three paths include the mental disciplines of right effort, meditation, and concentration.

According to Buddhism, this Eightfold Path, diligently and persistently pursued, will break the fetters that bind human beings to life, and hence to suffering. When these fetters are all broken, a person will achieve nirvana.[249]

(4) Nirvana. The Buddhist concept of Nirvana is not to be equated with heaven. Gautama insisted that even raising the question of what nirvana is like indicates that the desire for continued existence is still present. This desire is the unforgivable sin of Hinayana Buddhism. Buddhist writings would describe nirvana as a shattering state of neither existence nor nonexistence. This seeming

paradox is possible, in Buddhist thought, because the component parts or skandas still exist, but the original combination of skandas which constituted the distinct person is broken. This means that the individual does not have an ongoing conscious existence as the person he or she was before the nirvana experience.

According to most modern Buddhist groups, this state of nirvana can be reached in one's earthly existence. Parinirvana is a higher state and can be reached only after one dies. For the Buddhist, this is the ultimate or the eternal end.

It must be remembered that Gautama preached his concept of nirvana in a culture dominated by the Indian outlook of almost endless rebirths. He introduced a method which would break this chain of continuing eternal conscious existence as an entity, a soul, or personality. To the Buddhist the "end of becoming" is the most important and glorious goal possible. Nirvana is the breaking of the endless round of rebirths into conscious existence.[250]

(5) The Development of the Sangha of Monks. The attainment of these high Buddhist ideas by such a path would be possible only to people of keen intellect and strong powers of self-discipline. Such people must be able to separate themselves from ordinary life and devote themselves utterly to the effort. In other words, only capable people free to become monks could undertake this method of salvation.

Because of the conditions necessary for a serious pursuit of the Buddhist path to deliverance, a community of monks arose almost immediately. It was known as the Sangha, or congregation. Although a Buddhist monk is often called a priest by Westerners, the Sangha of monks is not a priestly group. Buddhism has no priesthood, no community standing between God and humans. Instead, the Sangha is a "community of seekers and strivers."[251]

In view of the difficult nature of Buddhism, the question will surely arise as to what Buddhism offers to the average person. The original form of Buddhism, known as Hinayana or Theravada, answers the question by saying frankly that the multitude in society have no chance of deliverance in a given lifetime. (The name *Hinayana,* in fact, literally means "little vehicle," or "few they be who are saved.") However, ordinary people may at least serve the Sangha of monks by providing food, clothing, and other necessities, and by venerating the monks and their preaching. By so doing, they may hope in a future birth to have the abilities and qualifications for becoming monks and thus seeking deliverance. However, even being a monk and diligently applying oneself to the rules and disciplines is itself no guarantee that deliverance will be attained.[252]

(6) The Canon of Holy Books. Hinayana has a definite canon, written down in Ceylon, in the Pali language, about 25 B.C. This canon is central and authoritative. Even though it is not conceived as a revelation, it is viewed and used in much the same way as conservative Christians use the Bible.

Hinayana Buddhism calls the canon the Tipitaka, or "Three Baskets." It consists of three parts. The "Teaching Basket" contains the alleged teachings, sermons, and dialogues of Gautama. The other two "baskets" contain rules for monks and psychological principles.[253]

(7) A Variation of Hinayana: Zen. Zen appeared in China in the sixth century and has exercised widespread influence from the thirteenth century. It teaches concentrated contemplation, by which adherents hope to attain satori, or enlightenment. Zen Buddhists give little place to logic, words, or letters; they stress "immediacy." They differ from teachers of the Hinayana form of Buddhism, to which they are much closer than to other varieties, "in positing an enlightenment or intuitive grasp of truth not only at the end of the Path, but here and now, as they persevere in the Path itself."

For a number of years, I have been taking study groups to Japan. For many women, a primary motivation for such trips is the opportunity to further their interest in flower arranging, tea ceremonies, and gardens. Few of these Americans realize that such famous cultural contributions are primarily an attempt to promote Zen satori or enlightenment.

Zen monks, in one medium after another, strive to create beauty by pruning away. They seek to allow a single simple core of exquisite naturalness and beauty to stand alone, free of entanglements. They claim that meditation on such an artistic creation should lead toward enlightenment.[254]

4. Modifications of Buddhism in Its Northern or Mahayana Form

The second major form of Buddhism is known as Mahayana (meaning large or great vehicle, or "wide is the gate and all may pass through it"). Mahayana candidly declares that few if any can pursue the way of Hinayana and full-time application as a monk. Therefore, it modifies Buddhism so as to open it to all persons. For the most part, Mahayana has developed where Buddhism has gone to an already highly developed civilization. It is the principal form of Buddhism in China, Korea, and Japan.[255]

(1) Basic Features of Mahayana Buddhism. Mahayana is almost infinite in variety. In each country where it is found, it has taken on a great many features from the religious, cultural, and ethnic characteristics of that society. Nonetheless, there are certain basic features of Mahayana which distinguish it from Hinayana Buddhism.

First, Mahayana has no canonical scripture. In its place, it features a classic religious document, the *Lotus Sutra,* or Lotus of the Good Law. This writing propounds all the major doctrines of Mahayana in fairly simple form.[256]

Second, Mahayana places heavy emphasis on Bodhisattvas, literally meaning "wisdom beings." (The historical Gautama Buddha, although respected, is relatively deemphasized.) Bodhisattvas are skilled, compassionate beings who are on their way to final enlightenment, but who delay for the purpose of helping others until all are enlightened. A Bodhisattva can come down in an apparition or ghost-like body to help the unenlightened in the form of a monk, abbot, orphan, beggar, prostitute, or rich man. Bodhisattvas cannot change karma or the law of judgment at a single stroke, but they can help a person make new resolutions and eliminate desire by their wise teaching and helpful experiences.[257]

Third, Mahayana is marked by an particular ornateness of religious symbols and buildings. Even though Buddhism ideally does not sanction the use of images, temples with images of the Buddha and often a series of pictures depicting events in Buddha's life abound everywhere, even in Hinayana Buddhism.[258]

Finally, Mahayana, being a religion for the masses, has much lower spiritual and moral standards than Theravada.

With its dimension of grace and its innumerable compassionate Bodhisattvas, the Mahayana stream of Buddhism softens the rigors of the founding tradition. It allays the severe loneliness of the individual path of the Hinayana version of the "Way." The goal of nirvana becomes more gently accessible, thanks to the concessions made to symbol and imagination and the means of grace which it approves and dispenses in rite and festival, in poem and legend, and in divine help from the Bodhisattvas.[259]

(2) Different Forms of Mahayana Buddhism. Mahayana Buddhism has developed in several different forms. In Tibet, it has fused with the Bon religion (a mixture of primitive Tibetan religion with Taoism) to form Lamaism. Among several distinctive features of this Tibetan variation is the way in which salvation is sometimes sought by the endless turning of a prayer wheel.

Another form of Buddhism developed in Tibet is Tantric Buddhism. It uses sacred and powerful words, gestures, and disciplined meditation. One of its guide books is the *Tibetan Book of the Dead,* which has had some influence on the "life after life" movement in the United States.

In China and Japan, Mahayana has frequently taken the form of Pure Land Buddhism. This version looks back to a Bodhisattva named Amitabha, or Amida Buddha, who long ago accumulated such a vast store of merit during his progress toward salvation (Buddhahood, or bliss) that he vowed to bestow on all who trusted in him an assured rebirth in his paradise far away in the western quarter of the universe. The only requirements were perfect faith and sincerity and the simple device of constantly repeating, "Hail Amida-Buddha."[260]

Japanese Mahayana Buddhism came from China by way of Korea five centuries after Christ. One popular form of Mahayana Buddhism in Japan involves a Bodhisattva whose features are to be seen all over Japan. This god, the compassionate Kannon, has a female form and is said to be modeled on an eighth-century empress of China.[261]

Another popular form of Buddhism in Japan is the Buddhist New Consciousness group, called Soka Gakkai in Japan and Nichiren Shoshu in America. In the thirteenth century, a zealous Japanese leader named Nichiren taught that all forms of Buddha-expression are unified in the *Lotus Sutra.* Nichiren taught that in chanting the essence of this sutra or teaching, a person can find practical and spiritual help here and now in a simple and almost immediate way. The teaching of Nichiren is the basis for the most spectacular religious movement in the twentieth century. From a few thousand in 1945, it has grown to twenty million claimed adherents worldwide.

The central emphasis of Nichiren Shoshu is on happiness. All three Buddha bodies or forms of expression—absolute essence, the mental world, and the material world—are seen as one, and a cause implanted in one of these worlds is thought to affect the others. For example, spiritual impulses produce material goods. The material benefits which derive from chanting are said by Nichiren Shoshu followers to be a practical proof that this unique spiritual-mental-material religion really works. (From the perspective of biblical religion, of course, Nichiren Shoshu falls far short. Christianity never equates the will of God for human life with immediate material satisfaction. In Nichiren Shoshu one does not find a transcendent and holy god who calls for repentance and change to conform to a prophetic way of life, such as that incarnated in Jesus Christ.)[262]

In the last century, Mahayana Buddhism has traveled to the United States from Japan and is by far the most popular form here. The major forms of Buddhism imported from Japan in the United States are Pure Land, Zen (a Hinayana form, as explained above), and Soka Gakkai.

5. Special Considerations for Christians in Approaching Buddhists

How can biblical Christianity reach out to a religion which is so varied in character and so extensively spread throughout the world? It should be remembered that it is intertwined with several civilizations and is a religion that has produced some of the most creative cultures in human history.

(1) Emphasis on the Christian Doctrine of the Person As an Eternal Personal Entity. Buddhism, from Gautama's day to the present, has had great difficulty getting people to accept as desirable the doctrine of no-soul. In fact, as we have noted, Mahayana Buddhism has had to modify this doctrine. An effective approach to sharing a biblical faith with a Buddhist is to emphasize the innate human longing for everlasting existence as an individual and to show how the Christian faith answers this longing.[263]

It is helpful to emphasize that Christians not only claim that God exists and once made a personal visit in human flesh; they also claim that Jesus was resurrected and forever remains in his risen form. The Christian faith further teaches that the Christian as well as Jesus maintains in resurrection life an identity that is continuous with mortal life, and that an individual's eternal existence can be good and desirable—in a suffering-free fellowship with God and other human beings.[264]

Buddhism's fundamental opposition to Christian faith is her rejection of the Christian proclamation that God raised Jesus. The Buddhist disputes the resurrection of Jesus because he believes there is no helper for humanity except humanity itself. The Buddhist, being fundamentally humanistic, believes that human beings cannot sustain their own personal identity. Yet because he is humanistic, the Buddhist believes that humans can liberate themselves from a state of dependence. Ultimately it is the Buddhist's sense of human sufficiency which must die in order for him or her to embrace the Christian faith.[265]

(2) Stress on God's Personal Existence and His Love for Humankind. Hinayana Buddhism is atheistic; it holds that there is no force, much less any intelligence or being, outside of humanity which can help humans in any way.

Here again, Buddhism is going against an intuition inherent in human nature. People sense that there is a spiritual world that lies beyond the visible, material world, and they also sense a need to depend on spiritual beings, or gods, or God, outside themselves. These natural human inclinations stand in favor of the Christian view of a personal God of love and power.[266]

(3) Introducing a God of Morality and Grace. An effective guide to Christianity for the Buddhist must be an introduction to a God who makes unequivocal moral demands but forgives and empowers human beings to live by those demands.

Despite the very high and noble ethic of the Eightfold Path and of other Buddhist teachings, there is nothing comparable to the biblical doctrine of sin and therefore no real sense of moral or immoral behavior. In Buddhism, all desire is considered evil, whether the desire is for something bad or sinful or for something good and noble and righteous. It is the desire itself, not the object of the desire, which is the block to salvation in Buddhism. Moreover, since in Buddhist teaching there is no such thing as personality, there can be no building of noble character. What seems to us to be noble, character-building ideals in Buddhism are to the Buddhist only the practical means to the end of deliverance from life and from rebirth.

Herbert C. Jackson maintains, therefore, that it is an essential part of the Christian mission to the Buddhist to emphasize three facts: (1) the value of good character itself, (2) the consequences of immorality, and (3) sin as separation from God.[267]

The Christian faith relates most vitally to the Buddhist in regard to the Buddhist concept of the wrongness of desire. Being innocent of desire, or guilty and frustrated in desire, is no part of the Christian case. The Christian does crucify selfishness and greed at the cross, but he or she rises from the resurrection experience with Christ as a new person with an ardent desire to be Christ's servant and fulfill his or her purpose in God's kingdom work. Grace enables the Christian to oust false desire so that he or she can develop right desire.[268]

(4) Establishing an Authentic Answer to the Buddhist Concern for Peace. Christianity must demonstrate its ability to produce integration and stability of personality and amicable and just relations among social groups. In particular, it must also seek a better position with reference to the annihilating character of warfare today. This is an important emphasis because of the Buddhists' longstanding interest in peace.

Christians who want to relate effectively to Buddhists cannot withdraw into a defensive shell and simply say, "The church cannot help what the government does, since we believe in the separation of church and state." Christianity must integrate with every area of life. Evidence must be given of its ability to create a society beneficial to mankind. This is important to a serious confrontation with Buddhism, perhaps more than with any other religion.[269]

Edmund Perry points out that the record of Christians in relation to Buddhist countries betrays the Christian's claim to be concerned for peace. This misrepresentation of Christ in the minds of Buddhists must die. Christians must demonstrate our concern for peace. Our mission to Buddhists must include evidence of our genuine repentance for betraying the Prince of Peace among the peace-making Buddhists.[270]

XII. What Is the Biblical Approach to the Native Religions of China?

1. The Importance of Studying Native Chinese Religions

Chinese civilization stands equal in significance and originality to the other great Asian civilization, the Indian. It should be noted, however, that in its early phase China differs deeply from India in its worldly, "secular" bent. Later China, through Buddhism, was deeply influenced and molded by Indian thought and religion. The civilization that is China's original creation, however, is also one of the truly remarkable expressions of the human mind.[271]

China is the birthplace of two of the world's religions, Confucianism and Taoism. Confucianism is more influential as an ethical system than as a religious cult. Taoism has tended, on the one hand, to become a philosophy or, on the other hand, to revert to magic and primitive religion.[272]

These two religions express a deep respect for nature that often tends toward nature worship, an ethical concern, and social emphasis. Despite the twentieth-century dominance of communism in the Chinese mainland, Hendrik Kraemer contends it is by no means certain that the communist drive for adherence to the infallible truth of Marxism has great chances of eradicating the grand cosmic, moral, and political Chinese conception of nature, humanity, and history.[273]

We must remember, of course, that Chinese religious practices continue in many places other than the Chinese mainland. The population of Taiwan, except for some mountain tribes, is almost entirely Chinese in origin, either from recent or older immigration. The people of Hong Kong and Macao, likewise, are predominantly Chinese. Hong Kong's population has been greatly swollen by a stream of refugees from Communist China.

In addition, there are Chinese minorities in the countries of Southeast Asia, such as Malaysia, Thailand, Indonesia, and the Philippines, as well as in Western countries such as the United States. In these expatriate communities of Chinese one can find the religion of pre-Communist China continuing—often, unfortunately with much of its superstitions.[274]

2. The Origin and Basic Concepts of Taoism

According to tradition, the founder of Taoism was Lao-Tzu, born about 604 B.C. in Central China. He wrote down his convictions in a book called the *Tao Te Ching*, or Classic of the Way and Virtue, which lays the foundations of philosophical Taoism.[275]

A basic teaching of Taoism concerns the Tao, or the Way, which is the ultimate cosmic principle. However, even to call it Tao is somehow to do it violence, for it is strictly ineffable, though in mystical ecstasy one can come into relation with it. Within the universe, the dialectical forces of Yin and Yang (male and female, day and night, summer and winter) are continually at work, and the Tao maintains them in unity and harmony. The ideal for human beings is the quietest approach of conforming to the rhythm of the universe.[276]

The Taoist teachers claimed that through the Tao one could overcome the destructive powers of nature. The Tao manifests itself in a process of antithetic but complementary rhythms, such as Yang and Yin, macrocosm and microcosm, which correspond with and counterbalance each other. To preserve the harmony of this primeval rhythm is the meaning of the natural and the human world. Humanity and the cosmos are one undivided unity of life. Therefore, the first commandment of all Chinese ethics is to live in harmony with Tao.

Imperial sanction was given to Taoism as a religion in the seventh century A.D. Gradually deities developed, with a Taoist Trinity of which Lao-Tzu was one. Monasteries and temples, priests and bishops, and heaven and hell were added to the basic concept of the Way.[277]

In the mid-1970s, American scientist and New Age leader Fritjof Capra entitled one of his books, *The Tao of Physics.* He contends that modern science supports the unity of all things, the nonexistence of an independent external world, and the unity of opposites.[278]

3. The Origin and Basic Concepts of Confucianism

Confucius, who was born about 551 B.C. is considered to be the greatest teacher of China. Through the centuries he profoundly affected not only Chinese culture, but also the culture of most of East Asia.[279]

(1) The Sacred Books of Confucianism. Our main sources for the teachings of Confucius are the Five Classics and the Four Books. The former writings are partly by Confucius himself and perhaps partly from before his time. The Four Books contain teachings and sayings of Confucius recorded by his disciples, though they also contain a good deal of material from after Confucius' time.

(2) The Ethical Emphasis of Confucianism. Though Confucius was apparently an agnostic, there is evidence that he had faith in the moral nature of the universe. This faith gave Confucius poise and confidence; he felt that heaven was back of him. Confucius' ethics were based upon this essentially religious attitude, coupled with a conviction that humanity is basically good. The basic idea is that what people need to function ethically is a proper environment and, especially, right example. Therefore, in applying ethics to politics, the relation of ruler to subject is exalted. The moral example of a virtuous ruler is of utmost importance.

But Confucius taught that there are other cardinal relationships: the relation of father and son, of elder and younger brothers, of husband and wife, and of friend and friend (or elder and junior). In each case, there is the relationship of superior and inferior which is fundamental to feudal society. But the moral responsibility and good example of the superior is fully as important as the obedience of the inferior. At the very heart of the Confucian system is filial loyalty and piety, which has contributed to the great strength of the family in China.

There are several key ideas expressing the Confucian ethic. Among these are propriety, humaneness, and reciprocity. The practical rule of reciprocity underlies human behavior. This law is to maintain balance and harmony in human relations. It means the "Golden Rule" of doing unto others as one would wish done to himself.[280]

(3) The Rational Emphasis of Confucianism. In Confucianism, the rational and the humanistic prevail. Indeed, Confucianism looks very much like "religion within the limits of reason alone." It was for this reason that all things Chinese were admired in eighteenth-century Europe, which also placed great emphasis on reason and humanism. Confucianism does recognize a God, but like the God of deism, he keeps discreetly in the background. In Confucian, anything savoring of mystery or of the numinous is avoided.[281]

(4) Influence and Development of Confucianism. Like Taoism, Confucianism inspired philosophical development, especially in the realms of the study of humankind, ethics, and political theory. Confucianism was also a religion. The emperors honored Confucius and erected Confucian temples in the various provinces of China. In these temples, offerings were made to the spirit of Confucius. Ceremonies were observed, and these became more and more elaborate over time.[282]

In China it has usually been considered permissible to profess more than one religion at a time. Thus the ideal would be to combine the reasonableness and humanity of the Confucian tradition with something of the depth and spirituality that have come from Taoism.[283]

4. The Influence of the Christian Faith on China and Its Native Religions

(1) Influence on the Taiping Rebellion. This rebellion, which took place in southern China from 1849–1865, was a colossal endeavor to overthrow the reigning Manchu Dynasty. Although eventually suppressed, it was an extraordinarily important event from a political and religious point of view because of its openness to Western spiritual influences. It built its program on a combination of Chinese and Christian regulative ideas.

The whole movement had its origin in a vision given to its founder, Hung Hsiu-chi'uan, which led him to study Christianity, seek contact with some missionaries, and ask for baptism. The content of his vision was that he was called by God to overthrow the Manchu Dynasty which, according to the Chinese way of thinking, had forfeited the Mandate of Heaven and had to be replaced. Hung Hsiu-Chi'uan believed he was called to establish a new state, called the Great Peace Heavenly State.

In its beginnings, the Taiping Rebellion was amazingly successful. It eventually suffered defeat through the military cooperation of the European powers with the tottering Manchu Dynasty. With few exceptions, the missionaries found the Taiping people wanting when measuring this imperfect but highly interesting Chinese version of Christianity with their Western Christian yardsticks. Nevertheless,

Hendrik Kraemer contends that this rebellion held great possibilities—cultural as well as religious. It could have meant a wholesome encounter of China with Western Christian concepts.

As a matter of fact, the Taiping Rebellion did result in increased contact with the West. It forced upon the leading officials and generals of the Manchu regime the necessity to study the Western craft of shipbuilding and manufacturing arms. This caused a going abroad of Chinese to Europe and America for purposes of study, first of a technical and military kind, but increasingly also of other kinds of Western knowledge.[284]

(2) Indirect Influence on the Twentieth-Century Chinese Revolution. Sun Yat Sen, who in 1911 succeeded where the Taiping Rebellion had failed in overthrowing the Manchu dynasty, briefly became the first president of the Chinese republic and was an important Chinese leader well into World War II. He contended that the only road to radical reform was through a transformation by political and social revolution. Educated in Christian schools and baptized a Christian, he had lived for a considerable length of time in Western countries and was heavily influenced by Western democratic ideas.[285]

(3) Influence of Missions. Christian missions was one of the significant agencies in making Western civilization with its spirit and achievements accessible to the Chinese. Unfortunately, the inevitable function of mediating Western culture as well as presenting the claims of the gospel increased the ambiguous position of missions in countries such as China. This ambiguity was created by the fact that the cultural services and religious purpose of the missionaries could never be separated from Western economics and political considerations.[286]

(4) Christianity and the Historical Roots of Communism. Finally, and paradoxically, the Christian faith influenced China through communism, which began its influence in the early twentieth century and finally took over the government of the Chinese mainland in 1949. Marxism and developed communist practice are violent and heretical embodiments of the Judeo-Christian tradition as well as Western idealism.[287]

5. Special Considerations for Christians in Approaching Followers of Chinese Native Religions

(1) Pointing Out the Flaws in Confucius' Understanding of Human Nature. It is generally accepted that Confucius had no understanding of the real sinfulness and corruption of the human heart. He held that mankind is good at heart, and that people only need wise instruction and proper relationships to make them what they ought to be. Set in a social context, this means that each social class will be good and virtuous if the class above it sets a good and virtuous example.[288]

Ethics are a form of human wisdom, never the expression of a personal divine will which is the measure and judge of all life and action. The whole spirit of Chinese civilization is that of humanism. In this idealism of harmony there is no real contrast between good and evil. Everything or every condition that breathes harmony is good. According to the Chinese idea of the natural order of the universe and the moral order of human life, there is no place for sin.[289]

(2) Pointing Out Inadequacies Concerning Salvation, the Life Hereafter, and a Personal God. Holding that the human problem is basically intellectual rather than moral, Confucius sought to make people virtuous by enlightenment. But he gave no answer to the basic questions of why people should want to be virtuous or what makes a person virtuous.

Remember, Confucius had no real faith in God. He recommended observing customary religious ritual without committing himself as to the real existence of gods or spirits. When asked about death, he replied that as we do not yet understand life, how can we know about death?[290]

The much-debated Chinese aversion to a personal conception of God has its deep roots in naturalistic monism. The conception of the divine as something wholly independent of nature or humanity is contrary to the Chinese view because, for the Chinese, nature and humanity are aspects of the totality of existence. The Chinese mind has therefore had difficulty with the idea of a transcendent God-Creator, who again and again takes the initiative and acts in history.[291]

XIII. What Is the Biblical Approach to the Native Religion of Japan?

1. The Importance of Studying Shinto

Culturally and religiously, Japan has been thoroughly influenced and molded by India and China as her fertile cultural "mothers." However, she shows her originality in two ways. First, she digested the rich Indian and Chinese nutrition in a peculiar or unique way. Second, Japan developed her own native religion, Shinto.[292]

Study of the Japanese people in their genesis and development leads to the unavoidable conclusion that they are a people with a highly distinctive character. The Japanese people with their unique capacity for single-mindedness (for good or for evil) occupy an important place in the world. The label "imitative" that is sometimes applied to them simply perpetuates misunderstanding.[293]

The national, genuinely Japanese religion, inherited from the pre-Confucian and pre-Buddhist past, goes under the name of Shinto. With an estimated membership of over forty million, Shinto presents the unique phenomenon of being the only "primitive" religion maintaining an independent and institutional existence in one of the most literate nations of the world.[294]

2. The Origin and Basic Concepts of Shinto

(1) An Overview of Shinto. Shinto, which means "Way of the Gods," is the native religion of the Japanese. It was originally a vague nature worship with general animistic and polytheistic elements. Interest in food production and fertility was dominant; thus deities and rites related to good production—agricultural deities, a storm-god, harvest festivals, and the like—predominated.

The one requirement for contact with deity in Shinto was purification. Defilements were many, and cleansing rites were of great importance. Places of worship were very simple; they were originally just roped-off places where food offerings could be made.[295]

Despite its primitive elements, Shintoism expresses a rich naturalist mythology. It has a deep sensitivity to nature in its many manifestations. This is one of the reasons why to this day Shinto is one of the main sources of the beauty and grace of authentic Japanese life and art.

For most Japanese, the question of monotheism or polytheism in Japanese religious life is quite irrelevant. A person worships in many forms the omnipresent and ever-active life which manifests itself equally in nature, human beings, and gods—one and, at the same time, many. The central significance of the notion of ritual purity, in which there is no distinction between ceremonial impurity and moral guilt, points to a bedrock in Japanese religious life of a primitive or archaic religion. In fact, in their history the Japanese seem to have retained the incapacity to discern or the reluctance to grapple with the problem of evil.[296]

(2) How Has Shinto Been Perpetuated in Modern Japan? There are two principal reasons for the continuance of this simple, primitive religion in the highly educated Japan of today.

In the first place, Shinto became closely associated with the imperial family and the Japanese nation, even to the point of deifying the emperor. In the eighth century A.D., two supposedly historical chronicles were produced which involved mythological accounts of the lineage of the emperor. He was represented as a direct descendant of the greatest deity, the sun goddess.[297]

In the second place, in the ninth century B.C., Shinto became closely associated with Buddhism. Buddhism had entered Japan in about the sixth century and became a prominent vehicle for the importation of the ancient and highly developed Chinese culture. The "marriage" of Buddhism and Shinto, in which the Shinto deities were identified as the appearance in Japan of the divine personages of Mahayana Buddhism, proved to be mutually beneficial. This union helped the Japanese accept Buddhism and served to insure Shinto's continuance into modern times.[298]

(3) What Is the Significance of Emperor Worship? Beginning about 1870, Shinto was developed as a patriotic cult of reverence for the emperor and for the deities responsible for Japan's origins and development. The Japanese idea of the emperor as the central figure in national life has primitive origins. It expresses the unbroken perpetuation of the sacral Chief-figure, which we know especially in Polynesian tribal structure. As we have seen, its mythological justification was the divine descent of the emperor from the Sun-Goddess, Amaterasu, whose worship became centralized in the national shrine in Ise in the sixth century B.C.

For the Japanese, therefore, emperor worship is rooted in cultural history in a profound way. Patriotism, which everywhere readily acquires some pseudoreligious undertones, is through Shintoism in Japan radically religious—in the sense of unconditional, absolute surrender and allegiance to an ultimate.[299]

3. The Continuing Significance of Shinto

After its defeat in World War II and the ensuing American occupation, Japan had to start afresh and learn the "democratic way." Under American pressure, the emperor in 1945 disavowed his "divinity" and official or state Shinto was abolished. However, it is generally accepted that this disavowal by the emperor did not alter anything in the hearts of the Japanese as to his real pivotal position in the Japanese "hierarchical way."[300]

New concern among Japanese Christians about the revival of state Shinto and the future of religious freedom was aroused with the death of Emperor Hirohito in 1989. The new emperor, Akihito, showed little interest in being declared divine. But the government-sponsored Shinto religious observances that began when the nation realized Hirohito was dying and were continued up to and after his funeral in February 1989 outraged many Christians, opposition parties, and factions opposed to the imperial system.

Most of these groups believe that such ceremonies are a violation of the Japanese constitution and also a threat to religious freedom. Particularly controversial is the "Great Rice-Tasting Ceremony" during which the new emperor presents rice to the gods and "communes" with the Sun Goddess. The ceremony is supposed to complete the new emperor's ascension to divinity; without it, officials insist, he is only a "half emperor." The United Church of Christ in Japan condemned this "sinister program" to use the death of Hirohito to revive imperial authority and its Shinto ideological buttress. And although surveys show that the majority of Japanese want the emperor system, only a very small group of hard-core rightists want him to be restored to the position of divinity he had before the war. Observers state that the Japanese enjoy their personal freedom and that expanding international contacts and the modern-minded new emperor likely will lead them forward, not backward.

The Japanese constitution adopted after World War II provides for the separation of religion and government. Shrine Shinto continues on the basis of voluntary support. Individual worshipers frequent the shrines, and various ceremonies are performed by the priests.

Sectarian Shinto consists of thirteen so-called Shinto sects. Many of these are very active in educational and social welfare work and missionary propagation.

Several of Japan's so-called new religions contain Shinto elements, but others are predominantly Buddhist in nature. Most of the new religions are syncretistic because they combine elements of several religions. Typical emphases are faith healing, the attainment of happiness and prosperity, and the divine nature of humankind.[301]

Hendrik Kraemer suggests that before the forum of the modern international world, the Japanese have sought to play the role of official neutrality in religious matters, yet that in their basic assumptions of life and their spontaneous emotional attachment to the emperor, Japan has changed very little. This lack of change is a cause for concern because behind Shinto is the mythological and metaphysical basis for a fervent "patriotic religion" that includes a world mission. This mission is to achieve Japan's "proper station," which is to create universal peace by drawing all men and all peoples into the "Way of the Emperor." And Shinto is the mythological and metaphysical basis of this fervent perspective.[302]

4. Special Considerations for Christians in Approaching Followers of Shinto

The biblical faith sees Shinto as it is expressed historically in Japan as idolatry—and of course the Bible specifically and clearly denounces idolatry. The biblical approach to Shinto, then, would be similar to the approach to any form of idolatry—pointing out the ineffectiveness of the idol and introducing the idol-worshiper to the true God, revealed in Jesus Christ, who alone is worthy of worship.

In the specific case of emperor worship, the close ties between this particular type of idolatry and national self-consciousness must be acknowledged; thus a proper understanding of religious liberty and separation of church and state should be encouraged in the modern Japanese state.

In all fairness, it should be admitted that nationalism in the U.S. and Europe often develops in a way which shows similarity and affinity to State Shinto, with its pseudoreligious or religious quality and atmosphere. Take for example the familiar school ceremonies in our country that center around the flag and the recital of central tenets of the Declaration of Independence and the Constitution. These ceremonies hold an almost sacred place in American life. And while there is nothing essentially wrong with ceremony in public life, in the minds of some people the line is easily crossed from respect of country to worship of country. And, of course, this tendency is not limited to the United States. The Communist countries also have their services of homage and veneration for the pictures of the great founding fathers and expounders of the "infallible" Communist faith.

The irony of our modern age is that our dereligionized, areligious or (think of the immense Communist area) antireligious world is bristling with clumsily camouflaged idolatry. This idolatry revolves around two centers: the idolatry of the inner, personal self and that of the collective self. In both cases, God is considered an annoying or infuriating nuisance, or as too contemptible to take any notice of, or simply as irrelevant.[303]

It should also be noted that neither in Shintoism nor in any other type of cult worship is there anything remotely comparable to the unique historical event of Jesus Christ which is both the origin and the substance of the gospel of the apostolic church. Therefore, the presentation of this unique historical event must take center stage in a presentation of Christianity.[304]

XIV. What Is the Biblical Approach to Organized Christianity?

An essential teaching of Christianity is that Christian churches in this world, with their all-too human elements, stand under the judgment of God, no less than other human structures and organizations, religious or secular. In this sense Christianity is "one of the religions," and must accept the fact that judgment is to begin at the house of God.

1. Distortion, Self-Criticism, and Renewal in the Christian Faith

Religion, in every concrete form in which it has appeared in history, including historical and empirical Christianity, has always had an ambivalent character. It is creative and destructive, salutary and corruptive, sublime and demonic.[305]

This ambivalence can be clearly seen in empirical or institutional Christianity, with its inextricable mixture of "true" Christians and Christians in name. In fact, the Evil One appears to be especially interested and active in tempting the church because of its potential power and grandeur. Satan is also active in regard to the church because the church is the Body of him "who came to destroy the works of the Devil" (1 John 3:8).[306]

The distortion of the authentic Christian faith has taken many forms, including institutional corruption, moral decrepitude, spiritual pride, and outright heresy. And yet, through the centuries, there has also been a self-corrective tendency that pulled the faith back to center.

Christianity is distinguished from other religions by the event which gave it birth. This means that it is itself continuously corrected and purified insofar as Christians habitually go back to that event and its biblical interpretation as their starting point, their touchstone, and their inspiration.[307]

This correction is necessary because of several factors. *First*, there is an inevitable tendency for the living experience of faith to harden into doctrinal formulae. *Second*, experience tends to become frozen and stagnant in institutional form. *Third*, the life of the church often comes to be bound by traditions that may or may not have anything to do with the heart of the faith.[308] *Fourth*, there is the distortion of emotional manipulation and disrespect for authentic traditions.

This Christian process of self-criticism and renewal can be seen in retrospect as one of the great spiritual happenings of our time. This emphasis can render immense service not only to the Christian faith but to all the other living faiths of the world.[309]

2. Distortions and Triumphs of the Christian Missionary Movement

When it comes to the relationship between Western Christianity and other religions, distortion in institutional Christianity has often taken the form of overidentification of the Christian religion with Western culture. Christianity has sometimes been presented as the religion of the victorious West and as the real secret of Western preeminence. This, of course, blurs the abiding, fundamental, and universal motive of Christian missions. It gives occasion to doubt whether a missionary is first and foremost an ambassador of Christ or of Western "Christian" civilization.[310]

Accordingly, Christian missions sometimes have become too closely identified with political and economic imperialism. A glaring example of this is the way in which Christian missions (Roman Catholic and Protestant) slowly penetrated into China in the wake of Western mercantile penetration. This penetration was related in a shameful way to the Opium War and other wars that humbled the proud people to the dust. Ardent as much missionary zeal was, it was often not coupled with wisdom and understanding of what really was happening to China from a Chinese point of view.[311]

However, even the personal failures and distortions of the spirit of Jesus that at times have characterized some missionary efforts cannot finally obscure the glory of the Christian missionary movement, which represents one of the most amazing human phenomena in world history as a whole.[312] When the missionary movement has acted according to its true nature as a disinterested service out of surrender to Jesus Christ, the Lord and Savior of the world, it has been unique in its power.

Through the ages, the missionary movement has inspired and sustained numberless men and women to lives of devotion, service, danger, and loneliness. These missionaries have been sensitive to the needs of the lowliest and most despised and downtrodden mass of humanity, faithfully persevering even when externally measurable results or success are not forthcoming. And it should be noted that when deeply committed Christians have been involved as a dynamic group, even a minority, its achievements have been sensational—quite out of proportion to the numbers of those engaged in the Christian enterprise.[313]

In fact, a Chinese woman, Han Suyin, has expressed her appreciation for the many missionaries pouring into Hong Kong after their expulsion from China by the Communist government.

> Here were the remains of a hundred years of missionary work in China. A hundred years of devotion, sacrifice and good works. For the glory of their God, in unselfish zeal, men and women of 29 denominations had gone to baptize the heathen, teach their variety of the Only Truth, heal the sick, feed the hungry, fulfill themselves and the will of their God. . . . In this room were the people who had worn down our traditions, broken our selfishness, awakened our social conscience, armed us with ideals, dragged our scholars from their poetic torpor and our peasants' superfluous babies from the cesspits, built our universities, our hospitals and our puritanism. They also had made New China. Although now we cast them out as instruments of foreign aggression, they have also made us. We were part of each other. And I was ashamed of my people. I was not ashamed of getting the missionaries out. Perhaps it was time they went; but I was ashamed of the way it was done.[314]

3. The Importance of the Separation of Church and State

An important issue related to the biblical worldview and the distortions of organized Christianity—or organized religion in any form—concerns issues of church and state. In a world of totalitarian tendencies, the need of a church which is committed to revealed values is especially great. The state, as one of the orders instituted or permitted by God, is entitled to human loyalty, but there is another loyalty which may not in any circumstances be circumscribed or compromised.[315]

It is its radical departure from the church-state union that gives importance to the American experiment of the separation of church and state. Stephen Neill suggests that the importance of church-state separation has not yet been adequately realized by historians outside the United States. What is granted to all forms of faith and of no-faith is not just toleration, but equality within the broad limits of the operation of the common law.

No solution of the relation of church and state is perfect. Even when there is no legal bond to the state, churches can become subservient to public opinion, to social pressures, and to the will of a majority. If the state is completely safeguarded against the influence of religion, it may become secularized, and government may come to be regarded as the field of the operation of unbridled power politics without reference to any higher laws and powers. Churches, even though they have no legal status, can organize themselves to bring considerable pressure to bear on any democratically elected government. Yet on the whole it must be recognized that the American experiment has worked well. The churches flourish. Deeply secularized as it is, the United States seems yet to regard itself as in some sense "a nation under God."[316]

XV. What Is the Biblical Approach to Mysticism?

Mysticism refers to that type of religion which puts an emphasis on immediate awareness of transcendent reality. Human beings are essentially mystical creatures, in that they tend to want to heighten their consciousness. Therefore the emphasis of mysticism exists in almost every religion, including Christianity, and also has adherents outside of organized faith.

1. Popular Kinds of Mysticism

(1) Nature and Introvertive Mysticism. Mysticism comes in several forms. One well-known type is known as nature mysticism, which looks upon nature and is seized with the profound unity of all things in the cosmos, to such an extent, perhaps, that distinctions between individual things virtually disappear.

Another type is known as introvertive mysticism. This more typical mysticism turns inward to the very center or ground of the self. It finds that the self is not an isolated self-contained entity, but is continuous with a universal spirit pervading all things.

Introvertive mysticism is itself of more than one kind. Some mystics use imagery to express their experiences. Erotic imagery is perhaps the commonest. This is not surprising, for marriage and the sexual relation is the most intimate union or communion between finite human beings. Thus it is well suited to represent that union of the soul with transcendent reality, which is in itself difficult to describe. But there are other mystics who avoid imagery, and whose experience of union with the transcendent seems to be more intellectual and even impersonal, in the sense of being unemotional.

The introvertive type of mysticism is well exemplified by Meister Eckhart, a thirteenth-century Dominican. Eckhart had the advantage of being an able philosophical theologian as well as a mystic, so that his theological opinions were fairly clearly set forth. His particular brand of mysticism championed a kind of pantheistic philosophical system influenced by Neoplatonism and Arabic and Jewish conceptions. He was accused of heresy by the church, although he proclaimed his orthodoxy, and many of his tenets were officially declared heretical after his death.[317]

(2) Drug Mysticism. Natural drugs have been used to induce states of mystical consciousness for centuries. Greek mystery cults as well as religious groups in Siberia and South America have used materials produced from hemp, datura, henbane, and mushroom. Indians in Mexico and the United States have used peyote for the same purpose, and this use in carefully supervised religious services has even been legalized. More recently, synthetic derivatives such as LSD and mescaline have been used for mystical and religious purposes.

There have even been numerous instances of people who have claimed to have mystical experiences through drugs. Novelist Aldous Huxley, for example, in his 1954 book, *Doors of Perception,* told of undergoing a mystical experience induced by mescaline which united him with ultimate reality.

Three years later, however, the prominent Oxford scholar, R. C. Zaehner wrote *Mysticism, Sacred and Profane,* in which he stated that Huxley's teaching about the relationship between drugs and mystical experience did not refer to an authentic Christian relationship with God. According to Zaehner, drug-induced experiences may have some similarity to a nontheistic, monistic mysticism, whose characteristics include cosmic oneness, transcendence of space and time, feelings of well-being, and increased sensory perception of color and sound. However, this type of mysticism is not in the biblical tradition, but more appropriate to India.[318]

2. Christian Mysticism

Prominent mystics in the general Christian tradition have lived in many places. Sören Kierkegaard represents Western Europe, as do Rudolf Otto and Friedrich Schleiermacher. Evelyn Underhill represents the British Anglo-Catholic tradition; others from that tradition are Elizabeth Fry, John Wilhelm Rountree, Emily Herman, and W. R. Inge. The British evangelical tradition is represented by Charles Haddon Spurgeon, William Booth, Andrew Murray, F. B. Meyer, George Matheson, and Hannah Whitall Smith. From the United States, the well-known Quaker Rufus Jones is an obvious choice. A Christian mystic from India is Sadhu Sundar Singh.[319]

According to Underhill, the Christian mystic is one for whom God and Christ are not merely objects of belief, but living facts experientially known. Inge states that Christian mysticism is fellowship with Christ, not as a figure in past history, but as a present, life-giving power and energy. And he claims that this is the mysticism of the apostle Paul, who used the formula "in Christ" or "in the Lord" one hundred sixty-four times in his writings.[320]

From the perspective of classical Christianity, nothing can displace the concrete historical figure of Jesus Christ from the central place in religious experience. In an authentic Christian mysticism there is a mutual abiding of Christ and the Father and the Christian disciple. Although there is personal fellowship, the biblical faith will not allow complete union and identification of the creature with the Creator (man with God). Individuality is heightened in Christian mysticism, not minimized.

In a sense, a certain mysticism is normative in the life of any Christian. In other words, some form of direct spiritual awareness of God is an important aspect of Christian growth. For the growing Christian, the study of the Bible and persons who have been successful in developing the inner spiritual life is important. The Christian faith cannot continue as a vital force without constant inner spiritual renewal through communion with God. In fact, all phases of Christianity are undergirded by inner renewal. In the words of Augustine, the famous fifth-century Christian mystic, "Thou hast made us for Thyself, O Lord, and we are restless until we rest in thee."[321]

Christian mysticism, however, seeks a balance between contemplation and ethical action. Such a mysticism is best engendered in a setting such as church, a Christian retreat, or a home. Physical worship aids may help the practice of Christian mysticism, but it is dependent for its origination and consummation on God's initiative and upholding power.[322]

3. The Difference between Christian and Non-Christian Mysticism

As we have seen, there are numerous classifications of mystics. In general, an authentic Christian mystic is seen as affirmative, theistic, active, and practical. This is in contrast to a type of non-Christian mystic who is negative, pantheistic, passive, and speculative.

The Christian mystic also emphasizes individual communion with God rather than personality loss and identifying union with an impersonal deity. The Christian mystic would say that any mystical absorption restricted to one's self or with nature or related to drugs falls short of biblical mysticism. The idea of a world force or an absolute is not the same as belief in a personal God.

Furthermore, the Christian mystic is a "reacting" type, in contrast to an "acting" type. "Acting" mystics regard their communion with God as a result of their own action, from which a reaction follows on the part of the transcendent. But "reaction" mystics see their communion with God as an experience in which they react or respond to God's initiative in coming to humankind in Christ. For the apostle Paul, for example, Christ held the initiative, and Paul's saving fellowship with God was a gift of God; it came by God's self-revelation and self-impartation. For the Christian mystic, the historical Jesus Christ and the Holy Spirit are the indispensable sources and constant prerequisites of Christian experience.[323]

XVI. What Is a General Biblical Approach to World Religions?

In the foregoing discussions of various world religions, I have discussed special considerations for Christians to keep in mind as they approach adherents of other religions for sharing and witness. In this section, it should be helpful to present suggestions for a biblical approach in a summary and systematic form.

1. The Pragmatic Approach

The pragmatic approach has as its chief aim the removing of mutual misunderstandings about the nature of authentic Christianity. This approach should be helpful to fruitful inter-religious contacts and witnessing.

It is important to point out that authentic Christianity is not sadistic, arrogant, or domineering. Salvation is by grace and not based on genius or place of birth. Christianity is not Western or Eastern. The gospel is a gift to be shared. Hell is to be proclaimed as a warning and an attempt to save people, not in a sadistic way to reach our own ends through threats and terror. We must always remember that although we witness to the gospel, we stand under the same judgment as do all men and women.

Biblical Christianity does not encourage ruthless conquest and exploitation of nature, although at times in history the institutional church has sanctioned both conquest and exploitation. Authentic Christianity is a realistic religion based on the doctrine that all humans—including people in power—are born with a proclivity or tendency toward selfishness. Thus Christianity must contend for structures of justice as well as for freedom and a divine redemption.

In such dialogue, a clear distinction will inevitably have to be made between what we may term "empirical Christianity" and the gospel. What Christians have made of their faith—or even of the gospel—is wide open to criticism, and we must always be ready to acknowledge this. We must equally allow the non-Christian participant to distinguish between the essence of his faith and its empirical manifestations.[324]

2. The Approach of Dialogue

This approach directly involves an open exchange of witness, experience, cross-questioning, and listening. However, the seriousness of true religion demands that one should avoid the temptation of letting such dialogue and relationship be based on the assumption that all religions are essentially one.[325] Such syncretism, or the combining of elements from various religious views tends to rob all religions of their distinctiveness. All dialogue, therefore, must begin with a clear grasp of presuppositions. These presuppositions must be analyzed and the implications noted.

It helps when Christians make it clear that they consider their faith not an achievement, but a gift of grace—a gift which excludes all pride but obliges Christians to speak gratefully of this Lord to all who will hear it. They can then make it clear that they are glad also to listen to their partners in dialogue and may learn much from the account of the others' spiritual journeys.

The dialogue will be all the richer if both persons give themselves as they are. For the Christian, that giving must include witness. It is possible for convinced Christians to enter into true dialogue with convinced Hindus or Muslims or Jews without giving up their basic convictions. The fact that Christians believe they know the source of divine truth does not mean that they have nothing to learn from people of other faiths.[326] In fact, nuances of their own faith are often perceived in such discussions.

In dialogue, the Christians will see anthropology or the understanding of man as a crucial future issue, arising out of the situation of modern secularism and the growth of Eastern religions in the West. There will also need to be a discussion of self-awakening over and against revelation as the true way to salvation. Christians will have to face squarely the issue of historical revelation, especially in its central tenet of the Incarnation, God's entering himself into history as a Person. There should be openness of mind and eagerness to learn, but no less an attempt to keep uncompromisingly in focus the true issues.[327]

3. The Personal Approach of Being and Witness

Perhaps the most needed approach in our time is not in terms of thinking, but in terms of being and personal witness. Could it not be that the best authentication of the Christian view is in this area of emphasis?

Much that has been called Christian is conditioned by traditions that are national, sectarian, or local rather than specifically Christian. But the biblical way of life is not static or status quo or simply the unfolding of human potential. Rather, Christianity calls for a prophetic way of life in keeping with God's dynamic purpose revealed in Jesus Christ. Furthermore, the Christian faith promises supernatural resources to carry out this unprecedented and custom-shattering Christian lifestyle.

The early Christians not only outthought, but also outlived and outdied the pagans. If we are to authentically present the claims of the gospel to those of other religious beliefs, we must do the same. This means that our concern for justice and our faithfulness to God's commands must rival that of the committed Muslim. Our belief in agape love's superiority to Eastern compassion must be demonstrated in unselfish service without racial discrimination. And our understanding and respect for the Jewish tradition must show that we truly appreciate our heritage. And then, we must honestly relate the experiences and relationship that lie behind our actions.[328]

The word *witness* has important theological roots and practical implications. The Christian faith is not just a body of theological propositions to be taught or learned. From a biblical perspective, the basic human problem is more than ignorance—it is rebellion against the holy creator God. The Christian remedy for this problem, therefore, involves knowledge of the saving acts of God in history and their theological meaning. But Christian salvation also involves a personal turning from self and from Satan and a commitment to God as he is revealed in

Christ. As we have already seen, not only the mind, but also the emotions and the will are involved in Christian conversion and the Christian life.

These theological truths mean that an important part of Christian witness and growth relates to the personal dimension as well as to the informational. It follows that an effective Christian witness will recognize the importance of the personal. The Christian response to the forward thrust of non-Christian religions will thus finally be founded on personal living and personal witness.

In the final analysis, the greatest service we can render to the world, Western and Eastern, is in being authentic followers of Jesus Christ and giving our personal witness and testimony as to what he has done in our lives. When that happens, Christ himself will bring the world to himself: "And I, if I be lifted up, will draw all men unto me" (John 12:32).

10

The Question of Faith and Reason and the Knowledge of God

Introduction: What Is the Dilemma of Faith in the Age of Reason?

Today, more than ever in the Western world, we are the children of the Enlightenment. Whether we like it or not, we as a people have come to put great faith in science, technology, philosophy, logical theories, psychological science, and mathematical logic. In addition, we are at the threshold of a great revolution created by the combination of the computer and electronics.

Advanced scientific views are seen as replacing backward religions, superstitions, and prejudices throughout the world. In the universities and colleges the new combination of scientific positivism and historicism has struck particularly hard at the Bible, questioning its accuracy and offering alternative naturalistic and seemingly scientific explanations for the rise of human religious beliefs.[1]

For many, the rise of the dominance of reason in the Enlightenment struck especially hard at the central belief of Christianity, which is the resurrection of Jesus Christ. Under the influence of certain canons of reason assumed by the historical-critical method, the resurrection lost its central position in the theological interpretation of both the apostolic kerygma or proclamation and the Christian faith. Since one canon of rationalistic historical criticism was that God does not intervene in the chain of secondary causes, miracles lost their status as historical events. Only those miracles for which a reasonable explanation could be given were granted historical status, such as certain miracles of healing that could be contained within the category of psychosomatic illnesses. Obviously, the resurrection fell outside that category and was judged to be merely a psychological miracle, a belief that arose within the minds of the first disciples.[2]

Since the Enlightenment, Christian scholars have attempted to show how one can still believe in Jesus Christ and not violate an ideal of intellectual integrity. Some attempted to preserve the Scriptures as revelation from God in a manner which could not be touched by historical criticism. Others said that even though the resurrection of Jesus happened in human time as an actual event within the world with an objective content, it remained an event not accessible to reason.

Still others say that faith must be based upon historical knowledge whose evidence is available for all to see.[3]

And so the question arises: How can the children of the Age of Reason and the computer-electronic revolution believe in God, know God and admit the divine authority of the Holy Scriptures?[4]

Is it rational for us to believe in God? Is it rational for us to place our confidence in him and his revelation to man? Can a person believe in God without performing a sacrifice of his intelligence? One cannot belong to the educated sector of modern Western society without having these questions come to mind.[5]

These questions are approached by Christians in a variety of ways. Some Christians engage in apologetics, that discipline which seeks to provide a rational justification for the truth claims of the Christian faith. They maintain that there are rational evidences for belief in God and the Christian faith. There are other Christians who contend that believing that God exists requires throwing overboard the demands of rationality, but they would nonetheless refuse to go along with the conclusion that we ought then to cease believing that God exists. Divine revelation, they say, has entered our existence, coming as an assault to our rationality. Accordingly, we must now choose by what principle we shall live our lives—reason or revelation. The believer has thrown in his lot with revelation, and rationality no longer has any claim on him. It is a matter of utter indifference to him whether his Christian convictions are rational.[6] Still other Christians believe that we should begin with divine revelation and then use reason to undergird, explicate and communicate our faith.[7]

In summary, it can be said that in Western culture, there are these three basic approaches, mentioned above, to the relation of reason and faith in regard to the existence and knowledge of God. It will be helpful to look at these approaches before we evaluate them in the light of the biblical worldview.[8]

I. What Is the Approach Which Advocates Beginning with Reason and then Turning to Faith or Revelation?

1. A "Two-Story" Approach

The first basic approach to the relation of faith and reason is to look at human reason as the "ground floor" of humanity's knowledge of God. This approach assumes that human reason was not seriously defaced in the Fall and thus is available as a foundation for approaching God, but that divine revelation must build the "second story," completing the structure of the knowledge of God. The tradition of scholastic orthodoxy, both Catholic and Protestant, takes this view, called philosophical or evidential theism, which sees reason as playing a creative and significant role in humankind's coming to faith.[9]

2. Thomas Aquinas's Development of This Approach

In the thought of the eminent medieval theologian Thomas Aquinas, reason has a creative role *prior* to faith. In other words, natural reason (the reason set forth in Aristotelian philosophy) can discover the laws of nature and the effects of God in nature, and this natural theology or natural knowledge of God is the condition or presupposition of faith. Aquinas also held that reason can to some degree prepare the way for faith, although the primary cause of faith is "God moving man inwardly by grace." In Aquinas's view, then, revelation enriches and completes reason rather than contradicting it. Reason deals with what can be demonstrated, whereas faith concerns that which is taken on authority.

Aquinas held that we cannot prove the God of revelation, but we can show that it is not unreasonable to posit the existence of a supreme power as the Author of nature. Philosophy thus can know the divine truth implanted in the natural order. Aquinas believed that it is possible for the Christian to convince an adversary of the validity of this type of divine truth by demonstrative arguments.[10]

In fact, Aquinas is famous for setting out five proofs (or, according to some scholars, one proof in four versions plus another proof) for the existence of God. They will be discussed in depth later in this chapter.

Aquinas taught that it is possible to begin with natural reason and advance by pure argument a part of the way to the saving truths of religion. For instance, human beings can prove that God exists and also that God is one and incorporeal (no bodily form). Other important religious truths, however, such as the Trinity, the Incarnation, and future life, are regarded as beyond the unaided grasp of human reason—though certainly not contrary to it. They are truths of faith or revelation. Thus Aquinas united the rationalist thought of Aristotle and medieval Christianity in a system of reason and revelation.[11]

Arthur Holmes points out, however, that Aquinas tended to overlook the personal side of truth. He believed that human reason is sufficiently independent of the moral will to proceed in a detached and objective fashion. In fact, he held that the intellect was the image of God in humankind, the part unsullied by our loss of moral likeness to God through sin. In his system, therefore, our knowledge of universal truths about nature and humankind and of what we can deduce with regard to God and morality remains intact, untouched by human sin. Sin may affect our willingness to act on what we know, but not our knowledge as such.[12]

Thus, according to Holmes, Aquinas can be criticized as a rationalist who makes reason autonomous and theoretical rather than a fully personal activity affected by man's sinful moral and religious condition. In fact, the autonomy of human reason is an important and perhaps unfortunate part of his gigantic legacy to the modern mind.[13]

3. The View of Karl Rahner

A number of Roman Catholic writers have updated the view of Aquinas. One of these is the Austian priest-theologian Karl Rahner, who has made a significant impact upon contemporary Catholic thought. Although standing within the tradition of Aquinas, he has also drawn heavily upon the philosophy of Martin Heidegger.

Rahner posits a universal prevenient grace which creates within human beings an openness to God and Christ. Human nature is such that it must look to grace for its fulfillment. Secular philosophy reflects this longing and seeking on the part of the natural human for the glory of God. In fact, it is even possible for a person to live up to the highest within himself without having a conscious knowledge of Christ; Rahner speaks of such a person as the "anonymous Christian." In his view, any person who completely accepts his own humanity and rationality has accepted the Son of Man, because in Christ God accepts humanity.[14]

However, says Rahner, this specific kind of natural theology does not stand on its own, nor can it be the sole foundation of Christian theology. Rahner holds that natural theology must be met, completed, and deepened by the teaching of the church and by the divine truth on which that teaching rests.

4. The Inductive View of the Princeton Theologians and Their Theological Descendants

The general emphases of Aquinas, including his five proofs for God, have been commended by later Protestant theologians and apologists, who see these proofs as creating a moral and logical disposition for the truth of the Christian faith. If one can prove that God exists, they say, one is halfway toward proving Christianity true. Accordingly, there has been a close relationship in the thought of some Protestant thinkers between philosophical evidences and Christian theology.[15]

For example, Charles Hodge, distinguished nineteenth-century professor of theology at Princeton Theological Seminary, and his colleague, B. B. Warfield, both sought to bring reason to the aid of faith. Hodge and Warfield alike believed that Christianity was placed in the world to reason its way toward dominion of the world.[16]

Like Thomas Aquinas and other Christian rationalists, Hodge saw reason as preparing the way for faith. He had a deep confidence in human mental faculties, and he believed such a confidence to be related to confidence in God. He was very sympathetic to the cosmological (first cause) and teleological (design) arguments for the existence of God. (These are discussed in more depth in section V of this chapter.)[17] Hodge affirmed a definite continuity between reason and revelation. Reason, he maintained, is even able to judge the credibility of revelation. Reason must also judge the evidence by which revelation is supported.

However, unlike his rationalistic forebears, and in agreement with thinkers of the later Enlightenment, Hodge defended induction over deduction. He strongly affirmed that our sensory perceptions are a reliable index to truth—that, in fact, our sensory perceptions have an exact correspondence to reality. He further believed that theology should not use the speculative deductive method of rationalistic philosophy, in which one starts out from principles and then proceeds to facts, but rather the inductive method, which derives principles from facts. The appropriate theological method is simply the inductive or scientific method applied to Scripture. Like the scientist, the theologian observes, arranges, and systematizes.[18]

Faith in Hodge's view had a decidedly intellectual character; he saw it as an intelligent reception of the truth on adequate grounds. He held that Scripture never demands faith "except on the ground of adequate evidence." The object of faith is the divinely revealed truth contained in Scripture. Faith involves an assent to the facts in Scripture and to their scriptural interpretation.[19]

As a Christian apologist who claimed to be objective, Hodge sought to resist many of the theological trends of the day, including Schleiermacher's subjectivism.[20] For Hodge, the primary characteristic of biblical truth is that it is propositional. One should detach subjective factors from the data of religion, and the data can then presumably be arranged with complete objectivity.

An important influence on the Princeton School of Hodge and Warfield was Scottish Realism, or Scottish Common Sense Philosophy, which was founded by Thomas Reid in the eighteenth century to refute both David Hume and Immanuel Kant. Reid tried to get behind the relativism of Hume and Kant to common-sense absolutes that all ordinary persons would accept. The first of these principles is that the mind truly knows objects as they are in themselves. Scottish Realists assumed that all persons think alike. They asserted that language is precise and literal and that all languages share a universal grammar.

These and other absolutist principles of Scottish Realism became important to the Princeton theologians in establishing religious certainty. They believed that a nineteenth-century American theologian could interpret the Bible with accuracy using a current dictionary and logic, without undue concern for historical or cultural context. In Hodge's own words,

> The Bible is to the theologian what nature is to the man of science. It is his store-house of facts; and his method of ascertaining what the Bible teaches, is the same as that which the natural philosopher adopts to ascertain what nature teaches.[21]

For the Princeton theologians, nature and the Bible are both systems which cross-reference so that we may enjoy a complete system of knowledge. This is not demonstrated from a study of either nature or Scripture, but is rather held as a necessary philosophical presupposition.[22]

Those of the Princeton school considered themselves to hold no special philosophy. They saw their own views as open-minded, unbiased, candid, objective, and scientific. Such a view worked well enough so long as there was a general consensus in the culture on certain metaphysical issues. But the new science following Darwin was excluding whole realms of religion and morality from "the facts." And evangelicals had developed no effective critique of the first principles on which scientific inquiry rested. They had failed to appropriate the insight of the great Puritan theologian Jonathan Edwards, who had pointed out that these first principles are metaphysical or based on faith principles.

There is no wholly neutral doctrine of knowledge that can settle disputes over what areas of human knowledge are factual and objective. Rather, a Christian view of knowledge should frankly begin, more or less as did that of Edwards, not only with common sense, but also with data derived from revelation. Our understanding of something of the full range of human knowledge is in important ways derived from our belief in a Creator who communicates to his creatures both in nature and Scripture. Commitment to such a view allows us to see in reality the evidences of spiritual things. Lacking such commitment, the modern agnostic sees the same phenomena, but does not apprehend their spiritual aspects.[23]

Since the time of Hodge and Warfield, other well-known writers and theologians have followed in their tradition of "reason and then faith." In his popular book *The Battle for the Bible*, Harold Lindsell, former editor of *Christianity Today*, seeks to keep Hodge's approach intact. Likewise, the late Francis Schaeffer, a popular Christian apologist, affirmed that he depended on J. Gresham Machen, a student of Warfield's at Princeton, as well as Warfield and Hodge themselves. Schaeffer's presuppositions are most evident when he connects science and religion. He alleges that it is a central purpose of the Bible to teach us what "has occurred in the cosmos."[24]

5. The "Rationalistic Idealism" of Gordon Clark

Clark, the late professor of philosophy at Butler University, stands in the tradition of rationalistic idealism and orthodox Calvinism. In stark contrast to Hodge, he disdains all empiricism and thereby reflects the earlier phases of the Age of Reason rather than its later ones. Clark is an avowed opponent of what he calls the "neo-orthodox irrationalism" of the early Barth and the subjectivism of emotional pietism.

Clark sees faith as an assent to propositional truth. Revelation is an axiom of reason, a datum accessible to reason. He regards the Bible as a verbal revelation from God; it represents the very mind or thought of God. In his view, we do not gain knowledge of God by an empirical encounter with the Bible as a historical record. What the Bible gives us is not so much a history of God's dealings with man as information about God.

Clark holds that we know the world not by means of our senses, but instead by innate ideas; these are to be found not simply in human minds, but in the mind of God, in whom we "live and move and have our being." Clark asserts that "our existence in the mind of God puts us in contact with the ideas in the mind of God." With many philosophical rationalists, Clark contends that universal and necessary truths cannot be justified on empirical grounds.

Accepting the label "rationalistic Calvinist," Clark has constructed a deductive axiomatic system. In his view, our logic and knowledge are identical with that of God, though this does not mean that we have as much knowledge as God. Our ideas participate in the very ideas of God. Clark holds that the image of God is logic or reason. The logical structure of reason is not affected by sin, although sin has implications for knowledge.

Clark has a deep affinity to both rationalistic philosophy and the older scholastic theology of Aquinas. He asserts that Aristotle's definition of God as "thought-thinking-thought" can be accepted because "God and logic are one and the same first principle." With Thomas Aquinas, he sees a harmony between faith and reason.[25]

In Clark's system, the task of apologetics is primarily negative—that of laying bare the contradictions and inconsistencies in all non-Christian positions through application of the law of contradiction. He asserts that the only position that comes through this process unscathed is biblical trinitarian Christianity. Farther than this, Clark believes, apologetics cannot go.[26]

As an unabashed rationalist who pursued truth with his mind, Clark was deaf to other dimensions of the philosophical enterprise. He was totally incapable of dealing sympathetically with, for example, a theologian like Karl Barth. On one occasion, a student who had read just about everything by Barth that had been translated into English was goaded by other students into attending one of Clark's classes on Barth. He was appalled to realize that Clark's negative pontifications were based exclusively on a reading of only one of Barth's earliest works. When the student pointed out in class discussion that Barth, in a more recent book, had changed his mind on a certain issue, Clark was nonplused; in his conception, changing one's mind was simply not how one operates. Having once made up his mind on an issue, after a full exercise of the intellect, he did not change it.

Clark had great influence on Edward Carnell and Paul Jewett of Fuller Seminary and on other prominent conservative leaders such as Carl F. H. Henry and Edmund Clowney. Later in life, Carnell saw weaknesses in Clark's approach. While Carnell did not turn his back on the law of contradiction, which was the formal basis of Clark's system of deductive rationalism, he became convinced that Clark was severely limited in his apologetical usefulness. The law of contradiction was the means by which one could ferret out the inconsistencies and illogicalities of opposing systems, and that, according to Clark, is the main task of apologetics; but Carnell was looking for something more positive.[27]

6. The "Historical Verification" Approach of Wolfhart Pannenberg

(1) The Approach. In recent years, Wolfhart Pannenberg, a professor at the University of Munich, has developed a "Reason and Faith" or evidential approach. In 1961, a circle of young theologians for whom Pannenberg served as the principal spokesman asserted in their manifesto, *Revelation as History,* that God makes himself known within history, that the horizon within which the theologian has to work is that of history itself, and that the full meaning of history itself is only opened up when history as a whole is seen in relation to God. Pannenberg laid great weight on the unity of universal history, which he maintained to be a necessary "postulate" for the work of the historian, and argued that ultimately such unity could only be located in a transcendent ground of all history, that is, in God.

Pannenberg also made much of the idea of the end of history, in whose light alone the meaning of history as a whole can be discerned, and he saw this end as revealed in the eschatological event of the resurrection of Jesus. Only in the light of this totality and this end could the real movement and goal of history itself be appreciated.

Conversely, in Pannenberg's view theology is grounded upon history and upon historically verifiable events—especially upon the Resurrection. His basic thesis is that reason precedes faith and provides the foundation on which faith rests. His thesis is not the traditional "I believe in order that I may know," but "I know, and so I believe."[28]

This approach is needed, according to Pannenberg, because theology has walled itself off against secular knowledge. Neo-orthodox theology has tended to flee into the harbor of supra-history (that which is "above" history), supposedly safe from the historical-critical floodtide, while existential theology withdrew from the course of objective history to the subjective experience of human authenticity. Theology's attempt at self-isolationism backfired, however, because the secular sciences turned upon it to criticize and contradict it.[29]

Therefore, if Christianity is to make any meaningful claim to truth, it must, according to Pannenberg, submit to the same procedures of testing and verification as are employed in the secular sciences. This method of verification will be indirect, however; for example, it will involve historical research. Since the Christian faith is based on a real past event, and since there is no way to know the past other than by historical-critical research, it follows that the object of Christian faith cannot remain untouched by the results of such research. A kerygmatic or proclaimed Christ utterly unrelated to the real, historical Jesus would be "pure myth," while a Christ known only through subjective encounter would be impossible to distinguish from "self-delusion." Therefore, the unavoidable conclusion is that the burden of proving that God has revealed himself in Jesus of Nazareth must fall upon the historian.[30]

In Pannenberg's view, without a factual foundation logically prior to faith, faith would be reduced to gullibility, credulity, or superstition. Only this evidential approach, in contrast to the subjectivism of modern theology, can establish Christianity's truth claim. Pannenberg also maintains that by concentrating on the Bible as the source and norm of truth, theology lost its broad perspective of universal truth. It landed in a ghetto, where it closed itself to the results of other sciences. It worked with its supernatural knowledge and found itself unable to defend it against the arguments from natural knowledge. This had the result of tending to make theology a blind faith, calling for a sacrifice of the intellect, and creating a tendency to ignore ordinary ways of seeing and hearing. Theology, Pannenberg contends, is mistaken when it rejects the postulate of verifiability.[31]

Pannenberg is calling for a rerouting of theology along an avenue different from that on which it has been traveling for the last fifty years. He does not want rationalism, but he does want respect for reasonableness instead of irrationalism and what amounts to a theological "monologue" in the midst of the "conversations" going on among the other disciplines.[32]

Even if faith is not the foundation of Christianity's truthfulness, this does not mean that faith is unimportant or without function for Pannenberg. He carefully distinguishes between historical certainty and the certainty of faith. Historical investigation does not result in a certainty that is sufficient to be a basis for action; faith does. History and faith are related, but not identical. Interpreting history as revelation involves an uncertainty built into the process of investigation. This uncertainty comes from viewing historical events as part of a now incomplete historical totality. Faith relies on the results of historical investigation, but acquires a certain independence of history by putting its trust in the God revealed in history rather than in the individual events themselves. Even where historical investigation calls into question interpretations upon which faith is built, faith anticipates future historical investigation which will vindicate it. It is not a faith built on an absolute certainty of historical investigation, but a faith in God's continued revelations in history.[33]

Basic to Pannenberg's view is the resurrection of Jesus, which is viewed as the authentication of his apocalyptic message and his ministry. His resurrection actualizes the end of history within history itself. The resurrection was the appearance of the God of the future.[34]

In a special way, therefore, Pannenberg has related his approach of reason and faith to Jesus. For him, the task of christology is to offer rational support for belief in the divinity of Jesus, for it is this which is disputed in the world today. Christology from "above" is unacceptable in that it presupposes the divinity of Jesus. However, christology viewed from "below" can construct from the life of the man Jesus of Nazareth a full christology, including his deity.[35]

(2) Evaluation of Pannenberg's Approach. In a world in which certain theologians have thought it necessary to surrender virtually all claims to the historical truth of the gospel in order to preserve the authority of the kerygma or proclamation, a theology trying to demonstrate the contrary is quite important. Pannenberg has perceived correctly that the surrender of such historical claims evaporates the Christian gospel into myth which may have meaning for one's individual subjectivity, but which asserts no claims concerning the universal truth of the gospel.[36]

A basic problem of Pannenberg's theology, however, is his attempt to make a transition from the probabilities of historical reason to the certainty of faith. By agreeing that historical reason produces only judgments of probability, while affirming that faith requires absolute trust, Pannenberg creates a dilemma in his theological system. How does one move from probability to certainty, from reason to faith? For if the full meaning of the Resurrection, namely, that it is the eschatological event in which God fully reveals himself in Jesus Christ, requires a step beyond historical knowledge, a leap which reason cannot fully warrant but faith demands, then Pannenberg himself is open to the charge of subjectivism that his entire theological proposal seeks to avoid. It may be that his approach provides a leap of faith which has greater historical warrant than in the case of Kierkegaard or Bultmann, and that may be an advantage, but it remains a leap toward certainty which the evidence established by historical reason cannot sustain.[37]

Pannenberg admits that psychologically one can believe in Jesus without first having established by reason the historicity of his claims and that, in fact, many persons have neither the time nor the competence to establish by reason the truth of the gospel. Although psychologically this may be the case, he still argues that knowledge logically precedes faith and leads into it. Thus Pannenberg maintains that the logical presupposition of faith is that its truth can be demonstrated. A moderate reading of this position would be that once faith exists, the believer can develop the logic of faith and give reasons for its existence. Here faith is assigned an essential role in acquiring knowledge. And in response to two critics, Pannenberg admits that "the movement of faith is already operative in the very perception of historical fact."[38]

Pannenberg recognizes that when the truth is presented, not all acknowledge it. But he ascribes this situation to the existence of subjective and irrational factors which cannot be removed by rational argument. Hence illumination or insight is necessary, but such insight is created not by faith, but by the truth itself, and occurs on the plane of reason. This understanding of illumination shifts the question of understanding God's revelation from one of sin and guilt to one of intellectual understanding. However, according to Scripture, it is not just irrational factors of various kinds which must be overcome for illumination to occur, but rather mankind's basic resistance to God himself.[39]

However, Pannenberg's chief emphasis is not only that the history of Jesus is logically prior to faith, but also that knowledge of that history produced by autonomous historical reason is logically prior to faith and leads into faith. Thus the dilemma mentioned above still exists.[40]

Pannenberg also downplays verbal revelation. However, he claims that human reason cannot decipher the meaning of revelatory events by inference from the events themselves, but instead requires a revelatory verbal context which has been accepted by faith as the true context for the understanding of the events recorded in the Bible.[41]

Pannenberg assumes that the only alternatives are faith grounded upon itself (subjectivism) or faith grounded upon historical events rationally known. There is, however, another possibility, as we will see in our third approach. Faith can be understood as correlated with revelation. Such correlation does not require a sacrifice of reason, but it does require a total surrender of the person to God and to his revelation. This revelation accepted by faith becomes, then, the arena within which and on the basis of which reason functions. The slogan "Faith and Reason" is not a declaration of irrationality, but rather provides the true understanding of the place of reason in the Christian faith.[42]

7. The Strengths and Weaknesses of the "Reason and Then Faith" Approach

Obviously, the "Reason and Then Faith" emphasis has made a significant contribution to Christian orthodoxy through the centuries. Its major weakness, however, as indicated by Holmes, is that it tends to confine knowledge to an objective awareness of true propositions and often fails to take into consideration the experience of the whole person. In most cases it accepts propositional truth independently of personal fidelity.

As we will see, it was against these limitations that many nineteenth- and twentieth-century theologians reacted; to an extent, the extremes of liberal theology began with the effort to give "equal time" to subjective experience. Unfortunately, in many cases the emphasis on the experiential as opposed to the propositional left people to distill doctrine from subjective religious experience rather than learning it from what the Bible teaches. In our day, for example, existential theology claims that Christian doctrine is primarily a human distillation from religious experience. And even in more conservative existential theologies, a separation of the personal and the propositional persists.[43]

The "reason and then faith" approach in its more modern incarnations corrects this liberal extreme. However, because it regards knowledge and truth alike as wholly propositional and not as personal or subjective, it still tends to reduce revelation to objectively true propositions apart from personal encounter.[44]

II. What Is the Approach Which Emphasizes That Faith Is All-Important and Reason Has Little Value?

This second view seeks to guard against the potential abuse of reason. In fact, a significant group of Christian thinkers have criticized in strong terms the use of reason in religious faith. Varying degrees of antagonism to reason are found among those who hold this view. Some say that faith and reason are completely opposed to each other and have no point of contact. Others affirm a limited purpose and use for reason, although within clearly defined limitations. This view is sometimes known as "fideism."

In looking at the work of this group of "antirationalists," it is important to remember that being antirationalist does not mean being irrational. The work of those covered in this section is coherent and analytical—indeed, rational. What they have in common is their emphasis that in religious matters, especially in the matter of knowing God, faith is all important and reason has limited value.[45]

1. The View of Tertullian

In the second century, the Latin writer Tertullian set forth the view that reason and faith are two separate, exclusive categories. He asked the celebrated question, "What has Athens to do with Jerusalem?"—using Athens to represent reason and Jerusalem to represent faith. His answer to his own question was "nothing." He denounced philosophy as the root of all heresy and insisted that worldly wisdom without faith was vain.[46]

2. The View of Martin Luther

Luther, in the sixteenth century, reacted against the use of reason and the emphasis of the medieval church on salvation through works (Luther considered rationalistic religious thinking as a form of work done to help attain righteousness).

Luther saw faith as standing in contradiction to reason. At one point, in fact, he called reason "the monster without whose killing man cannot live." His last sermon at Wittenberg has gone down in history as a classic invective against reason, which he called "the Devil's Whore." He referred to Aristotle, the Greek formulator of natural theology and the rational proof of God, as a "destroyer of pious doctrine," a "mere Sophist and quibbler," an "inventor of fables," "the stinking philosopher," a "billy-goat" and a "blind pagan." According to Luther's view, reason is incapable of discerning the things of faith. This is true because reason is exceedingly limited in its vision and also because reason is enslaved by the sinful human will.[47]

Luther did make a distinction, however, between natural reason and reason enlightened by faith. Reason by itself can know nothing about the plan of salvation, but faithful reasoning can tell us much about these matters. "Before faith and the knowledge of God, reason is mere darkness;" he wrote, "but in the hands of those who believe, 'tis an excellent instrument.'" And "all faculties and gifts are pernicious, exercised by the impious; but most salutary when possessed by godly persons." In a similar manner, Luther held that the works of the law avail nothing for our salvation, but that faithful doing is very necessary in the Christian life.[48]

As modern research has shown, Luther was not condemning reason as such; he himself employed it with great effect. The real target of his attacks was the abuse of reason, the situations where philosophy had crowded out the truth of the Christian faith. According to Luther, reason has its true function in grasping and evaluating what is set before it; but reason is not the sole criterion of truth.[49]

Faith, for Luther, is heartfelt confidence and trust in the mercy of God. It is *fiducia* (trust) much more than *assensus* (mental assent), although faith involves reason. In Luther's words, "There is a faith which believes what is said of God is true; there is a faith which throws itself on God." Luther believed strongly that only the latter is effectual for salvation.[50]

3. The View of Blaise Pascal

The prominent seventeenth-century French thinker Blaise Pascal can be considered a representative of the primacy of faith approach within the Roman Catholic Church. Pascal did not write in a systematic way. His ideas, thoughts, and inspirations often were written down on whatever was handy, sometimes in a legible hand and at other times in an illegible scrawl. Sometimes his writing was done in haste, and at other times he took time for deliberate composition. These scraps bound together in book form are called the *Pensées* (French for "thoughts"). What the *Pensées* lacked in order they atoned for in genius.[51]

Pascal was profoundly aware of the real nature of religion. His God was not the God of rationalist argument who is a mere hypothesis invoked to make other hypotheses feasible. He was convinced that God is not known in this way.[52]

Faith alone, according to Pascal, can lay hold of the self-revelation of God in Christ. Faith is an experience of the heart, which is the unitive center of personality. "This, then, is faith: God felt by the heart, not by the reason." Pascal is famous for saying, "The heart has its reasons which reason does not know."

It should be remembered, however, that when Pascal contrasts faith and reason he is thinking primarily of discursive or technical reason. Discursive reason proceeds syllogistically (following the laws of logic). But God is not the conclusion at the end of a syllogism. Faith is inward, spiritual, and intuitive, while reason is external, objective and geometric. Yet Pascal is not an irrationalist, for he himself was a scientist and mathematician and fully acknowledged that reason is very capable in spheres other than religion. The scientific method works quite well in the world of nature, but not in religion. Heart-knowledge, on the other hand, pertains only to God and His mercy.[53]

4. The View of Sören Kierkegaard

One of the most important intellectual and spiritual figures in the nineteenth century was the Danish philosopher Sören Kierkegaard. Kierkegaard was an especially significant exponent of the limitations of reason in religion. He scorned philosophy, renounced objectivity, and called the intellectual approach to Christianity paganism and blasphemy.

Like Marx, Kierkegaard began as a student of Hegel, but he ended up as a major philosophical opponent.[54] He regarded Hegel's speculative system as a complete falsification of the content as well as the form of Christianity, turning it into a system of thought instead of a way of life.

Kierkegaard regarded the Christian faith as essentially different from reason. He held that faith does not arise through intellectual understanding, but only through a decision of the will in the face of objective uncertainty. Christianity is essentially God's answer to the tragic problem of human life rather than to the perplexities of human thought.[55]

The important arguments of Kierkegaard against the rationalistic can be summarized as follows:

- An intellectual defense of God discredits God.
- Christianity requires a life commitment, not detached reflection.
- Faith in reason is idolatry. One insults God by attempting to prove his existence in his presence; this amounts to putting reason in the place of God.
- The rationalistic approach is uncertain and undermines faith.
- Human beings as finite creatures can never "prove" God, who is "wholly other" and beyond rational comprehension. If we are to know him, it will be because he reveals himself to the person who yields to God by faith.
- Doubt is not basically an intellectual problem, but rather a problem of sinful pride or rebellion.[56]

Kierkegaard did make room for certain uses of reason. In his system, reason can be used to expose humankind's limited horizon. It can point to its own limits by raising without answering the question of faith as implied in the actual situation of the existing individual. Reason used in this sense can both precede and follow faith in showing the limits of our understanding.[57]

Kierkegaard's view was extreme and one-sided in its emphasis, but it was valuable in clearly pointing out the basic limitations of reason in the realm of humanity's relation with God. He also rightly insisted that truly human knowledge must be fully personal if it is to be relevant to a unified human existence.[58]

Kierkegaard himself once described his work as "just a bit of cinnamon." And Colin Brown agrees, pointing out that cinnamon can be pleasant when used in small amounts to season a dish or correct its flavor, but a person cannot live forever on a diet of it. Similarly, Kierkegaard's work is helpful as a corrective but inadequate as a full philosophical diet. With changes, and taken out of context, certain of his ideas have been used by atheists like Sartre to lead to the conclusion that there can be no rational grounds for preferring belief to unbelief and that objective knowledge of God must be replaced by subjective knowledge of the human condition.[59]

5. The Presuppositional View of Cornelius Van Til

Van Til, for many years a professor at Westminster Seminary in Philadelphia, is among the most significant apologists in the conservative tradition of Dutch Reformed theology. For Van Til, natural theology, including the use of rational arguments for the existence of God, does nothing but lead to the idea of an impersonal "first cause," which falls far short of the living God of the Bible and experience.[60]

According to Van Til, for Christianity to require that the Christian faith have a rational foundation is tantamount to demanding that the Creator pass a test set up by the creature. "The only 'proof' of the Christian position is that unless its truth is presupposed there is no possibility of 'proving' anything at all."[61]

In thinking about God, Van Til states that we must either begin with God or with humankind. From Aristotle onward, secular philosophers (and Christians adopting their arguments) have begun with humankind. In contrast, asserts Van Til, authentic Christian thought must begin with the presupposition of a living, triune God who is perfect and self-contained.[62] The piecemeal approach of Christian evidences, in other words, is meaningless. A truly Protestant method of reasoning involves a stress upon the fact that the meaning of every aspect or part of Christian theism depends upon Christian theism as a unit.[63]

For Van Til, a confrontation between the Christian message and the non-Christian world must of necessity be a "head-on collision." It should be noted, however, that Van Til believes there is a common ground between the believer and the unbeliever. It lies in the sense of deity which is imprinted indelibly on the human soul and which natural, unredeemed man seeks to suppress but never quite manages to eradicate. This embryonic knowledge of God is the seed of a truly valid knowledge. However, it never blossoms into a right knowledge unless the person is regenerated by an act of God's special grace and thus brought into submission to the biblical God and his supernatural revelation.

Faith, thus, never grows out of rational evidence for God, the divinity of Christ, or the authority of Scripture. Rather, by an act of will, human beings must choose to accept the triune God of the Bible. This can only be done by regeneration of the soul and the creation of faith by the Holy Spirit. A non-Christian will accept the gospel if God pleases by his Spirit to take the scales from his eyes and the mask from his face. It is upon the power of the Holy Spirit that the witness relies when he or she tells people they are lost in sin and in need of a Savior.[64]

Van Til's presuppositional case for biblical theism claims to enable a person to know God as he really is and to know him with certainty. This view reflects the strong predestination emphasis of a rigid Calvinism.[65]

Van Til's influence on Christian apologetics has been considerable. Much in his approach is useful. He makes it clear that facts cannot be understood outside of some framework. In the case of Christian theism, this framework is the fact of God's existence; it is this fact that makes the world intelligible.

For Van Til, reasoning processes based on Christian presuppositions are sufficient means to truth. He admits that his reasoning is circular, but so, he asserts, is all reasoning. The scientific method, for example, begins by assuming the uniformity of nature, which it then "finds" in experimentation. In any system of thought the starting point, method, and the conclusion are always involved in one another. It is not strange, then, that Christians starting with the self-contained God as revealed in Scripture interpret everything by the inspired writings.[66]

Why start with Christian presuppositions rather than others? The Bible is accepted as self-authenticating. Van Til accepts Scripture to be that which Scripture itself says it is on its own authority. Christian philosophy, he asserts, rests upon its own self-authenticating biblical claims.[67]

III. What Is the Approach Which Affirms That We Should Begin with Faith, Then Use Reason (Faith Seeking Understanding)?

1. An Integrative Approach

As we have seen, both the "reason and then faith" approach and the "faith is all" approach to the question of the knowledge of God fail to address the whole of human experience. The "reason first" approach tends to reduce life to objective propositions and to ignore the reality of subjective religious experience. The "faith is all" approach, on the other hand, tends to stray too far from the biblical revelation and lead to a faith with no grounds in objective reality.

A satisfactory biblical approach would be one which avoids both extremes, which embraces and balances both the subjective and objective, the propositional and personal, putting each in its place and doing damage to neither. This approach, which could also be called "faith seeking understanding," sees a human person as a unity whose will and mind cannot be separated. If the will is wrong, then reason will be distorted in the area of faith and morals. But if we begin with faith, which is a realignment of the will, reason has a proper center, and the mind can be effective and fruitful in the religious sphere. This means that it is not a question of either faith *or* reason, but of both faith *and* reason. This is possible because of a "whole and part" relation in which the personal (faith) is the whole and the objective (reason) a part.[68]

2. The View of Augustine

The great church father Augustine, incomparably the greatest figure in the early, formative period of Christian thought, is the prototype of the "faith first" approach. Augustine sought to relate faith and reason very closely, yet he saw faith as being more decisive. His motto was "I believe in order to understand."

In other words, Augustine believed that before a person can come to a right understanding of God, that person must first believe in God's revelation in Jesus Christ. Reason apart from faith cannot bring us to a valid and saving knowledge of God. On the other hand, faith does not bring us perfect knowledge in all areas of life; it only sets us on the way. And faith itself is more than mere feeling; it must also involve intellectual assent: "No one indeed believes anything, unless he has first thought that it is to be believed."[69]

Reason, Augustine affirmed, is the instrument with which man interrogates and understands his experience. Hence experience must precede reason if reason is to have anything to work upon. Reason unfertilized by experience is as barren as the skill of a sculptor would be in a world devoid of wood or stone.[70]

Augustine held that faith is given by the Holy Spirit through the preaching of the gospel. However, that faith must be rationally appropriated or accepted by human beings. Once it is so appropriated, it then illumines a person's life and world: "For faith is understanding's step, and understanding is faith's reward."[71]

3. The View of Anselm

The eleventh-century theologian and scholar Anselm has given us another classic expression of faith in search of understanding. In his view, the knowledge of God does not come from a rational process which begins with everyday, external, and commonly accepted realities and then proceeds to demonstrate certain less evident, or perhaps even entirely unknown, truths. Rather, we find our inward experience of God, given in and through our self-consciousness, to be supremely revealing and significant among all other experiences, and then we go on to interpret all other experience in terms of it.[72]

For Anselm, God must necessarily be presupposed, not merely as a technical term in a rational argument, but also as the being addressed in our prayers. This means that the object of metaphysical thought and the object of religious worship are one and the same. God is akin not primarily to our thinking—which is only one particular function of our being—but to our being itself.

Decisively influencing Anselm's thought at this point is the biblical presentation of God as a dramatic figure. The Bible does not conceive of the absolute being as a supremely abstract, comprehensive idea, as Greek philosophy does. Rather, in the Bible God is seen as the Absolute Singular. He is known not by the speculative deduction of his attributes from the pure idea of him, but by meditation upon his recorded deeds in history and the inspired interpretation of those deeds.

It is no accident that Anselm expressed his view in a prayer found in his *Proslogian*: "I do not endeavor, O Lord, to penetrate Thy sublimity, for in no way do I compare my understanding with that; but I long to understand in some degree Thy truth, which my heart believes and loves."[73]

4. The View of Abraham Kuyper

In the nineteenth century, Abraham Kuyper, a noted Dutch evangelical, was an heir of this Augustinian-Anselmic tradition.[74] The point at which Kuyper departed most radically from American Common-Sense Realists such as Hodge and Warfield was his insistence that knowledge of God is founded not upon something prior to itself, but rather on God himself speaking to the minds of humans. This inspiration, the work of the Holy Spirit, communicates from God through Scripture to humans and provides its own certainty. This sense of God's inspiration of the mind of the sinner differs from the general principles of our consciousness in that it is not shared by all people.[75]

The crucial element making this immediate knowledge far less than universal is the presence of sin among humans. As much as anything, emphasis on the effects of sin separates Kuyper's thought from that of Hodge and Warfield. For Kuyper, unacknowledged sinfulness inevitably blinds one from true knowledge of God. Although all people have an innate sense of God, this natural relation is so broken and injured by sin as to be of no use in its present state as a foundation for knowing God. Only if one recognizes the brokenness of this relationship can one recognize this sense of God for what it truly is. Such a recognition, however, is not fully possible without God's inspiring communication of special grace.[76]

Hence, every effort to prove God to sinners who lack the essential foundation for such knowledge is bound to fail. Kuyper considered unrecognized human sinfulness a *preventative* to true knowledge of God, whereas the Common-Sense Realists of the Princeton School saw it only as an *inhibitive*. Sin indeed can stand in the way of an objective look at the facts, but the Americans remained confident in the possibility of an objective scientific knowledge available to all intelligent humans. Moreover, they saw no reason why knowledge of God could not be a form of such knowledge.[77]

Kuyper holds the view that God as revealed in Scriptures is known by us not as a conclusion of an argument, but as a primary truth immediately apprehended as the result of spiritual communication to the human consciousness. People whose hearts and minds are closed to this spiritual communication will not be convinced by arguments.[78]

Kuyper, in traditional Calvinist fashion, stressed that the Spirit works through Scripture and the body of believers, and that these authorities are susceptible to some testing, at least for consistency. Thus there is a place for reason after faith.[79]

For Kuyper, knowledge does not come in isolated packages, but is understood by subjects in the context of other beliefs the subject holds—beliefs determined either by the subjective urge to remake the universe in one's own image or by proper reverence for God. A person's thought is of a whole (is made up of a complex and vital relationship among ideas), so that sinfully determined basic first beliefs and commitments can pervade the rest of that person's intellectual activity. Sin creates a widespread abnormality. Trust in God provides us with some intuitive first principles of knowledge which are lacking in non-Christians. Christians should not be embarrassed to say frankly that this is the issue. If one trusts in God, one will view some evidence differently than will a person who basically denies God.[80]

Kuyper explicitly related his philosophy to its Christian assumptions, refusing to accept uncritically the Enlightenment ideal of one science for all humanity. Furthermore, he provided a basis for building a Christian intellectual outlook that can withstand the claims both of modern science and modern subjectivism. The general arguments for Christianity do not stand up as logically compelling unless one already grants certain assumptions about reality that virtually presuppose a benevolent Creator. Otherwise, alternative explanations can explain the phenomena as logically as can Christianity. Historical events are typically susceptible to more than one plausible interpretation. Furthermore, sinful people whose minds are adamantly closed to hearing God and his Word will be quick to point out the logical plausibility of the alternatives.[81]

Kuyper implemented his theories in 1880 with the establishment of the Free University of Amsterdam, an institution in which the theme of the fundamental differences between Christian and non-Christian thought was strongly expressed through most of the twentieth century.[82]

Kuyper's views are important for the survival of the Christian academic community in a secular setting because of his insistence that science cannot be regarded as a sovereign domain that sets its own rules to which Christians and everyone else must conform if they are to retain their intellectual respectability. As philosophers of science now are also recognizing, science itself is controlled to substantial degrees by assumptions and commitments. Christians, then, should be free to frankly state their metaphysical starting points and their assumptions and to introduce these into their scientific work in all areas of human inquiry. This means that they often employ underlying control beliefs that differ from those of non-Christians.[83]

5. The Approach of Karl Barth

Karl Barth stressed that Christian truth, including knowledge of God, must come from the Bible and not from any ontological or philosophical system. Barth knew, of course, that the theologian cannot be totally free from philosophical preunderstanding. But it is essential to Barth's whole approach that basic theological procedures and principles not depend on commitments that are not authenticated by Scripture.[84]

Barth, in fact, asserted that theology's only subject matter is God's Word. The Word is present in the church in a threefold form: the spoken Word, the written Word, and the living Word, Jesus Christ. God's message reaches Christians through hearing (preaching) and writing (through Scripture). Yet both of these flow from and point to Christ himself. Christ, Barth insists, is the source of the other two forms, yet we know him through them.

By equating the Word with more than Scripture, Barth sought to speak of God's revealing activity as personal and dynamic. Yet in Barth's conception, God's Word does not break forth in any way which is not dependent on the Bible. Although attempts to interpret Barth's statements about biblical authority have created endless controversy, in his actual theologizing Barth turned repeatedly to Scripture as his primary source and norm.[85]

It should be noted that, in an important sense, Barth was indebted to Enlightenment thinkers such as David Hume, Immanuel Kant, and the British analytic tradition in philosophy. By shattering the complacent acceptance of the rational approach to the knowledge of God, these thinkers forced theologians such as Barth to seek to work out the form and content of their theology in independence of speculative reason.

Barth contended that Hume and Kant, who had opposed the rational approach to the knowledge of God, were right for the wrong reasons! They were right in affirming that philosophical reasoning cannot bring a person to a true knowledge of God, but wrong in assuming that this was true because human knowledge could be obtained only through experiences. The real explanation, said Barth, is that human beings are sinners, and sinners by definition are rebels, and enemies, spiritually blind persons. For this reason, sinners can be reached by God only with a gospel, not through reason.[86]

According to Barth, it is theologically and spiritually confusing, if not totally chaotic, to affirm that we can know God both through natural theology and revealed theology. Barth does not see natural theology as only a case of bad logic or poor theology. Rather, he sees it as the act of the sinner's spiritual rebellion, the sinner's stronghold against the true knowledge of God in the revelation of God in Jesus Christ. In Barth's view, a saving knowledge of God is to be found only in Scripture—not in the natural world, the Jewish Torah, nor in the conscience of the Gentile.[87]

The later Barth (after 1932) was greatly influenced by the approach of Anselm, which he saw as a helpful lesson in the use of reason for purposes of clarification. According to Barth's interpretation of Anselm, once we have come to the knowledge of God through Jesus Christ, we may seek to understand in sharper lines the God in whom we believe.

From the perspective of conservative theology, Barth has many deficiencies. One weakness, according to Colin Brown, is that the later Barth was more interested in theological interpretation than in the historicity of the events he interprets. As discussed many times above, historicity is one of the unique claims of the Christian faith. Christianity is no mere esoteric, other-worldly religion; it claims to be grounded in history and experience. Key concepts such as the Resurrection are put forward in the New Testament as events in time and space, and they are subject to historical verification. Thus Barth's apparent indifference to the historical question causes him to ignore one of the important distinctives of the Christian faith.[88]

Bernard Ramm, however, contends that Barth knew there must be a real connection between history and Christian theology. He also contends that the notion that Barth could live with a theological history divorced from ordinary, empirical history is a preposterous notion, for too much theology of Scripture is tied into history. Furthermore, Barth did not believe that historical difficulties in Scripture invalidate its theology. According to Ramm, Barth attempted to come to terms with equal rights for all: (1) historical science as understood in modern times, (2) the actual nature of biblical history as it stands in the text, and (3) the theological integrity of the historical element in Scripture.[89]

Barth was convinced that faith is not dependent on science—in this case, historical science. Barth concentrated on the biblical material itself, on the reality that gets its validity through the biblical witnesses. "Seeking to understand, I must advance to that point where I stand before nothing but the mystery of the matter itself and not the mystery of the documents." This is not a retreat from the text of the Bible, but an intense concentration precisely on the deep content of the text.[90]

In any case, Barth's approach to faith and reason has much to commend it. He affirms that personal encounter is primary to knowledge of God, but he avoids extreme subjectivism by grounding that encounter in the revelation of the Word. He also made a place for God-given reason in clarifying what the Word reveals.

True, this is a preconceived worldview, but all humans, for good or ill, have preconceived views. For the Christian, the beginning is the primary datum of the Christian faith—God's revelation of himself in his Word. If the biblical datum is the guiding principle of the worldview, then reason can be utilized to positive effect.[91]

6. The View of Carl F. H. Henry

Henry holds a presuppositional view which is similar to that of Van Til. However, he has always been much more appreciative of the role of reason in the unregenerate. For Henry, as for Augustine, reason is the instrument which recognizes, organizes, and elucidates. But reason does not *verify* revelation. Revelation is the source of all truth and is its own verifying principle. As an instrument, reason must simply acquiesce in the Bible's claim to be the revelation of God, for the Bible is the axiom by which reason itself will ultimately be tested.[92]

Henry is careful to point out that reason and faith are not opposed to one another, but complementary. Faith without reason leads to skepticism; reason without faith does the same. And rationality permeates the revelational outlook.

We must remember that the Logos, or the wisdom of God incarnated, is at the beginning and center and climax of divine disclosure. God calls human beings to think his thoughts after him. But revelation lifts human reason beyond restrictions of intellects that are limited by human finitude and clouded by sin. Speculative arguments alone cannot provide the basis or the framework for the Christian worldview.[93]

7. The Cultural-Linguistic View of George Lindbeck

As indicated in earlier chapters, George Lindbeck of Yale has been an important figure in relating the enormous recent growth in the sciences of linguistics and cultural anthropology to biblical theology. In his *The Nature of Doctrine: Religion and Theology in a Postliberal Age,* he suggests that he has been inspired by both Wittgenstein and Barth in framing his cultural-linguistic approach, which stresses the very intimate connection between the language of a culture and the way it perceives reality.

For Lindbeck, the experience of becoming a Christian involves learning the story of Israel and of Jesus well enough to interpret and experience oneself and one's world in its terms. The proclamation of the gospel, then, is first of all the telling of the biblical story. Furthermore, this proclamation gains power and meaning insofar as it is embodied in the total gestalt of church life and action.[94]

Hauerwas and Willimon suggest that Lindbeck has made clear why we are no longer content, as pastors and theologians, to stand on the periphery, hat in hand, apologetically trying to translate our religious convictions into "rational" terms that "speak the language" of the world around us. Rather, we should now be ready to say that our Christian convictions lay down a program, a vision, a revealed paradigm for accommodating the world to the gospel. For as Lindbeck suggests, religion is not just a set of presuppositions to be believed or disbelieved, but rather a revealed way of life involving a set of skills that one employs in living. Such skills are acquired by learning the stories of Israel and Jesus well enough not only to interpret the world, but to do so in specifically Christian terms.[95]

8. The Approach of Millard J. Erickson as Applied to Christology

Millard J. Erickson of Bethel Theological Seminary has applied the "Faith and Reason" approach to the contemporary debate in christology.

The "faith only" approach to Christ taught by Emil Brunner and other existentialist theologians drew heavily upon the thought of Kierkegaard. According to this position, our knowledge of Jesus' deity is not grounded in any historically provable facts about his earthly life, but is a faith based upon the faith of the apostles as enunciated in the kerygma or proclamation.[96]

The "reason and then faith" approach used by Pannenberg is related in some ways to Thomas Aquinas; it seeks to demonstrate the supernatural character of Christ from historical evidences. Hence, the deity of Christ is not a presupposition, but a conclusion of the process. The appeal is to historical reason, not to faith or authority. As faith predominates in the former model, reason does here.[97]

Erickson, however, accepts the "faith and reason" approach which goes back, as we have seen, to Augustine. In this approach, faith precedes but does not remain permanently independent of reason. Faith provides the perspective or starting point from which reason may function, enabling a person to understand what he or she otherwise could not.[98]

When this model is applied to the construction of a christology, the starting point is the kerygma, the belief and preaching of the church about Christ. The content of the kerygma serves as a hypothesis or faith presupposition which is used to interpret and integrate the data supplied by inquiry into the historical Jesus. According to this position, the early church's interpretation of or faith in Christ enables us to make better sense of the historical phenomena than does any other hypothesis. This approach is not christology from below, which, ignoring the kerygma, leads to problems in attempting to understand the "mystery of Jesus." Nor is this approach an unsupported christology from above, constructed without reference to the earthly life of Jesus of Nazareth. Rather, it is tested and supported and rendered reasonable by the ascertainable historical facts of who and what Jesus was and claimed to be.[99]

This model follows neither faith alone nor historical reason alone, but both together in an intertwined, mutually dependent, simultaneously progressing fashion. Increased familiarity with the proclaimed Christ will enable us to understand and integrate more of the data of historical research. Similarly, increased understanding of the Jesus of history will more fully persuade us that the apostles' interpretation of the Christ of faith is true.[100]

There is a biblical basis for this approach. Some of those who knew Jesus' words and deeds very well did not necessarily arrive at an accurate knowledge of him. For example, the Pharisees saw Jesus perform miraculous healings through the power of the Holy Spirit (Matt. 12:22–32; Mark 3:20–30; Luke 11:14–23). Although they certainly were familiar with the Jewish traditions and presumably had observed Jesus for quite some time, their appraisal was, "He casts out demons by the power of Beelzebub." Somehow, they failed to draw the right conclusion, although they possessed a knowledge of the facts. And the Pharisees were not alone in not knowing Jesus; even those closest to Jesus failed to know him fully. Judas betrayed him. The other disciples did not realize the significance of his crucifixion and even his resurrection. The religious authorities obviously knew that the tomb was empty, but did not interpret this fact correctly.[101]

On a more positive note, there are also indications that when one comes to a correct perception of Jesus, it is on the basis of something more than natural perception. For example, when in response to Jesus' question, "Who do you say that I am?" Peter replied, "You are the Christ, the Son of the living God," Jesus commented, "Flesh and blood has not revealed this to you, but my Father who is in heaven" (Matt. 16:15–17). While there is a debate over the exact meaning of "flesh and blood," it is clear that Jesus is contrasting some sort of direct revelation from the heavenly Father with some purely human source such as the opinions of others.[102]

Another case in point is John the Baptist. In prison he began to wonder about Christ, and so he sent two of his disciples to ask the Lord, "Are you he who is to come, or shall we look for another?" (Luke 7:19). John may have been expecting some concrete historical event (perhaps his own release from prison?) as evidence that Jesus was indeed, as John knew him to be, the Christ. Jesus' answer was to point to the deeds he had been performing: "The blind receive their sight, the lame walk, lepers are cleansed, and the deaf hear, the dead are raised up, the poor have good news preached to them" (v. 22). The historical Jesus was the confirmation of the Christ of faith.[103]

In this approach, the two factors are held in conjunction: not the Jesus of history alone nor the Christ of faith alone, but the proclaimed Christ of the kerygma as the key that unlocks the historical Jesus, and the facts of Jesus' life as support for the message that he is the Son of God. Faith in the Christ will lead us to an understanding of the Jesus of history. It is a matter of "faith and reason."[104]

IV. What Is the Biblical Teaching on the Place of Reason and Faith in Relation to the Knowledge of God?

The three basic approaches to faith and reason have been described. It is appropriate, then, that the key ideas of the biblical perspective be presented as guidelines for evaluation of the various approaches to faith and reason.

1. God's Revelation as the Basic Source of Knowledge

(1) Self-Disclosure versus Human Discovery. The dominant message of the Bible in regard to the knowledge of God is that we do not discover God; rather, he reveals himself to us.

Discovery, in the modern sense of the word, is a human act of discernment. The initiative comes from the human discoverer, and the discovered object is relatively passive. Self-disclosure or self-revelation, however, is a voluntary act on the part of the one who is to be known.

The biblical teaching on revelation insists that we know God because he discloses or uncovers himself by his initiative. Without this initiative, there would be no knowledge of God—at least, not in a saving or redemptive sense.

A simple analogy of this is how a human person comes to know other persons. Without self-disclosure, the actual person cannot be known. He or she can be observed as a physical object, of course. As a falling body in a vacuum, for instance, a human being can be seen to have the same acceleration as a feather or a lead ball. But the person as a person remains inaccessible unless he or she chooses to reveal himself or herself.

Psychotherapists are quite familiar with this phenomenon, for psychotherapy and psychoanalysis depend upon human self-disclosure for their existence. Unless patients intentionally or unintentionally reveal themselves, therapists are helpless to treat the psychic sickness.[105] Similarly, unless God chooses to reveal himself to humankind, we are helpless to know him.

(2) Revelation versus Observation. Because knowledge of God must depend on God's intentional self-disclosure; scientific observation of the universe, including the moral and religious history of humankind, could never finally prove the existence or character of God. At best, these arguments for the existence and character of God can only make God a reasonable hypothesis.

If one is serious about knowing God, one must turn to the Bible, which is a result of the revelation of God in a series of self-disclosures in a continuous history—first to Israel and then to the new Israel, the church.[106]

2. The Acts of God as a Source of Knowledge

(1) Particular Events versus Abstract Truths. The Bible tends to be ultrapragmatic: It tells us nothing about God except his ways and his acts. What the Bible says God *is* really amounts to saying what he *does*. Descriptions of his nature are really descriptions of his function and behavior, and therefore the attributes or qualities ascribed to God are primarily descriptions of his acts. The Bible tells us nothing, and therefore we can know nothing significant, about the *being* of God. The only positive affirmations we can make are affirmations of the divine activity in relation to humankind and the world.[107]

In fact, as earlier chapters have shown, God's self-revelation in human history as recorded in the Bible is incredibly particularistic; that is, he reveals himself in the form of specific events rather than in the form of abstract truths. This particularism as seen in the histories of Israel and the church is as much a scandal to the modern mind as it was to the mind of Greek antiquity, for both tend to identify truth with the timeless and the universal.[108]

According to the biblical worldview, then, God is not Plato's "pure form," Spinoza's "universal substance," Paul Tillich's "object of ultimate concern," or Alfred North Whitehead's "value creating process." Rather, the Bible reveals him as the Definite One—the specific Person who reveals himself through specific events.[109]

The particularism of the Bible further insists that certain events within the history of God's dealings with Israel and the church are uniquely significant as conveyors of divine self-revelation. In the Jewish faith, this crucial event is the "event at Sinai"—a term that includes the whole complex of events beginning with the call of Moses and culminating in the "reception of the Torah." This "Sinai-event," according to Jewish thought, is that part of Jewish inner history which illumines the rest of it and makes it intelligible. Thus Exodus-Sinai is, for the Jew, the interpretive center of redemptive history. This is similar to the way in which the Incarnation, the Cross, and the Resurrection are central for the Christian.[110]

(2) God's Attributes and Qualities as Revealed by His Actions. Since in the biblical worldview God's self-revelation to us takes the form of specific acts, it follows that knowledge of God's attributes and of the qualities of his character is not attained primarily by abstract reason, but by inference from the observed activity of God in the governance of the world.

For instance, in the Old Testament, the Hebrew's understanding of God's power, holiness, and love came as a result of God's meeting them and choosing them in their weakness. He had shown his power over all human and natural powers in delivering them from oppression. Accordingly, in all subsequent events they could but recognize and acknowledge the one deity who had chosen and saved them. Wherever they were, or in whatever condition, he was to be found in their midst.[111]

Even the biblical accounts of the Creation, the Fall, the flood, and last things were undergirded by what God has done in history. They describe how the world must have begun and what the outcome of history must be in order to be consistent with God's experienced character and purpose. The beginning and end of history were interpreted by faith and revelation (not myth) and confirmed by the historical experience of God's people.

The language used of God by the Hebrews was inevitably concrete, historical, and based upon human analogy. To confess God meant to describe what he had done. The deepening of the language in the direction of the abstract was only gradually and partially accomplished when through the succession of historical events he revealed himself more clearly.[112]

(3) Biblical Dynamism versus Alternative Views. The dynamic moving vigor revealed by the biblical God stands in complete contrast to the Greek impersonal "first cause" and to the mystic's Source of illumination and beatification. It also contrasts clearly with every form of deism or philosophical abstraction. The God of the Bible is "the living God," in contrast to the dying-rising deities of the natural-cycle religions. He is the God of history, in bold contrast to the Greek and Hindu philosophies that teach that a deity involved in time and earthly life could be neither absolute nor good.[113]

The idols of the nations know nothing and can do nothing; Yahweh alone is the source of both creative and destructive activity. His directing presence is the comfort of the faithful, the terror of the wicked, and the problem for which Job seeks an answer (Job 7:17–21).

(4) Jesus as the Most Important Source of Knowledge. According to the biblical worldview, what God has done in Jesus is the most important thing human beings can know. Knowing the Incarnation, the Cross and the Resurrection is the only way we can sufficiently know God and his work and will. Only a high christology will adequately express what we know of God and should think of Christ.[114]

The concept of Christ as coeternal with the Father did not come from metaphysical speculations about his person. Rather, it came as a result of his unique and decisive work. The work of Christ drove the believer to develop a high theology about him. Remember, Paul was not a metaphysical speculator, but a proclaimer of what he knew in his conversion and Christian life and what he saw in his missionary activity. The unique and decisive work of Christ forced Paul to acknowledge Christ as God's Son.

3. Biblical Language as a Source of Knowledge

The very kinds of language used in the Bible can be an important source of knowledge about God's purposes and his relation to humankind. Rather than describing God in terms of abstract categories, the Bible describes him in concrete terms—making free and frank use of metaphor and anthropomorphic language.

As shown in chapter 3, the modern revolution in the philosophy of language has affirmed the value and importance of this kind of language in the Bible. It is possible to show that even what we regard as literal words and statements are actually expressions which were once metaphoric or symbolic in character. In other words, there are only two kinds of speech, live metaphors and dead metaphors. Since so-called literal expressions were once metaphoric, it follows that the metaphoric mode is more basic. This indicates that God-talk would have its deepest grounding in the metaphoric mode.[115]

The standard objection to this way of thinking is to claim that increased precision brings increased understanding. This would mean that nonmetaphoric speech is preferable to metaphoric, especially in theology. However, as Wittgenstein showed, such precision is neither possible nor necessary as an ideal for communication. There is no such thing as absolute precision of language; rather, there is only significant precision in the light of the context and purposes at hand.

When this understanding of the nature of language is brought to bear on the question of the meaning of religious and theological language, the results are as exciting as they are astounding. It is safe to say that the vast majority of Christian thinking about the function of God-talk has been predicated on the assumption, borrowed from Western philosophy, that the chief end of language is to transfer information in an abstract manner.[116]

On the other hand, both the Old Testament and Jesus used the metaphoric mode and the narrative or story method as the primary means of speaking about God, the kingdom, and faith. This approach always engages people at the concrete level where they live. It encourages people to see or walk forward to a richer understanding and commitment.[117]

In the Bible it is clear that God is not to be conceived as an abstract idea or principle. He is not apprehended primarily by means of an undefined, impersonal analogy or a technical definition. Rather, God is described in anthropomorphic terms, as a person possessing practically all human characteristics, including bodily form and personality, though excluding sex and physical needs. God is not described in the detached, technical language of science, but in expressive, ordinary language. He is portrayed through concrete metaphors as a living, active, forceful personality whom human beings can meet, know, and worship. He is One before whom they can bow in confession of sin and not be broken as before an inexorable law of fate. He is One in whom they can find both justice and forgiveness.[118]

Of course, anthropomorphism (God portrayed by human qualities) has its limits, which the Bible clearly defines. For example, as the second commandment shows, one is not to confine or materialize God (Exod. 20:4). God cannot be seen by human eye, and thus when he actually confronts humanity, his presence is hidden by a blinding brilliance, called his "glory," or by a cloud or smoke (Exod. 19:9). Indeed, as Hosea 11:9 clearly states, God is God and not a human. Nevertheless, God reveals himself as a personality whom humans can know and describe as being known in the language familiar to them.[119]

4. Obedience and Participation as a Source of Knowledge

(1) The Objective Detachment of the Greeks and Modern Science. The Greek and modern scientific way of knowledge is the way of objective detachment. In this method it is understood that the known reality, whether this refers to a thing or a person, always remains an object. The person seeking knowledge observes the object through the medium of the senses and more especially through the sense of sight. The subject must, as far as lies in his power, keep the greatest possible distance between himself and the object. He will master it only in so far as he restricts himself to observing it objectively. Knowledge, to the Greeks, is essentially detached, impersonal learning, the pure observation of things and persons which are assimilated by the mind through the medium of the idea. Furthermore, to the Greeks, the opposite of such knowledge can only be ignorance and error.[120]

(2) The Old Testament Combination of Objectivity and Encounter in Knowledge. The Old Testament view of knowledge does not exclude objectivity, but it goes beyond objectivity to stress involvement. In the Old Testament, "to know" certainly implies observation and intellectual grasp, but it also has another and far more significant meaning: to encounter, to experience, to share in. The Old Testament writers have a limited concern with grasping an object by means of the "idea" of it. Rather, they seek to allow themselves to be encountered by a reality which invades the inner recesses of the personality of the "subject" himself and draws him into its control.[121]

This approach involves a vital connection between the knowing "subject" and the known "object." From the Old Testament point of view, "to know" means to give one's consent to this personal commitment. It is not the intelligence alone which is involved; the will also comes into operation. Accordingly, in the Hebrew conception, the opposite of knowledge is not mere ignorance and error. Rather, lack of knowledge is related to disobedience, rebellion, or sin.

This conception of knowledge informs the biblical description of the relations between God and the people of Israel. For God to know Israel means not just that God knows Israel exists and is aware of what Israel has done, but that God pledges himself to Israel as a husband pledges himself to his bride. Similarly, for Israel to know God means not just that Israel is aware "there is" a God, but that Israel accepts God's covenant (Hos. 2:20), keeps his mighty acts constantly in mind (Deut. 11:2), ascribes glory to him, and obeys Him (Isa. 11:2).[122]

(3) The Place of Obedience in the New Testament Understanding of Knowledge. The New Testament retained the Hebrew conception of knowledge as involving

active participation. In particular, knowledge of God in the New Testament is the obedient recognition of the work of God, with the assumption that from now onward this work is fulfilled in Jesus Christ. The New Testament conviction is that Christ's work, completed but still hidden, will be gloriously revealed at the end of the ages for the salvation of those who believe. Then and only then will our knowledge of him be complete.

There was another wrinkle in the New Testament situation that affected the New Testament view of the knowledge of God. The apostolic message was addressed also to pagans. Thus it became necessary to pass on to these the knowledge of the divine acts of which they were ignorant. The knowledge imparted was at the intellectual level at first, but the texts make it quite clear that such knowledge could not remain at the theoretical level without becoming empty and meaningless (1 Cor. 13:2, 8, 9, 12). An intellectual awareness of the mighty acts of God is a necessary condition, but in no sense an all-sufficient condition of true knowledge. A saving knowledge always remains a gift of God bestowed through the Holy Spirit (1 Cor. 12:8) and received through faith acting in love (Phil. 1:9–11; Philem. 6).[123]

Excursus on the Liberation Theology Emphasis on Obedience and Participation as a Source of Knowledge

1. Definition and Perspective

It is significant that just at the time when traditional systematic theology is apparently declining in influence, many non-Western and minority groups have begun expressing their faith in nontraditional fashion. A number of scholars see a correlation between these so-called "liberation theologies" and the issue of obedience as a source of knowledge.

These so-called theologies of liberation come from three main groups: Latin Americans, Blacks, and women. In North America, "liberation theology" has also served as a designation for widely varied ideological and cultural movements, including some of the legitimate Protestant heirs of the social gospel and some of the more conservative social action emphases.[124]

Most liberation theologians emphasize the importance of participation and action as a source of understanding. This emphasis grows organically out of the nature of liberation theology. Liberation theologies are written from the standpoint of groups who feel themselves to be oppressed. Their proponents insist that the social location of the theologian is important, and they point out that the academic environment, where most traditional theology has been formulated, is largely a product of a social establishment. Academic theologians and their audiences almost always are white, male, and at least middle-class. The problems of being black, female, or poor do not touch them. Thus, according to liberation theologians, academic theology tends to perpetuate the interests and concerns of the establishment while neglecting those of the oppressed.

2. Methodology of Liberation Theology

In seeking to see life from the underside, liberation theologies are developing a new methodology. In a general sense it can be called inductive. It is experimental or participatory in nature.

Liberation methodology is not just a way of thinking, but an intertwining of action and reflection known as "praxis." This approach is opposed to the notion that truth can be discerned and articulated on an intellectual level removed from practical concerns. Instead, praxis originates as involvement in some concrete situation which people are trying to change. Thought arises as one element of these efforts toward change. It analyzes and criticizes these actions and that situation. Yet such thinking is always employed to further that process of change.

To the liberation theologian, then, truth is at the level of history, not in the realm of ideas. Reflection on praxis, on human significant action, can only be authentic when it is done from within, in the area of the strategic and tactical plane of human action.[125]

5. Sin and Rebellion as a Deterrent to Saving Knowledge (Problems with Natural Revelation)

In some circles there is a continuing interest in a natural or general revelation. This is a knowledge of God freed from all particular contexts and accessible to all humans simply because they are human. Proponents of this general revelation say that the heavens declare the glory of God to all alike. There is something in the human reason, conscience, or imagination that can lead a person to God if he or she will follow. And if there is such a "general" revelation, of what ultimate need or significance is the very different kind of special revelation to which Scripture testifies?[126]

It cannot be denied that human beings possess the basic capacity to know God and his ways. For since humankind was made for loving fellowship with God, such purpose in creation implies the possibility of direct knowledge and a personal relationship. Hence Scripture depicts Adam in familiar intercourse with God and enjoying full knowledge of his environment. But the fact that humankind rebelled against the living God changed the nature of that easy relationship and clouded the knowledge of God.[127]

One problem with general revelation from the biblical perspective is the fact that human beings are finite creatures and that, as a result, their view of things is conditioned by their particular position in the universe. Everything we human beings see, therefore, we see from our special perspective. Even if we could, as some idealist philosophers such as Hegel pretend, rethink God's thoughts, these thoughts would necessarily be relativized. They would also to some degree be falsified by our creaturely particularity.

From a biblical perspective, a much more important criticism of general revelation is the fact that despite the revelation of God in nature and conscience, human beings are sinners. Our sinful egocentricity distorts and perverts everything in the interests of the self and its idols. Sin blinds us and makes us deaf. Accordingly, sin leads humankind away from the knowledge of God and toward false doctrines and ideologies.[128]

It should be noted that although the effects of sin are pervasive, they do not touch all aspects of human thought in the same manner. Emil Brunner points out, for example, that the effect of sin on reason is a gradual one. The "objective" human reason becomes increasingly obscured and perverted by sin as it approaches closer and closer to the inner "subjective" core of existence. When it comes to the matter of a saving knowledge of God and therefore of an authentic knowledge of human nature, the incapacity of the unaided human reason is only too obvious.[129]

Nevertheless, since the essential nature of humankind has not been destroyed by sin, human beings remain religious and strive to relate their being to something ultimate beyond themselves. When they try to do this through their own powers, they fall into idolatry, or at best into some form of pantheism. On this level, the natural light of human reason is not merely insufficient, but actually delusive.[130]

Thus we see that human religious life is inadequate without God's rescuing special revelation. It is a more or less positive and a more or less negative answer to God's manifestation of his everlasting power and diversity in nature and conscience. All human beings are dimly aware of God, but in our selfishness and sin we pervert and distort this awareness. We invent gods in the likeness and image of humans and animals. We succumb to superstition and immorality. Without the light and salvation described in the Bible, humanity's effort to transcend self and reach what is beyond inevitably results in the conversion of the "wholly other" into an idolatrous god after humankind's own heart.[131]

V. What Is the Place of the Rational Arguments in Proving the Existence of God?

Since the time of the Greeks, there have been attempts on the part of philosophers and theologians to make use of rational arguments to prove the existence of God. As indicated earlier in this chapter, the use of reason alone in approaching God has been clearly shown to be limited, but the classical rational arguments nevertheless have some value.

1. The Origin and Development of the Rational Arguments

(1) The Place of Plato and Aristotle. The origin of natural theology, or the rational approach to the knowledge of God, is to be found in Greek thought. If Plato's interpretation of Socrates is historically accurate, then Socrates may be regarded as the first thinker in the Western world who argued for the existence of the soul and of God. These themes recur several places in Plato's writings. In the *Laws,* they are given a detailed analysis in a series of passages remarkable for the way they summarize most of the subsequent discussion of the issues.

Natural theology is taken up and given more systematic formulation in Book XII of Aristotle's *Metaphysics*. Aristotle's argument, like that of Plato, begins with the fact of motion and change in the universe. It then affirms the impossibility of an infinite series of "movers" and then proceeds to the conclusion that there must be a "first mover" that is itself unmoved. Similarly Aristotle argues from the basic idea of causality, and from the presumed impossibility of an infinite causal series, to a first cause. From Aristotle the conception of God as first cause and unmoved mover found its way into the mainstream of Western thought.

As the rational arguments emerged in medieval scholastic theology and in later thought, the list included four arguments: (1) cosmological, (2) teleological, (3) ontological, and (4) moral.[132]

(2) The Place of Thomas Aquinas in Developing the Arguments. Some light can be shed upon these arguments by a study of the historical situation which produced their use by Christian thinkers. Aristotle had been neglected in favor of Plato in the early church. His works were hardly available in Christian Europe during the medieval Dark Ages, although Islamic scholars utilized his work. Thus, until the early years of the thirteenth century, European Christendom knew little of Aristotle; the thought utilized by theologians was fundamentally Platonic. But at that time, knowledge of Aristotle seeped into Europe from Arabian culture, which had been brought to Spain.

The first impact of Aristotle was a stimulus to skepticism. In this situation of conflict, Thomas Aquinas undertook the task of mediation, attempting to show how the new categories of Aristotelian philosophy could be successfully employed to demonstrate the truth of orthodox Christianity. This spirit of mediation has led to the description of Thomas Aquinas as the first modernist.

What Aquinas did for the Christian faith at this important juncture can be seen in that context as a very bold, creative thing. He saw at once that a case must be made for God against this unrelenting, hostile pressure of skepticism brought about by Aristotelian philosophy. He chose to do this by meeting his adversaries on common ground, and thus proceeded to baptize Aristotle for the purpose at hand.[133]

In the hands of Aquinas, classical thought became not the opponent but the handmaiden of Christian doctrine. Aquinas did this not only in the *Summa Theologica*, where he set forth the grounds of belief for Christians themselves, but also in the *Summa Contra Gentiles*, where he undertook to prove God to those outside the household of faith. Under the guidance of Aquinas, philosophy, which had threatened to become the deadly enemy of Christian theology, became instead its auxiliary and ally.[134]

The five arguments of Thomas may be summarized as follows:

- Since motion exists, a first mover must be assumed.
- Since things are caused, a first cause must be assumed.
- Since contingent things exist, a necessary being must be assumed.

- Since varying degrees of perfection exist, an infinitely perfect being must be assumed.
- Since things show evidence of design, a designing intelligence must be assumed.

The first four arguments may be classified as varying formulations of the cosmological argument (first cause), since they argue from the world to God. The last is a formulation of the teleological argument, since it argues from the alleged fact of design in the world to a divine, designing intelligence.

From its inception, Thomism has been a formidable system. Proponents of Thomism regard it as the perennial philosophy, the definitive statement of the principles of universal rationality. In 1879, centuries after the time of Thomas Aquinas, Pope Leo XIII designated his teachings the official norm of Roman Catholic teaching and thought.[135]

2. The Value of the Cosmological Argument (First Cause)

As science, in the modern sense of the term, the Aristotelian-Thomist views of motion and cause are seriously defective. Their advocates answer this criticism by arguing that they were always meant as philosophy, not science. And as philosophy—a description of being in its most general terms—these conceptions still have validity.[136]

(1) A Definition of the Cosmological Argument. The essence of the cosmological argument is the contention that this world of contingent and mutable beings and things is not a self-explanatory world. We can only make sense of the undeniable fact that it exists by supposing that there exists also a noncontingent, or necessary, immutable reality which is responsible for its being. In other words, if the world exists, then God exists. And since the world manifestly *does* exist, of necessity, God exists also.

This simple hypothetical syllogism summarizes conveniently the bare form of the argument. Every concrete example of it, however, has to go beyond this bare form. Such a concrete example must indicate some specific type of relationship between God, the Necessary Being, and this contingent world that will show how he is responsible for it and will also substantiate the claim that presupposing divine existence will alone enable us to resolve the riddle of the universe.[137]

Essentially, the cosmological argument rejects a self-producing universe. Christian believers hold that the universe cannot be self-producing, self-governing, and self-authenticating. Instead, it depends on God for its beginning, remains within his control for its continuance, and groans and travails toward the realization of his purpose.

Science has not disproved this understanding of the cosmological argument. At the very least, we can say that the conception of the universe's being brought into existence by God's mighty act and of its being sustained throughout the ages by God's moving energy are not contrary to many theories of science which are being worked out in this atomic age. Of course, this does not mean that we have scientific proof of the existence of God or blueprints of his creative activity. It does mean, however, that we can confess God as Creator with a depth of meaning. We can call the world, as Isaiah did, to forsake its idols and lift up its eyes to him who did not create this universe in vain.[138]

(2) Relationship of the Cosmological Argument to the Doctrine of Creation. The biblical affirmation from Genesis to Revelation is rich in vivid and compelling statements of the central Christian theme of creation. There can be some value in the cosmological argument as it seeks to undergird this revealed truth.

It does this by pointing out that nature does not and cannot provide our minds with a complete explanation of itself. In fact, a careful study of nature discloses regularities and continuities which indicate the working of a power not confined to nature. If one begins with a consideration of physical events, it makes sense to believe that a being or at least a principle exists which bears a suspicious resemblance to what religious people call God.

Thus the cosmological argument, based firmly upon the Christian conviction that the world of nature is God's own creation, takes up the gauntlet which atheistic naturalism throws down to faith. Either nature is totally void of reasonable significance, or else it causes us to seek a meaning in a reality that is suggested by—though not included in—its constituent facts. In other words, we have to choose between God and nothing—or at least between God and some impersonal, immanent drive in nature.

The objection may rightly be raised, of course, that the cosmological argument does not express anything like the whole Christian doctrine of creation. Yet it does succeed in pointing up this doctrine for the special purpose of talking persuasively with unbelievers.[139] Many sensitive Christians see the cosmological argument as preparing the mind for faith. Although we must not look to such an argument to *produce* faith, it can nevertheless induce a frame of mind into which faith may come more properly and surely.

Evangelical Christians do not claim, as do many Roman Catholic philosophers, that the cosmological kind of argument, at its very best, demonstrates the bare existence of God beyond all rational doubt. We prefer to say that it makes the existence of God highly probable—much more probable, indeed, than any alternative hypothesis.[140]

3. The Value of the Teleological Argument (Design)

(1) A Definition of the Teleological Argument. The teleological argument is based upon the idea of design. Its fundamental contention is that the universe must be viewed as a highly complex mechanism and thus as the product of a designing mind. Plato used this argument in the *Timaeus*, in which he contended that the principle that "the mind orders all things" is the only one worthy of the world around us and the heavens above us. The teleological argument is also one of the five arguments taught by Aquinas. It was not, however, until the eighteenth century that the argument came into its own and achieved its height of popularity. As developed by William Paley in his *Natural Theology*, it became the foundation

of the deistic view of God. Paley likened the universe to a watch, the design of which involves a human designer. Hence, he argued, by way of analogy, the abundant evidence of design in the world proves that it must have a designer, who can be no other than God.[141]

(2) The Reformulation of the Argument. Charles Darwin's famous doctrine of natural selection is widely supposed to have destroyed the value of the teleological argument. By showing that variations in species come about by purely natural and even accidental causes rather than by special design, Darwin's ideas are thought to invalidate the argument that since nature manifests purpose and design, there must of necessity be a Designer.[142]

Since Darwin, however, the teleological argument for the existence of God has been reformulated by such scholars as Richard Taylor and F. R. Tennant in an attempt to account not only for change and order, but for the adaptive order of the world. This approach emphasizes the amazing manner in which one order of being is adapted to another. The particular adaptations without which human and animal survival in nature would be impossible are especially stressed in the reformulations. We are led to a sense of a wider design of deeper contrivance.[143]

In these more up-to-date versions of the teleological argument, we are reminded that there is still orderliness and beauty in nature. The earth, so far as we know, is unique in providing the conditions which make life possible. The inorganic world seems to be a preparation for the organic, and the lower stages of organic development appear to be a preparation for the higher.

Thus many modern scholars, standing in the midst of all the phenomena which make up this richly intricate universe, believe they live in an ordered cosmos. Many draw from this pageant of living forms, with its specialized organs and complex interactions, the impression that working through all this process is a purpose, a movement toward ends, that is not merely mechanical. To many, this force looks like an intelligent and creative God who is both rich in being and powerful. He is using this long complex process of development for the working out of universal ends and goals.

The prominent British theologian F. R. Tennant, in particular, has sought to demonstrate that the Christian worldview is the most probable of possible world explanations. He does this from the standpoint of objective reasonableness rather than subjective certitude. In other words, Tennant holds that no logical proof for the Christian worldview is possible, but that acceptance of Christianity is possible on the grounds of probability.[144]

(3) Limitations and Continuing Validity of the Teleological Argument. There are certainly limitations to the argument from design, even its more modern reformulations. As an argument for God, it runs headlong into the counterargument that nature shows nonpurposive as well as teleological or purposive tendencies. These arguments certainly cannot be ignored; they are undoubtedly strong enough to deny any clinching validity to the argument from design when it stands by itself. They make inappropriate the complacency with which some people have

used it. And even if purpose were proved, it would only prove a creator God—an arranger—not the personal and active God revealed in the Bible.[145]

And yet the teleological argument will always have some validity. For one thing, it has always been the rational argument with the greatest appeal for ordinary people. And although it is not a conclusive proof of God, it does add, along with the other rational arguments, to the cumulative evidence for our belief in God.[146]

4. The Value of the Ontological Argument

To the cosmological and teleological arguments, traditional theism has added two others, the ontological and the moral. The ontological argument was rejected by Thomas Aquinas, who held that it violated the inductive procedures of factual argument. For this reason, it has long been regarded with suspicion by Roman Catholic philosophy. It is, however, one of the most important ideas in Western philosophic and theological thought.[147]

First suggested in the writings of Augustine, the ontological argument was clearly expressed by Anselm in the eleventh century. Anselm had stated the cosmological argument in a document called the *Monologium*, but he sought a better proof for the existence of God. In the *Proslogium*, he undertook this task, motivated by a desire to understand what he believed. (He tells us that his first title for the *Proslogium* was *Faith Seeking Understanding.*)[148]

(1) A Definition of the Ontological Argument. Strictly speaking, the ontological argument is not a rational argument at all, but an affirmation that the idea of God involves his existence. It is an *a priori*, not an *a posteriori*, affirmation; it claims that the knowledge of God is not derived from sense experience, but is logically prior. This argument does not involve a dialectical process which begins with everyday, external, and common-sense things, whose reality is accepted at their face value by all mankind, and then proceeds to demonstrate certain less evident, or perhaps even entirely unknown, truths. Rather, it discovers our inward experience of God, given in and through our self-consciousness, to be supremely revealing and significant among all other experiences, and then goes on to interpret all other experience in terms of it. According to this argument, God is not known through nature, but nature is known in God.[149]

Anselm's object in formulating the ontological argument was to demonstrate not that God exists, but that all rational beings believe in his existence. The main outlines of the ontological argument are well known: God, as we know him in our minds, is a being than whom no greater can be conceived. But if what we have in our minds is simply an idea which may or may not correspond to some external reality, then clearly what we have in our minds is not God at all. For God is not a human idea which may, but conceivably may not, have any real counterpart. To suppose, for the sake of argument, that God may not exist is in fact to confess one's ignorance of the very meaning of the word. If God exists at all, he certainly does not exist, either in my mind or anywhere else, as an idea which can intelligibly be called in question. He is either a reality or a self-contradictory idea.[150]

(2) Criticism and Defense of the Ontological Argument. The criticism of the argument is also familiar. Anselm's contemporary, Gaunilo, contends that it can never be legitimate to suppose that an idea in the mind must necessarily have its counterpart in reality. He points out that if we have an idea in our minds of an island so perfect that none more perfect is conceivable, it by no means follows that such an island exists.

The essence of this objection is the obvious fact that existence is not a predicate. I neither add to nor subtract from, nor alter in any way, the content of an idea by either asserting or denying that it corresponds to a reality. Whether I say: "Unicorns are a figment of the imagination" or "Unicorns really exist," I mean the same thing by the word *unicorn* in either case. In other words, the content of an idea never includes its reference to reality.[151]

Anselm's reply to Gaunilo has the force of limiting his reasoning to just one unique object, namely a supremely great being. Clearly Anselm never intended to propose the view that all our ideas necessarily correspond to something real. On the contrary, his aim was to demonstrate that this necessary correspondence must be granted in one unique case—God.[152]

For Anselm, the idea of God is not an idea at all, in a conceptual sense, but a vivid apprehension. Indeed, a valid criticism of Anselm is that he made a mistake in trying to express in the uncongenial form of a dialectical demonstration a profound inward experience, which would perhaps be better communicated through the autobiographical, dramatic, and literary philosophical style of Augustine. The final testimony of Anselm is that if we retire sufficiently into the depths of ourselves, if we explore reality as we know it in the very act of living it, we will find ourselves face to face with the fact of absolute being and will find that absolute being is God. In Anselm's thought, what the ontological argument demonstrates is not the general validity of metaphysics, but the necessity of theism.[153]

J. V. Langmead Casserley, in defending Anselm's development of the ontological argument in a religious sense, points out that Anselm was influenced by the Bible's approach to the metaphysical theme of being in terms of the Absolute Singular. In this, he was really ahead of his time, for until the possibility of a real science of history and a valid logic of the singular had dawned upon the philosophic mind, this seemed like the very negation of rational method. Fortunately, the science of history has revived the concept of the singular and has brought forth new categories and intellectual methods. This was anticipated by Anselm's employment of the ontological argument to demonstrate the necessity not merely of metaphysics but of theism. Because Anselm was a biblical Christian, ultimate being for him was not universal but singular, so that any valid metaphysic in his view must necessarily take a theistic form, that is, must be more akin to history in its presentation of the Absolute than to abstract and discursive thought.[154]

In the classical metaphysics which the modern world has inherited from Plato, Aristotle, and Plotinus, absolute being must be conceived and defined if it is to be known at all in any significant sense. In contrast, in the philosophy of Augustine and Anselm, absolute being can only be apprehended and described. In the former of these two traditions, the function of reason is to discover, almost create. But in the latter tradition the vocation of reason is to apprehend, understand, and express a given experience which is prior to our reasoning and which provokes, stimulates, and disciplines our thought.[155]

In Anselm's view the existence of God is already given in our self-conscious experience, and the task of the Christian philosopher is to lay bare the latent meaning and implications of this basic apprehension. This approach confirms the implicit standpoint of the Bible, in which God is revealed supremely in a single course of historical events, in the history of Israel and the life of Jesus. The record of those events is found, by those who have tried to make it the stuff and basis of their personal lives, to be one which stretches and strains the latent capacities of human personality to the uttermost, and which calls on us to explore its depths.[156]

5. The Value of the Moral Argument

The moral argument will be discussed in detail in the chapter on the question of morality. However, a brief statement of this argument is in order in connection with the other arguments for the existence of God.

Among the widely different formulations of the moral argument, none is more famous or important than that of Immanuel Kant (1724–1804). In his *Critique of Pure Reason*, Kant severely criticized the cosmological, ontological, and teleological arguments.[157] Having removed these traditional arguments, at least to his satisfaction, Kant then set about constructing a new approach to theism, based upon moral experience, in his *Critique of Practical Reason*.

Kant held moral experience to be indubitable. This is, he conceived that there is an absolute and universal experience of obligation to respect persons—to treat human beings as ends rather than means. This being so, he asked the question: Upon what basis is moral experience intelligible or possible? His threefold answer was (1) freedom, (2) immortality, and (3) God. Thus it is in thinking out the consequences and implications of the indubitable fact that we are aware of and enjoy moral experience that metaphysical truths (such as the existence of God and the reality of human freedom and immortality) that are beyond the capacity of demonstrative metaphysics to prove may yet be recognized and believed.[158]

Many modern thinkers who have accepted Kant's criticism of demonstrative rationalist metaphysics as conclusive, or at least who have felt their force gravely weakened by the power of Kant's attack, have followed his lead in attempting to use the analysis of moral experience and its implications as a substitute for classical metaphysics in the philosophical approach to God and religion.[159]

It is significant to note that in Kant's last days, his view of God was significantly changing. Instead of just being an inference from or postulate of moral experience, he held, the reality of God is given directly and immediately in moral experience. God is not so much an inference from duty, but is experienced directly in the experience of duty.[160] In this approach moral experience is not just a point of departure for demonstrative argument, as in his *Critique of Practical Reason*. Rather, it is a supremely significant realm of experience in which our consciousness of duty is interpreted as a consciousness of a direct commandment from God.

4. A General Statement of the Significance of the Rational Arguments for God

The classical rational arguments have some value if they are seen as systematic attempts of reason to analyze and express critically the assumption of faith. They have an important ancillary position, but they are not fundamental. The life of religion is better expressed in prayer than argument.[161]

In other words, reason and rational arguments can lead the philosophical horse to water—but no farther. Whether a person participates in faith depends not just on what he thinks, but what he wills.[162]

A careful inspection shows that the rational arguments are circular; they assume what they seek to prove. Such reasoning, therefore, can never be more than probable. There is also the danger that faith will be distorted by the philosophical categories in which the rational arguments seek to express themselves, as was outlined in the discussion of Anselm and the ontological argument.[163]

Rational arguments can also become dangerous at the point that they assume that any human effort can successfully reduce God to a formula or an argument. This truth was effectively pointed out by the "faith only" tradition from Tertullian to Van Til. This tradition reminds us that, from the perspective of a personal God, attempts to prove God are almost an impertinence. For example, Sören Kierkegaard once stated that it is preferable to mock God rather than assume the disparaging air of importance with which one would prove God's existence. The existence or presence of a king is commonly acknowledged by an appropriate expression of subjection and submission—not by an attempt to prove that he does indeed exist! Similarly, in Kierkegaard's view, one best proves God's existence by worship and living.[164]

Finally, the late Professor Will Herberg of Drew University maintained that even if these rational proofs were to succeed in making their case, their success would be irrelevant to the biblical purpose. These arguments can prove no more than the probable validity of some ultimate metaphysical principle—a principle of perfection, a first cause, an unmoved mover, a demiurgic power, pure thought, or thinking itself.[165] They prove nothing about the existence of a personal God as he reveals himself in Scripture. Herberg maintained, moreover, that it is not helpful to attempt to deduce God from this given world or from the inner depths of the human consciousness. In these realities, after all, are mirrored our own confusions and limitations.[166]

5. The Biblical Type of Proof for God and His Power

Far more important than the classical rational proofs for God, according to Cherbonnier, is the proof inherent in the biblical message. Cherbonnier holds that the basic biblical question is whether or not God is trustworthy, and that once a person asks this question, he or she is prepared to receive the biblical proof for the existence of God. The ontological argument or any variation of the cosmological argument which presupposes an unbiblical conception of God is not valid. The final biblical proof is of a kind appropriate to a living God—the fulfillment of his promises. God's existence is proved not by philosophical arguments but by God himself as he fulfills his promises.[167]

The God of Jesus Christ can liberate human beings from the bondage of self by conferring upon them the one thing they cannot acquire by effort—agape love, which alone gives freedom. This gift of agape love results in a transformed heart and prepares humans to inherit the destiny originally prepared for them—the glorious liberty of the children of God. This transformed life is not a life of enslavement, but one of freedom. Agape love binds human beings together in a redemptive community.

So Christianity stands or falls not with rationalistic argument, but with the claim that God acted in history to fulfill his promises. Christ promised to forgive sins, incorporate men into a redemptive community, and bind up and renew men in agape love.[168] And that is the way he has acted, again and again, in the centuries that have followed his resurrection.

VI. What Is the Place of Reason, after Conversion, in the Life of a Christian?

1. The Role of Reason as an Inevitable Human Activity

Even if reason alone is insufficient to bring human beings to a knowledge of God, it will continue to have a role in the life of a Christian. This is true because human beings are creatures of both will and mind, of faith and reason. We are so constituted that we must think as well as act and feel; therefore our faith will necessarily have a rational component.

As long as human beings make assumptions of faith and think about them, the activity of criticism and appraisal will go on. The only alternative is a futile and frustrating attempt to put faith and reason in separate, watertight compartments. Such an attempt is disastrous to both faith and reason. It is significant to note that even those who have taken the "faith only" approach to the knowledge of God—for example, Luther and Kierkegaard—have made good use of reason in explicating their systems.

2. Rational Reflection as a Check upon Hasty, Superstitious, Illogical, or Contradictory Beliefs

Reason is more than just an inevitable human activity, however; it also serves several useful purposes in the context of faith. One of the most important of these purposes is to protect against false claims to revelation.

We know in advance that many alleged revelations are false, because there are absolutely contradictory claims. It cannot be true, for instance, that there is only one way by which human beings may be saved and, at the same time, many routes to salvation. However eager we may be for harmony and tolerance, we cannot be intellectually honest unless we face the fact that there is a real contradiction between conflicting claims. Therefore, the law of noncontradiction, a basic tool of logic, becomes a necessary tool of faith.[169]

If reason is not used in cases of contradictory claims to faith, there is little to prevent people from acting on blind credulity or choosing at random. In the words of Culbert Rutenber, "If it is nothing but a blind leap into the dark, then I might as well leap to Muhammad, or to Buddha, or to Mary Baker Glover Patterson Eddy and become a Christian Scientist." One way in which we can be rescued from blind credulity is by what Luther calls the negative function of reason. Reason has the negative function of pointing out where revelation has *not* taken place.[170]

No sane person tries to accept as authoritative revelation from God all writings which are self-declared to be such. The Koran, the Bhagavad-Gita, and *The Book of Mormon* cannot all be authoritative statements of the truth straight from the throne of God, yet each claims to be that. Not all self-proclaimed "revelations" can be true, for writings self-described as "revelations" contradict one another.

Few Christian writers have surpassed Tatian of the second century in their condemnation of reason as a guide in religion. Yet even Tatian reports that he used reason in his rejection of the pagan scriptures of the Romans and Greeks and the secret disclosures of the mystery religions. He reports that he reasoned that books and ideas which were so evil in many of their teachings and their effects on their devotees could not be of God. On the other hand, the superior qualities of the Bible commended it to his belief. Centuries later, reformer John Calvin officially recognized the necessity of such rational discrimination by including in his *Institutes of the Christian Religion* a chapter entitled "Rational Proofs to Establish the Belief of the Scripture."[171]

3. The Role of Reason in the Formulation and Communication of the Christian Faith

As soon as religious persons seriously try to communicate their faith to others, they necessarily involve themselves in reason. This is because such communication involves language, and all languages embody, in varying measure, a logical or rational structure. Without such structure, speech would be amorphous noise and written language would be meaningless scribbles on a page.

To communicate the Christian faith also involves the task of relating it to the many other aspects of culture, such as morality, art, science, and politics. Faith requires a language in which it can relate itself intelligibly and pertinently to the different areas and interests of culture, and the construction of such a language is one of the tasks of rational theology.[172]

4. The Role of Reason in Clarifying, Organizing, and Discovering the Implications of Revealed Truth

Even if a person has received a divinely revealed message, has recognized it as such, and has carefully distinguished it from false "revelations," that person is still not free of dependence upon reason. Reason will still be required to interpret the revelation and discover its implications for the ever-changing situations of everyday life.[173]

5. The Role of Reason in Removing Barriers to Faith

Those people who have difficulty coming to faith because of intellectual difficulties deserve our sympathy and respect, provided they are honest and sincere in their doubts. It is unwise or even immoral to urge such men and women to overcome their intellectual difficulties by suppressing them, even though suppression may seem to bear fruit in some cases. An act of faith which is only made possible by suppressing honest doubts will result in a life of faith which is continually weakened by the lurking presence of those same doubts.

It is far better to seek to dissipate doubts by careful intellectual analysis than to try to suppress them. In a way, rational theology may be likened to psychoanalysis. It seeks to disperse, by a process of patient and dispassionate analysis, the roots of doubt. It also deals with those half-concealed, sometimes altogether unconscious, intellectual difficulties which prevent persons from coming to God, and offering themselves to God, with their whole beings.[174]

6. The Role of Reason in Making Possible the Discussion and Comparison of Competing Views

We have noted throughout this study that a person's real choice is never "faith or no faith," but "which faith." An individual must choose from among the myriad faiths and philosophies that compete for the allegiance of mind and will.

Another important use of reason, therefore, is to facilitate the comparison of faith options by translating faith assumptions into a language in which meaningful discussion is possible. The task of rational analysis involves comparing the rational structures of differing views or orientations (for example, monism, naturalism, or agnosticism) with the Christian worldview and, in the process, showing the inadequacy of these alternative viewpoints. [175]

7. The Role of Reason in Showing the Unique Adequacy of the Christian Faith

In addition to making dialogue possible in the first place and showing the weaknesses of competing views, reason can effectively point out the unique adequacy of the Christian faith. Reason can show that the Christian hypothesis fits the facts of experience, as well as turning up new facts and illuminating particular areas of experience, in a way which cannot be matched by other worldviews.

George Marsden, professor at Duke University, points out that even if rational arguments are not compelling logically, they may have great psychological and even intellectual force, particularly for those who are wavering in their resolution to deny the presence of God and his Word. This is especially true if in fact Christianity accurately describes human conditions and needs and God's saving acts. For instance, if humans indeed have certain moral and religious sensibilities and needs to which the gospel best responds, then people might well be brought to some intuitive recognition of the suitability of Christianity to their conditions and needs by the use of rational arguments.

Compared with secularism, for instance, Christianity may be shown to be vastly superior in accounting for humans' actual sense of worth, of right and wrong, or of guilt—and of the need for redemption and new direction in their lives. How convincing such considerations will be depends of course on the psychological, intellectual, and spiritual condition of the person being addressed. Sin or commitments to other religions will blind many to any such considerations. For others, the Holy Spirit may use rational arguments to help remove such blinders and allow them to see their conditions and needs for what they really are.[176]

D. Elton Trueblood, in his book, *Philosophy of Religion*, attempts to use scientific methodology to show the adequacy of Christian theism. His procedure is to look at various types of human experience—scientific, moral, aesthetic, historical, and religious—and then to ask regarding each one, "If theism is true, what would we expect to be the case in this area of experience?" In each case, he hypothesizes an answer, then tests that hypothesis by examining the area of experience to see if the hypothesis is confirmed or not.[177]

Trueblood asks, for example, what kind of natural world we would expect to find if theism were true. His answer: an orderly cosmos of the sort science could investigate. Similarly, what would we expect to find in terms of moral experience? The answer: agreement among all morally sensitive persons on the general features of an objective moral order. Trueblood follows the same procedures for the other areas of experience. And he argues that in each case we do find a confirmation of Christian theism. In his opinion, therefore, theism can be shown to have a high degree of probability.[178]

In a similar approach, Edward J. Carnell gives considerable attention to working out the tests of a belief (or "presupposition" as he calls it). His conclusion is that the test of a belief is systematic consistency. This test looks for a systematic fitting of the facts and a consistency with other beliefs known to be true. Carnell argues that Christian theism passes these tests and so is rendered highly probable.[179]

VII. What Are Some Relevant Concluding Remarks?

We cannot finally argue people into Christianity. But we are charged with the responsibility for the proclamation and presentation of revealed truth in every way possible—including a rational or intellectual presentation.

The conversion of Augustine, one of history's most influential Christians, is a vivid example of the many instruments and methods God uses to reach even the most difficult people. Brilliant, headstrong, sensuous—Augustine was far from Christianity throughout the early part of his life. The story of the influences leading to his conversion in A.D. 387, at the age of thirty-three, is told in his *Confessions*, one of the great spiritual classics.

First, there was the constant witness of his Christian mother, Monica—her prayers and her persistent love.

Next, there was Augustine's disillusionment with other religions and philosophies he had tried—including Manicheism, which was a libertine religion, and Neoplatonism, which was somewhat like a fifth-century Christian Science.

In addition, there was the influence of the great Christian orator and preacher, Ambrose. Moving from his native North Africa to Milan, Italy, to pursue a career as a professional rhetorician, Augustine went to hear Ambrose, and God used Ambrose's skillful and enlightened guidance to remove many of the intellectual barriers that were keeping Augustine from Christianity.

The lives of simple Christians also influenced Augustine positively. To his amazement, he found ordinary church people living lives of victory over passions and lust, whereas he, with all his brilliance and education, continued to flounder.

Finally, God used the Holy Spirit, speaking through the Bible. Ambrose had given Augustine a New Testament. One day he was walking in the garden and sensed an inner voice telling him to open it and read. The New Testament fell open to Romans 13:14: "But put ye on the Lord Jesus Christ, and make not provision for the flesh, to fulfill the lusts thereof" (KJV). Like a little child, this brilliant young man dropped down to his knees and accepted Christ as his Savior and Lord. And he went on to guide and inspire Christians in the centuries to come.

In a similar manner, God continues to work through a variety of means to bring men and women to that saving and fulfilling knowledge of God in Christ and to a walk with him. The God-given gift of human reason can be an important—although certainly not the only—one of these means.

11

The Question of Human Morality

Introduction

1. The Difficulty and Complexity of the Question of Human Morality

We could well rephrase the title of this chapter to read, "The Difficulty of Relating the Biblical Worldview to Human Morality." This is because human morality is such a complex subject that there is wide disagreement as to what it entails—even among those who hold to the biblical worldview.

Conservative Christians, for example, are apt to accuse more liberal Christians of being "soft" on issues such as drinking, sexual morality, and personal piety. Liberal Christians tend to retort that conservatives are petty, legalistic, and unconcerned with social justice. And the issues which most concern either group seem to "shift" gradually over time.

Sophisticated intellectuals, on the other hand, are wont to assert that the modern world is too complex for ancient biblical ethics to have any relevance at all. How, they ask, does the Sermon on the Mount apply to a world confronted by the threat of nuclear war, ecologically destructive oil conglomerates, and brutal crime in the street?

2. The Urgency and Importance of the Question of Human Morality

It should be noted that morality and ethics are essentially synonymous. Morality relates to the evaluation of human conduct as right or wrong. Ethics or moral philosophy is concerned with both individual and social behavior in terms of right or wrong. Philosophical ethics approaches what man ought to do from what can be known by natural reason. Biblical ethics, in contrast, bases its approach to right and wrong on the revelation of God to humanity as described in the Bible.

Whatever it is called, few persons would doubt the urgency and importance of the question of morality and ethics. In fact, there is a growing concern worldwide about related issues.

On an educational tour to Mexico, I heard the head of the Department of Didactics at the National University of Mexico speak to a group of educators. He affirmed that of the twelve crucial questions facing Mexico, the most fundamental is the problem of moral corruption. He claimed that in his country there is an increasing tendency for people to seek power and easy money at every level of government and personal life.

And who among us can cast the first stone at a country like Mexico? For we in the United States face a looming AIDS problem, an epidemic of drug abuse and alcoholism, a spate of scandals both on Wall Street and in Washington, and countless other issues of morality—even reported widespread corruption in religious sectors. Individuals might argue over the extent and import of individual issues, but few would deny that the issue of morality—both public and private—is one of the most crucial questions facing the United States as well.

3. The Danger of Unreflective and Self-Serving Ideologies

Most people would agree that behind a person's moral perspective and decisions is a worldview or philosophy or belief system that determines his or her moral attitudes and decisions. But not all worldviews are equally beneficial to either individual or public well-being.

Some people adhere to an ideology, which is an orientation toward life and the world that seeks to advance the interests of a particular class or group in society. An ideology is an explanation of social-empirical reality that serves to reinforce certain vested interests. It is usually simplistic and refuses to see the whole picture of the situation by ignoring or hiding certain facts.

It is noteworthy, for instance, that ideologies or worldviews are more and more reflecting tribalistic or nationalistic loyalties rather than more comprehensive belief systems. People are giving their ultimate allegiance to race, nation, or ethnic heritage. We see this ideological thrust in such movements as pan-Arabism, Polish nationalism, Russian hegemonism, Zionism, Black African tribalism, Christian nationalism in South Africa, and communalism in India.[1]

Donald G. Bloesch contends that even among Christians, certain ideological conservatives and welfare liberals have become ideologues, and that their limited belief systems dominate their lives and unduly color their interpretation of the biblical worldview.[2]

The task of an authentic biblical vision is to recognize the ideological temptation and always to struggle against it. Ideology has its source not simply in finiteness or ignorance, but in people's inveterate tendency to justify self-interest. Thus ideology reveals the fact of corrupted will, which effects moral decisions.[3]

Alisdair MacIntyre contends that in the twentieth century we have—very largely, if not entirely—lost our comprehension, both theoretical and practical, of morality. If MacIntyre is correct, we live in a precarious situation. No wonder we hunger for comprehensive and balanced absolutes in such a world, for we rightly desire peace within ourselves and in our relations with one another. Granted, the world has always been violent, but when our own civilization seems to lack any moral guidelines or moral power, the question of human morality becomes especially urgent.[4]

4. The New Situation in Our World Concerning Competing Choices

According to Peter Berger, premodern people lived for the most part in a "given" world. That is, they had little choice about where to live, what vocation to enter, or whom to marry. Community mores were largely followed. In contrast, modern people find themselves confronted not only by many possible courses of action, but also by many possible ways of thinking about the world.

For example, in their groundbreaking book, *Habits of the Heart,* Robert Bellah and four other scholars show that white, upper-class Americans operate from any of several operative worldviews that are the heritage of our collective culture. One view, which the authors call utilitarian individualism, holds personal pleasure, happiness, and profit as primary life goals. A second view, described as expressive individualism, is interested primarily in self-realization and human potential. (One computer engineer, for example, reported that he divorced and entered a second marriage because he met a woman who "brings out the best in me.") A third view, called Jeffersonian republicanism, emphasizes that individuals should be concerned with the larger group welfare. The last view is the Puritan worldview, which affirms that a human being's chief end is to glorify God, be the instrument of his kingdom, and serve humankind.[5]

In the Far East, most countries were fairly well unified in terms of worldviews in earlier centuries. Then came the option presented by the Christian worldview and some secular views such as John Dewey's pragmatism. In the middle of the twentieth century, communism became a powerful option and in some countries a forced option.

In this modern context of competing choices, those who have a deep conviction that the biblical view of morality is the way for which humankind is made and the way which brings human fulfillment are called upon to incarnate and share the biblical perspective. They must show how the teachings of the Bible and of significant Christian thinkers can give us the ultimate guidelines for human morality.

In order to intelligently understand the people to whom they will witness and share, Christians should understand representative ethical systems followed in today's world. In addition, such a study will furnish a new understanding and appreciation of the biblical worldview by showing it in a broader perspective.

These tasks will provide the outline for our study. In our search for the answer to the question of human morality, we will analyze and evaluate representative secular views and then look at the biblical view and its exponents.

I. What Are the Moral and Ethical Views of Those in the Naturalist Tradition?

The biblical worldview is not the only view claiming to offer guidance in situations demanding moral choices or raising questions of ethics. Since ancient times, various naturalist worldviews have set forth principles for moral choices and actions. These views focus on the possibilities resident within humanity itself, with no transcendent reference. The appeal is to human reason as the final authority in the determination of the good. (Reason is here understood as any cognitive human faculty such as feeling, intellect, or mystical insight.)[6]

Secular or naturalistic moral philosophers are preoccupied with the fulfillment or well-being of the self rather than with the glory of God and service to mankind. Some who are close to mysticism may speak of "transcending the self," yet this is always for the sake of the self. The hallmark of the morally good life in the world of secular philosophy is inward satisfaction, peace of mind, and happiness in the sense of well-being.[7]

1. The Views of Ancient and Modern Elemental Naturalists (Cyrenaic View)

Humans, in contrast to animals, seem unable to live without some pattern of conduct. However, this pattern can be quite simple—a certain bent of will and conviction. Those who take this simplistic approach are called elemental naturalists. They are also called Cyrenaics, after the birthplace of the first proponent of this view, Aristippus, who lived in Cyrene, a Greek colony in North Africa, in the fifth century B.C. The Cyrenaic view teaches that the rule of human conduct is the performance of whatever yields the maximum momentary pleasure. This moment-by-moment devotion to subjective pleasure becomes the purpose of life.[8]

This is similar to the familiar modern beer ad that states, "You only go around once," or the Tennessee Saturday night crowd (notorious for spending a week's wages on Saturday night) who say that we live only for the pleasure of one night. Gourmets who fly to France for one gourmet meal could be seen as representatives of this view. So was the group of one hundred businessmen who, according to a San Francisco newspaper, were traveling around the world to engage in sexual orgies.

In the Cyrenaic view, since we can know only the sensation of the moment, pleasure as a past or future experience is nonexistent. Present pleasures differ only in intensity or degree. Physical or bodily pleasures are preferable to all others because they are more intense, more simple. No pleasure is bad, for pleasure is "the good," but weaker sensations are less desirable than intense pleasures.

Followers of this view hold that we are children of time, not of eternity, and that therefore we must seek joys within the compass of the momentary present. A life of pleasure, heedless and unthinking, undisturbed by reason, is the ideal of the pagan Cyrenaic spirit. "Eat, drink and be merry, for tomorrow we die" was the essence of the Cyrenaic credo.[9]

Several well-known writers of the modern period held philosophies that were essentially Cyrenaic in their emphasis on short-term pleasure. Nineteenth-century novelist D. H. Lawrence, for example, advocated finding pleasure in the intoxication of the senses and the intensity of passion: "My great religion is a belief in the blood, the flesh, as being wiser than the intellect. We can go wrong with our minds, but what our blood feels and believes and says is always true. . . . The real way of living is to answer one's wants."[10]

A more extreme modern expression was that of the eighteenth-century French novelist and soldier, the Marquis de Sade. He identified pleasure with pain and saw the highest pleasure in acts of violence and degradation. His ideal was the primitive savage, for he believed that the savage is most independent and closest to nature.[11]

The Cyrenaic approach is a species of simple or naïve naturalistic ethics. It affords no scientific or systematic discussion of the moral life. It also tends to run into difficulties, as the original Greek Cyrenaics discovered. The attempt to correlate sense flux with the maximum pleasure of the moment was thwarted by the disruptive fact that some pleasures caused disproportionate pain. (For example, physical exhaustion and mental sluggishness are the price of intemperate sex indulgence.) Furthermore, the Cyrenaics had to admit that maximal present pleasure often will undercut the possibility of maximal future pleasure. The Cyrenaics, therefore, had to develop an appeal beyond immediate sense experience to a principle of prudence. They were driven to acknowledge that the rational and moral life, which appeals to realities outside immediate experience, has a decisive relevance.[12]

2. The Views of the Ancient and Modern Hedonists (Long-Term Pleasure)

An ethical approach which has attracted much interest is hedonism, which argues that values may be defined in terms of pleasure. (The term *hedonism* is derived from a Greek word meaning "pleasure.") From the times of Democritus, Epicurus, and Lucretius in the ancient world to the days of Jeremy Bentham and John Stuart Mill in the modern world, hedonism has not lacked adherents. The basic premise of hedonism is that whatever a person values may be defined as that which gives that person pleasure or happiness. Hedonists argue that this is true for all people everywhere, whatever they say to the contrary! In fact, hedonists even suggest that pleasure ought to be the criterion of conduct.

(1) The View of Epicureanism (Intellectual and Long-Term Pleasure). The unresolved contradictions in the view of the Cyrenaics required a fundamental change of perspective. This came from the Greek philosopher Epicurus in the fourth century B.C. Like the Cyrenaics, Epicurus and his followers believed that pleasure was the supreme good of life, but they differed from the Cyrenaics in that they sought a higher justification of pleasure.[13]

Epicurus modified the Cyrenaic morality in two ways. First, he articulated a comprehensive worldview to go along with the basic moral outlook and to give human decisions a philosophical justification. His philosophy thus was the first materialistic view of life entitled to the designation of scientific or systematic naturalism. Second, he replaced the idea that short-term, immediately exhausted physical pleasures are the goal of life with another view of life—that of long-term, productive mental pleasures.[14]

Epicurus distinguished between various kinds of pleasures, ranking intellectual satisfaction above physical enjoyment. He also held that, while pleasure is ultimately reducible to the senses, reason must be the guide in regulating the life of pleasure and that the genuine life of pleasure must be a life of prudence, honor, and justice. The highest good, according to Epicurus, is the aesthetic self-enjoyment of the person of culture and refinement. He upheld the ideal of a state of repose and equilibrium, undisturbed by the discords and agitations of life.[15]

The Epicurean emphasis on long-term as against short-term pleasures intensified the moral tension already found in Cyrenaicism. The invitation to repress short-term, immediately exhausted fleshly pleasures for long-term, productive mental pleasures met with an almost insurmountable obstacle in the mind of Epicurus. For there is always the possibility that death would intervene to cheat Epicureans of remote pleasures, so that they would be deprived of both short-term and long-term gratifications. The consequence of this dilemma is pessimism. This is a development of Epicureanism which is not accidental, but which flows from its unresolved contradictions.

When a person is told that he or she may find meaning in life only by the pursuit of long-term pleasures, while being continually aware that death may come tomorrow and that time for physical gratification is short, the paralysis of the moral life is close at hand. The more expansive the "long view" of pleasures, the greater the threat, posed by nature, that their distant realization will be interrupted.[16]

(2) The View of Utilitarianism (Greatest Happiness for the Greatest Number). Utilitarianism is the modern revival of the ancient long-term pleasure principle of the ancient Epicureans. In fact, one of the chief exponents of utilitarianism, Jeremy Bentham (1748–1842) evaluated Epicurus as the only one among the ancients who had the merit of having known the true source of morality.[17] But this modern development imposed three modifications on the basic ideas of hedonism. It repudiates self-centeredness and champions altruism; it is optimistic, resisting any mood of pessimism and melancholy; and it is highly rationalistic and technically complex.

The proponents of utilitarianism held that the supreme aim of human conduct is not the pleasure of the individual—either short-term or long-term. Instead, conduct should be directed toward achieving the greatest happiness and the least pain for the greatest number of people.[18]

It is arguable that this altruistic aspect of utilitarianism reflects the influence of the Christian faith—for in many ways this influence separates ancient from modern history in the West. Even hedonism as an ethical philosophy could not escape the unique pervading influence of Christianity, with its concern for human welfare.

As indicated above, a prominent feature of utilitarianism is its strong emphasis on human beings as distinctively rational animals. Bentham even proposed a kind of "calculus" for the individual measurement of the probable pleasures attending alternate possibilities of moral action.[19]

It was utilitarian philosopher John Stuart Mill (1806–1873) who lifted to a yet higher dimension the significance of human reason as it applied to the pleasure principle. He emphasized the necessity of distinguishing qualitatively, not merely quantitatively, between pleasures. Mill also insisted upon an essential distinction between humans and the animals, asserting that human nature is too complex to be satisfied with "animal" pleasures.

Utilitarianism has shaped much of modern politics and economics in the democratic West. In the United States, for example, we base our economic policy on the belief that we should prosper in such a way so that everyone can realize a reasonable degree of happiness and freedom from poverty. The American Constitution speaks of the pursuit of happiness as an "unalienable" human right. Socialism, too, is often based on the idea that the goal of society is to banish poverty and free people for more happiness.[20]

Carl F. H. Henry points out that utilitarianism is too limited in its definition of pleasure. The biblical view would say that an inner spiritual quality and life beyond death are necessary to an adequate qualitative pleasure.[21]

However, the biblical view sees some positive aspects to hedonism, as well as the negative ones. It is obviously wrong from a biblical point of view for personal pleasure to be a person's supreme or final object—his or her reason for living. On the other hand, if fullness of personal life—affirmation of personality—be taken as the valid norm, it is plain to see that pleasures are important components of this ideal. They are, theologically speaking, part of God's good creation, and therefore intrinsically good, not evil. If the human good cannot be defined entirely in terms of pleasure, neither can it be defined without pleasure. In fact, from this perspective, happiness may well be regarded as a barometer of personal well-being. Wide occurrence of unhappiness may be understood as a danger signal, indicating the presence in a society of serious human evil. This may be taken as a positive aspect of the significance of such hedonistic philosophies as those of Bentham and Mill, which are in reality tools of social criticism.[22]

3. The Views of the Political Naturalists

(1) The View of Machiavelli. Although naturalistic philosophies and their attendant moral views were well represented in ancient times, the impact of Christian ethics upon the Western world subdued political naturalism as a moral and ethical force until around 1500 A.D., when it was revived by the Italian statesman and political philosopher Niccolo Machiavelli. Machiavelli's most influential work, *The Prince*, helped to mold the modern mind and, in consequence, modern history.

In *The Prince*, Machiavelli states that the successful ruler is a human lion (power) and fox (cunning)—keeping or breaking faith according to personal interest. Political expediency is placed above morality and the use of craft and deceit is endorsed to maintain authority and carry out government policies.[23]

Machiavelli holds up Cesare Borgia, the acknowledged son of Pope Alexander VI who forged a kingdom for himself by force and fraud, as an example of the kind of leader he was describing. Interestingly enough, however, Machiavelli's thought was more perfectly actualized by such twentieth-century dictators as Mussolini, Hitler, and Stalin. Mussolini, in fact, submitted a thesis on Machiavelli to fulfill the requirements of his doctoral degree.[24]

(2) The View of Thomas Hobbes. Thomas Hobbes (1588–1679) shares with Machiavelli the thesis that both human beings and the state are aspects of nature alone and hence can be understood only naturalistically. He also shared the idea that ends justify the means in government. Hobbes, in fact, developed the "might makes right" thesis long before Nietzsche and Hitler.

In Hobbes's approach, however, the people voluntarily transfer their rights to the ruler, because that is considered the only means of self-preservation. The state and all moral authority are rooted simply in the recognition that only government can keep people from destroying one another; therefore even the worst kind of government is "better than none." Since self-preservation is achieved through the sovereign state, that sovereignty must never be weakened.

In Hobbes's view, moreover, the orders of the ruler are to be obeyed for no other reason than the fact that what the ruler proclaims is for the good of the ruled. The "ought" has no eternal quality and has nothing to do with the voice of the people.[25]

Hobbes's thesis lacked an actual application whereby its historical consequences might be measured, except for the limited realizations of Charles I of Naples and Borgia. Today, of course, it is more obvious that power politics, instead of ministering to human self-preservation, often robs individual life of dignity and reduces it to being a pawn of the state. In resorting to an external sovereign will that maintains itself by fear and force, political naturalism directly contradicts the biblical teaching of God's supremacy. Christianity presents God as a loving Father concerned with each person rather than as an arbitrary tyrant.[26]

4. The Enlightened Naturalistic Egoism of Ayn Rand

The twentieth-century social philosopher Ayn Rand considered selfishness the highest virtue and rational selfishness the ground for ethical decision. The ethical system she advanced was enlightened naturalistic egoism—essentially, the ethics of self-preservation, with the added idea that to advance the self means to contribute indirectly to the good of the whole.

Self-love is considered a virtue, not a sin, in Ayn Rand's philosophy. Individualism is prized over collectivism. The ideal is not the welfare state, but the opportunity state—a place where each person is given the freedom to develop his or her talents and capabilities to the utmost.

This ethical philosophy, therefore, emphasizes liberty over justice and economic productivity over equality. Freedom is interpreted mainly in terms of opportunity for growth and development, unhampered by governmental and social restraint. Certain "natural rights" are respected, but the right of property is seen as among the most valuable.[27]

Ayn Rand's position stands in tension, if not outright conflict, with the New Testament ideal of self-sacrificing love. And yet there are those who are seeking to relate evangelical Christianity to Ayn Rand's ethics in order to provide the theoretical basis for an unrestrained free-enterprise capitalism.[28]

5. The Naturalistic Power-Ethics View of Nietzsche

The nineteenth-century philosopher Friedrich Nietzsche was an extremely influential exponent of a philosophy of power-ethics, the doctrine of human perfectibility through forcible self-assertion.

Nietzsche was vocally opposed to traditional morality in general and Christianity in particular, and he called for a complete transvaluation of traditional Hebrew-Christian values. In his *Ecce Homo,* for example, Nietzsche wrote, "Christian morality is the most malignant form of all falsehood. . . . It is really poisonous, decadent, weakening. It produces nincompoops, not men." Nietzsche, furthermore, discounted as futile the attempt to organize experience in terms of reason.[29]

Nietzsche's basic philosophy involved the "will to power," the self-assertive drive to live and attain power that exists in all individuals but is especially characteristic of the "superman," which Nietzsche conceived as an ideal or superior being, the final product of evolution. Behind this doctrine stand two influences—Schopenhauer's doctrine of the primacy of the will and Darwin's description of the mechanism of evolution. If life is an evolutionary struggle for existence in which only the fittest survive, strength becomes the primary virtue, and weakness the worst of faults.[30]

Carl Henry points out that Nietzsche's rejection of the biblical teachings concerning the strength of meekness, the force of love, the courage of forbearance, and the greatness of humility has thrown nations into disorder and decay. Through Adolf Hitler's adaptation of his philosophy, he is credited with influencing the buildup of the Third Reich and the start of World War II. And even today, Nietzsche's concept of power-ethics and ruthless self-assertion threatens to bankrupt civilization.[31]

6. The Political Naturalism of Karl Marx

(1) The Ethical Teachings of Marx. The ethical teachings of Karl Marx, even more than those of Nietzsche, have profoundly influenced modern history. Marx's *Communist Manifesto* projected a new social order whose controlling assumptions are not founded in religious or moral realities, but in emphases peculiar to the social sciences. It rejects any kind of supernatural moral order and has a specific hostility for the Christian ethic.[32]

Marx projected a moral theory which is consciously and deliberately relativistic; it regards ethical and religious sentiments alike as mere reflexes of the economic situation. It also sees specific ethical concepts or moral absolutes as the disguised tools of class interest, dismissing the idea of universally obligatory moral imperatives as "bourgeois ethics." In the Marxist view, law rests upon society, not society upon law. Accordingly, whatever contributes most efficiently to the proletarian aim is considered to be moral or ethical. The moral ideal thus becomes a floating propaganda weapon to promote class warfare.[33]

By its very nature, Marxism is utopian, projecting the vision of a social order free from strife and exploitation which can be ushered in by legislation or, failing that, by violent revolution. Marxism is essentially an Enlightenment creed, with its unwavering and unsubstantiated faith in the innate goodness of "the people" and its blindness to the corrupting influence of centralized power. It places its hope in the infinite possibilities resident in the human soul rather than in a divine promise to redeem humankind from its sin. It is obviously and deliberately in conflict with the biblical system of values.[34]

Nevertheless, as Christian sociologist and author Tony Campolo points out, Marxist thought has provided the most popular and powerful ideological alternative to the Christian faith since the Renaissance. Undoubtedly Christian thought has been and will be influenced significantly by dialectical tensions with Marxist ideologies. For better or for worse, the institutional forms of middle-class Christianity are being changed through conflict with its most formidable enemy of the twentieth century.[35]

For this reason, says Campolo, Western Christians would do well to listen to the Marxists. This would mean heeding the valid aspects of the Marxist critique —including the accusations that our ethical systems often are used as the tools of class interest rather than God-given guides for human behavior.[36] We would do well to purge ourselves of those accretions to our faith that are alien to the essence of the biblical message and only serve self-interest. At the same time, warns Campolo, we should listen to the Marxists in order to defend ourselves from their nonbiblical agenda. In reference to morals and ethics, this would mean guarding against the gradual acceptance of a relativistic and utilitarian system of ethics.

7. The Views of the Religious Naturalists

Religious naturalists see the order of nature not simply as an inexorable, necessary system, but as a divine rational necessity. Thus religious naturalism is a form of pantheism, the belief that God and nature are one. It conceives of nature as a necessary movement of events indifferent to the whims of the individual. Human existence and conduct, therefore, has significance and meaning only when it is in accord with this necessary system of nature.[37]

(1) The View of the Ancient Stoics. Zeno, a Greek philosopher of the late fourth and early third centuries B.C., founded the original Stoic school. He asserted that if we had absolute reason, we would know that everything occurs according to divine reason and hence for the best. This means that we should accept all the developments of life with equal readiness and not assert contrary preferences. Zeno held that there is a spark of pure reason in humanity, and that human beings are to order their lives by this divine reason. This means that human beings are to live "according to nature."

The Stoic rule of life, then, is a surrender to the unyielding firmness of the order of nature. The individual must find the "mind of nature" and cultivate an impassive disposition. *Apathy*—the suppression of all passion and emotion—thus becomes the key word of Stoic ethics.[38]

The Stoic philosophy universalizes conduct by stressing the importance of universal reason, which is considered humankind's only "fatherhood." Thus every decision of life is to be looked at rationally, from "the standpoint of the universe." All social and national differences between human beings are considered artificial.

Stoicism influenced a number of outstanding thinkers in the history of moral philosophy. In its ranks were the emperor Marcus Aurelius and the slave Epictetus. It remained, for the most part, a view of intellectuals.[39]

The line between Stoic and Christian ethics, however, is a sharp one. The Stoic doctrine negates the significance of individual personality. Its idea of the "universal brotherhood" of humankind means only that I must regard my blood brother in the same impersonal way that I do a stranger. This is far removed from the Christian doctrine of particular divine providence and of neighbor-love. The Stoic doctrine of moral apathy and stoicism in the experiences of life eliminates passion and compassion alike. Its call for resignation and desire for inner liberation from the world removes any ethical motive for transforming the world.[40]

(2) The View of Spinoza. The seventeenth-century Dutch philosopher Baruch Spinoza was a Jew who was in conscious revolt against the Hebrew tradition, and this revolt carried over into the realm of morals and ethics. In fact, one of Spinoza's major works is his *Ethics,* which is conceived much like a book of geometry. It begins with a series of definitions, which are supplemented by a set of axioms. Next is a set of propositions with their proofs. In Spinoza's naturalistic worldview, God is the sum total of nature, not an ethical personality outside it. He expounds this position with sophisticated finesse and thoroughness and seeks to make a place for ethics within it.[41]

Spinoza's view is similar to that of the Stoics in affirming that the life of resignation is the life of power, for it triumphs over circumstances, self, and others. He asserted that the only way to achieve the fulfillment of desire is to learn the mathematical structure of reality and to conform life to it. Ignorance of this structure is the cause of all disappointment. Human salvation from frustrated desires is achieved by the intellectual love of God, which consists of an acquiescence to the order of nature.

From the Christian point of view, then, the weaknesses of Spinoza's ethical views are similar to those of the Stoics. In the end, Spinoza's concepts reduce humanity to a fragment of impersonal reality. (The immortality Spinoza acknowledges is not that of an indestructible soul, but a relationship to the imperishable mathematical necessity of the universe.)[42] This, in turn, removes any incentive for involved caring or for positive ethical action.

8. The Views of the Empirical Naturalists

Empirical naturalists in the twentieth century share the concept that meaning is to be limited to the empirical content of experience. They differ among themselves, however, as to whether these ethics, based on experience, can become normative (as John Dewey's Pragmatism held) or whether they are only descriptive of personal attitudes and feelings (as held by the early logical positivists).

(1) The View of John Dewey (Pragmatism). John Dewey, the eminent twentieth-century educational philosopher, contended that morality should be given a scientific basis by bringing it within the scope of the experimental method. In his view, scientific knowledge should serve as the guide of conduct, and moral standards, in turn, should be discovered through the methodology of the natural sciences. This method affirms that whatever works is right. The test of the validity of ethical ideas is their workability; there are no permanent principles of morality.[43] Dewey did hold, however, that ethical statements can become normative if they are workable.

(2) The View of Logical Positivism. In the twentieth century, a revolution took place in the understanding of logic, mathematics, and geometry. Originally this movement was called logical positivism, then logical empiricism, and later linguistic analysis. Today it is generally called analytic philosophy. Earlier chapters of this book have outlined the influence of this view on the question of religious language. It has had many things to say about ethics, as well.[44]

From the inception of this new type of philosophy in the 1920s until the present, it has undergone many changes, including changes in ethical theory. We will look primarily at how this school looked at ethics prior to some of the later modifications.

Logical positivism specializes in the meaning of human communication and understanding. This means that it attempts to classify sentences, which in this specialized sense applies to formal statements of logic, mathematics, and geometry.

According to this branch of thought, if a sentence proposes to say something about the world, it is a material sentence. Material sentences are meaningful or meaningless; they make sense or they make nonsense. If something can be empirically verified about a sentence, the sentence is meaningful or it makes sense. Otherwise, a sentence is meaningless.

According to this criteria, the kinds of sentences that are made in the ethical area are seen as meaningless or senseless. That is, they can be grammatically correct, but they are meaningless from the standpoint of their logical character because they cannot be verified. According to this school, for instance, a sentence such as "It is wrong to lie" cannot be verified factually or empirically or experimentally. It is not a false sentence, but rather a meaningless or a nonsensical one.[45]

As shown in chapter 3, the shift from verificational analysis to functional analysis and the idea of language games eventually loosened up this older logical positivism to the point that even some Christian theologians believe that Christian ethics can be explained from the standpoint of analytical philosophy.[46]

9. The Ethical View of Jean Paul Sartre (Atheistic Existentialism)

One of the best known critics of biblical ethics in the twentieth century has been the French existential philosopher Jean Paul Sartre. A brief outline of his ethical philosophy will show his major conflict with Christian ethics.

For Sartre, there is no such thing as a fixed or established human nature. Instead, in their radical freedom men and women make themselves. There is no image of God in humanity which humanity in turn is to realize in religious and ethical life. There are no such things as innate moral ideas or natural law. Indeed, there is no God in the traditional Christian sense. If there were such a God, then human beings would be obligated to obey that God's moral principles. To obey somebody else is to lose one's freedom. Therefore, there cannot be both God and freedom—and according to Sartre, radical freedom is the basic status of the human condition.

According to Sartre, to make an ethical decision on the basis of force or coercion or demand is to be guilty of bad faith. When a person is faced with a moral question, there is really no right or wrong, as is taught in traditional ethics. There is only authentic choice, which is the real actualization of a person's freedom, or bad faith, which comes from coercion or force.[47]

For Sartre, then, no objective content is attached to the moral act. The existentialist formula is that human beings must choose. The content of what they choose would appear to be a matter of indifference. It is easy to see how such a view tends to lead to moral anarchy. Why would one ethical decision or one ethical content be more valuable than another? The Sartrean view would also lead to the notion that there is no objective reality beyond subjective existence.[48] On both points, it is clearly opposed by biblical faith.

II. What Are the Views of Representative Speculative Moral Philosophers in the Idealist Tradition?

As we have seen, naturalists over the centuries have seen human beings merely as rational animals trapped in the relativities of the space-time universe. For the most part, therefore, their ethical principles have been attempts to find and elaborate a rescuing and sustaining life principle.

Idealistic philosophies, on the other hand, affirm that it is impossible to develop such a rule or way of life on a naturalistic basis. It therefore repudiates naturalism as a falsification of reality.

For idealists of various traditions, reality involves more than space and time, and human beings are far more than just complex animals. Truth and morality, therefore, must include another dimension as well.[49]

1. The Ethical Views of the Classical Humanists

(1) The Platonic View. The ethical views of Plato and his teacher Socrates are based on the logical priority of an eternal, invisible, supernatural realm. This is an ultimate spiritual and mental reality beyond the natural world of space and time.

Plato affirms that man is superior to other creatures by virtue of a unique relationship to this supernatural world. As a bearer of divine reason, man transcends the space-time world and is destined for spiritual immortality beyond death. Plato, furthermore, teaches that certain distinctions of truth and morality are genuinely eternal and changeless. These distinctions are objectively addressed to human beings as fixed norms which they cannot violate without harm.

Plato's teachings emphasize that the happiness of the individual and society is based on harmony. The perfect, or just, state is one that has a right order headed up by a philosopher-king. Each class of society provides that society with a needed element. For example, the craftsmen provide, through their unity in diversity, the element of temperance. The warriors supply the state with courage, and the rulers provide wisdom.

Justice, in the Platonic view, is the proper relationship of all these virtuous elements within the whole. Justice is also the proper harmony of reason, will, and emotion in the individual life. This harmony is achieved by the enthronement of reason as the soul's seat of authority.

Platonic philosophy affirms the essential continuity of human and divine reason. On the spiritual side of their beings, humans are pictured as fragments of divinity. This teaching means that the problem of human morality can be reduced to one of forgetfulness or ignorance of the rational and moral norms which are always accessible to human beings on the basis of their intrinsic divinity.[50]

Plato taught that human beings require contact with the intellectual-moral-spiritual world that exists outside of, as well as within, humankind. He also held that humans can dimly recall previous existence in the world of spiritual ideals or forms. This view presupposes the preexistence of the soul, as well as its essential divinity.

Aristotle, the pupil of Plato, tended more toward the naturalistic tradition, identifying the end of ethics as personal "happiness." To Aristotle, happiness meant the exercise of natural human faculties in accordance with virtue, which he defined as the balanced and harmonious fulfillment of man's natural tendencies.

(2) The Difference between the Platonic and Biblical Views. The classical Greek view derives absolute moral principles from the nature of humanity in its present condition. This is based on the teaching that human beings are in fact a part of God. This clashes with the biblical view, which proclaimed to the Greco-Roman world that ethical standards are not to be based upon the human will, but upon the will of God, who is the Creator and Judge of humankind.

According to the Bible, human beings are made in the image of God, but they are not divine. The biblical worldview points out that sin enslaves the mind. It also contends that, for this reason, human beings need a special divine revelation for the normative definition of the content of morality. This, of course, is in direct contrast to Plato's teaching of the divinity of reason and the basic goodness of humanity.

Plato taught that humanity delights in the good, so much so that education in the truth will assure the performance of virtue. In contrast, the Bible teaches that human beings are fallen sinners inclined toward ethical disobedience and are thus in need of divine regeneration for the achievement of the good life.[51]

(3) The View of Erich Fromm. According to Donald Bloesch, twentieth-century psychoanalyst and author Erich Fromm is an example of classical humanism in our day. (Fromm, in fact, freely acknowledges his indebtedness to Aristotle and Plato.) Fromm opposes naturalism, which reduces humans to being the products of instinctual drives. He also criticizes nihilism, which considers the quest for meaning in life futile. He upholds the dignity and uniqueness of humanity.[52]

Like the classical idealists, however, Fromm sees the goal of the ethical life as happiness or well-being, which he interprets as the full realization of our creative potential. In Fromm's view, ethical norms are not derived from an authoritative divine revelation. Instead, they come from a rational analysis of the capacity of certain choices to promote "the optimum of growth and well-being and the minimum of ill-being."[53]

2. The Ethical Idealism of Kant

(1) Kant's Teaching and Emphases. In the eighteenth century, the German philosopher Immanuel Kant sought to preserve the classical Greek teaching that there is an absolute character to ethical norms. This emphasis was in specific opposition to that of his contemporary, David Hume. Hume had attempted to ground all experience, including morality, in nothing but sense impressions and therefore assigned a relative character to all moral judgments. Kant, in his publication, *Critique of Pure Reason*, struck hard against such a view, which he claimed reduced humanity from a rational and moral agent to merely a complex animal.

Kant insisted that the knowledge experience contains features which are not derivable from sensation. In the spheres of science and mathematics, for instance, truths are cast in a universal and necessary form which exceeds the limitations of sense experience. According to Kant, sensation supplies the content of knowledge, but reason supplies the form. Furthermore, it is only through the innate categories of reason that sensation becomes orderly and intelligible.

Kant held that although God and ethical ideals cannot be known through "pure reason," they must be at least postulated or assumed on the basis of "practical reason." In other words, although human beings are shut off from any direct knowledge of the metaphysical or divine world, they need not succumb to a skeptical and animalistic interpretation of life. For humankind is constituted not only by certain rational forms, but by a moral *a priori*—a basic sense of "I ought!"

This basic moral concept or law, which humans may disregard but never destroy, is what Kant termed the categorical imperative. The existence of the categorical imperative implies that, in our ethical life, we are to act toward others in a way which is so satisfactory that it can serve as universal law. Love can be universalized because love works for the good of all people. We are not to treat others merely as means, but always as ends.[54]

Kant thought that a categorical imperative is absolute; it applies unconditionally. For example, "Do not lie" is unconditional. It would be self-contradictory to imagine universal lying. If everyone lied, there could be no orderly system of communication; language would collapse, and therefore there could be no lying.

Kant taught that, from a practical perspective, God is presupposed by the moral law. It is not possible in our brief lives to achieve absolute goodness or moral perfection; we can only attain an approximation. In principle, however, the moral law makes absolute demands on us. And so the demands of moral law in practice indicate, therefore, that we should live on after death and that God should in the end match our virtue with full happiness. So God and immortality are practical outcomes of the demands of the moral law.[55] This argument, in essence, can be called the moral argument for the existence of God.

In his own way, Kant was profoundly religious. He said that the function of religion is to strengthen humanity's pursuit of the good in the face of moral weakness and even corrupt propensities. Kant frankly acknowledged the human need for divine assistance in fulfilling moral duties. According to John Macquarrie, in fact, it is little short of painful to see this great intellect struggling with the concept of divine grace as something he acknowledges to be necessary to the human condition, yet something for which his general philosophy (and perhaps also his temperament) cannot find a place.[56]

(2) Modern Adaptations of Kant's Moral Arguments. In the past century and a half, other philosophers and theologians have picked up the thread of Kant's thought where he left it and have developed it into that which some see as an even more convincing moral argument for the existence of God. Professor Sorley's Gifford Lectures, *Moral Values and the Idea of God,* represent a kind of climax in this intellectual development. Other popular exponents of the moral argument include A. E. Taylor and C. S. Lewis.[57]

These more recent scholars see Kant's contribution as twofold. First, he taught people to pay serious attention to the moral consciousness as a really significant part of experience. Second, he indicated the validity of postulational thinking—the progression from an undeniable experience to those deeper convictions which are required if the experience is not to be denied or made meaningless. The result of several generations of thought now makes it possible to present the moral argument for the existence of God in a form which is different from that in which Kant presented it, but which retains his most important insights.[58]

(3) The Weaknesses and Strengths of Kant's Moral Argument for God in Relation to the Christian Worldview. It should be noted that from a biblical standpoint there is much that is objectionable in Kant's view. He assumed humanity's moral continuity with the divine by venturing to postulate God in the moral image of man's ethical nature. His exclusion of any radical judgment or condemnation of human ideals from a divine standpoint rules out in advance the biblical doctrine of human sinfulness.[59]

Kant's view is antithetical in a specific way to the biblical view which bases ethics upon the general and special revelation of the will of God. In biblical ethics, humankind's knowledge of God's will always presupposes a theistic setting and rules out an autonomous ethic.[60]

Nevertheless, the moral argument can be shown to have several important strengths from a Christian point of view. The first of these strengths is its *existential or experiential emphasis*—its insistence that problems of the soul and of religion must be grounded in experience as well as theoretic reason.

In this emphasis Kant is preceded by Martin Luther, who in his *Commentary on the Letter of Galatians* rejected the competence of speculative reason to address the problems of the soul and instead stressed an orientation of active trust. In the century after Kant, Sören Kierkegaard picked up this experiential emphasis in opposition to the dominant philosophy of Hegel.

Another important strength of the moral argument from a Christian viewpoint is the *similarity of the moral experience to religious experience*. John Baillie contends, in fact, that moral experience is already a religious experience, that in our experience of a moral imperative we are actually and already being visited by God.[61]

In Kant's version of the moral argument there is, indeed, no thought of God as Savior, no hint of that personal relationship which the word *Savior* usually indicates when it is used by religious people. However, the fact that Kant's mind moved to the idea of God as the guarantor of the *summum bonum* must be significant. Surely there was operating in Kant's mind something of a direct religious sense of God as the supreme personal *Will*. This God not only makes an absolute claim upon man, but also, in and through that claim, discloses Himself as the only source and guarantor of humankind's highest good. If this is so, then it is incorrect to say that Kant's religion is nothing but morality. Instead, we should say that his morality is already in its deepest ground religious.

It must be granted that there is no self-evident logical necessity uniting the idea of God with the idea of unconditional values or moral absolutes. But for large numbers of people, there is a close correspondence between the idea of God and the idea of an unconditional demand upon the will—a connection which arises out of the deepest springs of religion in the human soul. Most people probably feel this connection in some degree, even when they theoretically repudiate a Christian view of the universe.

Kant rejected almost entirely both the evidence of nature and the evidence of religious experience, making the moral argument for theism the only one. From a Christian viewpoint, of course, this was a mistake and an unnecessary impoverishment. But the moral argument remains an argument which can help undergird the idea of a moral God.[62]

III. What Are the Views of Morality of Representative Nonbiblical Religions?

In chapter 9 of this book, we discussed in detail the general views of nonbiblical religions and gave a theological evaluation for each. This chapter will focus more specifically on the moral and ethical attitudes and teachings of these religions.

The major faiths have some things in common as far as moral conduct goes. For example, general proscriptions against stealing, lying, murder, and certain expressions of sexuality are found across the world. This commonality of emphasis appears to be necessary if there is to be a society at all, for the widespread breaking of such rules would lead to chaos. From a theological perspective, this can be accounted for by the concept of "common grace."[63] (This concept holds that all revelation of the good comes from God—some by general revelation or common grace to all humans, some by special revelation in the biblical tradition.)

On the other hand, religions differ considerably on more specific moral practices and even the specific expressions of the common categories. In sexual matters, for example, while almost all religions have general moral rules pertaining to sexual conduct, they vary widely on their judgments of particular practices. Christian men have only one wife at one time, and during much of the Christian era even divorce has been ruled out. The Muslim male, in contrast, may have up to four wives at one time, and divorce is built into the original legal system.

As for killing other people, some religions oppose it entirely, even in times of war. Others societies allow for the right of self-defense, and in war the killing of the enemy may be seen as a duty. Still others regard warfare as a natural means of spreading the domain in which the faith is exercised. (A notable example is the Islamic idea of the jihad, or holy war.)[64]

1. The View of Morality in Primitive Religions

God tends to have little to do with the standards or values adopted by the primitive society. Even if God is thought to be the ultimate upholder of the moral order, people do not consider him to be immediately involved in the keeping of it. Instead, it is the patriarchs (both living and dead), elders, priests, or even divinities and spirits who are the daily guardians or police of human morality.

Social regulations of a moral nature are related to the immediate contact between individuals, between humans, the living-dead (i.e. ancestors), and the spirits. Therefore, these regulations are on the human-to-human level, rather than on the God-to-human plane of morality.[65]

2. The Islamic Approach to Morality

Despite its widespread penetration into many countries by conquest, trade, and missionary activity, Islam remains a relatively homogeneous culture and religion. In fact, its most important division—that between the orthodox Sunna and the fundamentalist Shi'a—involves the question of how far it can adapt or make concession to Western ideas and culture.[66]

One reason for the relative uniformity of Islamic culture is its belief in a divinely instituted law. Early Islam saw itself as related to other revelations as given to such prophets as Noah and Jesus. However, the law as given by special revelation to Muhammad—which Islam claims was the final revelation—has its own unique features.[67]

According to Islamic thought, the radical transcendence of God means that moral law for humankind cannot be based on God's character—what he *is* by nature—because that nature is unknowable by humans. Moral law, therefore, must be based on the commands or decrees of God, which are found in the Koran. These commands are centered in the Five Pillars of Islam, which are the basic moral duties of every Muslim: recital of the creed, prayer, fasting, almsgiving, and pilgrimage. These basic laws, in their simplicity and universal application, make up the practice of Islam to the average Muslim.

Because strict monotheism is the heart of Islamic faith, the most heinous sins in Islam are those related directly to one's attitude toward God and toward the Muslim religion: polytheism, apostasy, skepticism, and impiety. In comparison, social sins and all subtler forms of evil pale into comparative insignificance.[68]

However, this does not mean that Islamic law ignores all other issues of wrong and right. To the contrary, Islamic law reaches out to cover countless details of everyday life, including such questions as finance, slavery, and ritual.

The reason behind such comprehensive application lies in both the Muslim concept of equality and community. In general, Islam is thought to apply equally to all human beings under Allah. The great difference between the numinous Allah and his humble worshipers gives the latter a sense of equality among themselves and of humility before God.[69]

Many critics allege that this concept of universal equality does not extend to women. And it is true that Islamic law and custom, stemming from the Koran and from developed tradition, impose a double standard on men and women. Men can have up to four wives at once, although women are forbidden to have more than one husband. In many countries, moreover, custom requires that women wear veils in public, although this practice is not laid down in Muslim revelation. Although women do have property rights and are protected by what in Muhammad's time was an enlightened system of divorce, most Westerners and some reforming Muslims think women's status is inferior. To an orthodox Muslim, however, Islamic law treats women and men as being fundamentally equal, albeit with separate natures and functions.[70]

Not only does Islam consider all humans under Allah brothers and sisters; it also believes that the Islamic community, brought into being under the leadership of Muhammad and spread throughout the world following his death, has a special blessing. This emphasis on community in Islam is seen in the requirement to give alms and thus help the poor brother or sister. It also is reflected in the close connection between Islam and the state and the requirement, when called on, to fight a jihad or holy war on behalf of the faith.

The Islamic aim is to build a society based on the revealed law of Allah. To accomplish this aim, all the levers of power, including war against the enemies of Islam, may be employed. Allah is, in essence, power—however much Allah may also be compassionate and merciful. Therefore, it is not surprising that the Muslim view of morality includes the use of earthly power as a way of expressing and strengthening Allah's dominion.[71]

3. The Hindu View of Morality

(1) The Importance of Traditional Culture in Hinduism. Hinduism, which retains a strong grip in India, as well as among overseas Indians from the Caribbean to South Africa and the South Pacific, is more a way of life than a form of thought. While Hinduism gives absolute liberty in the world of thought, it calls for a strict code of practice. The theist and the atheist, the skeptic and the agnostic may all be Hindus if they accept the Hindu system of culture and life. What is most important is conduct, not belief.[72]

(2) Morality and the Concepts of Dharma, Karma and Reincarnation. The Hindu view of morality is closely related to the concept of dharma. Every form of life, every group of people has its dharma, which is its essential character or the law of its being. Dharma also involves the concept of virtue, and it entails conformity with "the truth," which according to the Hindu mind is encapsulated in Hindu culture. Accordingly, vice or moral evil—called adharma—is defined as opposition to dharma, or disharmony with the truth which encompasses and controls the world.[73]

Dharma is not seen so much as a divine law or command as it is the fabric of the cosmos. Thus to follow dharma is to follow the natural bent of the universe, while to go against dharma is to be at cross-purposes with the general flow of things.

Closely related to dharma is the concept of karma, the mechanism which rewards good and punishes evil. According to the law of karma, moral acts (those that follow dharma, or custom) will bear positive fruit both in this life and in subsequent existences, while evil acts (those that violate dharma) will produce negative fruit. The concept of karma eventually came to be tied in with the idea of merit: The wise person acquires merit through his good deeds so that he may be reborn in more favorable circumstances.[74] This entire moral framework is built on the concept of reincarnation (many lives), which is the basic concept behind Hindu community life. According to Hindu philosophy, one's position in this life is determined by the good or evil which one practiced in previous lives. This idea helps to account for the caste stratification in India and Nepal (one's position in society is thought to be determined by one's conduct in past lives). It also explains why Hindu societies tend toward resignation in the face of oppression rather than revolution against the oppressors (future lives will bring retribution to the oppressors).[75]

An offshoot of Hinduism whose view of morality has been important in recent history is Jainism, which was founded by Mahavira, a contemporary with the Buddha, in revolt against the Indian caste system and the vague world spirit of the Hindus. Jainism is an ascetic faith whose rigid insistence upon not injuring living things (even insects and microbes) laid the foundation for much Indian thinking about nonviolence. Its teaching helped shape the thought of the great peaceful nationalist hero Mahatma Gandhi during his struggle for Indian rights and independence from British rule in the early part of the twentieth century. Small in numbers, the Jains are a prosperous and influential community.[76]

(3) The Basic Problem of the Hindu View of Morality. The basic problem with the Hindu approach to ethics and morals is that, in its monistic view, there is ultimately no difference between good and evil; they are merely different aspects of the one great evolving reality and purely relative.

According to Hindu belief, the opposites of cause and effect, substance and attribute, good and evil, and truth and error are due to the human tendency to separate related terms. This tendency can be overcome if we recognize that the opposing factors in each pair are mutually complementary elements based on one identity. If good and evil are both aspects of the One Great Reality, ultimately there is no sure way of deciding between what is good and what is evil. This means that in the Hindu way of thinking there is ultimately no difference between good and evil; they are purely relative. Evil, error, and ugliness are not ultimate. Evil has reference to the distance which good has to traverse. Ugliness is halfway to beauty. Error is a stage on the road to truth. All these opposite conceptions have to be outgrown to reach the final stage of nonbeing.[77]

4. The Buddhist View of Morality

As detailed in chapter 9, Buddhism is an amazingly successful missionary religion which has spread through Southeast Asian countries, into China via Central Asia, into Korea and Japan, and into Tibet. Although it has suffered extensively in the twentieth century under Marxist regimes,[78] its influence remains great throughout most of the East. There is no country to the east of India, apart from the Philippines, which has not been deeply affected by Buddhist culture and view of morality.[79]

(1) The Approach of Hinayana (Theravada or Southern) Buddhism. As mentioned in an earlier chapter, the code of morals in Hinayana Buddhism is summed up in the Eightfold Noble Path, which comprises right belief, right thought, right speech, action, means of livelihood, exertion, remembrance, and meditation. The goal of those who follow this path is nirvana, summed up as "the end of suffering by the elimination of personal and separative desire." The essence of Hinayana Buddhism can be summed up in the words:

> To cease from all sin
> To get virtue,
> To purify the heart.[80]

In Hinayana Buddhism, therefore, morality has to do not with obeying God, but with being wise; morality is seen as part of the general effort at self-purification. Whereas the model for the Christian, Jew, or Muslim is the obedient person of faith, such as Abraham, the model for the Buddhist is the person of superior insight, such as the Buddha.[81]

The Southern Buddhist emphasis on the Path to liberation helps to explain why Buddhism forbids taking "drugs and intoxicants" (the word covers liquor and other things). Liquor clouds the mind and also arouses anger—both of which are to be avoided by someone who seeks liberation. Clouding of the mind must be avoided because the task of the saintly person is to cultivate clarity of consciousness and self-awareness so that detached insight can be gained. Further, anger and allied emotions are the opposite of the peace which liberation should bring.

In Hinayana Buddhism monks and nuns are thought to have a much stronger chance of achieving nirvana because they have the discipline and concentration necessary to follow the difficult Eightfold Path. It is believed that ordinary laypeople may have to wait and get their chance in some future life; thus the teaching of karma and rebirth can project a person's career into the future beyond the grave. (However, as shown in chapters 8 and 9, the Buddhist interpretation of reincarnation differs from that of the Hindu and does not involve rebirth of the intact personality, but of a system of character traits.) The ordinary person gains merit by virtuous acts in this life and thus hopes for a better chance of achieving nirvana in the next life.

Indeed, the person who gives generously to the Buddhist Order and follows the moral Path may be reborn in a kind of heaven. This heaven, though, is not everlasting; it is not the final goal. This is true because, in Buddhism, a person's merit is in due course exhausted. At that time a person is obliged to disappear from paradise and be reborn in some other state. This is in accord with the Buddhist idea that all existence, including heavenly (and for that matter hellish) existence, is impermanent; only nirvana is the permanent, and it lies beyond existence, beyond this world and the next.[82]

In brief, Theravada Buddhism has traditionally seen morality as part of the path which leads to nirvana and as something which operates within a universe controlled by karma, the law of reward and penalty within the framework of the rebirth of character traits in different existences. In Theravada Buddhism, morality is seen as partly a matter of being prudent in the interest of achieving the state of final freedom and true happiness or at least attaining a better chance at nirvana the next time around. Morality also involves peace and, in some degree, withdrawal from the bustle of the world.[83]

This Buddhist emphasis on peace—even emptiness—and its tendency toward an "otherworldly" outlook has caused Buddhism from its inception to have difficulty with power. In fact, the issue of how power is used and, indeed, whether it can be used at all, is a basic problem of Hinayana Buddhist morality. This is true because, as in Hinduism, the concept of reincarnation dominates in Buddhist countries. The ideal is not social transformation but equanimity attained through detachment from the discords and sufferings of life.[84]

The dilemma of power is interwoven with the very origins of the Buddhist religion. In leaving his princely palace and setting out on the quest for truth through poverty and homelessness, the Buddha gave up all worldly power. In return he gained enlightenment, and in fact helped to shape the world that came after him. He was diplomatic in his preaching skills and kingly in his noble demeanor. But he was neither a diplomat nor a politician, still less a general. And his followers throughout the centuries have wrestled with the question of whether they can wield power and still follow their faith.

Three centuries after the death of Buddha, for example, the Indian emperor Ashoka, a follower of Buddha, destroyed a neighboring people in his pursuit of wider imperial power. However, he was so tormented by his aggressive actions that henceforth he tried to rule as a king of peace.[85]

(2) The Approach of Mahayana (Northern) Buddhism. As chapter 9 points out, Mahayana or Northern Buddhism is a form of Buddhism that relaxed the stringent requirements of salvation and thereby opened the religion to the masses. In a sense, Mahayana Buddhism developed out of a tension in original or Hinayana Buddhism between liberation and compassion.

As we have seen, the original emphasis in Buddhism is on right behavior as a means toward attaining nirvana or at least toward having a better chance of achieving it in another life. It is generally assumed that only a relatively few people have the strength and single-mindedness that are necessary to actually achieve salvation.

But alongside this strong emphasis on the right action of the few grew an emphasis on compassion for the suffering—a compassion that meant sacrificing oneself, even postponing nirvana, for the sake of serving one's suffering fellow beings. It was this concept of compassion and self-sacrifice that became the basis for Mahayana Buddhism.[86]

A distinctive characteristic of Mahayana Buddhism is a belief in Bodhisattvas, who are conceived as persons who have reached the peak of perfection (achieved Buddhahood), but who willingly forgo nirvana in order to help the less fortunate. Having attained a vast store of merit through his or her many lives of self-sacrifice, the Bodhisattva is in a position to distribute this immense surplus to others to help them on their way. Thus, the otherwise unworthy faithful person could, by calling on one of the Bodhisattvas, gain extra merit and thus draw closer to the goal of final release from suffering, although, as one Buddhist scholar observes, "Even a Buddha cannot help another being to salvation unless the latter's karmic merit is already ripened to such a degree that he can respond to a Buddha's teaching and influence."[87]

The Bodhisattvas, therefore, are figures of grace, and in some ways, the idea of the Bodhisattvas can be said to run parallel to Christianity. Instead of the idea of agape love, however, in Buddhism compassion is central.

In Mahayana Buddhism, the sharp division between nirvana and a worldly life was softened or called into question. It was thought possible for the Buddhist to pursue the ideal of imitating the Bodhisattva (indeed, of becoming a Buddha-to-be) through living the good life in this world.

Sometimes this idea had strange manifestations. In medieval Japan, for example, the warrior class came to see such disciplines as archery and swordplay as possible means toward the development of selflessness. In this manner, even warfare would be a means of gaining higher insight.

On the whole, however, the Mahayana Buddhists, like the Hinayana Buddhists, have been eager to minimize violence and promote peace.[88] Unlike the dynamic and politically oriented Islam, the Buddhist ethical system maintains a certain peaceful otherworldliness.

IV. How Would You Describe the Basic Biblical View of Human Morality?

In the Bible, ethical obligation is motivated not by the search for self-realization or social coherence, but by human response to the sovereignty of God. The whole of a person's life is to be presented in service to God as a "living sacrifice" (Rom. 12:1). Hence in the Bible ethics cannot be detached from theology. This is shown clearly in the close relationship between what Jesus designated as the first and second commandments: Human beings show their love to God by loving their neighbors (Mark 12:28–31). The context of ethical obligation is relationship to God. Apart from this relationship there is no biblical ethic.[89]

In the biblical faith, human beings are not related to abstract, timeless ethical principles which are discovered and refined by speculative reason. Rather, humans are related to the living God who makes a sovereign, personal claim upon their whole life. In this sense, the God of the Bible, is, in Pascal's words, "the God of Abraham, Isaac, and Jacob, and not the God of the philosophers and the scientists."[90]

1. Old Testament Origins of the Biblical View

(1) A Covenant-Based Morality. In the Old Testament story, the activity of God in his righteousness is the origin of human responsibility and freedom and therefore of morality. More specifically, God's actions in delivering his people out of slavery resulted in a covenant people who gladly served him and reflected his character as grateful servants.

To understand the Old Testament concept of biblical ethics, then, we must begin by exploring the relationship between God and humankind. And this demands a consideration of the covenant which God established with his people on the basis of his deeds in history.[91]

Clearly, the covenant between God and Israel was not a parity covenant—a bargain or commercial contract between equals. Rather, it was a relationship conferred upon a people by their Sovereign. And it was a covenant that required obedience: "All that the Lord has spoken we will do, and we will be obedient," Israel said in the ancient covenant ceremony (Exod. 24:7; cf. 19:5, 8).

We should note, however, the historical context of the making of the covenant. Its appearance in the Bible is preceded by a "historical prologue" which tells what God had done for his people. His "mighty acts" had delivered them at the time of the Exodus. Israel's whole existence, then, was dependent upon the sovereignty of God, and within the covenant he offered them the people found security and meaning in history.

It is important to emphasize, therefore, that God's acts in history provided the *motivation* for Israel's obedience and thus for human conduct. This obedience was not motivated by servile capitulation to the Sovereign's power, but by gratitude for his mighty acts of deliverance. This gratitude was expressed in every celebration of the Passover Feast. Israel was indebted to the Lord. This was the basis of the unconditional obligation expressed in the word *obedience.*[92]

Israel's obligation was to be expressed in social responsibility. For *covenant* as used in the Old Testament is a social term; it was made with a people, not just with a single individual. God's will for his creation is that human beings should find the fullness of life in communion with him and in community with one another.

From the biblical point of view, in fact, the loss of the intended community is the tragedy of human history as outlined in Genesis 1–11. The original community God created was destroyed because of humanity's estrangement from God and the consequent fracture of human relationships. God took the initiative, therefore, to reestablish community—first the community of the Old Covenant (Israel) and finally the community of the New Covenant (the church). Within this social context, human beings have access to God and are responsibly related to one another. In this sense, the Bible deals with social salvation. And the biblical view of morals and ethics is based on this community outlook.

As the great Hebrew prophets tirelessly pointed out, Israel's violation of its responsibility toward its fellow humans was a breach of Israel's relationship to God, and God's judgment of this violation was revealed in history (Amos 3:1–2). True, the covenant relationship began with God and rested upon his historical deeds of mercy, upon his "steadfast love" (*chesed*). But human beings were required in return to serve God by showing steadfast love to one another. So in a great prophetic passage, twice quoted in the New Testament, Hosea proclaims God's word: "I desire steadfast love and not sacrifice, the knowledge of God, rather than burnt offerings" (Hosea 6:6).[93]

The acts of God in history provide not only the motive, but also the *pattern* for human conduct. God teaches his people how they should serve him in the present through the remembrance of what he has done for them in the past. In other words, God's people know what "justice" is not by contemplating some abstract norm of justice, but by remembering how God delivered his people from oppression and bondage. Men know what "steadfast love" is by remembering and praising God for his great deeds of mercy.

Hence it is significant that Micah, after a summary of "the saving acts of the Lord" in which memory focuses primarily on the Exodus (Mic. 6:3–5), says: "He has showed you, O man, what is good; and what does the Lord require of you but to do justice, and to love kindness, and to walk humbly with your God?" (Mic. 6:8). In the relationship of the covenant, the human task is nothing less than "the imitation of God." It is, in the words of Martin Buber, "a following in God's footsteps and so serving His work in the world."[94]

Israel's ethic, then, is the ethic of the humble walk with God in willing obedience to his command. Specific commandments point beyond themselves to the one who commands, to the God who redeemed his people. This is evident in the case of the Ten Commandments, which formed the legal content of the ancient Mosaic covenant. The Decalogue is preceded by a brief historical prologue: "I am the Lord your God, who brought you out of the land of Egypt, out of the house of bondage," and it is set in the covenant form of "I and thou" address (Exod. 20:2).

God's revelation in the Ten Commandments was not primarily the disclosure of a set of laws or timeless ethical principles, but the disclosure of himself in personal encounter with Moses and his people in the event of the Exodus. The Ten Commandments then leave a wide area of freedom for responding to the claim of God in concrete, decisional situations.[95]

There are, of course, parts of the Bible that reveal a tendency toward understanding God's will in impersonal, legal terms, rather than in historical and personal terms. But the deepest motive and pattern of Israel's faith was not a legalistic doctrine of rewards and punishment or a service to God in order to receive blessings. Rather, the motive was an inner obligation written upon the heart by gratitude for God's acts of steadfast love toward his people (cf. Jer. 31:31–34).[96]

(2) A New Type of Obedience and Law. Because of the covenant relationship, the Israelite attained a new understanding of his work and of his use of earthly goods. Covenant theology meant that the Near Eastern common law that had been adopted by Israel had to be revised. For example, the law had to provide for the equality of all citizens before it. In Israel, all classes of society, no matter what their social status may have been, were included in the provision (Exod. 21:23–25; Lev. 24:19–22). The death penalty for embezzlement no longer applied in Israel, and the mutilation of the body as a legal penalty was abolished.

Since Israel had been redeemed from slavery in Egypt, the righteousness of God in the law was seen to be especially solicitous of the poor and the weak in society: "If you do afflict them, and they cry out to me, I will surely hear their cry" (Exod. 22:22).

This was an entirely new emphasis in law and morality for ancient times and was borne out in many specific moral and legal guidelines given in the Bible. The sojourner who does not have full civil rights and the widow and orphan who are defenseless against the powerful must not be oppressed in any way (Exod. 22:21–24). The poor person has the same right in court as the rich, and justice must not be taken from him or her (Exod. 23:6).[97] The poor person's need, moreover, must not become the occasion for profit. If he gives his clothing as a pledge of repayment, it should be returned to him before sundown because it is all he has to wear. When the poor person cries to God, God will hear him or her, for God is gracious (Exod. 22:21–27).

The Israelite attitude toward earthly goods is also determined by this new theology. Property belongs to God, who gives it to his people as a loan (cf. Lev. 25:23). There is no such thing as a natural and private right to the exploitation of property.[98]

(3) A New Meaning to Wisdom Literature. Israel, like most other societies of its time, had an active "wisdom" tradition. The "wise men" of Israel were a special class in the community, as distinct from priests and prophets. Their function was to give practical advice on the conduct of affairs in the community (Jer. 18:18; Ezek. 7:26). Although they came under the same prophetic condemnation as the priests (Eccles. 12:13–14), they nevertheless were considered an important source of knowledge by the people.

Three Books in the Old Testament Canon—Job, Proverbs, and Ecclesiastes—are products of this wisdom tradition; the anthology of epigrams in Proverbs seems to have been especially typical of their work. The primary source of their insight in such proverbs seems to have been observation, experience, and common sense. The teaching is chiefly practical, prudential, and utilitarian. Much of it is beautifully phrased, easily quoted, and exhibits a profundity of observation.

Like many sermons on character education in the past three generations, however, the wisdom teachings for the most part represent that which any person of good will can say, regardless of his theological affiliation or lack of it. Consequently, the close relation between Israelite wisdom literature and that of other countries, particularly of Canaan and of Egypt, is not surprising. In fact, other countries had a body of wisdom literature before Israel did, and undoubtedly many of Israel's proverbs were borrowed from the international collections. It is well that this is the case, for the proverbs indicate that a prudential, common-sense ethic, based upon broad experience, is by no means excluded from Israelite faith.[99]

The wisdom movement is deficient because its theological base and concerns tend to be too narrow. It represents an individualism in ethics and theology without a strong doctrine of society. However, in the canon of Scripture, Proverbs performs the important function of supplying an explication of the meaning of the law for individual life. In contrast, the bulk of Israelite law and prophecy held individual and social ethics together within the framework of covenant theology.[100]

It is important to notice, however, that Israel's covenant theology altered the inner meaning of the basic wisdom ethic. For example, a basic pattern in proverbial writing was to make clear what the good person should do by giving in contrast the manner of the bad person. And the biblical wisdom literature introduced a new kind of standard for this contrast of good and bad.

In Egyptian wisdom the contrast was between the silent person—one who is self-disciplined, patient, and self-controlled—and the passionate one—who is self-assertive, grasping, and arbitrary, disturbing the existing order and destroying the harmonious integration of society. In Israel, however, similar proverbs showed the basic contrast as being between the righteous or upright man and the wicked or foolish man. This presupposes an entirely different kind of judgment between good and bad: The righteous and the wicked are evaluated according to a given standard, which can only be the revealed law of

Yahweh. Thus the wisdom ethic in Israel cannot be conceived as unrelated to revelation. In fact, it rests squarely upon the peculiarly Israelite understanding of what constitutes good and evil.

This is the more clear when we observe that the motto of the wisdom movement in Israel seems to have been "the fear of Yahweh," which is the beginning of knowledge and wisdom (Prov. 1:7; 9:10). It is this holy reverence for Yahweh which is strength to the upright (Prov. 10:29), which produces righteousness (Prov. 14:2), which is a fountain of life (Prov. 14:27; cf. 19:23; 22:4). Thus Yahweh is in truth the source of wisdom (cf. Job 28) and the author of prudential morality. It is he who rewards the righteous and punishes the wicked.

It is also important to note that the extremely individualized perspective of the wisdom movement's doctrine of divine reward and punishment furnished the setting for theological controversy even in Old Testament times. In fact, the Book of Job was written specifically to deny that this doctrine is sufficient to explain all human suffering and to assert there is a deeper dimension in life. A major message of Job is that there is a mystery in the way God deals with human beings—a mystery which must be accepted humbly without loss of faith in God's providence.

Ecclesiastes represents a development in yet another direction—toward a denial of the whole belief in individual rewards and punishments in this life or hereafter. According to Ecclesiastes, God's moral government of the world, if it exists at all, is beyond our comprehension. The ordinary pursuits of human beings are vanity, emptiness, and weariness; they achieve no good end. The general view of this Book is that God's administration of the world cannot be understood by human beings. Whether one is righteous or wicked, wise or foolish, death is the great leveler in which both good and evil, love and hatred, perish (Eccles. 8:16–9:6). Nevertheless, according to Ecclesiastes, wisdom is indeed better than folly, and the proper life is one which enjoys the simple pleasures here and now in the fear of God, while avoiding self-assertive folly, pride, and rashness of spirit and action.[101]

2. The New Testament View

The New Testament presents both a renewal and fulfillment of the Mosaic covenant and a repudiation of the legalistic approach to reward and punishment that had grown up around the covenant. In the New Testament the activity of God culminating in Jesus Christ is the origin of an enlarged teaching about human responsibility, freedom, and human morality.

(1) A Kingdom-Based Morality. The ethic of Jesus, as set forth in the Sermon on the Mount, is a kingdom ethic. The sayings which are found in this "sermon" must be understood within the context of Jesus' vocation and his preaching concerning the nearness of the kingdom of God, the first signs of which were beginning to be seen in his ministry.

The message of Jesus brought to a climax the Old Testament motif of the kingship of God. Jesus proclaimed that God is King and that he is now beginning to inaugurate his kingdom in history. Hence men were called to serve the king—not in submission to an overwhelming assertion of power, but in gratitude for his grace and forgiving love.

On Jesus' lips, then, the call to discipleship and thus to a moral life was a call to decision, a call to grateful obedience, and a call to love God by showing love to the neighbor. Moreover, God's gracious actions were to be the pattern for human conduct: "Be ye perfect even as your Heavenly Father is perfect" (Matt. 5:48).[102]

(2) The Key to Moral Obedience. The New Testament then goes on to show how the moral life the Christian is called to is created and sustained by dependence on Christ as Lord. The Christian who acknowledges Christ's lordship is to possess the same mind and the same obedience demonstrated by Christ. The result is that such a Christian will act in love and without strife or vainglory. Instead of looking only to his or her own affairs, such a Christian will be humbly concerned with the lot of others. The "encouragement in Christ," the "incentive of love," and "participation in the Spirit" brings Christians together. They are to be "of the same mind, having the same love, being in full accord" (Phil. 2:2).

Acknowledgment of Christ's lordship is thus not an intellectual assent to a dogmatic proposition, but an active participation in the "mind of Christ" which results in community. It leads to an ethic which cannot be frozen into a system of law or justice because its essence is the free giving of self to those in need.[103]

To confess Christ is thus the most relevant political and social statement one can make. This confession does not always tell the Christian precisely how to act in a secular society. However, it does provide guidelines and the inner ground of all action and involves a participation in community living as a vocation to which one is called.[104]

The moral obedience of the Christians was also the expression of the Spirit's working. The sacrifices of the wealthy Christians in Acts, for instance, were the result of the work of the Spirit in the church. According to Paul, the redeeming grace of God through Christ frees the believer not only from the guilt of sin, but also from its grip on his life, so that he can and should produce the fruit of the Spirit: love, joy, peace, patience, kindness, goodness, faithfulness, gentleness, self-control (see Gal. 5:1, 13, 16–25).[105]

(3) The Uniting of Gospel and Law. The New Testament has a paradoxical position with regard to law. On the one hand, it states clearly that the law is of God and is to be obeyed as his will laid before us. Jesus himself said that his purpose was not to destroy the law, but to fulfill it. Furthermore, the Epistles, after theological exposition, generally conclude with specific ethical exhortations. Hence, in some manner, gospel and law appear to be joined together.

On the other hand, the freedom of Jesus in dealing with questions of law is evident. Paul taught, moreover, that the Christian has liberty in Christ and is no longer "under the law" (e.g., Rom. 6:14; Gal. 3:24–25; 5:18). These emphases would appear to set the law aside as the less-important focus of the Christian's attention.[106]

Nevertheless, Paul knew that so long as Christ's followers are ambiguously placed as citizens of heaven in a world very much under the sway of the old order, there must be some kind of law. This fact can be seen in the following emphases.

- *Without some law and order, life in a community of imperfect Christians and vast numbers of unbelievers is not possible.* This fact was probably one reason why Paul enjoined obedience to the Roman authorities. For Paul, it was clearly Roman law and not the law of Moses that was restraining current lawless tendencies.
- *Law elicits a knowledge of wrongdoing.* That is, the law brings to us indirectly a realization of our own sinfulness and helplessness in the face of evil. Paul says, "If it had not been for the law, I should not have known sin" (Rom. 7:7). He then goes on to give his classical account of the divided human heart apart from Christ.
- *Even for the committed Christian, fully conscious of his Christian liberty, law still provides useful guidance as to the best use of his freedom.* We can still learn a good deal about the Christian style of life from the law of Moses, if that law is studied in the light of Christ's coming and in the spirit of Christ.[107]

(4) Emphasis on Command Law Rather than Case Law. A helpful key to the paradox of freedom and law in the New Testament may be found in the distinction between the Old Testament concepts of case law and command law. "Case law" in this context refers specifically to the various particular and impersonal statutes and ordinances mediated to Israel by Moses (Exod. 21:1; Deut. 4:14) and developed by the Jewish teachers into a complex system of jurisprudence by the time of the New Testament. Command law, on the other hand, rested in God's direct exhortation, "Thou shalt," and involved inward and personal response to God's expressed purposes and will.

The Old Testament prophets had shown little interest in case law. They tended to be impatient with the mentality which lived and moved and had its being within legal systems and was concerned chiefly with what could be legally enforced. In the Book of Jeremiah, for example, God's law is his way (5:4–5; cf. 6:15); it is his words (6:19; cf. Isa. 1:10), not only those spoken to Moses, but also his living word transmitted by the prophets (cf. 25:3–7; 26:4–5). On the other hand, the professional handlers of the law do not know God; they have followed things which do not profit (2:8): "How can you say, 'We are wise, and the law of the Lord is with us'? But, behold, the false pen of the scribes has made it into a lie" (8:8).

The preoccupation with case law is thus seen by the prophets as a stultifying procedure. It enabled the legalist to forget that the primary content of the covenant was the inward, personal requirement: "Obey my voice, and I will be your God, and you shall be my people" (Jer. 7:23; 11:6–7; cf. 31:31ff.).[108]

Jesus' teachings showed the same exclusive concern with command law and impatience with case law, so that it was said that he taught "as one who had authority, and not as their scribes" (Matt. 7:29). Behind the teachings of Jesus is the continued insistence upon God's compelling will. For Jesus, obedience to God's will can spring only from inward and individual devotion which seeks first God's kingdom and his righteousness and which looks for "perfection" like that of the heavenly Father (Matt. 5:48; 6:33).

From Jesus' perspective, the legalists who concentrated on case law betrayed the weightier matters of the law by their exclusive endeavor to bind all life within a system of specific "dos and don'ts" (Matt. 23). Jesus protested whenever case law was used not as a guide to life, but as a power to coerce life. Hence the suspicion and fear many Jewish officials felt toward Jesus lay not so much in his exposition of command law as in his denial of the ultimate validity of case law.

The viewpoint expounded both by the prophets and Jesus implies that the individual members of the community possess a freedom for responsible decision amidst the details of daily life. This is true because they must seek first and continually to express the righteousness of God.[109]

The apostle Paul has considerable advice to give to specific problems, but his methodology is not that of case law. Rather, he continually reflects the spirit of the command law. In seeking to apply command law, Paul is quite conscious of the distinction between his opinion and God's Word. For this reason, Paul's method is very different from the legal practice of Judaism, wherein the application of command law took the form of enforced case law. The New Testament reasserts the absolute and compelling will of God for the community. It also emphasizes the free, responsible decision each individual must daily make if he or she has died with Christ and risen with him to new life.[110]

3. The Impact of the "Already-Not Yet" Kingdom View on Biblical Ethics

The community life of the New Testament church reflected a two-sided situation. On the one hand, it exhibited the ethics of a kingdom which had been foretold by the prophets and had actually dawned in Christ. On the other hand, it tells of the ethical life and decisions of a small, nonpolitical group which understood itself as living in the interval before the second coming of Christ, which was not yet realized. It is this expectation of a future consummation which gives the New Testament its urgency and intensity.[111]

We in the twentieth century are still living in the interim period, the period after the kingdom has come in Christ but before it has come in its final power and glory. It is a period in which, as the apostle Paul saw, we are engaged in a struggle against cosmic powers of evil. It is true that Christ won the decisive battle against these powers in his death and resurrection. In the interim period, however, these powers, though doomed, are only too evident in this world. The Christian life is properly regarded as a warfare against them (Eph. 6:12).[112]

Christian ethics today, therefore, has its place precisely in the field of tension between the old and the new aeons. Christian ethics and morality are not for the old alone, nor for the new alone, but for the time between the old and new. This "already-not yet" kingdom emphasis undergirds intense moral responsibility.[113]

4. The Biblical View of Human Responsibility and Freedom under the Covenant

The human capacity for genuine decision making is assumed in the Bible. Without this capacity, which entails both freedom and responsibility, there could be neither religion nor ethics nor moral decision. Human beings retain this freedom even under the bondage of sin, and God's providence is no denial of responsibility.

According to the biblical view, humanity possesses freedom and the power of decision because humans are more than merely part of nature. Instead, they have been given freedom by God as a part of God's own freedom. This freedom is part of the "image of God" in humankind, and it provides infinite potentiality for good and evil. This means that humankind transcends the limitations of all determinisms, including the scientific determinism of naturalist philosophy and the "idealistic" determinism of Socrates.

In fact, the watershed which separates Greek from biblical thinking can be summed up in the contrast between Socrates's claim that no human being knowingly does evil and the apostle Paul's declaration that human beings "are without excuse; for although they knew God they did not honor him as God or give thanks to him" (Rom. 1:20–21). The latter presupposes freedom, while the former precludes it. Contemporary naturalism, too, regards humanity as simply part of nature, and holds that humankind is inserted into a scheme of causal determinism that leaves no room for freedom, reason, or moral responsibility.

In the biblical view, every situation in which human beings find themselves has some margin of freedom of decision and responsibility. Humans possess a will which may be conditioned by external factors of nature and society and distorted by sin, but it still has some freedom for decisions. And along with decision-making freedom comes real responsibility. Such a responsible freedom is presupposed by key biblical words such as *sin, repentance, forgiveness, love* and *covenant*.

Consequently, the Bible, though not intentionally philosophical, contains by inference what is probably the most thorough understanding ever written of what it means to be a free agent. This is one more variation on Paul's thesis that "the foolishness of God is wiser than men."[114]

5. Idolatry as the Root Source of Moral Evil

Human beings are meant for fellowship with God; that is their "essential nature" in creation. Humans are meant to walk with their Creator in humility and love and to conduct their lives in the ever-present awareness of the divine source and center of their being. This is the significance of the biblical account of the blissful life in Paradise before the Fall. It is the normative condition of human existence, full of peace and harmony within and without.

This peace was lost and this harmony disrupted the moment the first humans, in the exercise of freedom, turned away from God and thus denied their own essential nature and the law of their being. Such is the meaning of sin—the "original" sin of Adam and Eve in Paradise and the sin of each of us throughout our lives.

But human beings cannot go on without some ultimate to give substance and meaning to life. Having turned away from the living God in the willfulness of sin, humankind is driven to seek for a ground of existence in what is not God. The result is idolatry.

Every human alive, by virtue of his or her freedom, has some focal point to which he or she stands in acknowledged or unacknowledged relation. Even such a cynic as Adolf Hitler, who claimed to be a law unto himself, superior to external constraint, appealed to the standard of "blood and soil."

The most important question that can be asked about a person therefore is, "What is the external criterion upon which his or her judgments of good and evil depend?" The answer to this question will shape all his decisions and thus the quality of that person's entire moral life.

To ask whether a person believes in "God" is consequently to misunderstand the issue. The proper question, as the biblical writers never forget, is rather: What (or who) is his or her god? As Martin Luther succinctly puts it, "Whatever, then, thy heart clings to and relies upon, that is properly thy god."

The most urgent question then is "Which is the *true* god?" The Bible proceeds from the recognition that life is a battle of the gods, or a battle between the true God and a host of pretenders. Hence Elijah's famous words: "If the Lord [Yahweh] is God, follow him; but if Baal, then follow him" (1 Kings 18:21).

In fact, the biblical concept of sin is that it is another word for allegiance to a false god. It is interchangeable with the word "idolatry." Hence Christian theology often equates sin with unbelief in the sense of trust in the wrong god.[115]

Of course, idolatry in modern terms is not simply worship of sticks and stones. And it is not necessarily the worship of something evil. More often, idolatry is the absolutization of the relative. That is, the object of idolatrous worship may well be something that is good in itself, but since it is not the true God, its goodness is necessarily only partial and relative. What idolatry does is to convert its object into an absolute, thereby destroying the partial good within it and transforming it into a total evil.

The vacuum created by the decay of traditional religion in our time has been filled by the abundance of things worshiped in place of God. Even the ancient nature cults find their representation in modern idolatry. (Note the cult of "life" as we find it under various guises in the Romantics, in Nietzsche, in the ecstatic worship of sex, and in the "dark forces" of instinct.) However, the dominant idolatries of our time are not so much the primitivistic cults of "nature" as the cults of collective society and objectified ideas. Race, nation, empire, class, state, party—even church and humanity—are among the gods who claim the allegiance of modern people. There are also science, culture, social reform, and progress. Each of these things represents a significant and valuable aspect of human life. However, each of them becomes delusive and demonic once it is absolutized and exalted into the god of our existence.

The ultimate imperative of biblical morality and ethics is, therefore, the affirmation of the Living God and the repudiation of idolatry. It is an imperative that is not really ethical at all, but religious: "Thou shalt love the Lord thy God with all thine heart, and with all thy soul, with all thy might" (Deut. 6:5).[116]

6. A Systematic Framework for a Biblical View of Human Morality

We have described the origin and development of the biblical view of human morality. It should be helpful to outline briefly six key ideas which provide a systematic background or framework for evaluating the various Christian approaches to Christian ethics or morality. These affirmations represent evangelical convictions:

- *Human beings are moral rebels who live in a world of fallen morality.* The world is under the sway of Satan.
- *If we are to have authentic ethics, they must come from a God who is above and outside this fallen world.* The good news of Christianity is that God has come into the world to reveal himself through the Hebrews, through Christ, and through the apostles. He has given us his self-revelation in mighty deeds and words through particular events and persons. Christian ethics comes primarily from this special revelation and not from man.
- *Christian ethics unmasks the revolt of general ethics against God.* There is some truth in secular ethics, since God reveals himself through common grace or revelation to humankind in conscience and nature. But the truth of secular ethics is distorted by sin.
- *Potentially, only Christian believers have full insight into authentic ethics.* It is the Christian's mission, therefore, to share these ethical principles and the realities of authentic morality with the world. Christians are to be a light in a dark world. They are to be salt for a decaying society. In a world of moral relativism, they are to hold up moral absolutes.
- *The practice of Christian ethics is not a burden, because doing the will of God will yield the greatest personal happiness as well as promote the general welfare.* Actual practice has shown this to be true. In fact, this moral contribution is one of the reasons our forefathers declared that churches and certain Christian institutions are tax-exempt.
- *The nature of agape love makes it morally impossible for the Christian to limit his love and concern only to friends and equals.* This means that Christians cannot withdraw from the world; they are to be concerned with both missions and cultural life. Christians do not envision a utopia before the return of Christ. However, they believe that the power of Christ, working through them, can infuse a new spirit into family life, labor relations, government, literature, music, the arts and all of culture. They also see that a part of their responsibility is to help maintain a framework of justice in the world.[117]

V. What Are Alternative Christian Approaches to Defining and Implementing Biblical Ethics?

Through the centuries, Christians have developed a variety of approaches for applying the biblical teachings on ethics and morality to the specifics of decision making in the world. In this section we will look at some of the common approaches—most of which have tended to stress one or more aspects of the biblical view to the neglect of others aspects. In the next section, we will describe an approach that more satisfactorily takes into account the entire biblical view.

1. The Natural-Law Approach to Biblical Ethics

The basic concept of natural law ethics is that moral absolutes are inherent in human nature and can be perceived and formulated by reason alone. According to John Macquarrie, such a doctrine claims that the basic ethical insights are in principle available to any rational human being, whatever his or her religion or ideology. In this first sense, natural law doctrine stands opposed to any attempt to tie ethics to some specific revelation. A second point about natural law is that it locates ethical norms in "nature" understood both as "human nature" and as that wider "nature" within which human life is set. This wider "nature" would perhaps be better called "reality," in the metaphysical sense of the term.[118]

(1) The Roman Catholic Version of Natural Law Ethics. The concept of natural law ethics is probably the most uniform constant in the history of ethics. It was propounded by the Greeks, accepted by most medieval Christians, modified one way or the other by the Reformers, and even today is part of the basis of law in countries that do not profess Christianity.[119]

In Christian circles, the concept of natural law has been particularly influential among Roman Catholic theologians. (It received special attention by Thomas Aquinas.) The Roman Catholic view is that the moral law of God is built into creation, and therefore into humanity, and is the universal moral law for the human race, applying to Christians and non-Christians alike.

For example, Roman Catholics hold that the idea that procreation is the purpose of human sexuality is derived from natural law, and that natural law can be applied to all people. So the Roman Catholic church feels free to prohibit birth control—not on the specific grounds that this prohibition is a matter of conscience with Roman Catholics, but that it is natural law and, as such, applies universally.

There is a hard line and a soft line about natural law in Roman Catholic moral theology. The hard line, as set forth in the Roman Catholic *Dictionary of Moral Theology*, tries to hold on to the strict Thomistic and medieval view: "Natural law is universal, immutable, not dispensable, and perceptible. It applies everywhere and for all men; it cannot change with the passage of time; no one can dispense from its observance; it may be understood or perceived by anyone who attains the use of reason; its observance obliges when it is perceived by a person who has the use of reason." The soft line, on the other hand, is taken by Roman Catholics who realize some of the problems in isolating specifics of natural law and who see the problem of so many variant ethical systems in the world.[120]

(3) The Protestant Versions of Natural-Law Ethics. There are a number of Protestant versions or adaptations of the natural-law approach. Some base natural law on human creation; being made in the image of God, human beings have impressed upon their mind a set of moral concepts. Others look at the Ten Commandments as not only projecting forward the kind of ethical life expected of Israel, but as a recovery of the natural law originally given to Adam.

Still others look at natural law not as so many specifics, but as a set of general rules, like rules of good health. By experience and reason, human beings learn that if they do certain things they get into trouble and if they do other things life goes better. Ethical systems diverge from one another only within certain limits, for society can exist only as people live within these semi-elastic limits. In light of this fact, it is argued that without some kind of natural law society is driven to a destructive ethical relativism or even to amoral nihilism.[121]

(4) The Problems of Natural-Law Ethics. According to Donald Bloesch, the problem with any natural-law theory is that it does not sufficiently take into consideration the effects of sin on the mind. Natural-law advocates hold that sin warps people more in the moral order than in the intellectual order. However, a look at philosophical history shows that every attempt to spell out the intellectual content of natural law has been historically and culturally conditioned. While all people seem to have a moral sense, when they begin articulating what this means, their own cultural and religious background proves to be determinative in their judgments.[122] Thus, the concept of a universally perceivable set of guidelines for morals and ethics established by unaided reason is suspect.

2. The Legalistic or Absolutist Approach

(1) Definition. One of the most common approaches to Christian ethics is to see the Bible as a total handbook or exhaustive dictionary of Christian ethics. This approach accepts the Bible as the infallible word of God speaking specifically to every moral situation. It sees potential ethical maxims lurking everywhere in Scripture, even in the most commonplace passages. According to this view, Christian conscience is bound not only to the clear ethical statements of Scripture, but also to all the maxims of Scripture which can be "decoded" from dozens of biblical passages that on the surface do not appear related to ethics and morality.[123]

(2) Weaknesses of the Legalistic Approach. One problem with such a use of the Bible for ethical direction is that it fails to see the progress of revelation in the historical development of Scripture. According to this approach the Word of God is one, and all parts that express God's will have equal authority. This means that a truth gleaned from some event in Judges binds the conscience as much as the specific exhortations of Romans 8. Such a treatment of Scripture not only violates the progressive character of the Bible, but makes Christian ethics arbitrary by taking the biblical teachings out of the context of the total message of the Bible as it is fulfilled or brought to a climax in Jesus Christ.

Another problem involved with this viewpoint is that it tends to put more weight for ethical decision on the Old Testament than the New, simply because the Old Testament is much longer than the New and therefore contains more material from which ethical direction can be derived. As a result, ethical maxims are drawn from the rich historical materials of the Old Testament and the more direct ethical teachings of the New Testament are neglected.

This use of Scripture leads to some arguments for ethical principles which many people would find odd. This approach attempts to judge the moral issue of birth control, for instance, from the actions of Onan. Or it attempts to defend a political theory by appealing to the political structures of the Old Testament. Or it takes the various rules of Leviticus and Deuteronomy and attempts to settle moral issues of the modern age from customs or practices of an ancient culture.[124]

In a recent theological lecture at Southwestern Seminary, Richard Mouw of Fuller Seminary listed several Scriptures which have been isolated from the total biblical teaching and used out of context to undergird certain attitudes and actions. We are not to seek to eliminate poverty, for example, because "the poor you will always have with you." We are not to be critical of any government actions, because "the powers to be are ordained of God." We are not to be concerned about the state of this world because Jesus' "kingdom is not of this world." Such a narrow, legalistic application of Scripture, of course, easily falls into the trap of neglecting the fundamental biblical message of the spirit of love, forgiveness, and help toward fellow sinners.

Religious legalism was a problem Jesus confronted in the Pharisees of his time, and it remains a problem among Christians today. It is important that the fundamental message of the Scriptures not be lost in the sticking to the "letter of the law" or even interpreting "law" out of situations that were not intended to be moral or ethical guidelines.

3. The Situation-Ethics Approach

The approach to biblical morality known as "situation ethics" first arose in the 1960s and achieved wide popularity over the next decade. Its best-known expositor was the British theologian John A. T. Robinson; its most incisive spokesman was the American professor of ethics at Boston's Episcopal Seminary, Joseph Fletcher. In this section our basic concern will be with Fletcher's opinions as reflected in his two basic books, *Situation Ethics* and *Moral Responsibility: Situation Ethics at Work.*[125]

(1) Reasons for the Popularity of Situation Ethics. The appeal of situation ethics when it first arrived on the scene is easy to understand, for it offered itself as a seemingly simple method of solving complex moral problems as well as claiming to be a correction for legalism. Situation ethics spoke to the mood of the hour in the 1960s and 1970s, when people were facing difficult moral choices and were restless with traditional morality.

In addition, the exponents of situation ethics had a lot to say about sex, which to most people was a very interesting subject, particularly when handled in a way that sounded permissive. In its rhetoric, situationism seemed to endorse the hunch which popular music and pulp writing so often expressed—that love will justify anything and that recognizing this made us both wiser and more humane than our parents.[126]

Although the moral climate changed somewhat in the 1980s, the decade when AIDS first made "safe sex" a household word, situation ethics still has influence and appeal. Fletcher's work in this area continues to be a point of departure for discussion and evaluation.

(2) Basic Concepts of Situation Ethics. Fletcher maintained that "the ruling norm of Christian decision is love: nothing else"; and he defined love as good will at work in partnership with reason, or reason calculating how love may best be served in any given situation. Ethical decision in turn is dependent on a rational calculation of consequences. The criterion is not the "right" or the "good" but what is "fitting" or contextually appropriate. The only intrinsic evil is malice; the only intrinsic good is love.

One well-known example of situation ethics given by Fletcher is the case of a German woman who was captured by the Russians in World War II while seeking food for her three small children. (Her husband had been taken to a P.O.W. camp in Wales.) In the prison camp, this woman—an active Christian—learned that she could be released as a liability if she became pregnant. Knowing the desperate plight of her children, she asked a camp guard to impregnate her. She was freed and returned home to search out her children in detention homes, then went to her pastor to ask if what she had done was acceptable in God's sight. Fletcher used this as an example of a situation in which love called for violation of the biblical teaching against adultery.[127]

Fletcher was not totally opposed to principles, but he understood them as guiding maxims, not as laws or precepts that are binding in all circumstances. In his view, principles can always be set aside in the name of love and rules can be discarded with a good conscience, so long as it can be shown that the welfare or happiness of the greater number of people is served. The ethics he proposed is relativistic, utilitarian, empirical, and existential.[128]

In Fletcher's view, neighbor-love is God's absolute and only demand in each situation. Despite what the simple reader of the Decalogue and the ethical parts of the New Testament might think, God does not require invariable performance of particular types of action, as such. God calls simply for love.

Fletcher also held that "old" Christian morality tends to lapse into Pharisaic legalism and therefore to sin against love. This is because it begins from the deductive, the transcendent, and the authoritative rules, which Fletcher opposed because he saw them being used in an arbitrary and inflexible manner. In his ethics, love dictates the breaking of accepted moral rules of "do this," "don't do that" type. According to Fletcher, these rules, both in Scripture and in life, are no more than rules of thumb or "maxims."[129]

Finally, Fletcher held that no situation ever faces us with a choice of evils. "The situationist holds that whatever is the most loving thing in the situation is the right and good thing. It is not excusably evil, it is positively good." According to this argument, Fletcher was ready to justify as positively good such acts as infanticide, abortion, "therapeutic" fornication, premarital sex, suicide, and euthanasia.[130]

(3) Evaluation of Situation Ethics. A careful evaluation of situation ethics as expounded by Fletcher reveals both strengths and weaknesses. Its primary strength is its provision of a necessary corrective to the all-too-common legalism which puts general principles before individual persons and whose zeal for God ousts neighbor-love from the heart. Situationists are right to stress that each situation is in some respects unique and that there are cases when the overall biblical injunction to love may outweigh the letter of the law.[131]

Situation ethics also has certain clear weaknesses from a biblical point of view. One is its neglect of guilt in the matter of ethical decisions. In Fletcher's approach, guilt has no place in ethical decision. We may be led to do some things universally deemed reprehensible, but with sorrow, not guilt; with regret, not remorse. If we reasoned wrongly concerning the outcome of a decision, it should be regarded as a mistake, not a sin.[132]

Another weakness of situation ethics is that it is too individualistic. If each person in each situation must make up his or own mind about the ethical or moral implications, then any concept of universal principle, eternal moral truth, or abiding ethical norms is shot down. Situation ethics fractures the Christian community, for it tends to isolate each individual on an ethical island of his or her own. Each individual makes moral decisions on the basis of love as he or she as a person understands love, not on the basis of a common moral heritage of the church as the Body of Christ.[133]

Still another weakness is that situation ethics neglects biblical guidelines. Although the New Testament does teach that love is the supreme ethic (Matt. 22:38–39, Rom. 13:10, 1 Cor. 13), it does not divorce love from specifics. Both Jesus and Paul added many other ethical norms to their belief in the centrality of love. In their minds, at least, there was no contradiction in asserting the primacy of love and then adding to that whatever you wish to call them—norms, principles, rules, moralisms, legalisms.

Situationists tend to label all law as "legalism," but this is not a true understanding of Scripture. The Hebrew word for law, *torah*, and the Greek *nomos* are much too broad in their meaning to be synonyms for legalism.[134]

Behind situation ethics's neglect of biblical guidelines is a fundamental misunderstanding of how the Bible relates love and law. In the Bible, neighbor-love is to be directed by law. There is no antithesis and possible clash between the claims of persons and of principles. Rather, the Bible assumes that we can only meet the claims of persons as we hold to the God-taught principles in dealing with them. These principles take the form of directives as to what should and should not be done to people.

The biblical approach to love and law, in a nutshell, is that God our Maker and Redeemer has revealed the unchanging pattern of response that he requires and that human beings need if they are to be truly themselves. The pattern is both an expression of God's own moral character—an indication of what he approves and disapproves—and a clue to human nature. By adhering to God's pattern, we express both our own true humanness and our true love for our neighbor.

Biblically, then, there is no antithesis between the motive of love and the divine directives which tell us what kinds of human action God approves and disapproves. The Bible does allow the fact that in some situations the task of love is to find how to do the most good and the least evil; doing nothing is rarely the answer! However, the evangelical Christian insists that evil remains evil, even when, being the lesser evil, it appears the only thing to do. In such a situation, we may have to choose an evil, but with heavy heart, and then seek God's cleansing of our conscience for having done it.[135]

(4) A Qualified Situation-Ethics Approach. A significant modification of the situation-ethics approach is that of the well-known ethicist John Bennett. Bennett agrees with Fletcher that love should be the guiding principle in person-to-person relations. However, he asserts, in the collective brutality of the social order, we need more developed and carefully thought-out principles than a simple admonition to "let love be the guide."

To meet such a need, Bennett suggests that we construct "middle axioms," which are concrete norms that mediate between the ethical ideal of sacrificial love and the existential and cultural realities. One arrives at these middle axioms through an empirical analysis of the cultural situation in light of the demands of love.[136]

Donald Bloesch, however, disapproves of this method. He points out that middle axioms or middle principles as conceived by ethicists might easily become ideological constructs that justify the special interests of a class or party within society. Feminists and black activists who clamor for affirmative action, as well as new religious rightists who press for prayer in the public schools and tax credits for parents with children in parochial schools are not necessarily being obedient to the divine commandment. Instead, they may actually be devising middle principles that can best advance the social agenda of their constituencies.

According to Bloesch, the biblical view of "good" is not the greater good of society rationally discerned or the happiness of the greatest number. Rather the good is how God's kingdom can best be served. As a means of guiding ethical behavior, Bloesch prefers the divine commandment which is not the outcome of rational deliberation. The divine commandment approach confronts people who are drifting in the wrong direction with the Word of God and calls for them to revise their presuppositions and conclusions.[137]

4. The Liberation-Ethics Approach

(1) The Liberation Theology Approach to Ethics. As shown in chapter 10, liberation theologies represent the viewpoint of groups who feel themselves to be oppressed and who identify particularly with biblical themes of justice for the poor and downtrodden. They also hold that academic theology is largely a

product of a social establishment and therefore tends to perpetuate the interests and concerns of that establishment while neglecting those of the oppressed. Their emphasis on the Bible's interest in the "underside" of history provides a helpful angle of vision for rediscovering certain dimensions of the gospel. And this emphasis also casts a new light on biblical ethics.

(2) The Methodology of Liberation Theology. In accordance with its "view from the underside," liberation theologies are developing a new methodology, which in a general sense can be called inductive. It is experimental in nature and closely connected with action.

In fact, liberation methodology is not just a way of thinking, but an intertwining of action and reflection known as "praxis." This approach is opposed to the notion that truth can be discerned and articulated on an intellectual level removed from practical concerns. Instead, praxis grows out of involvement in some concrete situation which people are trying to change. Thought arises as one element of these efforts toward change. It analyzes and criticizes these actions and that situation. Yet such thinking is always employed to further that process of change.

According to liberation theology, truth is found at the level of history, not just in the realm of ideas. In a broad sense, this is also a biblical emphasis. Reflection on praxis, on human significant action, can only be authentic when it is done from within, in the area of the strategic and tactical plane of human action.[139]

Liberation ethics, therefore, are based on this basic commitment to action. In fact, commitment to action in behalf of justice for the oppressed becomes the most important ethical norm, and failure to act becomes the most culpable sin. Choices of right or wrong must be made in light of the basic commitment to change, not necessarily on the basis of absolute moral law.

(3) Evaluation of the Ethical Views of Liberation Theology. To the credit of liberation theologians, they generally try to amass biblical support for their position. However, there is evidence that they are influenced as much by the Marxist dialectic of history as they are by the Bible. Many liberationists, by open admission, have accepted the Marxist prescription that the way to change the individual is to alter the social environment. This means that they place their primary hope in social revolution and education. The otherworldly and eschatological dimensions of the kingdom of God tend to be subordinated to this-worldly and utopian goals.[140]

For example, Gustavo Gutierrez, a prominent South American exponent of liberation theology, considers liberation from political and economic oppression "a salvation event . . . the historical realization of the Kingdom," and he redefines sin as "the abandonment of responsibility." According to much liberationist thought, human hope is in the promise of history rather than the personal return of Jesus Christ.

The mission of the church is drastically revised in this theology. Its task is no longer to convert people to the Christian religion, but to plant the seeds of liberation in the hearts and minds of the oppressed. The self-development of oppressed peoples of the Third World supplants the call to evangelize the non-Christian world.

The gospel itself is given a new meaning. No longer the good news of a substitutionary sacrifice by a God-Man, it now becomes a call to solidarity with the poor. Salvation is reinterpreted as deliverance from political oppression. Even Jesus' death on the cross is treated as a political event, a paradigm of revolutionary struggle.

Despite this flagrant distortion of biblical faith, liberation theology and the ethics it teaches cannot be lightly dismissed. It reminds us that the salvation Christ came to bring applies to the whole person—mind, soul, and body. It reclaims the theological truth that right understanding is inseparable from Christian practice. It emphasizes that faith, love, and justice belong together.

Yet liberation ethics can be faulted for politicizing the gospel. It confuses human justice with divine justification, and it tends to emphasize certain ethical emphases of the Bible without acknowledging some others. It entertains the dubious hope that the promise of the kingdom can be realized by social revolution. It fails to see that the way of the cross cannot ultimately be reconciled with the way of the sword.[141]

Excursus on the Contribution of Creation Ethics to the More Basic Kingdom Approach

1. The Importance of Creation Ethics

As we have seen, the concepts of the kingdom of God and the lordship of Christ have powerful ethical implications for the believer. Our moral and ethical decisions are to be made in light of our obedience to the King and our understanding of what his kingdom means.

But how can we relate kingdom ethics to non-Christians or to social ethics in a mixed society? In this area an emphasis known as creation ethics is helpful. This line of thinking, originating in the thought of Abraham Kuyper and elaborated by certain evangelical Anglicans such as J. I. Packer and Oliver Barclay and American Reformed scholars such as Arthur F. Holmes, provides the basic theme that lies behind the kingdom of God approach. This is true in the same way that the emphasis on God as Creator lies behind the truth that he is Savior.[142]

To some people, Christian ethics seem to be an arbitrary set of rules imposed by a remote God for no very good reason. To others, it seems that Christian morality is unrelated to reality—a set of norms imposed on the Christian for no reason than that God says so. If this is true, then the unbeliever would be right in feeling no obligation whatsoever to follow moral Christian standards.[143]

Advocates of creation ethics, however, believe that their approach shows us how and why Christian ethics should apply to *all* human beings.

2. The Difference between Creation Ethics and Natural-Law Ethics

On first glance, the creation approach would appear similar to the natural-law approach. But in contrast to natural-law ethics, which argues the correspondence of Christian and true human nature, and that this correspondence can be shown by a process of natural reason unaided by revelation, creation ethics affirms faith first. It holds that morality is to be framed by the biblical revelation and *then* justified and elucidated by the use of reason. It looks at the world as God's creation, and from that position it advocates moral imperatives that are both divine commands and also good sense.[144]

According to creation ethics, the Christian is first confronted with an overall understanding of the world and human life as expressed by the teaching of the Old Testament, Jesus, and the apostles. From this overall understanding, certain fixed points of right and wrong emerge. The Christian then has the opportunity and duty to try to show that the biblical framework is by far the best available and that, furthermore, the rights and wrongs which are a part of the biblical framework make excellent sense. Quite often we can show that the biblical way of morality is the best for humankind and that it has better rational justification than the alternatives. This broad undergirding can give confidence that the biblical way can be trusted at those points where no full justification is available, either rationally or in other ways, at least in our present state of knowledge.

3. Some General Characteristics of Creation Ethics

According to creation ethics, God's will creates and defines the good (for he alone is the measure of good). However, because he is both the Creator and the providential Ruler of his world, God commands only what corresponds both to humanity's God-given moral sense and to the good or benefit of mankind.

The God who created human beings knows exactly how human nature works best. It is his world, and he cares how it is used. Because he loves us and is a holy God, he commands only what is good. Christian ethics is given "that it may be well with us." Christians maintain that, by and large, it can be shown that adherence to Christian ethics will have this good result (Deut. 5:29).

This of course does not imply any one-to-one relationship between doing right and receiving human benefits. Particular acts of virtue do not always pay off. (For example, I may be maimed for life trying to help an old lady attacked by thugs.) The creation ethics contention is, however, that the observance of Christian ethics is in the long run, and in the community as a whole, for our own good.

In addition, of course, the Christian perspective includes the eternal dimension. "The good" is not just defined in terms of this life. What matters to the Christian and, much more important, what matters to God has other dimensions that cannot be exhausted in terms of the present, this-worldly, good of society.

Unfortunately the eternal dimension of the Christian perspective is too often used to escape the fact that Christian morality works best for this world, too. Creation ethics holds that in following the Christian way we are enabled to live as near as possible to the way in which we function best or the way we were created to live.[145]

4. A Sample Application of Creation Ethics

The basic arguments and methodology of creation ethics can perhaps best seen through a specific example—say, that of sexuality.

There are those in our culture who claim that there is no particular reason to play the game of sexual morality the Christian way. In fact, they say, it can be played any way so long as there is an agreement between those involved. For example, they assert, there is nothing sacred about monogamous or lifelong marriage. Some societies are polygamous, and other cultures, like much of the West today, follow a pattern of serial polygamy and polyandry—changing partners at intervals. Other groups pursue a more promiscuous pattern. What reasons could there be for following one pattern rather than another?

Creation ethics replies that, first of all, human nature is not infinitely plastic, and that certain actions do violence to human nature as it is. We have a definite psychological and biological makeup as well as a definite chemical makeup. So far, most people would agree. The Christian, however, goes on to say that God, because he sees the limitations of the human makeup and desires to protect us, has given us certain limits and ideals concerning sexuality.

Monogamous, lifelong marriage is a creation ideal; in other words, men and women are so made that they work best in such a relationship. Jesus himself, in commenting on the Old Testament law of divorce, appealed to this original creation ideal by referring back to what was "in the beginning" (Matt. 19). He stated clearly that God wants us to have, and therefore commands, what he created us to enjoy: lifelong partnership.

The creation ethicist, therefore, would argue that the biblical idea is the best and will prove to be the best for all human beings. This is true because the biblical view is the ideal of creation—or as near to that ideal as human sinfulness allows. (We should expect the creation ideal to be demonstrable to a substantial extent, but not necessarily capable of proof beyond doubt.)

God has been kind enough to give us certain basic rules (e.g., the Ten Commandments) which correspond to the way we are made. To behave in any other way is to court disaster in the long run. (In many instances this can be demonstrably proved by rational or scientific means; in other instances it cannot yet be conclusively proved.) Hence, following the "law of the Lord" is not only a matter of righteousness, but also a matter of wisdom (Ps. 119:97–104 and Ps. 19:7–11). In other words, God's way leads us to an understanding of how human nature and the world actually are and how life should be lived.[146]

5. Some Representative Divinely Given Structures

The creation approach to ethics is associated with the concept of the divinely given structures which are a part of God's creation. Among these structures are the following:

(1) Marriage and Sexual Fidelity. As we have already noted, marriage is part of the original creation. It is in itself a benefit, because it creates relationships which are capable of so much good, but it is also a necessity in light of human sinfulness. For who could have thought of such an effective means of curbing human selfishness. For two selfish people actually to live together in harmony for sixty years or more, sacrificing themselves in service to one another and to maddeningly self-centered children, is perhaps the most astonishing social achievement in the whole of creation.

But according to creation ethics, monogamous marriage is not merely expedient, or in a general sense a "good thing," but rather a basic part of the way human beings are made to function. Therefore, any departure from this creation ideal is a second best and an injury to the created order. The result is that marriage has to be thought of not only as one possible—or even the best—solution to the problems and the potential of sexuality. It should also be seen as a part of the ideal structure of society. To attempt to get away from this ordinance is a very sad deprivation.[147]

A related issue within the structure of marriage and sexual mores is that of fornication. Creation ethics points out that the biblical admonition against fornication reflects the basic needs of the human being as created by God. First Corinthians 6 implies this by stating that fornication is an insult and injury to the personality ("sin against his own body," where body means the person).[148]

(2) The State. The state is also considered by the creation ethicists as a part of the providential order. It may have a wide variety of forms within certain limits, but the question must always be what the best forms are, not whether we can dispense with the state altogether. First Peter 2 is even clearer about the importance of the state than Romans 13 because it was written under persecution.[149] The Old Testament likewise stressed the importance of a framework of government.

(3) Truthfulness and Honesty. Ephesians 4:25–30 provides another example of a created structure—that of truthfulness. Here we are told that everyone is to "speak the truth with his neighbor" (with non-Christian as well as Christian). Two reasons are given for this admonition. The first reason is that "we are members one of another"—part of a social community whose solidarity is undermined by lies. The second reason given is that not being truthful would "grieve the Holy Spirit of God."

Creation ethicists point out that practical experience clearly undergirds the creation ideal in this instance. A school, a family, or a wider community in which truthfulness cannot be assumed is as we all know, impoverished. At best, it is extremely inconvenient and destroys good personal relationships, as well as wasting a lot of time and effort.

It is important to note that the creation ideal of truth applies to all purposes —"good" ones as well as "bad" ones. This means that we should not easily excuse lies told for the purposes of accomplishing good. There may be cases when it might be absolutely necessary, as for instance in a "just" war, but even these "necessities" must be carefully scrutinized in light of the biblical structure of truth.

To lie in order to get Bibles into the Soviet Union, for example, may seem excusable from a traditional Christian point of view, but in the long run it may work against the very kind of mutual trust and respect which is necessary if our talk about biblical "truth" is to be credible. The duty to spread the truth does not overrule creation-based responsibilities but has to be worked out within that creation framework (see also 1 Tim. 5:8 and Matt. 15:5–6).

This raises an important point about structures. According to creation ethics, we must beware of destroying or weakening the structures of society, not only because they are in themselves positive goods for the community, but because we need to use them to be God's witnesses. If we believe communism to be wrong, for instance, we must show that we are not antisocial (lying is basically antisocial) and that we do not lie when we offer the truth of the Bible.[150]

Similarly, we are to refrain from stealing—both for social reasons and because of our relationship to God. Whether we like it or not, we are in a society, and stealing injures all social relationships. It is perhaps possible to have a society that does not respect honesty, but it would be a sadly deprived community. God has made us "members one of another" and intends for us to live in respect for that fact of creation.[141]

(4) The Sabbath. According to creation ethics, the sabbath is related to the way we are made; we need a prescribed day of rest from our daily activities. Jesus reflected this fact when he stated that "The sabbath was made for man."[152]

(5) Prohibition of Murder. Murder is forbidden in the Bible for many reasons, but one of the most important is violence tends to beget violence. Creation ethicists claim that this is a basic part of the created order: "Whoever sheds the blood of man, by man shall his blood be shed" (Gen. 9:6). Therefore, "all who take the sword will perish by the sword" (Matt. 26:52).[153]

5. The Long-Range Applicability of Christian Ethics

It is not always possible to prove convincingly the positive value of Christian morality. In the area of sex ethics, for instance, people in the West have not lived long enough with the alternatives to a Christian view to see how alarmingly inferior the modern, secular alternatives are.

The creation approach maintains that on serious examination over a period of time, the Christian approach to morality can be shown to be extraordinarily fitting to the way things really are. Far from being alien, or arbitrary, Christian ethics are exactly fitted to the creation as we find it. In this sense they correspond to what is truly natural—not necessarily to what people like to do or find it "natural" to do.

This explains why many aspects of Christian ethics are also held by other religions and philosophies. This is logical if they are a result of a right understanding of human society and can be seen to be so to a considerable extent by any wise man. Any rational reflection on man and society produces some of the same "obvious" points: that there must be a basic morality; that it must include qualities such as justice, truth, and respect for life.

According to creation ethics, the Christian can recommend these moral teachings without reference to revelation, but he can go much further on the basis of revelation. He knows that they are commanded, but he can also recommend them in terms of an understanding of the world and of man as he is and is intended to be and to live.[154]

6. The Continued Validity of Creation Ideals in Light of the Fall

Creation ethics holds that creation ideals are appropriate even in the face of human sin and selfishness—that the Fall does not negate the value of basic created structures. Some have argued that, after the Fall, God's original ideals have little significance and may have to be abandoned because of people's "hardness of heart"—as Moses did in the matter of divorce (Matt. 19:8–9). But Christ himself made it plain in that very context that God's ideal does stand firm. This means that the creation ideal is still the standard to which we should seek to adhere, even if public legislation (the law of Moses) no longer enforces it.

It is true that sin and its indirect effects complicate matters, making it much more difficult to get anywhere near the ideal. Because of sin, it is necessary to introduce into the biblically ordained structures certain functions that would otherwise have been unnecessary. For example, the state (which would have been necessary in any case) cannot concentrate exclusively on its positive tasks, but has to spend a great deal of its time in restraining and punishing evil.

But creation ethics holds that when all these and other effects of sin have been mentioned, the creation ideal still is the best for the whole of God's creation. Human beings still function best when they get as close to it as they possibly can, and Christian morals are the way to do just that. (It is of course true that the effects of the Fall are dramatically matched and overcome by the gospel and the work of the Holy Spirit.)[155]

7. How Christian Ethics Transcend Alternative Views

As mentioned above, the creation ethics approach also maintains that Christian ethics transcend non-Christian frameworks or worldviews. Some non-Christians contend that the worldview of Christian ethics is only rational within a Christian framework—just as, say, Marxist ethics are rational within a Marxist framework.

Creation ethics contends, however, that the Christian approach transcends particular worldviews. By and large, around the world, the basic set of principles which the specific Christian commands protect is recognized as in practice the best. This realization comes after other policies deduced from a non-Christian philosophy have been tried and found wanting.

For instance, the non-Christian, on the whole, realizes the importance of truth and honesty in society; even Communist societies have become quite puritan about such things as marriage and sexual ethics. The Soviet attack on the family as too "bourgeois," a characteristic of the early Marxist revolution, for instance, was soon given up, and Communists today are often more strict on sex ethics than so-called Christian societies, even if their reasons are somewhat utilitarian.

It is of course theoretically possible for a group to live by values and morals that are directly contrary to Christian ethics. And certain revolutionary groups from time to time have quite deliberately chosen a system of ethics that deplores most of what is valued by Christian ethics and society in general—a system that applauds murder, dishonesty, untruthfulness, indiscriminate sex, the dissolution of family life, and despises work and concern for others.

But Christian ethicists hold that such practices in the larger society are almost always self-destructive. A minority group in revolution against society can practice within a wider community that lives by the moral law, but life becomes unbearable if these views are put into practice as a majority. As soon as it is tried even up to a point, people are driven back to the old fixed points, as has happened to a remarkable extent in the Soviet Union. Even for the non-Christian, therefore, creation ethics can be shown to be applicable, because they are intrinsically related to the way human beings are made.

There is another very important point. Non-Christians often accept many more positive, ethical standards than their theories would justify; in other words, their morality is better than their theories. When a Christian appeals to a non-Christian—presents the Christian ethic and invites the non-Christian to admit that it is incomparably the best for all men—the Christian does not usually have to start from nothing and build up by pure reasoning. Instead, quite often there is in the other person's consciousness an awareness of moral truth, and this moral truth already corresponds in some degree to the Christian revelation. If it does not already correspond in any articulate sense, Christian ethics are often quickly acceptable to a surprising degree once they are properly understood. They are seen to be creation ethics, exactly tailor-made for man as he is.[156]

VI. What Is a Christian Approach to Ethics That Strikes a Balance between Legalism and Situation Extremes?

In a way, the entire history of Christian ethics has been an attempt to strike a satisfactory balance between the specific principles given through divine revelation, the observations of human reason, and the biblically ordained impulse of love. And most of the alternative approaches outlined above tend to err too far toward one of these emphases—toward rationalism, which holds that the best way to live can be determined by human reason alone; toward legalism, which tends to make keeping the law a condition for being in God's favor; or antinomianism, which tends to discard the restraints of the law in a celebration of Christian freedom.

Accordingly, through the centuries there has arisen a mediating approach which specifically aims at a balanced view of Christian ethics that takes divine revelation seriously without abandoning human reason, degenerating into legalism, or falling into the trap of "anything goes." This approach can be called the love-and-revealed-principles approach.

1. Christian Leaders and Movements Who Have Contributed to This Approach

Those who have taken this approach have differed among themselves in specific emphases, particularly as these differences pertain to the specific relationship of reason, the law, and love. But they all contend that we need definite biblical guidelines to help spell out in concrete ways how to express Christian love. Like T. B. Maston, they have affirmed that while the Bible is not a rule book we can consult for every imaginable problem or situation, obvious principles which have proven valid through the centuries should not be discarded simply because they are either commandments or prohibitions. All hold that we should be able to recognize their worth, apply them to our age and culture, and obey them accordingly.[157]

(1) Martin Luther. Luther basically saw the law as the "hammer of judgment" that convicts us of sin and thereby prepares us to hear the good news of God's mercy. The chief purpose of the law is to condemn us and to drive us to despair. Because Christians are still sinners, they constantly need to be directed by the law back to Christ.

A continual subject of debate in scholarly circles is whether Luther held to a third function of the law—that of providing a specific pattern for the moral Christian life. Helmut Thielicke and Paul Althaus contend that the idea of the law as pattern and guide for the Christian life is definitely present in Luther's theology. After all, Luther himself declared, "The law is to be retained by the believers so that they might have a pattern for doing good works."[158]

Luther tried to make a place for keeping the commandments of God. However, this emphasis was definitely subordinated to the demands of love, which sometimes contradict the letter of the commandment.[159]

(2) John Calvin. Luther's fellow reformer John Calvin, on the other hand, believed that the principal use of the law is to serve as a guide for conduct. (The other two uses are to bring us to humility and repentance and to restrain our rapacity.) Calvin argued that the Decalogue is designed to form us and prepare us for good works.[160]

For Calvin, the Christian life is not freedom *from* the law but freedom *for* the law; Christian liberty does not annul the demands of the law but enables us to obey them. Therefore, one who has been touched by the grace of God does not flee from the law, but lovingly embraces it. Calvin saw the Christian as free from the rigid requirements and consequent burden of the law, but not from its abiding intention. He reminded his readers that our Lord did not come to abolish the law but to fulfill it (Matt. 5:17). (Because of this emphasis, those in the Calvinist tradition have tended to drift toward legalism, whereas those in the Lutheran tradition have sometimes fallen toward antinomianism.)[161]

(3) The "Left Wing" of the Reformation (Baptists). The third strand of the Reformation tradition—sometimes called the "left wing" of the Reformation or given the generic term "baptists," included such traditions as the Anabaptists, the Swiss Brethren, and the Mennonites. This tradition stressed that the person of Christ and his teachings became a "new law" which is in discontinuity with the old law. There was also an emphasis on soul competency, discipleship, and community.

Historically, the baptist tradition has insisted that the church should build its theology and ethics from the New Testament. They reject the procedure which develops its ethic from the Old Testament, prunes off the ritualistic and cultic elements, and then adds the New Testament materials. To the contrary, Christian ethics is to start with the New Testament, and anything used in the church from the Old Testament must first be assessed in the light of the New Testament.[162]

Through the centuries, a legalism based on this "new law" has been a constantly recurring temptation among the heirs of this branch of the Reformation. However, this was countered by their staunch adherence to the gospel as the forgiveness of sins and to "grace alone" as belonging to the heart of the Christian message.[163]

Historically, baptists have said that the New Testament is their rule of faith and practice. This was never meant to disqualify the Old Testament or to be some kind of a new version of Marcion (a heretic of the second Christian century who divorced the New Testament from the Old). According to Bernard Ramm, this emphasis on the New Testament as the rule of faith and practice was an attempt to counter the parts of Roman Catholic theology substantiated by tradition and questionable interpretations of the Old Testament. It also sought to correct the Protestant theologians who were using the Old Testament in a way that was not in agreement with New Testament teachings.

(4) Karl Barth. Much of Karl Barth's work in ethics was aimed at ending the division of ethics and theology which had been part of the legacy of Kant. Barth returned ethics to the territory of theology by including ethics in his fundamental doctrine of God, rather than under the doctrine of sanctification, as had been customary throughout most of Christian history.[164]

In contrast to classical Reformed Protestantism (the Calvinist and Lutheran traditions), Barth affirmed basically two uses for the law: to prepare the way for the gospel and to guide our response to the gospel. Barth maintained that the gospel has priority over the law—that we first hear the gospel and then are able to understand the law. This emphasis that the gospel is *before* the law is in contrast to Calvin's emphasis on the law *with* the gospel and Luther's on the law *before* the gospel. Barth reminds us that even the Decalogue begins with a historical prologue, the announcement of inconceivable grace. The evangelical indicative—the priority of the gospel—is prior to the moral imperative.

In Barth's theology, when the commandments of God are viewed in the light of the gospel, they become permissions rather than simply prohibitions. "You shall not" becomes "You need not." The law is a permission because it both orders human beings to live in response to the gospel and gives them the freedom to do it. In commanding, God provides the power to obey. The law is to be seen as an opportunity for service, and therefore it becomes a privilege. We are invited, not ordered, to care for our neighbor in love.[165] Our motivation for obedience to the law is gratitude for the love of God revealed in the gospel and clarified by the law.

Just as the law of God is reinterpreted as the law of freedom in Barth's theology, so sin is also given a new meaning. No longer the transgression of an external moral code, as in legalistic religion, sin is now viewed as the breaking of a personal relationship. It is the refusal to let the Spirit have his way in our lives.[166]

Barth held that the divine commandment always directs us to Christ, for he is the supreme and definitive manifestation of God's grace. We are called to pattern our lives after his example. This does not mean that we must copy the historical details of his lifestyle, but it does mean that we are to look to Christ's life and death in determining our response to ethical issues in the present.[167]

(5) Carl F. H. Henry. Carl Henry takes a more literalistic stand regarding the commandments of God revealed in the Bible; he holds that they are absolutely binding on all people. He specifically addresses the relativistic claims of situation ethics by asserting that love is not a norm that stands in juxtaposition or tension with God's commandments, but rather is the way we apply the commandments to the situation in which we live.[168]

Henry is adamant that we must uphold moral standards as well as the gospel of love. He insists that the doctrine of redemption does not relax the believer's obligation to the divine commandments, nor should it weaken his motivation to observe them: "Christian ethics is not left to chart its course of divinely approved conduct by self-reflection alone, or by an immediate spiritual impression traced to 'encounter' (with Christ)." It is "through an objective Divine outline alone that [one] can discriminate between right and wrong directions of love in action. The biblically revealed ethic of principles, commandments, examples, and applications provides such a content." Henry is here referring primarily to the Sermon on the Mount, but he would also readily include the Decalogue.[169]

(6) Other Representatives. Donald H. Bloesch, a professor at the University of Dubuque, is another representative of the love-and-revealed-principles approach. A notable example of his work in ethics from this perspective is found in his *Freedom for Obedience.* Bernard Ramm of the American Baptist Seminary of the West is also a significant writer in this tradition.[170]

Excursus on Dispensational Ethics

1. Definition and Origin

Presenting a radically different understanding of law and gospel is dispensational fundamentalism, a strand of theology that has had a considerable impact on the American scene. This view portrays the Christian life as the separated life—separated from the sin of the world unto godliness and holiness. It claims that the "man of faith" is no longer under the Jewish law, which belongs to an older dispensation, but is now under the gospel. It also holds that the people of God are called out of the apostate church as well as the world enters the last days.[171]

According to C. C. Ryrie, unsystematic dispensational ideas can be found from the time of the church fathers on, but dispensationalism as a system did not begin to develop until the early part of the eighteenth century, when it appeared in the writings of Pierre Poiret, John Edwards, and Isaac Watts. Though these men set forth dispensational schemes, it was not until the nineteenth century that the concept was fully systematized.[172] The dispensational system in its basic form arose in England among the Plymouth Brethren, and was taught with widening influence by John Nelson Darby (1800–1882) and also by William Kelley (1821–1906). In America it received the support of James M. Gray, Arno C. Gaebelein, L. S. Chafer, and many others.[173]

2. Central Idea of Dispensationalism

The classic or original systematized dispensationalism is represented by Cyrus Ingerson Scofield (1843–1921), founder of Dallas Theological Seminary. Through titles and marginal notes in the *Scofield Reference Bible* (1917), which popularized the views of Darby, Scofield and his associated editors conveyed their theology to millions. The "pattern for the ages" that they traced in the Bible embodied a complex premillennial eschatology "simplified" into a scheme of sevens (seven dispensations, seven judgments, seven—plus one—covenants).[174]

Scofield depicts Jesus as forthrightly political, proposing to set up the kingdom of heaven (to be distinguished from the kingdom of God) as an earthly institution. But because the Jews rejected Jesus' offer, he made a pivotal (if "temporary") reversal of field, offering instead a salvation for individuals that would be only loosely related to the original "kingdom of heaven" once proposed. This arrangement was to last until the end of the age, when Christ's Second Advent would finally inaugurate the establishment of the postponed kingdom on earth.

The Sermon on the Mount (and with it Jesus' central teaching on nonviolence) was to be law for *the coming* kingdom, and its requirements apply directly only to that coming time, not to the present age. This means that peace as Scripture teaches it may now consist in peace between individuals and God or in an "inner peace," but the present age will be characterized by wars and rumors of wars. While wars are the mark of an unconverted age, at least no hint in Scofield warns the reader against taking part in them, although of course it remains true that "the poor in spirit, rather than the proud, are blessed."[175]

3. The Dispensationalist View of Ethics

From the dispensational perspective, the law and the gospel are separated, for they signify two contrasting dispensations. The gospel is not found in the Old Testament, nor does the church have its beginning in Israelite history. Law and grace are mutually exclusive. To Scofield, "It is . . . of the most vital moment to observe that Scripture never, in any dispensation, mingles these two principles. Law always has a place and work distinct and wholly diverse from that of grace."[176] Similarly, Hal Lindsey believes that "to mix these principles robs the law of its bona fide terror and grace of its creative freeness."[177] When one is under grace, one is no longer under the Mosaic law. The gospel signifies freedom from the law, though sometimes in this kind of theology the gospel is unwittingly transposed into a new law.[178]

A distinction is also made between the church age and the kingdom age, which is seen as being entirely in the future. The first or church age represents the present dispensation between the resurrection of Christ and his second coming. The second or kingdom age will begin when Christ ushers in his millennial reign at his second coming. In this scenario, the epistles of Paul pertain primarily to the church age and the Gospels primarily to the age of the kingdom. The teachings of Jesus form part of the law of the old dispensation, but they are also to be applied in the millennial kingdom. They are beneficial to the Christian in this present age but are not of primary significance.[179]

The original—what some call extreme—form of dispensationalism rigidly distinguishes the dispensation of law (Sinai to Calvary) from the dispensation of grace (Calvary to the second advent) both chronologically and in principle and spirit. The principles of the two dispensations are held to be diametrically opposed, and the subsequent dispensation of a thousand-year kingdom-rule is assertedly predicated on law. Christ's teachings are assumed to be divided in their application, some applying to the legal kingdom age and some to the present church age of grace. For example, the Sermon on the Mount is held to be legal in character; the King "sets forth the nature of the proposed Kingdom and the laws by which He will govern the earth when He re-establishes and occupies the throne of David."[180] "As a rule of life, it is addressed to the Jew before the cross and to the Jew in the coming Kingdom, and is therefore not now in effect . . . The Sermon . . . both by its setting in the context and by its doctrinal character . . . belongs for its primary application to the future kingdom age."[181]

The Sermon on the Mount is not given as the standard of Christian experience and work. It will be fulfilled literally, but not until the age in which we live has come to its close and the Lord Jesus shall be dealing with his people Israel. The Christian is held to be free from the Sermon as such "because the day of . . . application has not yet come to the earth."[182] In its primary and literal significance, the Sermon on the Mount is directed to the millennial kingdom as its governing code of laws, and not to Christian conduct in this life.[183]

4. Strengths of Dispensationalism

There is no one theology that has universal authority among all who identify themselves as dispensationalists. Whereas some would see the mission of the church exclusively in terms of heralding the gospel of free grace to a lost and dying world, others would make an attempt to unite evangelism with discipleship, the proclamation of the New Testament church with the teachings of Jesus.[184]

The Plymouth Brethren, the original propagators of dispensationalism, emphasized the free grace of God as the only source of salvation, acknowledged the radically new character of the gospel, and saw the Christian life as one of Christian liberty. They also have New Testament warrant for their contention that when a church becomes apostate it is then the obligation of Bible-believing Christians to protest. While some mainline denominations have reduced the gospel to a set of ethical principles, dispensationalists have, for the most part, remained true to the New Testament and Reformation teaching that the gospel is basically the proclamation of God's reconciling action in Jesus Christ to save sinners from sin, death, and hell.[185]

C. C. Ryrie, a prominent leader in more moderate dispensational circles, maintains that dispensationalists show strength in teaching that salvation is always through God's grace. The basis of salvation in every dispensation is the death of Christ; the requirement for salvation in every age is faith; the object of faith is the true God; but the content of faith changes in the various dispensations.[186]

5. Weaknesses of Dispensationalism

Dispensationalists have been accused of both a new legalism and antinomianism. By championing freedom from the Mosaic law, they seem to leave the Christian without any guidelines except love. On the other hand, by emphasizing the binding character of the Pauline commands (such as women keeping silent in the churches), they sometimes lapse into a legalistic orientation.[187]

Some critics of dispensationalism have detected similarities to Marcionism. The radical dispensationalists, like the Marcionites, elevate the Pauline epistles and call into question the Christian significance of the Old Testament. They also tend to deemphasize the historical Jesus.[188]

Donald G. Bloesch takes issue with dispensationalists in their elevating to the level of dogma such marginal doctrines as the millennium, the pretribulation rapture of the saints, and the great tribulation, as well as such questionable doctrines as the restoration of glory to Israel as a political entity. At times, Bloesch points out, these themes become the primary content of their sermons on Christ and his kingdom. Bloesch also takes exception to dispensationalist tendency to separate the two Testaments, thereby losing sight of the Reformation's insight into the one covenant of grace with two manifestations. In addition, he points out that churches who separate themselves too readily from the mainstream of Christianity lose the opportunity to be instruments of renewal to the whole church.[189]

According to James McClendon, the charted pageant of kingdoms, judgments, and apocalyptic splendors is pushed away to history's rim, leaving the present an age in which "wars and rumors of wars" persist unchecked. Pessimism about the present is coupled with hope for a "first resurrection" (other millenarians have called this "the rapture") that will translate dead and living saints out of earth's penultimate terrors.[190]

2. The Love-and-Revealed-Principles Approach to Finding the Will of God

(1) The Basis of Christian Morality. Despite the differences of their approach, the various exponents of the love-and-revealed-principles approach to ethics agree on the broader points of how God's will is to be found and followed. More specifically, all would affirm the fact that Christian morality is rooted in the righteous will of God and the redeeming work of Christ.

Certainly, this grounding includes a powerful message of love. We are to love our neighbor radically for his or her own sake, with no prudent regard for self; only such a radical love can break the vicious circle of greed and selfishness. However, we need definite biblical guidelines and principles to spell out in concrete ways how to express Christian love, remembering that the one absolute norm is Jesus Christ, who is both promise of hope and empowerment and command for moral action.

The love-and-revealed-principles approach advocates obedience rather than rational calculation. Thielicke describes its salient thrust: "We are forbidden to ask what the result will be when I keep this or that commandment, e.g., the command to do what is right even though the long-range possibilities of service seem thereby to be reduced if not shattered. We simply have to do what is right in the situation which is before us."[191]

(2) The Biblical Guidelines. The love-and-revealed-principles approach finds in the Bible, especially in the New Testament, guidelines for the kinds of moral action that are appropriate for a Christian.

The Bible particularizes moral principles in a preliminary way in the Ten Commandments. These fundamental commandments reflect the moral character of God. The Psalms and the prophets gave more moral principles. In addition, the prophets are helpful examples of the application of God's principles to specific moral problems of a particular time. We can get general guidance in a book like Amos, for example.

The Sermon on the Mount is the New Testament statement of the ideals of God's will, which with God's help we can seek to approximate.[192] If properly understood, the Sermon on the Mount also shows that additional dimensions must be added to the basic "dos and don'ts" of moral behavior. Keeping the "letter" of the law is not enough, nor is "external" conformity to law sufficient. The inward motivation must be as right as the external deed. To have an inward motivation that conflicts with the act done is hypocrisy. Right acts must grow out of the proper motivation, and wrong inward feelings can be sin as much as overt transgressions. In modern terms, the Sermon on the Mount could be said to be an exposition of morality as the harmony of life and action. The person acceptable to God is the person whose motivation is proper and whose external actions are right. How we think, how we feel, and how we evaluate our thinking and feelings internally are as important to ethics as is conforming to proper ethical norms.[193]

(3) A Christological Emphasis. The love-and-revealed-principles approach holds that it is important to see the progressive nature of revelation from the Old Testament to the New Testament with its christological center. It must be remembered that the New Testament is the ethical center of gravity in the Bible and therefore that whatever is said in the Old Testament must be evaluated from the perspective of the New Testament.[194] (On the other hand, the New Testament must be seen in light of its historical context—the Old Testament. Principles are to be sought in the midst of a historical situation.)

More specifically, the love-and-revealed-principles approach utilizes a christological interpretation of Scripture in determining biblical norms. Such a position includes within itself the priority of the New Testament over the Old but attempts to make those principles more systematic and usable.

Christian ethics has always affirmed that in Jesus Christ, whose teaching was sanctioned by the one perfect, sinless life, we have the supreme ethical teacher of the human race. Therefore the New Testament makes constant appeal to the moral perfection of Jesus as the example for Christians (1 Pet. 2:21, 1 John 3:16, Heb. 12:3, Phil. 2:5, Rom. 8:29, 1 Cor. 15:49, 2 Cor. 3:18, 2 Cor. 8:9, Acts 20:35, and Col. 3:10). Notably, however, the primary emphasis of the love-and-revealed-principles approach is not on the fact that Jesus lived the perfect life, but on the fact that Christ reflected the right kind of values, the right nature of the good, the right attitudes toward all classes of people, and preeminently the way of love in all ethical confrontations.

By using the christological criterion, ethical statements of the Old Testament as well as incidents with proposed ethical content are not accepted at face value. If they contradict the ethics suggested by the whole life of the Son of God, they are considered not binding on Christians. That part of the Old Testament which can be binding to Christians must pass the christological test.

The first advantage of this position is that it represents a corrective for many of the historical abuses of Scripture. A christological ethic will be more humane, more tolerant, and more considerate of persons and situations than legalistic systems.

An important point to consider in terms of the christological basis for ethics is that such an ethic must be built from the Christ of the total witness of the New Testament. Jesus should not be cut down to our likings, presuppositions, and sentimentalities. Many groups have failed at this point in the past, for the temptation is always to remake God in our image. However, the Jesus Christ of a christological ethic should be no more a neo-orthodox Jesus than a liberal or a fundamentalist Jesus. He can only be the Jesus of the whole of the New Testament.[195]

(4) The Uses of Evangelical Casuistry. Even the most literal interpreter of the Bible will admit that Scripture does not give particular advice on how Christians should react in certain specific circumstances of their lives. Certain issues such as AIDS, nuclear war, global warming, wiretapping—or even such mundane questions as whether to keep extra change returned by a vending machine—were simply not part of the experience of biblical writers and were not addressed specifically.

Those who hold to the love-and-revealed-principles approach affirm, however, that the proper Christian response to these particular situations can be derived from both specific biblical commands and its general principles. The process of applying these general principles and commands to general situations is known as casuistry.

Donald Bloesch describes a particular form of casuistry, which he terms "evangelical casuistry." Whereas the word *casuistry* can be defined as the attempt to apply general ethical norms to specific situations, evangelical casuistry is more specifically the attempt to discern God's will for a specific situation. In this case, we do not begin with abstract norms, but with God's self-revelation in Jesus Christ, which exemplifies and embodies the norms and principles of both the Old and New Testaments.

Evangelical casuistry focuses on directives given by the Spirit of God to the church that enable us to act both faithfully and intelligently in our specific situations. Thus the commandments of God are applied to the way we live in the world of our time.[196]

Evangelical casuistry presupposes that the Bible not only gives us specifics but it teaches us how to think ethically. It teaches us how to discern the will of God in areas where specifics are not given. When used in this way, the Bible can become a living guide for all generations and all cultures.

Narcotics, for example, are not mentioned in Scripture. However, what Scripture says of strong drink and about the body as the temple of the Holy Spirit will give us some guidance on this subject on a personal level. So will the strong biblical teachings against idolatry, exploitation of the poor, honesty, and other teachings on a societal level.[197]

The principle of evangelical casuistry also separates specific actions in the Bible from overarching commandments and principles. Nonresistance to evil, for example, is not a universal principle that holds true for all situations. It can be shown to have its origin in a divine commandment given in the context of the preaching of Jesus to his disciples concerning the new life in the kingdom of God (Matt. 5:38–42). That it is not a general principle, however, is made clear by the fact that Jesus took up a whip and drove the money changers out of the temple (John 2:15). Evangelical casuistry shows that nonresistance to evil is a derived ethical ideal that pertains to some, but not all situations.[198]

Evangelical casuistry also assumes that when the Bible is used properly, it allows for creative compromises which lead toward the moral ideal rather than away from it. Paul's admonition to women to keep silent in the churches is that kind of creative compromise. This teaching signified a temporary solution to a problem that was getting out of hand, that is, worship services constantly being interrupted by women glossolalists (1 Cor. 14).

In a more modern setting, creative compromise based on evangelical casuistry can be seen in the example of treating heroin addicts with methadone. Methadone is a synthetic narcotic drug not nearly as injurious as heroin. Those unable to break completely with drugs are given one that enables them to make some progress toward a substance-free existence. Similarly, Roman Catholic leader Theodore Hesburgh's advocacy of laws that would severely restrict abortions but allow for some exceptions also reveals an effort toward a creative compromise that takes into consideration the realities of the cultural situation.

This kind of creative compromise can be developed only when it is based on the divine commandment. The divine commandment contains two aspects: the ideal or goal toward which the Spirit of God would direct us and the concrete steps toward this goal. Just as God's permissive will leads to his ultimate or perfect will, so a creative compromise will, it is hoped, lead toward the fulfillment of the great commandment of love toward God and neighbor.

The creative compromise in conflict situations is not an accommodation to evil but an acceptance of a solution that falls short of the ideal of love. This solution nonetheless has God's sanction and is therefore covered by justifying grace. In conflict situations, Christians are never called to compromise their faith. However, they may be called upon to temporarily fall back from the ideal in order to be obedient to the interpretation of God's will in that particular situation. While obedience to the divine commandment is always good and never evil, in a conflict situation it may involve us in acts that fall short of the goal toward which God beckons us.[199]

3. The Love-and-Revealed-Principles Approach to Finding Empowerment to Do God's Will

As any practicing Christian is aware, morals and ethics involve more than just determining what is right and wrong. Biblical ethics involve *doing* what is right, not just *knowing* what is right. Even the apostle Paul confessed ruefully that, because of sin, "I do not do what I want, but I do the very thing I hate. . . . I can will what is right, but I cannot do it" (Rom. 7:15, 18–19). And this is the experience of all Christians throughout much of our lives. A key moral and ethical issue, then, is how Christians can be empowered to follow Christian morals and ethics.

(1) Vital Union with Christ. While in one sense the climax of biblical ethics is reached in the life and teachings of Jesus, in another sense the biblical ethic attains its most significant development in the post-Resurrection period. This is particularly true of the emphasis that daily Christian living is a natural outgrowth of a vital, life-changing union with the resurrected Christ.

This perspective is particularly prominent in Paul's Epistles and in 1 John. The movement from within the Christian experience outward is such a natural expression of the vital relationship with the resurrected Christ that the outer expression, in turn, becomes a proof of the inner relationship.[200]

The apostle Paul teaches that a Christian has no ethical power without a vital union with Christ by the Holy Spirit. There is no sinless perfection for the Christian. But there is the possibility of progressive spiritual growth.

(2) Prayer. In addition to the enabling power of union with Christ, Christian ethics is impossible without prayer. Without divine help, we cannot begin to practice agape love. Prayer also helps keep each of us alert to our unique destiny as a child of God. It quickens the relation between our moral nature and God. Prayer is the very lifeblood of Christian morality.[201]

(3) Bible Study and Community in Church Fellowship. As detailed in earlier chapters, thinkers such as George Lindbeck, Stanley Hauerwas, and William Willimon (professor at Duke Divinity School) have been at the forefront of a movement emphasizing the importance of the church community and of "Christian formation" in empowering the individual Christian.

Lindbeck suggests that a religion can be viewed as a kind of cultural and linguistic framework or medium that shapes the entirety of one's life and thought—including ethical norms. Becoming a Christian, therefore, involves more than just an initial decision; it also involves learning the story of Israel and of Jesus and the "language" of Christianity well enough to interpret and experience oneself and one's world in its terms. The proclamation of the gospel, as a Christian would put it, is thus first of all the telling of the story. Furthermore, this proclamation gains power and meaning insofar as it is embodied in the totality of church life and action.[202]

Hauerwas, following Lindbeck's lead, contends that the vision that shapes the moral life of Christians is not primarily the timeless vision of beauty or goodness, but a narrative vision. It is based on the Christian story in which present-day Christians must participate if they are to develop character conformable to Christian faith.

Both Lindbeck and Hauerwas stress that being Christian is much like learning a language. Learning a language means learning certain words, grammar, and syntax that enable us to say certain things and not say others. The enculturation that this language provides gives us a new perspective on life and forms us into a particular person. The church encompasses our life in a similar way. In fact, the first task of the church is formation rather than education—not just "bringing out," but "bringing to." The task of Christian educators, therefore, is not just to develop an individual's potential, but to induct Christians into the faith community, to give them the skills, insights, words, stories, and rituals they need to live this faith in a world that neither knows nor follows the One who is truth.

All of this means that the church plays a crucial role in empowering Christians for the ethical life. Both Willimon's *The Service of God* and Hauerwas's

The Peaceable Kingdom are preoccupied with the church. They state strongly that the quality of life required of Christians is too difficult and peculiar to survive without the church.

According to this viewpoint, individual ethical decisions are indeed important, but decisions that are not reinforced and reformed by the community tend to be short-lived. A Christianity without Christian formation is no match for the powerful social forces at work within our society. Formation implies the existence of an intentional, visible community made up of people who are willing to pay the price of community.[203]

4. Theological Encouragements to Human Morality

(1) The Promise of Ultimate Success in the Life Beyond. Although the primary motive for the Christian's ethical acts is gratitude to Christ, the Christian is also encouraged by God's promise of the ultimate success of his kingdom and the promise of spiritual reward. In fact, C. S. Lewis states that one aspect of our reward will be in the form of a greater capacity to receive the gifts of God.

The promise of the second coming of Christ and the hope for the new heaven and the new earth are incentives to urgency in our practice of Christian morality.[204] Evangelical theology calls for a robust faith—a faith that seeks for justice in the spirit of love. At the same time, it is acutely conscious that the only justice realizable in this world is a proximate one. It acknowledges that this world is a "vale of tears," that the Christian life is a life under the Cross.

Evangelical theology is a theology of the Cross, but it makes a place for a theology of glory as well. The glory that is to come can be anticipated now in moments of faith and surrender to God. Paul declares that God "has put his seal upon us and given us his Spirit in our hearts as a guarantee" (2 Cor. 1:22; cf. Eph. 1:13, 14).

On the basis of the biblical promises, Christians have the confidence that the perfect fellowship of love will be realized beyond this world. It will come in God's own time and in his own way. Yet even now we can set up signs and parables of the coming of the kingdom through moral actions in daily life. Because the biblical promises include the millennial hope, we can look forward to the realization of some of these promises in earthly history. Yet even these are only tokens of the glory to come—the new heaven and the new earth that signify both the crown of creation and the apex of redemption.[205]

(2) The Final Judgment. Some theologians tend to downplay the motivation of fear as unworthy of the Christian. But the clear biblical message is that the God we worship is not only our heavenly Father but also our Lord and King. He is not only love and mercy but also majesty and holiness. He not only creates light but also brings about darkness (Isa. 45:7). He not only saves from judgment but also executes judgment. He not only raises up, but also casts down and destroys. Jesus cautioned his hearers to be watchful and vigilant lest they be found wanting when the Lord appears on the day of reckoning (Matt. 25:1–13).[206]

In fact, the New Testament is very strong in its emphasis on the relevance of final judgment to morality. The New Testament has no doubt of the reality of such a judgment. It appears in many parables, including that of the sheep and goats, where the criterion of judgment is explicitly ethical. It appears in straightforward statements such as the apostle Paul's declaration, "For we must all appear before the judgment seat of Christ, so that each one may receive good or evil, according to what he has done in the body" (2 Cor. 5:10), and our Lord's warning that "The Son of man . . . will repay every man for what he has done" (Matt. 16:27). In Revelation it appears in the form of vivid pictures—the great white throne, city gates closed to evildoers, and a lake burning with fire and brimstone.

Some set all this aside as part of outmoded Jewish apocalyptic writing. But even in those parts of Jesus' teaching where the apocalyptic language is not evident, there is much emphasis on final rewards and punishments. The notion of a final judgment is far too explicit and widespread throughout the whole New Testament to be explained away as a concession to ancient forms of thought or language. It is a fundamental part of the apostolic *kerygma* or preaching.[207]

There are certain considerations which may help us to appreciate the teaching of a final judgment as an incentive to good conduct. Such a doctrine brings home to us the gravity of moral choices. It assures us that our choices of right or wrong are no mere short-term policies without any permanent significance; they are important factors in the ultimate destiny of ourselves and of the universe.

Our Lord had no scruples about encouraging his disciples in ways of good by the assurance that their rewards would be great in heaven. There is a practical realism in this teaching which takes us as we are—creatures who are motivated by the anticipation of rewards and the fear of consequences.

The teaching about the Last Judgment gives final assurance of the moral nature of the universe. The ultimate demands of God's moral order renews our gratitude to Christ for his vicarious death, which frees us from guilt and preserves the moral order.[208]

The teaching about the Last Judgment in the New Testament also bears witness to the fundamental righteousness that is at the heart of the universe. However honestly human beings have held that goodness is to be sought for goodness' sake, they have never been content to believe that the good will always suffer and that the wicked will prosper permanently. The Bible teaches that when the whole story of the universe is viewed from the angle of eternity, moral evil and ultimate destruction are inseparably bound together. We have glimpses of this both in the biblical apocalypses and in the hard facts of history. Moral goodness and humanity's ultimate welfare are also inseparably linked. In the biblical conception of judgment, the vindication of goodness is always included.[209]

VII. Conclusion

We began this chapter with a citation of the difficulties, complexities, and urgency of the question of human morality. With natural human resources, Christian morality is difficult—even impossible. But the triune God has come to humanity in Christ and the Holy Spirit to restore our destiny and give us a vision of the way of life for which we are made.

This way of life is not a way of drudgery. It does not call for the music of life to be stopped, but rather for celebration of the good life of joy and fulfillment. In the words of Karl Olson, "Come to the Christian party." The Christian way begins with a personal commitment to Christ as sin-bearer, risen Lord, Master, and Teacher. Then it continues in the active church relationship and in a life of spiritual discipline and joy.

12

The Question of the Arts, Culture, and Worship

I. What Is the Importance of Concern with the Arts, Culture, and Worship?

Since World War II, the social sciences have emphasized that a given group of people orient themselves in the world by a complex of symbols—including artifacts, words, events, and rites. The totality of this orientation is a group's culture.

"The arts" constitute an important facet of a given culture. By "the arts," I am referring to that part of life which expresses itself in the creative, the imaginative, and the dramatic. This, of course, includes the traditional "fine arts," such as music, painting, literature, sculpture, and architecture. It obviously includes the "lively arts," such as drama and ballet. And in our day it definitely includes the "popular arts," such as movies, television, and radio. In fact, even TV commercials have become art forms of a sort. And the very popular music videos make use of a variety of art forms.

Worship, as the reverent love and allegiance accorded to God, involves ceremonies and the utilization of art forms. Although Christian groups differ in their practices, such art forms as music, painting, speech (such as sermons), sculpture, architecture, drama, religious dance, television, and radio are utilized in worship.

The biblical worldview, as we have noted in chapter 1, does not allow the Christian to withdraw from the world. This means that Christians should be concerned with an appropriate biblical relationship to the arts, culture, and worship.

1. The Importance of the Arts in Human Life

Art is as persistent in history as humankind itself. The earliest artifacts included stone axes, with which primitive man is supposed to have clobbered his neighbor, but also included delicate and beautiful cave paintings.

We find art among the civilized and uncivilized. It belongs to Pablo Picasso and Piet Mondrian and also to the Indians in the great rain forest. It belongs to Béla Bartók and Arthur Honegger and to the pygmies in central Africa. At this moment, around the world, there are thousands of people sitting before blocks of wood or stone, at musical instruments, at a writing desk—or even a computer—going through the mysterious experience of "creation."[1] (I remember a day I spent in the Dahlem Museum in West Berlin. In the course of that day, I viewed works of art from Africa, the Far East, the South Seas, and South America. I remember being almost overwhelmed by the sometimes grotesque, but still strikingly beautiful, arts and artifacts from these countries.)

Art belongs to both the old and the young. Wolfgang Amadeus Mozart began composing at five, and Raphael was a busy and successful painter at seventeen; yet Giuseppe Verdi composed *Falstaff* and *Othello* not long before he died at almost eighty. Art is a product of every creed and philosophy, of the bohemian Amedeo Modigliani, the atheist A. E. Houseman, and the religious Michelangelo and Rembrandt van Rijn. Art is coincident with humanity and universal in origin and significance.[2]

In contemporary life, the arts are becoming even more powerful. Essayist Susan Sontag goes so far as to claim that contemporary art forms are modifying our sensibility or consciousness. She maintains that the new cinema, painting, music, drama, and literature are so powerful that they give rise to something like an exaltation, commitment, and captivation; artists play a decisive role in our lives for good or evil.[3] This is also the view of media commentator Marshall McLuhan, who has called our era the "image age."[4]

As we move further into a technological age, we feel in a new way the necessity of art in our lives. Governing powers become more remote as they proliferate, until we are content to be ruled by people we scarcely know and can hardly influence. The oncoming revolution involving electronics and computers, while offering further material wealth, threatens increasing depersonalization.[5]

But through the arts, we can still experience values other than those imposed upon us.[6] In the arts we can still find a kind of excellence not predicated on success in a materialistic society. It should be noted, however, that because of economic and other considerations, a considerable amount of today's art is directed, at least partially, toward serving commercial purposes. Many creators of these art forms such as movies, television programs, graphic arts, and studio music are quite skilled and dedicated artists, but their "patrons" are commercial interests.

2. Reasons Conservative Christians Are Suspicious of the Arts

Historically, conservative religious people, especially Protestants, have been suspicious of the arts—especially the visual arts and drama. Since the days of the Exodus, when the Israelites worshiped the golden calf, people in the biblical tradition have been aware of the tendency of men to worship what their hands have made.

The Protestant reformation was particularly strong in renouncing the arts, partially because of the way the arts had been used in the medieval church. In the middle ages, the visual arts had been widely used in churches, but they were used in many cases to present legends, romances, fables, astrology, and extrabiblical material about Mary. The reformer John Calvin, therefore, was vehement in denouncing religious imagery as absurd fiction.

Other religious groups over the years continued the suspicion toward the arts. The Puritans were afraid of most art forms. Church edifices were oftentimes as austere as barns. Psalms were sung without instrumental music. The Puritans did not reject art because it was lacking in power. Rather they were so conscious of its awe-inspiring character that they feared its power. They rejected the visual image and developed the verbal image to its fullest possibilities.

Charles Finney, prominent evangelist of another generation and the first president of Oberlin College, said that all dramatists and actors are "triflers and blasphemers of God." And Karl Barth reiterated Calvin's emphasis when he pointed out the danger of idolatry inherent in any use of images.

There is some justification for these misgivings about the arts. Is it not true that many artists participate in and dramatize the human rebellion against God? The world of creative imagination, like all of us, is deeply involved in the general corruption of humankind.

William Muehl of Yale contends that artistic skills can become the media of self-destruction and the corruption of others. In fact, artistic genius may have even greater possibilities for demonic influence than other types of genius.

Literary and dramatic artists, for example, have complete control over both the internal development of their characters and the context of that development. In the writing of history, objective data keeps statements under some kind of control: It can be shown that Louis XVI was not a genius at statecraft and that Marilyn Monroe was not a withered hag. But in many art forms, the artist is a god; he or she is master of both character and continuity. The artist can make villains exciting and good people dull. (Look what artists have done to ministers!) He or she can show scoundrels full of compassion and make faithful husbands objects of ridicule.

The artist can mix the component elements of life in unrealistic and even irresponsible ways. It is a sign of our times, however, that a person is called an "antiquarian" if she or he even suggests that the world of creative imagination is also deeply involved in the fall of humanity.[7]

The most dangerous form of sin is to claim that reality is wholly defined by one's own vision and totally subject to one's own manipulation. Because an artist has peculiar abilities, he also is most vulnerable to that sin.

3. A Suggested Approach to the Arts, Culture, and Worship for Christians

The problems mentioned about the power and danger of the arts must not keep Christians away from the arts. A force as powerful as the arts must not be ignored by biblically responsible people. I would like to suggest that we approach the arts by asking and seeking to answer five questions:

- What does the Bible have to say about the arts, culture, and worship?
- What are the implications of the biblical patterns of thinking for the significance and place of art forms?

- What are the contributions the arts can make to Christianity and to Christian people (why Christianity needs the arts)?
- What are the possible contributions the Christian perspective can make to the arts (why the arts need Christianity)?
- What are the limitations of the arts from the Christian perspective?

II. What Does the Bible Have to Say about the Arts, Worship, and Culture?

1. The Significance for Art and Culture of the Biblical View of Nature

Most art forms are related to "this empirical world," even if they point to a reality beyond this world. It is important, therefore, that a worldview conducive to art should not depreciate this world in favor of a view which sees this world as semi-illusory or a realm to be escaped through mystic contemplation or detachment. An appropriate view of nature for art should not see the physical or the material as inherently evil.

(1) The Biblical World-Outlook versus the Greco-Oriental Outlook. As we have seen in earlier chapters, the "higher" spiritual approaches of humankind fall into two main groups—the biblical or Hebraic and the Greco-Oriental. Both approaches agree in affirming some absolute or ultimate reality.

According to the Greco-Oriental (mystical or philosophic) approach, this ultimate reality is a primal impersonal force—an all-engulfing divine quality, the ground and end of all. It is an ineffable, impassive divine substance. Whether one names it Brahman or the All-Soul or Nature (as Spinoza does) or nothing at all (as is the way of many mystics) does not really matter. What is meant is very much the same in all cases. There is some ineffable, immutable, impassive divine substance that pervades the universe—or rather *is* the universe insofar as the latter is at all real. This view, of course, is pantheism: All is "God." Greco-Oriental religion, whatever its specific form, irresistibly tends toward a pantheistic position.[8]

The biblical view, in contrast, sees God as neither a metaphysical principle nor an impersonal force, but as a living will, an active being endowed with personality. God is a transcendent Person. He has created the universe, but he is not continuous with it. The phenomena of nature are his creatures and serve him.[9]

These contrasting views of God result in different attitudes toward life, the world, culture, and the arts. The Greco-Oriental view finds life and history semimeaningless and therefore seeks the unchanging reality behind the empirical world. To the Buddhist theologian, the Hindu mystic, or the Platonic philosopher, the empirical world is illusion—an unreal, shifting flux of sensory deception. Only the Absolute, which is beyond time and change, is real. Life and history are therefore essentially meaningless. True knowledge, saving knowledge, consists in breaking through the "veil of illusion" of empirical life—sweeping this shadow world aside in order to obtain a glimpse of the unchanging reality it hides. This is the way of salvation and artistic truth. In fact, if one accepts this view, one tends to argue that the nonmaterial arts of music and poetry are superior to the material arts of painting, sculpture, architecture, and dance.[10]

According to the biblical view, however, the empirical world is real and significant, but not self-subsistent, since it depends on God. Life and history are real and meaningful since God operates and reveals himself in them. God plunges into human history and this world and personally encounters human beings in their activity. Humans can establish genuine personal relations with God. Humanity is made in the image of God and is meant to be creative. In fact, there is a significant similarity between humanity's composing and God's creating. Humanity's embeddedness in the physical creation and its creaturely vocation and creaturely end within that creation are where we must begin if we are to describe how the Christian sees the arts.[11]

(2) The Biblical View of Nature versus the Romantic View of Nature. The Romantic movement in literature, the visual arts, and music began in the eighteenth century and reached its full fruition in the early part of the nineteenth century. William Wordsworth and Samuel Taylor Coleridge are well-known literary representatives of this movement, which has had tremendous influence on later generations.

The Romantics looked at nature as kind and benevolent, the supreme object of adoration. According to the Romantics, nature had an immanent order which was complete in itself.

In contrast, the biblical writers repudiated nature as an object of adoration and worship, although they acknowledged that nature has power, beauty, and grandeur. The key to the biblical view of nature is that it, like humanity, is a creation and servant of God. Nature is our sister, not our mother—and certainly not our god! Isaiah 66:1 has God saying that "Heaven is my throne and the earth my footstool."

Humanity and earth are equally creations of God. Order is given to nature by the will of God (Isa. 40:22–24), and nature is constantly dependent on him (Prov. 8:29). (It is significant that Psalm 104, that great nature poem, is a hymn to God rather than an ode to the cosmos.) Alfred North Whitehead calls this the doctrine of imposed law versus the immanent law of the Greek philosophers.[12]

For the Bible, the beauties of the world issue from the grandeur of God. "All thy works shall give thanks to thee" (Ps. 145:10). Nature is not a part of God, but a creation of and a fulfillment of his will.

The Jews began with God as a Living Person and not as a cosmic force. This view came about because of God's loving acts of concern and his compassion. God had come to Abraham and to Egypt and had delivered a helpless people.[13] Within a weak and oppressed group there suddenly appeared power. To the civilized world, the God of Israel could have been nothing more than the minor deity of a minor people. But to Israel, he was the Lord who had delivered her from bondage. He had given her a land of milk and honey, and in doing so had shown his power over nature, Pharaoh, and the armies of Canaan.[14]

(3) How the Biblical View of God's Immanence in Nature Explains the Artistic

Experience of Discovery and Inspiration. According to the Hebrew view, God is transcendent but discloses himself immanently in history and in nature and in conscience (Rom. 1:19–20). The following verses reflect this view: "In him we live and move and have our being" (Acts 17:28); "He is before all things, and in him all things hold together" (Col. 1:17); "[Christ] reflects the glory of God . . . upholding the universe by the word of his power" (Heb. 1:3). Thus God is seen as being in constant dialogue with humanity, revealing his everlasting power and divinity, his wrath, and his redemption in Christ.[15]

Christian teaching describes the immanence of God as constituted by a life-force that runs through all creation. This is not pantheism. The creature is from God; it is not God in itself. God does not depend upon the universe for his existence. Yet the universe remains in existence, not simply because God first created it and now commands it to exist, but because it draws its power to exist from the life-stream that flows through it from God.

The biblical view of transcendence and immanence helps to explain the basis of inspiration which comes to artists, poets and musicians. Many artists report that for them the process of creativity is something far closer to discovery than to invention. But even discovery is not an adequate expression of the situation, since this word suggests that the artist is active in relation to a wholly passive environment. More often, we are told, it is as though the artist did not choose, but was chosen. The relation is not that of calm and deliberate choice, but of submission to a spell. The beautiful is not something the artist seeks, but something which claims him or her.

Composers, painters, poets—all these and many more—know what it is to feel this claim and not to be their own masters. The greatest lovers of beauty, including those who have been most successful in helping their fellows to see it or to see more of it, have repeated endlessly that, instead of their finding beauty, it has found them. For example, John Keats, the British poet, said that he often was not aware of some thought or expression until after he had written it down, when it then seemed rather the production of another person.

True, the artist, poet, or musician has his disciplines, and his or her conscious mind must work upon the material. However, unless that elusive something from the depths is present, the artist's production will be no more than a design in color, a scrap of verse, or a collection of musical notes. In other words, without the "gift" of inspiration, the skeleton and the flesh are there, but the life is absent.[16]

It could be said that the artist, poet, or musician is one whose physical or mental makeup gives him frequent and dynamic experiences of the immanent stream of life flowing from God. In a sense, the artist sees "the soul of things" and struggles to present that soul to others. If we are receptive, those of us who listen to, or look at, or otherwise contemplate the finished work can also find a response arising within us as we, too, experience something of "the soul of things."

This idea of inspiration does not make God the author of all aesthetic creations and responsible for their expressions. The stream of life is the raw stuff, and in making his contact with it the poet or artist has a glimpse of the soul of things. But the artist's appreciation of what he or she sees is colored by his or her own moral character.

Inspiration of this kind, therefore, is no guarantee of moral worth. And indeed, some great works of art have been created by people with less than noble character. It is said that George Gordon, Lord Byron, wrote some of his best poems after nights of self-indulgence. The great composer Richard Wagner, who certainly saw the soul of things, also maintained the loosest possible ideas of marriage and love. Some inspired poems and works of art are even immoral in themselves, but they are nonetheless powerful, because their creator has built them from the life-stream of God's immanence. Just as a scientist can direct the awesome power of atomic energy to a good or evil end, an artist can make of the "raw stuff" of the universe something either good or evil.

This view also explains some things about certain kinds of modern art that many of us find discordant and difficult to understand. Where these forms are serious and not mere affectation, it is possible that their producer has given them to us insufficiently filtered—has let them emerge directly from too deep a level of the mind. According to this theory, some modern art can be compared with unintelligible tongues, which cannot emerge coherently, as opposed to prophecy, which comes from the depths in an intelligible form. John Dillenberger, on the other hand, sees some abstract art as an attempt to present the world anew to us, freed of forms that once had power but have become banal.

Another possible explanation for inspired art that is discordant and difficult is that the inspired person, seeing into the "soul of things," may perceive something negative about the corporate life of his or her day. For example, if one lives in a community that is frustrated, self-centered, embittered, and puzzled, something of this disharmony may be contained in the vision that comes. The soul that is seen is a disordered soul: The life-force is running through crippled creatures. Thus the productions of poetry and art will carry in them the discord and ugliness that is at the heart of the community.[17]

(4) The Biblical Explanation of the Meaning of Natural Beauty. The created order is beyond all question saturated with beauty; in fact, the beauty of nature has been a major impetus for the arts throughout history. Yet the beauty of nature raises a question which no thoughtful mind can brush to one side. Why is nature, even in its most secret recesses, uniformly beautiful, so that wherever humanity strikes into it, beauty is disclosed to his delighted mind? The biblical view helps explain this by making clear Who the source of natural beauty is—God.

Lord Balfour once said that natural beauty is a revelation from spirit to spirit.[18] And this testimony has received the corroboration of other sensitive minds. Speaking of Balfour's testimony, William Temple testified as follows: "For what my own experience may be worth, it entirely confirms his interpretation!"[19]

Elton Trueblood contends that the reverence which so many feel when confronted by beautiful scenes in nature is not intelligible or defensible on any other than theistic grounds. There is nothing worthy of reverence about a rock or even a great pile of rocks. Indeed, the entire aesthetic experience is a cheat and a delusion unless beauty is a revelation from spirit to spirit. If it is such a revelation, it all makes sense. In short, the aesthetic experience is what we should expect to find if theism is true.[20]

The words of Calvin are helpful in this respect: "We see the 'hands and feet' of God actually before our eyes in the works of creation. The minds of men, therefore, are blind to this light of nature which shines forth in all creatures until being irradiated by the Spirit of God they begin to understand what otherwise they cannot comprehend. . . . We have in this world a conspicuous image of God . . . a theater of divine glory."

(5) The Call for Sensitive Earth Management. Several implications can be drawn from the biblical view of nature as it relates to art and culture. In the first place, because nature is our fellow creature, our sister, we should relate to it in love and care. In the words of Revelation, we should "hurt not the earth, neither the sea, nor the trees" (Rev. 7:3).

This is an especially important word in the twentieth century, when human beings have developed the means to manipulate the natural world on an unprecedented scale. Joseph Sittler affirms that "Science has enabled man to move in on the realm of nature and virtually take it over." However, in her "pathetic openness to glorious use as well as to brutal rapacity" our sister nature reminds us of our common parentage and linked destiny.

In spite of the fact that we are to relate to nature as a fellow creature and as a way of seeing God, the biblical worldview holds that nature cannot finally reveal the inner nature of God. For one thing, nature has many characteristics—not just beauty. Even the ancient polytheists recognized this fact. There were two kinds among the nature gods they worshiped. On one side was the Mother Goddess and the god of healing. But on the other side were the more somber gods of Baal and Enlil. These gods of storm were the personification of the hidden, uncontrollable, amoral depths of nature.[21]

According to the biblical worldview, God is finally known in a saving way not through nature, but in his concrete acts in history as the Lord who led Israel from Egypt and as the Father of Jesus Christ.

2. The Biblical View of Worship

(1) The Polytheistic View of Worship. Beneath the surface of pagan religion was the dark, mysterious world of magic, divination, and demons. Pagan worship, for the most part, was rooted in magic. In worship, the pagan priests conjured up incantations and used exorcisms. Diviners used the livers of animals and the flight of birds to guide the people.[22]

In polytheism, the great cultic festivals centered in three major celebrations. There was the New Year Celebration, in which the divine battle against the chaos that constituted creation was refought and rewon and the security of society in nature reestablished for the ensuing year. Then there was the marriage rite in the spring, when the rain and vegetation god was reunited with the goddess of fertility. In the fall, there were rites incident to the revival of the rain god after his death in the summer's drought.

Basic to these celebrations was sympathetic magic. In them, the people acted ritually—taking on the form or the identity of the gods. By acting out the divine elements, human beings by a willed exercise sought security and integration within nature. A human being in a drama taking the part of a god was thought to become that god temporarily, and his actions became the actions of the god. He thus created anew the orderly world in the battle against chaos, and he secured the revival of nature in spring and fall.[23]

(2) The Old Testament View of Worship. In Israel, by contrast, the basis of worship was historical memory, spiritual communion, and obedience. Magic was forbidden as a part of the abomination of the nations. The Old Testament makes it clear that the God of Israel cannot be tricked or coerced or influenced by magic. He will make his will known when, where, and how he chooses through his prophets.

Unfortunately, there were some lapses and carry-overs from paganism in the Old Testament. Saul, for instance, went to the witch of Endor and engaged in spiritualism. (Saul also died prematurely.)

Even David inquired of Yahweh by means of the Urim and Thummim—the sacred dice carried by the chief priest. And there was the continual problem of discerning true prophecy from false prophets who practiced a pagan type of divination.[24]

There are, of course, examples of magical thinking which exist in many forms to this day. But the important thing in Israel was that the worship of God cut the ground from beneath the magical approach to deity, so that the world of the occult was no longer the center or basis of worship.

The true prophet as God's spokesman was no soothsayer in possession of numerous ritual incantations. He was possessed by God, and there existed between him and his Lord a fellowship of understanding and conscious communion. This is the opposite of the automatic efficacy that is expected when ritual is used in paganism—where the ritual itself is said to evoke a specific response.

In other words, the worship of God in Israel had a far deeper basis than it had in paganism. In Israel, spiritual attitude was all-important. Unless human beings can bow in humble contrition and reverence before God, there can be no such thing as worship. God's first requirement is reverence.

The second requirement is faith, trust, and love. This means to believe God, to accept his promises with a grateful heart, and to act obediently in love without anxiety. The man possessed of such fear and faith has nothing whatever to be afraid of, except sin.[25]

The biblical faith was a remarkable and unique thing in the ancient world. It was rooted in a knowledge of the divine nature and purpose which through Christ has become the basis of the Christian's faith and worship.

In Israel, the official festivals betray no hint of sympathetic magic. In Israel's worship, some of the annual festivals were retained, but their meaning was transformed; they were "historicized" to relate to the great redeeming acts of God (Deut. 5:3; 16:16; 26:3–11).

The spring festival, for instance, became the Passover and the associated Feast of Unleavened Bread. These were related to the historical events of deliverance from Egyptian bondage. The Feast of Pentecost later in the spring commemorated the receiving of the Law. (Later, in New Testament time, this festival came to be associated with the coming of the Holy Spirit.)

The feast of ingathering in the autumn became the Feast of Tabernacles, which commemorated the booths in which Israel had to live in the wilderness after the Exodus (Lev. 23:43). Exodus relates the Sabbath to the Sinai covenant (Exod. 31:12–17).

Although there were a variety of motives behind the Hebrew festivals, the dominating tendency was toward historical commemoration. They were not the reenactment of a drama in which by sympathetic magic and human identification with the divine the harmonious integration of nature and society was thought to be achieved.

In the worship of the Israelite and the Christians, primary attention is focused upon the great redeeming acts of God. In worship these historical events are rehearsed and the worshiper joins himself by sympathetic imagination with the original participants and understands that these acts were done for him or her also (cf. Deut. 5:3; 26:3–11). The worshiper then gives thanks and praise to God for what God has done and solemnly renews his covenanted vows.

The spiritual process in biblical worship thus involves a combination of historical narration with participations by means of memory and imagination. Illumination is derived from the continued working of God's Spirit. There is praise and thanksgiving and a solemn renewal of covenant as the worshiper again faces his own life.

This type of worship avoids the pitfalls of magic and mysticism. It combines the historical past, present, and future in the conception of God's gracious and continuous direction of human life.[26]

(3) The New Testament Approach to Worship. The New Testament church was aware of itself as a new community which was created by the historical work of Christ and the actualizing power of the Holy Spirit. This New Testament community and its worship is to be sharply contrasted with the mystery cults, with their dying-rising gods from whose flesh power was transferred to the believers in cultic ceremonies. Central in the New Testament church was the function of history and of a living historical memory in the creation, preservation, and renewal of life and community.[27]

The community thus formed by the historical work of Christ and the Holy Spirit was united in the central act of worship, which was a confessional recital of what had happened, accompanied by expressions of joy, praise, and thanksgiving. New Testament worshipers also gave interpretative statements or expositions of the meaning of what had been confessed, and they reaffirmed loyalty to the Lord, who was the community's Ruler.

The New Testament Christians really believed that they had been saved by Christ through his historical work and his indwelling Spirit. Christ's salvation had made them into a people and had bound them to himself. And this belief was kept alive as the chief constituting factor of community life because it was kept central in worship.[28]

The New Testament writers do not make a special point of the "real presence" of God in practices such as the Lord's Supper. God is the living God; Christ is the living Christ; and both are present in the work of the Spirit. The biblical writers took for granted the presence of Christ because they had a real doctrine of the Spirit. Therefore, in talking of the Lord's Supper, they stressed the elements of memorial and communion in the new Covenant.[29]

Thus we see that the New Testament emphasis is not upon the outward, magical ritual so characteristic of pagan cults. Rather, the emphasis was upon forgiveness, inner purification, and a personal attachment of the most intimate kind.[30]

The emphasis upon faith and obedience and on the leading of the Spirit makes it certain that the mainstream of the New Testament is not magical, nor is it corrupted by the idea of the automatic effectiveness of external rites correctly performed. The apostolic Church shows no real support for the idea that God can be subdued or controlled by outward conformity or observance.[31]

In the New Testament, a life led by the Spirit has an inwardness, a vitality, a personal quality, and a moral responsibility. This Spirit-led life is thus set apart from the realm of magic, even when that magic is decked out in the attractive garb of allegedly sacramental observance.[32]

The symbol is worthless without that which is symbolized. That which is symbolized is more important for the Bible than the symbol. The Bible finds peril in a symbol which becomes an end in itself. Yet the Bible does not despise symbols when they are charged with meaning.

The Lord's Supper, for example, is an act which symbolizes the constant renewal of our surrender to Christ and the renewal of his work in us. If it represents this, it has meaning when it marks the experience of that renewal. However, it is futile and worse if it replaces the experience.[33]

(4) The Pagan Polytheistic View of the Place of Worship. From the pagan perspective, the temples of the gods were manor houses where the gods lived with their families and servants, both divine and human. Food and drink oblations were provided for the god and offered before their likeness in the temple (idols). Gifts were brought when people came to see the god. From Egyptian and Mesopotamian archaeology we are now informed that the ancient polytheist took the phrase, "house of god," in a literal sense.[34]

But, we ask with our logical minds, how could a god dwell in a house? The original, basic feature of a great polytheistic deity was his personification of a principal or major element in nature: sky, storm, sun, moon, Venus, earth, water, fertility, death, and so on. How could an all-pervasive or cosmic deity be localized in a temporal, earthly building and particularized in the form of a statue (the idol)? This is difficult for us to understand.

The idea becomes a little clearer when we see that the temple was filled with cosmic symbolism, so that it became a microcosm of the macrocosm—it reflected the universe in which the deity lived. In fact, the building, which was like or which symbolized the universe, in some measure was thought to *be* the universe. Thus a cosmic deity could "dwell" in the structure without being confined to or by it. Similarly, the idol was like the god; therefore, on the principle of "like is like," the god and the idol were considered to be identical. One could meet the god "face to face" by appearing before the idol—without the idol's in any way so particularizing the deity that the deity was confined to the spot where the idol was placed.

In polytheism, then, the temple was an all-important link between heaven and earth. The welfare of society was utterly dependent upon the integration with the world of nature and deity, established by its cultic rites. Accordingly, the pagan priests achieved a large measure of control over society, and this control was increased by economic means. The priests, especially in Egypt and Mesopotamia, owned large tracts of land and exercised economic as well as spiritual influence.[35]

(5) The Old Testament View of the Place of Worship. Israel, in its early days as a people, adopted outward forms of worship from surrounding cultures. However, the meaning and nature of Israel's view were changed under God's guidance.

As for the Israelite sanctuary itself, both the nomadic tent shrine (the tabernacle) and the Solomonic temple were interpreted originally very much as pagan shrines were interpreted. They were "the house," or "the house of the Lord." They thus localized the Lord of the whole earth in the midst of his people. The Solomonic temple was filled with the same rich cosmic symbolism as were the pagan temples. For example, the great bronze laver in the courtyard was named "the sea" symbolizing the primeval deep.[36]

But we have sufficient evidence to indicate that Israelite theology was of such a nature as to cause a problem with these pagan conceptions that the temple was God's dwelling place. Some of the leaders of Israel rejected the notion that God could be confined to the temple. This is clearly seen, for example, in Solomon's prayer of dedication of the temple (1 Kings 8:27–30), which clearly rejects the whole attempt to localize God or to consider his temple as a dwelling. The temple instead is simply a place where God's Name abides.

There can be no doubt that the idea of the Name in connection with the temple was used to separate the building's significance entirely from the priestly attempt to explain God's presence in terms of "dwelling." The temple is important, but not because it is God's house in any literalized sense. Rather, the temple is God's gracious condescension to human need. It symbolizes his nearness and provides the assurance that prayers directed toward it will be heard and answered. The temple was a house of prayer in this theology (cf. Isa. 56:7).[37]

According to this view, there were indeed places of worship, but they were not the ultimate dwelling place of Yahweh. Rather, they were simply places where he revealed himself. Wherever his chosen people were, he could be found. His dwelling place was properly in heaven, from which he came down to earth (Exod. 19:11, 18, 20).[38]

The Israelite priests were aware of the problem of the transcendent God in any sense being localized in an earthly abode. So they did not use "dwell" when speaking of God's presence on earth. Instead they used the archaic term "to tent" or "to tabernacle." God never dwells on earth as does man, he "tabernacles" in the midst of his people. The tabernacle was primarily a tent of revelation where God had graciously allowed his presence, hidden by his shekinah, or glory, to tabernacle and there be met (Exod. 25:22; 29:42–43; 30:36).[39]

Even in the economic life of the nation, the Israelite temple could achieve no importance like the pagan temple. It could own no land, but had to be supported solely by the gifts of the worshipers.

The Old Testament writers carefully avoided the literalism of paganism. Their views prepared the way for the later conception of the synagogue and church as places where God may be worshiped, though his physical being is in no way permanently resident there.

It should also be noted that Israel's attachment to God in election and covenant demanded a spiritual type of worship and obedience for which the temple was not an adequate means of expression. Consequently, both the prophets and Jesus could envision God's actual destruction of the temple precisely in order that a proper worship might be ordained (Jer. 7:1–15; Mark 13–14; John 2:19).[40]

(6) The New Testament View of the Place of Worship. In the New Testament era, worship in spirit and truth took the place of temple worship. In the story of the clearing of the temple (John 2:13–22), the evangelist shows that the Person of Christ, who died and rose again, has taken the place of temple worship. In place of the Jewish Temple worship comes that worship in which the crucified and risen One assumes the central place which the temple holds in Jewish worship. In John 4:1–30, "worship in Spirit and in truth" also takes the place of temple worship.[41]

The glory, the shekinah of God, is no longer to be found in the temple. But as John 1:1–14 proclaims, this divine glory has now appeared in the incarnate Word, Jesus Christ. Since Christ—not the temple—is the center of all worship, worship is no longer geographically limited; instead, all worship becomes worship in the "spirit."[42]

3. The Significance of the Biblical View of Symbols for Worship and the Arts

(1) The Pagan View of Symbols. For centuries, human beings have sought to create visual symbols of God in which his presence could be enshrined or confined. This attempt represents what is known as the *real* symbol view. A real symbol is a visible object that represents something invisible. It is something present which represents something absent. It is assumed that the divine resides in the symbol or that the symbol partakes of the reality of the divine.[43]

For example, a physical image of a god is a *real* symbol. The god and the image are closely identified; the person who has the image is believed to have the god, for the god resides in the image. This can be seen in the idea that when a victor nation carries off the god-image of the conquered nation, he deprives the vanquished nation of the presence and aid of their god.

In the fifteenth century B.C., for example, a statue of the goddess Ishtar of Nineveh was carried with great pomp and ceremony from Mesopotamia to Egypt. This act was obviously for the purpose of letting Egypt enjoy the blessings which the goddess by her presence would bestow upon the land.[44]

(2) The Biblical View of Symbols. The Bible, by contrast, teaches the *conventional* symbol view. A conventional symbol is a symbol whose substance is not endowed of the entity. Rather, it suggests that entity by reason of relationship, association, or convention. An example is a flag, which is usually related to a country.[45]

The Old Testament writers specifically opposed the alliance of religion and art in images, just as Moses opposed the creation of the golden calf. In fact, the second commandment specifically forbids the making and worshiping of images and idols: "You shall not make for yourself a graven image, or any likeness of anything that is in heaven above, or that is in the earth beneath, or that is in the water under the earth; you shall not bow down to them or serve them; for I the Lord your God am a jealous God" (Exod. 20:4). The same emphasis is continued in the prophets. For the Israelites there was to be no veneration of images, no physical embodiment of supreme mysteries.[46]

This is not to say that the Bible prohibits art; in fact, the descriptions of the building of the temple and the tabernacle contained detailed descriptions of the beautiful objects created to be part of the worship of the Lord. Gene Vieth, a well-known evangelical writer in the field of Christianity and the arts, has attempted to explain the seeming contradiction between the second commandment and these descriptions. He points out that the second commandment did not prohibit art in itself, but the worship of art—what Vieth terms the "mystification" of art.

Vieth cites the example of the brazen serpent in this context. This snake was an image, but it was employed as an instrument in Israel's relationship to God (Num. 21:6–9). Centuries later, King Hezekiah destroyed the bronze serpent because the people "burned incense to it" (2 Kings 18:4). The bronze serpent had become an idol and therefore was a violation of the second commandment.[47]

According to the biblical view, God manifested himself in events, not in things, and these can never be captured or localized in things. It is significant that Mount Sinai, the place on which the supreme revelation occurred, did not retain any degree of holiness in the biblical mind. It did not become a shrine, a place of pilgrimage.[48] And in the New Testament, as we have seen, the architectural symbol of God's presence, the temple, was not needed in and of itself. God has spoken primarily through the historical event of Christ (John 1:1–18) and the inspired apostolic writers.

In the biblical view, physical objects—bread, trumpets, palm branches—can be instruments of worship, but not objects of worship. They are not given homage; they are not symbols in themselves. The Bible says that the image and shape of the scrolls or the cross do not convey to us any inspiration beyond reminding us of their function and our obligation. The Bible itself is to be read, not gazed at. There is no inherent sanctity in ritual objects. Ritual art is enhancement of doing a religious act. It adds to the pleasure of obedience. Art objects have religious function—they are not religious substitutes. The purpose is not in direct contemplation—but to add pleasure to obedience and delight to fulfillment.[49]

(3) The Biblical Response to the Modern Symbolic View of Religion. An understanding of this biblical view of symbolism in worship and the arts is helpful in responding to a modern emphasis that religion itself is largely symbolic. This view had its origins in the eighteenth century. As shown in chapter 11, Immanuel Kant sought to demonstrate that it is utterly impossible to attain knowledge of the world as it is because knowledge is always in the form of categories in the mind, and these categories, in the last analysis, are only representational constructions. In other words, Kant argued that only symbolic knowledge is possible.

This view has been carried over into religious truth. Many modern thinkers hold that while our knowledge of God is not objectively true, it is still symbolically true. For many, then, religion has become largely an affair of symbols. Translated into simpler terms, this view regards religion as a fiction, but sees it as useful to society or to man's personal well-being. Thus, although there may be no personal God, we must go on worshiping his symbol.[50]

The person who holds the biblical worldview, however, is not satisfied to worship a symbol. If God is only a symbol, then religion is futile. What is the value of searching for a goal that will forever remain unknown?

Moreover, if God has no mercy and offers no light to those who grope for him, does he deserve humanity's desperate efforts to reach him? Just as truly loving another person means loving not a symbol or idea of that other person, but the person himself or herself, so loving and fearing God means not being satisfied with worshiping a symbol or worshiping symbolically.

According to the biblical view, symbols are means of communication; they communicate or convey to us what they represent. In order to understand or appreciate a symbol, then, we must be in possession of what the symbol stands for. In order to prove the validity of symbols in general and in order to judge the adequacy of particular symbols, we must possess a knowledge of the symbolized object that is independent of all symbols. To justify and to judge symbols, we are in need of nonsymbolic knowledge.[51]

The Bible is not a religion of a vague symbol or an unknown God. Biblical religion is built upon a rock of certainty that God has made known his will to his people.[52] All symbols in worship or any other area of life are secondary to that central truth.

(4) The Biblical Emphasis that Symbols Are Secondary to Concrete Obedience to God in Life. The prophets and Jesus teach that God does not finally desire

only symbols—but concrete, real living. True religion is not essentially speculative or artistic, but grounded in insight, faith, and dedication. Symbols are of auxiliary importance.

Since Christ has come, biblical religion has had a minimum of ceremony and a maximum of living observance. This is even true of Jewish religion, in which there is also a minimum of show, of ceremonialism. Ceremonies are for the eye, but biblical religion is an appeal to the spirit. Biblical observance is a response to God and his acts—not a search for God. Symbols have a psychological, not an ontological status.[53]

(5) The Danger of Symbolism from the Biblical Perspective. In the past, even in the Christian church, symbols have often come to serve as a substitute for faith, for insight, and for immediate perception. In fact, the Reformation was in part a reaction against the tendency in medieval Christianity for symbolism and ceremony to smother the immediacy of faith.

With the increasing exposure of the public to the arts, many people are becoming more interested in the ceremonial and the symbolic. The question is whether this craving for ceremony is truly an expression of a more profound care for the will of God[54] or simply an aesthetic preference.

Visual symbolism in worship tends to reduce observance to ceremony and theology to aesthetics. Symbols are aesthetic objects—they please the senses, but make few moral or ethical demands. They are ideas which offer enjoyment but do not call for commitment. Faith tends to die in an overdose of symbols. Symbols undermine the certainty of history, in which God speaks through events and commands.

The uniqueness of the Bible is not in its symbolism; the religions of Egypt, Rome, and India were also rich in symbolism. They lacked, however, the knowledge of "the living God." The uniqueness of the Bible is in disclosing the will of God in plain words, in telling us of the presence of God in history, rather than in symbolic signs or mythic events.

It is crucial to remember always that God is not a symbol—but real. Man-made symbols cannot redeem us. Instead, for a symbol to be meaningful, it must always point to and communicate the event. An example of such a meaningful symbol is found in Jeremiah 19:1, 10–11: "Thus said the Lord: 'Go, buy a potter's earthen flask. . . . Then you shall break the flask in the sight of the men who go with you, and shall say to them, "Thus says the Lord of hosts: So will I break this people and this city, as one breaks a potter's vessel, so that it can never be mended."'"

Now, this is not to say that symbols are "off limits" for Christians. Christianity can have and use symbolic objects—such as crosses, lambs, doves, and the like. But these images must always point back to the historical past and to the concrete acts of God and humans in history—not to themselves.

This view is in contrast to some contemporary writers such as W. T. Stace and Aldous Huxley, who claim that modern religious consciousness must dissolve connections with time and space. In such a view, religious knowledge is not tied to historical fact, but to certain mystical symbols.[55] There is no check on the truth of such mystical symbols; they are ambiguous. But biblical symbols are inseparably connected with definite words spoken and deeds done. They thus preserve both the rational element, without which all discourse degenerates, and the factual element, without which theology becomes a fairy tale.

The relatedness and function of such biblical symbols can be seen in Isaiah's going barefoot and naked as a sign of the coming captivity of Egypt, in Jeremiah's wearing the yoke to symbolize Judah's impending subjection to Babylon, and in Ezekiel's lying on his side for forty days to represent the duration of Judah's captivity.[56]

All this discourse on symbolism relates directly to the use of the arts in worship. The arts—visual, musical, dramatic, and so on—can continue to function as a powerful means of expression, since they appeal to the whole person—not just the intellect. However, those who hold the biblical worldview will not mistake this means for an end. The biblical person should not be so impressed with the way artists express themselves that they neglect what they are saying and fall into a dubious worldview.[57]

4. The Positive and Evaluative Approach of the Bible toward Culture and Art Forms

The Bible deals with human life on earth. It portrays humanity as the crown of God's creation. Human beings are made in the image of God and are to be supreme over created things. Yet, this sovereignty is subject to the overlordship of God. Human beings must create in obedience to God and not exploit creation for their own ends.[58]

This basic fact of creation gives a key to the overall biblical approach toward culture and civilization in general. This in turn casts light on the biblical view of the arts, which are the fruits of human culture.

(1) Old Testament Perspectives on Culture and the Arts. The Old Testament reveals a continuing tension between different views of culture and civilization and the gradual establishment of the Davidic view of culture under God's control as dominant.

The first of these views of culture is the *nostalgic* view, which looks back to the wilderness period as the golden age of fellowship between God and Israel. The prophets portray the wilderness as the place of direct worship with God. Hosea, Micah and Jeremiah at times express this attitude (Jer. 2:2, 3; 35:6–10). Although they did not call for a return to the conditions of the wilderness, they held it up as an ideal (Hosea 2:14, 20; Ezek. 20:35, 36).[59]

The second recurring view of civilization to recur in the Old Testament is the *pessimistic* view, in which every cultural development is shown to be accompanied by some sort of spiritual lapse.

In the early parts of Genesis, for example, every development seems to be accompanied by increased wickedness and unhappiness. By the very juxtaposition of traditional stories, the biblical writer presents his view of the progress of civilization—which is rather gloomy. In Genesis 4 the separation of nomadic and agricultural pursuits is accompanied by the first murder. The building of the first city is accompanied by the story of Lamech, whose vengeful life is the picture of humanity's ultimate degradation in a life apart from God. At the close of the flood story (Gen. 8), we are told about the introduction of vineyard culture, one of the basic industries of the Palestinian and Syrian areas. And this is accompanied by the picture of the good man, Noah, drunk! The distribution and blessing of the nations in Genesis 11 is accompanied by the Tower of Babel story, in which humankind thrusts its creation into heaven itself, saying, "Let us make a name for ourselves" (v. 4).[60]

The thread of the pessimistic view of culture continues through the Old Testament. Even the reign of Solomon, which has long been known as glorious, is shown to lead to idolatry, profligacy, and heartlessness. The extreme statement of the biblical condemnation of civilization is found in Ezekiel's withering prophecies about Tyre (26–28).

According to this view of culture, civilization at each stage is seen as being accompanied by its spiritual problems. The meaning of the whole is that culture knows nothing whatsoever of its responsibility to its sovereign Creator. Later the pessimistic view developed into the idea that all things may be the occasion of evil, although they are yet part of the purpose of God for man. (This analysis of culture is similar to that made by Paul in Romans 1.)[61]

Thus the Old Testament has a remarkable doctrine of the fall of civilization. Civilization is not in itself sinful. Yet, like individual humans, human civilization desires to be free of God and even to be God. So civilization and culture, which can and should mean so much to humanity, drive humanity to self-destruction. Thus civilizations eventually fall.

This means that, according to the Old Testament, all human institutions and cultures are impermanent. The implication is that God's people must not become too identified with any civilization. God's people must be faithful to God and thus abide the fall of civilization. In modern times, Reinhold Niebuhr held a similar view. For Niebuhr, history is a perennial tragedy—the story of human hubris (pride) and divine nemesis. The world is most accurately portrayed as a tower of Babel in which our infinite possibilities are time and again subverted by sin.[62]

The third view of civilization found in the Old Testament was the Davidic picture of a civilization and culture under *God's control*. Later in Jewish history, the people looked for a return of the Davidic era. The reign of David made their nation, they affirmed, and gave them a chance to fulfill their destiny among the nations.

David was a Shepherd-King under the rule of God. Jesus used this idea. The Shepherd watches his sheep—so justice and mercy are given and human beings can dwell in peace. These are the conditions and guarantee of any worthy civilization. The Davidic ideal is not a reign of splendor or a regression to the primitive, but a time of dignity and brotherliness (Amos 9:11–15; Zech. 3:10).[63]

(2) General New Testament Perspectives on Culture and the Arts. Almost no precise information can be found in the New Testament about culture and civilization, and still less on the arts. There are reasons for this. One reason is the humble station of most of the early Christians. Another is the fact that the New Testament encompasses a far shorter period of time than the Old Testament, and the entire New Testament period was dominated by one overarching culture, that of the Roman Empire. A much more important reason, however, was the view of the early church that the Second Coming was imminent. In view of the immediate return of Christ, institutions and culture were seen to have no ultimate value.

Yet the New Testament displays no basic hostility to culture. The early Christians recognized the validity of an effective framework for life.[64] However, the early Christians did not accept the cultural framework unconditionally—but only so far as they were able to do so without being disloyal to the gospel. The early Christians thus advocated neither asceticism nor complete surrender to the enjoyments of life.

Even though art and literature are not mentioned explicitly in the New Testament, it is reasonable to assume that the view of the early Christians toward these subjects would be similar to their view of the state. That is, they can be accepted and appreciated positively—but only if they are limited to their own affairs and remain neutral in religious affairs. If art, culture, or the state make religious claims, they are demonic and must be resisted by the Christian.

It is interesting to note that, in spite of persecutions, the church remained remarkably loyal to the state throughout the first two centuries of its existence. Paul, for example, urged the Romans to "be subject to governing authorities. . . ." (Rom. 13:1). The early church father Polycarp, who was himself condemned to death by the state, echoed Paul in writing that the Christian must give loyal obedience to the authorities so long as they do not attack his faith and do not force him to say, "the emperor is God." We find the same loyalty in the early Christian apologists, from Justin Martyr to Tertullian. They vie with one another in denying that they are anarchists or revolutionaries. They remind their readers that they pray for the emperors and acknowledge their authority.

Even in relation to cultural institutions that were contrary to Christian principles—slavery is a notable example—Christians did not start by attacking the outer framework of injustice. They began not by suppressing or reforming the existing social framework, but by observing the fullness of love toward all their brethren inside the existing framework. In this way, they created a new community, the church, alongside the social institutions of the world. They believed that when Christian brethren really attained this love one toward the other, evil institutions such as slavery would collapse automatically, even outside the church. They did not in the least approve of slavery; they did not recommend its preservation. But they did not want to destroy the social framework before changing human hearts, just as they did not approve of the zealots and their religious war against the Roman state.[65]

At times, of course, the early Christians rejected civilization if it was bound up with idolatry. When pagan institutions were rejected, it was not because they were not Christian. (We have seen that they do not have to be Christian to be acceptable.) Rather, such institutions were rejected because they had religious pretensions. Only on this basis did the early Christians feel they must reject the surrounding civilization. In such cases, acceptance—even passive acceptance—would entail the surrender of faith in Christ.

In the ancient world, many human activities were impregnated with religion: literature, the theater, the market (the meat market in particular), and military service. Contact with the dominant culture was, therefore, far more often a defiling influence for those early Christians. This situation helps us to understand the wildly uncompromising attitude of a man like Tertullian in the second century, who disapproved of so many professions that Christians were forced to ignore his proscriptions in order to make a living.

In his treatise, *De Idololatria,* Tertullian forbade Christians to be merchants, since commerce proceeds from avarice. He condemned almost all the artisan trades: carpentry, joinery, tilery, carving, and sculpture, because they all had associations with idolatry. And he demanded that Christians should not be schoolteachers, because mythology formed part of the curriculum.

Furthermore, Tertullian protested above all against Christian participation in pagan festivals that had a religious character (in this, of course, he was being faithful to apostolic precepts). Tertullian was willing to make certain concessions, however; he allowed participation in pagan festivals that did not involve the worship of an idol but merely honored in a simple, human way a nondeified mortal.[66]

The state and dominant culture were stoutly opposed by the early church when Christians were forced to worship the emperor. From the earliest times, and in spite of their overall loyalty, Christians proved unyielding on this point. If worship of the emperor had not existed, it is highly probable that there would have been no persecutions or martyrdoms. But once the state ceased to be neutral, resistance was inevitable. Acknowledging but one Lord, the Christian could not possibly confess, "Kyrios Kaisar—Caesar is Lord." (According to the account of the martyrdom of Polycarp, the officer who arrested this bishop of the church asked him: "What is there so terrible in saying 'Kyrios Kaisar'?")

If the Roman state had taken the trouble to study Christian principles, it would have realized that the members of the church were, in fact, its most loyal subjects and that their resistance would come to an end once they were excused from participating in worship of the emperor. But the Romans were determined to interpret the Christian attitude as one of revolt and anarchy. This was a gross mistake, which led to two centuries of martyrdom.[67]

(3) The Culture of the New Testament Church. In addition to their attitude toward existing forms of culture and civilization, the early Christians also created new forms of culture and civilization. The new sociological pattern of the church, with a unique discipline distinct from the jurisdiction of the state, is one example.

Despite certain resemblances to the minor literature of the time, the four Gospels represent a unique departure unparalleled in secular literature. Unintentionally, the early Christians, who had no literary pretensions of any kind, created a new genre. The Gospels were a specifically Christian work of art, which in essence had nothing in common with the art of the ancient world, despite certain similarities of form.[68]

There were times, of course, when the early Christians allowed themselves to be influenced by pagan elements which were incompatible with Christianity. One of the clearest examples of this influence was that of the Gnostics, who tried to establish a kind of universal synthesis of wisdom and religion. What this implied was an attempt to fuse the gospel with the whole of pagan culture, including its religious pretensions. It meant abandoning the fundamental Christian position without which Christianity ceases to be Christian. Ever since the first two centuries, most Christians have, with a sure instinct, recognized this danger. The triumph of the Gnostic movement would have meant the end of Christianity.

At the other extreme we find, from the second century onward, an ascetic reaction against the "temptations" of civilization and culture. In the middle of the second century, for example, a Christian called Montanus tried to root out all the influences of ancient civilization from the church, which was by now already all too comfortably established in the world.

This attempt was no more in accordance with the wholesome directives of Paul and the other apostles than the opposite extreme of Gnosticism. According to these Christian leaders, the Christian era had already begun, and the church had to continue living within the framework of the world so long as God willed, with their eyes set on a future world which God himself would establish. The Montanists wrongly advocated an escape from the world.[69]

Tertullian, whose hatred of pagan civilization is described above, ended by foundering in Montanism. Sadly, his attitude far exceeded that of the New Testament. The apostle Paul, judging from his attitude to the problem of meat sacrificed to idols, would very likely have been more prepared to compromise than was Tertullian. By recommending a flight from the world, Tertullian desired to protect the Christian from all conflicts. According to the New Testament, however, the Christian should not evade necessary conflicts but endeavor to resolve them on the basis of the gospel.[70]

Tertullian's hatred of pagan civilization blazed most violently of all in regard to the games and public shows to which he devoted a whole treatise. He was absolutely uncompromising on this point. It would have been useless to retort, as did some later opponents of such rigor, that David had danced before the ark and that Paul had not shrunk from comparing the Christian life to a race (1 Cor. 9:24). Tertullian would not have been convinced by such arguments. For him, one spectacle alone was legitimate: the Last Judgment.

Another church father, Tatian, was opposed to all Greek literature. According to him, it was one mass of impurities, with no good qualities at all. Plato was a drunkard, Diogenes a bluffer, Aristippus a rake and a hypocrite, Aristotle a flatterer, and so on. This is hardly a point of view that is dominant in the Bible, as we will note in the next section.[71]

(4) The Positive Biblical View of Culture and the Arts. On the whole, the biblical view toward culture and the arts can be seen to be positive. There are two main grounds for this conclusion:

First, both the Hebrews and the early Christians borrowed freely from surrounding communities, adapting outside material to the specific purposes of the covenant people. In some of its forms, for example, Israelite poetry borrowed many features from Canaanite literature, including a metrical scheme and climactic or repetitive rhetorical structure. The Psalms are now known to swarm with words, phrases, and allusions which were taken from the works of Canaanite poets. Psalm 29, for example, has been shown to be fundamentally Canaanite in diction and imagery; it was probably adapted by an Israelite poet from a hymn to Baal and put into a biblical framework in a context of divine inspiration.

The material in the Book of Proverbs is another vivid example of divinely guided cultural adaptation. Such proverbs arose within a "wisdom" movement in which no tension existed between Israelite, Egyptian, Canaanite, Edomite and other adherents to the epigrammatic teaching of prudential ethics. While in Israel the theological basis of wisdom became "the fear of the Lord," the proverbs nevertheless were drawn for the most part from an international movement concerned with the character education of the individual.

The institution of kingship was acknowledged to be a direct borrowing from pagan society (e.g., 1 Sam. 8:4), although in Israel the interpretation of the office was acclimatized to the community faith. If kingship counted in Egypt as a function of the gods and in Mesopotamia as a divinely ordained political order, the Hebrews knew that they had introduced it on their own initiative, in imitation of others, and under the strain of an emergency. Kingship never achieved a standing equal to that of institutions which were claimed to have originated during the Exodus and the desert wandering.

As explained above, the Solomonic temple, when seen as being in some manner an abode of deity or a "house of God," was a foreign importation which required reinterpretation in Israel. Like kingship, however, the temple never became an indispensable institution of community life, important though it was conceived to be (cf. Jer. 7).[72]

In the New Testament, as well, there was a viable and positive relation between the new people of God and their environment. The apostle Paul used Cynic diatribe and Stoic terms. And the evangelist John employed the Greek term *logos* for the Word which was coexistent with God and had now become flesh (John 1).

In doing this, John exhibited an extraordinary theological adaptation of his environment, reinterpreting the conception in Christian terms. On the one hand, the use of the term would immediately recall to those trained in Greek philosophy a wealth of context on which entirely new light was now shed. On the other hand, for Eastern readers the concept of the personified divine

Word had a long history in the Semitic world. Indeed, the conception, as John uses it, has its closest kinship with Judeo-Hellenistic literature and behind that with two millennia of usage in the Near East. Yet this divine, creative word of long history was now focused in the person of Christ.

Despite this freedom of adaptation, however, Christianity, under divine guidance and inspiration, was kept free from the pagan mythologies, astrology, and magic which tended to accompany the borrowed material. Faith in Christ was power over the spirits of darkness.[73]

The *second* ground for concluding that the biblical view of culture is positive is found in the New Testament's originality, independence, and fine sense of balance and proportion. The New Testament reveals that the early Christian community possessed the means of living in a positive relation to the world. It had independent judgment, which enabled it either to reject or affirm specific elements, while never losing the balance needed to preserve its own distinctiveness and inner power.

The scene of calling for both the community and the individual was in the world. Therefore, a positive approach to the world and those outside the Christian community was necessary. God is Lord of the world and is engaged in the struggle to extend his sovereignty over it.

This positive relationship requires that God's people both reject and accept earthly culture and masters. Our work is for the Lord and our eye must be single; the motivation of decision must be derived from the singleness of obedience (Matt. 6:24). But when the surrounding culture does not interfere with that single purpose, it can be embraced and influenced.

The Christian community's obedience thus leaves individuals in a responsible relationship to the world here and now, for they are called upon continually to make decisions in keeping with their calling. To obey the divine Master in the earthly position wherein one is called is a precarious type of existence in which choices and judgments must be made. It sometimes seems easier and safer to withdraw. But the New Covenant instead calls Christians to encounter and engage the world around them. The Christian life is risky because there are no detailed rules. Christians have a revealed order to follow, a revealed and inferential pattern, but not a legalistic guide to protect them from decisions.

The New Testament perspective on culture means that individuals can live creatively, though insecurely, in the world. And they can live without fear, because they have a kingship, a means of judgment, a perspective, and a knowledge concerning the present and future relation of the world to its true sovereignty. In the words of one early Christian, "Live in the world, but as a stranger; as a stranger, but in the world."

(5) Views toward Arts and Culture in Subsequent Christian History. In subsequent Christian history, various persons and groups have sought to follow these New Testament guidelines with varying success. John Calvin's ideal was to establish a holy community in which both church and state cooperate

to fashion a social order where the glory of God is served in every area of life. Both church and state are to stand under the revealed law of God; the church interprets this law to the state, and the state in turn applies this law to life in society.

The holy community is not itself the kingdom of God, which is fundamentally a spiritual kingdom, but it can be a means by which the kingdom of God is extended in the world. Indeed, Calvin taught that we, as humans transformed by grace, can extend and advance the kingdom of God through the preaching of the Word, prayer, church discipline, the sacraments, and works of social service.

Centuries later, Karl Barth called for a transformation of the cultural vision in the light of the divine promise and commandment. At the same time, Barth sharply stressed that no cultural achievement may identify with the coming kingdom of God. For Barth, Jesus Christ is the humanizer of culture. It is through his grace, which is always redemptive and never simply preservative, that men and women can move toward a more just and humane society.

Though influenced by Barth, Jürgen Moltmann, the well-known twentieth-century German theologian, has turned in another direction. Moltmann takes a positive view of culture, but he is also acutely aware of the lingering shadow of exploitation and oppression that hangs over human cultural achievements. The division Moltmann sees in history is between the oppressors and the oppressed, and this is why Moltmann belongs in the larger circle of liberation theology. What Jesus Christ gained for us is the promise of a new world; we still wait for its fulfillment. But we can do more than wait: We can join the human struggle for liberation and thereby pave the way for the kingdom. The lordship of Christ takes effect only where it is acknowledged and realized in acts of compassion, service, and social action.

Prominent evangelical scholar Donald Bloesch urges that the first responsibility of Christians is to bring people into a saving relationship with Jesus Christ. We cannot realize our humanity in the way God intended until we come to a right knowledge of the living God and what he has done for us in Jesus Christ. Bloesch does not call for an imperial church, which imposes its peculiar beliefs upon an unwilling people, but for an obedient church, which tries to live in the light of God's promise and in fidelity to his commandment. The weapons of the church are spiritual: the Word of God, prayer, and works of mercy. It is not by law or coercion that people are brought into the kingdom, but by the preaching and hearing of the word of God and by deeds of love.

According to Bloesch, the Christian protest is not to be against the secular culture, for culture deserves a certain autonomy, but against secularism, the enthronement of cultural values and ideas. Bloesch further emphasizes that the Christian church is not anticultural but transcultural. It is not iconoclastic but transformative. Its aim is not to tear down but to refocus. Civilization is something to be appreciated, even celebrated, but worldliness is something to be spurned and fought. Christ does not call us out of the world; he sends us into it—but to conquer, not to succumb (cf. John 17:15–19).[74]

III. What Are the Implications of the Biblical Pattern of Thinking for the Significance and Place of Art Forms?

1. The Dominance and Importance of Hebrew and Greek Patterns of Thinking in the West

Underlying the "Life We Prize," to use an expression coined by Elton Trueblood to refer to Western civilization, we find two basic patterns of thinking—the Hebrew and the Greek. There are obviously influences from the East, such as the Hindu influence on Emerson and transcendentalism. However, for our purposes we will emphasize the two dominant influences.

In Christian intellectual history, both Hebrew and Greek patterns are encountered. Sometimes they are harmonized, as in the case of Augustine, and sometimes they are found in disharmony, as with Tertullian. The Roman Catholic church has tended toward the Greek pattern with its emphasis on the *visual,* the *contemplative,* and the *logical.* The Protestant Reformers, especially Luther, tended toward the Hebrew pattern, with its emphasis on *speaking, hearing,* the *dynamic* and the *psychological.*[75]

It is obvious that these two patterns of thinking are not mutually exclusive, but complementary. However, let us remember that Christianity arose on Jewish soil. Jesus and the apostles were firmly rooted in the Old Testament and lived primarily in its world of images.[76]

Some contemporary scholars of significance contend that the New Testament thought-world is essentially Hebraic, whatever it may owe to Hellenistic influences. According to Oscar Cullmann, we must reckon with Greek influence upon the origin of Christianity from the very beginning. But the Greek ideas should be subordinated to the total view of Hebrew history.[77]

Tragically, many educated men and women are lacking in an appreciation of the Hebrew roots of Christianity. In the words of President Howard Lowrie of the College of Wooster, "It is surely our Hebrew heritage which is most sorely neglected in our contemporary cultural self-understanding." This statement by a prominent educator points up the fact that the unique value of Hebrew thinking is misconstrued by a majority of scholars. It is often mistaken for primitive thinking, as though it were prelogical. And it *is* prelogical to the extent that it stands closer to natural life than the subtle, lifeless, unimaginative and almost fossilized abstractions of some highly scientific thinking. However, as we shall see, the Hebrew writers have given expression to profound and meaningful truths in simple and unadorned language.[78]

In the light of the importance of both the Hebrew and Greek patterns of thinking, it should be helpful to survey the way in which these patterns affect the significance and place of art forms. My concern is to discriminate for the purposes of comprehension. Both methods or patterns are valid and necessary, and both Hebrew and Greek thought must pay the price of one-sidedness for their great achievements. We need to know both Greek and Hebrew thinking, and ideally there should be a synthesis between them. But Christians should bear the burden of the Hebraic gap in our cultural self-understanding in a way secular people are unable or unwilling to do. This approach will have a special importance for those of us who are presumedly seeking to live under the dominance of the biblical worldview and who accept the inspired normativity of the biblical view.[79]

Excursus on the Sources of This Emphasis

The emphases of this section largely follows the thinking of Thorlief Boman, lecturer at the University of Oslo in Norway, who theorized that special characteristics of the Hebrew mentality affected its view of beauty: the Hebrew propensity for dynamic rather than static thinking, perception through the Hebrew's use of all the senses rather than merely through sight, and the Hebrew lack of concern for form in perception.[80] According to Boman, Western scholars have difficulty accepting this different approach to beauty because their epistemological and philosophical foundations rest upon the Greek tradition.

Boman's ideas have been accepted by many. In *The Gift of Art: The Place of the Arts in Scripture*, Gene Vieth's approach rests upon the foundation of Boman's conclusions.[81] Old Testament scholar Hans Walter Wolff, in his discussion of the beauty of the body in *Anthropology of the Old Testament*, also owes much to Boman's study.[82]

Samuel Terrien, long-time professor of Old Testament at Union Seminary in New York City, though not dependent on Boman, reached a similar conclusion regarding the nature of the perception of beauty in Israel. For Terrien, "seeing" in the Old Testament involves a wide range of sensations; it is more than visual.[83]

A recent Old Testament scholar who deals extensively with beauty in the Old Testament is Claus Westermann. He follows Boman in suggesting that the perception of beauty in Israel was different from the perception and expression of beauty among the Greeks. He emphasized the difference between a view of reality as "being" among the Greeks and as "becoming" among the Hebrews.[84]

Boman's theses have not been universally accepted. However, even prominent British theologian James Barr, who in *The Semantics of Biblical Language* protested Boman's use of linguistic evidence in theological discussion, did not assert that he thought Boman's contrast was invalid, but simply suggested that the contrast could be outlined and accepted without reference to supposed differences between the Hebrew and Greek languages.[85]

2. The Methods of Thinking Developed by the Hebrews and the Greeks

(1) The Hebrew Approach. Hebrew thinking can be characterized as dynamic, vigorous, and passionate. This is revealed by the Hebrew language, where the verbs always express a movement or an activity. Ultimate reality can only be thought of as a person who is predominantly in movement and activity.[86]

(2) The Greek Approach. In contrast, Greek thinking, especially as portrayed by many of the pre-Socratics and Plato, is static, peaceful, moderate, and harmonious. For these ancient Greek philosophers, true *being* is that which is immovable and immutable. All *becoming* is mere appearance, and all sense impressions are deceptive.

There are some exceptions to this approach. One was the Greek philosopher Heraclitus, with his more dynamic understanding of reality as symbolized by fire. We do not know the reason that this philosopher differed so from the mainstream of Greek thought; perhaps he was subject to oriental influence. At any rate, Plato openly declared that he could not understand the teaching of Heraclitus.

The Dionysian or ecstatic emphasis in Greek culture is also different from the dominant Apollonian or rational emphasis. Nikos Kazantzakis's contemporary novel, *Zorba the Greek*, is a modern expression of this ancient emphasis. In Kazantzakis's story, the controlled, Apollonian professor finally asks at the end of the story for the lively Zorba, the Dionysian, to "teach me to dance."

Even Plato recognized that the things of sense possess a certain reality or being. However, the general emphasis of classical Greek thought is that the spiritual world, the world of the "ideas" or "forms," is the highest reality, because the world of appearance is perishable and transitory. As we shall see, these ideas have important implications in relation to art forms.[87]

3. The Significance of the Hebrew and Greek Understandings of Beauty as They Relate to Art Forms

(1) The Greek (Platonic) Idea of Beauty. We can perhaps best understand the Platonic idea of beauty by realizing why Plato thought a geometric figure was so beautiful. The beauty of the geometric figure is related to the clarity, facility, and elegance with which the figure reveals the range of mathematical ideas.

For the Greek in the Platonic tradition, beauty is spirituality revealed in material objects. One may note this in looking at a Greek statue of a nude woman. There is no gross sensuality there. Kenneth Clark has made this point in his well-known book entitled *The Nude*. The material or the so-called sensuous is minimized, and the spiritual is magnified.[88]

A work of art according to the Greek artist is perfect when it portrays the ideal form which is to be found in the individual and suppresses all the peculiar features in the model. This accounts for the greatness of Greek art, but also accounts for its tendency toward an impersonal character. Many Greek statues and paintings have expressionless faces because they are not simple imitations of nature nor even representations. They are *idealized* types.

The basic Greek idea of beauty was developed by Plato in his *Symposium*. According to Plato, beauty is first discovered in a beautiful figure. Then we learn to understand that the beauty of one body is the sister of the beauty of any other body; it would be unreasonable not to observe the beautiful as a beauty always remaining the same. When we have understood this, we love every beautiful figure, when we used to love one only. Then we begin to treasure more highly the value of the soul than the beauty of the body, so that we also love the one who has the beautiful soul but a less beautiful body. The beautiful is eternal, without birth or death, and it neither waxes nor wanes. The beauty is not a body or a part of a body nor anything corporeal. It is the beautiful in itself. It is the *form* beauty.[89]

This Platonic approach, therefore, is called formalism. In its metaphysical interpretation, formalism stresses the primacy of abstract conception and definition. The idea is that since material reality is logically and ontologically dependent on formal or conceptual reality, true and great art must be that which most nearly mirrors the perfect and unchanging abstract relationship among qualities. This interpretation would suggest that it is only by focusing on the formal qualities of works of art that we can ascertain their true worth. This is true because it is only these features that can be universally valuable across different times and cultures.[90]

(2) The Hebrew Idea of Beauty. For the Hebrew, on the other hand, the beautiful is that which fulfills its *purpose*. "How beautiful are the feet of those who preach good news" (Rom. 10:15). Purpose implies power and authority and movement. Therefore the Israelite finds beauty in that which lives and moves and exudes power and authority.

Furthermore, it is not form which mediates the experience of beauty as for the Greeks, but the sensations of light, voice, sound, tone, smell, and taste. When we have become familiar with this idea, it does not strike us as offensive that "The divinity smells with pleasure the smoke of sacrifice" (Gen. 8:21), and that "the prayers of the saints rise like incense to the presence of God" (Rev. 5:8).[91]

The Song of Solomon teaches us the basic Hebrew concept that a person's beauty is found in his or her preeminent *qualities*, which are expressed by means of the body. In the Song of Solomon, the maiden is described as having a neck like the tower of David. The tower image is a way of expressing the trait that was important for the purpose in mind—in this case, the proud inaccessibility and virginity of a pure maiden.[92]

The colors of nature are less important for the Israelite than for the Greek. If white and red were most preferred for the Hebrews, this is connected with the fact that they come closest to light and fire and therefore provide the most illumination. In the Hebrew conception, God did not surround himself with colors, but surrounded himself with *light* as a mantle. Yahweh's glory appeared on the top of the mountain like a devouring *fire*. In contrast to the Greeks, the Hebrews did not feel that the beautiful needed to have a graceful harmonious form.[93]

It is not difficult in this connection to see the inner relationship between the Hebrew biblical mentality and the modern Post-Impressionistic and Expressionistic art: All are essentially dynamic. Roger Ortmayer and Harvey Cox see a recovery of biblical emphases in the return of the liturgical dance in worship services.[94]

As we have seen, the Hebrews found the highest beauty in the formless, dreadful fire and in the life-giving light. Protestants, in their attempt to return to the biblical worldview, were attracted to Rembrandt, who appeared to reflect a biblical emphasis when he used light to express holiness and divine glory.

The commandment against the making of images meant that, for the Hebrews, there was to be no portrayal of God through sculpture or painting. The Hebrews did not even make visual images in their imagination of God. The images of God which the Hebrews held in their mind were mobile, dynamic, and auditory. This means that their conception of God had to do with God's dynamic qualities.

For example, in Psalm 18 many parts of God's body are described. Surely these references to bodily members are not to be construed as actual descriptions. Rather, they are figurative expressions which describe God's qualities with poetic license. The reference to God's arm refers to his might. His hand signifies power. When it is indicated that God is like a bull, this would describe God's potency or power, not his appearance. God's hand which covered Moses, as described in Exodus 33, is not to be conceived visually, as though God had a huge hand. That would be just as grotesque an image as a visual conception of a woman having a neck like a tower. God's hand appears here as his powerful means of protecting Moses from danger. God does not necessarily possess a human hand.[95]

These Hebrew emphases give us a clue as to the art forms which are most compatible with the biblical worldview. The sermon, music, and drama are surely more basic than static visual forms such as painting and sculpture.

Here also we see the reason why so much theological criticism has been brought against movies such as Cecil B. DeMille's *The Ten Commandments.* In this movie, an attempt is made to visualize God in a way that is contrary to the Hebraic mind. Nothing is left to the imagination. *The Ten Commandments* is an example of a Western mind trying to portray the unique Hebrew type of thinking.

On the other hand, John Killinger's emphasis on dynamic yet controlled spontaneity in worship is congenial with the biblical emphasis. At the Wailing Wall in Jerusalem, the Hebrews never stop moving as they pray. This emphasis is also congenial with the use of consoles to provide lighting, music, and other effects. Perhaps space should be allowed in worship centers for more movement. The tactile emphases in certain art forms also seem appropriate.[96]

Since the sermon and drama have been mentioned as uniquely effective art forms for a biblical worldview, it is interesting to note the way in which the Hebrew speaker used language. He sought to awaken feelings and passions in the listeners. He came to his point immediately and then repeated himself. He used language to challenge listeners to do something in obedience to God's will. For the Hebrew, it is by doing the right thing that we learn the truth. We know God as we keep his commandments.

To achieve his purpose, the Hebrew emphasized description. That is the reason for so many images and comparisons in the Hebrew language. Since the images are not meant to be precise, many are used, and they are piled one upon the other. In contrast, the Greek speaker sought to use logically grounded arguments. His speech was arranged with skillful beauty and architectural style. He emphasized clarity and exactness.[97]

4. The Significance of the Hebrew and Greek Understandings of Time and Space as They Relate to Art Forms

(1) The Greek View of Time and Space. Time for the Greeks is the realm of decay and change and thus the enemy of harmony, symmetry, and perfection. Hebrew thinking moves in *time*, while the Greeks employ *space* as their thought form.

For Plato, time is only a pictorial, moving imitation of immovable and unalterable eternity, which represents perfection. Time is more destructive than constructive. That which exists eternally, such as a geometrical proposition, does not belong to time. The Greek gods in the divine world had to be conceived as exempt from all time and change because time and change were synonymous terms. (This concept has influenced Christian theology. Think, for instance, about the arguments which have gone on for centuries in theological circles over the unchangeableness of God.)[98]

Once again, we see why the Greeks were interested in sculpture and architecture. Through these media they could portray the form which was behind the sensuous and the changing.

There is some similarity between the Greeks and Zen Buddhism in terms of art emphases. The work of the Zen painters does not attempt to represent nature itself, but to express the spiritual essence behind nature. They try to see in a flower or spray of bamboo the eternal which is behind or underlying humanity and nature.[99]

Most people who travel in the Far East are fascinated by the numerous Buddhist statues. I find that many do not understand that Buddha is purposely portrayed in an impersonal or impassive manner in order that the spiritual reality behind the figure might be portrayed.[100]

(2) The Hebrew View of Time and Space. For the Hebrews, God was interested primarily in *time*. He created in time and acted in time. Time for the Hebrews is important because it is a container of God's revealing events. God revealed himself when he acted in time and history. Paul said, "In the fullness of time, God sent Christ."[101]

Paul Tillich sees Abraham as the archetypal Jew who was called into a redemptive time emphasis away from a bondage to cultic space in Ur of Chaldees. The true purpose of the Jews, according to Tillich, is to scatter out over the pagan world as people of ethical and religious conviction and mission in time. They are not to be comfortable in pagan space. They are primarily a people of time, not of space. Time implies direction and purpose and something new.[102]

The Hebrews gave special attention to the peculiarity of events—and what is time but the stream of events. The Greeks developed definite verb forms which could express the distinction between past, present, and future. The Hebrews did not. In fact, the Indo-Germanic framework of three time spheres (past, present, and future) is quite foreign to the Hebrew notion of tense. (The Indo-Germanic view of time was developed in Western Europe from Greek, Roman, Germanic, and other sources.) We are accustomed to saying, for example, that the future lies "before" us and the past lies "behind" us, when it is clear that time neither lies nor stands, but goes, comes, and becomes. To follow the Hebrew conception, we should say, "the future is coming" rather than "lies before us." Time is not some kind of abstract measure which has to be filled. Rather time is identical with the occurrence that fills it.[103]

Sören Kierkegaard has recovered for us the essentially Hebraic idea that to be a true Christian means to leap across and forget the centuries in order to become contemporaneous with Jesus and his disciples and then in that situation make a decision for Christ as the Son of God. The Hebrews have made a great contribution to the understanding of history because they can experience contemporaneity with the action under discussion. This gives us some clue as to why the reenactment of the Passover has been so meaningful to the Hebrews through the centuries.[104]

(3) The Hebrew View of Boundaries and Its Implications. It is characteristic of the Hebrews that form was an indifferent matter for them to the extent that they did not emphasize *outline* or *contour*. The Israelites were interested primarily in the *content* of the shape, not in the outline or form of the shape. In their view, the beauty of human appearance is not in the form of the body or part of the body but in the peculiar properties which appearance betrays in various ways. Apocryphal stories say that the apostle Paul was quite ugly and unharmonious in his physical appearance. This would have constituted no great difficulty for the Hebrews. But for the Greeks, such as we find at Corinth, a person of harmonious and symmetrical speech and appearance such as Apollos would be more attractive to the people.

Ordinarily when we draw a tree trunk, we first of all draw an outline. In contrast, the Israelites tended to experience objects in terms of color and shadow, texture and temperature; they were not particularly concerned with the contours. Therefore, they did not employ words to express this notion.[105]

Boman suggests that the Hebrews probably had something that is quite significant for philosophy in their ability to dispense with boundaries. Some of the greatest philosophical problems with which the Western mind is faced are related to the problem of the boundaries of time and space.[106]

It is quite significant that Einstein, who gave us the great breakthrough in the relativity of time and space, was a Jew. It is also significant that Karl Marx, who had Jewish roots, gave us a breakthrough in formal economics, and Sigmund Freud, who was of Jewish background, gave us a breakthrough in formal psychology. Their thinking ignored the boundaries of their disciplines and opened the way for creative new synthesis.

(4) The Implications of the Hebrew View of Time and Space for Architecture, Drama, and Painting. In relation to architecture, the Hebraic approach would mean that a biblically oriented artist would not be too concerned with the straight line which is rationally perfect. Actually our experience of God's providence and grace is not symbolized by a straight line. A straight line may be good to symbolize a factory but does not necessarily express the deepest and truest

facets of our biblical tradition. An experience of God's grace actually involves a world where there are not always straight lines, in the sense of everything's being rational or deductively logical.[107]

Some contemporary churches are seeking to portray a new dynamic use of space in the realm of architecture. The Church of the Holy Whale, the First Presbyterian Church at Stamford, Connecticut, has done this by a new "creased paper" method of concrete construction which assumes irregular or jagged shapes.

The famous chapel designed by L. E. Corbusier at Ronchamps in France also captures many of the new dynamic developments in architectural design. This building is extremely "irrational" in design and profoundly impressive and compelling in its impact. It has been suggested that this building is a reflection of the irregularity and mysterious character of man's psychic and religious life. Discontinuity, the possibility of revelation, the unexpected grace of God, inexplicable providence, and elusive mystery are all incarnate in this building.[108]

It is only fair to remember that the Greeks not only used verticals and horizontals in the Parthenon, but slightly curved lines to express energy. Nevertheless, the Greek influence on architecture emphasized the idealized type. The Greek temples were not copies of anything in nature, but they exhibit the balance, symmetry, and proportion which the Greek mind abstracted from nature.

Insofar as it had this Greek emphasis on balance and proportion, there is a relationship between Gothic architecture and Greek thinking. Similarly, in literature, the great poet Dante echoed the Greek emphasis upon form.

Undoubtedly, our architecture should symbolize our theological perspective. We must not organize space falsely or tell a lie about our convictions. The architecture of the churches says more to the public world and to ourselves about the theology of a church and its mission than we realize. With informed architects and clergy and lay leadership, remarkable results can be achieved. The new materials, light and color possibilities, and better theological identity afford exciting possibilities.

Expressionism in drama and literature and other arts is also relevant in this connection. The Expressionists or Post-Impressionists were artists who wanted to do more than contemplate the surface of things. They wanted to look within their characters, treat them subjectively, tap their streams of consciousness if need be, and penetrate into their innermost beings.[109]

And I think we can also see that Expressionism as a type of painting has relevance in this connection. In Van Gogh's painting, violent colors, crude forms, and restless rhythms reveal man's inner life. Painters such as Gauguin turned back to older, primitive and more exotic forms in order to find a medium of expressing the inner dynamic forces of reality.

(5) The Greek and Hebrew Views of the Eternal World and "This" World. According to Plato, human beings achieve their highest when they absorb and realize in themselves as much of the eternal world as possible. According to the Bible, however, human beings achieve their highest when they repent and

are restored as they were at creation. Here is an exceedingly important point for those seeking to live according to the biblical worldview.[110]

The context of Greek thought and of much Christian thought which follows Greek thought is the "upward and downward" emphasis. The salvation principle is that of ascent to union with God. Mystical union is the end result of the religious discipline—not understanding or necessarily redemptive action.[111] This is the context within which most of our ecclesiastical symbols have acquired their form and definition. It is foolish for persons seeking to follow the biblical pattern to even discuss the place of symbolism as long as we allow this "upward and downward" context to remain unchallenged.[112]

As over against this Greek "upward and downward" motif, the motif of the Bible is that of "journey and return" after the redemptive pattern of the Prodigal Son. It is the context of human revolt against God, of God's redemptive love plan, and of human response and return.[113]

Instead of mystical withdrawal into other-worldly absorption, the biblical movement is one of redemptive experience with God in the context of history. In the Bible the purpose of the great religious experiences was not just seeking a mystical union with God, but also securing a knowledge of one's vocation. This is true in the experience of Moses, Isaiah, Jeremiah, and Paul. This experience always ended with an emphasis on "send," "go," and "do." It was God's way of turning a person around in his tracks and confronting him with his job.[114]

If God revealed himself to the nation Israel through actions by which he leads the people of Israel consciously toward a purpose, the life of humanity must have a final great end in which God's highest thoughts and purposes are to be worked out. Hence, in the framework of Hebrew thought, eschatology is just as necessary a conclusion as immutable eternity is for the Greeks. The biblical worldview emphasizes philosophy of history and purpose and renews the dimension of eschatology. The world had a beginning and will have an end. Humanity will reach a goal.

Whereas the Greek spatial concept emphasizes the "beyond," the Hebrew time emphasis tells of the end of history. In fact, Karl Marx unwittingly revealed his Jewish heritage in his emphasis upon philosophy of history. In fact, much of that which is powerful in Marxism has been adapted from the Hebrew-Christian philosophy.[115]

One corollary of this Hebrew emphasis is that negation of this world and withdrawal, which are sometimes identified with religion, are to be shunned. Rather, it is a biblical principle that we are to engage in a positive calling to create, under God, as God creates and to form on the finite level as God forms infinitely. In fact, in the biblical pattern guilt arises from not creating or from willing against one's calling or creating outside the context of grace and God's Lordship.

5. The Biblical View of Tragedy

It should also be noted that the biblical view is different from the tragic view of life. The tragic authors hold that human frustration is the ultimate law of life, whether due to the jealousy of the god as in some Greek drama or to a built-in metaphysical necessity as in Schopenhauer.

The Bible, however, holds that it is rebellion and idolatry rather than an inscrutable fate which is responsible for human catastrophe. According to the tragic view, the downfall of human greatness is inevitable, built into the nature of the universe, but the Bible insists that it is due to man's rebellion against God and misplaced allegiance. The human situation is actually more tragic for being avoidable. Not only does the Bible hold human beings responsible for their fate, but it says evil can be transmuted into good.[116]

It is important to note that much modern drama—like much drama over the centuries—is a representation of the ancient Greek tragedies. As Emil Brunner has pointed out, however, it is not by chance that a Christian tragedy does not exist. Christian faith and the tragic understanding of life are irreconcilable.[117]

6. Summary: The Importance of the Hebrew Way of Thinking for an Approach to Art and Culture

It is hoped that what has been said does not imply that we have ignored general revelation or common grace. The reason which we can establish in mathematics, logic, or in the physical world does intimate a divine wisdom in the background, and thus the Greeks had a partial and important insight in their observations. But it is readily seen that such a general revelation is inadequate for the fullest understanding of the nature of a personal God and our relation to him. This understanding could only come when the personal God chose to act and speak in the context of time and history and when a person sympathetically participates in response to these events.

Surely both the Hebrews and the Greeks as well as the Romans have made magnificent contributions to our Western civilization. We are grateful for these contributions. We will always have somewhat of a synthesis between them, following the example of such great thinkers as Augustine and Kant. But there are large segments of reality not to be grasped by formal, logical thinking. This area, which is more related to time than space, is the realm of religion and morals whose locale is most prominently in the innermost depths of man. It is Faith (Revelation) and Reason—not Reason and then Faith (Revelation). A thrilling challenge of our time is the task of pointing out the implications of the biblical worldview for the dynamic areas of contemporary art forms and culture and for personal and corporate Christian living.[118]

IV. What Are the Contributions the Arts Can Make to Christianity and Christian People? (Why Christianity Needs the Arts.)

As we have noted, art is universal. As far as we can discover, all of the peoples of the earth are involved in some type of art, such as music, poetry, role-playing, sculpture, or painting.[119]

Through the ages, philosophers and theologians have attempted to explain the human urge to participate in artistic creativity and the human love of the various art forms. There are at least three classic answers to the question of the meaning of art:

- Art is a form of creating, making, or constructing.
- Art affords pleasure, satisfaction, and joy.
- Art is a distinctive form of expression or communication.

Each of these meanings suggests contributions that the arts can make to Christianity.

1. The Importance and Possibility of Bringing Order and Renewal to the Chaos and Boredom of Life

(1) The Importance of Order. Human beings are born into a chaos of impressions and experiences. To live constructively, we must cope with this chaos through some type of orientation.

Artists are more than imitators or expressers of emotion. They construct material into structured or ordered form. An art form is fundamentally a structure with its own independent existence and value. From one perspective, an artist is a person who sees chaos, but in some way makes sense out of it.

Although biography is not creative art in the strict sense, it illustrates the deep appeal exerted by form when imposed upon experience. Contemporary biography helps to illustrate how literary artists bring order to a chaos of events. Older types of biography tended to stick to facts more than seek out key ideas in a life to portray the meaning of that life. The so-called new biography—taking its cue from the novel and drama—searches for the pivotal clues that establish a true (or more authentic) portrait. (A good portrait painter or photographer does the same.) Interestingly, John follows this "newer" technique in his Gospel.[120]

(2) The Importance of Renewal. The artist helps to renew life. We need a world that is constantly renewed, for yesterday's wonderful tends to become today's commonplace. In the words of Whitehead, "the freshness of being evaporates under mere repetition."[121]

It has been suggested that the first requirement for an artist is that he or she be a pioneer. Sallie TeSelle, professor at Vanderbilt Divinity School, sees the artist as one who awakens our faculties of perception and helps us see what we have not seen before. Thomas Moran did that for the West and the Yellowstone Park area. Karl Barth suggests that the music of Mozart helps us understand the goodness of creation. More recently, the film, *Chariots of Fire,* was helpful to many of us because of its visual and musical freshness, as well as its boldness in presenting a fair presentation of an authentic Christian in a major motion picture.

Post-Impressionist art, such as that of Van Gogh, helps us to see beneath the surface of nature. Surrealism, introduced in the early part of the twentieth century, helps us to realize that we are more than rational persons, and that the subconscious is very important in our lives. And even Pop Art, the 1960s phenomenon that involved the realistic representation of soup cans, adhesive bandages, and other relics of everyday life, was a fresh reaction against abstract art; it called us to come back again to the concreteness of life.

2. Art as a Source of Pleasure and Joy

In recent years the artistic world has been confronting us with a so-called "new aesthetics" or theory of beauty. The new aesthetics wants to leave the categories of meaning and hope to others. The artist says, "I want to put an emphasis on the sensuous surface and sound of things: the fantastic colors of psychedelic experience, the fresh voices of electronic music and light shows."[122]

Christians may well have problems with this perspective if this is all there is to art. But the artist's emphasis on the inherent worth of nonpragmatic pleasure and joy has helped Christians to examine or reexamine their own resources in this regard.

Jürgen Moltmann suggests, for example, that God created the world as a playground for his pleasure, and he made human beings for the specific purpose of glorifying God and enjoying him and his creation forever. It was God's good pleasure for his Son to become human in order to redeem and restore us to God's favor and fellowship. Since the Cross and the Resurrection, Christians have special reasons for joy and celebration.[123]

As early as 1950, E. J. Carnell of Fuller Seminary was speaking out for the constructive possibilities of television as a medium of relaxation and pleasure. Human nature craves fun and laughter, and television can help provide that dimension to human life.

The Christian community is ideally a place of joy, happiness, and celebration, as well as a place for evangelism, education, and Christian social-ethical activities. Within the Christian perspective, there is a legitimate place for leisure, relaxation, and entertainment. Even theology can be seen as an art form, especially in terms of the great theological systems which have been developed by Henry, Barth, Tillich, and others.[124] Many theologians, as well as laypersons, find joy and pleasure in their study of the harmony, order, and insights found in significant theological systems.

Through the centuries, many have seen human worth in terms of what human beings produce. It is true that the vocation of a worker is one part of humankind's God-ordained purpose and dignity, and John Calvin's contention that we should glorify God through our work is an appropriate one. Martin Luther, however, emphasized another dimension. Human beings are not just what they produce. Christian persons find their deepest sense of worth in the fact that God loves them and Christ has died for them. They are accepted and loved as they are. Christians therefore have reason to be joyful. Their religion is not just an opiate to compensate for unbearable conditions, but a true source of joy. And that joy is for now, as well as the future. It is true that we anticipate the joy of heaven. But we can also have joy and festivity in the present.[125]

3. The Arts as a Source of Rest and Re-Creation

The concept of rest is an idea closely related to the biblical idea of the quiet of the Sabbath. All work, manual or mental, tends to produce a certain amount of tension in life. It is important, therefore, to balance our work with rest.

As we move further into the technological age, we feel in a new way the necessity of art as a form of rest in our lives. Art forms seem especially helpful to urban people who do not live in immediate touch with the relaxing perspective that comes by being close to nature. Noteworthy are the crowds thronging museums on Sunday afternoons in urban centers. For these people, art has become a means of re-creation and rest.[126]

At least some types of art can spiritualize the physical and sensualize the spiritual. For example, sexuality without spirituality is little more than animal life. A book on poetry by Professor McGill of Princeton is entitled, *Celebration of the Sensual*. Here the word *sensual* does not relate to sexual life in particular, but refers to attempts to spiritualize or give perspective on the concrete stuff of life. Here again, art forms bring re-creation and new meaning to what could be humdrum lives.

4. The Arts as a Means of Raising the Ultimate Questions to Which the Biblical Faith Speaks

In the contemporary secular world, artists force people to stop and ask, "Who am I, what is my destiny, what is my purpose?" French writer Denis de Rougemont suggests that art forms are "calculated traps to force us to meditate." Paul Tillich and Nathan Scott, professor at the University of Virginia, see art forms, especially literature and certain types of visual arts, as asking the questions of human existence that the Christian faith is prepared to answer.[127]

Many art forms fall into this category. In recent years I have seen a number of plays and movies which forced me to consider certain basic questions. The play, *Agnes of God*, raised the problem of innocence and responsibility. *Amadeus* raised the question of the justice of a God who gives talent to a person whose personal life is disordered and profane. The movie, *Witness*, which deals with the Amish people, raises the problem of technology and what it is doing to the human spirit.

These contemporary works are in a tradition of modern literature which has forced people to face such problems as guilt (Albert Camus, *The Fall, The Plague*), isolation (Franz Kafka, *The Castle*), original sin (William Golding, *The Lord of the Flies*), and the meaning of success (Arthur Miller, *The Death of a Salesman*).

In some cases, the arts spell out in dramatic fashion the full implications of what it means to live in a world without God. If a young person wants to know the full implications of atheism, for instance, let him or her study Sartre's *No Exit* or *Nausea*, with their statement "Hell is other people"![128]

Some scholars suggest that the Theater of the Absurd, dominated by such playwrights as Samuel Beckett, Eugene Ionesco, and Harold Pinter, also shows us the full implications of life without God. Human actions are seen as irrational and senseless. Communication is no longer possible. In his play, *The Lesson*, Ionesco shows the absurdity of language. Pinter, in *Homecoming*, shows the breakdown of the institution of marriage. Francis Schaeffer suggests that such stark views may prepare some people to look again at the Christian vision.[129] Others see some forms of absurd theater, such as *Waiting for Godot*, as having considerable positive value in itself. In any case, the absurd dramatists shock us out of our complacency.[130]

A number of contemporary artists have made us realize that the most basic question now being raised is, "Does life have any meaning at all—now or ever?" In my book, *Christianity and Contemporary Art Forms*, I have described this as hunger art. There is always a possibility of an opening for more constructive approaches to life as humanity realizes the emptiness of life without God.[131]

5. Art Forms as Revealers of Christian Distortions and Inconsistencies

Art forms, especially literature and drama, are often effective instruments to point out how Christian practice distorts the Christian ideal and is inconsistent with the avowed Christian faith.

The use of satire and irony, for example, is often quite effective in exposing the dismal asceticism and cult of ugliness in some religious circles. George Bernard Shaw did this in earlier years in England. In other cases, the social immoralities of caste and irresponsible wealth, as sanctioned by religion, are held up for examination. Who can forget Sinclair Lewis' exposure of fraud in evangelism in *Elmer Gantry*?

It is true that some modern agnostic writers ridicule restricted views of Christianity which religious leaders themselves are opposing. It is also true that some attacks on Christian patterns of life may be rooted in positivist, hedonist or Marxist presuppositions. There are, however, many artistic indictments of religion which direct themselves not at the Christian faith itself but at its distortions and betrayals.

The great American novelist William Faulkner, for example, sees and exposes some of these distortions. With a gift for satire and the grotesque, Faulkner scrutinizes the practices of fossilized Southern religion. The whole fable of Faulkner's *The Sound and the Fury* points toward a healthful order of values which has been violated. This kind of diagnosis of religion and culture is far more searching and illuminating than is possible in traditional theological discussions.[132]

6. The Arts as Facilitators of Christian Communication

Communicating the Christian faith calls for far more than mental assent to an intellectual body of doctrine. It is centered around a person, Jesus Christ, and a relationship to a person involves the emotions and will as well as the mind. For Christian communication to be effective, therefore, it needs to awaken people to their need of Christ. Then there must be the presentation in an appealing manner, either directly or indirectly, of the Christian faith. Artists who specialize in reaching people through their senses as well as their minds can teach Christians a great deal concerning dynamic, concrete, and symbolic communication.

An art form such as drama, through dramatic conflict, can arouse and provoke an audience to deep emotional levels. Sören Kierkegaard, a genuine literary artist as well as a philosopher, used a variety of indirect literary devices such as paradox, irony and dialectic to stir, provoke, and arouse his readers. T. S. Eliot used dramatic conflict in *The Cocktail Party* to help secular audiences discover for themselves their emptiness and need of spiritual help. Flannery O'Connor, the significant Christian writer from Georgia, used a similar approach in many of her stories.[133]

In the same *The Sound and the Fury* mentioned above, William Faulkner presents some of the positive resources of the Christian faith. This is done through an account of a church service in the last section of the book, especially in the sermon of the black preacher from St. Louis. Here Faulkner sets forth the life-giving mystery and the perennial vigor of the Christian faith among the poor in spirit, contrasting this against the way religion is used by some of the more affluent. (Faulkner's techniques remind us again that effective art forms in the twentieth century must be realistic, expressionistic, and utilize the best technical methods.)

Of course, the literary arts are not the only possible vehicles for authentic Christian communication. Music has great emotional power. Few sermons or doctrinal presentation have the power to describe the sorrow and joy of the crucifixion and resurrection as well as music. This is one reason why music is still so important in portraying the message of the Book of Revelation. Recently I was in a meeting where my brother Russell Newport sang "The Holy City," by Gaul, and I realized anew that music communicates the Christian message in unsurpassable power.

In the area of preaching, the classic means of Christian communication, ministers are now learning to wrap biblical truth in story and story form. This development is closely related to the emphasis on narrative theology and the metaphoric mode described in chapter 3.

Evangelical groups have come to power and influence in American religious life. This means that they have the responsibility to understand and create and utilize new and constructive art forms. The power and value of the arts call for conservative Christian people to give up their fear of the arts. (These groups are especially impoverished in regard to the visual arts.)

We also need to develop an appropriate theology of architecture. More flexibility is possible with new materials and methods of construction. Buildings can be erected which express the theology of the particular church and which identify with the area where the church is located. Appropriate forms of sculpture can be used even in evangelical churches. (I tried to express this possibility in an address I made in Alexandria, Louisiana, at the dedication of a large, semiabstract sculpture entitled "Angels.") Banners can add color and festivity. Visual symbols can be used in ways which do not violate biblical guidelines.

7. The Arts as Helpers for Understanding and Interpreting the Bible

Devout biblical scholars are emphasizing that the Bible's meaning and purpose can be impaired or misconstrued if it is taken in a mechanically literal way or if the dramatic parts are not taken seriously. Martin Luther was aware of this, too; he urged the young people of his time to study literature, drama, and poetry as an aid to a proper understanding of the Bible.[134]

In the case of the Book of Revelation, for example, perceptive interpreters and devout literary scholars affirm that failure to see the Book in its historical context and as a literary whole has resulted in a literalistic distortion of the book. They say we should learn to appreciate Revelation as an inspired book of artistic images and aesthetic visions full of wonder, judgment, truth, and hope. For example, behind the vision of Christ coming on a white horse in Revelation 19, we catch the significant truth that there will be ultimate victory and that Christ's presence in power will inaugurate the last great stage of his kingdom.[135]

In my commentary on the Book of Revelation, *The Lion and the Lamb*, I devote thirty-five pages to the importance of the artistic and literary background of Revelation. To see the biblical books as literature does *not* contradict the idea that the literary visions are inseparably connected with God's past actions in history and his promised actions in the future.[136]

In a similar vein, Randolph Klassen suggests that Genesis 1 was intended by the Spirit of God to be read or sung by believers in adoring tribute to the wonderful Creator. To force Genesis 1 into categories of technical scientific precision is like trying to interpret Rembrandt's *Night Watch* by a chemical analysis of the oil paint.

Artists can help us appreciate the beauty of the Song of Solomon, the poetry of the prophets, and the magnificent art in Ezekiel's vision. And I wonder if we have fully appreciated the drama of Job and the satire of Jonah. In the New Testament, we are coming to appreciate even more the drama of Mark and the artistry of John's Gospel.

As suggested in an earlier chapter, Roland Frye sees in John Calvin's doctrine of accommodation a helpful approach to the Bible for the conservative mind. Frye understands Calvin as suggesting that it was a part of God's wisdom that he raised up people who told the story of God's redemptive work in history in a way "sufficiently dramatic" to catch the attention of people in every succeeding generation. Technical reports would have attracted little attention beyond a restricted circle of specialists. The Bible is faithful to events and to its redemptive purpose, but it is given to us in dramatic form so that its message can reach a wide audience and convey an indelible impression.[137]

8. The Importance of Christians' Encouraging Art and Media Education and Criticism and Art Exposure and Experience

Obviously, art is both subjective and objective. And not all art is acceptable from a Christian perspective. But in light of the above arguments, Christians can benefit from exposure to the arts and use of the arts.

This may not come naturally, especially for those who have shied away from the arts in the past. But artistic perception, ability, and appreciation can be developed. In painting, we can learn of color, form, and balance. Although art appreciation is a highly individual pursuit, there are nevertheless standards of meaning, truth and greatness. (For Nicholas Wolterstorff, a work of art has merit if it is unified in character, is internally rich, and has intensity.)[138]

V. What Are the Possible Contributions the Christian Perspective Can Make to the Arts? (Why the Arts Need Christianity.)

1. A Dynamic Theological and Philosophical Backdrop for Artistic Creations and Life in General

It is the Christian contention that the biblical worldview can provide rich soil for the production of dynamic art forms. The biblical vision states that human beings, including artists, have a vocation and are to be subcreators under God.[139]

The following are some aspects of the biblical vision that can help provide a rich background for artistic creation:

(1) The Biblical Emphasis on the Goodness of Physical Creation. Many worldviews devalue the physical side of God's creation. This devaluation has taken the vague and curious form, so characteristic of American culture, that "spiritual values" are more desirable than "material values."

Every such form of devaluation flies in the face of God's affirmation of his creation. The sheer physicality or materiality of something is never a legitimate ground for assigning to it a lower value in our lives. The important concern is the manner in which the physical or material is used.

So the artist who sees life and reality as a Christian will not despise the creation in which he finds himself or herself. He will not see it as something from which to be liberated. And though the artist may on occasion produce highly intellectual, even perhaps conceptual, art, he will not do so because he wants to free himself from the constrictions of his materials. Instead, he will see the world as a storehouse of materials out of which he can select to do his work. He will think of those materials as something whose potentials are to be realized rather than as something constricting the scope of his own self-expression.[140]

One's attitude toward the physical also incorporates an attitude toward oneself. We are not angels hovering lightly over the earth. A denigration or downplaying of the physical implies denigration of oneself. Correspondingly, any denigration of art on account of its physicality is a form of self-denigration. To denigrate the ballet, for example, because it so intimately involves the body, is to denigrate a whole dimension of oneself.[141]

Earthly existence is one of God's favors to us. When the Christian affirms the goodness of the physical creation, he is not just praising its magnificence. He is saying that the physical creation is good for human beings, that it serves human fulfillment. Earth is humankind's present home, the world our present dwelling place. This view is good soil for art.[142] However, even though the Bible affirms the goodness of the physical, it never implies that the physical is all there is to life, which is an assumption of much contemporary art.

(2) The Biblical Emphasis on the Incarnation. Although a Christian aesthetics or theory of beauty, from a theological perspective, is concerned with the arts relating to portraying God's good creation, humanity made in the image of God, the Fall, and redemption, it finds its center of gravity in the doctrine of the Incarnation. The material earth not only comes from the hand of God, but is radiant with God's presence. This means that philosophical idealism, which plays down the material earth, is not possible for the artist, a fact which Plato recognized.

It is essential to any artist that he or she be free to find meaning and expression in the material world. The Christian artist goes further in seeing that the physical and the material were also judged worthy to contain Jesus Christ. The material world is thus radiant with both the glory of the creation and the new creation that proceeds from the Incarnation.[143]

The biblical worldview thus undergirds all art that seeks to probe into the reality of God's creation. Naturalism and Expressionism can teach us much about the earth. Cubism, abstract art, and action painting (painting done in dynamic manner without formal patterns) can reveal the creative power of humanity made in the image of God. Expressionists can reveal man's alienation, cruelty, and despair. But in the Incarnation there is the additional insight that undergirds a holy naturalism.[144]

Although there are relatively few explicit Christian artists of prominence, there are some who set forth facets of biblical perspective in implicit or veiled terms. For example, within the last few decades in the area of literature and drama, one can think of Graham Greene, T. S. Eliot, Christopher Fry, and Walker Percy. More explicit or open Christian artists include Charles Williams, Alan Paton, C. S. Lewis, François Mauriac, Dorothy Sayers, Philip Turner, and Flannery O'Connor. William F. Lynch calls for the Christian doctrine of the Incarnation to be taken as the fundamental model for literary imagination.[145]

(3) The Biblical Emphasis on the Importance of Vocation Under God's Authority. The Bible affirms humankind as having a responsible vocation under the guidance and authority of God. We are to subdue the natural world for the sake of human livelihood and delight and also for the sake of honoring God.

This vocation applies to the artist. The artist takes a blob of clay and shapes it into a vase that is a thing of beauty and delight. He takes a disorderly array of pigments and a piece of canvas and orders them into a painting richly intense in color and evocative of some aspect of God's creation. The artist, when he brings forth order for human benefit or divine honor, shares in man's vocation to master and subdue the earth.[146]

But there is more to human responsibility than responsibility with respect to nature. We have responsibilities with respect to each other: We are to love our neighbor as ourselves. This presupposes that each is to love himself. To neglect becoming what one can become, to squander one's life instead of nourishing one's potential—that is to fail in one's responsibility to God. Each of us is to seek his or her own fulfillment. But equally, each is to exhibit solidarity with the other. We are to stand in our neighbors' stead, to love them as they love themselves and to seek their fulfillment as they seek their own. Indeed, in seeking the welfare of others, we will find our own welfare. This calling also applies to the artist as a person.[147]

Another phase of human responsibility and vocation calls for us to acknowledge and praise God. Once again, the artist is to share in this human responsibility to honor God with images of glory and songs of thanksgiving.

Art plays and is meant to play an enormous diversity of roles in human life. Works of art are instruments by which we praise our great men and women, express our grief, evoke emotion, and communicate knowledge. Works of art are the objects of actions—such as contemplation for the sake of delight. Works of art can be accompaniments for everyday actions such as rocking infants or background for eating meals.[148]

It is at this point that the Christian conception of the artist differs most sharply from that of post-Enlightenment Western secular society. The Christian sees the artist as a responsible agent before God who shares in our human vocation. Western secular society sees the artist as freed from all responsibility—an exceptional person who struggles simply to express himself or herself in untrammeled freedom. Indeed, it is often suggested that an artist who so much as thinks in terms of responsibility will be stifled in terms of the flow of creativity.[149]

(4) The Biblical Emphasis on the Enjoyment of God and His Creation. In addition to the emphasis on responsible action as a human vocation, delight or enjoyment is an important emphasis. This joy or delight comes in a multiplicity of forms, among them the joy of aesthetic satisfaction. Aesthetic joy is not the only form of joy worth man's pursuit, but it is a valid form of joy. For the artist, in particular, there is the additional joy which he experiences in creating his work.[150]

(5) The Biblical Emphasis on Redemption and Renewal. The Christian worldview, however, speaks of more than creation. It also speaks of redemption. Admittedly, there are those who perceive the message of the Christian gospel as the message of escape from our creaturely earthly existence. But the Christian drama tells of the renewal of human existence. This means that humanity may attain fulfillment both in the present and in the future. Artists are called to be God's agents in this cause of renewal. This means that art thus gains new significance. Art can serve as an instrument in our struggle to overcome the fallenness of our existence, while also affording us delight, which anticipates the kingdom beyond.[151]

(6) The Biblical Provision of Metaphysical and Spiritual Depth for Art. Behind the surface of the Christian drama is theological and metaphysical depth, realism and underlying purpose. There is a total vision of both beauty and ugliness and possible redemption. For example, there is beauty in Jesus on the cross from the eternal perspective. In fact, from the Christian view, the cross is a way of spiritual accomplishment and a prelude to resurrection and renewal.

The Christian is convinced that profound artistic life will wither in societies which have a reduced spiritual and metaphysical depth. In such societies, art tends to degenerate into mere cleverness and virtuosity which cannot move the heart. Grand passions originate from spiritual depth and tensions, and the biblical worldview can provide that kind of depth in society.

2. A Crystallization, Historicization, and Fulfillment of Fundamental Archetypes or Universal Myths

The Christian view would accept the fact that, by common grace, all people have spiritual longings and create religious myths. There is truth in the Jungian view which identifies these "archetypes" as fundamental and universal symbolic patterns latent in all people. Religious phenomenologists such as Mircea Eliade have discovered these motifs in both primitive and sophisticated societies. Such images as creation, a fall, a hero figure, a dying and rising god, the demonic, yearning for paradise, rebirth, and resurrection are in all people's mythic consciousness.

It is the Christian contention that these mythical longings and images are crystallized, historicized, and fulfilled in the biblical view. Around Christ, these images are reconstituted in a powerful way as the Incarnation, the Messiah, the New Covenant, the Word, the Cross, and the Kingdom. These master images, as transformed by Christ and the Bible, afford artists dynamic and balanced themes of universal interest and power.[152]

3. The Challenge of Rigorous Christian Evaluation and Discrimination

(1) The Need for Evaluation. Christians will grant the importance of form as opposed to content in a work of art. A film, for example, should be assessed on the quality of its script, casting, action, location, camera work, color, sound, editing, and dramatic performances. Such stylistic analysis is important to advancing the art of the cinema.

Christians contend, however, that art forms are never neutral. Films, for example, grip the imagination, portray a worldview, and create certain emotions. There is more than just the aesthetic experience in encountering art forms; they reflect world visions or views. Amos Wilder and Jacques Maritain suggest that all imaginative creations offer particular views of reality. Accordingly, Christians hold that a film, a drama, or any work of art can and should be assessed on the relative truth or falsity of its overall theological or philosophical statement as well as on its form.[153]

Unlike the nineteenth-century poet and critic Matthew Arnold, Christians do not see artists as priests and art galleries as worship centers. They do admit that artists have power, however, and that therefore the views of artists are especially important. For this reason, artistic worldviews need to be analyzed and the implications brought out in the open. Amos Wilder calls such analysis a "testing of the spirits."[154]

(2) The Importance of the Evaluation of Influential Art Forms. Almost any kind of art form is open to responsible Christian evaluation—for example,

church music. Scotty Gray, professor of church music at Southwestern Seminary, maintains that there is a disappointing emphasis on the superficial, on immediacy, and on passivity in much contemporary church music. This type of music contributes little to understanding and living the Christian faith, and may even give a very distorted concept of what is involved in Christian discipleship.

Gray believes, however, that there are unprecedented possibilities to be realized by thoughtful and diligent people who are willing to be informed and take the lead in realizing the deeper potentials in music in the church. Don Hustad calls for a balance between the physical, intellectual, and emotional elements in church music, as well as genuine creativity.

The vast field of secular literature is even more needful of careful evaluation from a Christian point of view—especially the tragic stream of exploitive and sexual writing that began in the eighteenth century with the work of Marquis de Sade. Even today, de Sade is a spokesperson of a subculture which wants freedom for sex to operate without moral and social controls. This type of person wants this sensual subculture to become the dominant culture. Every character who passes through the pages of de Sade's works either defiles someone else or is defiled. No one ever loves, and no one lives outside the categories of lust, murder, or theft. De Sade broke with the moral consensus of the Judeo-Christian tradition and introduced a literary tradition of erotic cruelty and perverse admiration of crime.[155]

Some would place the American author, Norman Mailer, in this same stream. One of Mailer's books, *An American Dream*, has as its theme murder and sex and the virility and excitement which come from the combination of both. Edmund Fuller suggests that Mailer has helped to revive the "whorehouse" mystique. The brothel is seen as woman's true vocation and as man's true haven. In Mailer's books, women are not people, but objects.[156]

Violence, death, sexual murder, and numerous other sexual perversions are celebrated with intensity in William Burroughs's *The Naked Lunch*—not to mention heroin, morphine, LSD, and any other drug available. The deliberate hanging of naked youths to cause them to have sexual emissions is one of the main themes of this highly lauded novel.[157]

These are only a few examples of the powerful and ideologically influential books which represent the theme of absolute liberty to describe and even to celebrate any perverse sexual experience. According to these writers, a person has a right to his or her perversions and should seek to widen the range of possible experiences. Some observers, such as Leslie Paul, suggest that the continuation of this trend will tend to undercut the Judeo-Christian consensus, which has been so important in our culture. In such circumstances, responsible Christian evaluation is urgently needed.[158]

Of course, we should be careful in discriminating between authentic artists and cheap purveyors of sleaze. However, even true artists are capable of holding irresponsible worldviews and are not immune to evaluation from the point of view of content. Ultimate issues are at stake. The very power of art forms calls for a rigorous Christian discrimination at every level.

Both the professional theologian and Christian layperson should feel an obligation to evaluate art forms in terms of biblical criteria. It is to be hoped, of course, that such will be an informed evaluation. Christians should view films, for example, with a solid grasp of what human nature is and what truth is. Great caution and theological sensitivity are needed.

(3) The Urgency of Christian Evaluation of Mass Media. William F. Fore, a prominent leader in the field of Christian communication, affirms that increasingly the mass media, which are different from other art forms in terms of their group creation and mass appeal, provide the myths, symbols, and images for the majority of American people. These myths tell us who we are and what we should do. They tell us who has power and what is right and permissible.[159]

This is not to say that the media are all bad. We have already noted relaxation as a positive contribution of the media; education, in the form of news programs and documentaries, is another. We can still suggest, however, that the media provide a kind of religious framework for many people—a system of values and belief. They establish many of the myths which we uncritically assume as given in our lives. Marshall McLuhan identifies these myths as an invisible but nevertheless manipulative environment.

Much of the media's influence is exerted through the seven million advertising messages that go out each day. Gregor Goethals, a well-known writer in the field of communication theory, points out that the power of commercial television is to indoctrinate us into a public system of symbols. (Whoever had the image of people ecstatically soaping up in their showers before the commercials showed us the exhilaration of being clean?) If we do not critically evaluate the symbols of American television, we constantly risk the danger of becoming prisoners of illusion.[160]

But the content of the programming needs to be evaluated along with the commercial messages. What about the soap operas—those addictive blends of lust, treachery, and melodrama? Most soap operas portray wrong glamorously, and the characters are nearly all unhappy. Even prime-time television (many of whom are also billed as "soaps") are heavy with irresponsible sex, exploitive violence, lying, cheating, and stealing.

An example of the values imparted by the mass media is the belief that material happiness is the chief end of life and that immediate gratification of wants is crucial. As a result of this basic value, authentic sexuality is often transformed into sex appeal, and the value of self-respect into pride. Authentic will-to-live is made into will-to-power. Recreation is changed into competition. Rest is made into escape.

It should be obvious that the authentic Christian tradition stands opposed to most of the values created by the media world or at least reflected by this world. Instead of power over individuals, the Bible calls for justice and righteousness, kindness and humility (Amos 3, Mic. 6). Instead of power over nature to consume and waste, Genesis 1–3 tells us to guide and transform nature in harmony with the whole of creation—for God's glory and man's good. Over against narcissism (self-love), immediate gratification and creature comforts are the words of Jesus: Leave self behind, and take up your cross (Matt. 16:24).

Jesus saw wealth as secondary to people and spiritual purposes. He made it clear in his parables that the man with his big barns might gain the world but still lose his soul. And this is not just a New Testament emphasis. The Hebrews saw all wealth as belonging to God and symbolized this by the Jubilee, which meant that every fifty years, personal wealth was to be returned to the community (Lev. 25).

The Bible does not see humankind as basically good, but as rebellious participants in pride and will to power who are in need of redemption. And in contrast to the general media message, the Bible clearly states that happiness consists in appropriating divine resources to form the kingdom of God within one's self and among one's neighbors.[161]

A new and rapidly developing phenomenon in the mass media is the development of religious television networks with strong charismatic emphasis and often emphatic political views. The emphases of these programs must be carefully and critically evaluated. To what extent do they uncritically accept many of the underlying assumptions of the media (images of prestige and power, and of sex and escape)? Jerry Shoals, in his book *That Primetime Religion*, feels that many of these television evangelists bring unbaptized pagan elements into the sanctuary and home.

And then there are the religion-for-money programs. All too easily, the concept of "seed-faith"—"You give to us, and you will get more for you"—comes to look like any other self-centered and materialistic media game.

All of these myths reach us less at the intellectual level than at the level of dream and fantasy. This image-symbol-subconscious level is obviously more powerful than the intellectual level.

Who is to counter the pervasive and harmful media myths? Marshall McLuhan calls on artists to create a kind of "antienvironment" to reverse the indoctrination of the mass media. But Robert Bellah in *The Broken Covenant* calls for the urgency of the perspective supplied by prophetic religion. Many of the media myths are obviously contrary to the historic Christian ideals. The arts and America can profit if Christian leaders revive in Christian people the ability to identify myths and evaluate them from a biblical perspective.

Most cultural analysts say that the place to counteract the media myths is where people meet face-to-face in small groups. This is precisely where the Christian churches and Christian groups have strength. Here is where media and art evaluation can and must take place.

Such a critical media analysis is not easy. Media evaluation would have a different focus for different groups. Among the poor, for example, media evaluation could help people define their real problems and outline their constructive role in society. It would help middle-class people understand ways they are manipulated by society, as well as helping them establish more authentic values and develop lifestyles in keeping with their own Christian goals rather than media goals.[162]

The Russian writer Alexander Solzhenitsyn, in his addresses in the United States in the late 1970s, called for the West to recover its prophetic and biblical heritage. In a response to Solzhenitsyn's challenge, University of Chicago church historian Martin Marty suggested that there is actually nothing which would prevent the people of this country from reappropriating our moral and prophetic heritage. The heritage has been the basis for many of our people acting out of reserves of mercy and sacrifice. Of course we cannot return (and would not wish to return) to the state-endowed and privileged church of earlier centuries. Furthermore, we cannot teach religion in our public schools in such a way as to compel faith. Marty suggests, however, that there are many other outlets for the nurture and development of the classic biblical vision apart from the context of a religious uniformity with actual or implied coercion.

Christian people live by hope. We know that people and societies are sinful, and that the mass media oftentimes reflect this Adamic way. Christians affirm, however, that we have been given a vision. Futurist Alvin Toffler has asserted that Americans are starving for positive images of the future, and Nathan Scott suggests that it is time for the realistic and revelatory "Art of the Fall" to give way to that to which it is always pointing, the "Art of the Redemption." Christians should stand ready to share with artists the positive images which they have found in the Christian vision.[163]

VI. What Are the Limitations of the Arts from the Christian Perspective?

Christianity is more than art. It is redemptive, ethical, and practical as well as aesthetic.

Art symbols should not be converted from means of communication to false centers of worship. In fact, art presents the constant temptation to identify the Holy God of the universe with the beautiful.

According to Novak, a primary aim of the aesthetic conscience is to create a work of harmony, balance, and pleasure. In its higher ranges, the aesthetic conscience often pursues beauty at any cost, independent of honesty, courage, freedom, community, and other human values. It prefers form, sweetness, and ecstasy. In its lower forms, the aesthetic conscience is often the pursuit of novelty, sensation, and peace-of-mind adjustment.

It is more comfortable to live with an art form than with the Holy God of the universe. Many sophisticated people who are interested in the arts are not prophetically inclined or ethically concerned. In fact, some artistic types, like many of us, are downright unethical when it comes to anything which will affect their own private economic or personal interest. There are many people in America who are interested in the arts, but who are not interested in an authentic religion which forces them to face the ethical and practical challenge of the God of Jesus Christ.

The annals of the arts are filled with the stories of those who put their art in the place of God and who suffered accordingly. In the twentieth century, Pablo Picasso is recognized as the foremost genius in painting. However, according to Arianna Huffington in *Picasso: Creator and Destroyer*, Picasso used his painting to combat nature, human nature, and the God who created it all. In his advanced age he was filled with despair and fueled by hatred.

For Friedrich Schelling, the German philosopher, artistic genius is almost identical to God. In fact, the more creative an artist, the more he or she is tempted to confuse himself with God. Jaroslav Pelikan suggests that composer Richard Wagner came close to this position. Friedrich Nietzsche, more profoundly than anyone in his time, attempted to find God in the subtle stirring of the beautiful. Despair and madness finally came when Nietzsche realized that the authentic God refuses to be taken captive even by the beautiful.[164]

VII. What Are Summary Guidelines for a Christian Relationship to the Arts?

1. The Importance of Maintaining a Positive Relationship between the Arts and the Christian Faith

For the Christian, in the area of the arts and the media, there is danger lurking in the shadows. But as we have seen, there is also the need for and the possibility of a positive relationship.

Christianity should seek to understand the nature and purposes of art. It should recognize artistic values and contributions. It should not seek to suppress authentic art or oppose legitimate artistic freedom. At the heart of the Christian vision, however, is a realization that even art cannot be allowed to be the master.

2. The Importance of the Christian Artistic Life's Being Pursued under Revealed Guidelines

In one of his books, a prominent literary figure tells of two Englishmen standing on the shores of the Atlantic, getting ready to sail to a distant land. One is an artist and the other is a Christian.

The artist says, "Let us sail; let us experience the wild blue yonder; let us take risks; let us live sensuously and dangerously."

The Christian responds, "I want to sail. I am adventurous, too. I want to experience life in its fullness. But I want to take my map. This map is composed of the experiences of men who have safely sailed the seas before. It has guidelines prepared by the master Pilot."

To leave the story, Christians would agree that life should be dramatic and exciting. Life should be explored in its depth and height and breadth. But there are guidelines for Christians which they believe reflect revealed insights and sources of power and perspective. They will sail with these guidelines in hand and heart.

Christians need the arts. But Christian people also affirm the importance of the map provided by their ancient yet always contemporary prophetic religion for the exciting journey of the creative and worthwhile life.

Selected Bibliography

I. Introduction

1. Worldviews and Ultimate Questions

Dooyeweerd, Herman. *In the Twilight of Western Thought.* Philadelphia: Presbyterian & Reformed, 1960.

Evans, C. Stephen. *Philosophy of Religion: Thinking About Faith.* Downers Grove, IL: InterVarsity, 1985.

Hasker, William. *Metaphysics: Constructing a World View.* Downers Grove, IL: InterVarsity, 1983.

Holmes, Arthur F. *Contours of a World View.* Grand Rapids, MI: Eerdmans, 1983.

Hutchison, John A. *Faith, Reason, and Existence.* New York: Oxford Univ. Press, 1956.

Kaufman, Gordon. *Relativism, Knowledge and Faith.* Chicago: Univ. of Chicago Press, 1960.

Macquarrie, John. *In Search of Humanity: A Theological and Philosophical Approach.* New York: Crossroad, 1985.

Wild, John. *Human Freedom and Social Order.* Durham, NC: Duke Univ. Press, 1959.

Zuurdeeg, Willem F. *An Analytical Philosophy of Religion.* New York: Abingdon, 1958.

2. The Biblical Worldview

Cherbonnier, Edmond La B. "Biblical Metaphysic and Christian Philosophy." *Theology Today* 9 (1953).

———. *Hardness of Heart.* Garden City, NY: Doubleday, 1955.

———. "Is There a Biblical Metaphysic?" *Theology Today* 15 (January 1959):454–469.

———. "Jerusalem and Athens." *Anglican Theological Review* 36 (October 1954):251–271.

Cohen, Arthur A. *The Natural and the Supernatural Jew: An Historical and Theological Introduction.* New York: Pantheon, 1963.

Filson, Floyd. *The New Testament Against Its Environment: The Gospel of Christ the Risen Lord.* London: SCM, 1950.

Henry, Carl F. H. *God, Revelation and Authority.* Vol. 1, *God Who Speaks and Shows: Preliminary Considerations.* Waco, TX: Word, 1976.

Heschel, Abraham J. *God In Search of Man.* New York: Meridian, 1959.

Hodges, H. A. *Christianity and the Modern World View.* London: SPCK, 1962.

Hodgson, Leonard. *Towards a Christian Philosophy*. London: Nisbet & Co., 1946.
Holmes, Arthur F. *All Truth Is God's Truth*. Grand Rapids, MI: Eerdmans, 1977.
McIntire, C. T. *The Legacy of Herman Dooyeweerd: Reflections on Critical Philosophy in the Christian Tradition*. Lanham, MD: Univ. Press of America, 1985.
Niebuhr, Reinhold. *The Self and the Dramas of History*. New York: Scribner's, 1955.
Rust, Eric C. *Salvation History: A Biblical Interpretation*. Richmond, VA: John Knox, 1962.
Thomas, Owen C. *William Temple's Philosophy of Religion*. London: SPCK and Seabury, 1961.
Tresmontant, Claude. *Christian Metaphysics*. Translated by Gerard Slevin. New York: Sheed & Ward, 1965.
———. *A Study of Hebrew Thought*. Translated by Michael Francis Gibson. New York: Desclee, 1960.
———. *The Origins of Christian Philosophy*. Translated by Mark Pontifex. New York: Hawthorn, 1963.
Wright, G. Ernest. "Archaeology, History and Theology." *Harvard Divinity Bulletin* 28 (April 1964): 85–96.
———. *The Biblical Doctrine of Man in Society*. London: SCM, 1954.
———. *God Who Acts: Biblical Theology as Recital*. Chicago: Alec R. Allenson, 1952.
———. *The Old Testament Against Its Environment*. Naperville, IL: Alec R. Allenson, 1957.

3. Comparison and Evaluation of Worldviews

Bendall, Kent, and Frederick Ferre. *Exploring the Logic of Faith*. New York: Association, 1962.
Brown, Colin. *Philosophy and the Christian Faith*. London: Tyndale Press, 1969.
Carnell, Edward John. *Christian Commitment: An Apologetic*. New York: Macmillan, 1957.
———. *A Philosophy of the Christian Religion*. Grand Rapids, MI: Eerdmans, 1952.
Craig, William Lane. *Apologetics: An Introduction*. Chicago: Moody, 1984.
Cunningham, Richard B. "A Case for Christian Philosophy." *Review and Expositor* 82 (Fall 1985): 493.
———. *The Christian Faith and Its Contemporary Rivals*. Nashville: Broadman, 1988.
Dyrness, William. *Christian Apologetics in a World Community*. Downers Grove, IL: InterVarsity, 1983.
Emmet, Dorothy M. *The Nature of Metaphysical Thinking*. London: Macmillan, 1953.
Geisler, Norman. *Christian Apologetics*. Grand Rapids, MI: Baker, 1976.
Howe, Frederic R. *Challenge and Response: A Handbook of Christian Apologetics*. Grand Rapids, MI: Zondervan, 1982.
Lewis, Gordon R. *Testing Christianity's Truth Claims*. Chicago: Moody, 1976.
Lovejoy, Arthur. *The Great Chain of Being*. Cambridge, MA: Harvard Univ. Press, 1948.
Richardson, Alan. *Christian Apologetics*. New York: Harper, 1947.
Woodfin, Yandall. *Why Be a Christian?* Layman's Library of Christian Doctrine. Nashville: Broadman, 1988.
———. *With All Your Mind: A Christian Philosophy*. Nashville: Abingdon, 1980.

II. The Meaning of History

Baillie, John. *The Belief in Progress*. London: Oxford Univ. Press, 1950.
Bebbington, D. W. *Patterns in History: A Christian View*. Downers Grove, IL: InterVarsity, 1979.

Berkhof, Hendrikus. *Christ, the Meaning of History.* Translated by L. Buurman. Richmond, VA: John Knox, 1966.

———. *Well-Founded Hope.* Richmond, VA: John Knox, 1969.

Butterfield, Herbert. *Christianity and History.* London: G. Bell & Sons, 1950.

Campolo, Anthony. *Partly Right.* Waco, TX: Word, 1985.

Casserley, J. V. Langmead. *Toward a Theology of History.* New York: Holt, Rinehart & Winston, 1965.

Cohen, Morris R. *The Meaning of Human History.* Chicago: Open Court, 1961.

Driver, Tom F. *The Sense of History in Greek and Shakespearean Drama.* New York: Columbia Univ. Press, 1961.

Ellul, Jacques. *Jesus and Marx: From Gospel to Ideology.* Grand Rapids, MI: Eerdmans, 1988.

Erickson, Millard J. *Christian Theology,* Vol. 2. Grand Rapids, MI: Baker, 1984.

Guinness, Os. *The Dust of Death.* Downers Grove, IL: InterVarsity, 1973.

Hunt, R. N. Carew. *The Theory and Practice of Communism: An Introduction.* New York: Macmillan, 1951.

Newport, John P. *Paul Tillich.* Makers of the Modern Theological Mind. Waco, TX: Word, 1984.

———. *The Lion and the Lamb.* Nashville: Broadman, 1986.

Niebuhr, Reinhold. *Faith and History.* New York: Scribner's, 1949.

Peters, Ted. *Futures—Human and Divine.* Atlanta: John Knox, 1978.

Richardson, Alan. *History Sacred and Profane.* Philadelphia: The Westminster Press, 1964.

Rust, Eric C. *Towards a Theological Understanding of History.* New York: Oxford Univ. Press, 1963.

Shinn, Roger Lincoln. *Christianity and the Problem of History.* New York: Scribner's, 1953.

Wacker, Grant. *Augustus H. Strong and the Dilemma of Historical Consciousness.* Macon, GA: Mercer Univ. Press, 1985.

III. Religious and Biblical Language

Albright, William Foxwell. *History, Archaeology and Christian Humanism.* New York: McGraw-Hill, 1964.

Casserley, J. V. Langmead. *The Christian in Philosophy.* New York: Scribner's, 1951.

Dodd, C. H. *The Bible To-day.* Cambridge: Cambridge Univ. Press, 1962.

Erickson, Millard J. *Christian Theology.* Vol. 1. Grand Rapids, MI: Baker, 1983.

Ferre, Frederick. *Language, Logic and God.* New York: Harper, 1961.

Frye, Roland M. *Perspectives on Man: Literature and the Christian Tradition.* Philadelphia: Westminster Press, 1961.

Gilkey, Langdon. *Naming the Whirlwind: The Renewal of God-Language.* Indianapolis: Bobbs-Merrill, 1969.

Gill, Jerry H. *Faith in Dialogue: A Christian Apologetic.* Waco, TX: Word, 1985.

Hauerwas, Stanley. *The Peaceable Kingdom: A Primer in Christian Ethics.* Notre Dame, IN: Univ. of Notre Dame Press, 1983.

Henry, Carl F. H. *God, Revelation and Authority.* Vol. 3, *God Who Speaks and Shows: Fifteen Theses, Part Two.* Waco, TX: Word, 1979.

Hordern, William. *Speaking of God: The Nature and Purpose of Theological Language.* New York: Macmillan, 1964.

Lindbeck, George A. *The Nature of Doctrine: Religion and Theology in a Postliberal Age.* Philadelphia: Westminster, 1984.

Newport, John P. *What Is Christian Doctrine?* Nashville: Broadman, 1984.

Ramsey, Ian T. *Religious Language*. London: SCM, 1957.

Tilley, Terrence W. *Story Theology*. Wilmington, DE: Michael Glazier, 1985.

———. *Talking of God*. New York: Paulist, 1978.

Williamson, Wm. B. *Ian Ramsey*. Makers of the Modern Theological Mind. Waco, TX: Word, 1982.

Wright, G. Ernest. "History and Reality: The Importance of Israel's 'Historical' Symbols for the Christian Faith." In *The Old Testament and the Christian Faith*, edited by Bernard W. Anderson. New York: Harper, 1963.

IV. Science and Origins

Bube, Richard H. *The Human Quest: A New Look at Science and Christian Faith*. Waco, TX: Word, 1971.

Geisler, Norman. "Creationism: A Case for Equal Time," *Christianity Today* (19 March 1982).

————, and J. Kerby Anderson. *Origin Science: A Proposal for the Creation-Evolution Controversy*. Grand Rapids, MI: Baker, 1987.

Gilkey, Langdon. *Creationism on Trial: Evolution and God at Little Rock*. Minneapolis: Winston, 1985.

Henry, Carl F. H. God, *Revelation and Authority*, Vol. 6, God *Who Stands and Stays, Part Two*. Waco, TX: Word, 1983.

Hooykass, R. *Religion and the Rise of Modern Science*. Edinburgh: Scottish Academic Press, 1972.

Hummel, Charles E. *The Galileo Connection: Resolving Conflicts Between Science and the Bible*. Downers Grove, IL: InterVarsity, 1986.

Hyers, Conrad. *The Meaning of Creation: Genesis and Modern Science*. Atlanta: John Knox, 1984.

Kuhn, T. S. *The Structure of Scientific Revolutions*. Chicago: Univ. of Chicago Press, 1970.

Newbigin, Lesslie. *Foolishness to the Greeks: The Gospel and Western Culture*. Grand Rapids, MI: Eerdmans, 1986.

Noll, Mark A., and David F. Wells, eds. *Christian Faith and Practice in the Modern World: Theology from an Evangelical Point of View*. Grand Rapids, MI: Eerdmans, 1988.

The Proceedings of the Conference on Biblical Inerrancy 1987. Nashville, TN: Broadman, 1987.

Ramm, Bernard L. *The Christian View of Science and Scripture*. Grand Rapids, MI: Eerdmans, 1954.

Richardson, Alan. *The Bible in the Age of Science*. Philadelphia: Westminster, 1961.

Rust, Eric C. *Science and Faith*. New York: Oxford Univ. Press, 1967.

Torrance, Thomas F. *The Christian Frame of Mind*. Colorado Springs, CO: Helmers & Howard, 1988.

V. Miracles, Providence, and Intercessory Prayer

Brown, Colin. *Miracles and the Critical Mind*. Grand Rapids, MI: Eerdmans, 1984.

———. *That You May Believe: Miracles and Faith, Then and Now*. Grand Rapids, MI: Eerdmans, 1985.

Farmer, H. H. *The World and God*. London: Nisbet & Co., 1936.

MacArthur, John F., Jr. *The Charismatics: A Doctrinal Perspective*. Grand Rapids, MI: Zondervan, 1978.

Monden, Louis. *Signs and Wonders: A Study of the Miraculous Element in Religion*. New York: Desclee, 1966.
Mullins, E. Y. *Why Is Christianity True?* Philadelphia: Judson, 1905.
Peters, George W. *Indonesia Revival: Focus on Timor*. Grand Rapids, MI: Zondervan, 1973.
Smedes, Lewis B., ed. *Ministry and the Miraculous*. Pasadena, CA: Fuller Theological Seminary, 1987.
Thielicke, Helmut. *Man in God's World*. New York: Harper, 1963.
Trueblood, David Elton. *The Logic of Belief: An Introduction to the Philosophy of Religion*. New York: Harper, 1942.
Warfield, B. B. *Counterfeit Miracles*. Carlisle, PA: Banner of Truth, 1918.
———. *Miracles: Yesterday and Today, True and False*. Grand Rapids, MI: Eerdmans, 1954.
Wright, J. Stafford. *Man in the Process of Time*. Grand Rapids, MI: Eerdmans, 1956.

VI. Cosmic Evil and the Demonic

Bridge, Donald, and David Phypers. *Spiritual Gifts and the Church*. Downers Grove, IL: InterVarsity, 1973.
Collins, Gary R. *Can You Trust Psychology?* Downers Grove: InterVarsity, 1988.
Hammond, Frank, and Ida Mae Hammond. *Pigs in the Parlor: A Practical Guide to Deliverance*. Kirkwood, MO: Impact, 1973.
Jacobs, Donald R. *Demons*. Scottdale, PA: Herald, 1972.
Johnson, Walter C. "Demon Possession and Mental Illness." *Journal of the American Scientific Affiliation* 34 (September 1982): 149–54.
Kallas, James. *Jesus and the Power of Satan*. Philadelphia: Westminster, 1968.
———. *The Real Satan: From Biblical Times to the Present*. Minneapolis: Augsburg, 1975.
Koch, Kurt E. *Christian Counseling and Occultism*. Grand Rapids, MI: Kregel, 1965.
Ladd, George Eldon. *Jesus and the Kingdom*. New York: Harper, 1964.
Langton, Edward. *Essentials of Demonology*. London: Epworth, 1949.
Lewis, C. S. *The Screwtape Letters*. New York: Macmillan, 1970.
Mascall, Eric Lionel, ed. *The Angels of Light and the Powers of Darkness*. London: Faith Press, 1955.
McAll, R. Kenneth. "The Ministry of Deliverance." *Expository Times* 86 (1975): 296–98.
Montgomery, John Warwick, ed. *Demon Possession*. Minneapolis, MN: Bethany, 1976.
Newport, John P. *Demons, Demons, Demons*. Nashville: Broadman, 1972.
———. *Christ and the New Consciousness*. Nashville: Broadman, 1978.
Oates, Wayne. *The Psychology of Religion*. Waco, TX: Word, 1973.
Peck, M. Scott. *People of the Lie: The Hope for Healing Human Evil*. New York: Simon & Schuster, 1983.
Philpott, Kent. *A Manual of Demonology and the Occult*. Grand Rapids, MI: Zondervan, 1973.
Southard, Samuel, and Donna Southard. "Demonizing and Mental Illness: The Problem of Identification, Hong Kong." *Pastoral Psychology* 33 (Spring 1985): 173–88.
Virkler, H. A. "Demonic Influence and Psychopathology." In *Baker Encyclopedia of Psychology*, edited by David G. Benner. Grand Rapids, MI: Baker, 1985.
Warner, Timothy M. *The Power Encounter in World Evangelization*. Grand Rapids, MI: Baker, projected for 1990.
Wink, Walter. *Unmasking the Powers: The Invisible Forces That Determine Human Existence*. Philadelphia: Fortress, 1986.
Wright, J. Stafford. *Mind, Man and the Spirits*. Grand Rapids, MI: Zondervan, 1971.

VII. Personal Evil and Suffering

Beker, J. Christiaan. *Suffering and Hope*. Philadelphia: Fortress, 1987.
Bloesch, Donald. *The Ground of Certainty*. Grand Rapids, MI: Eerdmans, 1971.
Bowker, John. *Problems of Suffering in Religions of the World*. Cambridge: Cambridge Univ. Press, 1970.
Brightman, Edgar S. *A Philosophy of Religion*. Englewood Cliffs, NJ: Prentice-Hall, 1940.
Cairns, D. S. *The Riddle of the World*. New York: Round Table, 1938.
Conner, W. T. *The Faith of the New Testament*. Nashville: Broadman, 1946.
Davis, Stephen T., ed. *Encountering Evil: Live Options in Theodicy*. Atlanta: John Knox, 1981.
Farmer, Herbert H. *Towards Belief in God*. New York: Macmillan, 1943.
Geisler, Norman L. *The Roots of Evil*. Grand Rapids, MI: Zondervan, 1978.
Hick, John. *Evil and the God of Love*. New York: Harper, 1966.
Lewis, C. S. *The Problem of Pain*. London: Collins, 1940.
Marty, Martin E. *Health and Medicine in the Lutheran Tradition: Being Well*. New York: Crossroad, 1983.
Peake, Arthur S. *The Problem of Suffering in the Old Testament*. London: Dalton & Kelly, 1904.
Proudfoot, Merrill. *Suffering: A Christian Understanding*. Philadelphia: Westminster, 1964.
Ramm, Bernard L. *The God Who Makes a Difference*. Waco, TX: Word, 1972.
Robinson, H. Wheeler. *The Religious Ideas of the Old Testament*. London: Duckworth, 1952.
———. *Suffering, Human and Divine*. New York: Macmillan, 1939.
Stewart, James S. *The Strong Name*. New York: Scribner's, 1941.
Wenham, John W. *The Enigma of Evil*. Grand Rapids, MI: Zondervan, 1985.
Whale, J. S. *The Christian Answer to the Problem of Evil*. 4th ed. London: SCM, 1957.

VIII. Death and the Life Beyond

Albrecht, Mark, and Brooks Alexander. "Thanatology: Death and Dying." *Journal of the Spiritual Counterfeits Project* (April 1977).
Aldwinckle, Russell. *Death in the Secular City*. Grand Rapids: Eerdmans, 1972.
Anderson, Ray S. *Theology, Death and Dying*. New York: Basil Blackwell, 1986.
Bertocchi, Peter Anthony. *Introduction to the Philosophy of Religion*. Englewood Cliffs, NJ: Prentice-Hall, 1951.
Bloesch, Donald G. *Essentials of Evangelical Theology*. Vol. 2, *Life, Ministry and Hope*. San Francisco: Harper, 1979.
Chandler, Russell. *Understanding the New Age*. Dallas: Word, 1988.
Hendricks, William L. *A Theology for Aging*. Nashville: Broadman, 1986.
Henry, Carl F. H. God, *Revelation and Authority*. Vol. 4, *God Who Speaks and Shows: Fifteen Theses, Part Three*. Waco: Word, 1979.
Hick, John H. *Death and Eternal Life*. New York: Harper, 1976.
Jüngel, Eberhard. *Death: The Riddle and the Mystery*. Philadelphia: Westminster, 1974.
Kantonen, T. A. *Life After Death*. Philadelphia: Muhlenberg, 1962.
Koestenbaum, Peter. *Is There an Answer to Death?* Englewood Cliffs, NJ: Prentice-Hall, 1976.
Ladd, George Eldon. *I Believe in the Resurrection of Jesus*. Grand Rapids, MI: Eerdmans, 1975.
———. *The Last Things*. Grand Rapids, MI: Eerdmans, 1978.

MacGregor, Geddes, ed. *Immortality and Human Destiny: A Variety of Views*. New York: Paragon House, 1985.

May, William. "The Sacral Power of Death in Contemporary Experience." In *Perspectives on Death*, edited by Liston O. Mills. Nashville: Abingdon, 1969.

Moody, Dale. *The Word of Truth: A Summary of Christian Doctrine Based on Biblical Revelation*. Grand Rapids, MI: Eerdmans, 1981.

Phipps, William E. *Death: Confronting the Reality*. Atlanta: John Knox, 1987.

Scott, Nathan A., Jr., ed. *The Modern Vision of Death*. Richmond, VA: John Knox, 1967.

Stendahl, Krister, ed. *Immortality and Resurrection*. New York: Macmillan, 1965.

Thielicke, Helmut. *Death and Life*. Philadelphia: Fortress, 1970.

———. *Living with Death*. Grand Rapids, MI: Eerdmans, 1983.

Torrance, Thomas F. *Space, Time and Incarnation*. London: Oxford Univ. Press, 1969.

———. *Space, Time and Resurrection*. Grand Rapids, MI: Eerdmans, 1976.

IX. Religion and World Religions

Anderson, J. N. D. *Christianity and Comparative Religion*. Downers Grove, IL: Inter-Varsity, 1970.

Aldwinckle, Russell F. *Jesus—A Savior or the Savior?* Macon, GA: Mercer Univ. Press, 1982.

Bonino, Jose Miguez. *Doing Theology in a Revolutionary Situation*. Philadelphia: Fortress, 1975.

Copeland, E. Luther. *Christianity and World Religions*. Nashville: Convention Press, 1963.

Cragg, Kenneth. *The Christ and the Faiths: Theology in Cross-Reference*. London: SPCK, 1986.

Farmer, Herbert Henry. *Revelation and Religion: Studies in the Theological Interpretation of Religious Types*. London: Nisbet and Co., 1954.

Hick, John. *God and the Universe of Faiths*. New York: St. Martin's Press, 1973.

Jackson, Herbert C. *Man Reaches Out to God*. Valley Forge, PA: Judson, 1963.

Kraemer, Hendrik. *Religion and the Christian Faith*. Philadelphia: Westminster, 1956.

———. *Why Christianity of All Religions?* Translated by Hubert Hoskins. Philadelphia: Westminster, 1962.

———. *World Cultures and World Religions: The Coming Dialogue*. Philadelphia: Westminster, 1960.

Neill, Stephen. *Christian Faith and Other Faiths: The Christian Dialogue with Other Religions*. London: Oxford Univ. Press, 1961.

Newport, John P. *Christ and the New Consciousness*. Nashville: Broadman, 1978.

————, ed. *Nineteenth Century Devotional Thought*. Nashville: Broadman, 1981.

Perry, Edmund. *The Gospel in Dispute*. Garden City, NY: Doubleday, 1958.

Smart, Ninian. *The Phenomenon of Religion*. New York: Macmillan, 1973.

Smith, Wilfred Cantwell. *Toward a World Theology*. London: Macmillan, 1980.

Visser 't Hooft, W. A. *No Other Name*. London: SCM Press, 1963.

Vos, Johannes G. *A Christian Introduction to Religions of the World*. Grand Rapids, MI: Baker, 1965.

Wright, G. Ernest. *The Challenge of Israel's Faith*. Chicago: Univ. of Chicago Press, 1944.

Zaehner, R. C. *Mysticism, Sacred and Profane*. New York: Oxford Univ. Press, 1971.

X. Faith and Reason

Braaten, Carl E., and Philip Clayton, eds. *The Theology of Wolfhart Pannenberg*. Minneapolis: Augsburg, 1988.

Carnell, Edward John. *An Introduction to Christian Apologetics: A Philosophic Defense of the Trinitarian-Theistic Faith.* Grand Rapids, MI: Eerdmans, 1948.
Casserley, J. V. Langmead. *Graceful Reason: The Contribution of Reason to Theology.* Greenwich, CT: Seabury, 1954.
Cherbonnier, Edmond La B. *Hardness of Heart.* Garden City, NY: Doubleday, 1955.
Hazelton, Roger. *On Proving God.* New York: Harper, 1952.
Herberg, Will. *Judaism and Modern Man.* New York: Farrar, Straus & Young, 1951.
Holmes, Arthur F. *Faith Seeks Understanding.* Grand Rapids, MI: Eerdmans, 1971.
Hutchison, John A. *Faith, Reason, and Existence.* New York: Oxford Univ. Press, 1956.
Jenkins, Daniel. *Believing in God.* Philadelphia: Westminster, 1952.
Kroner, Richard. *Speculation and Revelation in Modern Philosophy.* Philadelphia: Westminster, 1961.
Nash, Ronald H. *Faith and Reason: Searching for a Rational Faith.* Grand Rapids, MI: Zondervan, 1988.
Patrick, Denzil G. M. *Pascal and Kierkegaard.* Vol. 2. London and Redhill: Lutterworth Press, 1947.
Plantinga, Alvin, and Nicholas Wolterstorff, eds. *Faith and Rationality: Reason and Belief in God.* Notre Dame: Univ. of Notre Dame Press, 1983.
Ramm, Bernard. *After Fundamentalism: The Future of Evangelical Theology.* San Francisco: Harper, 1983.
Ruegsegger, Ronald W., ed. *Reflections on Francis Schaeffer.* Grand Rapids, MI: Zondervan, 1986.
Van Til, Cornelius. *The Defense of the Faith.* Philadelphia: Presbyterian & Reformed, 1955.
Wolfe, David L. *Epistemology: The Justification of Belief.* Downers Grove: InterVarsity, 1982.
Wright, G. Ernest. *The Rule of God: Essays in Biblical Theology.* Garden City, NY: Doubleday, 1960.

XI. Morality

Anderson, Bernhard W. "The Biblical Ethic of Obedience." *The Christian Scholar,* 39, no. 1 (March 1956): 66–71.
Baillie, John. *Our Knowledge of God.* London: Oxford Univ. Press, 1939.
Bloesch, Donald G. *Freedom for Obedience: Evangelical Ethics in Contemporary Times.* San Francisco: Harper, 1987.
Fletcher, Joseph. *Situation Ethics: The New Morality.* Philadelphia: Westminster, 1966.
Henry, Carl F. H. *Aspects of Christian Social Ethics.* Grand Rapids, MI: Eerdmans, 1957.
———. *Christian Personal Ethics.* Grand Rapids, MI: Eerdmans, 1957.
Kaye, Bruce and Gordon Wenham, eds. *Law, Morality and the Bible.* Downers Grove, IL: InterVarsity, 1978.
Lewis, C. S. *Mere Christianity.* New York: Macmillan, 1953.
Lillie, William. *Studies in New Testament Ethics.* Philadelphia: Westminster, 1961.
Macquarrie, John. *In Search of Deity: An Essay in Dialectical Theism.* New York: Crossroad, 1984.
Maston, T. B. *Biblical Ethics.* Cleveland, OH: World, 1967.
McClendon, James William, Jr. *Ethics: Systematic Theology.* Nashville: Abingdon, 1986.
O'Donovan, Oliver. *Resurrection and Moral Order: An Outline for Evangelical Ethics.* Grand Rapids, MI: Eerdmans, 1986.
Ramm, Bernard. *The Right, the Good and the Happy.* Waco: Word, 1971.

Smart, Ninian. *Worldviews: Crosscultural Explorations of Human Beliefs.* New York: Scribner's, 1983.

Thielicke, Helmut. *Theological Ethics.* Vol. 1, *Foundations.* Grand Rapids, MI: Eerdmans, 1966.

XII. The Arts, Culture, and Worship

Boman, Thorlief. *Hebrew Thought Compared with Greek.* Philadelphia: Westminster, 1960.

Cherbonnier, Edmond La B. "Biblical vs. Mystical Symbolism." *The Christian Scholar,* 39, no. 1 (1956).

Cullmann, Oscar. *Christ and Time: The Primitive Christian Conception of Time and History.* Philadelphia: Westminster, 1950.

———. *Early Christian Worship.* London: SCM, 1953.

———. *The Early Church.* Edited by A. J. B. Higgins. Philadelphia: Westminster, 1956.

Dixon, John W. *Nature and Grace in Art.* Chapel Hill, NC: Univ. of North Carolina Press, 1964.

Fuller, Edmund. *Man in Modern Fiction.* New York: Random House, 1958.

Hazelton, Roger. *A Theological Approach to Art.* Nashville: Abingdon, 1967.

Hurley, Neil P. *Theology Through Film.* New York: Harper, 1968.

Johansson, Calvin M. *Music and Ministry: A Biblical Counterpoint.* Peabody, MA: Hendrickson, 1984.

Kilby, Clyde S. *Christianity and Aesthetics.* Downers Grove, IL: InterVarsity, 1961.

Küng, Hans. *Art and the Question of Meaning.* Translated by Edward Quinn. New York: Crossroad, 1981.

Lynch, William F. *Christ and Apollo: The Dimensions of the Literary Imagination.* New York: Sheed & Ward, 1960.

Moltmann, Jürgen. *Theology of Play.* Translated by Reinhard Ulrich. New York: Harper, 1972.

Nathan, Walter L. *Art and the Message of the Church.* Philadelphia: Westminster, 1961.

Newport, John P. *Christianity and Contemporary Art Forms.* Waco, TX: Word, 1979.

Scott, Nathan A., Jr. *The Broken Center.* New Haven, CT: Yale Univ. Press, 1966.

Sherrell, Richard E. *The Human Image: Avant-Garde and Christian.* Richmond, VA: John Knox, 1969.

van der Leeuw, Gerardus. *Sacred and Profane Beauty.* New York: Holt, Rinehart & Winston, 1963.

White, James F. *New Forms of Worship.* Nashville: Abingdon, 1971.

Whittle, Donald. *Christianity and the Arts.* Philadelphia: Fortress, 1967.

Wilder, Amos Niven. *Theology and Modern Literature.* Cambridge: Harvard Univ. Press, 1967.

Wolterstorff, Nicholas. *Art in Action: Toward A Christian Aesthetic.* Grand Rapids, MI: Eerdmans, 1980.

Wright, G. Ernest, and Fuller, Reginald H. *The Book of the Acts of God: Christian Scholarship Interprets the Bible.* Garden City, NY: Doubleday, 1957.

Notes

Preface

1. John P. Newport, *The Lion and the Lamb* (Nashville: Broadman, 1986).

Chapter 1

1. Owen C. Thomas, *William Temple's Philosophy of Religion* (London: SPCK and Seabury, 1961), 151.
2. Gordon Kaufman, *Relativism, Knowledge and Faith* (Chicago: Univ. of Chicago Press, 1960), 101.
3. Robert Bellah, et al., *Habits of the Heart: Individualism and Commitment in American Life* (Berkeley: Univ. of California Press, 1985), 219.
4. Langdon Gilkey, *Naming the Whirlwind: The Renewal of God-Language* (Indianapolis: Bobbs-Merrill, 1969), 305–413.
5. Dorothy M. Emmet, *The Nature of Metaphysical Thinking* (London: Macmillan, 1953), 194.
6. Thomas, *William Temple*, 155.
7. John A. Hutchison, *Faith, Reason, and Existence* (New York: Oxford Univ. Press, 1956), 28–29.
8. Kaufman, *Relativism*, 90.
9. William Hordern, *Speaking of God: The Nature and Purpose of Theological Language* (New York: Macmillan, 1964), 78.
10. Claude Tresmontant, *The Origins of Christian Philosophy*, tr. Mark Pontifex (New York: Hawthorn, 1963), 8–9.
11. Arthur Lovejoy, *The Great Chain of Being* (Cambridge, Mass.: Harvard Univ. Press, 1948), 157.
12. Richard B. Cunningham, "A Case for Christian Philosophy," *Review and Expositor*, 82 (Fall 1985): 493.
13. James William McClendon, Jr., "What Is 'Baptist' Theology?" (n.d.): 5.
14. Ibid.
15. Cunningham, "Case for Christian Philosophy," 496.
16. Ibid., 493.
17. Ibid., 493–494.

18. McClendon, "What Is 'Baptist' Theology?" 6.

19. H. A. Hodges, *Christianity and the Modern World View* (London: SPCK, 1962), 8.

20. G. Ernest Wright, "Archaeology, History and Theology," *Harvard Divinity Bulletin*, 95.

21. Hodges, *Christianity*, 16–17.

22. Ibid., 17.

23. Tresmontant, *Origins*, 17–18.

24. Ibid., 25.

25. Cf. Herman Dooyeweerd, *In the Twilight of Western Thought* (Philadelphia: Presbyterian & Reformed, 1960), vii, ix–x.

26. Cf. Karl Barth, *Church Dogmatics*, vol. 2, pt. 1 (Edinburgh: T & T Clark, 1957).

27. Ibid.; cf. G. C. Berkouwer, *The Triumph of Grace in the Theology of Karl Barth* (Grand Rapids, Mich.: Eerdmans, 1956).

28. Reinhold Niebuhr, *The Self and the Dramas of History* (New York: Scribner's, 1955), 77–78.

29. Ibid., 88; for a symposium critique of this approach see Owen C. Thomas, ed., *God's Activity in the World (The Contemporary Problem)* (Chico, Calif.: Scholars, 1983).

30. Wright, "Archaeology," 88.

31. Ibid.

32. Ibid., 89.

33. Ibid., 95.

34. Ibid., 96.

35. Arthur A. Cohen, *The Natural and the Supernatural Jew: An Historical and Theological Introduction* (New York: Pantheon, 1963), 301, 304.

36. Abraham J. Heschel, *God in Search of Man* (New York: Meridian, 1959), 200, 204, 230.

37. Terrence W. Tilley, *Story Theology* (Wilmington, Del.: Michael Glazier, 1985), 35.

38. Ibid., 11, 12.

39. Ibid., 25, 26.

40. George A. Lindbeck, *The Nature of Doctrine: Religion and Theology in a Postliberal Age* (Philadelphia: Westminster, 1984), 33.

41. Ibid., 121.

42. Ibid., 121–122.

43. Ibid., 128.

44. Ibid., 34.

45. Ibid., 36.

46. Hodges, *Christianity*, 11.

47. Lindbeck, *Nature of Doctrine*, 132.

48. Ibid., 133–134.

49. Cunningham, "Case for Christian Philosophy," 501.

50. Leonard Hodgson, *Towards a Christian Philosophy* (London: Nisbet & Co., 1946), 12; Cunningham, "Case for Christian Philosophy," 501.

51. Eric C. Rust, *Salvation History: A Biblical Interpretation* (Richmond, Va.: John Knox, 1962), 19–20.

52. Robert E. Patterson, ed., *Science, Faith and Revelation* (Nashville: Broadman, 1979), 205.

53. Ibid., 206, 210.

54. Ibid., 210–211.
55. Rust, *Salvation History,* 10.
56. E. Y. Mullins, *Freedom and Authority in Religion* (Philadelphia: Griffith & Rowland, 1913), 382.
57. Patterson, *Science,* 218.
58. Rust, *Salvation History,* 12.
59. McClendon, "What Is 'Baptist' Theology?" 11–12.
60. Cunningham, "Case for Christian Philosophy," 495.
61. Ibid., 495–496.
62. Ibid., 496.
63. John Smith, *Reason and God* (New Haven, Conn.: Yale Univ. Press, 1961), 152.
64. Cunningham, "Case for Christian Philosophy," 499.
65. Ibid.
66. Edmond La B. Cherbonnier, *Hardness of Heart* (Garden City, N.Y.: Doubleday, 1955), preface.
67. Edmond La B. Cherbonnier, "Biblical Metaphysic and Christian Philosophy," *Theology Today* 9 (1953): 363–364.
68. Ibid.
69. John Wild, *Human Freedom and Social Order* (Durham, N.C.: Duke Univ. Press, 1959), 61–62.
70. Ibid., 84.
71. Wright, "Archaeology," 88.
72. Eric C. Rust, *Evolutionary Philosophies and Contemporary Theology* (Philadelphia: Westminster, 1969), 34–35.
73. Ibid., 36.
74. John Macquarrie, *An Existentialist Theology* (London: SCM, 1965), 89.
75. L. Russ Bush and Tom J. Nettles, *Baptists and the Bible* (Chicago: Moody, 1980), 297.
76. Patterson, *Science,* 213.
77. Ibid., 213–214.
78. Gordon R. Lewis, *Testing Christianity's Truth Claims* (Chicago: Moody, 1976), 21, 23, 25, 31.
79. William Dyrness, *Christian Apologetics in a World Community* (Downers Grove, Ill.: InterVarsity, 1983), 23–51.
80. Ibid., 53–69.
81. Ibid., 38–40.
82. Carl F. H. Henry, *God, Revelation and Authority,* vol. 1, *God Who Speaks and Shows: Preliminary Considerations* (Waco, Tex.: Word, 1976).
83. Carl F. H. Henry, *Christian Personal Ethics* (Grand Rapids, Mich.: Eerdmans, 1957), 15.
84. Carl F. H. Henry, *Aspects of Christian Social Ethics* (Grand Rapids, Mich.: Eerdmans, 1964), 9.
85. Arthur F. Holmes, *All Truth Is God's Truth* (Grand Rapids, Mich.: Eerdmans, 1977), 125–128.
86. Ibid., 102–113.
87. Edmond La B. Cherbonnier, "Is There a Biblical Metaphysic?" *Theology Today* 15 (January 1959): 454–469; Cherbonnier, "Jerusalem and Athens," *Anglican Theological Review* 36 (Oct. 1954): 251–271.

88. Kent Bendall and Frederick Ferre, *Exploring the Logic of Faith* (New York: Association, 1962), 166–172.

89. Emmet, *The Nature of Metaphysical Thinking*, 200.

90. Ibid.

91. Reinhold Niebuhr, *Faith and History* (New York: Scribner's, 1949), 151-152.

92. Ibid., 165–170.

93. Edward John Carnell, *A Philosophy of the Christian Religion* (Grand Rapids, Mich.: Eerdmans, 1952), 44–45

94. Ibid., 47–329; and Edward John Carnell, *Christian Commitment: An Apologetic* (New York: Macmillan, 1957), 302–303.

95. Thomas, *William Temple*, 157.

96. Robert D. Linder, "Religion and the American Dream: A Study in Confusion and Tension," *Mennonite Life*, 38, no. 4 (Dec. 1983): 17; and cf. Christopher F. Mooney, *Religion and the American Dream: The Search for Freedom Under God* (Philadelphia: Westminster, 1977).

97. John P. Newport, "Humanism and the Future: A Tentative Proposal for an American Solution," *Liberal and Fine Arts Review*, 4, no. 1 (Jan. 1984): 56–57.

98. Niebuhr, *The Self*, 175–177.

Chapter 2

1. Eric C. Rust, *Towards a Theological Understanding of History* (New York: Oxford Univ. Press, 1963), 5–6.

2. R. G. Collingwood, *The Idea of History* (London: Oxford Univ. Press, 1946), 24–25.

3. Bernard Ramm, *After Fundamentalism: The Future of Evangelical Theology* (San Francisco: Harper, 1983), 72–73.

4. Herbert Butterfield, *Christianity and History* (London: G. Bell & Sons, 1950), 17.

5. Ibid., 23.

6. Arthur W. Munk, *History and God* (New York: Ronald Press, 1952), 8–11.

7. Ramm, *After Fundamentalism*, 81.

8. Bernard Ramm, "Biblical Faith and History," *Christianity Today* (1 March 1963): 524.

9. Ramm, *After Fundamentalism*, 83–86.

10. Ibid., 521.

11. Ibid., 521, 523.

12. Ibid., 524; cf. Oscar Cullman, *Christ and Time: The Primitive Christian Conception of Time and History* (Philadelphia: Westminster, 1950), 231–242.

13. D. W. Bebbington, *Patterns in History: A Christian View* (Downers Grove, Ill.: InterVarsity, 1979), 17.

14. Ibid., 21.

15. Ibid., 22–24; cf. Arend Th. Van Leeuwen, *Christianity in World History* (London: Edinburgh House, 1965), 188.

16. Ibid., 24–25; cf. Mircea Eliade, *Cosmos and History* (New York: Harper, 1959), 112–115.

17. Ibid., 25.

18. Paul Tillich, *Systematic Theology*, vol. 3 (Chicago: Univ. of Chicago Press, 1963), 351ff.

19. Bebbington, *Patterns in History*, 25–26.
20. Ibid., 26.
21. Ibid., 27–28.
22. Rust, *Towards a Theological Understanding*, 21; cf. John Baillie, *The Belief in Progress* (London: Oxford Univ. Press, 1950), 46–47.
23. Ibid., 21; cf. Tom Driver, *A Sense of History in Greek and Shakespearean Drama* (New York: Columbia Univ. Press, 1960), 27–30.
24. Bebbington, *Patterns in History*, 30; cf. Baillie, *Belief in Progress*, 48–49.
25. Rust, *Towards a Theological Understanding*, 54–55.
26. Bebbington, *Patterns in History*, 33.
27. John Baillie, *The Belief in Progress* (London: Oxford Univ. Press, 1950), 50–51.
28. Paul Tillich, *Theology of Culture*, ed. Robert C. Kimball (New York: Oxford Univ. Press, 1959, 1965), 34.
29. Reinhold Niebuhr, *Faith and History* (New York: Scribner's, 1949), 157–158.
30. Driver, *A Sense of History*, 37.
31. Ibid., 38–39.
32. Bebbington, *Patterns in History*, 38; Rust, *Towards a Theological Understanding*, 22.
33. Rust, *Towards a Theological Understanding*, 22–23.
34. Cf. Oswald Spengler, *The Decline of the West*, vols. 1 and 2 (New York: Knopf, 1926, 1928).
35. Rust, *Towards a Theological Understanding*, 23.
36. Spengler, *Decline of the West*, 2:17.
37. Rust, *Towards a Theological Understanding*, 24–25.
38. Bebbington, *Patterns in History*, 40.
39. Ibid., 40.
40. Ibid., 41.
41. Ibid., 41–42.
42. Ibid., 100–105.
43. Baillie, *Belief in Progress*, 64–73.
44. Ibid., 115–116.
45. Bebbington, *Patterns in History*, 82–83; Rust, *Towards a Theological Understanding*, 37–38.
46. Bebbington, *Patterns in History*, 83.
47. Rust, *Towards a Theological Understanding*, 38.
48. Bebbington, *Patterns in History*, 83.
49. J. B. Bury, *The Idea of Progress* (London: Macmillan, 1920), 290.
50. Bebbington, *Patterns in History*, 84.
51. Baillie, *Belief in Progress*, 138–139.
52. Ibid., 138–142.
53. Ibid., 144–145.
54. Ibid., 146.
55. Eric C. Rust, *Evolutionary Philosophies and Contemporary Theology* (Philadelphia: Westminster, 1969), 88, 92–93; cf. Henri L. Bergson, *Creative Evolution* (New York: Modern Library, 1944), 166–167, 182, 194.
56. Samuel Alexander, *Space, Time and Deity*, vol. 2 (London: Macmillan, 1920), 346.
57. Baillie, *Belief in Progress*, 148.
58. C. Lloyd Morgan, *Emergent Evolution* (London: Williams & Norgate, 1926), 33, 36, 209.

59. Alfred North Whitehead, *Adventures of Ideas* (New York: Macmillan, 1933), 354.

60. Alfred North Whitehead, *Process and Reality* (London: Cambridge Univ. Press, 1929), 448.

61. Rust, *Evolutionary Philosophies*, 113.

62. Ibid., 118–119.

63. Alan Richardson, *History Sacred and Profane* (Philadelphia: Westminster, 1964), 290.

64. Bebbington, *Patterns in History*, 119.

65. Richardson, *History Sacred and Profane*, 290.

66. Ibid., 290–292.

67. Rust, *Towards a Theological Understanding*, 56; cf. Georg W. F. Hegel, *The Philosophy of History* (New York: Dover, 1956).

68. Richardson, *History Sacred and Profane*, 291.

69. Ibid., 291.

70. Rust, *Towards a Theological Understanding*, 57.

71. Ibid., 57–58.

72. Ibid., 58.

73. Richardson, *History Sacred and Profane*, 291–292.

74. Rust, *Towards a Theological Understanding*, 45–46.

75. Bebbington, *Patterns in History*, 91.

76. Rust, *Towards a Theological Understanding*, 45.

77. Rust, *Evolutionary Philosophies*, 61.

78. Anthony Campolo, *Partly Right* (Waco, Tex.: Word, 1985), 145.

79. Karl Marx and Frederick Engels, *The German Ideology*, 3rd rev. ed. (Moscow: Progress Publishers, 1938), 58–60.

80. Stephen Neill, *Christian Faith and Other Faiths: The Christian Dialogue with Other Religions* (London: Oxford Univ. Press, 1961), 153–154; R. N. Carew Hunt, *The Theory and Practice of Communism: An Introduction* (New York: Macmillan, 1951), 9–11.

81. Baillie, *Belief in Progress*, 133; Rust, *Evolutionary Philosophies*, 69–70; Hunt, *Communism*, 14–28.

82. Bebbington, *Patterns in History*, 121.

83. Rust, *Evolutionary Philosophies*, 65–66; cf. Ludwig Feuerbach, *The Essence of Christianity* (New York: Harper, 1957).

84. Cf. W. H. Shaw, *Marx's Theory of History* (London: Hutchinson, 1978).

85. Bebbington, *Patterns in History*, 123–125.

86. Campolo, *Partly Right*, 151, 153, 156; cf. Karl Marx, *Capital* (New York: Modern Library, 1936).

87. Bebbington, *Patterns in History*, 129–130.

88. Ibid., 131–132.

89. Ibid., 132–133.

90. Ibid., 135.

91. Neill, *Christian Faith and Other Faiths*, 159–160.

92. Bebbington, *Patterns in History*, 138–139.

93. Campolo, *Partly Right*, 148.

94. Bebbington, *Patterns in History*, 139.

95. Campolo, *Partly Right*, 146; Neill, *Christian Faith and Other Faiths*, 176.

96. Neill, *Christian Faith and Other Faiths*, 165.

97. Ibid., 166; cf. William Hordern, *Christianity, Communism and History* (New York: Abingdon, 1954), 96–117.

98. Ibid., 167, 169–170.

99. Ibid., 164–69.

100. Bebbington, *Patterns in History*, 19.

101. Ibid., 92–93; Grant Wacker, *Augustus H. Strong and the Dilemma of Historical Consciousness* (Macon, Ga.: Mercer Univ. Press, 1985), 16.

102. Wacker, *Strong*, 10–11; cf. H. Stuart Hughes, *Consciousness and Society* (New York: Random House, 1958).

103. Robert H. Wiebe, *The Search for Order* (New York: Hill & Wang, 1967), ch. 2.

104. Wacker, *Strong*, 32–33.

105. Bebbington, *Patterns in History*, 93–94; Rust, *Towards a Theological Understanding*, 10.

106. Rust, *Towards a Theological Understanding*, 9; cf. Max H. Fisch and Thomas G. Bergin, eds., *The New Science of Giambattista Vico* (New York: Cornell Univ. Press, 1948).

107. Bebbington, *Patterns in History*, 107–108.

108. Ibid., 109.

109. Ibid., 110; cf. Hans P. Rickman, ed., *W. Dilthey: Selected Writings* (Cambridge: Cambridge Univ. Press, 1976).

110. Rust, *Towards a Theological Understanding*, 10.

111. R. G. Collingwood, *Idea of History*, 214.

112. Bebbington, *Patterns in History*, 112–113.

113. Wacker, *Strong*, xiii–xiv.

114. Rust, *Towards a Theological Understanding*, 10–12.

115. Bebbington, *Patterns in History*, 113–114.

116. Ibid., 114–116.

117. Alvin Toffler, ed., *The Futurists* (New York: Random House, 1972), 4.

118. Bertrand de Jouvenel, *The Art of Conjecture* (London: Weidenfeld & Nicolson, 1967), 18–19.

119. Os Guinness, *The Dust of Death* (Downers Grove, Ill.: InterVarsity, 1973), 55–74. For details about the extensive bibliography on futurology see Toffler, ed., *The Futurists*; Edward Cornish, ed., *The Study of the Future* (Washington, D.C.: World Future Society, 1977); Ted Peters, *Futures—Human and Divine* (Atlanta: John Knox, 1978).

120. Ibid., 41–42.

121. Cf. Tom Sine, *The Mustard Seed Conspiracy* (Waco, Tex.: Word, 1981); Stephen Davis, *The Jesus Hope* (Downers Grove, Ill.: InterVarsity, 1974); Peters, *Futures—Human and Divine*; Guinness, *Dust of Death*; Donald E. Hoke, *Evangelicals Face the Future* (South Pasadena, Calif.: William Carey Library, 1978). For an evangelical evaluation of the New Age movement, see Douglas R. Groothuis, *Unmasking the New Age* (Downers Grove, Ill.: InterVarsity, 1986) or Russ Chandler, *Understanding the New Age* (Waco, Tex.: Word, 1988).

122. Hendrikus Berkhof, *Well-Founded Hope*, (Richmond, Va.: John Knox, 1969), 71–72, 81–82.

123. Hendrikus Berkhof, *Christ, the Meaning of History*, tr. L. Buurman (Richmond, Va.: John Knox, 1966), 21–22; H. A. Hodges, *Christianity and the Modern World View* (London: SPCK, 1962), 16–17.

124. Bernard J. Cooke, *The God of Space and Time* (New York: Holt, Rinehart & Winston, 1969), 70–72.

125. Rust, *Towards a Theological Understanding*, 214–215.

126. Berkhof, *Christ*, 37–39.

127. G. Ernest Wright, "The Faith of Israel," in George A. Buttrick, ed., *The Interpreter's Bible*, vol. 1 (New York: Abingdon, 1952), 376–378; Driver, *Sense of History*, 43–44.

128. G. Ernest Wright, *The Old Testament Against Its Environment* (Naperville, Ill.: Alec R. Allenson, 1957), 47–50.

129. Ibid., 53–54.

130. G. Ernest Wright, *God Who Acts: Biblical Theology As Recital* (Chicago: Alec R. Allenson, 1952), 113.

131. Wright, *Old Testament Against*, 59–60.

132. Ibid., 64–68.

133. Ibid., 71–72.

134. Floyd V. Filson, *The New Testament Against Its Environment: The Gospel of Christ the Risen Lord* (London: SCM, 1950), 49–51; Rust, *Towards a Theological Understanding*, 207.

135. Rust, *Towards a Theological Understanding*, 207–208.

136. G. Ernest Wright, *The Biblical Doctrine of Man in Society* (London: SCM, 1954), 79–84; Filson, *New Testament Against*, 52.

137. Filson, *New Testament Against*, 54–56.

138. Ibid., 66–68.

139. Ibid., 76.

140. Berkhof, *Christ*, 104–108.

141. Ibid., 113–121.

142. Ibid., 122–123.

143. Wright, *Biblical Doctrine of Man*, 134–137.

144. Berkhof, *Christ*, 174–175; Anthony A. Hoekema, "History: God's Game Plan," *Christianity Today* (2 May 1980): 29.

145. Hoekema, "History," 29.

146. Berkhof, *Christ*, 184–187.

147. Ibid., 84–85.

148. Ibid., 88–89.

149. Ibid., 89.

150. Ibid.

151. Ibid., 90–91.

152. Ibid., 91–92.

153. Ibid., 95–97.

154. Ibid., 98.

155. Ibid., 99–100.

156. Eric C. Rust, *Salvation History: A Biblical Interpretation* (Richmond, Va.: John Knox, 1962), 264; Berkhof, *Christ*, 129–130. Cf. Johannes Munck, *Paul and the Salvation of Mankind* (Richmond, Va.: John Knox, 1959); John P. Newport, *The Lion and the Lamb* (Nashville: Broadman, 1986), 185–187.

157. Berkhof, *Christ*, 131.

158. Ibid., 141–151.

159. Ibid., 153–157; John P. Newport, *The Lion and the Lamb* (Nashville: Broadman, 1986), 294–300.

160. Bebbington, *Patterns in History*, 56–57; cf St. Augustine, *The City of God* (New York: Modern Library, 1950).

161. Rust, *Towards a Theological Understanding*, 238–239.

162. Ibid., 249; Bebbington, *Patterns in History*, 60; John M. Headley, *Luther's View of Church History* (New Haven, Conn.: Yale Univ. Press, 1963), 224–267.

163. Ibid., 239.

164. Ibid., 250.

165. Baillie, *Belief in Progress*, 186–235.

166. Niebuhr, *Faith and History*, 235–243.

167. Rust, *Towards a Theological Understanding*, 252–256.

168. Bebbington, *Patterns in History*, 166.

Chapter 3

1. David Hume, *An Enquiry Concerning Human Understanding*, vol. 12 (Oxford: Clarendon, 1902), 165.

2. John Passmore, *A Hundred Years of Philosophy* (London: Duckworth, 1957), 369.

3. A. J. Ayer, "The Vienna Circle," in Alfred Jules Ayer et al., *The Revolution in Philosophy* (London: Macmillan, 1956), 70.

4. Millard J. Erickson, *Christian Theology*, vol. 1 (Grand Rapids, Mich.: Baker, 1983), 131.

5. Carl F. H. Henry, *God, Revelation and Authority*, vol. 3, *God Who Speaks and Shows: Fifteen Theses, Part Two* (Waco, Tex.: Word, 1979), 348.

6. G. E. Moore, *Philosophical Studies* (Paterson, N.J.: Littlefield, Adams, 1959).

7. Ludwig Wittgenstein, *Tractatus Logico-Philosophicus* (London: Routledge & Kegan Paul, 1958) 4.112, 4.116; also Erickson, *Christian Theology*, 1:131.

8. Erickson, *Christian Theology*, 1:133.

9. Jerry H. Gill, "Wittgenstein and Religious Language," *Theology Today*, 21 (April 1964): 62; also Ludwig Wittgenstein, *Philosophical Investigations*, tr. Gem Anscombe (New York: Macmillan, 1953), 36.

10. Erickson, *Christian Theology*, 1:134.

11. William Hordern, *Speaking of God: The Nature and Purpose of Theological Language* (New York: Macmillan, 1964), 49–52.

12. Ian T. Ramsey, "Contemporary Empiricism," *The Christian Scholar*, 43 (Fall, 1960): 177–178.

13. William B. Williamson, *Ian Ramsey*, Makers of the Modern Theological Mind (Waco, Tex.: Word, 1982), 15–32.

14. Ibid., 111–123.

15. Ian T. Ramsey, *Religious Language* (London: SCM, 1957), 14–15.

16. Erickson, *Christian Theology*, 1:148.

17. Ramsey, *Religious Language*, 15–28; Williamson, *Ramsey*, 123–128.

18. Ramsey, *Religious Language*, 28–37.

19. Ibid., 38–48.

20. Ibid., 49–89.

21. Frederick Ferre, "Mapping the Logic of Models in Science and Theology," *The Christian Scholar*, 46 (Spring 1963): 25.

22. Jerry H. Gill, *Faith in Dialogue: A Christian Apologetic* (Waco, Tex.: Word, 1985), 122–123.

23. Ibid., 123.

24. Ibid.

25. Ibid.

26. Ibid., 124.
27. Ibid., 126.
28. Ibid.
29. Ibid., 127.
30. Cf. George A. Lindbeck, *The Nature of Doctrine: Religion and Theology in a Postliberal Age* (Philadelphia: Westminster, 1984), 20–22; Stanley Hauerwas, *The Peaceable Kingdom: A Primer in Christian Ethics* (Notre Dame, Ind.: Univ. of Notre Dame Press, 1983), 61–63.
31. Lindbeck, *Nature of Doctrine*, 33–34.
32. Roland M. Frye, *Perspectives on Man: Literature and the Christian Tradition* (Philadelphia: Westminster, 1961), 25.
33. J. V. Langmead Casserley, *The Christian in Philosophy* (New York: Scribner's, 1951), 190–195.
34. Ibid., 39–41.
35. Ibid., 57, 69.
36. John Calvin, *Commentaries of John Calvin*, vol. 6, *Commentary on Isaiah* (Grand Rapids, Mich.: Eerdmans, 1947–50), 1.
37. Casserley, *Christian in Philosophy*, 182.
38. J. V. Langmead Casserley, "Event-Symbols and Myth-Symbols," *Anglican Theological Review*, 38, no. 2 (April 1956): 243.
39. C. H. Dodd, *The Bible To-day* (Cambridge: Cambridge Univ. Press, 1962), 111–112; and John P. Newport, *What Is Christian Doctrine?* (Nashville: Broadman, 1984), 36–42.
40. Dodd, *The Bible*, 112–113.
41. Dodd, *The Bible*, 113; and Newport, *Christian Doctrine*, 70–71, 106–107.
42. Dodd, *The Bible*, 110–111.
43. Newport, *Christian Doctrine*, 149.
44. Dodd, *The Bible*, 116–117.
45. Ibid., 117–118.
46. Ibid., 100–102.
47. Ibid., 101.
48. Ibid., 102.
49. Ibid., 102–105.
50. Casserley, "Event-Symbols," 243; cf. also J. V. Langmead Casserley, *Apologetics and Evangelism* (Philadelphia: Westminster, 1962), 104–106.
51. Casserley, *Apologetics*, 109–110; cf Alan Richardson, *History Sacred and Profane* (Philadelphia: Westminster, 1964), 195–212.
52. Ibid., 110.
53. Casserley, *Christian in Philosophy*, 239–240.
54. Ibid., 240–242.
55. Amos N. Wilder, "Contemporary Mythologies and Theological Renewal," *Journal of Religious Thought*, 27 (Autumn–Winter 1970): 6–7.
56. Cf. discussion in William Foxwell Albright, *History, Archaeology and Christian Humanism* (New York: McGraw-Hill, 1964), 51–53, 66–67.
57. B. A. G. Fuller, *A History of Philosophy* (New York: Henry Holt & Co., 1955), 182–183.
58. Albright, *History*, 70–71.
59. Ibid., 68, 85–89.

60. G. Ernest Wright, *God Who Acts* (London: SCM, 1952), chaps. 2–3.

61. G. Ernest Wright, "History and Reality: The Importance of Israel's 'Historical' Symbols for the Christian Faith," in Bernard W. Anderson, ed., *The Old Testament and the Christian Faith* (New York: Harper, 1963), 194–195. Cf. also Gordon D. Kaufman, *Systematic Theology—A Historicist Perspective* (New York: Scribner's, 1968); Wolfhart Pannenberg, *Revelation in History* (New York: Macmillan, 1968); and Richardson, *History Sacred and Profane.*

62. G. Ernest Wright, *The Old Testament and Theology* (New York: Harper, 1969) 46–69.

63. Otto Piper, *Biblical Theology of the New Testament* (Princeton, N.J.: Princeton Theological Seminary, n.d.), 76.

64. Ibid., 77, 82.

65. Claude Tresmontant, *A Study of Hebrew Thought*, tr. Michael Francis Gibson (New York: Desclee, 1960), 146–147.

66. Ibid., 3–16.

67. Ibid., 17–38.

68. John Calvin, *Commentary on Genesis* (Edinburgh: Calvin Translation Society, 1844–1855), 1:15–16.

69. Claude Tresmontant, *The Origins of Christian Philosophy* (New York: Hawthorn, 1963), 19–21.

70. Henry, *God, Revelation and Authority,* 3:389.

71. Ibid., 401.

72. Ibid., 458.

Chapter 4

1. Charles E. Hummel, *The Galileo Connection: Resolving Conflicts Between Science and the Bible* (Downers Grove, Ill.: InterVarsity, 1986), 9, 13.

2. Mark A. Noll and David F. Wells, eds., *Christian Faith and Practice in the Modern World: Theology from an Evangelical Point of View* (Grand Rapids, Mich.: Eerdmans, 1988), 239; cf. also Don Cupitt, *The Sea of Faith: Christianity in Change* (London: British Broadcasting Corporation, 1984), 79.

3. Hummel, *The Galileo Connection,* 13.

4. Ibid., 14; Conrad Hyers, "The Fall and Rise of Creationism," *The Christian Century* (24 April 1985): 411.

5. Hyers, "Fall and Rise of Creationism," 411.

6. Hummel, *Galileo Connection,* 14; Hyers, "Fall and Rise of Creationism," 411.

7. Hyers, "Fall and Rise of Creationism," 411.

8. Ibid.

9. Hummel, *Galileo Connection,* 19.

10. Hyers, "Fall and Rise of Creationism," 412.

11. Hummel, *Galileo Connection,* 19; Hyers, "Fall and Rise of Creationism," 412.

12. Hummel, *Galileo Connection,* 16.

13. Ibid., 17; cf. John Dillenberger, *Protestant Thought and Natural Science* (Garden City, N.J.: Doubleday, 1960), 21–28, 75–93 and Alan Richardson, *The Bible in the Age of Science* (Philadelphia: Westminster, 1961), 9–23.

14. Thomas F. Torrance, "Theological Scientific Inquiry," *Dedication Addresses: The Center of Theological Inquiry: Reports from the Center,* Number 2 (1985), 8.

15. Hummel, *Galileo Connection,* 158; Richard H. Bube, *The Human Quest: A New Look at Science and Christian Faith* (Waco, Tex.: Word, 1971), 56.

16. J. Kenneth Eakins, "The Relationship of the Bible to Natural Science," *The Proceedings of the Conference on Biblical Inerrancy 1987* (Nashville: Broadman, 1987), 358.

17. Ibid.

18. Hummel, *Galileo Connection,* 158–159.

19. Cf. T. S. Kuhn, *The Structure of Scientific Revolutions* (Chicago: Univ. of Chicago Press, 1970); Ian G. Barbour, *Issues in Science and Religion* (Englewood Cliffs, N.J.: Prentice-Hall, 1966), 141–144.

20. Noll and Wells, *Christian Faith,* 253–256.

21. W. Newton-Smith, "In Defence of Truth," in U. J. Jensen and R. Harre, eds., *The Philosophy of Evolution,* (Brighton: Harvester, 1981).

22. Noll and Wells, *Christian Faith,* 252–253.

23. Ibid., 261.

24. Lesslie Newbigin, *Foolishness to the Greeks: The Gospel and Western Culture* (Grand Rapids, Mich.: Eerdmans, 1986), 70; cf. Stanley Jaki, *The Road of Science and the Ways to God* (Chicago: Univ. of Chicago Press, 1978).

25. Newbigin, *Foolishness,* 71.

26. Ibid., 71–72.

27. Hummel, *Galileo Connection,* 160; cf. Jaki, *The Road of Science.*

28. Cf. R. Hooykass, *Religion and the Rise of Modern Science* (Edinburgh: Scottish Academic Press, 1972).

29. Dillenberger, *Protestant Thought and Science,* 128–132; Hooykass, *Religion and the Rise of Modern Science,* 135–160.

30. Hummel, *Galileo Connection,* 166.

31. Ibid., 169.

32. Noll and Wells, *Christian Faith,* 260.

33. Hummel, *Galileo Connection,* 166–167.

34. Ibid., 167; cf. Bernard Ramm, *Special Revelation and the Word of God* (Grand Rapids, Mich.: Eerdmans, 1961), 79–83.

35. Barbour, *Issues in Science and Religion,* 216–219.

36. Ibid., 158–59; Hummel, *Galileo Connection,* 168.

37. Malcolm Jeeves, *The Scientific Enterprise and Christian Faith* (Downers Grove, Ill.: InterVarsity, 1969), 74–78.

38. Hummel, *Galileo Connection,* 169.

39. Ibid., 170.

40. Ibid.; cf. I. H. Marshall, *Biblical Inspiration* (Grand Rapids, Mich.: Eerdmans, 1982), 91.

41. Eakins, *Proceedings 1987,* 357.

42. Hummel, *Galileo Connection,* 170–172.

43. Ibid., 200.

44. Ibid., 200–201.

45. Hyers, "Fall and Rise of Creationism," 414; cf. also Conrad Hyers, *The Meaning of Creation: Genesis and Modern Science* (Atlanta: John Knox, 1984), 50–56.

46. Hyers, "Fall and Rise of Creationism," 414.

47. Ibid.

48. Hummel, *Galileo Connection,* 202–203.

49. Ibid., 205, 214–216.
50. Ibid., 15.
51. Ibid., 174–176.
52. Eakins, *Proceedings 1987,* 357.
53. Hummel, *Galileo Connection,* p. 176–177; cf. Bernard Ramm, *The Christian View of Science and Scripture* (Grand Rapids, Mich.: Eerdmans, 1954), 65–77 and Hooykaas, *Religion and the Rise of Modern Science,* 117–124.
54. Ibid., p. 177–178; cf. Jeeves, *The Scientific Enterprise,* 13–14.
55. Ibid., 227–228; cf. Jeeves, *The Scientific Enterprise,* 90-91, 96–97; William C. Dampier, *A Shorter History of Science* (New York: Meridian, 1957), 120–122.
56. Edwin A. Olson, "Hidden Agenda Behind the Evolutionist/Creationist Debate," *Christianity Today* (23 April 1982): 27; Hummel, *The Galileo Connection,* 228–229; Bube, *The Human Quest,* 45–46; Eric Rust, *Science and Faith* (New York: Oxford Univ. Press, 1967), 146–148.
57. Jeeves, *The Scientific Enterprise,* 100–103.
58. Hummel, *Galileo Connection,* 229.
59. John C. Greene, *Science, Ideology and World View: Essays in the History of Evolutionary Ideas* (Berkeley: Univ. of California Press, 1981), chap. 7.
60. Eakins, *Proceedings 1987,* 358.
61. Noll and Wells, *Christian Faith,* 254–255.
62. Hummel, *Galileo Connection,* 239–240; Rust, *Science and Faith,* 147–159; G. A. Kerkut, *Implications of Evolution* (New York: Pergamon Press, 1965), 6, 157.
63. Ramm, *The Christian View of Science and Scripture,* 280–293.
64. Ibid., 284–285; Hummel, *Galileo Connection,* 232–233.
65. Benjamin B. Warfield, "On the Antiquity and Unity of the Human Race," in Samuel G. Craid, ed., *Biblical and Theological Studies* (Philadelphia: Presbyterian & Reformed, 1952), 238.
66. George F. Wright, "The Passing of Evolution," in *The Fundamentals,* vol. 4 (Los Angeles: Bible Institute of Los Angeles, 1917), 72.
67. James Orr, *The Christian View of God and the World* (Grand Rapids, Mich.: Eerdmans, 1948), 99.
68. Millard J. Erickson, *Christian Theology,* vol. 2 (Grand Rapids, Mich.: Baker, 1984), 481.
69. David L. Dye, *Faith and the Physical World: A Comprehensive View* (Grand Rapids, Mich.: Eerdmans, 1966), 147–148.
70. Erickson, *Christian Theology,* 2:481.
71. Hummel, *Galileo Connection,* 241–242.
72. Erickson, *Christian Theology,* 2:483.
73. Carl F. H. Henry, *God, Revelation and Authority,* vol. 6, *God Who Stands and Stays, Part Two* (Waco, Tex.: Word Books, 1983), 222–223.
74. Erickson, *Christian Theology,* 2:479–480.
75. Hummel, *Galileo Connection,* 242–243.; cf. also Hyers, *Meaning of Creation,* 23–29; Henry M. Morris and John C. Whitcomb, Jr., *The Genesis Flood* (Philadelphia: Presbyterian & Reformed, 1961); Henry M. Morris, *The Remarkable Birth of Planet Earth* (San Diego: Creation-Life, 1972); Henry M. Morris, *The Twilight of Evolution* (Grand Rapids, Mich.: Baker, 1963); Henry M. Morris, *History of Modern Creationism* (San Diego: Creation-Life, 1984); Henry M. Morris, *Creation and the Modern Christian* (San Diego: Creation-Life, 1985).

76. Norman L. Geisler, "Creationism: A Case for Equal Time," *Christianity Today* (19 March 1982): 27; cf. Norman Geisler, *Is Man the Measure?: An Evaluation of Contemporary Humanism* (Grand Rapids, Mich.: Baker, 1983).

77. Ashley Montagu, ed., *Science and Creationism* (Oxford: At the University Press, 1984), 365–397.

78. Norman Geisler, "What Didn't Happen at Little Rock," *Eternity* (May 1982): 22.

79. Ibid., 23.

80. Ibid.

81. Hummel, *Galileo Connection*, 244; J. C. Whitcomb, Jr., and H. M. Morris, *Journal of the American Scientific Affiliation* 16 (June 1964): 60.

82. Hummel, *Galileo Connection*, 244–245.

83. Davis Young, "Genesis: Neither More nor Less," *Eternity* (May 1982): 16; cf. Davis A. Young, *Christianity and the Age of the Earth* (Grand Rapids, Mich.: Zondervan, 1982).

84. Hyers, "Fall and Rise of Creationism," 412–413.

85. William James, *The Varieties of Religious Experience* (New York: Penguin, 1982, first published 1902), 122.

86. Hyers, "Fall and Rise of Creationism," 413.

87. Young, "Genesis," 18–19.

88. Hyers, "Fall and Rise of Creationism," 413; cf. Conrad Hyers, *The Meaning of Creation* (Atlanta: John Knox, 1984), 23–29.

89. Ibid., 414–415; also Henry M. Morris, *The Remarkable Birth of Planet Earth* (Minneapolis: Bethany, 1972), viii, 84.

90. Hyers, "Fall and Rise of Creationism," 415.

91. Ibid.

92. Ibid.

93. Young, "Genesis," 19.

94. Hummel, *Galileo Connection*, 212.

95. Young, "Genesis," 15–16.

96. Hummel, *Galileo Connection*, 212.

97. Young, "Genesis," 15.

98. Ibid., 16; James I. Packer, "The Challenge of Biblical Interpretation: Creation," *The Proceedings of the Conference on Biblical Interpretation 1988* (Nashville: Broadman, 1988), 29–30.

99. Young, "Genesis," 16.

100. Hummel, *Galileo Connection*, 249–250.

101. Erickson, *Christian Theology*, 2:482.

102. Ibid., 482–484; cf. also Ramm, *Christian View of Science and Scripture*, 102–117; Davis A. Young, *Creation and the Flood: An Alternative to Flood Geology and Theistic Evolution* (Grand Rapids, Mich.: Baker, 1977); Robert C. Newman and Herman J. Eckelmann, Jr., *Genesis One and the Origin of the Earth* (Grand Rapids, Mich.: Baker, 1977); Pattle P. Pun, *Evolution: Nature and Scripture in Conflict?* (Grand Rapids, Zondervan, 1982).

103. Hyers, *Meaning of Creation*, 80–85.

104. Jerry H. Gill, *Faith in Dialogue: A Christian Apologetic* (Waco, Tex.: Word, 1985), 21; Karl Barth, *Church Dogmatics*, vol. 3, pt. 2, ed. G. W. Bromiley and T. F. Torrance, tr. G. W. Bromiley, et al. (Edinburgh: T & T Clark, 1936–1969); Bernard Ramm, *After Fundamentalism: The Future of Evangelical Theology* (San Francisco: Harper, 1983), 152–154.

105. Ibid., 21–22; Hummel, *Galileo Connection*, 259.

106. Ibid., 261–262; Bube, *The Human Quest*, 124–126; D. M. MacKay, "Complementary Descriptions," *Mind* 66:390–394; T. F. Torrance, *The Ground and Grammar of Theology* (Belfast: Christian Journals, 1980), 128–145.

107. Ibid., 251–252; Bube, *The Human Quest*, 206–209.

108. V. Elving Anderson, "Evolution, Yes; but Creation Too," *Christianity Today* (8 October 1982): 39–40.

109. Ibid., 40.

110. Ibid.

111. Ibid.

112. Warfield, "On Antiquity and Unity of Human Race," 238.

113. Bertram S. Kraus, *The Basis of Human Evolution* (New York: Harper, 1964), p. 282; Erickson, *Christian Theology*, 2:484–486.

114. Hummel, *Galileo Connection*, 264.

115. Newbigin, *Foolishness*, 93–94; Hummel, *Galileo Connection*, 264–265.

116. Noll and Wells, *Christian Faith*, 262.

117. Hummel, *Galileo Connection*, 216–219.

118. Rust, *Science and Faith*, 201–270.

119. Ibid., 20, 267–275.

Chapter 5

1. David Hume, "Of Miracles," *An Enquiry Concerning Human Understanding* in E. A. Burtt, ed., *The English Philosophers from Bacon to Mill* (New York: Random House, 1939), 657; cf. N. Smart, *Philosophers and Religious Truth* (London: SCM, 1969), 25–49.

2. Eric C. Rust, *Science and Faith* (New York: Oxford Univ. Press, 1967), 295; Colin Brown, *Miracles and the Critical Mind* (Grand Rapids, Mich.: Eerdmans, 1984), 47–77.

3. Alan Richardson, *An Introduction to the Theology of the New Testament* (London: SCM, 1958), 12.

4. Millard J. Erickson, *Christian Theology* , vol. 1 (Grand Rapids, Mich.: Baker, 1983), 407.

5. Ibid., 387.

6. Ibid., 403–404.

7. Bernard Ramm, *The Christian View of Science and Scripture* (Grand Rapids, Mich.: Eerdmans, 1954), 90.

8. Stephen Neill, *Christian Faith and Other Faiths: The Christian Dialogue with Other Religions* (London: Oxford Univ. Press, 1961), 125; David Elton Trueblood, *The Logic of Belief: An Introduction to the Philosophy of Religion* (New York: Harper, 1942), 265.

9. Ramm, *Christian View*, 90–91.

10. Charles E. Hummel, *The Galileo Connection* (Downers Grove, Ill.: InterVarsity, 1986), 195.

11. Ibid., 196.

12. Ibid., 187.

13. Ibid., 188.

14. Ibid., 196.

15. David Elton Trueblood, *Philosophy of Religion* (New York: Harper, 1957), 215.

16. Erickson, *Christian Theology*, 1:406–408; cf. C. S. Lewis, *Miracles* (New York: Macmillan, 1947), 59–61.

17. Richard H. Bube, *The Human Quest: A New Look at Science and Christian Faith* (Waco, Tex.: Word, 1971), 116.

18. Trueblood, *Philosophy of Religion*, 216.

19. Hummel, *Galileo Connection*, 196; cf. Alan Richardson, *History, Sacred and Profane* (Philadelphia: Westminster, 1964), 211–212; Lewis B. Smedes, ed., *Ministry and the Miraculous* (Pasadena, Calif.: Fuller Theological Seminary, 1987).

20. Cf. John F. MacArthur, Jr., *The Charismatics: A Doctrinal Perspective* (Grand Rapids, Mich.: Zondervan, 1978), 74.

21. Ibid., 74.

22. Ibid., 75.

23. Ibid., 74.

24. Erickson, *Christian Theology*, 1:395.

25. MacArthur, *Charismatics*, 76.

26. Ibid., 75.

27. Ibid., 75.

28. Erickson, *Christian Theology*, 1:409.

29. Ibid., 387–388; Smedes, *Ministry and the Miraculous*, 45–47.

30. Carl F. H. Henry, *God, Revelation and Authority*, vol. 6, *God Who Stands and Stays, Part Two* (Waco, Tex.: Word Books, 1983), 459.

31. Erickson, *Christian Theology*, 1:403.

32. Ibid., 398.

33. Ibid., 402–403.

34. Henry, *God, Revelation and Authority*, 6:465.

35. Erickson, *Christian Theology*, 1:395.

36. Rust, *Science and Faith*, 279–280.

37. Ibid., 285–287; Gordon D. Kaufman, *Systematic Theology* (New York: Scribner's, 1968), 299–313.

38. Erickson, *Christian Theology*, 1:403–404; Smedes, *Ministry and the Miraculous*, 47–49.

39. Henry, *God, Revelation and Authority*, 6:471–472.

40. Erickson, *Christian Theology*, 1:405–406.

41. Ibid., 406; Henry, *God, Revelation and Authority*, vol. 4, *God Who Speaks and Shows: Fifteen Theses, Part Three* (Waco, Tex.: Word, 1979), 482.

42. Ibid.

43. Helmut Thielicke, *Man in God's World* (New York: Harper, 1963), 103–104.

44. Rudolf Bultmann, *Kerygma and Myth: A Theological Debate*, ed. H. W. Bartsch (New York: Harper, 1961), chap. 1.

45. Bube, *Human Quest*, 46–47.

46. B. B. Warfield, *Miracles: Yesterday and Today, True and False* (Grand Rapids, Mich.: Eerdmans, 1954), 3, 6.

47. B. B. Warfield, *Counterfeit Miracles* (Carlisle, Penna.: Banner of Truth, 1918), 25–26.

48. Edward John Carnell, *An Introduction to Christian Apologetics: A Philosophic Defense of the Trinitarian-Theistic Faith* (Grand Rapids, Mich.: Eerdmans, 1948), 272, 269.

49. Louis Monden, *Signs and Wonders: A Study of the Miraculous Element in Religion* (New York: Desclee, 1966), 25–26; Brown, *Miracles and the Critical Mind*, 216–218.

50. Ibid., 60.

51. Ibid., 70ff.
52. Ibid., 94, 343.
53. J. Stafford Wright, *Man in the Process of Time* (Grand Rapids, Mich.: Eerdmans, 1956), 83; Smedes, *Ministry and the Miraculous*, 38–39.
54. Brown, *Miracles and the Critical Mind*, 137–139.
55. David duPlessis, "Pentecost Outside Pentecost" (pamphlet, 1960), 6.
56. MacArthur, *Charismatics*, 13; John L. Sherrill, *They Speak with Other Tongues*, (Old Tappan, N.J.: Revell, 1964), 60.
57. George W. Peters, *Indonesia Revival: Focus on Timor* (Grand Rapids, Mich.: Zondervan, 1973), 61–63.
58. MacArthur, *Charismatics*, 180.
59. Sudhir Kakar, *Shamans, Mystics and Doctors: A Psychological Inquiry into India and Its Healing Traditions* (Boston: Beacon Press, 1983); Ari Kiev, ed., *Magic, Faith and Healing: Studies in Primitive Psychiatry Today* (New York: The Free Press, 1974).
60. MacArthur, *Charismatics*, 188.
61. Colin Brown, *That You May Believe: Miracles and Faith, Then and Now* (Grand Rapids, Mich.: Eerdmans, 1985), 189.
62. Ibid., 190–192.
63. Ibid., 198–199; cf. Smedes, *Ministry and the Miraculous*, 30–32.
64. Ibid., 196.
65. Ibid., 205.
66. Ibid., 209–210.
67. Ibid., 211.
68. Ibid., 215.
69. Ibid., 219–221.
70. Cf. Peters, *Indonesia*, 60–61.
71. A detailed report of a task force of twelve Fuller Seminary professors is found in Smedes, *Ministry and the Miraculous*, 15–17; cf. also "Fuller Seminary Releases Study on the Miraculous," *Christianity Today* (6 February 1987): 44.
72. "Fuller Seminary Releases," 31.
73. Ibid., 32, 33, 51.
74. Ibid., 48, 57.
75. MacArthur, *Charismatics*, 84.
76. E. Y. Mullins, *Why Is Christianity True?* (Philadelphia: Judson, 1905), 170–187.
77. MacArthur, *Charismatics*, 84.
78. Ibid., *Charismatics*, 142.
79. Ibid., 200–203.
80. Henry, *God, Revelation and Authority*, 6:482.
81. H. H. Farmer, *The World and God* (London: Nisbet & Co., 1936), 261–265.
82. Ibid., 266–268.
83. Henry, *God, Revelation and Authority*, 6:482.
84. Trueblood, *Philosophy of Religion*, 217.

Chapter 6

1. M. Scott Peck, *People of the Lie: The Hope for Healing Human Evil* (New York: Simon & Schuster, 1983), 182; cf. Jeffrey Burton Russell, *The Devil* (Ithaca, N.Y.: Cornell Univ. Press, 1977).

2. Kenneth L. Woodward with David Gates, "Giving the Devil His Due," *Newsweek* (30 August 1982): 72; Walter Wink, *Unmasking the Powers: The Invisible Forces That Determine Human Existence* (Philadelphia: Fortress, 1986), 1.

3. Wink, *Unmasking the Powers*, 3.

4. Ibid., 9–10.

5. Ibid., 28.

6. Edward Langton, *Satan, A Portrait* (London: Skeffington & Son, 1945), 117; Malachi Martin, *Hostage to the Devil* (New York: Reader's Digest, 1976).

7. Wink, *Unmasking the Powers*, 41.

8. Arthur Lyons, *The Second Coming: Satanism in America* (New York: Dodd, Mead, 1970), 197.

9. John Warwick Montgomery, ed., *Demon Possession* (Minneapolis: Bethany, 1976), 256–257.

10. Wink, *Unmasking the Powers*, 2, 4.

11. Peck, *People of the Lie*, 183–184.

12. Jeffrey Burton Russell, *Satan* (Ithaca, N.Y.: Cornell Univ. Press, 1981), 222.

13. Eric Lionel Mascall, ed., *The Angels of Light and the Powers of Darkness* (London: Faith Press, 1955), 1.

14. Wink, *Unmasking the Powers*, 6–7; cf. John P. Newport, *Demons, Demons, Demons* (Nashville: Broadman, 1972).

15. Montgomery, *Demon Possession*, 34–35, 326.

16. Peck, *People of the Lie*, 203.

17. Montgomery, *Demon Possession*, 34–35.

18. Edward Langton, *Essentials of Demonology* (London: Epworth, 1949), 63–67.

19. George Eldon Ladd, *Jesus and the Kingdom* (New York: Harper, 1964), 83–97.

20. Ibid., 6, 49, 52, 77, 610.

21. Ibid., 401–402.

22. Ibid., 608, 610, 628.

23. James Kallas, *Jesus and the Power of Satan* (Philadelphia: Westminster, 1968), 202–215.

24. Eric Rust, *Towards a Theological Understanding of History* (New York: Oxford Univ. Press, 1963), 125.

25. Os Guinness, *The Dust of Death* (Downers Grove, Ill.: InterVarsity, 1973), 277–280.

26. Peck, *People of the Lie*, 183.

27. William L. Hendricks, *A Theology of Aging* (Nashville: Broadman, 1986), 163–164.

28. Peck, *People of the Lie*, 210.

29. Millard J. Erickson, *Christian Theology*, vol. 1 (Grand Rapids, Mich.: Baker, 1983), 451.

30. Hendricks, *Aging*, 164.

31. Peck, *People of the Lie*, 205.

32. C. H. Dodd, *The Authority of the Bible* (London: Nisbet & Co., 1928), 236–237.

33. Langton, *Essentials*, 160.

34. Cf. Rudolf Bultmann, *Primitive Christianity in Its Contemporary Setting*, tr. R. H. Fuller (New York: Thames & Hudson, 1956).

35. Kallas, *Jesus and the Power of Satan*, 202–215.

36. Wink, *Unmasking the Powers*, 41–42.

37. Ibid.

38. Selby Vernon McCasland, *By the Finger of God* (New York: Macmillan, 1951), 136.

39. Wayne Oates, *The Psychology of Religion* (Waco, Tex.: Word, 1973), 259.
40. Ibid., 260.
41. Ibid., 261.
42. Peck, *People of the Lie*, 185.
43. Cf. Montgomery, *Demon Possession*, 223.
44. Kurt E. Koch, *Christian Counseling and Occultism* (Grand Rapids, Mich.: Kregel, 1972), 322–323; Donald G. Bloesch, *The Reform of the Church* (Grand Rapids, Mich.: Eerdmans, 1970), 134.
45. Wink, *Unmasking the Powers*, 38.
46. Ibid.
47. Montgomery, *Demon Possession*, 342.
48. Ibid., 342–343.
49. R. H. Robbins, *The Encyclopedia of Witchcraft and Demonology* (New York: Crown, 1959), 180–189.
50. Grillot De Givry, *Witchcraft, Magic and Alchemy* (New York: Bonanza, 1970), 25–39.
51. Montgomery, *Demon Possession*, 342–343.
52. Ibid., 343.
53. Frank Hammond and Ida Mae Hammond, *Pigs in the Parlor: A Practical Guide to Deliverance* (Kirkwood, Mo.: Impact, 1973), 111–121. Other charismatic authors dealing with this subject include Don Basham, Kenneth Hagin, Gordon Lindsay, and Derek Prince. Cf. Don Basham, *Deliver Us from Evil* (Washington Depot, Conn.: Chosen, 1972).
54. Ibid., 47–52.
55. Ibid., 84–85.
56. Donald Bridge and David Phypers, *Spiritual Gifts and the Church* (Downers Grove, Ill.: InterVarsity, 1973), 66.
57. Peck, *People of the Lie*, 193.
58. Ibid.
59. Wink, *Unmasking the Powers*, 43.
60. Ibid., 52.
61. Ibid., 53.
62. Ibid.
63. Ibid.
64. C. S. Lewis, *The Screwtape Letters* (New York: Macmillan, 1970), 3.
65. Mascall, *Angels of Light*, 13–14.
66. Ibid., 14–16.
67. Ibid., 16–17.
68. Smedes, *Ministry and the Miraculous*, 72–73.
69. John A. Sanford, *Evil: The Shadow Side of Reality* (New York: Crossroad, 1981), 118.
70. Peck, *People of the Lie*, 206.
71. Ibid., 206–207.
72. Erickson, *Christian Theology*, 1:448, 450.
73. James Kallas, *The Real Satan: From Biblical Times to the Present* (Minneapolis: Augsburg, 1975), 110.
74. Ibid., 110–111.
75. Wink, *Unmasking the Powers*, 42.
76. Ibid.

77. Ibid., 42–43.
78. Ibid., 43.
79. Ibid., 50–51.
80. Ibid.; cf. H. G. Baynes, *Germany Possessed* (London: Jonathan Cape, 1941).
81. Ibid., 51–52; cf. Martin Luther King, Jr., "A Prophecy for the '80s: Martin Luther King's 'Beyond Vietnam' Speech," *Sojourners* 12 (January 1983), and Ernest Becker, *The Denial of Death* (New York: Free Press, 1973), 133.
82. J. Stafford Wright, *Mind, Man and the Spirits* (Grand Rapids, Mich.: Zondervan, 1971), 132.
83. Peck, *People of the Lie,* 190.
84. Donald G. Bloesch, *The Reform of the Church* (Grand Rapids, Mich.: Eerdmans, 1970), 131–133.
85. Koch, *Christian Counseling and Occultism,* 217–218.
86. Peck, *People of the Lie,* 210.
87. Bloesch, *Reform,* 133.
88. Peck, *People of the Lie,* 190.
89. Ibid.; cf. Kent Philpott, *A Manual of Demonology and the Occult* (Grand Rapids, Mich.: Zondervan, 1973), 116–118, and Newport, *Demons, Demons, Demons,* 77.
90. Colin Brown, *That You May Believe: Miracles and Faith, Then and Now* (Grand Rapids, Mich.: Eerdmans, 1985), 211.
91. Ibid., 212.
92. Bridge and Phypers, *Spiritual Gifts,* 68–69.
93. Bloesch, *Reform,* 132.
94. Peck, *People of the Lie,* 191–192.
95. Ibid., 192–193.
96. Wink, *Unmasking the Powers,* 59.
97. Smedes, *Ministry and the Miraculous,* 74
98. Ibid., 60.
99. Ibid., 60–61.
100. Ibid., 61.
101. Ibid., 64.
102. Ibid.
103. Donald R. Jacobs, *Demons* (Scottdale, Pa.: Herald, 1972), 39–40.
104. Peck, *People of the Lie,* 207–208; M. Scott Peck, *The Road Less Traveled* (New York: Simon & Schuster, 1978), 51.
105. Peck, *People of the Lie,* 208.
106. Jacobs, *Demons,* 40–41.
107. Peck, *People of the Lie,* 185.
108. Ibid., 185–186.
109. Ibid.
110. Ibid., 199; Smedes, *Ministry and the Miraculous,* 74.
111. Ibid., 208.
112. Ibid., 185–186.
113. Koch, *Christian Counseling and Occultism,* 277–278; Philpott, *Demonology and the Occult,* 11–12.
114. Peck, *People of the Lie,* 189.
115. Ibid., 187.
116. Ibid., 188.
117. Wink, *Unmasking the Powers,* p. 65.

118. Ibid.
119. Ibid., 65–66.
120. Ibid., 67–68.
121. Ibid., 68.
122. Bloesch, *Reform,* 134.
123. Montgomery, *Demon Possession,* 86–87.
124. Kallas, *Real Satan,* 111.

Chapter 7

1. Cf. Germaine Bree, *Camus* (New Brunswick, N.J.: Rutgers Univ. Press, 1959).
2. Stephen T. Davis, ed., *Encountering Evil: Live Options in Theodicy* (Atlanta: John Knox, 1981), 7.
3. John Macquarrie, *In Search of Humanity: A Theological and Philosophical Approach* (New York: Crossroad, 1985), 224.
4. J. Christiaan Beker, *Suffering and Hope* (Philadelphia: Fortress, 1987), 16.
5. Davis, *Encountering Evil,* 6.
6. Beker, *Suffering and Hope,* 16.
7. Ibid., 20–21.
8. Herbert H. Farmer, *Towards a Belief in God* (New York: Macmillan, 1943), 241–242.
9. David Elton Trueblood, *Philosophy of Religion* (New York: Harper, 1957), 232–233.
10. Ibid., 231–232.
11. Macquarrie, *In Search of Humanity,* 223.
12. John Hick, *Evil and the God of Love* (New York: Harper, 1978), 3–4.
13. Ibid., 4.
14. Ibid., 6.
15. J. A. Hutchison, *Faith, Reason, and Existence* (New York: Oxford Univ. Press, 1956), 144; J. S. Whale, *The Christian Answer to the Problem of Evil,* 4th ed. (London: SCM, 1957), 11.
16. Trueblood, *Philosophy of Religion,* 233ff.
17. Norman L. Geisler, *The Roots of Evil* (Grand Rapids, Mich.: Zondervan, 1978), 15.
18. Robert Ernest Hume, *The World's Living Religions* (New York: Scribner's, 1944).
19. Geisler, *Roots of Evil,* 16.
20. Swami Vivekananda, *Vedanta Philosophy* (New York: Baker & Taylor, 1913).
21. Mary Baker Eddy, *Science and Health with Key to the Scriptures* (Boston: Trustees under the Will of Mary Baker Eddy, 1934), 71.
22. Ibid., 348, 378.
23. Millard J. Erickson, *Christian Theology,* vol. 1 (Grand Rapids, Mich.: Baker, 1983), 420.
24. Ibid., 421; Geisler, *Roots of Evil,* 17.
25. Winston L. King, *Introduction to Religion* (New York: Harper, 1968), 272–273.
26. Arthur Schopenhauer, *The World as Will and Idea,* vol. III, tr. R. B. Halden and J. Kemp (London: Routledge & Kegan Paul, 1883, 1948), 376–401.
27. Rudoslov A. Tsanoff, *The Nature of Evil* (New York: Macmillan, 1931), xiv.
28. Andrew M. Fairbairn, *The Philosophy of the Christian Religion,* 8th ed. (New York: Macmillan, 1947), 125.
29. Donald Bloesch, *The Ground of Certainty* (Grand Rapids, Mich.: Eerdmans, 1971), 105.

30. Ibid.

31. Ibid., 106; Hick, *Evil and the God of Love*, 26–27.

32. Ibid.

33. Georg W. F. Hegel, *Lectures on the Philosophy of Religion*, tr. E. B. Speirs and J. B. Sanderson, vol. 3 (London: Kegan Paul, Trench, Trubner, 1895), 48.

34. Erickson, *Christian Theology*, 1:414–415.

35. Geisler, *Roots of Evil*, 18.

36. Hick, *Evil and the God of Love*, 38, 39.

37. Samuel M. Zwemer, *Islam, A Challenge to Faith* (New York: Student Volunteer Movement, 1907), 96.

38. Armand Maurer, "Scotism and Ockamism," *A History of Philosophical Systems*, ed. Vergilius Ferm (New York: Philosophical Library, 1950), 222.

39. Hick, *Evil and the God of Love*, 124–125.

40. Martin E. Marty, *Health and Medicine in the Lutheran Tradition: Being Well* (New York: Crossroad, 1983), 56; Dorothee Soelle, *Suffering* (Philadelphia: Fortress, 1975), 17–28.

41. Hick, *Evil and the God of Love*, 123–124; Edward A. Dowey, *The Knowledge of God in Calvin's Theology* (New York: Columbia Univ. Press, 1952), 213–216.

42. Bernard L. Ramm, *The God Who Makes a Difference* (Waco, Tex.: Word, 1972), 125.

43. Ibid.

44. Harold S. Kushner, *When Bad Things Happen to Good People* (New York: Avon, 1981), 134.

45. Edgar Sheffield Brightman, *The Problem of God* (New York: Abingdon, 1930), 17.

46. Edgar S. Brightman, *A Philosophy of Religion* (Englewood Cliffs, N.J.: Prentice-Hall, 1940), 336–337, 245, 314.

47. Hick, *Evil and the God of Love* 39.

48. Brightman, *Problem of God*, 183.

49. King, *Introduction to Religion*, 273–274.

50. Ibid., 276.

51. Bloesch, *Ground of Certainty*, 116, 117.

52. Ibid.

53. Ibid., 118.

54. Beker, *Suffering and Hope*, 28–29.

55. H. Wheeler Robinson, *Suffering, Human and Divine* (New York: Macmillan, 1939), 33–34.

56. Ibid., 34.

57. Ibid., 35; Beker, *Suffering and Hope*, 58.

58. Robinson, *Suffering, Human and Divine*, 34ff.

59. Beker, *Suffering and Hope*, 34–35.

60. Ibid., 35–36.

61. Ibid., 36.

62. Robinson, *Suffering, Human and Divine*, 38.

63. A. B. Davidson, *The Books of Nahum, Habakkuk, and Zephaniah* (Cambridge: Cambridge Univ. Press, 1899), 93; Albert C. Knudson, *The Religious Teaching of the Old Testament* (New York: Abingdon-Cokesbury, 1918), 286.

64. Ramm, *The God Who Makes a Difference*, 142.

65. Robinson, *Suffering, Human and Divine*, 43.

66. Ibid., 42–46.

67. H. Wheeler Robinson, *The Religious Ideas of the Old Testament* (London: Duckworth, 1952), 176.

68. Robinson, *Suffering, Human and Divine,* 192–193.

69. J. H. Bernard, *The Second Epistle to the Corinthians,* in *The Expositor's Greek Testament* (Grand Rapids, Mich.: Eerdmans, n.d.), 112.

70. A. B. Davidson, *The Theology of the Old Testament* (Edinburgh: T & T Clark, 1949), 287.

71. Ramm, *The God Who Makes a Difference,* 138.

72. W. T. Conner, *The Faith of the New Testament* (Nashville: Broadman, 1946), 100–101.

73. Arthur S. Peake, *The Problem of Suffering in the Old Testament* (London: Dalton & Kelly, 1904), 119.

74. Beker, *Suffering and Hope,* 41.

75. Ibid., 42, 52.

76. Ramm, *The God Who Makes a Difference,* 145–146.

77. Robinson, *Suffering, Human and Divine,* 82–87.

78. Alvin Plantinga, *God, Freedom and Evil* (Grand Rapids, Mich.: Zondervan, 1985), 204–205.

79. D. S. Cairns, *The Riddle of the World,* (New York: Round Table, 1938), 311.

80. John W. Wenham, *The Enigma of Evil* (Grand Rapids, Mich.: Zondervan, 1985), 204–205.

81. Norman L. Geisler, *The Roots of Evil* (Grand Rapids, Mich.: Zondervan, 1978), 71.

82. Ibid., 73–74; also James S. Stewart, *The Strong Name* (New York: Scribner's, 1941), 142.

83. Macquarrie, *In Search of Humanity,* 230.

84. Trueblood, *Philosophy of Religion,* 255.

85. Alan Richardson, *The Gospel and Modern Thought* (New York: Oxford Univ. Press, 1950), 192ff.

86. Robinson, *Suffering, Human and Divine,* 131.

87. Ibid., 88; Geisler, *Roots of Evil,* 75–76.

88. Carl F. H. Henry, *God, Revelation and Authority,* vol. 6, *God Who Stands and Stays, Part Two* (Waco, Tex.: Word, 1983), 271.

89. Trueblood, *Philosophy of Religion,* 253–254.

90. Stewart, *Strong Name,* 138–139.

91. Bernard Ramm, *The Christian View of Science and Scripture* (Grand Rapids, Mich.: Eerdmans, 1954), 335.

92. Geisler, *Roots of Evil,* 74.

93. Hick, *Evil and the God of Love,* 309–310.

94. Ibid., 312.

95. Ibid., 313–314.

96. Wenham, *The Enigma of Evil,* 205; C. S. Lewis, *The Problem of Pain* (London: Collins, 1940), 117–132; Robert E. D. Clark, *The Universe: Plan or Accident?* (London: Paternoster, 1949), ch. 16.

97. Trueblood, *Philosophy of Religion,* 251–252.

98. Henry, *God, Revelation and Authority,* 6:280.

99. G. Ernest Wright, *The Biblical Doctrine of Man in Society* (London: SCM, 1956), 43.

100. Trueblood, *Philosophy of Religion,* 252.

101. Hick, *Evil and the God of Love,* 266.
102. Ibid., 270–271.
103. Ibid., 272.
104. Ibid., 274–275.
105. Wenham, *Enigma of Evil,* 52.
106. Ibid., 53.
107. Ibid., 251.
108. Bloesch, *Ground of Certainty,* 122.
109. Ibid., 118–119.
110. Ibid., 122–123.
111. Davis, *Encountering Evil,* 82.
112. Wenham, *Enigma of Evil,* 51.
113. Ibid.
114. Bloesch, *Ground of Certainty,* 120.
115. Ibid., 120–121.
116. Wright, *Biblical Doctrine of Man,* 66.
117. Wenham, *Enigma of Evil,* 56.
118. Beker, *Suffering and Hope,* 60.
119. Ibid., 61.
120. Ibid., 61–62.
121. Wenham, *Enigma of Evil,* 74, 76–77.
122. Herbert H. Farmer, *Towards a Belief* 245.
123. Ibid., 245–246.
124. Wenham, *Enigma of Evil,* 58, 68.
125. Ibid., 68–69.
126. Ibid., 69.
127. Ibid., 70.
128. Robinson, *Suffering, Human and Divine,* 168–172, 184.
129. Beker, *Suffering and Hope,* 62–63.
130. Ibid.
131. Henry, *God, Revelation and Authority,* 6:303.
132. William Dyrness, *Christian Apologetics in a World Community* (Downers Grove, Ill.: InterVarsity, 1983), 162.
133. Ibid., 162–163.
134. Beker, *Suffering and Hope,* 91.
135. P.T. Forsyth, *The Justification of God* (London: Independent, 1948), 53.
136. Stewart, *Strong Name,* 163.
137. Beker, *Suffering and Hope,* 91.
138. Ibid., 58.
139. Robinson, *Suffering, Human and Divine,* 150–158.
140. Wenham, *The Enigma of Evil,* 170.
141. Frank Louis Mauldin, "God's Transformation of Evil and Suffering," *Search* (Fall 1984): 49–50.
142. Stewart, *Strong Name,* 169–170.
143. Ramm, *The God Who Makes a Difference,* 132.
144. Ibid., 132–133.
145. Ibid., 134.
146. Mauldin, *Search,* 50–51.

147. Ibid., 51; also Robinson, *Suffering, Human and Divine*, 160.
148. Macquarrie, *In Search of Humanity*, 224.
149. Stewart, *Strong Name*, 165.
150. Robinson, *Suffering, Human and Divine*, 191–193.
151. Beker, *Suffering and Hope*, 65.
152. Ibid.
153. Ibid., 48.
154. Ibid., 50.
155. Stewart, *Strong Name*, 168.
156. Dyrness, *Christian Apologetics*, 160–161.
157. Ibid., 161–162.
158. Walter von Loewenich, *Luther's Theology of the Cross*, tr. Herbert J. A. Bouman (Minneapolis: Augsburg, 1976), 13ff, 119–123.
159. Marty, *Health and Medicine*, 60.
160. Ibid.
161. Andre Dumas, *Dietrich Bonhoeffer, Theologian of Reality* (New York: Macmillan, 1971), 203–207.
162. Edmund Bergler, *The Basic Neurosis* (New York: Grune & Stratton, 1949).
163. Beker, *Suffering and Hope*, 78–79.
164. Ibid., 49.
165. Ibid.
166. Ibid.
167. Ibid., 49–50.
168. Ibid., 50.
169. Frederick von Huegel, cited by D. Elton Trueblood, *The Logic of Belief* (New York: Harper, 1972), 280.
170. Hutchison, *Faith, Reason, and Existence*, 148–149.

Chapter 8

1. William L. Hendricks, *A Theology for Aging* (Nashville: Broadman, 1986), 25.
2. John Macquarrie, *In Search of Humanity: A Theological and Philosophical Approach* (New York: Crossroad, 1982), 233.
3. Carl F. H. Henry, *God, Revelation and Authority*, vol. 4, *God Who Speaks and Shows: Fifteen Theses, Part Three* (Waco, Tex.: Word, 1979), 602.
4. Macquarrie, *In Search of Humanity*, 234.
5. Mark Albrecht, *Evangelical Newsletter* 4 (21 October 1977).
6. David H. C. Read, "Secular Apocalyptic," in Geddes MacGregor, ed., *Immortality and Human Destiny: A Variety of Views* (New York: Paragon, 1985), 186.
7. Ibid., 190.
8. Eric C. Rust, *Towards a Theological Understanding of History* (New York: Oxford Univ. Press, 1963), 208.
9. Hendricks, *Theology for Aging*, 25.
10. Emil Brunner, *Eternal Hope* (Philadelphia: Westminster, 1954), 91–92.
11. Cf. Ernest Becker, *The Denial of Death* (New York: Free Press, 1973), 11–24.
12. Ray S. Anderson, *Theology, Death and Dying* (New York: Basil Blackwell, 1986), 32.
13. Becker, *Denial of Death*, 175.
14. Anderson, *Theology, Death and Dying*, 105.

15. Michael Simpson, *The Facts of Death* (Englewood Cliffs, N.J.: Prentice-Hall, 1979), 5, 264.

16. William E. Phipps, *Death: Confronting the Reality* (Atlanta: John Knox, 1987), 174.

17. Anderson, *Theology, Death and Dying,* 23.

18. Ibid., 2.

19. Ibid., 24.

20. John H. Hick, *Death and Eternal Life* (New York: Harper, 1976), 437.

21. Anderson, *Theology, Death and Dying,* 59.

22. Macquarrie, *In Search of Humanity,* 233–234.

23. Phipps, *Death,* 7.

24. David Hendin, *Death As a Fact of Life* (New York: Norton, 1974), 100.

25. Alan Harrington, *The Immortalist: An Approach to the Engineering of Man's Divinity* (New York: Random House, 1969), 3.

26. Millard J. Erickson, *Christian Theology,* vol. 3 (Grand Rapids, Mich.: Baker, 1985), 1168.

27. Jessica Mitford, *The American Way of Death* (New York: Simon & Schuster, 1963).

28. Anderson, *Theology, Death and Dying,* 34, 16.

29. Erickson, *Christian Theology,* 3:1168–1169.

30. Henry, *God, Revelation and Authority,* 4:602–603.

31. Helmut Thielicke, *Living with Death* (Grand Rapids, Mich.: Eerdmans, 1983), 29ff.

32. William May, "The Sacral Power of Death in Contemporary Experience," in Liston O. Mills, ed., *Perspectives on Death,* (Nashville: Abingdon, 1969), 172ff., 168ff.

33. Ibid., 170.

34. Phipps, *Death,* 155.

35. Gilbert E. M. Ogutu, "An African Perception," in MacGregor, ed., *Immortality and Human Destiny,* 105.

36. Phipps, *Death,* 155–156.

37. Hendricks, *Theology for Aging,* 27.

38. Henry, *God, Revelation and Authority,* 4:603.

39. John Lewis, *The Life and Teachings of Karl Marx* (New York: International, 1965), 273.

40. Russell Aldwinckle, *Death in the Secular City* (Grand Rapids, Mich.: Eerdmans, 1972), 32–33.

41. Macquarrie, *In Search of Humanity,* 249.

42. Ibid.

43. Manfred Kerkhoff, "MesoAmerican Ball Games," in MacGregor, ed., *Immortality and Human Destiny,* 170.

44. Macquarrie, *In Search of Humanity,* 249–250.

45. Henry, *God, Revelation and Authority,* 4:598, 608.

46. Peter Anthony Bertocchi, *Introduction to the Philosophy of Religion* (Englewood Cliffs, N.J.: Prentice-Hall, 1951), 528–529.

47. Phipps, *Death,* 171.

48. Immanuel Kant, *Foundations of the Metaphysics of Morals,* tr. L. W. Beck (Indianapolis: Bobbs-Merrill, 1959).

49. O. J. West, *Psychical Research Today* (London: Duckworth, 1954), 11.

50. Robert A. Morey, *Death and the Afterlife* (Minneapolis: Bethany, 1984), 175–176.

51. Anderson, *Theology, Death and Dying,* 106.

52. Ibid., 106–107.

53. Morey, *Death and the Afterlife,* 179.

54. Ibid., 179–180.

55. William James, *Human Immortality* (New York: Houghton Mifflin, 1899), 488–489.

56. Anderson, *Theology, Death and Dying,* 107.

57. Phipps, *Death,* 171; C. J. Ducasse, *A Critical Examination of Belief in a Life After Death* (New York: Charles C. Thomas, 1961), 276–299.

58. Anderson, *Theology, Death and Dying,* 104.

59. Ernst Haeckel, *The Riddle of the Universe* (New York: Harper, 1900), 201, 210.

60. T. A. Kantonen, *Life After Death* (Philadelphia: Muhlenberg, 1962), 11–12.

61. Hendricks, *Theology for Aging,* 18.

62. William Hasker, *Metaphysics: Constructing a World View* (Downers Grove, Ill.: InterVarsity, 1983), 69–70.

63. Ibid., 70.

64. Ibid., 58, 60.

65. Edgar S. Brightman, *A Philosophy of Religion* (New York: Henry Holt & Co., 1925), 395.

66. H. R. Mackintosh, *Immortality and the Future* (New York: George H. Doran, 1917), 107.

67. Macquarrie, *In Search of Humanity,* 7.

68. Ibid., 49.

69. Ibid., 50.

70. Ibid.

71. Cf. Jacob Neusner, *The Way of Torah: An Introduction to Judaism* (Encino, Calif.: Dickenson, 1974).

72. Anderson, *Theology, Death and Dying,* 6.

73. Neusner, *Way of Torah,* 56.

74. Emil Fackenheim, *God's Presence in History: Jewish Affirmations and Philosophical Reflections* (New York: New York Univ. Press, 1970), 84.

75. Anderson, *Theology, Death and Dying,* 6, 7, 126.

76. Ibid., 127.

77. Ibid.

78. Ibid., 57–58.

79. Hasker, *Metaphysics,* 65; cf. Oscar Cullmann, "Immortality of the Soul or Resurrection of the Dead," in Krister Stendahl, ed., *Immortality and Resurrection* (New York: Macmillan, 1965), 9–53.

80. Erwin Rohde, *Psyche* (London: Kegan Paul, Trench, Trubner, 1925), 342.

81. Harold R. Willoughby, *Pagan Regeneration* (Chicago: Univ. of Chicago Press, 1929), 100–101.

82. George Galloway, *The Idea of Immortality* (Edinburgh: T & T Clark, 1919), 104.

83. Henry, *God, Revelation and Authority,* vol. 6, *God Who Stands and Stays, Part Two* (Waco, Tex.: Word, 1983), 502.

84. Macquarrie, *In Search of Humanity,* 250.

85. Kantonen, *Life After Death,* 13.

86. A. E. Taylor, *Plato, The Man and His Work* (London: Methuen, 1948), 177.

87. Dale Moody, *The Word of Truth: A Summary of Christian Doctrine Based on Biblical Revelation* (Grand Rapids, Mich.: Eerdmans, 1981), 500.

88. Phipps, *Death,* 161.

89. Moody, *Word of Truth,* 500.

90. Ibid.
91. Anderson, *Theology, Death and Dying,* 8.
92. Ibid., 58.
93. Macquarrie, *In Search of Humanity,* 250.
94. Anderson, *Theology, Death and Dying,* 59.
95. Ibid.
96. Brightman, *Philosophy;* Kantonen, *Life After Death,* 14.
97. Anderson, *Theology, Death and Dying,* 7.
98. Ibid.
99. Ibid., 23.
100. Ibid., 8–9.
101. Ibid., 9.
102. Hick, *Death and Eternal Life,* 332–333.
103. Ibid., 337.
104. Ibid., 338–340.
105. Ibid., 339.
106. Ibid., 344–346.
107. Ibid.
108. Anderson, *Theology, Death and Dying,* 23.
109. R. C. Gordon-McCutchan, "Transmigration in the Transcendentalists," in MacGregor, ed., *Immortality and Human Destiny,* 22.
110. Russell Chandler, *Understanding the New Age* (Dallas: Word, 1988), 45–46.
111. Gordon-McCutchan, "Transmigration," 24–27.
112. Ibid., 28–29.
113. Ibid., 31–35.
114. Ibid., 21–22.
115. Chandler, *Understanding the New Age,* 205–207.
116. Anderson, *Theology, Death and Dying,* 106.
117. Phipps, *Death,* 172.
118. Ibid., 172–173.
119. Hick, *Death and Eternal Life,* 404.
120. Ibid.; Phipps, *Death,* 173.
121. Hick, *Death and Eternal Life,* 404.
122. Grace Rosher, *Beyond the Horizon* (London: James Clark, 1961), 28.
123. Ibid., 405–406.
124. John H. Hick, *Death and Eternal Life* (New York: Harper), 129, 130.
125. Brooks Alexander, "Theology from the Twilight Zone," *Christianity Today* (18 September 1987): 24.
126. Irving Hexham and Karla Poewe, *Understanding Cults and New Religions* (Grand Rapids, Mich.: Eerdmans, 1986), 20.
127. J. Stafford Wright, *Mind, Man and the Spirits* (Grand Rapids, Mich.: Zondervan, 1968), 106.
128. Ibid., 112.
129. Phipps, *Death,* 158; Anderson, *Theology, Death and Dying,* 107–108.
130. Chandler, *Understanding the New Age,* 262–263.
131. Walter A. Elwell, ed., *Evangelical Dictionary of Theology* (Grand Rapids, Mich.: Baker, 1984), 926.
132. Phipps, *Death,* 159.

133. Elwell, *Evangelical Dictionary,* 926.
134. Phipps, *Death,* 159–160.
135. Elwell, *Evangelical Dictionary,* 926.
136. Phipps, *Death,* 160.
137. Ibid.
138. Ibid., 160–161.
139. Elwell, *Evangelical Dictionary,* 926.
140. Hick, *Death and Eternal Life,* 456.
141. Anderson, *Theology, Death and Dying,* 112.
142. Elwell, *Evangelical Dictionary,* 926.
143. Albrecht, *Evangelical Newsletter;* Anderson, *Theology, Death and Dying,* 108. Cf. also Elisabeth Kübler-Ross, *Death, the Final Stage of Growth* (New York: Macmillan, 1975) and *Questions and Answers on Death and Dying* (New York: Macmillan, 1974); Raymond Moody, *Life after Life* (New York: Bantam, 1977) and *Reflections on Life after Life* (New York: Bantam, 1978).
144. Albrecht, *Evangelical Newsletter.*
145. Mary Jo Meadow, "Proto-Religious Views of Death," in MacGregor, ed., *Immortality and Human Destiny,* 91.
146. Ibid.
147. Nicholas F. Gier, "Humanistic Self-Judgment," in MacGregor, ed., *Immortality and Human Destiny,* 10; cf. Maurice Rawlings, *Beyond Death's Door* (Nashville: Thomas Nelson, 1978).
148. Ibid., 11; cf. Kenneth Ring, *Life at Death: A Scientific Investigation of the Near-Death Experience* (New York: Coward, McCann & Geoghegan, 1980), 193–194, 249.
149. Phipps, *Death,* 53.
150. Ibid., 54–55.
151. Meadow, "Proto-Religious Views of Death," 92.
152. Albrecht, *Evangelical Newsletter.*
153. Phipps, *Death,* 19.
154. Mark Albrecht and Brooks Alexander, "Thanatology: Death and Dying," *Journal of the Spiritual Counterfeits Project* (April 1977): 6; Gier, "Humanistic Self-Judgment," 12.
155. Stephen Board, "Light at the End of the Tunnel," *Eternity* (July 1977): 17.
156. Phipps, *Death,* 162–163; cf. George Kuykendall, "Care for the Dying: A Kübler-Ross Critique," *Theology Today* 38 (April 1981): 44.
157. Board, "Light at End of Tunnel," 30–32.
158. Albrecht and Alexander, "Thanatology: Death and Dying," 14.
159. Board, "Light at End of Tunnel," 32–33, 48.
160. Anderson, *Theology, Death and Dying,* 10.
161. Hick, *Death and Eternal Life,* 97.
162. Peter Koestenbaum, *Is There An Answer to Death?* (Englewood Cliffs, N.J.: Prentice-Hall, 1976), 7.
163. Koestenbaum, *Is There an Answer?,* 11.
164. Elwell, *Evangelical Dictionary,* 503.
165. Ibid., 503–504.
166. Macquarrie, *In Search of Humanity,* 238.
167. Ibid., 239.

168. J. Glenn Gray, "The Problem of Death in Modern Philosophy," in Nathan A. Scott, Jr., ed., *The Modern Vision of Death* (Richmond, Va.: John Knox, 1967), 66.
169. Ibid., 67.
170. Anderson, *Theology, Death and Dying,* 11–12.
171. Ibid., 33.
172. Henry, *God, Revelation and Authority,* 6:501–502.
173. Anderson, *Theology, Death and Dying,* 11–12.
174. Ibid., 30–40.
175. G. Ernest Wright, "The Faith of Israel," in George A. Buttrick, ed., *The Interpreter's Bible,* vol. 1 (New York: Abingdon, 1952), 370.
176. Ibid., 370–371; Anderson, *Theology, Death and Dying,* 42–43.
177. Thielicke, *Living with Death,* 32.
178. Anderson, *Theology, Death and Dying,* 45.
179. Ibid., 46–47.
180. Ibid., 48.
181. Ibid., 57.
182. Karl Barth, *Church Dogmatics,* vol. 3, pt. 2, tr. Harold Knight et al. (Edinburgh: T & T Clark, 1960), 632.
183. Ibid., 51.
184. Ibid., 55–56.
185. Barth, *Church Dogmatics,* vol. 3, pt. 2, 628.
186. Anderson, *Theology, Death and Dying,* 56–57.
187. Erickson, *Christian Theology,* 3:1171.
188. Kantonen, *Life After Death,* 17–18.
189. Erickson, *Christian Theology,* 3:1173.
190. Ibid., 3:1173–1174.
191. Anderson, *Theology, Death and Dying,* 84–85.
192. Ibid., 86–87.
193. T. F. Torrance, *Space, Time and Resurrection* (Grand Rapids, Mich.: Eerdmans, 1976), 164.
194. Anderson, *Theology, Death and Dying,* 89–90.
195. Torrance, *Space, Time and Resurrection,* 79, 98–99.
196. Anderson, *Theology, Death and Dying,* 92–93, 96.
197. Ibid., 97–98.
198. Ibid., 98–99.
199. Elwell, *Evangelical Dictionary,* 939–940.
200. Ibid., 940.
201. Ibid., 940–941.
202. Ibid.; cf. Archibald M. Hunter, *The Work and Words of Jesus* (Philadelphia: Westminster, 1973, rev. ed.), 123.
203. Elwell, *Evangelical Dictionary,* 941.
204. Brunner, *Eternal Hope,* 143.
205. James Denney, *Jesus and the Gospel* (New York: A. C. Armstrong, 1909), 106.
206. Walter T. Conner, *The Resurrection of Jesus: A Message of Hope and Cheer* (Nashville: Sunday School Board of the Southern Baptist Convention, 1926), 20–21.
207. Laurence W. Miller, *Jesus Christ is Alive* (Boston: W. A. Wilde, 1949), 15.
208. Moody, *Word of Truth,* 502–503.
209. Wright, "Faith of Israel," 370–371.

210. Anderson, *Theology, Death and Dying,* 114.
211. Ibid., 115–116.
212. Moody, *Word of Truth,* 507–508.
213. Erickson, *Christian Theology,* 3:1198.
214. Kantonen, *Life After Death,* 43–44.
215. Erickson, *Christian Theology,* 3:1199.
216. Hick, *Death and Eternal Life,* 295.
217. Erickson, *Christian Theology,* 3:1199.
218. Ibid.
219. Ibid., 1174.
220. Ibid., 1175.
221. Kantonen, 32.
222. Ibid., 32–33.
223. Erickson, *Christian Theology,* 3:1183.
224. Kantonen, 35.
225. Ibid.
226. Ibid.
227. Anderson, *Theology, Death and Dying,* 116.
228. Ibid., 117.
229. James I. Packer, "The Challenge of Biblical Interpretation: Eschatology," in *The Proceedings of the Conference on Biblical Interpretation 1988* (Nashville: Broadman, 1988), 201.
230. Erickson, *Christian Theology,* 3:1177.
231. Ibid., 3:1179.
232. Ibid., 3:1180.
233. Ibid., 3:1181.
234. Ibid.
235. Anderson, *Theology, Death and Dying,* 117–118.
236. Torrance, *Space, Time and Resurrection,* 102.
237. Anderson, *Theology, Death and Dying,* 118.
238. Packer, "Challenge of Biblical Interpretation," 194–195.
239. John P. Newport, *What Is Christian Doctrine?,* Layman's Library of Christian Doctrine (Nashville: Broadman, 1984), 34–36.
240. Thomas N. Finger, *Christian Theology: An Eschatological Approach,* vol. 1 (Nashville: Thomas Nelson, 1985), 101–102.
241. Ibid., 102.
242. Jürgen Moltmann, *Theology of Hope* (New York: Harper, 1967), 16.
243. S. G. F. Brandon, *The Judgment of the Dead: The Idea of Life After Death in the Major Religions* (New York: Scribner's, 1967).
244. Anderson, *Theology, Death and Dying,* 68.
245. Ibid., 68–69.
246. Ibid., 69, 72.
247. Cf. Leon Morris, *The Biblical Doctrine of Judgment* (Grand Rapids, Mich.: Eerdmans, 1960); Kantonen, *Life After Death,* 45–46.
248. Kantonen, *Life After Death,* 45.
249. Hendricks, *Theology for Aging,* 19.
250. Kantonen, *Life After Death,* 47; Rust, *Towards a Theological Understanding,* 260.
251. Kantonen, *Life After Death,* 48.

252. Ibid.
253. Erickson, *Christian Theology*, 3:1235.
254. Ibid.
255. Henry, *God, Revelation and Authority*, 6:508.
256. Ibid., 6:509.
257. Ibid.
258. Packer, "Challenge of Biblical Interpretation," 200–201.
259. Kantonen, *Life After Death*, 50, 51.
260. Packer, "Challenge of Biblical Interpretation," 196.
261. Rust, *Towards a Theological Understanding*, 264.
262. Ibid., 265.
263. George Eldon Ladd, *Jesus and the Kingdom* (New York: Harper, 1964), 333.
264. Kantonen, *Life After Death*, 53.
265. Ibid., 52.
266. Ibid., 320.
267. John P. Newport, *The Lion and the Lamb* (Nashville: Broadman, 1986), 310, 312, 320.
268. Henry, *God, Revelation and Authority*, 6:513.
269. Erickson, *Christian Theology*, 3:1231–1232.
270. Ibid., 3:1232.
271. Hendricks, *Theology for Aging*, 27.
272. Erickson, *Christian Theology*, 3:1232.
273. John Baillie, *And the Life Everlasting* (New York: Scribner's, 1933), 281.
274. Erickson, *Christian Theology*, 3:1233–1234.
275. Finger, *Christian Theology*, 1:166–167.
276. Thielicke, *Living with Death*, 81–82.
277. Anderson, *Theology, Death and Dying*, 81–82.
278. Ibid., 138–139; cf. J. Robert Nelson, *Human Life—A Biblical Perspective for Bioethics* (Philadelphia: Fortress, 1984), 107–110.
279. Hendricks, *Theology for Aging*, 23–24.
280. Henry, *God, Revelation and Authority*, 4:604.
281. Hendricks, *Theology for Aging*, 23.
282. Anderson, *Theology, Death and Dying*, 140.
283. Sandol Stoddard, *The Hospice Movement: A Better Way of Caring for the Dying* (Briar Cliff Manor, N.Y.: Stein & Day, 1978), 166.
284. Anderson, *Theology, Death and Dying*, 149–150.
285. Ibid.
286. Ibid., 151, 153.
287. Ibid., 146–147
288. Ibid., 154, 156.
289. Ibid., 157.
290. Phipps, *Death*, 68.
291. Ibid., 69.
292. Ibid., 72.
293. A. Venkoba Rao, "Suicide in India," in Norman L. Farberow, ed., *Suicide in Different Cultures* (Baltimore: University Park, 1975), 233.
294. Phipps, *Death*, 68.
295. Hendricks, *Theology for Aging*, 278.

296. Phipps, *Death*, 73–75.
297. Ibid., 86.
298. Ibid.
299. Ibid., 85.
300. Ibid., 85–86.
301. Hendricks, *Aging*, 278.
302. Anderson, *Theology, Death and Dying*, 133.
303. Ibid., 133–134.
304. Ibid., 135.
305. Hendricks, *Theology for Aging*, 28.
306. Henry, *God, Revelation and Authority*, 6:492.
307. Ibid., 6:492–493.
308. Ibid., 6:493–494.
309. George R. Beasley-Murray, *Highlights of the Book of Revelation* (Nashville: Broadman, 1972).

Chapter 9

1. Hendrik Kraemer, *Religion and the Christian Faith* (Philadelphia: Westminster, 1956), 37. For a helpful study of world religions from a Christian perspective, cf. Yandall Woodfin, *With All Your Mind* (Nashville: Abingdon, 1980), 147–172.
2. Johannes G. Vos, *A Christian Introduction to Religions of the World* (Grand Rapids, Mich.: Baker, 1965), 9.
3. Ibid., 11; Clyde F. Crews, *Ultimate Questions: A Theological Primer* (New York: Paulist, 1986), 73.
4. John Macquarrie, *In Search of Humanity: A Theological and Philosophical Approach* (New York: Crossroad, 1985), 199; cf. David B. Barrett, *World Christian Encyclopedia* (New York: Oxford Univ. Press, 1982).
5. Ibid., 200.
6. Friedrich Schleiermacher, *On Religion: Speeches to its Cultured Despisers*, tr. John Oman (New York: Harper Torchbooks, 1958), 1–118.
7. Friedrich Schleiermacher, *The Christian Faith* (Edinburgh: T & T Clark, 1928), 126, 133; Macquarrie, *In Search of Humanity*, 201–202.
8. Macquarrie, *In Search of Humanity*, 202.
9. Rudolf Otto, *The Idea of the Holy* (London: Oxford Univ. Press, 1931), 75, 8, 88, 31, 140ff.
10. Cf. Mircea Eliade, *The Sacred and the Profane*, tr. W. R. Trask (New York: Harcourt, Brace & World, 1959); Eliade, *Myth and Reality*, tr. W. R. Trask (New York: Harper, 1963); Kenneth L. Woodward, "A Scholar's Sacred Quest," *Newsweek* (15 July 1985): 63.
11. Woodward, "Scholar's Sacred Quest," 63.
12. Macquarrie, *In Search of Humanity*, 214–215.
13. William Dyrness, *Christian Apologetics in a World Community* (Downers Grove, Ill.: InterVarsity, 1983), 144–145.
14. Sigmund Freud, *The Future of an Illusion*, tr. W. D. Robson-Scott (Garden City, N.Y.: Doubleday, 1957); Crews, *Ultimate Questions*, 76.
15. Freud, *Future of an Illusion*, 82.
16. Dyrness, *Christian Apologetics*, 139.

17. Mark A. Noll and David F. Wells, eds., *Christian Faith and Practice in the Modern World* (Grand Rapids, Mich.: Eerdmans, 1988), 339.

18. B. F. Skinner, *Beyond Freedom and Dignity* (New York: Vintage, 1971), 27, 136; Dyrness, *Christian Apologetics,* 141.

19. Dyrness, *Christian Apologetics,* 142.

20. Émile Durkheim, *The Elementary Forms of the Religious Life* (New York: Macmillan Free Press, 1965).

21. Jerry H. Gill, *Faith in Dialogue: A Christian Apologetic* (Waco, Tex.: Word, 1985), 51–53.

22. Dyrness, *Christian Apologetics,* 149.

23. Ibid., 170.

24. Ibid., 170–171; cf. Jose Miguez Bonino, *Doing Theology in a Revolutionary Situation* (Philadelphia: Fortress, 1975).

25. Crews, *Ultimate Questions,* 75; Noll and Wells, eds., *Christian Faith and Practice,* 271.

26. J. N. D. Anderson, *Christianity and Comparative Religion* (Downers Grove, Ill.: InterVarsity, 1970), 56.

27. Macquarrie, *In Search of Humanity,* 220–221;

28. Daniel L. Pals, "Is Religion a *Sui Generis* Phenomenon?" *Journal of the American Academy of Religion,* 55 (Summer 1987): 271.

29. Ibid., 278.

30. Ninian Smart, *The Phenomenon of Religion* (New York: Macmillan, 1973), 52.

31. Macquarrie, *In Search of Humanity,* 220–221.

32. John Macquarrie, *Theology, Church and Ministry* (New York: Crossroad, 1986), 125.

33. Ibid., 126–127.

34. Ibid., 127.

35. Kenneth Cragg, *The Christ and the Faiths: Theology in Cross-Reference* (London: SPCK, 1986), 5.

36. Macquarrie, *Theology,* 127–128, 130.

37. Ibid., 128, 130–131, 138.

38. Joseph M. Kitagawa, "Tillich, Kraemer, and the Encounter of Religions," in James Luther Adams et al., eds., *The Thought of Paul Tillich* (San Francisco: Harper, 1985), 204–207.

39. John Newport, *Christ and the New Consciousness* (Nashville: Broadman, 1978).

40. Cragg, *The Christ and the Faiths,* 321–322.

41. Ibid., 6–7.

42. Ibid., 319.

43. Hendrik Kraemer, *Why Christianity of All Religions?* tr. Hubert Hoskins (Philadelphia: Westminster, 1962), 51–52.

44. Gill, *Faith in Dialogue,* 96.

45. Anderson, *Christianity and Comparative Religion,* 12.

46. William Ernest Hocking, *Re-Thinking Missions: A Laymen's Inquiry After One Hundred Years* (New York: Harper, 1932), 325.

47. Ibid., 327.

48. Hendrik Kraemer, *Religion and the Christian Faith* (Philadelphia: Westminster, 1956), 63, 73, 222–224.

49. Arnold Toynbee, *Christianity among the Religions of the World* (New York: Scribner's, 1957).

50. Hendrik Kraemer, *World Cultures and World Religions: The Coming Dialogue* (Philadelphia: Westminster, 1960), 328–330.

51. Anderson, *Christianity and Comparative Religion*, 15; and D. H. Lawrence, *The Man Who Died* (London: Secker, 1931), 148.

52. W. A. Visser 't Hooft, *No Other Name* (London: SCM, 1963), 48–49.

53. Vos, *Christian Introduction to Religions*, 30.

54. Anderson, *Christianity and Comparative Religion*, 107–108.

55. Ibid., 108; David Elton Trueblood, *Philosophy of Religion* (New York: Harper, 1957), 224–228..

56. W. Cantwell Smith, *The Faith of Other Men* (New York: New American Library, 1965), 124.

57. R. Panikkar, *The Unknown Christ of Hinduism* (London: Darton, Longman & Todd, 1965), 54.

58. John Hick, *God and the Universe of Faiths* (New York: St. Martin's, 1973), and *God Has Many Names* (London: Macmillan, 1980).

59. Herbert Henry Farmer, *Revelation and Religion: Studies in the Theological Interpretation of Religious Types* (London: Nisbet & Co., 1954).

60. Kraemer, *Religion and Christian Faith*, 237–321, 441.

61. Ibid., 6–7.

62. G. Ernest Wright, "The Faith of Israel," in George A. Buttrick, ed., *The Interpreter's Bible*, vol. 1 (New York: Abingdon, 1952), 357–358.

63. G. Ernest Wright, *The Old Testament Against Its Environment* (Naperville, Ill.: Alec R. Allenson, 1957), 16–17.

64. Ibid., 18–20; and Wright, "Faith of Israel," 358.

65. Wright, "Faith of Israel," 358.

66. Wright, *Old Testament Against*, 20–22.

67. Wright, "Faith of Israel," 359.

68. Ibid., 359–360.

69. Edgar Allen Poe, "To Helen," in Norman Foerster et al., eds., *American Poetry and Prose* (New York: Houghton Mifflin, 1970), 350.

70. Floyd V. Filson, *The New Testament Against Its Environment: The Gospel of Christ the Risen Lord* (London: SCM, 1950), 29–30.

71. Kraemer, *Religion and Christian Faith*, 283–285.

72. Ibid., 293–295.

73. Ibid., 277.

74. Filson, *New Testament Against*, 91.

75. Ibid., 93.

76. G. Ernest Wright, *The Biblical Doctrine of Man in Society* (London: SCM, 1954), 95.

77. Kraemer, *Religion and Christian Faith*, 298–299.

78. Wright, *Old Testament Against*, 20.

79. Ibid., 361.

80. Edmund Perry, *The Gospel in Dispute* (Garden City, N.Y.: Doubleday, 1958), 83–84.

81. Ibid., 86–87.

82. Ibid., 96–97.

83. Ibid., 106.

84. Ibid.

85. Eric Rust, *Salvation History* (Richmond, Va.: John Knox, 1962), 263–264.
86. Ibid., 264.
87. Oscar Cullmann, *Christ and Time: The Primitive Christian Conception of Time and History* (Philadelphia: Westminster, 1950), 162–166.
88. Rust, *Salvation History*, 266–267.
89. Ibid., 305.
90. Edmund Davison Soper, *The Religions of Mankind* (New York: Abingdon, 1921), 55.
91. Luther E. Copeland, *Christianity and World Religions* (Nashville: Convention Press, 1963), 13.
92. William Howells, *The Heathens: Primitive Man and His Religions* (Garden City, N.Y.: Doubleday, 1948), 7.
93. Stephen Neill, *Christian Faith and Other Faiths* (London: Oxford Univ. Press, 1960), 126.
94. Herbert C. Jackson, *Man Reaches Out to God* (Valley Forge, Pa.: Judson, 1963), 28.
95. Ibid.
96. Howells, *The Heathens*, 26.
97. Jackson, *Man Reaches Out to God*, 26.
98. Ibid., 34.
99. W. T. Harris and E. G. Parrinder, *The Christian Approach to the Animist* (London: Edinburgh House, 1960), 30.
100. W. Schmidt, *The Origin and Growth of Religion*, tr. H. J. Rose (London: Methuen, 1931), 88, 191–192.
101. Ibid., 198.
102. Jackson, *Man Reaches Out to God*, 29.
103. Ibid., 30.
104. Eugene A. Nida and William A. Smalley, *Introducing Animism* (New York: Friendship, 1959), 28.
105. Jackson, *Man Reaches Out to God*, 32.
106. Ibid., 32–33.
107. E. D. Soper, *The Philosophy of the Christian World Mission* (New York: Abingdon Press), 162.
108. Stephen Neill, *Christian Faith and Other Faiths*, 143.
109. Ibid., 148.
110. Ibid., 149.
111. G. F. Vicedom, *Church and People in New Guinea* (London: Lutterworth, 1961).
112. Neill, *Christian Faith and Other Faiths*, 143–150.
113. Perry, *Gospel in Dispute*, 148, 109.
114. Ibid., 110–113.
115. Cragg, *The Christ and the Faiths*, 15.
116. Ibid., 160.
117. Krister Stendahl, "Judaism and Christianity: Then and Now," *Harvard Divinity Bulletin*, 28 (October 1963): 6.
118. Vos, *Christian Introduction to Religions*, 70.
119. Rust, *Salvation History*, 130–131.
120. Vos, *Christian Introduction to Religions*, 70–71.
121. Rust, *Salvation History*, 134.

122. Ibid., 141–142.
123. Vos, *Christian Introduction to Religions,* 72; Wright, *Old Testament Against,* 75; Jacob Neusner, *Way of Torah,* 99.
124. Neusner, *Way of Torah,* 43.
125. Ibid.
126. Ibid., 44.
127. Ibid., 81–82.
128. Ibid., 74–75.
129. Vos, *Christian Introduction to Religions,* 74.
130. Neusner, *Way of Torah,* 76.
131. Ibid., 74–76, 78; Vos, *Christian Introduction to Religions,* 73.
132. Martin Goldsmith, "Jews and Christians," in Robin Keeley, ed., *Eerdmans' Handbook to Christian Belief* (Grand Rapids, Mich.: Eerdmans, 1982), 322.
133. Russell F. Aldwinckle, *Jesus—A Savior or the Savior?* (Macon, Ga.: Mercer Univ. Press, 1982), 39.
134. Cragg, *The Christ and the Faiths,* 113, 15.
135. Aldwinckle, *Jesus,* 39.
136. Rust, *Salvation History,* 147–148.
137. Ibid., 148.
138. Cragg, *The Christ and the Faiths,* 104–105.
139. Ibid., 105.
140. Ibid., 110–111.
141. Ibid., 112.
142. Franz Rosenzweig, *The Star of Redemption,* tr. W. W. Hallo (New York: Holt, Rinehart & Winston, 1970), 341, 346; Nahum Glatzer, *Franz Rosenzweig: His Life and Thought* (New York: Farrar, Straus & Young, 1953); Will Herberg, *Judaism and Modern Man* (New York: Farrar, Straus & Young, 1952).
143. Cragg, *The Christ and the Faiths,* 121.
144. Ibid., 129.
145. Hans Joachim Schoeps, *The Jewish-Christian Argument* (New York: Holt, Rinehart & Winston, 1963), 4.
146. Cragg, *The Christ and the Faiths,* 132.
147. Leo Baeck, *This People Israel: The Meaning of Jewish Existence,* tr. A. H. Friedlander (New York: Holt, Rinehart & Winston, 1965), 141.
148. Cragg, *The Christ and the Faiths,* 162.
149. Ibid.
150. Ibid., 164.
151. Ibid.
152. Ibid.
153. Perry, *Gospel in Dispute,* 133.
154. Ibid.
155. Karl Barth, *Dogmatics in Outline* (New York: Philosophical Library, 1949), 81.
156. Ibid., 80; and Perry, *Gospel in Dispute,* 135.
157. Barth, *Dogmatics in Outline,* 81; and Perry, *Gospel in Dispute,* 137–138.
158. Kenneth Cragg, *The Call of the Minaret* (New York: Oxford Univ. Press, 1956), 74.
159. Ibid., 75.
160. Perry, *Gospel in Dispute,* 149–150.
161. Jackson, *Man Reaches Out to God,* 50.

162. Ibid., 50–51; Carl F. H. Henry, *Confessions of a Theologian* (Waco, Tex.: Word, 1986), 392.
163. "Moslem Furor Astounds West," *The Dallas Morning News* (19 February 1989): 17A.
164. John P. Newport, "Humanism and the Future: A Tentative Proposal for an American Solution," *Liberal and Fine Arts Review*, 4 (January 1984): 54–55.
165. Richard N. Ostling, "Americans Facing Toward Mecca," *Time* (23 May 1988): 49.
166. Ibid., 49–50.
167. Ibid., 50.
168. Hendrik Kraemer, *World Cultures and World Religions*, 269.
169. Kenneth L. Woodward et al., "The Minority That Iran Persecutes," *Newsweek* (24 March 1980): 61.
170. John P. Newport, *Christ and the New Consciousness*, 66.
171. Cragg, *The Christ and the Faiths*, 30–31.
172. Perry, *Gospel in Dispute*, 152.
173. Stephen Neill, "God in Other Religions," in Keeley, ed., *Eerdmans' Handbook to Christian Belief*, 196–197.
174. Cragg, *The Christ and the Faiths*, 14.
175. Jackson, *Man Reaches Out to God*, 59–60.
176. Ibid., 62–63.
177. Ibid., 63–64; John B. Noss, *Man's Religions* (New York: Macmillan, 1956), 687–688.
178. Vos, *Christian Introduction to Religions*, 64.
179. Copeland, *Christianity and World Religions*, 101–102.
180. Jackson, *Man Reaches Out to God*, 65.
181. Perry, *Gospel in Dispute*, 153.
182. Abdullah Yusuf Ali, *The Holy Qur'an, Text, Translation, and Commentary* (New York: Hafner, 1946), 268.
183. Cragg, *The Christ and the Faiths*, 13.
184. Anderson, *Christianity and Comparative Religion*, 47.
185. Perry, *Gospel in Dispute*, 155, 157.
186. Neill, "God in Other Religions," 196.
187. Cragg, *The Christ and the Faiths*, 54–55.
188. Ibid., 55.
189. Ibid., 55–56.
190. Kraemer, *Why Christianity?*, 61–62.
191. Perry, *Gospel in Dispute*, 151.
192. Ibid., 162.
193. Ibid., 164–165.
194. Anderson, *Christianity and Comparative Religion*, 49–50.
195. Ibid., 89–90.
196. Ibid., 90.
197. Cragg, *The Christ and the Faiths*, 14.
198. Ibid., 87–88.
199. Jackson, *Man Reaches Out to God*, 65.
200. Neill, *Christian Faith and Other Faiths*, 61.
201. Jackson, *Man Reaches Out to God*, 68.
202. Kraemer, *Why Christianity?*, 84.

203. Cragg, *The Christ and the Faiths,* 45–46.
204. Ibid., 90–92.
205. Jackson, *Man Reaches Out to God,* 66.
206. Ibid.
207. Ibid., 67.
208. Ibid., 85–86.
209. Vishal Mangalwadi, "How Hindus See Jesus," in Keeley, ed., *Eerdmans' Handbook to Christian Belief,* 107.
210. Copeland, *Christianity and World Religions,* 37.
211. Jackson, *Man Reaches Out to God,* 87.
212. Perry, *Gospel in Dispute,* 191.
213. John P. Newport, *Christ and the New Consciousness,* 12–13.
214. Dyrness, *Christian Apologetics,* 95.
215. Ibid., 95–97.
216. Perry, *Gospel in Dispute,* 182.
217. Dyrness, *Christian Apologetics,* 98.
218. Ibid.
219. Perry, *Gospel in Dispute,* 187–188.
220. Dyrness, *Christian Apologetics,* 98–99.
221. John Macquarrie, *In Search of Deity: An Essay in Dialectical Theism* (New York: Crossroad, 1984), 249.
222. Newport, *Christ and the New Consciousness,* 32–35.
223. Macquarrie, *In Search of Deity,* 249.
224. Dyrness, *Christian Apologetics,* 100.
225. Ibid., 100–101.
226. Ibid., 101.
227. Ibid., 102.
228. Cragg, *The Christ and the Faiths,* 177; Jackson, *Man Reaches Out to God,* 86.
229. Cragg, *The Christ and the Faiths,* 177.
230. Jackson, *Man Reaches Out to God,* 98.
231. Cragg, *The Christ and the Faiths,* 201–202.
232. Perry, *Gospel in Dispute,* 223.
233. Ibid., 199–200.
234. Jackson, *Man Reaches Out to God,* 80–81.
235. Vos, *Christian Introduction to Religions,* 43.
236. Perry, *Gospel in Dispute,* 196–197.
237. Cragg, *The Christ and the Faiths,* 264.
238. Jackson, *Man Reaches Out to God,* 69.
239. Perry, *Gospel in Dispute,* 20–21.
240. Jackson, *Man Reaches Out to God,* 71.
241. Perry, *Gospel in Dispute,* 198.
242. Jackson, *Man Reaches Out to God,* 71.
243. Perry, *Gospel in Dispute,* 199.
244. Jackson, *Man Reaches Out to God,* 72.
245. Perry, *Gospel in Dispute,* 200.
246. Jackson, *Man Reaches Out to God,* 72.
247. Ibid., 72–73.
248. Perry, *Gospel in Dispute,* 205.

249. Jackson, *Man Reaches Out to God,* 73–75.
250. Ibid., 75–76.
251. Ibid., 76–77.
252. Ibid., 77–78.
253. Ibid., 79–80.
254. Anderson, *Christianity and Comparative Religion,* 57; Newport, *Christ and the New Consciousness,* 54–55.
255. Jackson, *Man Reaches Out to God,* 77–78.
256. Ibid., 78.
257. Newport, *Christ and the New Consciousness,* 52.
258. Jackson, *Man Reaches Out to God,* 79.
259. Cragg, *The Christ and the Faiths,* 259–260.
260. Anderson, *Christianity and Comparative Religion,* 66.
261. Macquarrie, *In Search of Deity,* 250.
262. Newport, *Christ and the New Consciousness,* 52, 56.
263. Jackson, *Man Reaches Out to God,* 81–82.
264. Perry, *Gospel in Dispute,* 211.
265. Ibid., 223–224.
266. Jackson, *Man Reaches Out to God,* 82.
267. Ibid., 83.
268. Cragg, *The Christ and the Faiths,* 282.
269. Jackson, *Man Reaches Out to God,* 84.
270. Perry, *Gospel in Dispute,* 223.
271. Hendrik Kraemer, *World Cultures and World Religions,* 172–173.
272. Copeland, *Christianity and Comparative Religions,* 63.
273. Kraemer, *World Cultures and World Religions,* 198.
274. Copeland, *Christianity and Comparative Religions,* 75–76.
275. Ibid., 66.
276. Macquarrie, *In Search of Deity,* 251.
277. Copeland, *Christianity and Comparative Religions,* 67.
278. Kraemer, *World Cultures and World Religions,* 175; Fritjof Capra, *The Tao of Physics* (Berkeley, Calif.: Shambhala, 1975), 25.
279. Copeland, *Christianity and Comparative Religions,* 68.
280. Ibid., 68.
281. Macquarrie, *In Search of Deity,* 250.
282. Copeland, *Christianity and Comparative Religions,* 70.
283. Macquarrie, *In Search of Deity,* 251.
284. Kraemer, *World Cultures and World Religions,* 180–181.
285. Ibid., 185.
286. Ibid., 181–182.
287. Ibid., 198.
288. Vos, *Christian Introduction to Religions,* 48–49.
289. Kraemer, *World Cultures and World Religions,* 176.
290. Vos, *Christian Introduction to Religions,* 49.
291. Kraemer, *World Cultures and World Religions,* 176.
292. Ibid., 172.
293. Ibid., 200–201.
294. Copeland, *Christianity and Comparative Religion,* 115.

295. Ibid., 115–116.
296. Kraemer, *World Cultures and World Religions*, 205.
297. Copeland, *Christianity and Comparative Religions*, 116.
298. Ibid., 116–117.
299. Kraemer, *World Cultures and World Religions*, 206–207.
300. Ibid., 225.
301. Copeland, *Christianity and World Religions*, 117–118.
302. Kraemer, *World Cultures and World Religions*, 225–226.
303. Ibid., 227.
304. Anderson, *Christianity and Comparative Religion*, 45.
305. Kraemer, *Religion and Christian Faith*, 38.
306. Ibid., 336–337.
307. Anderson, *Christianity and Comparative Religion*, 32.
308. Neill, *Christian Faith and Other Faiths*, 209–210.
309. Ibid., 218.
310. Kraemer, *World Cultures and World Religions*, 95.
311 Ibid., 92.
312. Neill, *Christian Faith and Other Faiths*, 218.
313. Ibid., 219.
314. Ibid., 220.
315. Neill, *Christian Faith and Other Faiths*, 216.
316. Ibid., 97.
317. Macquarrie, *In Search of Deity*, 193–194.
318. Newport, *Christ and the New Consciousness*, 156–157; R. C. Zaehner, *Mysticism, Sacred and Profane* (New York: Oxford Univ. Press, 1971), 198–207; Weston La Barre, *The Peyote Cult* (New York: Shocken, 1969).
319. John P. Newport, ed., *Nineteenth Century Devotional Thought* (Nashville: Broadman, 1981), 10–11.
320. Ibid., 93–95, 9–10.
321. Newport, *Christ and the New Consciousness*, 157–158.
322. Geoffrey Parrinder, *Mysticism in the World's Religions* (New York: Oxford Univ. Press, 1976).
323. Newport, ed., *Nineteenth Century Devotional Thought*, 10; Donald G. Bloesch, *The Crisis of Piety* (Grand Rapids, Mich.: Eerdmans, 1968), 95–124.
324. Anderson, *Christianity and Comparative Religion*, 28.
325. Kraemer, *World Cultures and World Religions*, 356.
326. Anderson, *Christianity and Comparative Religion*, 27–28.
327. Kraemer, *World Cultures and World Religions*, 368–369.
328. Newport, *Christ and the New Consciousness*, 167.

Chapter 10

1. Alvin Plantinga and Nicholas Wolterstorff, eds., *Faith and Rationality: Reason and Belief in God* (Notre Dame, Ind.: Univ. of Notre Dame Press, 1983), 219, 221.
2. Ibid., 265–266.
3. Ibid., 266–267, 271, 273.
4. Bernard Ramm, *After Fundamentalism: The Future of Evangelical Theology* (San Francisco: Harper, 1983), 40.

5. Ibid., 8; William Lane Craig, *Apologetics: An Introduction* (Chicago: Moody, 1984), xi; Norman Geisler, *Christian Apologetics* (Grand Rapids, Mich.: Baker, 1976), 7.
6. Plantinga and Wolterstorff, *Faith and Rationality*, 135–136.
7. Walter A. Elwell, ed., *Evangelical Dictionary of Theology* (Grand Rapids, Mich.: Baker, 1984), 915.
8. Ibid.
9. John A. Hutchison, *Faith, Reason, and Existence* (New York: Oxford Univ. Press, 1956), 137.
10. Donald Bloesch, *The Ground of Certainty* (Grand Rapids, Mich.: Eerdmans, 1971), 177–178; Thomas Aquinas, *Summa Theologica*, in A. C. Pegis, ed., *The Basic Writings of Thomas Aquinas* (New York: Random House, 1945), 2:1116.
11. Hutchison, *Faith, Reason, and Existence*, 136–137.
12. Arthur Holmes, *All Truth Is God's Truth* (Grand Rapids, Mich.: Eerdmans, 1977), 41.
13. Ibid.
14. Karl Rahner, *Theological Investigations*, vols. 1–3, tr. Cornelius Ernst (Baltimore: Helicon, 1961–65).
15. Ramm, *After Fundamentalism*, 158.
16. William Dyrness, *Christian Apologetics in a World Community* (Downers Grove, Ill.: InterVarsity, 1983), 17; B. B. Warfield, *Selected Shorter Writings*, vol. 2 (Philadelphia: Presbyterian & Reformed, 1973), 120.
17. Bloesch, *Ground of Certainty*, 182.
18. Ibid., 182; Elwell, *Evangelical Dictionary*, 514.
19. Bloesch, *Ground of Certainty*, 182–183.
20. Charles Hodge, *Systematic Theology*, vol. 1 (London: Clark, 1960), 3–4.
21. Ibid., 1:10.
22. Jack Rogers, ed., *Biblical Authority* (Waco, Tex.: Word, 1977), 15–46.
23. Plantinga and Wolterstorff, *Faith and Rationality*, 242, 246, 247; Norman Fiering, *Jonathan Edwards's Moral Thought and Its British Context* (Chapel Hill, N.C.: Univ. of North Carolina Press, 1981).
24. Ronald W. Ruegsegger, ed., *Reflections on Francis Schaeffer* (Grand Rapids, Mich.: Zondervan, 1986), 63.
25. Bloesch, *Ground of Certainty*, 183–184; Ronald H. Nash, ed., *The Philosophy of Gordon H. Clark* (Philadelphia: Presbyterian & Reformed, 1968), 67, 406.
26. Rudolph Nelson, *The Making and Unmaking of an Evangelical Mind: The Case of Edward Carnell* (New York: Cambridge Univ. Press, 1987), 36, 64, 129.
27. Ibid., 36–37, 64, 129.
28. Craig, *Apologetics*, 14; Alasdair I. C. Heron, *A Century of Protestant Theology* (Philadelphia: Westminster, 1980), 112; Plantinga and Wolterstorff, *Faith and Rationality*, 304.
29. Craig, *Apologetics*, 15.
30. Ibid.; Wolfhard Pannenberg, *Jesus—God and Man*, tr. L. L. Wilkins and D. A. Priebe (London: SCM, 1968), 27–28.
31. Craig, *Apologetics*, 15; G. C. Berkouwer, *A Half Century of Theology* (Grand Rapids, Mich.: Eerdmans, 1977), 160–163.
32. Berkouwer, *A Half Century of Theology*, 176.
33. Stanley N. Gundry and Alan F. Johnson, eds., *Tensions in Contemporary Theology* (Grand Rapids, Mich.: Eerdmans, 1977), 160, 163.

34. Ibid., 222.

35. Pannenberg, *Jesus—God and Man*, 34; Millard J. Erickson, *Christian Theology*, vol. 2 (Grand Rapids, Mich.: Baker, 1984), 668.

36. Plantinga and Wolterstorff, *Faith and Rationality*, 304.

37. Ibid., 306–307.

38. Ibid., 308.

39. Ibid.

40. Ibid., 308–309.

41. Ibid., 311.

42. Ibid.

43. Holmes, *All Truth*, 75–76.

44. Ibid., 76.

45. Elwell, *Evangelical Dictionary*, 915.

46. Colin Brown, *Philosophy and the Christian Faith* (London: Tyndale, 1969), 13.

47. Bloesch, *Ground of Certainty*, 178–179; Brown, *Philosophy and the Christian Faith*, 43; B. A. Gerrish, *Grace and Reason: A Study of the Theology of Luther* (New York: Oxford Univ. Press, 1962), 1–2.

48. Bloesch, *Ground of Certainty*, 179; Thomas Kepler, ed., *The Table Talk of Martin Luther* (Cleveland, Ohio: World, 1952), 49.

49. Brown, *Philosophy and the Christian Faith*, 44.

50. Bloesch, *Ground of Certainty*, 179.

51. Bernard Ramm, *Types of Apologetic Systems* (Wheaton, Ill.: Van Kampen, 1953), 17–18.

52. Brown, *Philosophy and the Christian Faith*, 59.

53. Bloesch, *Ground of Certainty*, 179–180; Blaise Pascal, *Pascal's Pensées and the Provincial Letters* (New York: Random House, Modern Library, 1941), 95.

54. Richard Kroner, *Speculation and Revelation in Modern Philosophy* (Philadelphia: Westminster, 1961), 304–305.

55. Cf. Denzil G. M. Patrick, *Pascal and Kierkegaard*, vol. 2 (London and Redhill: Lutterworth, 1947), 221–251.

56. C. G. Rutenber, God *and Modern Doubt: Holland Foundation Lectures, 1953* (Fort Worth: Baptist Book Store, 1953), 15–18.

57. Bloesch, *Ground of Certainty*, 181.

58. Holmes, *All Truth*, 44.

59. Brown, *Philosophy and the Christian Faith*, 131–132.

60. Ibid., 245–246; Cornelius Van Til, *The Defense of the Faith* (Philadelphia: Presbyterian & Reformed, 1955), 175–180, 302–356.

61. "At the Beginning, God: An Interview with Cornelius Van Til," *Christianity Today* (30 December 1977): 19.

62. Brown, *Philosophy and the Christian Faith*, 246–247.

63. Van Til, *Defense of the Faith*, 132.

64. Brown, *Philosophy and the Christian Faith*, 249.

65. Van Til, *Defense of the Faith*, 132.

66. Dyrness, *Christian Apologetics*, 62–63; Gordon R. Lewis, *Testing Christianity's Truth Claims* (Chicago: Moody, 1976), 139.

67. Lewis, *Testing Christianity's Truth Claims*, 139–140.

68. Holmes, *All Truth*, 75–77.

69. Erich Przywara, *An Augustine Synthesis*, 4th ed. (New York: Sheed & Ward, 1945), 61.

70. J. V. Langmead Casserley, *The Christian in Philosophy* (New York: Scribner's, 1951), 43.

71. Przywara, *Augustine Synthesis*, 52.

72. Casserley, *Christian in Philosophy*, 59-60.

73. Ibid., 61–68.

74. Bloesch, *Ground of Certainty*, 79.

75. Plantinga and Woltorstorff, *Faith and Rationality*, 248.

76. Abraham Kuyper, *Encylopedia of Sacred Theology: Its Principles*, tr. J. Hendrik De Vries (New York: Scribner's, 1898), 359.

77. Plantinga and Wolterstorff, *Faith and Rationality*, 249.

78. Ibid., 250–251.

79. Ibid., 251.

80. Kuyper, *Encyclopedia*, 553–563.

81. Plantinga and Wolterstorff, *Faith and Rationality*, 253, 256–257.

82. Ibid., 254.

83. Ibid., 255–256

84. Karl Barth, *Dogmatics in Outline* (New York: Harper, 1959), 9–14.

85. Thomas N. Finger, *Christian Theology: An Eschatological Approach*, vol. 1 (Nashville: Thomas Nelson, 1985), 96.

86. Ramm, *After Fundamentalism*, 160.

87. Ibid., 161–162.

88. Brown, *Philosophy and the Christian Faith*, 257–258.

89. Ramm, *After Fundamentalism*, 74–75, 79.

90. Berkouwer, *A Half Century of Theology*, 131–132.

91. Brown, *Philosophy and the Christian Faith*, 260.

92. Carl F. H. Henry, *God, Revelation and Authority*, vol. 1, *God Who Speaks and Shows: Preliminary Considerations* (Waco, Tex.: Word, 1976), 199–200.

93. Ibid., 200–201.

94. George A. Lindbeck, *The Nature of Doctrine: Religion and Theology in a Postliberal Age* (Philadelphia: Westminster, 1984).

95. Stanley Hauerwas and William H. Willimon, "Embarrassed by God's Presence," *Christian Century* (30 January 1985): 98–100; William H. Willimon, "Making Christians in a Secular World," *Christian Century* (22 October 1986): 914–918.

96. Erickson, *Christian Theology*, 2:673.

97. Ibid.

98. Ibid.

99. Ibid., 673–674.

100. Ibid., 674.

101. Ibid.

102. Ibid.

103. Ibid., 674–675.

104. Ibid., 675.

105. Albert T. Mollegen, "A Christian Understanding of Revelation," *The Christian Scholar* 39 (March 1956): 19.

106. Ibid., 20.

107. Will Herberg, *Judaism and Modern Man* (New York: Farrar, Straus & Young, 1951), 247–248.

108. Ibid., 246.
109. G. Ernest Wright, *The Rule of God: Essays in Biblical Theology* (Garden City, N.Y.: Doubleday, 1960), 3–4.
110. Herberg, *Judaism and Modern Man*, 251.
111. G. Ernest Wright, "The Faith of Israel," in George A. Buttrick, ed., *The Interpreter's Bible*, vol. 1 (New York: Abingdon, 1952), 352.
112. Ibid., 353.
113. Ibid., 362.
114. Floyd V. Filson, *The New Testament Against Its Environment: The Gospel of Christ the Risen Lord* (London: SCM, 1950), 20.
115. Jerry H. Gill, *Faith in Dialogue: A Christian Apologetic* (Waco, Tex.: Word, 1985), 122–123.
116. Ibid., 123.
117. Ibid., 124.
118. Wright "Faith of Israel," 363.
119. Ibid.
120. J. J. Von Allmen, ed., *A Companion to the Bible* (New York: Oxford Univ. Press, 1958), 221.
121. Ibid., 221–222.
122. Ibid., 222.
123. Ibid.
124. James William McClendon, Jr., *Ethics: Systematic Theology* (Nashville: Abingdon, 1986), 264, 82–84.
125. Russell, *Human Liberation in a Feminist Perspective: A Theology* (Philadelphia: Westminster, 1974), 54; Jose Miguez Bonino, *Doing Theology in a Revolutionary Situation* (Philadelphia: Fortress, 1975), 88, 72.
126. Herberg, *Judaism and Modern Man*, 252.
127. Ibid., 253.
128. Ibid.
129. Emil Brunner, *Man in Revolt* (Philadelphia: Westminster, 1947), 529.
130. Herberg, *Judaism and Modern Man*, 254.
131. Ibid., 256.
132. John A. Hutchison, *Faith, Reason, and Existence*, 93–96; cf. Yandall Woodfin, *With All Your Mind* (Nashville: Abingdon, 1980), 38–59; Ronald H. Nash, *Faith and Reason: Searching for a Rational Faith* (Grand Rapids, Mich.: Zondervan, 1988), 105–176.
133. Roger Hazelton, *On Proving God* (New York: Harper, 1952), 170–171.
134. Ibid., 172.
135. Hutchison, *Faith, Reason, and Existence*, 133–144.
136. J. V. Langmead Casserley, *Graceful Reason: The Contribution of Reason to Theology* (Greenwich, Conn.: Seabury, 1954), 62–63.
137. Casserley, *Christian in Philosophy*, 82–83.
138. Hazelton, *On Proving God*, 95–97.
139. Ibid., 98–100.
140. Casserley, *Graceful Reason*, 67.
141. Eric C. Rust, *Religion, Revelation and Reason* (Macon, Ga.: Mercer Univ. Press, 1981), 93.
142. Rutenber, *God and Modern Doubt*, 11–12.
143. Hutchison, *Faith, Reason, and Existence*, 154–155.

144. D. E. Scudder, *Tennant's Philosophical Theology* (New Haven, Conn.: Yale Univ. Press, 1940), 215–239; F. R. Tennant, *Philosophical Theology*, vol. 2 (Cambridge: Cambridge Univ. Press, 1930), ch. 4.

145. Hutchison, *Faith, Reason, and Existence*, 155.

146. Daniel Jenkins, *Believing in God* (Philadelphia: Westminster, 1952), 26.

147. Hutchison, *Faith, Reason, and Existence*, 140.

148. Ibid.; St. Anselm, *St. Anselm*, tr. Sidney Norton Deane, (Chicago: Open Court, 1910), 2.

149. Carl F. H. Henry, *Notes on the Doctrine of God* (Boston: W. A. Wilde, 1948), 52; Casserley, *Christian in Philosophy*, 59.

150. Casserley, *Christian in Philosophy*, 60–61.

151. Ibid., 61–62.

152. Hutchison, *Faith, Reason, and Existence*, 141; Casserley, *Christian in Philosophy*, 62.

153. Casserley, *Christian in Philosophy*, 63.

154. Ibid., 66–67.

155. Ibid., 68.

156. Ibid., 69.

157. Hutchison, *Faith, Reason, and Existence*, 141.

158. Ibid., 141–142; Casserley, *Christian in Philosophy*, 128.

159. Casserley, *Christian in Philosophy*, 128.

160. Hutchison, *Faith, Reason, and Existence*, 143.

161. Ibid., 156–158.

162. Edmond La B. Cherbonnier, "Is There a Biblical Metaphysic?" *Theology Today* 15 (January 1959): 466.

163. Casserley, *Christian in Philosophy*, 63–69.

164. Herberg, *Judaism and Modern Man*, 67; Sören Kierkegaard, *Concluding Unscientific Postscript* (Princeton, N.J.: Princeton Univ. Press, 1944), 485.

165. Herberg, *Judaism and Modern Man*, 35.

166. Ibid.

167. Cherbonnier, "Is There a Biblical Metaphysic?" 462.

168. Cf. Edmond La B. Cherbonnier, *Hardness of Heart* (Garden City, N.Y.: Doubleday, 1955), 48–57; Cherbonnier, "Is There a Biblical Metaphysic?" 466–468; Cherbonnier, "The Theology of the Word of God," *The Journal of Religion*, 33 (January 1953), 29.

169. David Elton Trueblood, *Philosophy of Religion* (New York: Harper, 1957), 32.

170. Rutenber, *God and Modern Doubt*, 43.

171. L. Harold DeWolf, *A Theology of the Living Church* (New York: Harper, 1953), 34–35.

172. Hutchison, *Faith, Reason, and Existence*, 130–131.

173. DeWolf, *A Theology*, 35.

174. Casserley, *Graceful Reason*, 158.

175. Hutchison, *Faith, Reason, and Existence*, 156–157.

176. Plantinga and Wolterstorff, *Faith and Rationality*, 255.

177. David L. Wolfe, *Epistemology: The Justification of Belief* (Downers Grove, Ill.: InterVarsity, 1982), 34–35.

178. Ibid., 35; Trueblood, *Philosophy of Religion*, 74–89.

179. Edward John Carnell, *An Introduction to Christian Apologetics: A Philosophic Defense of the Trinitarian-Theistic Faith* (Grand Rapids, Mich.: Eerdmans, 1948), 56–62.

Chapter 11

1. Donald G. Bloesch, *Freedom for Obedience: Evangelical Ethics in Contemporary Times* (San Francisco: Harper, 1987), 250, 252, 279.
2. Ibid., 252–254.
3. Ibid., 250–251.
4. Alasdair MacIntyre, *After Virtue* (Notre Dame, Ind.: Univ. of Notre Dame Press, 1981), 2.
5. Robert N. Bellah, et al., *Habits of the Heart: Individualism and Commitment in American Life* (Berkeley: Univ. of California Press, 1985), 3–51.
6. Bloesch, *Freedom for Obedience,* 20.
7. Ibid., 25.
8. Carl F. H. Henry, *Christian Personal Ethics* (Grand Rapids, Mich.: Eerdmans, 1957), 24, 26.
9. Ibid.
10. Arnold Lunn and Garth Lean, *The New Morality* (London: Blandford, 1964), 80.
11. Bloesch, *Freedom for Obedience,* 28–29.
12. Henry, *Christian Personal Ethics,* 26–27.
13. Ibid., 28.
14. Ibid., 31.
15. Bloesch, *Freedom for Obedience,* 28, 36.
16. Henry, *Christian Personal Ethics,* 35.
17. Jeremy Bentham, *An Introduction to the Principles of Morals and Legislation* (Oxford: Clarendon, 1892), ch. 2.
18. Henry, *Christian Personal Ethics,* 37.
19. Ibid., 40.
20. Ninian Smart, *Worldviews: Crosscultural Explorations of Human Beliefs* (New York: Scribner's, 1983), 115.
21. Henry, *Christian Personal Ethics,* 47.
22. John A. Hutchison, *Faith, Reason, and Existence* (New York: Oxford Univ. Press, 1956), 79–80.
23. Ibid., 52.
24. Ibid., 52–54.
25. Ibid., 54–55.
26. Ibid., 56–57.
27. Ayn Rand, *For the New Intellectual* (New York: Signet, 1963), 123; Ayn Rand, *The Virtue of Selfishness* (New York: Signet, 1964), 32.
28. Bloesch, *Freedom for Obedience,* 178.
29. Friedrich Nietzsche, *A Genealogy of Morals* (New York: Macmillan, 1924), 166; Friedrich Nietzsche, *Anti-Christ* (New York: Knopf, 1920), 230.
30. Henry, *Christian Personal Ethics,* 60–61.
31. Ibid., 65.
32. Ibid., 66–67.
33. Ibid., 67–72.
34. Bloesch, *Freedom for Obedience,* 255.
35. Campolo, *Partly Right,* 145–146.
36. Ibid., 146.
37. Henry, *Christian Personal Ethics,* 73–74.

38. Ibid., 75.
39. Ibid., 76.
40. Ibid., 76–79.
41. Ibid., 80.
42. Ibid., 81, 83.
43. Ibid., 88.
44. Bernard L. Ramm, *The Right, the Good and the Happy* (Waco, Tex.: Word, 1971), 69–70.
45. Ibid., 70–71.
46. Ibid., 72.
47. Ibid., 73–74.
48. Henry, *Christian Personal Ethics*, 127–128.
49. Ibid., 97.
50. Ibid., 100, 103.
51. Ibid., 105–107.
52. Bloesch, *Freedom for Obedience*, 174.
53. Erich Fromm, *The Revolution of Hope* (New York: Harper, 1968), 91.
54. Henry, *Christian Personal Ethics*, 108–110.
55. Smart, *Worldviews*, 125–126.
56. John Macquarrie, *In Search of Deity: An Essay in Dialectical Theism* (New York: Crossroad, 1984), 9–10.
57. W. R. Sorley, *Moral Values and the Idea of God*, 2nd ed. (Cambridge: Cambridge Univ. Press, 1921); David Elton Trueblood, *Philosophy of Religion* (New York: Harper, 1957), 107.
58. C. S. Lewis, *Mere Christianity* (New York: Macmillan, 1953); Trueblood, *Philosophy of Religion*, 107.
59. Henry, *Christian Personal Ethics*, 111–112.
60. Ibid., 114.
61. John Baillie, *Our Knowledge of God* (London: Oxford Univ. Press, 1939), 166–167.
62. David Elton Trueblood, *The Logic of Belief: An Introduction to the Philosophy of Religion* (New York: Harper, 1942), 177–178.
63. Smart, *Worldviews*, 117.
64. Ibid.
65. Colin Chapman, *The Case for Christianity* (Grand Rapids, Mich.: Eerdmans, 1981), 140.
66. Smart, *Worldviews*, 41–42.
67. Ibid., 120.
68. Chapman, *Case for Christianity*, 157–159.
69. Smart, *Worldviews*, 119.
70. Ibid., 119–120.
71. Ibid., 120–121.
72. Chapman, *Case for Christianity*, 145.
73. Ibid.
74. Smart, *Worldviews*, 118.
75. Bloesch, *Freedom for Obedience*, 261.
76. Smart, *Worldviews*, 44.
77. Chapman, *Case for Christianity*, 146, 150.
78. Smart, *Worldviews*, 43.

79. Ibid., 42.
80. Chapman, *Case for Christianity,* 145.
81. Smart, *Worldviews,* 117.
82. Ibid., 118–119.
83. Ibid., 119.
84. Bloesch, *Freedom for Obedience,* 261.
85. Smart, *Worldviews,* 121.
86. Ibid., 124.
87. Bloesch, *Freedom for Obedience,* 40–41.
88. Smart, *Worldviews,* 124.
89. Bernhard W. Anderson, "The Biblical Ethic of Obedience," *The Christian Scholar,* 39, no. 1 (March 1956): 66.
90. Ibid., 67.
91. Ibid.
92. Ibid., 68.
93. Ibid., 68–69.
94. Ibid., 69; Martin Buber, *The Prophetic Faith* (New York: Macmillan, 1949), 102, 114.
95. Anderson, "Biblical Ethic of Obedience," 69.
96. Ibid., 70.
97. G. Ernest Wright, "The Faith of Israel," in George A. Buttrick, ed., *The Interpreter's Bible,* vol. 1 (New York: Abingdon, 1952), 383.
98. Ibid.
99. Ibid., 381.
100. Ibid., 382.
101. Ibid., 381–382.
102. Anderson, "Biblical Ethic of Obedience," 70.
103. G. Ernest Wright, *The Biblical Doctrine of Man in Society* (London: SCM, 1954), 102.
104. Ibid.
105. Filson, *New Testament Against Its Environment* (London: SCM, 1950), 81.
106. Wright, *Biblical Doctrine of Man,* 103.
107. William Lillie, *Studies in New Testament Ethics* (Philadelphia: Westminster, 1961), 73–75.
108. Wright, *Biblical Doctrine of Man,* 104–105.
109. Ibid., 105.
110. Ibid., 105–106.
111. Ibid., 106–107.
112. Lillie, *New Testament Ethics,* 144–145.
113. Helmut Thielicke, *Theological Ethics,* vol. 1, *Foundations* (Grand Rapids, Mich.: Eerdmans, 1966), 43.
114. Edmond La B. Cherbonnier, *Hardness of Heart* (Garden City, N.Y.: Doubleday, 1955), 29–38.
115. Ibid., 40–42.
116. Will Herberg, *Judaism and Modern Man* (New York: Farrar, Straus & Young, 1951), 94–96.
117. Henry, *Christian Personal Ethics,* 145–235.
118. Macquarrie, *In Search of Deity,* 217.
119. Ramm, *The Right,* 37.

120. Ibid., 37–38; F. Cardinal Roberti, *Dictionary of Moral Theology* (Westminster, Md.: Newman, 1962), 697.

121. Ibid., 38.

122. Bloesch, *Freedom for Obedience*, 173.

123. Ramm, *The Right*, 32.

124. Ibid., 32–33.

125. Joseph Fletcher, *Situation Ethics: The New Morality* (Philadelphia: Westminster, 1966); Joseph Fletcher, *Moral Responsibility: Situation Ethics at Work* (London: SCM, 1967).

126. James Packer, "Situations and Principles," in Bruce Kaye and Gordon Wenham, eds., *Law, Morality and the Bible*, (Downers Grove, Ill.: InterVarsity, 1978), 151.

127. Fletcher, *Moral Responsibility*, 163–164.

128. Bloesch, *Freedom for Obedience*, 49.

129. Packer, "Situations and Principles," 158–159.

130. Fletcher, *Situation Ethics*, 37–38, 65–66, 74, 98, 126–127, 163–165.

131. Packer, "Situations and Principles," 160.

132. Bloesch, *Freedom for Obedience*, 49–50.

133. Ramm, *The Right*, 61–62.

134. Ibid., 63.

135. Packer, "Situations and Principles," 163–164.

136. Bloesch, *Freedom for Obedience*, 56.

137. Ibid.

138. Leonardo Boff and Clodovis Boff, *Salvation and Liberation*, tr. Robert R. Barr (Maryknoll, N.Y.: Orbis, 1984).

139. Letty M. Russell, *Human Liberation in a Feminist Perspective: A Theology* (Philadelphia: Westminster, 1974), 54; and Jose Miguez Bonino, *Doing Theology in a Revolutionary Situation* (Philadelphia: Fortress, 1975), 88, 72.

140. Bloesch, *Freedom for Obedience*, 179–180.

141. Ibid., 180–181; Gustavo Gutierrez, *A Theology of Liberation*, tr. Sister Caridad Inda and John Eagleson (Maryknoll, N.Y.: Orbis, 1973), 177.

142. Oliver Barclay, "The Nature of Christian Morality," in Kaye and Wenham, eds., *Law, Morality and the Bible*, 149–150.

143. Ibid., 125.

144. Ibid., 126, 128–129.

145. Ibid., 129–131.

146. Ibid., 131–133.

147. Ibid., 133.

148. Ibid.

149. Ibid., 133–134.

150. Ibid., 134–135.

151. Ibid., 134.

152. Ibid.

153. Ibid., 134–135.

154. Ibid., 135–134.

155. Ibid., 136–137.

156. Ibid., 139–140.

157. William M. Pinson, Jr., comp., *An Approach to Christian Ethics: The Life, Contribution and Thought of T. B. Maston* (Nashville: Broadman, 1979), 109.

158. Paul Althaus, *The Theology of Martin Luther* (Philadelphia: Fortress, 1970), 272.
159. Bloesch, *Freedom for Obedience,* 111.
160. Ibid., 112.
161. Ibid., 113.
162. Ramm, *The Right,* 50–51; James William McClendon, Jr., *Ethics: Systematic Theology* (Nashville: Abingdon, 1986), 28–35.
163. Bloesch, *Freedom for Obedience,* 113–114.
164. Bernard Ramm, *After Fundamentalism: The Future of Evangelical Theology* (San Francisco: Harper, 1983), 146–147; McClendon, *Ethics,* 41–45.
165. Bloesch, *Freedom for Obedience,* 119.
166. Ibid., 120.
167. Karl Barth, *Church Dogmatics,* vol. 2, pt. 2, G. W. Bromiley and T. F. Torrance, eds. (Edinburgh: T & T Clark, 1957), 566–583.
168. Henry, *Christian Personal Ethics,* 357.
169. Ibid., 301, 375.
170. Cf. Bloesch, *Freedom for Obedience,* 55; Ramm, *The Right.*
171. Bloesch, *Freedom for Obedience,* 121.
172. C. C. Ryrie, "Dispensation, Dispensationalism," in Walter A. Elwell, ed., *Evangelical Dictionary of Theology* (Grand Rapids, Mich.: Baker, 1984), 322.
173. Henry, *Christian Personal Ethics,* 286.
174. McClendon, *Ethics,* 304–305.
175. Ibid., 305.
176. Bloesch, *Freedom for Obedience,* 121; C. I. Scofield, *Rightly Dividing the Word of Truth* (Neptune, N.J.: Loizeaux, 1896), 34.
177. Hal Lindsey, *Satan Is Alive and Well on Planet Earth* (Grand Rapids, Mich.: Zondervan, 1972), 179.
178. Bloesch, *Freedom for Obedience,* 122.
179. Ibid.
180. William L. Pettingill, *The Gospel of the Kingdom* (Findlay, Ohio: Fundamental Truth Publishers, n.d.), 58.
181. L. S. Chafer, *Systematic Theology* (Wheaton, Ill.: Van Kampen), 5:97ff.
182. Henry, *Christian Personal Ethics,* 287; Donald G. Barnhouse, *His Own Received Him Not, But . . .* (New York: Revell, 1933), 38.
183. Henry, *Christian Personal Ethics,* 287.
184. Bloesch, *Freedom for Obedience,* 122.
185. Ibid., 122–123.
186. Ryrie, "Dispensation, Dispensationalism," 322.
187. Bloesch, *Freedom for Obedience,* 122.
188. Ibid.
189. Ibid., 123.
190. McClendon, *Ethics,* 318–319.
191. Thielicke, *Theological Ethics,* 1:615.
192. Henry, *Christian Personal Ethics,* 278–326.
193. Ramm, *The Right,* 42–43.
194. Ibid., 33.
195. Ibid., 34–35.
196. Bloesch, *Freedom for Obedience,* 55–56.
197. Ramm, *The Right,* 36.

198. Bloesch, *Freedom for Obedience*, 65–66, 203–204.
199. Ibid., 204.
200. T. B. Maston, *Biblical Ethics* (Cleveland, Ohio: World, 1967), 285.
201. Henry, *Christian Personal Ethics*, 573–583.
202. George A. Lindbeck, *The Nature of Doctrine: Religion and Theology in a Postliberal Age* (Philadelphia: Westminster, 1984).
203. Stanley Hauerwas, *The Peaceable Kingdom: A Primer in Christian Ethics* (Notre Dame, Ind.: Univ. of Notre Dame Press, 1983), 102–115.
204. Henry, *Christian Personal Ethics*, 549–572.
205. Bloesch, *Freedom for Obedience*, 99.
206. Ibid., 152.
207. Lillie, *New Testament Ethics*, 147–148.
208. Henry, *Christian Personal Ethics*, 549–572.
209. Ibid., 148–150.

Chapter 12

1. Clyde S. Kilby, *Christianity and Aesthetics* (Downers Grove, Ill.: InterVarsity, 1961), 10–11.
2. Ibid., 11.
3. Susan Sontag, *Against Interpretation* (New York: Dell, 1966), 293–304.
4. Marshall McLuhan, *Understanding Media* (New York: McGraw-Hill, 1964).
5. E. William Muehl, "The Aesthetic Heresy," *Reflection* (November 1968): 1–2, 4.
6. Roger L. Shinn, *The Existentialist Posture* (New York: Association, 1959), 97–98.
7. Muehl, "Aesthetic Heresy," 1, 2, 4.
8. Will Herberg, *Judaism and Modern Man* (New York: Farrar, Straus & Young, 1951), 48.
9. Ibid.
10. Ibid., 49; Nicholas Wolterstorff, *Art in Action: Toward a Christian Aesthetic* (Grand Rapids, Mich.: Eerdmans, 1980), 69.
11. Wolterstorff, *Art in Action*, 68–69.
12. Abraham J. Heschel, *God in Search of Man* (New York: Farrar, Straus & Young, 1959), 93.
13. Ibid., 95.
14. Ibid., 21.
15. Hendrik Kraemer, *Religion and the Christian Faith* (Philadelphia: Westminster, 1956), 308–309.
16. J. Stafford Wright, *Man in the Process of Time* (Grand Rapids, Mich.: Eerdmans, 1956), 67.
17. Ibid., 68–72; John Dillenberger, *A Theology of Artistic Sensibilities* (New York: Crossroad, 1986), 1246; cf. Yandall Woodfin, *With All Your Mind* (Nashville: Abingdon, 1980), 121–124.
18. A. J. Balfour, *Theism and Humanism* (New York: George H. Doran, 1915), 90.
19. William Temple, *Nature, Man and God* (New York: Macmillan, 1934), 253; Woodfin, *With All Your Mind*, 116–118.
20. David Elton Trueblood, *The Logic of Belief: An Introduction to the Philosophy of Religion* (New York: Harper, 1942), 193–194.

21. G. Ernest Wright and Reginald H. Fuller, *The Book of the Acts of God: Christian Scholarship Interprets the Bible* (Garden City, N.Y.: Doubleday, 1957), 30.

22. G. Ernest Wright, "The Faith of Israel," in George A. Buttrick, ed., *The Interpreter's Bible,* vol. 1 (New York: Abingdon, 1952), 375.

23. Ibid., 376–377.

24. Ibid., 375–376.

25. Ibid., 376.

26. Ibid., 377–378.

27. Wright, *The Biblical Doctrine of Man in Society* (London: SCM, 1954), 67–68.

28. Ibid., 68.

29. Wright, *Biblical Doctrine of Man,* 68–69.

30. Ibid., 70.

31. Floyd V. Filson, *The New Testament Against Its Environment: The Gospel of Christ the Risen Lord* (London: SCM, 1950), 94–95.

32. Ibid., 95.

33. Rowley, *Unity of the Bible,* 158.

34. Wright, "Faith of Israel," 378.

35. Ibid., 379.

36. G. Ernest Wright, *The Rule of God: Essays in Biblical Theology* (Garden City, N.Y.: Doubleday, 1960), 69.

37. Ibid., 70–71.

38. Wright, "Faith of Israel," 378.

39. Ibid., 379.

40. Ibid.

41. Oscar Cullmann, *Early Christian Worship* (London: SCM, 1953), 73, 80–81.

42. Ibid., 73–74, 117.

43. Abraham J. Heschel, *Man's Quest for God* (New York: Scribner's, 1954), 117–118.

44. Ibid., 118–120.

45. Ibid., 118.

46. Ibid., 119–120.

47. Gene Edward Vieth, Jr., *The Gift of Art: The Place of Arts in Scripture* (Downers Grove, Ill.: InterVarsity, 1983), 107–109.

48. Edmond La B. Cherbonnier, "Biblical vs. Mystical Symbolism," *The Christian Scholar,* 39, no. 1 (1956): 37.

49. Heschel, *Man's Quest,* 121–125.

50. Ibid., 127–130.

51. Ibid., 129.

52. Ibid.

53. Ibid., 132–136.

54. Ibid., 142.

55. Cherbonnier, "Biblical vs. Mystical Symbolism," 33, 40–41; Paul Tillich, *The Religious Situation* (New York: Meridian, 1956), 89.

56. Cherbonnier, "Biblical vs. Mystical Symbolism," 33, 36, 43.

57. Ibid., 43.

58. Stephen Neill, "Civilisation," in Alan Richardson and W. Schweitzer, ed., *Biblical Authority for Today,* (Philadelphia: Westminster, 1951), 323–326.

59. Ibid., 327–328.

60. Wright, *Rule of God,* 31–32.

61. Neill, "Civilisation," 328–330.

62. Ibid., 331–332; see Reinhold Niebuhr, *Moral Man and Immoral Society* (New York: Scribner's, 1932), 256, and *Beyond Tragedy* (New York: Scribner's, 1937), 186, 193, 224; also Donald Bloesch, "God the Civilizer," in Mark Noll and David F. Wells, eds., *Christian Faith and Practice in the Modern World* (Grand Rapids, Mich.: Eerdmans, 1988), 182–183.

63. Neill, "Civilisation," 332–334.

64. Oscar Cullmann, *The Early Church*, ed. A. J. B. Higgins (Philadelphia: Westminster, 1956), 195–198.

65. Cullmann, *The Early Church*, 201–204.

66. Ibid., 203–204.

67. Ibid., 204.

68. Ibid., 204–206.

69. Ibid., 206–207.

70. Ibid., 208.

71. Ibid., 208–209.

72. Wright, *Biblical Doctrine of Man*, 153–156.

73. Ibid., 157–158.

74. Ibid., 160–164; Bloesch, "God the Civilizer," 180–181, 188–194; see Jürgen Moltmann, *Theology of Hope*, tr. James W. Leitch (New York: Harper, 1965), *The Church in the Power of the Spirit*, tr. Margaret Kohl (New York: Harper and Row, 1977), and *Religion, Revolution and the Future*, tr. M. D. Meeks (New York: Scribner's, 1969).

75. Thorlief Boman, *Hebrew Thought Compared with Greek* (Philadelphia: Westminster, 1960), 12.

76. Ibid., 17.

77. Cf. Oscar Cullmann, *Christ and Time: The Primitive Christian Conception of Time and History* (Philadelphia: Westminster, 1950), 54–59.

78. Hugh R. Harcourt, "The Hebraic Void in the University," *Theology Today*, 20, no. 3 (October 1963): 360–361.

79. Ibid., 360–361.

80. Boman, *Hebrew Thought*, 74.

81. Vieth, *The Gift of Art*, 63–66.

82. Hans Walter Wolff, *Anthropology of the Old Testament*, tr. Margaret Kohl (Philadelphia: Fortress, 1974), 69–73.

83. Samuel Terrien, *The Elusive Presence: The Heart of Biblical Theology* (San Francisco: Harper and Row, 1978), 127.

84. Claus Westermann, *Creation*, tr. John J. Scullion (Philadelphia: Fortress, 1974), 63–64.

85. James Barr, *The Semantics of Biblical Language* (London: Oxford Univ. Press, 1961; London: SCM, 1983), 6, 14.

86. Boman, *Hebrew Thought*, 27–28, 47–48.

87. Ibid., 51–55.

88. Ibid., 85–86; cf. Kenneth Clark, *The Nude: A Study in Ideal Form* (Garden City, N.Y.: Doubleday, Anchor, 1956).

89. Boman, *Hebrew Thought*, 86.

90. Jerry H. Gill, *Faith in Dialogue: A Christian Apologetic* (Waco, Tex.: Word, 1985), 81–82.

91. Boman, *Hebrew Thought*, 87.

92. Ibid., 88.
93. Ibid., 89.
94. John P. Newport, *Christianity and Contemporary Art Forms* (Waco, Tex.: Word, 1979), 100–101.
95. Boman, *Hebrew Thought,* 101–102., 103–104.
96. Cf. Newport, *Contemporary Art Forms,* 102–103.
97. Boman, *Hebrew Thought,* 68–69.
98. Ibid., 127–128.
99. John P. Newport, *Christ and the New Consciousness* (Nashville: Broadman, 1978), 54–55.
100. Ibid., 50–52.
101. Boman, *Hebrew Thought,* 138–139, 171; Harcourt, "Hebraic Void," 360.
102. Paul Tillich, *Political Expectation,* James Luther Adams, ed. (New York: Harper and Row, 1971), 152; John P. Newport, *Paul Tillich,* Makers of the Modern Theological Mind, Robert E. Patterson, ed. (Waco, Tex.: Word, 1984), 185–186.
103. Boman, *Hebrew Thought,* 139–140, 144ff., 155–156.
104. Ibid., 147–148.
105. Ibid., 155–157.
106. Ibid., 157–160.
107. John P. Newport, "Religion, Architecture and the Arts in the 1980s," *Faith & Form,* 13 (Spring-Summer, 1979): 19.
108. Ibid.; Newport, *Paul Tillich,* 228–229.
109. Newport, *Paul Tillich,* 230–232.
110. Herberg, *Judaism and Modern Man,* 121–124, 127.
111. Ibid., 52; Boman, *Hebrew Thought,* 54.
112. F. Ernest Johnson, ed., *Religious Symbolism* (New York: Harper, for the Institute for Religious and Social Studies, 1955), 238.
113. Ibid.
114. Herberg, *Judaism and Modern Man,* 203–204.
115. Ibid., 228, 234–235.
116. Harold Ehrensperger, *Religious Drama: Ends and Means* (Nashville: Abingdon, 1962), 69–70.
117. Ibid., 69–72; Emil Brunner, *Christianity and Civilisation,* vol. 2, *Specific Problems* (London: Nisbet & Co., 1949), 78–79.
118. Boman, *Hebrew Thought,* 207–208.
119. Wolterstorff, *Art in Action,* 1.
120. Kilby, *Christianity and Aesthetics,* 12–13.
121. Alfred North Whitehead, *Science and the Modern World* (New York: Macmillan, 1948), 201.
122. Nathan A. Scott, Jr., "The Collaboration of Vision in the Poetic Act: Its Establishment of the Religious Dimension," *The Christian Scholar,* 45 (December 1957): 282–283, 279; Sontag, *Against Interpretation,* 1–14; Hans Küng, *Art and the Question of Meaning,* tr. Edward Quinn (New York: Crossroad, 1981), 9–25.
123. Jürgen Moltmann, *Theology of Play,* tr. Reinhard Ulrich (New York: Harper and Row, 1972), 15–24.
124. Karl Barth, *Church Dogmatics,* vol. 3, pt. 4, ed. G. W. Bromiley and T. F. Torrance, eds., tr. MacKay, et al. (Edinburgh: T & T Clark, 1961), 374–385.
125. Moltmann, *Theology of Play,* 47–48.

126. Brunner, *Christianity and Civilisation*, 2:85.

127. Denis de Rougemont, "Religion and the Mission of the Artist," in Stanley R. Hopper, ed., *Spiritual Problems in Contemporary Literature* (New York: Harper, 1952), 176; also Rollo May, *Love and Will* (New York: Norton, 1969), 322–223; cf. Newport, *Paul Tillich*, 225-233.

128. Francis A. Schaeffer, *The God Who Is There* (Downers Grove, Ill.: InterVarsity, 1968), 30–43.

129. Ibid., 126–130.

130. Newport, *Contemporary Art Forms*, 69–73.

131. Ibid., 84-91.

132. Amos Niven Wilder, *Theology and Modern Literature* (Cambridge, Mass.: Harvard Univ. Press, 1967), 125.

133. Nathan A. Scott, Jr., "The Theatre of T. S. Eliot," in Nathan A. Scott, Jr., ed., *Man in the Modern Theatre* (Richmond: John Knox, 1965), 13–39.

134. Martin Luther, "Letter to Eoban Hess, March 29, 1523," *Luther's Correspondence*, vol. 2, tr. and ed. Preserved Smith and Charles M. Jacobs (Philadelphia: United Lutheran, 1918), 176–177.

135. Roland Mushat Frye, *Perspective on Man: Literature and the Christian Tradition* (Philadelphia: Westminster, 1961), 34–37.

136. John P. Newport, *The Lion and the Lamb: The Book of Revelation for Today* (Nashville: Broadman, 1986), 38–77.

137. Frye, *Perspective on Man*, 38–39.

138. Wolterstorff, *Art in Action*, 164–168.

139. Ibid., 68–69.

140. Ibid., 69–70.

141. Ibid., 71.

142. Ibib., 72.

143. John W. Dixon, *Nature and Grace in Art* (Chapel Hill, N.C.: Univ. of North Carolina Press, 1964), 79.

144. Ibid., 198–201.

145. William F. Lynch, *Christ and Apollo: The Dimensions of the Literary Imagination* (New York: Sheed & Ward, 1960), 45–65.

146. Wolterstorff, *Art in Action*, 77.

147. Ibid.

148. Ibid., 4.

149. Ibid., 78.

150. Ibid., 79, 82, 83.

151. Ibid., 84.

152. Amos Niven Wilder, "Art and Theological Meaning," in Nathan A. Scott, Jr., ed., *The New Orpheus: Essays Toward a Christian Poetic* (New York: Sheed & Ward, 1964), 414.

153. Richard E. Sherrell, *The Human Image: Avant-Garde and Christian* (Richmond: John Knox, 1969), 26; cf. Jacques Maritain, *Creative Intuition in Art and Poetry* (New York: Pantheon, 1953); Nathan A. Scott, Jr., *The Broken Center* (New Haven, Conn.: Yale Univ. Press, 1966), 201; Nathan A. Scott, Jr., "Collaboration of Vision in the Poetic Act," 281.

154. Nathan A. Scott Jr., "The Relation of Theology to Literary Criticism," *The Journal of Religion*, 33 (October 1953), 269; cf. also Northrup Frye, *Anatomy of Criticism: Four Essays* (Princeton, N.J.: Princeton Univ. Press, 1957), 7.

155. Leslie Paul, *Eros Rediscovered* (New York: Association, 1970), 158–161.

156. Edmund Fuller, *Man in Modern Fiction* (New York: Random House, 1958), 101–105.

157. Paul, *Eros Rediscovered*, 166–167.

158. Ibid., 167.

159. William F. Fore, "Mass Media's Mythic World: At Odds With Christian Values," *Christian Century* (19 January 1977): 33.

160. Cf. Neil P. Hurley, *Theology Through Film* (New York: Harper, 1968), 9–11.

161. Fore, "Mass Media's Mythic World," 33–34.

162. Ibid., 33.

163. Scott, *The Broken Center*, 1–24.

164. Jaroslav Pelikan, *Fools for Christ: Essays on the True, the Good, and the Beautiful* (Philadelphia: Muhlenberg, 1955), 118–144.

Index of Names

Index of Select Subjects